Malinowski

Malinowski

Odyssey of an Anthropologist
1884–1920

MICHAEL W. YOUNG

Yale University Press
New Haven and London

For information about this and other Yale University Press publications, please contact:
U.S. Office: sales.press@yale.edu yalebooks.com
Europe Office: sales@yaleup.co.uk www.yalebooks.co.uk

Set in Bembo by SNP Best-set Typesetter Ltd., Hong Kong
Printed in Great Britain by Biddles Ltd, Kings Lynn

Library of Congress Cataloging-in-Publication Data

Young, Michael W., 1937–
    Malinowski : odyssey of an anthropologist, 1884–1920/Michael W. Young.
        p.   cm.
    Includes bibliographical references and index.
    ISBN 0–300–10294–1 (cl: alk. paper)
    1. Malinowski, Bronislaw, 1884–1942.   2. Anthropologists—Poland—Biography.
3. Anthropologists—Papua New Guinea—Biography.   4. Ethnology—Papua New
Guinea.   5. Papua New Guinea—Social life and customs.   I. Title.
    GN21.M25Y68 2004   301′.092–dc22   2004001545

A catalogue record for this book is available from the British Library

10 9 8 7 6 5 4 3 2 1

For Helena, who made it possible

Contents

Part II   1910–1914

List of Illustrations

Figures

Maps

Plates between pages 258–9

Plates between pages 514–15

Acknowledgments

Helena Wayne, Malinowski's youngest daughter and literary executor, invited me to write this biography. She gave me unrestricted access, not only to her father's papers, but also to many other biographical materials that she had accumulated over a period of two decades. They included notes of interviews she had conducted, in person or by correspondence, with a number of Malinowski's pupils, friends and colleagues. This is, therefore, an authorized biography informally commissioned by Helena with her sisters' approval. It is also fully authorized in the sense that Helena read and implicitly endorsed the final draft. Should this suggest a hagiographic compact between us, I hasten to say that nothing could be further from the truth. Inevitably, during our many conversations I was influenced by her attitude towards her father, but this does not mean that I surrendered my impartiality as an outsider. Indeed, at times Helena took a more uncompromising view of his shortcomings than I was inclined to do, and I can recall conversations in which I found myself in the curious position of defending him against her critical judgement. Nor was Helena able to peer over my shoulder as I wrote. She lived in England, I lived in Australia. Between 1998 and 2002, when most of this book was written, we communicated only by letter and telephone, and then infrequently. There are passages in this biography which, as I wrote them, I felt sure Helena would wish me to remove or modify. But not once did she take me to task for presenting her father in an unfavourable light; not once did she ask me to withdraw anything I had written. The reader may judge whether this was owing to my tact or to her magnanimity, but I have not knowingly exercised self-censorship and her forbearance has been greater than I had any right to expect.

It is a pleasure, then, to acknowledge Helena's cordial assistance. Not only did she read the text from the first sentence to the last, but also – as a former journalist – she generously rendered sub-editing service by correcting typos and factual errors, identifying solecisms, and bringing to my attention obscure or inelegant phrasing. I thank her warmly, too, for sharing with me her knowledge, wisdom, good humour, and the rare pleasure of laughter at the foibles of her father. It is perhaps unusual to dedicate a biography to the daughter of its subject, but I do so as a token of my respect, gratitude and affection.

Belatedly, I thank Helena's sisters, the late Józefa Stuart and the late Wanda Shortall, for their gracious hospitality in Long Island and New York, and for the frankness with which they talked to me about their father. Although they had read some of my earlier essays about him, neither had read any of the present text. I acknowledge their assistance with sadness and remorse, for they did not live to see this book.

I must also record my gratitude to those, also deceased, who granted me more or less lengthy interviews during the early 1990s: Bill Epstein, Raymond and Rosemary Firth, Hans Khuner, Ashley Montagu and Isaac Schapera.

I tender very special thanks to my friend and unofficial editor Roger Averill, who read the penultimate draft of this book with such scrupulous care and critical acumen. His remarkable skill as a reader saved me from many infelicities of style, while his detailed comments on certain chapters led me to reconsider incautious statements. Of great assistance, too, was his blue pencil during my increasingly desperate attempts to cut surplus fat from the text. For this onerous editorial work I cannot thank him enough, or for the encouragement with which he boosted my flagging confidence.

Special thanks are also due to those who read and commented helpfully on the drafts of various chapters, or otherwise contributed significantly to my research: Robert Baldock, Linus Digim'Rina, Don Gardner, Katy Gillette, Terry Hays, Barbara Holloway, Grażyna Kubica, Maria Lepowsky, Gilbert Lewis, Martha Macintyre, Shelley Mallett, the late Will Stober, Borut Telban, Tim Troy, Don Tuzin, Jim Urry and Ron Waterbury.

A work of this weight and length of gestation required a considerable amount of material and intellectual support. To begin with the bread and butter, I am especially grateful to the Department of Anthropology in the Research School of Pacific and Asian Studies at the Australian National University for their long-term financial support and for permission to conduct 'fieldwork' in so many archives and libraries outside the ambit of the Pacific-Asia region. I am also grateful to the Wenner-Gren Foundation for Anthropological Research for the Regular Grant that enabled me to travel in Europe, the United States and Mexico.

I acknowledge with thanks many helpful archivists, librarians and researchers in the following institutions: the British Library of Political and Economic Sciences at the London School of Economics (especially Angela Raspin and Sue Donnelly); the Bodleian Library, Oxford; Cambridge University Library; the Ethnography Department of the British Museum, London; the Jagiellonian University Library, Cracow; the Library of Congress, Washington D.C.; the Matlock Library, Adelaide; the Menzies and Chifley libraries at the Australian National University; the Michael Somare Library at the University of Papua New Guinea; the Mitchell Library, Sydney; the National Archives of Australia in Canberra and Melbourne; the National Archives of Papua New Guinea, Port Moresby; the National Library of Australia, Canberra; the National Museum of Victoria, Melbourne; the Pimlico Branch of Westminster Public Library, London; the Pitt Rivers Museum, Oxford; the Royal Anthropological Institute Library in the Museum of Mankind, London; the South Australian Museum, Adelaide; the Staff Office of the London School of Economics; the Tatra Museum in Zakopane; Trinity College Library, Cambridge; the University of Melbourne Archives; and Yale University Library, New Haven.

For permission to quote extensively from Malinowski's *Argonauts of the Western Pacific* (1922), *The Sexual Life of Savages* (1932 edition), *A Diary in the Strict Sense of the Term* (1967), and from Helena Wayne's *The Story of a Marriage* (1995), I must thank Routledge. I thank also Cambridge University Press for permission to quote from Ellen et al (eds), *Malinowski between Two Worlds* (1988), and from Thornton and Skalník (eds), *The Early Writings of Bronisław Malinowski* (1993). I also thank Northwestern University Press for permission to quote from Daniel Gerould's edition of *The Witkiewicz Reader* (1992).

In the course of working on this book I have benefited from the expertise of a great many people. It is a pleasure to acknowledge all those, from so many countries, who answered my questions, offered insights into aspects of Malinowski's life and works, directed me to particular sources, or provided me with their own writings in draft or finished form. For these kind services I thank: Stephanie Anderson, Chris Ballard, John Barnes, Jeremy Beckett, Joanne Williams Bennett, Jonathan Benthall, Harry Beran, Bruce Berman, Kevin Birth, Basia and Marian Bosowski, Erik Brandt, Richard

Broinowski, Susan Drucker Brown, Lucy Burke, Patrick Burke, Shirley Campbell, Matthew Ciolek, Paul Cocks, Hal Conklin, Dave Cooper, Barry Craig, Jay Craig, Tim Curtis, Wojciech Dąbrowski, Fred Damon, Allan Darrah, Donald Denoon, Jerzy Domaradzki, Elizabeth Edwards, Roy Ellen, Judith Ennew, Richard Eves, Colin Filer, Andrzej Flis, the late Anthony Forge, Jim Fox, the late Derek Freeman, Margaret Gardiner, the late Alfred Gell, the late Ernest Gellner, Daniel Gerould, Patrick Glass, Geoff Gray, Chris Gregory, Murray Groves, Ramachandra Guha, Ranajit Guha, Chris Hann, Christine Helliwell, Gil Herdt, Les Hiatt, Robin Hide, Melinda Hinkson, Garrick Hitchcock, Harry Jackman, Michael Jackson, Jan Jerschina, Margaret Jolly, Alun Gwynedd Jones, Christine Jourdan, Ian Keen, the late Roger Keesing, Marian Kempny, Klaus-Peter Koepping, Susanne Kuehling, Adam Kuper, Jean La Fontaine, Jerry Leach, Ariane Lewis, Nico Lewis, John Liep, Peter Loizos, Anthony Low, Nancy Lutkehaus, Angela MacAdam, Stuart Macintyre, the late Ken Maddock, Piero Matthey, Grant McCall, the late Anna Micińska, John Middleton, Jadran Mimica, Don Mitchell, Michael Moran, Howard Morphy, John Morton, Mark Mosko, Janusz Mucha, John Mulvaney, Hank Nelson, Don Niles, Andrzej Nowakowski, George and Gwen Nurse, Michael O'Hanlon, Eugene Ogan, Doug Oliver, the late Nigel Oram, Anna Paini, Andrzej Paluch, Andrew Pawley, Nic Peterson, Krystyna Pisarkowa, Anton Ploeg, Johanna Raines, Greg Rawlings, Barnett Richling, Kathy Robinson, Arturo Alvarez Roldán, Nicolas Rothwell, Irving Rouse, Sandra Rouse, Alan Rumsey, Ian Scales, Sławomir Sikora, Peter Skalník, Hal Scheffler, Jim Specht, George Stocking, Jr, the late Ian Stocks, Marilyn Strathern, Walker Stuart, Stanley J. Tambiah, Bob Tonkinson, Ron Vanderwal, Eric Venbrux, Gerry Ward, the late Annette Weiner, James Weiner, the late Gehan Wijeyewardene, James Woodburn, Terence Wright, Jenny Young and George Zubrzycki.

I have been well served by a number of translators, especially Basia Plebanek, who made a line-by-line check of Norbert Guterman's translation of *A Diary in the Strict Sense of the Term* against the Polish original and restored passages censored by Malinowski's widow. Basia also translated dozens of pages of manuscripts, fieldnotes and journal jottings, and I thank her for her skill and infinite patience. I must also thank Marc Heine, who was commissioned by Helena Wayne to translate the early diaries. For their translations of sundry unpublished Polish correspondence I thank Matthew Ciolek, Daniel Gerould, Grażyna Kubica, Annamaria Orla-Bukowska and Elizabeth Tabaka.

For research assistance, and technical and administrative support I wish to thank Ann Buller, Fay Castles, Ben Cauchi, Bob Cooper, Petra Engelbrecht, Martina Piercy, Emmerentia van Rensburg, Jackie Sheehy, Ernest Sprules, Basil Wilson, Judith Wilson and Ria van de Zandt.

To Elizabeth Brouwer, who shared so many of my journeys in Malinowski's tracks, who discussed with me so many aspects of his life, who nudged me to write when procrastination was getting the upper hand, and who has been an exacting critical reader of so many of my chapters, I offer my love and heartfelt thanks.

Not least, I want to thank my sister, Margaret Watkis, and my sons, Julian and Rafael, who have listened to me talk about Malinowski for as long as they can remember. Their love and moral support means a great deal to me.

M. W. Y.
Pimlico, London
November 2003

A Note on Orthography and Pronunciation

Polish orthographic conventions have been followed except in a couple of cases: Kraków and Warszawa appear as Cracow and Warsaw. The approximate pronunciation of Bronisław Malinowski's name is Bronis-*waav* Malin-*of*-ski. Once he had begun to write in English, he replaced the 'ł' in Bronisław with 'l', which elicits 'Bronis-*law*' rather than 'Bronis-*laav*' in Anglophone speakers. In addition, Americans are inclined to mispronounce Malinowski as Malin-*ow*-ski. I believe this book would read quite differently if one's inner ear heard an open '*ow*' instead of a narrow '*of*' (or '*off*') in the middle of his name.

Malinowski's grandfather's name, Juljan, and his father's, Lucjan, can be rendered by the more familiar Julian and Lucian. The pronunciation of his mother's maiden name, Łącka, presents particular problems for English speakers, but '*Wonska*' comes close, especially if the '*on*' is slightly nasalized. Of the other Polish names which occur frequently in this book, Józefa sounds like '*Yusefa*', while it is the second syllable in Helena that takes the stress. Stanisław Witkiewicz is approximately 'Stanis-*waav* Vit-*kee*-eh-vich'; Staś is 'Stash'; Żenia is 'Zhenia'; Tośka is 'Toshka'.

Malinowski's Kiriwinian orthography is somewhat anomalous by modern standards, but I have not changed it except when rendering a few place names. As in Italian and Spanish, vowels in Kiriwina (Kilivila to modern linguists) are voiced with a full, open value. Stress, sometimes barely perceptible, usually falls on the penultimate syllable, though in longer words it falls on the anti-penultimate syllable. 'Omarakana', for instance, is lightly accented on the second 'a'.

Introduction

Sixty years after his death, Malinowski remains a fascinating figure. If Charles Darwin is the archetypal biologist, Bronislaw Malinowski is the archetypal anthropologist – the Polish aristocrat who invented the rigorous rite of passage called ethnographic fieldwork and revolutionized social anthropology in Britain. He has been cast as William the Conquerer to Sir James Frazer's King Harold, a king-slayer who inscribed a Domesday Book for the Trobriand Islands of Melanesia.

His times were momentous, encompassing two world wars and the birth of modernism. He was a contemporary of modernist icons such as T. S. Eliot, James Joyce, Franz Kafka, John Maynard Keynes, D. H. Lawrence, Robert Musil, Ezra Pound, Lytton Strachey and Ludwig Wittgenstein. Like many of these men, he chose exile, straddled two or more worlds, and bridged the cultural currents of the nineteenth and twentieth centuries. A true, if ambivalent, cosmopolitian, he was born a citizen of the Austro-Hungarian Empire, became a Polish citizen in 1920, a British citizen in 1931, and was contemplating United States citizenship at the time of his death in 1942. Besides Poland, England and America, he lived and worked in Australia, Papua (ex-British New Guinea), Italy, Africa and Mexico.

A legendary Malinowski inhabits the folklore of the discipline, enlivening classrooms and lecture halls wherever anthropology is taught. (His provocative definition of the subject as 'the study of man embracing woman' still elicits groans from first-year university students.) Adam Kuper sees in his myth the exemplary tale of a prophet: 'The false start, then the illness and conversion, followed by migration; the earth-shattering calamity – no less than a world war – leading to isolation in the wilderness; the return with a message; the battle of the disciples.'[1] The messianic hero is the complete ethnographer who is empathetically at home with the savage, speaking his language and living (almost) as he does. This modern ethnographer descends from the missionary's verandah and pitches his tent in the middle of the native village, where he stays and stays, enduring sickness and sexual privation, loneliness and boredom, in pursuit of 'the Ethnographer's final goal', which is 'to grasp the native's point of view, his relation to life, to realize *his* vision of *his* world'.[2] Such heroic endurance in the winning of ethnographic riches is rewarded by an elevation in status, the acclaim of colleagues and the sweet envy of rivals.

Caricatures of this popular image of Malinowski and his works have appeared in George Perec's novel *Life: A User's Manual*, in Umberto Eco's short story 'Industry and Sexual Repression in a Po Valley Society' and in the American television series *Young Indiana Jones*. In an 'encyclopedic tour of the fabled South Seas', Tony Wheeler of the *Lonely Planet Guide* presents a lay version of the legend:

> Anthropologists are often a colorful lot, but it would be hard to find a more colorful character than Bronislaw Malinowski. Born in Kraków, Poland, Malinowski had the good fortune to be in the right place – Australia – at the wrong time – the start of World War I. He avoided internment as an enemy national in exchange for a spot of self-exile in the remote Trobriand Islands, east of Papua New Guinea. There Malinowski set to work studying the islanders, their intricate trading rituals, their yam cults, and – the subject that always seems to intrigue anthropologists most – their sexual habits.[3]

A kernel of mundane truth lies in this romantic shell. Although Malinowski was neither the first ethnographer in the Trobriands nor the first Western anthropologist to spend a year or more among a 'primitive' people documenting their customs and learning their language, it is true that his myth has long served social anthropology as a validating charter for its methods of fieldwork. He was one of those paradigmatic figures who, through a serendipitous combination of talent, training and timing, personify historical trends. He rode the wave of a disciplinary advance to professionalism that had begun at the end of the nineteenth century and gathered momentum by the time he proclaimed his functionalist revolution in the early 1920s. He embodied a scientific ideal: that of a more exact knowledge of 'primitive' societies in particular and human culture in general. Of course, Malinowski could also be understood in household terms as a great man, an exemplary self-mythologizing hero whose legend was embroidered by

many of his pupils. Speaking on their behalf, Hortense Powdermaker con-
ceded simply: 'We were all, probably, more successful because of the myth
than we would have been without it.'[4]

The posthumous publication of his New Guinea fieldwork diaries in
1967 brought Malinowski fresh notoriety. A raw and nakedly honest
account of his tribulations, with its Conradian subtexts, its Oedipal anguish
and Dostoevskian moods, *A Diary in the Strict Sense of the Term* provoked
charges of misanthropy and racism. It sensationally debunked his own myth
of empathetic rapport with his Melanesian subjects and revealed how temperamentally unsuited he was to the protracted, coalface fieldwork that he
advocated. In a bemused review of the *Diary*, Clifford Geertz denounced
this 'archetypal fieldworker' as a 'crabbed, self-preoccupied, hypochon-
driacal narcissist, whose fellow-feeling for the people he lived with was
limited in the extreme'. Yet for Geertz (too young to have known
Malinowski) there was an enormous paradox: how could such a disagreeable man have been such a great ethnographer? 'What saved him,' Geertz
surmised, 'was an almost unbelievable capacity for work.'[5] The work was
expiatory, the result a prodigious corpus of ethnographic data. Although
it scandalized the profession in the late 1960s and helped precipitate a crisis
of anthropological conscience in the 1970s, the *Diary* became an iconic text
that endorsed the postmodern and post-colonial preoccupations of subsequent decades, serving as a charter for a more self-consciously reflexive and
interpretative anthropology, one that rejected positivist scientific pretensions
and embraced a more humanistic agenda.

Odyssey of an Anthropologist covers the first thirty-five years of Malinowski's
life and seeks to explain why, and how, he became an anthropologist. It
traces his intellectual and sentimental journey from his birthplace in the
capital of the imperial Austrian province of Galicia to the Mediterranean
and the Canary Islands, to Leipzig and London, to Warsaw and Zakopane,
to Ceylon (Sri Lanka), Australia, colonial Papua and the Trobriand Islands
– and finally to the moment when he sailed for England, laden with the
ethnographic riches that would secure his legacy.

It is important to demystify Malinowski's achievements as a fieldworker,
and my narrative reveals to what degree they were flawed or exaggerated
– and, conversely, to what extent they have been underestimated. I devote
eight chapters, almost a third of the book, to his Papuan fieldwork. Such
detailed treatment is warranted, I believe, by its legendary status. Above all,

I want to show that so much more was happening in Malinowski's life during the various phases of his fieldwork than the dedicated accumulation of anthropological data. He accomplished his fieldwork in the teeth of a discouraging array of obstacles – social, political, psychological and medical. Tenacity of purpose saw him through in the end, but it was a close thing. It was also largely happenstance (missed boats, absent missionaries and the like) that led him to the Trobriands in the first place and kept him there long enough to make the kind of discoveries that laid the groundwork for his fame.

If Malinowski had been *only* a consummate professional ethnographer and a charismatic academic leader whose contributions remain relevant today, he would hardly justify such a bulky biography. There are, however, so many extracurricular activities worth the telling, so many more aspects to his private life and public career. I have made no attempt to separate these two conventional facets of his existence, for he lived his anthropology to an extraordinary degree, and it would not have been true to the spirit of Malinowski's life to distinguish sharply between his private and public selves. He became a vocal popularizer, pundit and public intellectual who was invited to pronounce on the most debated issues of the interwar period: sex, marriage, birth control, the family, eugenics, religion, the rise of Fascism, mobilization and war. Malinowski held firm opinions, and he wrote wittily and lectured tirelessly to propagate them. At the time of his death he was a controversial international celebrity: a cosmopolitan humanist dedicated to the fight against totalitarianism.

While this biography can be read *inter alia* as a critical evaluation of Malinowski's place in the history of anthropology, this task has already been accomplished by more able historians. I could not hope, for example, to surpass the scholarly depth and scope of George Stocking's *After Tylor*, which situates Malinowski at the centre of the broad historical tradition of British anthropology between 1888 and 1951. Expositions and critiques of Malinowski's theories and of his work more generally are legion, and the secondary literature continues to grow. While this is the first full-scale biography of Malinowski to be published, many valid biographical essays exist.[6] It would have hindered my narrative immeasurably, and added inordinately to its length, to engage with this vast literature at every turn. I have adhered quite firmly to the historicist principle that only Malinowski's coevals deserve a place in this biography. The principle necessarily excludes myself as author, and I have resisted the temptation to argue with my own contemporaries. I reserve for an epilogue to the second volume some reflections on Malinowski's intellectual legacy and a consideration of his posthumous reputation.

If this is not, in the strictest sense, an intellectual biography, then what is it? One of my rejected subtitles was 'The Savage Pole', which quotes Malinowski's ironic self-deprecation in acknowledging that, despite his aspiration to be British, he despised the empire-building game of cricket. Other discarded subtitles were 'The Making of an Anthropologist' (too pedestrian) and 'Portrait of the Anthropologist as a Young Man' (too obviously Joycean). Whatever its shortcomings, *Odyssey of an Anthropologist* invokes the classical image of fateful, adventurous voyages; it also points the way to *Argonauts*. Malinowski's life was indeed one of restless journeying: an interminable, migratory search for knowledge of self and others, for love and fame, for elusive health and happiness. Because he fancied himself as the Conrad of anthropology – although he rightly suspected that he was closer to being its Zola – and because I have sought to describe the intricate interplay of his life and his works, this might best be characterized as a literary biography.

It is also a resource for scholars to use as they see fit. I have paid particular heed to the historical record, and in the degree that the biography is based on verifiable documentary evidence it is scientific. Mindful of the critic Desmond MacCarthy's axiom that a biographer is 'an artist who is on oath', I have invented no facts, confected no imaginary conversations, conjured no hypothetical events. Some readers may regret the dearth of speculative interpretation in my account, but in reflecting Malinowski's obsessive interest in his own psyche, this is inevitably a psychological biography. It has been said that all modern biography is written in Freud's shadow. I acknowledge this, but in attempting to explain the behaviour of a self-confessed neurotic I have called upon Freudian insights only when Malinowski himself appeared to endorse them. More generally, I have sought to present his point of view, '*his* vision of *his* world', and have tried to view my subject 'in the round and not in the flat' – as Frazer wrote of Malinowski's Trobriander – to give full recognition to the fact that he was 'a creature of emotion at least as much as of reason'.[7]

The private diaries that Malinowski kept intermittently between 1908 and 1918 presented me with thorny problems of biographical narration. They are so embarrassingly rich in confessional material, so revelatory of his introspective, multifaceted character, it seemed best in the end to recount the events of Malinowski's life during these crucial years according to the scripts his diaries dictated. His voice, his vision of his world, had to prevail in the telling of his story; besides, this narrative device most accurately renders the full stretch and flavour of Malinowski's thinking and feeling. I judged it even more necessary to quote generously from the early diaries that are inaccessible to the Anglophone reader, though they have recently been published in their original Polish.[8]

The diaries help to illuminate Malinowski's ethnographic style and field techniques. He once noted that his diary was complementary to his ethnography, which was as close as he came to an admission (made by later generations of anthropologists) that ethnography is implicity informed by autobiography as much as it is by explicit theory and method. Reciprocally, Malinowski applied rudimentary functional analysis to the understanding of his own life, and I show that his use of what he called 'synoptic charts' was biographical before it was ethnographical and pedagogical. 'Integrate fragmenting themes,' he urged himself, and it is surely an obligation of his biographer to try to integrate his career and his character in order to indictate how the latter shaped his particular mode of anthropological thinking.

There is a complex relationship to be explored, then, between Malinowski's living, thinking and writing. Readers will differ in their opinions as to how I have tilted the balance between life and works. Some may think that I have devoted a disproportionate amount of space to Malinowski's love affairs, however revealing they were of the man. But, beginning with his adoring mother, women played a strikingly influential part in Malinowski's life, and when he was in love he could think of little else. His romantic passions consumed his time as well as his heart, and for good or ill they inflected his work. I have heeded Lytton Strachey's warning that 'discretion is not the better part of biography', and my subject, after all, was the author of *The Sexual Life of Savages* and a friend and admirer of Havelock Ellis.

Malinowski's obsession with his own moral character is evident from his diaries, which famously conclude with the despairing judgment: 'Truly I lack real character!' In any conventional sense, of course, he most certainly did not, and of his paradoxical character there is an abundance of anecdotal evidence. He appealed and appalled in about equal measure, but few could remain unresponsive to his protean personality. Another of his flippant definitions of anthropology was 'the study of rude man by rude men', and his colleagues did indeed find him rude as well as charming. On first meeting him, Ruth Benedict wrote to Margaret Mead: 'He has the quick imagination and by-play of mind that makes him a seven-days' joy.' But Robert Lowie recalled Malinowski's 'adolescent eagerness to shock the ethnological bourgeois', and Ashley Montagu remembered how his 'ornery sense of humour and his occasional hapless aspersions did not sit well with some of his colleagues and students'.[9] Undoubtedly, Malinowski made enemies as easily as he made friends. He could be moody, irritable, hypersensitive, self-absorbed, vain, petulant, foul-mouthed, sentimental and melancholic. But he could also be gregarious, emotionally generous, deeply courteous and scintillatingly eloquent. He was a demonically hard worker whose zeal galvanized those around him.

For readers curious about my credentials for writing this biography, I offer some autobiographical details (with apologies for any hint of self-mythologizing). Half a century ago, following an undistinguished school career in Manchester, I sailed for Australia aboard an Orient Line steamer. Knowing nothing of anthropology and never having heard the name Malinowski, I had no inkling that some forty years earlier he had sailed the same route on a ship of the same line that called at the same ports: Naples, Port Said, Aden, Colombo, Fremantle, Adelaide, Melbourne and Sydney. After crossing the Tasman to New Zealand, I spent two carefree years working in offices, warehouses and factories, on wharfs and sheep farms. While hitch-hiking one day, I met a young anthropologist who told me intriguing stories about the Maori. The voyage back to England took me the breadth of the South Pacific, and although the ship called only at Fiji and Tahiti, I became, rather like Malinowski at the same age, enchanted by the tropics – by coral reefs and turquoise lagoons, golden beaches stretching beneath coconut palms, and frangipani-scented girls with flawless chocolate skins.

My real engagement with Malinowski began on 1 October 1960 – memorable because it was my first day as an undergraduate student at University College London. I had enrolled for the BA honours course in anthropology, and was immediately advised to immerse myself in some classical ethnography; Malinowski's *Argonauts of the Western Pacific* and *The Sexual Life of Savages* were mentioned. I dutifully began to read these books and the Exotic and the Erotic soon coloured the grey October mornings of Bloomsbury's Gower Street. As my first essay topic I chose to write on the chiefly political system of the Trobriands, but I confess that – although I clutched *Argonauts* to my bosom in the chilly corridors of University

College as Malinowski had hugged *The Golden Bough* on the steps of the medieval Jagiellonian – I did not feel then as he had felt about Frazer, 'bound to the service' of Malinowskian anthropology. Fate, however, decreed otherwise.

Two of my teachers at UCL, Daryll Forde (chair of the anthropology department) and Phyllis Kaberry, had known Malinowski personally. At the London School of Economics, where I also attended lecture courses, I met two other pupils of Malinowski: Raymond Firth and Lucy Mair. While Malinowski's Melanesian monographs had warmed me, I was soon required to enter the more rigorous African worlds of Radcliffe-Brown, Evans-Pritchard and Meyer Fortes. My anthropological apprenticeship thus benefited from the double intellectual inheritance of that clannish era of British anthropology – that of the two founding fathers, Malinowski and Radcliffe-Brown.

In late 1965, after completing a master's thesis on African divine kingship, I sailed with my bride for Australia. I had taken up Phyllis Kaberry's suggestion of applying for a scholarship at the Australian National University (ANU) with a view to working in Papua New Guinea. I joined an anthropology department whose foundation professor had been Siegfried Nadel, another of Malinowski's pupils, in a research school whose first director had been Raymond Firth. My chief academic supervisor was Ann Chowning, a pupil of Ward Hunt Goodenough, who had been one of Malinowski's pupils at Yale; my other supervisor was Bill Stanner, who had attended Malinowski's seminar at the LSE. I thus came to do fieldwork in the Malinowskian mode on Goodenough Island in eastern Papua, one hundred miles to the south of the Trobriands.

In October 1966, accompanied by my wife and infant son, I made my first visit to the Trobriands. We stayed with the Australian doctor on the government station at Losuia and accompanied him on his medical rounds of villages on Kiriwina Island. I took notes and photographs but neglected to ask if anyone remembered Malinowski. On a much later trip to Kiriwina in June 1989, I spent a week as the guest of my PhD student Linus Digim'Rina in his natal village of Okeboma where we witnessed a spectacular yam festival. Again, I was preoccupied with present rather than past events and asked only cursory questions concerning Malinowski. Many villagers knew of his books by reputation (especially *Argonauts* and *Sexual Life of Savages*) though it seemed that very few had tried to read them. A few years later, however, Linus was able to record legends about Malinowski in

Oburaku, the lagoon village where he had spent three miserable months in early 1918.

In October 1970, almost ten years to the day after I began to read anthropology, I took up a teaching appointment in the faculty of archaeology and anthropology at the University of Cambridge. I was heir to the position of Reo Fortune (a maverick pupil of Malinowski in the 1930s) who had retired the previous year. Other senior members of the faculty who had been taught by Malinowski were Audrey Richards, Meyer Fortes and Edmund Leach. It had taken me a decade to become a fully fledged social anthropologist by the orthodox academic route, including the *rite de passage* of fieldwork in an exotic location.

Professor Meyer Fortes proposed that I offer a postgraduate seminar on Malinowski; this obliged me to read more of his works, many hitherto unfamilar to me. Towards the end of the three years that I taught this course, Adam Kuper, editor of Routledge's anthropology series, invited me to compile a Malinowski reader designed for an undergraduate market. I duly produced a 'digest' of Malinowski's Trobriand ethnography, comprising selections from his major works repackaged as a single monograph. By the time it appeared I had already resigned my Cambridge position and returned to the ANU where I resumed research and writing on Goodenough Island and neighbouring areas.

Malinowski's ghost continued to haunt me, and during this period I wrote a book about the biographical uses of mythology in Kalauna. In examining the life-history narratives of several leading magicians, I stretched Malinowski's conception of 'living myth' by demonstrating that not only were certain Kalauna myths charters for magical systems of knowledge, but also blueprints for the construction of their owners' personal identities.

Inadvertently, I had become an expert on Malinowski, and invitations to write articles or collaborate in making television films about him landed on my desk with disconcerting frequency. In September 1984, I attended the centennial celebrations of Malinowski's birth in Cracow. The Polish scholars who convened the symposium were intent upon rehabilitating him in his native land after forty years of official disparagement by the Communist regime. I joined an international band of Malinowski scholars in the Jagiellonian's Collegium Novum (where in November 1908 Malinowski had received his doctorate *summa cum laude* from Emperor Franz Josef's representative) to watch Sir Raymond Firth, Malinowski's most eminent surviving pupil, ceremonially conferred with an honorary degree. My only contribution to this grand occasion was an article that I distributed among my Polish colleagues; it answered a question they had probably never thought to ask: 'Why did Malinowski go to the Trobriands?'

My next major excursion into Malinowskiana was at the suggestion of an American colleague, Terry Hays. He pointed out that Malinowski's first New Guinea monograph, *The Natives of Mailu*, was virtually inaccessible, languishing as it did in the obscure *Proceedings* of an Australian Royal Society. Routledge agreed to publish an edition, which I annotated and introduced. Work on this book led me to correspond with Malinowski's youngest daughter and literary executor, Mrs Helena Wayne. We had first met in 1978 at a King's College, Cambridge conference on the Kula (the main subject of *Argonauts*), and subsequently at the centenary celebration in Cracow. I enjoyed her lively reminiscences about her father – though she was only seventeen when he died – and I learned that when her step-mother died in 1973 Helena had dashed to Mexico to retrieve what remained of Malinowski's papers. It was there that she discovered her parents' correspondence and several of her father's private diaries.

Out of the blue, in November 1991, Helena wrote to me with a simply worded invitation to write a full-blown biography of her father. She had abandoned her own plan of writing a memoir and was working instead on her parents' correspondence (published by Routledge in 1995 as *The Story of a Marriage*). She assured me that I would have unrestricted access to all her father's papers, including English translations of his unpublished diaries.

I was awed by the invitation, for I could think of several more likely candidates – Polish, British and American – for such a daunting task. I was also concerned that such a monumental assignment would create distortions in my long-term ethnographic projects in Vanuatu and Papua New Guinea. To bide time while I considered Helena's proposition, I wrote to two eminent Malinowski scholars for their advice. Sir Raymond Firth replied with a mere hint of equivocation: that insofar as a full biography was needed, I was 'probably the best person to do it'. Professor George Stocking, who had spent longer poring over Malinowski's archived materials than anyone else I knew, brushed aside my doubts and encouraged me to meet the challenge. I accepted Helena's invitation on my fifty-fifth birthday.

For several years thereafter I made an annual pilgrimage to the London School of Economics, where I ploughed steadily through the interminable archive boxes containing Malinowski's papers – two hundred of them and still counting. It is an unruly archive, incompletely catalogued. Malinowski saved almost every document that came his way – including menus, leaflets, invoices and tickets – and had the inconsiderate habit of scribbling field-notes and lecture notes on the backs of important letters. Each box sprang a fresh surprise. By comparison, the leaner, more organized archive in the Sterling Library at Yale was a model of accessibility and I worked though it within a month.

A reading knowledge of Polish would certainly have been an advantage in this enterprise, but I made only the most perfunctory attempt to acquire one. In justification, I plead that Malinowski practically ceased to write in his mother tongue after completing his habilitation thesis in 1914. Nor did he speak Polish in the home. Helena wondered 'why there was so little Polishness in the household in which my sisters and I grew up?' She supposed 'it must have been because we did not learn the language'.[10]

In September 1995, Helena invited me to Oberbozen in the Italian Tyrol, where I sampled the air that had invigorated the Malinowski family and visiting pupils during the summers of the 1920s and early 1930s. At Villa Malinowski I slept soundly in his old bed and sat thoughtfully at his desk on the verandah overlooking the ethereal Dolomites. The following year I accompanied Helena on a visit to Poland, a trip fortuitously funded by the publisher's advance on *Malinowski's Kiriwina*, my book about his fieldwork photography. We stayed with distant relatives on Malinowski's mother's side and explored Warsaw, Cracow and Zakopane, the scenes of his turbulent youth. Other incidental journeys I made in his footsteps were to places where he had lived in England and Australia. In Papua New Guinea I was already familiar with Port Moresby, Samarai, Suau, Woodlark, Dobu and the Trobriands, though I never managed to set foot on Mailu, the site of his apprentice fieldwork. More recently, I visited Oaxaca in Mexico and university campuses in the USA where he had taught – Berkeley, Tucson and Yale.

A Selective Łącki-Malinowski Genealogy

Magdalena Montreil (1789–1854) m. Jan Ignacy Łącki (1786–1855)

Leoncjusz m. Julia Landie (1818–1903) (1813–1884)

Aniela (1823–1897)

Karol m. Paulina Dunin-Szpotański (1825–1907) (1829–1909)

Eleonora m. Leopold Łącki (1821–1904) (1801–1871)

Julijan Malinowski (1816–?) m. Ewa Górska

Alfons (1850–1918)

Helena

Lucjan (1839–1898)

Józefa m. Lucjan (1848–1918)

Kazimierz (1857–1920)

Władysław m. Eleonora Staszewski (1847–1912) (1850–1924)

Józefa m. Bronisław Wolf (1847–1908) (1862–1930)

Bronisław m. Elsie Masson (1884–1942) (1890–1935)

Roman m. Stefania Wolski (1877–1952) (1887–1945)

Maria m. Stefan Kobyliński (1889–1942) (1885–1960)

Zygmunt (1883–1912)

Zdzisław m. Maria Beski (1886–1926) (1881–1945)

Stanisław m. Eugenia Brzeziński (1871–1950) (1884–1953)

Józefa (1920–2002)

Wanda (1922–2003)

Helena (1925–)

3 children

2 children

3 children

3 children

Edward m. Karolina Błotnicki (1852–1915) (1862–1942)

Maria m. Ryszard Błotnicki (1859–1933) (1854–1917)

Jadwiga m. Kazimierz Jezierska Roman (1861–1929) (1857–1930)

Władysław (1902–?)

Helena

Stanisław (1895–1955)

Maria (1893–1955)

Ryszard (1890–1916)

Kazimierz Tadeusz (1887–1966) m. Maria Miłkowska

Marian m. Jadwiga Joachim Dubowski (1886–1975) (1881–1942)

1 child

1 child

2 children

2 children

Adam (1910–?) and 5 siblings

Julia (1847–1879)

Maria m. Edward Rakoczy (1855–1930) (1857–1893)

Maria (187?–1900)

Stanisław m. Janina Marchwicki (1883–19??)

Stanisław Juliusz

3 children

Part I

1884—1910

Chapter 1

Father and Son

'A special passion'

Why did Bronislaw Malinowski become an anthropologist? This deceptively simple question is not easily answered. But if I could put the question to Malinowski's ghost it would be in a more indirect form: 'Why did
you give no credit to your father for your choice of career?' The bare facts
are these. Lucjan Malinowski was a university professor, an eminent linguist,
ethnographer and folklorist. He died when the boy — his only child — was
not quite fourteen. Fathers are role models for their growing sons, and
should they die before their sons attain adulthood they are apt to be idealized and loved beyond the grave. Yet Lucjan is almost completely absent
from his son's public and private reminiscences.

As to why he took up anthropology, Malinowski himself was inclined to
offer different explanations on different occasions. Most famously, there was
his public declaration, made in Liverpool in November 1925:

> If I had the power of evoking the past, I should like to lead you back
> some twenty years to an old Slavonic university town – I mean the town
> of Cracow, the ancient capital of Poland and the seat of the oldest uni-
> versity in Eastern Europe. I could then show you a student leaving the
> medieval college buildings, obviously in some distress of mind, hugging,
> however, under his arm, as the only solace of his troubles, three green
> volumes . . . *The Golden Bough*.

He had been 'ordered to abandon for a time' his laboratory research
'because of ill-health', but was 'allowed to follow up a favourite line
of study'. Reading this 'English masterpiece in the original' changed
Malinowski's life:

For no sooner had I begun to read this great work, than I became immersed in it and enslaved by it. I realized then that anthropology, as presented by Sir James Frazer, is a great science, worthy of as much devotion as any of her elder and more exact sister studies, and I became bound to the service of Frazerian anthropology.[1]

Although this is a compelling conversion myth it is unreliable history. Malinowski was already fully embarked upon his British career when he spoke these words, and the circumstances of his claim – delivery of the Frazer Lecture at a time when he was busily promoting his functional revolution – suggests a strategic investment of personal myth into a flattering tribute to British anthropology's most distinguished figure. The title of Malinowski's lecture, aptly enough, was 'Myth in Primitive Psychology', and it expounded his seminal theory of myth-as-charter. Myths, legends and all stories about the past, including history, serve a legitimating function in the present. Thus the irony of his introducing a lecture about the function of myth with a primitive charter myth about himself, the function of which was to assert his affiliation to the British academic establishment.

As an eminence himself, Malinowski was sometimes obliged to concoct concise autobiographies (for *Who's Who*, *Current Biography* and the like) and he enjoyed toying with different views of his personal history on such occasions – again, no doubt, fully aware that his own stories about his past were being created with present purposes in mind. In his fiftieth year he submitted the following as part of a *curriculum vitae* for a visit to South Africa.

> Owing to [a] breakdown in health, [he] travelled in the Mediterranean, North Africa and Canary Islands for two years, and decided to take up the study of exotic cultures and peoples. Like his friend and countryman, Joseph Conrad, acting on the principle that if [one is to be] an anthropologist, then [be] a British anthropologist.[2]

Certainly, a penchant for travel and, latterly, an acquired British identity were two components of Malinowski's dedication to anthropology. There is another reference to his illness here, but no mention of Frazer; instead an invocation of Conrad's name as a romantic avowal of his own Polish roots and, of course, as a reminder of Malinowski's purported claim to be anthropology's Conrad.

Yet another autobiographical sketch survives which dwells on his early experiences of travel and exposure to a variety of languages and cultures, inducing in him the sense of a 'double life'. It concludes (I paraphrase his handwritten notes): 'Almost everyone has travelled to some extent and even lived abroad. Some throw themselves into their surroundings with a special passion. This is the making of an anthropologist.'

Whence the 'special passion'? Is it sparked in childhood? If so, to what degree are parents responsible for influencing their child's adult choices? Without becoming distracted by the problem of how biographers are to understand childhood – how much interpretative weight early experiences can be made to bear; to what extent such events shape or determine the career patterns, and the sexual and familial configurations of adult life – one might simply observe that in the construction of biography (a literary arti-fact that predicates the internal coherence of any given life) a teleological element is inescapable: *this* childhood led to *that* adulthood. This does not mean that a single luminous thread can or should be identified in every life. A subject's sense of personal destiny notwithstanding, it is a suspiciously simplistic biography that presents a given life as an inexorable, unilinear development from cradle to grave.

There is a weak or minimalist position on these matters which accepts that while certain childhood events and experiences may be significant they are unlikely to be wholly determinative of adult personality. There is also the strong position taken by psycho-biographers, associated with Freud and his followers, for whom infancy and childhood are the *fons et origo* of all adult character formations, and hence of biographical directions. In this phi-losophy, the child is indeed father to the man. Although inclined to adopt the weaker position, I am uneasily confronted by the fact that, like many intellectuals of his time, Malinowski found Freud revelatory. He felt, as his own daughter was to put it, that the Oedipal hypothesis 'explained so much in his complex and often tortured personality'.[3]

Bronislaw Malinowski's earliest years in Poland left few detectable traces. To employ his own distinctions in the phases of a child's development as 'defined by biological and sociological criteria',[4] almost nothing is known about his infancy (from birth to weaning) or his babyhood (until roughly the age of six). Of the third stage, his childhood ('the attainment of rela-tive independence . . . the beginning of schooling'), something can be recovered from school records and his own autobiographical notes. Con-cerning adolescence (the last phase, 'between physiological puberty and full social maturity . . . the time of secondary and higher schooling') there are some useful fragments: a handful of official documents (the bulk of the family papers was destroyed in 1915 by rampaging soldiers and vengeful peasants), a few published reminiscences from others now long deceased, a score of letters, the occasional recollection in his own published writings and the rare, incandescent memory-burst in his personal diaries.

A noble ethos

Malinowski was proud of his noble ancestry. To the supremely class-conscious British he often claimed to be an aristocrat ('with his Polish aristocratic background, he prided himself on his good horsemanship', wrote his pupil Hilda Beemer Kuper, recalling his visit to Swaziland[5]). His pride in origins sometimes manifested itself as snobbery, sometimes as arrogance and condescension, and sometimes as disdain if not contempt for servants, peasants and other members of the 'lower orders'. Strictly speaking, however, he was not a Polish aristocrat but a member of the richly assorted class of nobility and landed gentry called *szlachta*.

Like many members of the *szlachta* Malinowski could rightly claim to belong to a named clan or heraldic line. The intricate coat of arms of the clan Poróg-Malinowski that graces the armorial manuals was probably a late elaboration of an originally simple crest based on equestrian symbols. It consists of a blue shield emblazoned with a silver horseshoe, surmounted by a golden Maltese cross; there is a helmet on top of the shield and a golden coronet on top of that. The crest that rises above the coronet is a cartoon-like profile of a dog's head between two buffalo horns.[6] Malinowski had a simplified version of the same coronet (minus the dog and horns) embossed on his visiting card, its five prongs topped by three flowers and what appear to be two ripe poppy seeds. This crest served as his 'blazon of exile'.[7]

Polish social hierarchy is complex and deeply rooted in the feudal past. The pre-feudal clan, each with its own battle cry and heraldic device, preceded the emergence of the Piast Polska kingdom in the tenth century. Poróg, the title of Malinowski's clan and presumably the name of a founding ancestor, was one such battle cry.[8] During the half-millennium of Piast rule, the clans disappeared as social units but persisted to some extent in ideology, and knights and other nobles continued to call themselves by their ancient battle cries. As long as the Poróg lived in one region the use of Christian or nicknames would have been sufficient to identify individual members, though in documents the name of a village owned by a noble was commonly used. One of the Pobógs, let us say Bronisław, owned a village of serfs called Maliny (literally, 'Raspberry'). He would be identified as Bronisław of Maliny – not yet a proper name, but a designation that indicated the origin of the individual called Bronisław. This appellation later became a regular name as a result of internal migration. So a nobleman who moved from Maliny to a village called, say, Borowki was called Malinowski of Borowki ('Malinowski' being the adjectival form of Maliny). The phrase 'of Maliny' was finally dropped at the beginning of the nineteenth century and the adjectival form then persisted as a family name.[9]

It was the Republic of Nobles (1569–1795) that saw the rise to supremacy of the *szlachta*. This became the largest franchised class in Europe, comprising over 10 percent of the population. As well as their absolute control of the peasantry, they now governed the monarchy through parliamentary elections. The Polish nobility thus anticipated the English and American revolutions in bringing their kings and queens to heel. By the middle of the eighteenth century, however, enormous disparities of wealth and power had appeared among the *szlachta*: a majority of them owned a village or (like Malinowski's grandfather) a part of one, the middle nobility held several villages, and the most powerful nobles of all (rich barons like the Radziwiłłs and Zamoyskis) owned vast territories. As Polish society became ossified the republic fell into economic decline, inviting invasion. The first of three Partitions by the neighbouring kingdoms of Russia, Prussia and Austria occurred in 1772, followed by a second in 1793. Two years later, following an anti-Russian insurrection, came the final Partition which abolished the very state of Poland. The legal status of the *szlachta* was annulled by the new powers and nobles lost their political and economic privileges.

Despite the fall of the *szlachta* as a governing class, the 'noble ethos' lived on into the nineteenth century and beyond, and would have filtered into the consciousness of the young Malinowski. Under foreign rule the ex-nobility shared the burdens of oppression with the common people and persecution helped forge a new Polish national unity. Norman Davies writes:

In this way the ex-*szlachta* became the pioneers of the new intelligentsia; the former 'noble nation' was transformed and expanded to include all social classes of the new, universal Polish nation; and the *kultura szlachecka* – with its ideals of exclusivity, equality, unanimity, resistance, and individualism – continued to provide the guide-lines for Polish social and political thought. . . . Two hundred years after the abolition of the *szlachta* most people in Poland are content to think of themselves as honorary nobles.[10]

It is not too fanciful to see reflections of these noble ideals in the life and work of Bronislaw Malinowski. Equality underlay not only his belief in the essential unity of humanity (without which he could never have contemplated a career as an anthropologist), but also his treatment of women as equals – for, unusual in Europe until the twentieth century, *szlachta* women held property in their own right. His daughter Helena wrote that he 'expected women to be intellectually equal to men' and he gave her 'the gift of never feeling that women are inferior'.[11] Unanimity was a *szlachta* value that, joined to resistance and equality, informed Malinowski's endorsement of the concept of liberal democracy. It was a value fiercely opposed to absolutism and totalitarianism, both of which spelt slavery. 'Freedom is an indispensable ingredient of civilization' and 'The absence of political freedom destroys all other liberties' were among Malinowski's last published dicta.[12] Finally, Malinowski's anthropology enshrined individualism. His pragmatic functionalism boiled down to the biologically based needs of individuals. Abstract systems and structures held little charm for him, and theories that invoked a group mind or collective consciousness were anathema. Even misplaced concreteness in the use of standard anthropological terms could offend him: responding to a statement that 'the clan rears its offspring', he scoffed: 'Whoever heard of a clan wiping a baby's bottom!'

The emancipation of the peasantry caused the ruin of many nobles. Thousands abandoned the countryside and joined the new class of intelligentsia in the cities. Two failed rebellions against Russia (in 1830–31 and 1863–64) further impoverished the *szlachta*, and many who had retained estates saw them confiscated by the tsar. Malinowski's paternal grandfather was among those forced to leave the countryside and find work in the towns.[13]

It was to this social category of intelligentsia rather than to the gentry that Malinowski felt he owed allegiance. This was apt to be misunderstood by his British and American academic colleagues, for there was no corresponding category in Britain or the United States. The Polish *inteligien-*

cja (a term borrowed from the Russian) was defined by its self-conscious duty to treasure, protect and augment Polish culture.

Cracow could rightly claim to be the cultural capital of the divided nation. Between 1815 and 1846 it had been a free city, a nominally autonomous republic. It was then forcibly incorporated into the Austrian province of Galicia, the poorest of the three Partitions. Cracow was 'swallowed but not digested', as Swift once said of Poland as a whole. With the granting of internal autonomy to Galicia in 1868, however, Cracow could begin a cultural revival and again play host to subversive political movements. In addition to its excellent university – which celebrated its six-hundredth anniversary in 1900 – it could boast liberal newspapers, theatres, cabarets and busy coffee shops in which the city's intellectuals argued the evenings away. When Malinowski was of an age to join them, Cracow was a city of almost forty thousand people and a proud bastion of Polish culture.

Educating Lucjan

The Malinowskis were from the province of Lublin in eastern Poland. Juljan, Malinowski's grandfather, was born in 1816, the year after the establishment of the Russian-dominated Congress Kingdom of Poland. From his father (whose name is forgotten), Juljan had inherited part of the village and estate of Jaroszewice near the town of Bełżyce. The estate was confiscated following the November insurrection of 1830, though Bronislaw Malinowski hinted that its loss was also owing to mismanagement.

More is known about Juljan's mother's ancestors than about Malinowski's paternal line. Juljan's maternal grandmother's family traced descent from Stanisław Koźmian in the late seventeenth century. The Koźmians belonged to the upper tier of the landed gentry (referred to jokingly as 'one *szlachta* and a half') and became active in the political and cultural life of Poland in the eighteenth century.[14] Malinowski's grandfather married Ewa, née Górska, the granddaughter of a Koźmian. Despite this noble connection, Juljan became impoverished following the loss of his estate and was obliged to become a civil servant.

Born of this family at Jaroszewice on 16 July 1839, Lucjan Feliks Jan Malinowski was their first child. Juljan and Ewa also had a daughter, Helena (who died young), and another son, Alfons Alfred, who was born in 1850. After schooling in Lublin, Alfons studied medicine and practised as a doctor in Warsaw, where according to one account he became director of a children's hospital. Although he married, Alfons fathered no children and, as Lucjan had only one child, Bronislaw was to become the sole descendant of the Malinowski line. Alfons and his elder brother do not appear to have been particularly close. In addition to the eleven-year age difference between them, they pursued different careers and dwelt for most of their lives in different parts of the divided country. Malinowski probably saw little of his paternal uncle, but he remembered him fondly as a man 'with the most brilliant intellect, beautiful character and most aristocratic manners, but no will power'.[15] When Alfons died in 1918 he left his nephew 3,000 roubles (then worth about £300) and two-thirds of his remaining estate, to be inherited after the death of his wife. Malinowski calculated the latter to be worth about £6,000, a small fortune; but in 1927, when his aunt finally died, inflation had reduced the value of the inheritance and Malinowski (already established in London by that time) relinquished it in favour of his aunt's sisters in Poland.[16]

Lucjan Malinowski, Bronislaw's father, was taught at home before attending primary school in Tomaszów.[17] In 1852 he entered a gymnasium in Lublin, but had to interrupt his studies after two years because his father could no longer afford the fees. During the next four years Lucjan earned his own living: first as a scribe for the local town council, then as a minor civil servant, and finally as a tutor to the sons of a local dignitary. Having saved enough money to resume his studies at the Lublin gymnasium, Lucjan spent three more years there, leaving in 1861 with top marks in every subject. Thus he became independent of his father at an early age and financed his own schooling. His obituarist makes no further mention of the impoverished parents, the implication being that from the age of fifteen Lucjan made his own decisions.

Although his was a generation of social revolutionaries and Poles were to be found on every barricade in Europe, Lucjan Malinowski appears to have kept his head well down. His attendance in 1862 at the recently opened Szkoła Główna (Main School) in Warsaw was timely, for it was in existence for only seven years. The January Rising of 1863–64 was suppressed by the tsar's army and was followed, as usual, by executions and deportations. Among the thousands of Poles sent to Siberia during the early 1860s were Apollo Korzeniowski with his wife and their son Józef (later known as Joseph Conrad), and the family of Stanisław Witkiewicz, the father of Staś, Malinowski's best friend. The façade of the Congress Kingdom was dismantled, and the Partition forcibly reunited with the Russian Empire. During this terrible time of unrest, Lucjan's tactic 'was to concentrate on his studies and to try to dissuade others from getting involved with extremist trends'.[18]

Whether he liked it or not, however, his academic career was intimately bound up with the imaginary nation's fortunes. Since Partition, the preservation of Polish culture had been an important plank of political strategy. Norman Davies puts it pithily: 'Culture became the invisible nation's greatest treasure and last line of defence.'[19] Education had been the chief concession won by the Sejm parliament when it was forced to sign the Partition treaties in 1773, and it remained at the forefront of national concern. 'Polish culture, Polish educational enterprise, and the Polish intelligentsia survived, bruised but intact, from the Partitions to the "explosion" of Independence in 1918.'[20] Davies likens the transmission of educational institutions during this period to a relay race, in which each runner carried the torch of learning for a brief stage before handing it on. Always under threat of closure by the reigning authorities, the schools and universities rose and fell in tempo with the insurrections, suppressions and persecutions.

In 1862 it was the Szkoła Główna in Warsaw that emerged to carry the torch for a brief but brilliant period, until the Jagiellonian University was re-Polonized following the granting of autonomy to Galicia in 1868. The Galicians then carried the torch for the next forty years, a period that covers Malinowski's own education in Cracow. Just as Malinowski might have considered himself fortunate to have been born in Cracow at a time when it could boast the best and most liberal educational institutions in Poland, so his father had been lucky enough to attend Warsaw's Szkoła Główna. Lucjan graduated from the historical-philological faculty in 1867 with a master's degree. Two years later the school was closed by the Muscovite authorities and converted into a Russian university, but during its short existence the Szkoła Główna educated many of Poland's best minds.[21]

On graduating, Lucjan secured a grant to continue his studies in philology. First he spent a year in Germany at the universities of Jena and Berlin, where he learned the principles of linguistics and comparative grammar; next he spent a couple of years at the universities of St Petersburg and Moscow, where he studied Slavonic philology and early Slav Church palaeography. Encouraged to study Polish dialects, Lucjan spent the summer of 1869 in Silesia visiting sixty localities. This field trip enabled him to gather a great deal of linguistic material, including folklore, legends and songs, many of which remained unpublished at the time of his death. Lucjan described some of his experiences – covering a period of just twelve days – in the form of an ethnographic diary, which he published in 1892 as 'Letters from an Ethnographical Journey to Silesia'.[22] As do many ethnographers, he discovered that his objectives, indeed his very presence, were apt to be misunderstood: 'the simple folk (and the police, too) just could not understand that he really was pursuing a line of research and was not a spy or a secret agent.'[23]

In 1870–72 Lucjan taught Polish literature and classical languages at the prestigious St Anne's Gymnasium in Cracow. The Germanic-Latin curriculum followed a German model under Germanic-type discipline, but by this time it was no longer taught in the German language. By an extraordinary coincidence that would have delighted Malinowski, it seems that Lucjan's brief period at St Anne's coincided with the equally brief attendance of a twelve-year-old boy who would become Joseph Conrad.[24]

Impatient to resume his academic career, in the spring of 1872, Lucjan left for Leipzig University where he took courses in philology and comparative grammar. (Five years earlier Friedrich Nietzsche had also studied philology at Leipzig.) Lucjan quickly completed a doctoral dissertation based on his field research into Silesian dialects. Although only fifty-five pages in length, in the judgment of his obituarist it was 'an epoch-making achievement' that 'set up a model of how results should be presented' and 'initiated a scientific approach to Polish dialectology'.[25] In short, Lucjan broke new ground in methodology. The ancient pattern of peripatetic learning that Lucjan Malinowski followed in the years 1867–72 was common in a nation centred at the crossroads of Europe, and the Polish education authorities sensibly encouraged it. A generation later, his son would pursue his post-doctoral education in similar fashion, even to the extent of studying at Leipzig.

Lucjan returned to Warsaw in August 1872 to take up a new appointment at the so-called Third Gymnasium, where he taught classical languages for five years. As a teacher 'he was extremely popular and evolved a method of teaching which kept his pupils interested and keen – he never gave them homework, but went over and over the lessons with them in class, drawing every pupil into discussion and questions'.[26] This description could almost serve for the Socratic method Malinowski practised on his pupils at the London School of Economics many years later.

By the age of thirty-eight, Lucjan had achieved academic distinction and was appointed to the chair of Slavonic philology at the Jagiellonian University, a position he held until his death. In his personal file in the university archives is a formal reference from the director of the Warsaw gymnasium. It reads more like a police report, stating in bald and curiously negative terms that Lucjan Malinowski held no property, possessed no orders or decorations (though later he would be made a Knight of the Order of St Stanisław), and that he was a bachelor. His political record was clean. Concerning his occupation, he had 'never been dismissed from service', nor did he ever 'outstay his leave of absence'.[27]

During the next two decades Lucjan consolidated his academic career: teaching, examining, publishing, serving on various committees of the university and the Academy of Sciences and Arts (to which he was elected in 1880), and acting as dean of the university's faculty of philosophy – a position about which he was ambivalent. 'I cherish the position and dull responsibilities of a dean,' he told his Czech friend Jarosław Goll.[28] He had met Goll, a poet and professor of history at Charles University, during a visit to Prague in 1880.

With 'great clarity of exposition', Lucjan lectured on Polish grammar and on the Old Slavonic, Russian, Czech, Serbian and Lithuanian languages. His linguistic seminars, the first in Poland, were devoted to the analysis of texts, as presented by students in the dialects of their districts of origin. He also conducted seminars on palaeography, for one of his pet projects was the compilation of a Polish dictionary that would include vocabulary from the fourteenth to the sixteenth centuries. Lucjan trained many pupils who also became distinguished linguists, the most eminent being Jan Bystroń and Kazimierz Nitsch.[29] The latter was especially close to Lucjan, and he eventually succeeded to his Jagiellonian chair. Nitsch was also one of Malinowski's personal tutors, for whom he developed a lasting affection.

A brilliant linguist and diligent ethnographer, then, who made observations on all aspects of rural life, Lucjan Malinowski was something of a pioneer who eventually earned the accolade of 'founder of Polish dialectology'.[30] His field research in Silesia and subsequent work on folklore and dialectology coincided with the stirrings of the Young Poland movement of cultural revitalization and was given impetus by a surging interest in Slavonic origins. Whether wittingly or not, Lucjan catered to a felt need for Polish scholarship. Nationalism might be better served through this means than by the revolutionary political activism that had so disastrously failed earlier in the century.

In 1911, Lucjan's son, who was then at the University of London, reviewed a Polish work on comparative Slavonic folklore for the English journal *Folk-lore*. After briefly surveying the field (and pointing to a convergence between folklore and ethnology as 'comparative sciences'), Malinowski sketched the history of systematic folklore studies in Poland, beginning in 1802. On reaching the last decades of the century, he listed researchers from Warsaw, Cracow and Leopol (Lwów); and there under Cracow, alongside the names of two of his pupils, is 'Prof. L. Malinowski'.[31] This modest mention of his father's work is the only one that Bronislaw Malinowski ever made in print.

'A double life'

In a tantalizingly brief and incomplete sketch for an unidentified biographical purpose, Malinowski noted:

> Brought up in R.C. faith & owing to early illness, in Tatry Mountains age fr. 4–10. From child[hood] Polish, French, & and their dialects. A double life, at least. . . . Mixed with the mountaineers, speaking their gwara (dialect) looking after sheep & cows, running away for days, learnt fairy tales, legends of good old days of banditry.[32]

This romantic memory of a childhood spent in the Tatras – the spectacular alpine region south of Zakopane – adopting the life and language of the Carpathian 'mountaineers', or Górale, is corroborated in part by Lucjan's letters to Jarosław Goll. Another autobiographical sketch survives, handwritten and telegraphic in format, but probably the most detailed one Malinowski ever made. It is embedded in a comprehensive, seven-page synopsis of an introduction to a textbook that he had been invited to write by an American publisher in the early 1930s. One of its working titles was 'The A.B.C. of Culture: A Text-Book of Comparative Anthropology and Sociology'. In outlining his Introduction, Malinowski proposed to include three sections devoted to his own experiences. The first was to be entitled 'Culture as Personal Experience', the second 'Living a Culture versus Studying It' and the third 'Cultural Reality in Fieldwork'. Under the first heading he offers an impressionistic account of his childhood; to be more precise, he evokes those experiences he judged to be relevant to his later career as an anthropologist. Within the space of a couple of dense and cryptic foolscap pages there are more clues to Malinowski's experience of childhood than in any other source.[33] What follows is an edited version of his telegraphic notes.

'Ponice idyll,' he began, referring to a village of several hamlets near Rabka, in the Beskidy region south of Cracow.[34]

As a child, between the ages of four and eight, I lived intermittently in a secluded Carpathian village among the peasantry. It was an Arcadian valley. My memories are vague, but my mother helped me to recover them. . . . I remember my contemporaries telling 'fairy tales' about stone houses and stone churches with stone steeples; there was a mythology about paved roads and carriages. . . . That urban world was familiar to me, but unknown to my friends. It was my first experience of duality, of the multiplicity of the world of culture. . . . The hamlets comprised a dozen houses and a wooden church; the priest led his flock in the worship of a local saint. Family life was simple, honest, rude. On Sundays family councils convened at which difficult matters – rows and problems to do with sex – were solved by patriarchal deliberations under the old pear tree. There was a public house kept by a memorable Jew, the only vil- lager in touch with the outer world. Gendarmes visited periodically, but their appearance was regarded as a calamity. . . . The local economy was potatoes, oats and sheep. . . . How strange it is now that there seemed to be no money! A vanished world!

He contrasted this rural idyll with his other life:

When I was eight we returned more or less permanently to the town, though I also stayed on the country estates owned by my mother's father, brothers and sisters. In Cracow we lived in an old stone building, a prop- erty of the University. It was a shabby-genteel existence, withal a truly cultured world not without dignity and heroism (see J. Conrad's recol- lections).[35] We belonged to the dispossessed, impoverished small Polish nobility, shading into the *inteligiencja*. . . . Family tradition linked us with Warsaw and Paris; we spoke and read French . . . and hankered after things French. This was a third cultural medium for me. France seemed a Promised Land, but it was a false and unreal Gallicism.

Summarizing his two worlds of rough peasant hamlet and genteel *szlachta* town, he wrote:

By the time I was eight I had lived in two fully distinct cultural worlds, speaking two languages, eating two different kinds of food, using two sets of table manners, observing two sets of reticencies and delicacies, enjoying two sets of amusements. I also learned two sets of religious views, beliefs and practices, and was exposed to two sets of morality and sexual mores (see *Sex and Repression* [sic]).[36]

Malinowski then generalized his earliest experiences of cultural diversity. He was evidently seeking to formulate, for the didactic purposes of his book, how he acquired a predilection for the study of anthropology:

As a child I was surrounded by racial and cultural differences. They formed part of the background of my earliest experiences. There were the lowland peasants of the plains, an inferior 'caste' of *chłopi* [peasants] described in the works of [Władysław] Reymont, and there were the Carpathian mountaineers, the Górale. There were also Jews and Russians and Austrian Germans. . . . The Jews were always on the social horizon with their different religious and occupational character. They looked different. They wore 'corkscrews' and long gabardines. They also smelled differently, of garlic, onions, goose and goat, and they were afflicted with scabies. . . . But every child brought up within a national minority in the U.S.A. must have had experiences similar to mine: living at home within a transported, migrant culture and at school in the American culture.

We need not quibble here over Malinowski's facts (he was apparently in Rabka only between the ages of two and five), or quarrel with his lightly theorized description of what today would be called multiculturalism. What matters is his overall perception of the elements that constituted his childhood experiences. For we should view these memories through the theoretical lens of his own teaching, that accounts of the past are invariably constructed to serve the present. In this light, looking back in his late forties, he assembled selective childhood memories into a pattern that explained and 'legitimated' his calling as an anthropologist. The other two sections of his proposed introduction to the textbook accomplish this in an even more obvious way, for in them he describes the beginnings of his anthropological career and his first experiences of fieldwork. In other words, these sketchy memoirs are part and parcel of the charter myth that created the heroic ethnographer of British social anthropology.

Evading father's gaze

There is a lacuna in these accounts, one revealing of Malinowski's strategy of self-construction. It is the omission of any mention of his father. There is, in fact, just one parenthetical reference to him, buried in the last page of his synoptic notes. Malinowski reprises Górale family life as characterized by 'cohesion, strength, devotion, reliance' and 'the patriarchal obedience of children'. To this he appended a subversive comment that speaks volumes: 'I knew that I could evade [the] eye of my father.' If Malinowski knowingly suppressed any mention of his father, then the implication is clear. Dare one say what Malinowski appeared to deny by his silence on the matter: that he followed in his father's footsteps by becoming a methodologically astute, linguistically alert, text-gathering, fieldworking ethnographer? His genius lay precisely in his remarkable linguistic aptitude allied to the equally remarkable range and acuity of his ethnographic observation, talents that he creatively united in a fruitful theoretical vision for a scientific anthropology. It must surely have occurred to him that he had inherited his father's abilities. For the sake of his self-serving myth of the Great Ethnographer, however, 'following in father's footsteps' was a less than compelling narrative theme. It not only lacked dramatic impact, it denied the premise of self-creation.

A portrait of Lucjan Malinowski hangs in the Jagiellonian University. The painting reveals a square-faced man of fifty, conventionally jacketed in black, with a full moustache and a straggling white beard, fashionably forked.[37] What was this stolid-looking paterfamilias like as a person?

In all the personal diaries Malinowski kept – covering ten years and amounting to several hundred pages – he refers to his father only once, on the last page of the last diary. Even then Lucjan was recalled to his son's memory only by the painful image of his dead mother: 'All the tender feelings of my childhood come back: I feel as when I had left Mother for a few days, returning from Zwierzyniec with Father.'[38] Similarly, in the immense correspondence between Malinowski and Elsie Masson, only twice does he refer directly to his father: once in relation to his mother and once in relation to his eldest daughter. On the first occasion, significantly, it is his mother's loss of her husband rather then his own loss of a father that he recalls.[39] All the intimate sources testify to Malinowski's enduring love for his mother; regarding his father they are silent, evasive or frank about his dislike of him.

Audrey Richards (pupil, colleague and staunch friend of the family) told Malinowski's youngest daughter, Helena, that her father 'often and forcibly disparaged Lucjan to her, saying he was stern, distant and did not try to understand his son'.[40] Helena herself remarks that her father 'felt much closer to his mother's family than to the Malinowskis, as indeed he felt incomparably closer to his mother than to his father'. The absence of the father from the son's life was amplified in the following generation: 'I really don't remember hearing anything about my Polish grandfather when I was a child . . . whereas our Polish grandmother was a real "presence" to us children.' The Malinowski daughters remember their father telling them that his father never played with him as a boy. An aloof figure, then, one might surmise that Lucjan was strict and staid, humourless if not dour, preoccupied with his career and *dignitas*. But his letters to Jarosław Goll reveal a more human personality: a man who is anxious, weary and lonely, yet not without a mordant sense of humour and a full measure of paternal pride, concern and deep affection for his only son.

Let us accept the invitation in Malinowski's autobiographical notes to consult *Sex and Repression in Savage Society*, the polemical work he wrote in the early 1920s to challenge Freudian doctrine concerning the universality of the Oedipus Complex. We find in this book a caricature of a Polish father behind which may well lurk the cool, remote and authoritative parent that he knew:

> In the wealthy classes of Western civilization, the child is well separated from his father by all sorts of nursery arrangements. Although constantly with the nurse, the child is usually attended to and controlled by the mother, who, in such cases, almost invariably takes the dominant place in the child's affections.[41]

Although the Malinowskis could not afford a nurse, there is some autobiographical colouring to this picture, and probably even more in the additional touches:

> The father, on the other hand, is seldom brought within the child's horizon, and then only as an onlooker and stranger, before who [sic] the children have to behave themselves, show off and perform. He is the source of authority, the origin of punishment, and therefore becomes a bogey. Usually the result is a mixture; he is the perfect being for whose

benefit everything has to be done; and, at the same time, he is the 'ogre' who the child has to fear and for whose comfort, as the child soon realizes, the household is arranged. The loving, sympathetic father will easily assume the former role of a demi-god. The pompous, wooden, or tactless one will soon earn the suspicion and even hate of the nursery.[42]

Malinowski was inclined to see his own father in the second of these guises: pompous, wooden, tactless. In a lighter vein, in a later article he contrasted the impunity with which his youngest daughter called him an 'ass' with the punishment he would have received had he spoken thus to his own father.[43] The point was a general one ('times have changed'), but it bears an autobiographical impress. He proposed that the father in America and Britain was 'in process of losing his patriarchal position' which would lead to the obliteration of the Oedipus Complex. Future generations, he conjectured facetiously, 'will only know a weak and henpecked father. For him the children will feel indulgent pity rather than hatred and fear.'[44]

Malinowski continues sketching his picture in *Sex and Repression*, attending now to the later stage of a son's development:

> The father sees in the son a successor, the one who is to replace him. ... He becomes therefore all the more critical, and this influences his feelings in two directions: if the boy shows signs of mental or physical deficiency, if he is not up to the type of the ideal in which the father believes, he will be a source of bitter disappointment and hostility. On the other hand, even at this stage, a certain amount of rivalry, the resentment of future supersession, and the melancholy of the waning generation lead again to hostility. Repressed in both cases, this hostility hardens the father against the son and provokes by reaction a response in hostile feelings.[45]

While this statement may be taken to be a gloss on orthodox psychoanalytical doctrine, it does not directly cite Freud. In view of Malinowski's authorship, then, one might suppose that he is drawing on his own experience, perhaps in imagining that his father had been disappointed in him because of his sickly constitution. But he is also extrapolating beyond his own experience, for his father died before the postulated appearance of that 'resentment' and 'melancholy', and, indeed, before his son was old enough to be regarded as a rival or a threat.

Given the boy's perception of a distant and 'wooden' father, one might also surmise that Malinowski had difficulties with the role of fatherhood himself. He had no sons, however, and he believed that, in principle, there were fewer grounds for paternal conflict with daughters: 'The father's feeling towards the daughter – a repetition of himself in feminine form – hardly fails to evoke a tender emotion, and perhaps also to flatter his vanity.'[46] But he cannily acknowledged that his father's treatment of him influenced his own behaviour towards his three daughters. With respect to nine-year-old Józefa, the eldest, he told his wife: 'At times I catch myself in moments of paternal gaucherie which remind me of my father's rather unfortunate treatment of myself and then I try to unstiffen and above all to drop that surface touchiness.'[47] For their part, his daughters are unanimous in their claim to have been far, far closer to their mother than they were to him, somewhat undermining his theoretical deduction that 'the father cling[s] more tenderly to the daughter than to the son, while with the mother it is the reverse'.[48] His daughters blame him not so much for neglect or indifference – he loved and cared for them as best he could, and they agree that he could be tremendous fun – but for his frequent absences during their childhood and later for his persistent irritability and periodic withdrawal into brooding secrecy. Like father, like son – as he grew older he became more like the Lucjan he remembered.

One might also imagine that Malinowski sought fatherly qualities in certain older men. Warmly sympathetic father-figures did indeed appear at crucial moments of his career, when he was in need of material help, intellectual encouragement and academic patronage. He was good at ingratiating himself with such paternal surrogates – the Rev. Stefan Pawlicki, Sir James Frazer, Edward Westermarck, Alfred Haddon, Charles Seligman, the list is long – and there was something manipulative about his cultivation of their friendship. But it is also true that he allowed such friendships to ripen, and he continued to enjoy his relationships with many such men long after they had ceased to provide him with fatherly support. Conversely, he could vehemently disagree with them, in some instances to the point of poisoning the relationship. The archaic Freudian plot of father-slaying is discernible in Malinowski's career no less than in his psyche.[49] Should this seem a rash judgment, there is all the evidence one might wish that Malinowski himself toyed with a starkly Freudian reading of his Oedipal impulses.

Oedipus sighted

In an unpublished footnote questioning the phenomenon of repression that he drafted for *Sex and Repression* Malinowski 'confessed' to his notepad:

> Re Oedipus Complex. Reason why I adopted it. Incest dreams very fre-
> quently & very distressing. A large circle of friends − mind you in a
> country where [there is] far less repression. Direct incest interests. . . .
> Father hatred. Strong attachment to M[other] − inferiority to father.
> Death wishes. F. speaks about his death. Desire. Dreams of his death.
> Aft[er] death very strong conscience. Further back. Attachment to
> mother. Desire to go to bed. Same dreadful feeling when [I] leave [her]
> as when violently in love etc. Not repressed. Composed out of elements
> very distinct in memory.[50]

Could any biographer, even one sceptical of Freud's brand of psychological determinism, expect more? The classic syndrome is complete: father-
hatred, incestuous desire for mother, feelings of inferiority with respect to
father, guilt over father's early death, separation anxiety associated with
mother. Yet Malinowski is at pains to point out that none of this inflam-
matory psychic 'material' was repressed − he had actually begun the note
by chiding leading psychoanalysts, Freud included, for their lack of moral
courage in failing to admit publicly to their own deep, dark desires. In the
interrupted thought about his 'large circle of friends' he was probably
remembering how, in contrast to their Viennese cousins, the Polish acquaintances of his youth were open and frank about such matters. By the same
token, however, we cannot attribute to repression Malinowski's silence
about his father in his personal diaries. And in the light of his Freudian confession (even if it was only to himself), the almost total omission of the
father from the son's personal history cannot be taken to mean that
Malinowski had terrible memories to hide. Rather, Lucjan was deemed an
irrelevance and simply forgotten. Metaphorically speaking, this particular
Oedipus did not put out his own eyes.

Or did he? Freudians would doubtless spin their double-headed penny
and say that denial of repression is simply evidence of a deeper repression;
that the 'distressing' memories Malinowski is offering as proof of his lack of
repression are in fact 'screen' memories that conceal something worse. The
proof of this lies in the phenomenon called 'the return of the repressed'.

Is it not a curious fact that in a salient strand of his anthropology Malinowski appears to have directed keen attention to paternity in the abstract, away from his own 'dead, yet flesh-and-bone' father? Having made strident claims that 'primitives' were ignorant of biological paternity, he wrote social fatherhood (indeed, writ it large as a 'principle of legitimacy') into his kinship theory. He became an international authority on sexuality, wrote articles on kinship and marriage for the *Encyclopaedia Britannica*, and contributed greatly to the cross-cultural study of parenthood and the family. Can we detect in this theoretical preoccupation with the anthropology of the family (in which fatherhood is notoriously ambiguous and ambivalent if not actually denied) a Freudian nod in the direction of massively repressed memories concerning his own father? At the very least, we may suppose that such powerful and troubling feelings recalled by Malinowski stirred and spurred him into obliterating his father's footsteps even as he trod in them. Here was a man who made of ethnographic fieldwork a new art (and a new scientific fetish), a man whose mastery of spoken vernaculars allowed him to contribute significantly to linguistic theory. In both endeavours the son outshone the father.

Earlier, I outlined Lucjan Malinowski's academic career in order to establish two things. First, that while it conformed to the general pattern of his age he made the most of some unusual opportunities; second, that it undoubtedly set a model for his son to emulate. Malinowski's implicit denial of this was abetted by an obfuscation made possible by his voluntary exile. Had he remained in Poland he would not have been allowed to forget that he was his father's son, even to the extent of 'succeeding' to a professorship at the Jagiellonian University. When Malinowski declined a chair of ethnology created for him in 1922, one of his reasons could well have been that he did not want to be seen to be following so closely in Lucjan Malinowski's imposing footsteps. To change the metaphor, he could best evade that paternal gaze by staying well out of sight.

The parallels between the lives of father and son that the latter was keen to deny extend to the manner and timing of their deaths. Both men died in their fifty-eighth year. The *Polish Biographical Dictionary* passed clinical judgment on Lucjan: 'Hard work in the different fields in which he was involved was the cause of the early ruin of his organism and his heart disease.'[51] Just forty-four years later this would also serve as a diagnosis for his son.

Chapter 2

Mother Love

Maternal origins

'I am happy!' Lucjan Malinowski announced to Jarosław Goll at the beginning of July 1882. 'For a week I have been engaged to the most perfect of all Polish women – one I have loved for sixteen years. Her name is Józefa Łącka.'[1] If he had met her as early as 1866, it must have been while Lucjan was a student at the Szkoła Główna. Obviously, he had been in no hurry to declare himself during the subsequent years of study abroad and teaching in Cracow. Then he rediscovered the charms of Warsaw: 'There are salons, hospitality, life. It is slightly frivolous, superficial, but as far as life is concerned even Parisians are impressed by Warsaw.'[2]

So it was six years after taking up his professorship at the Jagiellonian that, on 3 April 1883 in Warsaw, Lucjan married Józefa Eleonora Zenobia Łącka. He was forty-four; she was thirty-five. In June a bemused Lucjan told his Czech friend he was convinced that the calling of professor was no match for the duties of a married man: 'I haven't done anything for two months.'[3] The couple's only child was born in the parish of St Stephan in Cracow on 7 April 1884. He was christened Bronisław Kasper Malinowski, nicknamed Bronio or Bronek. Appropriately, his patron saint, St Bronisława, was female. Soon after his birth, Józefa took him to Warsaw for the entire summer and autumn while Lucjan remained in Cracow. Thus began a pattern of regular and lengthy separations from his father. When mother and infant returned to Cracow, Lucjan was pleased to see that Bronio already had his first tooth, less pleased to observe that he appeared to have been spoiled by his mother's family. 'He is a house tyrant, who, if brought up in that way any more, would grow into a great scamp.'[4]

Józefa came from a large and well-to-do family that still retained property. The Łąckis were *szlachta* gentry, less *déclassé* than the landless and comparatively impoverished Malinowskis. It would therefore be truer to say that Bronislaw Malinowski was born into his mother's large family rather than into his father's, which by this time consisted only of the two brothers. Józefa was born in 1848, the second child of Leopold Łącki and Eleonora Łącka, who were actually – though apparently not scandalously – blood relatives. Leopold (1801–71), Malinowski's maternal grandfather, held respectably high government office, initially as counsellor to the attorney general of the Kingdom of Poland, later as state counsellor and member of the senate.[5] Eleonora (1821–1904) was Leopold's second wife. His first had died after having borne eight children, all of whom, astonishingly, had also died. So it must have been with remarkable resilience – the triumph of hope over experience – that Leopold Łącki remarried. Perhaps it was excessive caution (as well as great courage) that led him to choose as his second wife his own niece, the daughter of his elder brother, Jan Ignacy Łącki (1786–1855).

Jan, a government official, and his wife, Magdalena Katarzyna Monfrell, had four daughters. Julia (1818–1903) married Leoncjusz Landié, a banker. It was Eleonora (1821–1904), the second daughter, who married her uncle Leopold. The third daughter, Aniela, did not marry, devoting much of her life to caring for the father of a fiancé who never returned from Siberian exile. The youngest daughter, Paulina (1829–1909), married Karol Stanisław Dunin-Szpotański, an official of the insurance commission in Warsaw. Between them, the three married daughters produced twelve children, seven females and five males, and in the next generation there were sixteen, eight of each sex, who were, of course, Malinowski's first and second cousins. There can be no doubt that Malinowski's maternal relatives provided a large and nourishing network that compensated for the dearth of paternal kin.

A family historian, Adam Dubowski (great-grandson of Paulina Łącka and Karol Szpotański), has drawn up a six-generation genealogy with a marked matrilineal bias – as if he too were more interested in his mother's line than his father's. The implication is that the women descended from ancestor Jan Ignacy Łącki were of higher social standing than the men who married them – though all could claim to be *szlachta*. The matrilineal tendency of the three original daughters' families (the Landiés, Łąckis and Szpotańskis) was reinforced by the Łącki brother who married his own niece. This tilt towards matriliny is perhaps also an artifact of demography, since in four generations the daughters reproduced more readily than their brothers. Malinowski's mother bucked the wider family trend by having only one child, and a boy at that. But in Malinowski's own generation seven of his eight female cousins reproduced, whereas only three of his seven male cousins did so. Malinowski himself exemplified the family tradition by fathering three daughters. In the sixth generation (that of Malinowski's grandchildren), the trend was finally reversed with the birth of fourteen females to twenty-five males. By this time, of course, the three matrifocal families had become widely dispersed, and today their members can be found in California, New York, England, Switzerland and Germany, as well as in various towns and cities in Poland.

Norman Davies alludes to a developing tradition of 'strong-minded' Polish noblewomen in the era of the Partitions, when the menfolk were obliged to work and fight for the foreign emperors who ruled them. Such women, equal to men under the law with respect to property and there-fore secure in their inheritance, were 'the mothers and grandmothers who brought up the children at home, who proved to be the guardians of the nation's most precious property – its culture'.[6] There seems to have been something of this tradition of strong-minded, culture-bearing women among the noble families of the Landiés, the Łąckis and the Szpotańskis. Certainly, Malinowski's own mother was one. Although there is no evidence of soldiering in her family, grandfather Jan and father Leopold were in 'foreign service' to the tsar, for the government they served in Warsaw was a puppet regime. It does not impugn their patriotism as Poles to point out that they and their descendants somehow managed to retain some of their land and avoid Russian persecution during the nineteenth century. Perhaps, like Lucjan Malinowski, they kept their heads down.

Eleonora had married her father's brother in 1847; he was twenty years her senior and predeceased her by more than thirty years. There were five children of this marriage. The eldest, Bronisław (1847–1908), became the owner of a cardboard factory; he married Józefa Wolf (1862–1930) and they had two daughters, Eugenia (Genia) and Maria (Mania). Cousin Genia was exactly the same age as Bronio, and they played together as children; she married at eighteen and by the time Bronio was entering university she was pregnant with her first child. The second of Leopold and Eleonora's children was Józefa; how she was educated and what she did until she married Lucjan Malinowski are minor mysteries. Her sister Eleonora (1850–1924), their mother's namesake, was the third child. She married a lawyer, Władysław

Staszewski, and their three childen were all born within a few years of Malinowski. Zygmunt (who died in 1912), Stefania (later Wolska) and Marja (later Kobylińska) were Bronio's other first cousins. Marja, or 'Cousin Mancia', was his favourite, and she wrote many affectionate letters to him during the 1920s until she became disheartened by his infrequent replies.

Józefa's younger brother was Kazimierz (1857–1920), the 'Uncle Kaź' of Malinowski's diaries, though there was another Uncle Kazimierz (Szpotański), who worked in the Bank of Poland, and *his* son, Kazimierz-Tadeusz, who was three years younger than Malinowski. Uncle Kaź, Malinowski's mother's brother, had graduated from Riga polytechnic in chemical engineering. He never married and what he did for a living is uncertain, though he embarked upon some 'silly industrial enterprise' (in Bronio's phrase) which led to bankruptcy in 1912 and cost his sister Józefa dearly.

Malinowski's early childhood was thus surrounded and supervised by numerous maternal kin. He had one living grandmother and her three sisters; a mother and her sister and two brothers; his mother's seven cousins; his own five first cousins and ten second cousins. The sense of being an only child must have been diluted by the awareness of so many relatives, though most of them lived in the Warsaw region and he would not have seen them very often. Of all these maternal relatives none left Poland except on short visits, yet none is so well known in their homeland as Bronislaw Malinowski, who spent more than half his life abroad.

Childhood

Józefa Malinowska's granddaughter Helena describes Józefa as 'a woman of outstanding intellect, great determination and utter devotion to her gifted son'.[7] She was undoubtedly a cultivated woman who had been soundly educated, perhaps at home, perhaps at a convent boarding school.[8] Her second language was French, as it was for most educated Poles of the nineteenth century (recalling her son's charge of 'false Gallicism'). Józefa also spoke German and probably some Russian and Italian; she would have learned Spanish during the long period she spent with Bronio in the Canary Islands. Although she spoke only a little English, she learned to read it – as family legend has it – to help her son. A small notebook has survived in which she had transcribed, in an exquisite hand, excerpts from Spencer and

Gillen's *The Native Tribes of Central Australia* and Frazer's *The Golden Bough*.[9] This could only have been done for her son's benefit.

A photographic portrait of Józefa as a young woman shows her in a ruffle-fronted blouse with a high lace collar, above which a serious, wanly pretty face looks to one side. Her fashionable coiffure is complex: fair hair swept gently from the face and over the ears to fall below her neck in ringlets; atop her head is a thick braid. Her eyes are slightly hooded, limpid perhaps; her lips are full and cupid-bowed. Bronio inherited these lips, which his friend Stanisław Ignacy Witkiewicz described as 'like a strange fruit freshly cut open'.[10] Józefa fattened with age, 'wearing her grey hair back in a tight bun, but she kept her upright carriage and her face retained its good looks, the broad brow, penetrating eyes and large well-shaped mouth'.[11]

The only surviving source concerning Bronio's infancy and early child-hood is his father's letters to Jarosław Goll. We learn that his mother was unable to breast-feed him beyond two weeks, and thereafter he was fed by a series of wet nurses.[12] For his baptism, held in Cracow on 26 April 1885, a 'whole pack' of relatives from Warsaw came to stay with the Malinowskis in their small apartment at 12 Podwale Street. Lucjan flippantly described the ceremony. 'Now my son has decided to . . . assent to the truths of the Christian religion – with some reservations, however. When the priest asked him whether he renounced Satan and his ways, the boy without hesitation decisively answered: *ne* (n.b. in Czech!). My son is *Der Geist der stets verneint*, a trait inherited in part from his father.'[13] There is a hint of paternal pride in the joke that his tiny son was already endowed with 'a spirit that always says "no"'.

It soon became clear to his parents that Bronio's health was extremely delicate. At fourteen months he was 'so sick . . . there was almost no hope for him to live'. His mother took him to Zakopane for the summer, which 'proved to be miraculous' for his recovery.[14] At twenty-two months, Bronio could walk and talk and even make up rhymes.[15] Later that year, the child was stricken with 'dysentery', but he was 'cured by the air' of Zakopane and Rabka, where the family also spent the following summer.[16] Bronio fell sick again just after he turned four. 'He had a few fits or convulsions and is still very irritated, capricious.'[17] The doctors recommended 'absolute peace', so mother and son returned to the 'Ponice idyll' recalled in such detail by Malinowski some fifty years later. The pattern of separations, of evading his father's eye, was now well established.

'I am a poor man, a grass widower. I am keeping two houses,' lamented Lucjan in October 1888. After leaving Ponice his wife and son spent most of the year in Zakopane, with periods at 'Janiszów', the Łącki estate near Warsaw.[18] For the next few years, Lucjan joined them in Zakopane at Christmas, Easter and for the long summer vacation. 'My life is divided into two parts,' he wrote to Goll in July 1889: '1. living in Zakopane, and 2. longing for Zakopane, or rather for my family which is staying there.' It was an annual round of absences and reunions that Malinowski would replicate in his own marriage.

In 1889 Bronio was 'thriving', though his 'nerves' were so sensitive that Lucjan was reluctant to submit him to the discipline of learning. 'He is our only satisfaction,' he told Goll. 'We won't leave him a fortune, but we want to assure his health.'[19] Lucjan's own health was now precarious, and at the insistence of his wife he spent a month in Dr Chramiec's hydropathy clinic in Zakopane. He did not regret it, he told Goll after returning to his dreary Cracow routine. 'My nerves are calmer. Moreover, I still keep to their diet: only milk and water. No vodka, beer, coffee, tea do I take into my mouth. Sometimes I take a little wine. I write about this in such detail because it is a crucial issue for me.'[20]

Since his wife and son were now spending most of the year in Zakopane Lucjan decided to make a proper home there. The resort town's popularity had boomed in 1890 following its purchase by Count Zamoyski, Galicia's richest magnate. There was a fresh influx of visitors as casinos, hotels and new villas were built. Lucjan bought a 0.3 hectare plot on Chramcówki street and Józefa now had another excuse for staying in Zakopane: to supervise the building of a house.[21] She encountered many problems and construction was delayed for so long that Lucjan wryly proposed to name his villa 'Nuisance'.[22] By the time the eleven-room house was completed in June 1892 he had sunk 9,000 Austrian crowns into it.

Bronio had whooping cough in May, though it was perhaps for reasons of his own health that Lucjan decided to rent out his new house and travel with his son across the breadth of Poland and Prussia to the East Frisian island of Juist. Józefa joined them a few weeks later, having visited her ailing mother in Warsaw. Bronio was now eight years old, and this was perhaps the first lengthy period that he spent alone in his father's company. It must also have been his first sight of the sea and his first experience of life on a small island. Juist was 'a wonderful place for seabathing,' according to Lucjan, although he felt the 'awful boredom' of the resort.[23]

At the beginning of 1893 Bronio suffered another health crisis. It began with a sore throat and high temperature, followed a few days later by vomiting and acute stomach pains. Six doctors, 'internists and surgeons', debated his case. 'They wanted to do a laparotomy, but peritonitis had developed and that stopped them. The boy was lying as a corpse – ready for a coffin.' Then an abscess developed and the surgeons operated in order to drain it. Five weeks after the onset of his illness Bronio's condition began to improve, though he still had the draining tube in his belly. 'We had a hard time,' Lucjan told Goll, who had earlier lost a son of his own. 'Before and after the operation it was very close to catastrophe. . . . What we have passed through, my wife and I, you can understand!'[24]

By 1894, Lucjan was tired and frustrated. 'I have been a professor for seventeen years and I am weary of it,' he wrote to Goll, listing his burdensome duties. 'I have gathered [research] material for twenty years and do not know whether I will be able to publish it. This thought poisons my life.'[25] He was beginning to suffer from congestive heart failure and spent the following summer immobile in Juist. Back in Cracow he wrote to Goll: 'I am fifty-six, and the hope is rather small that the heart will regain the necessary energy, and when the heart stops working, everything stops.'[26] A few days later he wrote to say that his health had improved. But what kind of health is it, he asked bitterly, when you are told 'you can't drink this; you can't eat that; don't go upstairs, walk slowly, don't get excited, speak only a little, work only a little, avoid violent movements, don't carry heavy things, don't bend down. In a word: wrap yourself in cotton wool, have yourself stuffed and put in a glass case.'[27]

Because of the altitude of Zakopane, Lucjan was forbidden by his doctors to stay there for more than a few days at a time. The house in which he had planned to spend his retirement was now denied him. His heart disease entailed even longer separations. 'Is it strange to you that I am spending my vacations apart from my family?' he wrote to Goll in the summer of 1897. Zakopane was 'excellent' for his son, however, who had recently climbed Czerwony Wierch – a Tatry ridge of over 6,000 feet – with his cousin Zygmunt and a young teacher. 'The result: Zygmunt is ill, and Bronislaw is swearing that he will never again go to the mountains. For such boys of fifteen and thirteen years these climbs are too arduous.'[28] Lucjan's final letter to Goll mentioned his hopes for Bronio. 'My boy is very talented and I would like to make him a [professional] man, but children are in this world to achieve their own goals, not for their parents' comfort, ergo. . . .'[29] The note of sad resignation was prophetic. Lucjan died three months later, on 15 January 1898.

The 'old stone building' belonging to the Jagiellonian University in which the Malinowski family lived its 'shabby-genteel existence' is situated in the small market square of Mały Rynek; this lies immediately behind Rynek Główny, the spacious medieval market square of central Cracow. Number 8 Mały Rynek is a sturdy, empire-red building attached at one end to the fifteenth-century church of St Barbara. Today Malinowski's old home is a convent; then it was an 'academic dormitory' or hostel for impoverished students over which, from 1892, Lucjan presided as warden. Following his death, Józefa remained in the apartment as a 'house-mother' to the students. She had taken Bronio to Warsaw for the summer, and her family had urged her to stay. Bronio could study privately in Warsaw and return to Cracow to take his exams. Józefa was tempted, but decided that as long as she was still needed at the Mały Rynek dormitory she and her son would remain in Cracow.

Bronio recalled staying frequently at the country estates of his maternal kin. The one he visited most was 'Janiszów', near Warsaw, where his grand-mother Eleonora lived until she died in 1904. Thereafter it appears to have been occupied by the Staszewskis (Józefa's sister's family) and perhaps her unmarried brother, Uncle Kaź. In addition to the manor house and stables, there were cattle and a farmyard with pigsties and hen coops. From the remote world of the Trobriand Islands on Christmas Eve, 1917, Malinowski looked back nostalgically to Poland, where 24 December was 'the most festive day of the year'.

> In the evening, when the first star appears, we sit down to a meal – it is called the Vigil-meal – and it is a fast day: we eat only fish, but none the less it is always a very crack sort of supper. Then comes the Xmas tree, a spruce sapling [which] is always mysteriously lit (there are many small candles on it) by some parent or uncle and you enter the drawing room with *éblonissement* [dazzle] and with a feeling that something almost supernatural has happened. . . . I have some dim visions of such won-derful moments with my parents and my uncles about me. Then you go to the midnight mass, during which X-mas carrols [sic] are sung, and for the next few days there is a lot of eating, no school of course, and a happy time altogether.[30]

Bronio recalled his first love at the age of five. Dzinia (short for Jadwiga) was a girl of his own age, a daughter of Henryk Sienkiewicz, the Nobel laureate novelist.[31] Long before he found fame, Sienkiewicz was a school friend of Bronio's uncle Alfons and as an indigent student he used to live in grandfather Juljan's household. Another young love was Misia, the daughter of Józef Kallenbach, a philology pupil of Lucjan Malinowski. 'Your unfaithful child-fiancée,' Bronio's mother teased him in 1915 when, already married for some years, Misia gave birth.[32] As a boy, Bronio was evidently liked and admired by girls, and does not appear to have been shy. Janina Landié, his second cousin, remembered how he used to visit Warsaw for Easter. He usually stayed with her grandmother (Julia Landié, Józefa's mother's sister) but often called at the house of his widowed uncle Edward, whose daughter Janina was a year older than Bronio: 'I loved to chat with him. . . . I remember us reading together and discussing the works of Heine, whom we both admired. Bronek was full of enthusiasm and I cherish the memory of the hours we spent together in purely "intellectual" conversation.'[33] Another woman who remembered him as an adolescent was Zofia Krzyżanowska. Bronio used to practise the violin with her brother in their parents' apartment on Basztowa, the broad street that curves around the northern swathe of the Planty. Still a child herself, Zofia was impressed by Bronio's charm, his beautiful smile 'and the way he treated children kindly'.[34] As a violinist, his mother told Goll, 'he is talented to some extent, but without work his lessons go only fairly well. Yet he listens to music with great delight and doesn't miss a concert.'[35]

'Men of knowledge'

The Malinowskis would have entertained friends and university colleagues in the Mały Rynek apartment, and there young Bronio would have listened to their conversations. The Jagiellonian professors, according to Witold Truszkowski, 'formed quite an exclusive clan . . . which was not easy to penetrate'.

A high level of scientific achievement in a candidate was not enough; what was also considered was a high moral standard, relevant social prominence and sociability, the proper upbringing of children and a sense of patriotism. These requirements were important because the intention was to create an elite which was to influence young people. The professors' wives played a prominent role in this clan. They often met and constituted a great university aristocracy, which passed judgements on professors and candidates. Woe betide those who became notorious![36]

Prominent among Lucjan's friends were August Witkowski, Lothar Dargun, Stanisław Estreicher and Karol Potkański. Malinowski would later say that he had fallen under their intellectual spell. Witkowski was the senior professor of physics, a particularly strong field at the Jagiellonian around the turn of the century. He had studied under Helmholtz in Lwów and Berlin, and later at Glasgow under Lord Kelvin. He worked on the thermodynamic properties of gases, and his experimental physics laboratory at the Jagiellonian was the first to be built in Poland.[37] The Witkowski family and the Malinowskis were close, so close that August became a godfather to baby Bronislaw. This fact alone may have disposed Malinowski to take the study of physics seriously. When he called the roll of the Cracovian 'men of knowledge' who had most influenced him, Witkowski's name was first; and on learning of his death in 1914 Malinowski shed tears for him.

Lothar Dargun was a professor of law with an interest in ethnology, particularly in the origins and evolution of the family and forms of property. Against the prevailing view (promoted by Henry Maine, Friedrich Engels, Carl Starke and Edward Westermarck), Dargun believed that individual ownership preceded communal ownership. He was also interested in the cultural phenomenon of war and its effect on the development of law.[38] In 1913 Malinowski wrote an essay in German on the sociology of the family in which he addressed some of the issues close to Dargun's heart. He also cited Dargun's work approvingly – though not uncritically – concerning 'the functional dependence of the kinship relations on jural, moral and economic factors'.[39] Although not converted to Dargun's views on the sociology of the family, Malinowski was clearly influenced by them. When he came to think about primitive law, and later still about warfare, it is fair to suppose that Dargun's arguments formed part of the bedrock position from which Malinowski wrote. Likewise the views of Stanisław Estreicher, who succeeded Dargun as law professor at the Jagiellonian of which he also became rector. 'A man of many interests, a bibliographer, publicist and writer, [who] influenced students of various university faculties by his good sense and erudition.'[40] It was Estreicher, on behalf of the Academy of Arts and Sciences, who saw Malinowki's only Polish book through the press following his departure for Australia in 1914.

Karol Potkański was a historian with an even broader range of interests, which encompassed the entire spectrum of human sciences (archaeology, physical anthropology, linguistics, ethnology, sociology and psychology) and which would have qualified him in Britain or America as a general anthropologist. Viewing history as the process of change in social structures, Potkański used the comparative method to demonstrate general laws of social development.[41]

In addition to these three men, there were others whom Malinowski acknowledged as having influenced his youthful thinking, though they properly belonged to his years at university: Stefan Pawlicki (a philosopher and theologian), Marian Zdziechowski (a philosopher who wrote on the 'psychology of Slavonic peoples') and Władysław Matlakowski (a surgeon and ethnographer of the folk culture of the Górale).[42] Towards the end of his life, Malinowski eulogized this eminent group of proto-anthropologists: 'The array of men of knowledge, writers and artists remains before my eyes. . . . From today's perspective I can see the greatness and real goodness of that Polish culture, focused as it was in this small segment of the national life.'[43]

Even before he entered university, then, Malinowski was disposed to take a general interest in philosophy, psychology and the evolution of law, as well as a particular interest in linguistics, folklore and ethnology. We cannot rush to judgment at this point, however, and assume that the course of his later career was set even before he began his university studies. Malinowski would spend much of his time during the following years studying mathematics and the natural sciences.

Schooling

A faded portrait photograph of Bronio survives, taken when he was about eleven. He is wearing a high-collared, military-style tunic, the uniform of the Sobieski Gymnasium. His solemn, cherubic face has the dark, intense stare of his father and the full, pouting lips of his mother. His hair is cut short and parted neatly on the left.

It was in early 1895, just before he turned eleven, that Malinowski entered what was reputed to be the best secondary school in Galicia. This, to give it its full name, was the King Jan III Sobieski Imperial and Royal Gymnasium. Of Bronio's primary schooling nothing is known, apart from a stilted self-appraisal of 1907, written in German and in the third person: 'During his school years, from the very start, his progress was appraised by his teachers as good or very good, both academically and in his morals.'[44] Some, if not all, of his early tuition was at the hands of private tutors. 'He learns very easily,' his father told Goll.[45]

According to one account he attended the school for only one academic year (1899–1900), being obliged by his poor health to complete the remaining terms as an extramural pupil.[46] Feliks Gross (perhaps misreading the same source) believed it was only in his fourth year (1898–99) that Malinowski spent the full year at school.[47] But scrutiny of the school records reveals a far more complicated story. In his own summary version, Malinowski stated that he attended the gymnasium 'in the years 1895 to 1901 . . . partly as a regular pupil and partly privately'.[48] Before examining Malinowski's record, however, something must be said about the Sobieski Gymnasium and its curriculum.

Feliks Gross, who attended the gymnasium fourteen years after Malinowski, characterized its regime as 'demanding and difficult':

> The entire curriculum consisted of required courses, no electives . . . if you failed in only two subjects you had to repeat not a term but the entire year; if you repeated and failed again, you were out. The faculty and administration were quite severe. School infractions were punished by *carcer* – hours of additional attendance; one had to copy an ancient text.[49]

Gross is making an implicit comparison with the American high-school system, but actually the gymnasium rather resembled an English public school, designed to prepare sons of the elite for university and professional careers. Like all such schools, it was conservative in curriculum and despotic in discipline, the more so in that it conformed to the same Germanic model as the gymnasium in which Lucjan Malinowski had taught a generation earlier. The curriculum appears to have changed little during that time: religious instruction, Latin, Greek (from Form III), Polish, German, geography and history (linked as a single subject), mathematics, and natural sciences. Neither French nor English was taught. In some years pupils also took gymnastics – Bronio did so for one year – and for at least two years he was taught 'history of the fatherland' (Austria, perhaps, not Poland). In the final years there was an introduction to philosophy. With these few exceptions, the syllabus did not vary from one year to the next. At the end of their eighth year, pupils took their *Matura*, or matriculation, which involved written examinations in every subject except religious instruction.

Almost needless to say, Malinowski was a brilliant student. He had an aptitude for concentration and dedicated study, and a truly remarkable flair for languages. His own modest assessment of his early scholastic achievement is perfectly accurate: 'He passed the secondary school certificate with excellent results, and in the subsequent years the subjects he pursued for his examinations were rewarded with "very good" or "excellent".'[50] In fact, his gymnasium record shows that, by subject, 'excellent' outnumbered 'very good' in every semester but two of his six years. The seven papers he took for the *Matura* in May 1902 earned him 'excellent' and 'very good', and he matriculated with honours.

A legend has grown up around Malinowski's absences from school, and like most legends it exaggerates. It is true that his school career was shorter than most: instead of the full eight years (sixteen semesters), Bronio attended for only six. He enrolled halfway through Form I (in February 1895) and left at the end of the first semester of Form VII (in December 1900). It is also true that he was absent a good deal, though if the gymnasium's records are to be believed, not as often as legend would have it. Absences were recorded in terms of class hours per semester, and I calculate that over the six years of his schooling Malinowski was absent for only 14 percent of the optimum number of class hours.[51]

It is the pattern of absences that is of greater interest, however. Bronio achieved perfect attendance in only three of his twelve semesters, but there was great variation from semester to semester and from year to year. The absences began in 1896, when he was twelve and lost two weeks owing to measles. One of the longest absences of his school career – of about seven weeks – was recorded in the second semester of Form III, that is, during the first half of 1897. His father's letters refer to no illness, but rather to the boy's staying in Zakopane with his mother and a Silesian teacher who was coaching him in German. There was also a plan to send him to Germany with his mother the following year 'for a thorough education'. Lucjan was inclined to be scornful of Polish schools, which he said were 'full of pedagogical and didactic dilettantes'.[52]

The next significant absence, of about two weeks, was during the second part of the 1897–98 year. This was probably connected with his father's death, which occurred just before the semester began. His teachers' assessments for that semester suggest no disturbance of his scholastic application. 'Diligence' remained 'Good' and his 'General Mark' was 'Excellent', as it was for most of the nine subjects of the syllabus. His academic performance, in short, seems to have been unaffected by Lucjan's sudden demise. Indeed, measured by the number of 'excellents', Form IV was the most distinguished of his school career.

His mother claimed some credit for this when she wrote her own report card on Bronio for Jarosław Goll:

> He is talented, clever and sharp-witted, but lazy and lacking conscientiousness. It seems that it is I who am to be blamed for his faults. His being the only child I was taking care of him too much, I was making his education too easy. Until the end of his fourth form I was learning all his subjects with him, and only in the fifth form was he left to his own resources. Therefore he is starting to work better. If he doesn't always like to work, he passionately enjoys reading and serious conversation. If a book is too difficult for him he cannot eat or sleep.[53]

During this year, 1898–99, Bronio missed about five weeks of schooling, owing perhaps to his deteriorating eyesight. 'My son grows and thrives,' his mother wrote to Goll. 'But his sight is very weak and this makes me immensely worried. Now only fifteen years old he wears glasses.'[54] In Form VI Bronio was absent from school for about eight weeks – a quarter of the school year. As we shall see, this was owing to another major health crisis. Autumn 1900 was Bronio's last semester at the gymnasium; he began Form VII but did not complete the year.

The stark exactness of the gymnasium's record of absences is like a photographic negative that needs to be reversed to produce a more lifelike and positive image. Bronio's absences from class translate into presences at home with his mother in Mały Rynek, or with tutors in Zakopane or Warsaw. Almost two decades later, having recently learned of his mother's death, Malinowski's memories of school lead directly to memories of her:

> My time at the gymnasium; I recall Szarlowski and other teachers, but Sz. most vividly of all. Planty [public gardens in Cracow], morning moods, going back home. At times I see Mother still alive, in a soft gray hat and a gray dress, or in a house dress, or in a black dress, with a round black hat.[55]

'Owing to illness'

Malinowski's wretched health was a determining factor in his life and, he
believed, the explanatory key to his inconsistent character. 'Owing to illness'
became a familiar refrain, as he sought to explain a particular course of
action or to excuse himself from some disagreeable task. Like his heroes
Conrad and Nietzsche, he learned to use his ill-health strategically. It was
owing to illness, he tells us, that he was taken to 'an Arcadian valley' and
introduced to the double life of the ethnographer; it was owing to illness
that he turned to the consolations of *The Golden Bough* and became 'bound
to the service' of anthropology; it was owing to illness that his ethnographic
fieldwork in New Guinea took the particular course that it did, permitting
the serendipitous discovery of functionalism; and it was owing to illness that
he found himself in any number of places that significantly shaped his
life – among them, the Canary Islands, Oberbozen and the United
States.

The extent of Malinowski's hypochondria will become evident, but it is
unclear what exactly was wrong with him. He was by no means puny, and
at 5 feet 10 inches he was above average height. On the basis of what he
told an American doctor in 1938 the latter reported to a colleague: 'His
forebears were not particularly strong people, of a rather nervous type and
belonged to the lesser Polish aristocracy.'[56] (One can imagine the expletive
with which Malinowski greeted this aspersion!) Fortunately, a more detailed
diagnostic inventory exists. In 1932, Malinowski spelled out his early
medical history for the New Lodge Clinic in Windsor. 'General debility in
childhood, convulsions, constant trouble with digestion and respiratory
organs.'[57] At the age of eight, he continued, he was operated on for an
intestinal abscess on the left side, leaving an 'open wound with drainage of
pus'. When he was sixteen, he reported, he was operated on again for septic
appendicitis, leaving another open wound 'with secondary abscesses
forming in the iliac region'. This event conforms with his Form VI school
record, for it was a year of lengthy absences amounting to eight weeks. But
it was during the following year that a more insidious illness overtook him.
Curiously, Malinowski does not mention this in his medical history, though
it effectively ended his school career.

During the latter half of 1900 his eyes deteriorated alarmingly – though
he felt no pain – and the doctors feared he would lose his sight altogether.[58]
His mother wrote about the 1900–01 crisis to Jarosław Goll. 'I cannot

express what I was going through, death is better than such an awful invalidism! Now, thank God, it is much better, and the doctors promise to save
his eyes, but the treatment will last a very long time.' He was being treated
in Warsaw between periods of rest in the country. Her eighty-year-old
mother, with whom they were staying, 'was so depressed by her grandson's
illness that she suffered a light paralytic fit'. Caught between her 'seriously
ill mother' and 'the son in hospital on the other side of Warsaw', a distraught
Józefa suffered 'such anxiety, such worry!'[59] Bronio's treatment – which
mainly consisted of seclusion in a darkened room – was effective, and in
July Józefa reported that the threat of blindness was over. She planned to
take him to Trenczyn in Hungary (now in Slovakia) to bathe in the sulphur
springs.[60]

The eye affliction was congenital, perhaps, though in one retrospective
medical view it could have been scrofula 'caused by an infection of tuberculosis, which was widespread in Cracow at that time and which caused
allergies, chronic conjunctivitis and other diseases'.[61] Malinowski's daughter
Helena disputes this diagnosis, however, as a thorough medical examination
at the Mayo Clinic in 1938 revealed no tubercular lesions anywhere in his
body. Whatever the cause, Malinowski remained severely myopic throughout his life. He was unfit for military service and he never mastered the
typewriter or learned to drive a car.

The immediate consequence of his semi-blindness was an inability to
read. Family legend has it that 'Józefa forbade her son to peruse books;
she read everything to him herself, did lessons with him and devoted all
of her time to the boy'.[62] Malinowski's daughter Helena adds: 'He could
never have completed his schooling, which he did brilliantly despite
these handicaps, without her, and he never forgot it.'[63] There is Józefa
Malinowska's own testimony that until the end of Form IV she had 'made
his education too easy' by studying every subject with him. She then left
him to cultivate his own study skills; but scarcely two years passed before
she took up the task of reading to him in his darkened room. This practice
continued for some years after his recovery. In early 1903 she told Goll: 'I
want to go with my son wherever he needs to go for his studies, all the
more so because he needs me as a reader.'[64] Not only would Malinowski
never forget his mother's selfless dedication to his learning, he would recreate didactic situations of similar intimacy with the women he loved.
Studying *à deux*, shoulder-to-shoulder, was for him an eroticized intellectual pleasure.

'A fanatical devotion'

The intimate intellectual explorations with Mama helped to make his relationship with her the most important in Malinowski's life for many years to
come. Elsie Masson, his wife-to-be, understood this: 'I am sure she was far,
far more important to you than most mothers are to sons because you
thought and worked together.'[65] Paul Khuner, the Viennese Jewish friend to
whom Malinowski dedicated *Sex and Repression in Savage Society*, noted a
less benign effect: 'It seems to me that you have developed few purely emotional attachments in your life, it probably was all centred on your mother.'[66]

In Malinowski's synopsis of the fourth developmental stage of the human
child (I cite only those features characteristic of what he called the 'educated classes' in 'modern civilized communities'), adolescence is the period
'between physiological puberty and full social maturity . . . the time of
secondary and higher schooling. . . . This is the period of complete
emancipation from the family atmosphere.'[67] In the light of this definition,
Malinowski's own adolescence must have seemed a frustrating period of
arrested development. Worse, at sixteen, owing to illness it culminated in
regression. His secondary schooling was interrupted, not by the death of
his father (an event that might even have had the effect of maturing him
precociously), but by a serious illness followed immediately by an acute
physical and social handicap – semi-blindness no less. This could only have
had the dire psychological effect of stultifying the normal trajectory of adolescent development, undermining its gains and even plunging him back
into the bosom of his family – that is, into the care of his doting mother.

He had already passed through the pubescent phase of being embarrassed
by female relatives:

> Who of us does not remember the pangs of ineffable shame when, jaun-
> tily going along with our school fellows, we suddenly met our mother,
> our aunt, our sister, or even our girl cousin and were obliged to greet
> her. There was a feeling of intense guilt, of being caught *in flagrante delicto*.
> Some boys tried to ignore the embarrassing encounter, others more brave
> blushed crimson and saluted, but everyone felt that it was a shadow on
> his social position, an outrage on his manliness and independence.[68]

At sixteen, instead of 'complete emancipation from the family atmosphere',
Bronio was reclaimed by it, and owing to illness his adolescence entailed
a series of helpless surrenders to Mother's care: 'her existence was like

an atmosphere around me, that I breathed and lived in.' She was a 'mother in the full sense of the word, from whom one has taken all ideas and feelings in childhood and youth and who loved one beyond everything with a fanatical devotion.'[69] A fine and sincere tribute, but in the circumstances of his adolescence we may well imagine that his mother's 'fanatical' attentions presented (as Wengle has put it) 'a threat to the autonomy of Malinowski's nascent and developing self'.[70]

What moods and dispositions might this humiliating situation of thwarted development have fostered in an already vulnerable youth? Any number of defensive postures, probably, and in later life Malinowski displayed an impressive range of them: from extreme touchiness to hypochondria and general pessimism; from acute sensitivity to his own and others' moods, to morbid introspection in which his very sense of self came under threat of dissolution – his diaries refer repeatedly to 'the abyss' and 'the void'. A correlative of the sense of his own importance and a narcissism reinforced by his mother's 'fanatical devotion' was a brittle and permeable ego. Here is just one telling citation from his Trobriands diary describing what he diagnosed as neurasthenia: 'Over-all mood: strong nervous excitement and intellectual intensity on the surface, combined with inability to concentrate, superirritability and supersensitiveness of mental epidermis and feeling of permanently being exposed in an uncomf. position to the eyes of a crowded thoroughfare: an incapacity to achieve inner privacy.'[71]

It would not do to lay the blame for these quirks of Malinowski's psyche on the frustrated development of his adolescence, or specifically on the circumstances that encouraged his mother to prolong his childhood dependence upon her, but the pattern is suggestive. Given the obstacles he had to overcome – the betrayal of his body, the continuing need for maternal nurture – it is to be expected that he devised mental escape routes and enjoyed surrogate conquests of the imagination in order to emancipate himself from oppressive maternal bonds. Denied external independence he could at least cultivate internal autonomy. Owing to illness, he was in no position even to attempt to reject his mother's love – intensified as it must have been following the death of his father – but he could accommodate it by taking it for granted. He was free to fortify his inner self with dreams, fantasies and secret ambitions, and his consolations would lie in the unfettered life of the mind.

So the son's maturity, one might surmise, was in part achieved despite his mother, with the help of secrets he kept from her – and, of course, with much help from his friend Staś Witkiewicz, his partner in imaginary crime. In later years Bronio secured his independence by a habitual but necessary duplicity. He would call upon his mother's aid frequently in his pursuit of scholarship and profess his deep love for her, but he would also keep her at an emotional distance. We should note, however, that in his diaries he affectionately referred to her as 'Mamusia' or 'Mama', translated better by 'Mummy' than by the misleadingly formal 'Mother' of the published *Diary*. 'I recall the countless occasions when I deliberately cut myself off from Mother [*Mama*], so as to be alone, independent – not to have the feeling that I am part of a whole. . . . I never was open with her, I never told her *everything*.'[72]

He was uncomfortable with his duplicity and he yearned to unify himself, to be 'part of a whole' which included his mother. He intellectualized the problem as an ethical one, the solution to which was integration: 'Twinges of conscience result from lack of integrated feelings and truth in relation to individuals. My whole ethics is based on the fundamental instinct of unified personality. From this follows the need to be the same in different situations.'[73]

When he learned of his mother's death, the shock, grief and remorse annulled his duplicity and he regressed to the state of a vulnerable child: 'All the time I feel grief and desperate sadness, such as I felt as a child when I was separated from Mother for a few days.'[74] He was then a world and a war away from Poland, and news of her death reached him in the Trobriands five months after the event. He recorded his first reaction in his diary: 'Went into the thicket and burst into tears.'[75] Then he sat in his tent and wrote to Elsie Masson:

> My mother was infinitely more to me than the best mother I have seen and I never appreciated it and I was a very bad son. I feel terrible remorse mixed with my grief. . . . In my childhood and youth she was the first to influence me and the foundations of all I possess mentally were laid by her. But she had an entirely different character [to me]: her capacity for loving and the depth of her feelings, their permanence and intensity was immense.[76]

Chapter 3

Early Travels

'An enthusiasm for the exotic'

Cracow could boast excellent rail connections: north to Warsaw, Lithuania, the Baltic and St Petersburg; east to Lwów, the Ukraine and the Black Sea; southwest to Vienna, Trieste, Venice, Genoa and the Mediterranean; west to Wrocław (Breslau), Dresden and Leipzig; northwest to Poznań and Berlin, and beyond to Hamburg and the North Sea. By the time he was seventeen – the age at which Joseph Conrad left Cracow to go to sea – Malinowski would have travelled along all of these routes.

Twenty-seven years separated these two men. In April 1884, when Malinowski was born, Conrad, orphaned when he was twelve, was in Bombay and about to sign onto the *Narcissus*. Ten years earlier, he had boarded the Vienna Express in Cracow, 'as a man might get into a dream'.[1] His intention was not simply to go to sea: it was to free himself from his past, from his debilitating illnesses, his unfinished schooling, his well-meaning but uncomprehending guardians, and from his self-doubts. We might imagine that Malinowski left Cracow for similar reasons. The difference was that Conrad's departure had greater finality, for Malinowski returned to his home city many times, tugged at by maternal ties. Coincidentally, at the moment when Conrad did at last return to Cracow – on the eve of war in July 1914 – Malinowski was sailing for Australia into his own inadvertent exile. Exile, of course, was one of the mortal conditions that both men suffered and shared with so many other European intellectuals of the age.[2]

These parallel, recursive themes of two compatriot lives lived a generation apart are significant only because they intimate a fateful pattern, a Nietzschean *amor fati* that both men seemed determined to embrace. We can only guess how much Malinowski knew about Conrad's life as he was living his own – probably very little until one day in 1913 when they met in the Kentish countryside. Malinowski's admiration for Conrad could then begin to nourish his reading of his own life: 'if a seaman, then an English seaman', for which Malinowski would substitute 'anthropologist'.[3] He too could contemplate becoming a celebrated Polish–British writer with 'an enthusiasm for the exotic': an explorer of outposts of empire from which he would return with strange tales.

In a famous, if apocryphal, claim, he aspired to become the Conrad of anthropology.[4] The outline of a youthfully romantic myth of travel and adventure was perhaps already beginning to form, and would take firmer shape once he recognized Conrad as a model with whom to identify. In yet another of Malinowski's brief and undated excursions into autobiography (again written in the third person) we read, as variations on a now familiar theme:

> After graduating his health gave way and the next three years he spent on the shores of the Mediterranean, visiting North Africa, Asia Minor, and the Canary Islands. With the practical gift for languages of his countrymen, he spoke from childhood, in addition to Polish and its various peasant dialects, German, French, and Russian. During these three years he acquired Spanish and Italian & was thus everywhere in his travels able to study the peoples among whom he lived. He had, moreover, like his distinguished countryman, Joseph Conrad, whose acquaintance he was afterwards to make, an enthusiasm for the exotic that led him at this time to desert the sober sciences of mathematics, physics and chemistry for the humanistic study of anthropology. It was not altogether a new interest; in his childhood, spent in the Carpathian mountains, he had lived among the rude mountaineers and shepherds who. . . .[5]

Here the page ends; if there was a second one, it is lost. But this is the most focused and finished fragment in the record, and it might well have been titled 'Why Bronislaw Malinowski Became an Anthropologist'. Let us note first that the health crisis and the ensuing period of travel (the latter having expanded to a round three years) are now temporally positioned *after* Malinowski's graduation from university in 1906. The elements of a nascent, euhemerist myth of the birth of the Ethnographer are all here ('old Polish nobility' was mentioned in an earlier paragraph): the illness, the educative travel, the extraordinary command of languages (here modestly attributed to all Poles), the turn from 'sober sciences' to a romantic pursuit of the exotic (vindicated by the example of Conrad himself) in the guise of anthropology.

In his memoir of the young Malinowski, Feliks Gross asks the rhetorical question:

> How did it happen that in this northern city [i.e. Cracow] – so far from the tropics, distant in history, interest, and space from what was falsely considered at that time 'a romance of the colonies,' that here, in a rather medieval urban setting, you find a young man who dedicated his life primarily to the anthropology of the Pacific?[6]

The question itself is ambiguously posed, for Malinowski did not dedicate himself to anthropology or to the Pacific while he was actually in Poland. To the extent that ethnology interested him during his student years in Cracow it was, as he said in his public dedication to Frazer, 'a favourite side line of study' – not necessarily even his favourite. But Gross has a point when he tries to answer the question from his own experience of being a pupil at the Sobieski Gymnasium. He writes that 'there was a passionate interest – more than an interest – a fascination with the unknown, with undiscovered lands and their inhabitants':

> When we were 11 or 12 years old, we got out school atlases for our first geography classes . . . On some maps we found white spots. This was the mark to indicate that the region was still unknown, untraveled. That was what we were looking for. It made us think that perhaps there was a place where we would be the first visitors . . . And I think Malinowski, like many others, was fascinated by the romance of the unknown, not solely by anthropology itself.[7]

Wittingly or not, Gross must be alluding here to the passage in Conrad's *A Personal Record* in which the novelist, as a child of nine or ten, stares at a map of Africa and, putting his finger on a blank space at the heart of the continent, declares: 'When I grow up I shall go there.'[8] As indeed he did. Or perhaps Gross was recalling *Heart of Darkness* (that subtext of Malinowski's first New Guinea diary), in which Conrad, in the voice of his narrator Marlowe, says:

> 'Now when I was a little chap I had a passion for maps. I would look for hours at South America, or Africa, or Australia, and lose myself in all the glories of exploration. At that time there were many blank spaces on

the earth, and when I saw one that looked particularly inviting on a map . . . I would put my finger on it and say, "When I grow up I will go there".'

The romance of travel, exploration and discovery on the edges of empire – whether or not Malinowski imbibed it, as Gross had, from reading Alexander Humboldt and other explorers – was in the very air of modernism that Polish intellectuals breathed at the turn of the century. The allure of the exotic unknown was something Malinowski was later to note in his diaries, but he controlled it by intellectual analysis – as he sought to control most of his impulses – and there is no sense in which he might be said to have been impelled or *driven* by it. The seductive call of the wild was an aesthetic experience he could cultivate and indulge in mildly, but it could not be the main motive force of his ambition, and to suggest that it led him to anthropology is as misleading as the claim that it was Conrad's 'enthusiasm for the exotic' that led him to become a novelist. Exoticism, in short, is not a sufficient explanation for Malinowski's choice of career.

When he had fully embarked upon that career he proved to be neither an intrepid explorer nor a discoverer of lost tribes. While in New Guinea he had some unique opportunities to venture, if not directly into those tantalizing blank spots on the map of which the hinterland was largely composed, then at least into the ethnographically uncharted areas adjacent to them. But Malinowski declined (for perfectly good reasons, let it be said) even this adventurous option. With one exception – the Amphlett Islands, to the south of the Trobriands – his field sites in New Guinea were places that had already been lightly scratched by previous ethnographers, and all had been more or less thoroughly missionized. Throughout his life Malinowski was nervously restive and rarely content to remain in one place for long. As his diaries attest with their litanies of frustrations, his was not the kind of psychological disposition conducive to contented travel. A lifelong traveller, certainly, and one initiated into its charms and its boredoms at an early age, but not one who travelled simply to fulfil an ambition. His ambitions lay elsewhere than in those blank spots on the map.

Postcards

Considering their limited means, Józefa Malinowska and her son managed to do a remarkable amount of travelling, though they were obliged to travel third class and seek modest lodgings. Józefa received a widow's pension from the university but it was hardly sufficient to meet the expense of travel abroad. Presumably she raised some money from her own family, and on at least one occasion a friend of her dead husband, Dr Dobrski, came to the rescue. Beginning in 1901 with a visit to the Dalmatian coast and culminating in 1907–08 with a prolonged stay in the Canary Islands, mother and son 'made shorter and longer journeys south in search of mild climates and sun'.[9] Concerning their other destinations the sources are scanty and it is impossible to reconstruct their itineraries with any precision. Exactly when, for example, they first went to the Algerian spa town of Biskra is uncertain, but it is likely that they spent some months there in 1903 and again in 1904.[10] Faded group photographs suggest that their travels in North Africa were organized by Cook's Tours. Malinowski's autobiographical jottings are unhelpful or inconsistent on the matter of dates, and he states only that he had spent 'almost a year in Mohammedan countries: 9 months in Africa and 2 months in Turkey'.[11] He gives no indication of how many trips were involved and, as was his habit in later years, he probably exaggerated the duration.

Some overseas trips can be roughly dated from the trails left by postcards sent to his friend Józef Litwiniszyn. In 1903 mother and son were in Palestine, Tunis and Palermo. In 1904 they visited Naples and Algiers. (A photograph survives of Malinowski precariously seated upon a camel.) There are no postcards from Biskra, but it was accessible by rail from both Tunis and Algiers. Undated cards from Finland, Egypt and Malta have also survived. It was in Malta, he later recalled, that he first saw the Union Jack fluttering in the breeze; the second time was in Gibraltar while en route to the Canaries.[12] In April 1906, mother and son visited Florence, Pisa and Rome. There are few other traces of the long and companionable voyages Malinowski made with his mother. He would, many years later, tell Feliks Gross that some of his happiest days were spent in Cetinje in Montenegro, 'a romantic kingdom, famous among the stamp collectors, and ruled by King Nikita', but he gave no date for this excursion to the Balkans.[13] On the way to Australia in June 1914, Malinowski wrote to his mother that the typical 'oriental aroma' of Port Said reminded him of Tunis and Tangier.[14] Writing to her from Anuradhapura in Ceylon, he compared the Sinhalese scene unfavourably with the Arab towns they had known: 'A street in Tunis, Tetuan, Biskra or Tangier is much more lively, singular and interesting.'[15]

Malinowski's reference to spending 'almost a year in Mohammedan countries' was made to support a wider claim that he had been exposed at an early age to other ways of life, including other religions. He had been confronted, too, with local forms of Roman Catholicism in Poland, Spain, France and the Canary Islands.[16] In an illustration of his 'naïve conviction' from the time when he was 'a believing, practising Christian' he told one audience how he needed to visualize concretely the abstract dogma of Creation. 'And aided, I think, by some pictures, I perceived the ship of God, the Father, floating above the dark waters of the primeval ocean.'[17] His own father appears to have been a freethinker, and although he probably concealed his doubts from his son, he confessed them to Jarosław Goll: 'I know only that I cannot pray, I do not believe it would be reasonable. All this [religious belief] is an anthropomorphism and that's it.'[18]

The Catholic faith into which Malinowski was born ceased to have any outward hold on him from about the age of sixteen. It was then (as he told his eldest daughter) that he had first questioned the existence of God. He recalled travelling on a train and falling into conversation with a young Jew, who told him that he was an atheist. Until that moment Malinowski had not realized that one could live without a god and organized religion. It came as a revelation, he implied, though there must have been a series of influences or events that brought him to that conscious questioning of a hitherto taken-for-granted faith. In any case, he was to become a 'humble agnostic' rather than a 'confident atheist'.[19] His mother was devout, however, and his quiet apostasy must have saddened her. 'He is eager for life and people, which makes me scared sometimes,' she told Goll in 1899. 'He is not going to become a priest, for sure.'[20]

'No language, no penetration!'

'The practical gift for languages' that Malinowski claimed was uncommonly bounteous, even for a Pole. Later, Charles Seligman would wonder whether there was any anatomical basis for his remarkable talent ('if there is any actual macroscopical difference in your left temporal convolutions').[21] It has been said of Joseph Conrad, exposed as a child to native Polish, home-learned French, and the Russian and German of the occupiers, that he was 'enmeshed in language shifts' and that 'such cross-fertilization was excellent preparation for a man who would create a distinct cadence and rhythm in

English'.[22] This might have been even truer for Malinowski with his child-hood experience of rural Polish dialects.

He spoke Polish, French and German from childhood; later he learned Italian, Spanish and English. During his early travels he would have polished up his French in Algeria and Tunisia. Was he also tempted to learn some Arabic, or a smattering of Turkish in Constantinople? As well as practising Italian while in Istria and Dalmatia, did he also struggle with Slovene and Croat? He was studying the classics during his first visits to the Mediterranean – Homer and Horace, Thucydides and Tacitus. And behind all these tongues, ancient and modern, were the dialects he had picked up in the hamlets of Ponice and the alpine pastures of the Tatras. Yet beyond enumerating the languages at his command Malinowski gives few clues to his experience of learning them. Polish and French he learned at his mother's knee, German in his classroom in Cracow, and a smattering of Russian on the streets of Warsaw.[23] But the English vernacular, which was to become by far the most important language to him, he learned (initially at least) from the lips of female friends. According to Raymond Firth, Malinowski's recipe for learning a European language 'was to invest in an armful of novels and read through them with minimal resort to grammar or dictionary'.[24]

Language acquisition would become the central plank of his ethnographic method. 'Three-quarters of the success in fieldwork depends on the right equipment and attitude to language,' he told his students in 1932.[25] Language mastery was also the most obvious key to his achievement as an anthropologist. 'No language, no penetration!' he declaimed in his notes towards the unwritten textbook. His young playmates in Ponice and the Tatras were the children of peasants and Górale highlanders through whose eyes he learned to see the wonders of the city to which he really belonged. Another reconstructed childhood memory specifically refers to such early lessons in comparative linguistics:

> I discovered when very young that certain things could not be expressed in the dialect of the Górale. There was no vocabulary for refinements, abstractions and sophistications; the rude, clipped grammar was unsuited to clear and cogent reasoning. On the other hand, it permitted strong, direct speech. It was best for swearing and expressing the crudities of life.[26]

Malinowski would later take a mischievous pride in his ability to swear colourfully and comprehensively in several different languages.[27]

Some part at least of Malinowski's sense of leading a 'double life' as a child must have come from his juggling of linguistic codes. His extraordinary ability allowed him to talk his confident way into a vernacular; he actively and interactively pursued its idioms until the language spoke through him as it would through a native speaker. In a revealing lecture on 'Speech and Mental Processes' delivered in London in 1935 he explained:

> In learning my Trobriand language I found that I acquired it rather as a child does; I learnt a few words and then these began to multiply. I did not use the academic approach which is summed up by 'language expresses mental processes'. I was unable to get inside the mental processes of the natives. I had to learn to behave like the native in personal and social intercourse. Through this I learned how they think, day-dream. I learned the language by a pragmatic approach to being rather than by merely getting the contents.[28]

Although greatly oversimplified, here is the notion that one who learns a language as a child does so through imitation and practical interaction; one learns to *inhabit* the language as a mode of thought and a way of being. On this occasion, Malinowski summed up his approach in a dictum that, despite appearances, owed nothing at all to his Viennese-British contemporary Ludwig Wittgenstein (whom he probably did not know and almost certainly did not read): 'We cannot speak of the meaning or symbolism of words outside their social and cultural contexts.'

Dreaming the Adriatic

Malinowski referred to his youthful journeys only fleetingly in autobiographical notes or in casual asides in his diaries and letters. There is a singular exception to be found among his papers. Some twelve years after the event, in February 1913, Malinowski recalled in vivid detail visits to the Dalmatian coast and Venice. His literary vehicle was an essay in the form of a letter to Aniela Zagórska, a friend from Zakopane, three years his senior, who had taught him some English. Through her father, Aniela was a distant cousin of Joseph Conrad. It was with Aniela and her mother (Karol Zagórski had died in 1899) that Conrad and his family stayed during their ill-timed visit to Zakopane in July 1914. He cherished the Zagórska women as his closest living relatives in Poland, and during the 1920s Aniela translated several of his novels into Polish.

It was on his return to London from Poland in January 1913 that Malinowski decided to write his epistolary essay for Aniela. To complicate the plot, he had only recently concluded a brief and unsatisfactory love affair with Karola Zagórska, Aniela's younger sister. At this time he must have known of the Zagórska sisters' relationship to Conrad, though it seems he had not yet met the famous novelist (nor, indeed, had Aniela). He was to do so later in the year, the introduction being effected by yet another woman, known to us as 'Tośka' in the published diaries. Thus was Malinowski's relationship to Joseph Conrad mediated, initially at least, by three young Polish women.

Malinowski's unfinished, and presumably unsent, epistolary essay is supposedly an answer to Aniela's question as to why he first went to London.[29] But towards the end of the piece he digressed on his first experiences of the Mediterranean and Italy. The writing is self-consciously literary – the inscription of a twenty-nine-year-old man reflecting upon the experiences of his seventeen-year-old self. The autumn to which he refers can only be that of 1901, when he was recovering from his eye affliction. As a memoir, it has profoundly nostalgic as well as romantic overtones; it is in part a meditation on the Mediterranean of antiquity, which to the author is doubly removed in time and as elusive as a dream.

I still remember the indescribable impression that I had on my first visit to the Mediterranean. Sitting on the seashore, in a marvellous bay, where in the midst of a grove of stone-pines and long avenues of aloes and *erica arborea* no one disturbed the beauty and solitude of [those] autumn days, I read the *Odyssey*, in Greek, in preparation for the *Matura*. . . . When I felt stronger, I went with Mother into the town of Lussin Piccolo [now Mali Lošinj in Croatia]. . . . I remember one moonlit evening, when I reached the harbour rather late, just after sunset. The town is very empty, almost dead; on the still water barques with dark sails roll in the soft, warm air; the smell of olive oil frying and the rapid, mocking, rounded speech of the Italians; from afar a song can be heard: '*Ninetta mia, Son' barcarola – Sono del'arte e Sono gentile – Nell' mia barca se vuoi venire – Sull'alto mare andaremo. . . .*' I remember this moment vividly, its smell and its melody – which even today evokes the essence of that period: an unconscious, longed-for grasp of things Italian in an idealized form of

my own, which reality subsequently destroyed. . . . I was very taken up
then with the poetic beauty of Homer's *Odyssey*. The sounds of Greek
being scanned, only half comprehensible to me – or rather totally foreign
to me *as a language*, as a tool for the direct expression of inner content
– were therefore associated then in a strangely plastic fashion with a
whole accumulation of exuberantly developing impressions and sensations. Poetry in a language which one does not know well, in which one
feels more than understands [each] word; in a language not defiled by
commonplaces and daily use, has a particular magic and power of its own.
It is like a language made up of proper nouns, individually signifying as
many states of mind.[30] Of course, poetry in one's own, native language
is *the* completely and properly understood poetry, but the other kind has
a value of its own, too. For me, certain catchwords in the *Odyssey* had
the kind of concrete shape into which the wave of life which then spilled
over me from the deepest sources, had become crystallized. Besides the
language, along with the sounds I was also fascinated by the images which
were slowly opening out before me, by the theme of the adventures of
the divine wanderer and, especially, the scene of these adventures – the
sea. With an indescribable longing I let my thoughts and eyes run out
through the narrow outlet of the bay, onto the vast, violet sea; I glided
across its vast, smooth surface, far off, all the way to the shores of Italy,
rounded Italy and went off in the direction of Sicily, the land of Polyphe-
mus; and far off, in the opposite direction, to the waters of the Pont,
where Odysseus's wanderings began and to the shores of Eygpt, where
the lotus-eaters dwelt. . . . And I simply did not wish to believe that that
water, above which I was sitting, which came up to my feet, was part of
the very same sea which vanishes further off in the mists of legend,
becomes myth, barely within the grasp of the imagination. And later, after
a few weeks' stay in Cigale, I boarded ship and went south, to pursue the
shadows of my mind – a vain pursuit! . . . I well remember my feelings
as I awoke during the approach to Ragusa [now Dubrovnik]. . . . For the
first time I had a distinct feeling that I was on the waters of the magnificent Mediterranean basin, in which the entire culture of the ancient
world was nurtured, where on just such a bright and sunny morning
Roman [sic] triremes sailed along the bright, sparkling shore. We were
travelling then along the coast of Dalmatia, stopping at all the major ports
in turn and visiting them. This journey made a strong impression on me,
perhaps precisely because I was prepared for it by a long yearning, an

inner stillness, in which those things without shape and without content, but so immensely powerful, those gleams that foreshadow *life*, are able to develop freely. The first port, the town of Zara [now Zadar] interested me immensely as the first specimen that I had seen of a small Italian town. I observed the dark, narrow back-streets where people walked quietly, as if down paved corridors, the little churches hidden picturesquely in amongst the houses, the life, the dirty and *lazzarone*-like [sic] incarnation of all those thoughts and daydreams without form, or rather of a vague, unintegrated form, which I had experienced so many times in connection with that magical name *Italy!*

In this essay Malinowski discovers a form of evocative travel writing, in a distinctly modernist style, in which physical place and psychological state melt into one another. Locations are strung upon threads of introspection and imagination. (Later, he would write in his New Guinea diary: 'I dissolved into the landscape.') There is a dream-like, stream-of-consciousness quality to the writing, technically supported by the absence of paragraphing and the incantatory repetitions. The words 'dream' and 'dreaming' occur on every page. Memories seamlessly flow from the shores of the Adriatic to the canals of Venice.

In the passage's content we glimpse some of the turns of Malinowski's romantic imagination: promises of bliss that reality cannot honour; the vain pursuit of the mind's shadows; the power of language – even when imperfectly understood – to conjure compelling images; the tangible sea of the present merging mistily into that legendary sea sailed by Odysseus. In short, he is writing about the Adriatic of his daydreams, a romantic creation of language and imagination that must ultimately be betrayed by experience. Appropriately, he was reading the *Odyssey* while sitting on the shores of Homer's wine-dark sea, and the passage suggests that blind Homer was his companion – being read to him by his mother – throughout their Mediterranean voyaging. One might wonder whether the title *Argonauts of the Western Pacific*, which spirits the Aegean to the Solomon Sea, was privately meant to commemorate these classical voyages of discovery he had made with his mother.

In this light, let us review Joseph Conrad's youthful fascination with the Mediterranean. In 1906 he wrote: 'I yet longed for the beginning of my own obscure Odyssey, which, as was proper for a modern, should unroll its wonders and terrors beyond the Pillars of Hercules.'[31] The stuff of a teenager's daydreams, indeed, revisited a generation later by Malinowski, whose meditation on the Bay of Cigale reflects with eerie precision Conrad's confession in *The Mirror of the Sea*: 'The charm of the Mediterranean dwells in the unforgettable flavour of my early days, and to this hour this sea, upon which the Romans alone ruled without dispute, has kept for me the fascination of youthful romance.'[32]

Although Malinowski had yet to meet Conrad at the time he wrote his travel essay, he was quite likely to have had his older fellow exile vaguely in mind – if only because Conrad's cousin, Karola Zagórska, was distressingly in his thoughts. But whether deliberate or inadvertent, there are discernible Conradian echoes in his essay. These may be unwonted artifacts of multiple translations, for we are reading in English what Malinowski wrote in Polish after (we must imagine) he had read Conrad's Polish-flavoured English. Although Malinowski's unedited manuscript is probably a second draft, it was never given the final polish that would prepare it for publication. Stylistic comparison with Conrad's 'impressionism', therefore, must be invidious. The sentence structures are less complex and ornate than those of Conrad; but Malinowski's sometimes acute, sometimes vague psychological perceptions, his aesthetic concern with phrasing and his predilection for the long sentence insistently suggest Conrad's literary influence.

Venice by the back door

Conrad's dream-like train journey from Cracow on the Vienna Express took him to Marseilles; Malinowski's took him, in the late summer of 1902, to Venice. This 'most improbable' island city with its breathtaking vista of the Piazza San Marco should be approached only from the sea – so said Thomas Mann's Aschenbach: 'to come to Venice by the station is like entering a palace by the back door.'[33] Like so many other visitors, Malinowski was overwhelmed by his first impression of the floating stones of Venice, by the way the city seems to envelop you like a dream.

Such an incarnation in stone of one's dim and diffuse thoughts, such an integration into a living whole of whatever there is of a land of dreams, constitutes one of the greatest charms of travel for me. In these impressions, which always arrive unexpectedly, a journey can be really beautiful; just like love, which creates in life that for which we long, but in which we almost do not dare to believe. Sometimes this incarnation of a daydream appears so suddenly, so unexpectedly, strikes a mind tired and buried under the dust of trivial expressions, by so powerful a cascade of stimulating and creative beauty, that it is like a dream incarnate; it possesses at one and the same time the mysterious charm of a dream and the life-brimming intensity of consciousness.

Again, along with the incantatory repetition of the word 'dream', this passage has a Conradian vagueness, something indefinable and portentous on the edge of awareness. But abruptly Malinowski switches to sharper, quasi-ethnographic observations on the wearying reality of rail travel, and on entering the magnificent palace of Venice by the back door:

Tired out from visiting Vienna in the dry and sweltering September days, worn out by walking through the Postojna caves [in Slovenia], late in the afternoon Mother and I boarded a train for Venice. . . . I fell into a state of passive exhaustion and nervous excitement; the monotonous clack of the wheels against the rails, the dirty, flickering light of the lamp, the hoarse voices in which one always speaks in order to shout above the din of the train, the dirty yellow interior of the third-class carriage – these are the external features of the well-known railway atmosphere. . . . The Venice railway station, the porters, the swarm of hotel servants, all helped to accentuate the immensely banal form in which I first found myself on the lagoon. From the station one comes out directly onto the Canal Grande. I was suddenly struck by the silence of the clear, moonlit night. In the silver, bluish light, the yellow lights of the lanterns, their reflections sputtering on the gently rippling water. The water laps softly against the stone steps and this murmur seemed so strange to me, immediately told me so much about the deepest essence of Venice – about the white marble, drenched in green water, about the waves of the lagoon, in which the Gothic tracery of the palaces is reflected and which farther off bathe the little fishing villages and sands and flat silty coast. We got into a gondola, which carried us for a while along narrow side canals, [and] at times emerged once again onto the Canal Grande. Shapes well known to me, conjured up from the shadows, appeared before me; I heard their names with a tremor, with a strange feeling of joy, as if I were experiencing a great moment, as if these great things were only now being realized. . . . I was simply brimming over with enthusiasm. The Chiesa degli Scalzi, the Palazzo Vendramin-Calergi, the Palazzo Foscari – to this day I remember the names from that night.

Malinowski's introspective travelogue ends abruptly at this point.

During the years of travel with his mother he realized some of his day-dreams and liberated his imagination from the cloistered confines of Cracow. Józefa Malinowska appears to have deliberately sought to broaden her son's horizons in this way. Their journeys together were an extension of his education and they helped to build 'the foundations of his very cosmopolitan nature'; but they were also a part of a long process of alienating himself from Poland. He would say later that from about the age of sixteen 'he had begun to "leave" Poland, to cut ties with his native land'.[34] A Gypsy-Pole, he remained an avid but ambivalent traveller for the rest of his life.

Chapter 4

Essential Friendships

Snapshots

Malinowski sat the comprehensive matriculation examination at the Sobieski Gymnasium and on 30 May 1902 was awarded the *Matura* with honours. He spent most of the following summer with his mother and her family at their Janiszów estate and attended the wedding of his favourite cousin, Genia. Mother and son then went back to Trenczyn for the sulphur baths, and in September to Venice and Lake Garda.[1] On 6 October he entered the Jagiellonian University.

After leaving their accommodation in Mały Rynek, Malinowski and his mother lived in various apartments in central Cracow. To eke out her widow's pension Józefa sometimes took in her son's friends as boarders. One was Józef Litwiniszyn (recipient of those postcards from exotic places), who recalled that Józefa Malinowska became a surrogate mother to him. Another occasional boarder was Stanisław ('Staś') Ignacy Witkiewicz, Malinowski's best friend. Yet another boarder had been a friend of Bronio and Staś since boyhood: Władysław Matlakowski, the son of Lucjan's surgeon-cum-ethnographer colleague, who later published a memoir that offers some intimate glimpses of the Malinowski *ménage* around 1905. The apartment they shared was close to the railway station in Radziwiłłowska Street: 'Our two second-storey rooms were in the annexe which practically adjoined the railway line so that every morning we were awakened as by an alarm clock by the passage of the Cracow–Lwów express clattering by at 7.30 a.m.'[2]

Like the other young men, Matlakowski was charmed by his landlady, rather less so by her son:

> Madame Malinowska . . . was a person of exceptional sweetness and she
> kept traces of her beauty into old age; the oval of her face and the outline

of her mouth were especially charming. Bronek resembled his mother but lacked her gentleness and his prominent chin indicated a strong character and even ruthlessness. . . . She spoke slowly, had a pleasant voice and she mouthed her words distinctly. Bronek, on the contrary, spoke, as it were, filtering his words through clenched teeth.

Matlakowski recalled how Malinowski, in order to ease the strain on his troublesome eyes, 'evolved a very odd way of working':

> He would lie in a semi-recumbent position on his bed, his head covered with blankets; a colleague from the university, named Siebodziński, would read to him. From time to time Bronek would uncover his head sufficiently to peer at mathematical formulae, after which he would resume his former position. At times he would get very angry and shout: 'Read properly! Repeat it again! Show me!' and he would slip his head from under the blanket. It really did require his exceptional gifts to study mathematics in this manner.

And also, one imagines, exceptional patience on the part of his lector. Despite Malinowski's imperious manner he was 'greatly admired' by poor Siebodziński, who was given dinner for reading to him. 'Bronek was a very decent chap really, but he wished to pass himself off for a cynic and a tough. Also, he was conceited and his attitude to us was friendly but patronizing; he only regarded Staś as his equal.'

These unflattering anecdotal recollections are echoed in the views of some of Malinowski's seniors, notably Staś's father, whose photographs of the two youths are as revealing as his opinions. One such photograph, taken in Zakopane in 1902, conveys some of their comradely solidarity. They are standing outdoors in the same rather formal pose, dressed in identical dark tunics and trousers. Both look unsmilingly at the camera, heads tilted slightly to the left, hands in tunic pockets. Malinowski's broad forehead is crowned by a full head of hair and he wears dark round spectacles. One can see the cynic and the tough of Matlakowski's description, and if he weren't so youthful he would appear sinister. Staś's face is finely chiselled and wanly handsome.[3] If this photograph represents their complicit seriousness — it is suggestive too of their elitism — there are others that capture their playfulness. Staś's father also took a photograph of them by the edge of a forest in the winter of 1902. Staś sits Buddha-like in the snow, about to be assaulted by a bearded man with a pointed stick. (Witkiewicz would become notorious for such theatrical foolery in later years.) Malinowski is grinning at the camera from under a hat pulled low over his eyes. Although he is peripheral to the main action, he and Staś seem to be wearing identical hats and jackets and both sport boyish moustaches. These two photographs, counterpointing solemnity and frivolity, subtly express the young men's complementarity, their difference within their similarity. They *appear* kindred, almost identical, but the photographer also catches disparities of demeanour.

Complementarity was a key to the famous friendship between these 'two wilful and demanding temperaments'.[4] It was intensely ambivalent, characterized by discord as well as deep affection. Only a year apart in age, both gifted with quick and questing intellects, there was a streak of sibling rivalry in Bronio and Staś's companionship. Even as he pronounced it bankrupt in October 1914, a dejected Malinowski referred to it as his 'most essential friendship' and in a striking mathematical image reflected: 'A friend is not merely an added quantity, he is a factor, he multiplies one's individual value.'[5] Much later, on being told the tragic circumstances of Staś's death, Malinowski wrote: 'Indeed, he was the only man I ever met in my life whom I knew from first and last to be a real genius.'[6]

Fathering genius

Stanisław Ignacy Witkiewicz was born in Warsaw on 24 February 1885 into a well-connected Polish-Lithuanian family (the Witkiewiczs were related to Józef Piłsudski, Poland's dictatorial president between the wars). Like Malinowski, Staś was an only son. Stanisław Witkiewicz senior (1851–1915) was an eminent critic, landscape painter and folklorist whose architectural designs became fashionable as the 'Zakopane style'. Handsomely bearded and sweetly charismatic, he was also something of a national sage who preached 'a patriotic gospel of creative renewal through a return to native Polish arts and crafts'.[7] Staś's mother was Maria Pietrzkiewiczówna, a music teacher who had graduated from the Warsaw conservatoire. Witkiewicz was an iconoclast, a romantic individualist who believed that his son should be freely allowed to develop his own personality and talents, unhampered – undisciplined as it turned out – by conventional schooling.

In 1890, the same year that Lucjan Malinowski bought land there, the Witkiewicz family moved to Zakopane to help ameliorate the father's tuberculosis. Spectacularly situated at the foot of the Tatras, this health resort was already known as the summer capital of Poland and it became increasingly accessible after the rail link to Cracow was opened in 1899. It was settled by artists, writers, musicians and other members of the intelligentsia. According to Karol Estreicher, son of Stanisław, whom Malinowski so admired, 'it was round Witkiewicz that the elite of the day gathered: the best minds, artists, scientists, aristocrats.'[8] As frequent residents in Zakopane during the 1890s, the Malinowskis must have been among this elite, and young Bronio would have been a familiar figure in Jedrzej Slimak's cottage on Krupówki, rented by the Witkiewiczs. Like Malinowski, Staś was exposed during childhood to the 'folkways' of the local highlanders. A Górale bard named Jan Krzeptowski Sabała became a close friend of the Witkiewicz family and a godfather to Staś. Sabała was romanticized as 'the Homer of Zakopane', 'a killer of bears, wanderer of the Tatra forests, sometimes a companion of robbers'.[9] Staś's godmother was the Polish-American actress Helena Modjeska, 'star of two continents', and an old flame of his father.

The boy was 'devilishly talented' – a prodigy in fact. He was barely five when his doting father observed him 'sweating over painting and drawing'. At six his mother taught him the piano and he soon began to improvise and compose.[10] He was seven when he began to study astronomy and natural history, and created his own little 'Tatra museum' for his collections of insects and rocks. According to Matlakowski, Staś learned to read and write 'without anyone's help', and even began to read Shakespeare's plays, lent to him by Matlakowski senior, who was then working on a translation of *Hamlet*.[11] By the time Staś was eight he had not only discovered theatre but had written (and published on his own hand-printing press) a dozen short plays with titles such as 'Cockroaches', 'Comedies of Family Life' and 'Squabbles about Stench'. In these fledgling dramas, Daniel Gerould finds a range of devices used later by the mature playwright (famous by then as Witkacy): 'accelerating action erupting in sudden violence; unexpected surprise endings; comic use of names, foreign phrases, and detailed stage directions; made-up words; off-hand dialogue full of non-sequiturs, deflation, and anti-climax; and the use of the author himself and his own personal experiences – as well as of his reading – as material for his dramas.'[12] Malinowski, too, was written into several of the later plays as a foil for Witkacy's own ideas.

Stanisław Witkiewicz believed that schools were stiflingly conformist and he would not entrust to them the education of his precious, precocious son, though when Staś was twelve, his father reluctantly yielded to his wish to attend secondary school in Lwów. Otherwise Staś was privately taught at home. Beginning in 1900, he spent several summers in Lithuania, staying at the country estate of his father's sister, Aniela Jałowiecka. There he enjoyed painting (in his own phrase) 'the melancholy lakes of Lithuania'. These holidays gave Staś a taste of adult independence and played an analogous role to the lengthy excursions abroad that Malinowski would make a few years later. A remarkably candid correspondence between father and son began during their first unaccustomed separation, and it would continue intermittently until Witkiewicz senior's death.[13] In 1902 Staś exhibited two of his Lithuanian landscapes, which were judged to be the best works in the Zakopane exhibition; and in the same year he wrote two brief philosophical treatises, one on dualism and the problem of free will, the other on Schopenhauer. These early exercises would almost certainly have been sparked by discussions with his philosophically inclined friends, Malinowski and Leon Chwistek.

Staś took his *Matura* in June 1903. 'I hope that by this,' he wrote impishly to his aunt Aniela, 'I shall gain more respect in the family and, what is more important, that Daddy will no longer skimp me jam.'[14] Father, however, was unimpressed: '"Certificate of Maturity" indeed! So I who never got it am immature still.'[15] A few weeks later he wrote to his son:

> One has to aim at objectives that lie beyond life's tollgate: . . . in intellectual ideas, to reach into infinity, in social notions, to go to the extreme limits of boundless omnipotent love. Let no caste limitations stick to you, no professional prejudices, no petty individual and class egotisms. The social system which one should accept should go further than the dreams of today's socialists. . . . Live in the future. Keep your place always at the top from which you can see the furthest horizons and prepare the wings of your thoughts and deeds to fly beyond them. . . . And be good in life, bright, compassionate, magnanimous, openhanded. My dear, be happy.[16]

Lofty sentiments and moral precepts worthy of Polonius (and Nietzsche), yet conveyed with such affectionate concern and passionate idealism. (Did Lucjan Malinowski ever speak to his son in this manner?) But Witkiewicz senior's combination of permissiveness and moral exhortation eventually backfired, and Staś rebelled. Continually urged to create himself, he resorted to disguise and artifice. His childhood playmate, the novelist's daughter Maria Sienkiewicz, recalled how he was 'always playing some role or other.

He was never himself. . . . And he was singularly nasty to his father. . . . Staś himself later said when he was grown up that he blamed his father for not beating him.'[17]

Malinowski and Staś were not only fierce friends but also practised correspondents, though the balance of letters was always wanting on Bronio's side. The first surviving missive from Staś is from his aunt's estate in Lithuania, and was written between 10 and 15 September 1903 – within a few weeks of the homiletic letter from his father. The latter's idealized image of his son contrasts starkly with the son's 'wicked' self-image. The first part of Staś's letter details frantic travel plans: 'I'm going to Cracow for the winter. Don't go to Catánia [Sicily] yet. We'll see how it will work out for us here together. Maybe that's presumptuous (as Prince Patrykowicz would say).' This is just one of many fantasy names and imaginary identities that enliven Staś's correspondence, and Malinowski probably responded in kind. Staś's verve, ebullience and gross frivolity ('my erotomania is quiescent for the present') would also characterize his novels and plays. 'Write me a long letter,' he urges Malinowski:

> Don't worry about the style, just grub around in your inner self. Your divagations in that department are a source of exquisite pleasure to me. Don't concoct any theory about my 'brutality'. At least don't you, of all my friends, engage in that nonsense. There's only one recollection that should make you blush, that is, when you once called my attention to the fact that Miss Ewa had scrambled egg around her mouth and you gave me a green, inquisitorial look from behind your dark glasses. Whenever I remember that, I double up with laughter.[18]

As well as wordless jests, they were obviously accustomed to sharing their most intimate thoughts. Grubbing around in their inner selves was what these young men did for much of the time (Staś with the principled encouragement of his father as a means of discovering his 'soul'), so much so that brooding introspection became for both of them a lifelong habit.

There was something in the relationship between his son and Bronio that caused Witkiewicz senior disquiet. As early as 1900 he had referred to Malinowski in a letter as 'Lord Douglas' (Oscar Wilde's nemesis, son of the ninth Marquess of Queensberry).[19] Although he was doubtless following Staś's lead in the use of this sobriquet, it is difficult to resist the inference that Witkiewicz suspected his son and Malinowski of experimenting dangerously with (in Lord Alfred Douglas's notorious phrase) 'the love that dare not be named'. In a number of letters between 1900 and 1912 the father hinted at the concern he felt, though he tried to maintain a conciliatory tone. 'I have sympathy for Bronio, and whenever you write well of him, I am glad,' he wrote in 1905. But he added another gentle warning: 'Like you, he [Malinowski] is in the process of self-creation, and may be passing through phases that could arouse apprehensions as to whether he is the best companion for you.'[20] Staś was already disinclined to listen to such advice though he, too, wanted to be conciliatory, and in June of that year he asked his father's frank opinion on 'the question of Bronio'. The reply equivocated:

> Strictly speaking, I know him only superficially. I know the outward form of his intelligence, which is easily oriented towards diverse subjects in accordance with a very adroit dialectical approach. He gives the impression of one who keeps his thoughts and words independent of external as well as inner emotional influences. . . . This is his outward appearance. In addition I know of a few cynical letters. This cynicism, in such a person as Bronio, can only be a purely dialectical expression, and will be a hindrance in his life.[21]

His meaning is not entirely clear (several translators have wrestled in despair with the passage), though he appears to be commending Malinowski on the flexibility and nimbleness of his intellect while condemning him for aloofness and cynicism. This judgment is perceptive in its narrow way: Malinowski was indeed a divided self whose intellect must often have seemed to operate independently of what he was feeling. Witkiewicz senior's view agrees, to some extent, with that of Karol Estreicher. Malinowski was 'a studious boy, not gifted with imagination [*fantazja*] who learned well but who was reluctant to disclose his intentions. . . . He did not say what he thought; he was reserved in order to act ruthlessly afterwards, disclaiming any responsibility.'[22] Again the charge of secrecy, if not duplicity. But it is a strange observation that Malinowski was 'not gifted with imagination', scarcely an evaluation with which posterity could concur. Estreicher was perhaps using as his yardstick the wantonly fantastic imagination of Staś Witkiewicz. As for Malinowski's purported cynicism, it was not obvious to his later associates (nor is it evident in his diaries), so it may well have been a youthful pose ('a purely dialectical expression') that he outgrew. Curiously, though, when their relationship was suffering its deepest crisis and hung by a mere thread Staś wrote reproachfully to Malinowski:

> What a frightful liar you are when you say that I taught you cynicism. It was you who taught me to regard everything including oneself with cynicism. Think that over for a moment. A convenient attitude: to have a total lack of faith in any noble impulses whatsoever and your cold ironic smile, and the conviction that at bottom human motives are always petty and mean. If one wishes to see life that way, it's quite easy. Flowers grow in the swamp. One can look at them, without sticking one's nose in the mud.[23]

Months before receiving this painful letter, Malinowski had already committed to his diary a summary judgment on his friend: 'I respect his art and admire his intelligence and worship his individuality, but I cannot stand his character.'[24]

An independent judgment of Staś's character was pronounced in 1921 by an older contemporary, the critic and poet Taduesz Boy-Żeleński:

> Witkiewicz is by birth, by race, to the very marrow of his bones an artist; he lives exclusively by art and for art. And his relationship to art is profoundly dramatic; he is one of those tormented spirits who in art seek the solution, not to the problem of success, but to the problem of their own being.[25]

Staś's dedication to art eventually had an antagonistic and even alienating effect on Malinowski, who would need to seek in science a complementary solution to the 'problem' of his own being.

Zarathustras of Zakopane

Heavily colonized by the intelligentsia, Zakopane exhibited Cracow's vibrant modernism. Its cultural pretensions became as rarefied as its mountain air. During this heady period, *la belle époque* of Zakopane, the intelligentsia deliberately courted the local highlanders to contrive a fertilization of fine arts by folk crafts. As in Cracow, the flirtation between intellectuals and peasants was consummated in the marriages of several artists and writers to peasant women. Witkiewicz senior was himself a paragon of this aspect of the neo-Romantic Young Poland movement, which esteemed Polish folk culture as an authentic source of national culture. He wanted a rural life for his son: 'It is my dream that you should live in the Tatras. Not as a tourist, a mountain-climbing bourgeois – I want you just to live there and paint it, not as a study of the foreground and background, but as an expression of them and of yourself.'[26] Staś did indeed live for most of his life in Zakopane, glorying in its 'granite giants reflected in blue lakes'.

Important though Malinowski and Staś were to one another during their youth, they were not exclusive companions. Indeed, their friendship was complicated and enriched by a third party: Leon Chwistek, son of Dr Bronisław Chwistek, the director of a Zakopane sanatorium. Leon's mother was an artist who taught her son at home until he entered the Sobieski Gymnasium. Born in the same year, Chwistek and Malinowski went through school and university together. In this respect it was Witkiewicz, a year younger, who was the odd man out; but from another perspective it was Malinowski, for Chwistek had artistic flair and aspired to become a painter, though he never achieved such fame as Witkiewicz. From yet another point of view, it was Chwistek who was the outsider on account of his comparatively lowly social origins. In addition to their needle-sharp intellects, however, the three companions had much in common: literary proclivities, an infatuation with 'fantastic subjects' and a passion for philosophy. Eventually, all three men achieved posthumous national fame of the kind commemorated by postage-stamps portraits.

The personal chemistry of their triangular relationship was complex. Malinowski seems to have treated Leon Chwistek with less respect than he gave to Staś, and apparently regarded him as boastful and arrogant (defences deployed by Chwistek, perhaps, to compensate the sense of social inferiority that Staś played upon). Malinowski was also inclined to side with Staś during their frequent arguments. Basing his account on Chwistek's own recollections in the 1930s, Karol Estreicher writes of their adolescence in Zakopane:

> They all read to each other their plays and poetry, and wrote pseudo-scientific treatises. . . . The boys' literary imagination was constantly aroused and stimulated by a symbolically tainted kind of eroticism – symbolism being then in its heyday. Dreams of success, power and fame were interwoven with boyish reveries about love rather naïvely conceived as some sort of sensual folly.[27]

A few lines of verse in Malinowski's unmistakable hand have survived which appear to apostrophize Chwistek, though the punning title is 'Chlystek' ('whipper-snapper'). In view of Chwistek's portly figure there can be little doubt that he was the butt of the poem. It includes the following malicious lines: 'O you horrible meatball/ Sizzling on the frying pan of cosmic possibilities/ Your flesh is stuck together . . ./ Like the magma of a volcano that never erupts.'[28]

Chwistek eventually became a distinguished Formist painter and theoretician of art as well as a mathematician, logician and philosopher. As a logician he won the respect of Bertrand Russell, who helped him secure a professorship at the University of Lwów in 1929.[29] Before that he had taught at his alma mater, the Sobieski Gymnasium, where Feliks Gross was among his pupils. It was from Chwistek that Gross first learned about Malinowski. In opposing Fascism during the 1930s, Chwistek moved to the radical left, learned Russian and spent World War II in the Soviet Union. He died in Moscow in 1944.

Another close friend of Malinowski and Staś was Tadeusz ('Tadzio') Szymberski, a once-popular but now forgotten poet and playwright. Tadzio married a painter named Zosia (whom Staś detested), and they went to live in Paris where Malinowski visited them frequently between the wars. The couple were impoverished, however, and Zosia was mentally unstable. Helena Wayne remembers Tadzio Szymberski as her 'ideal of a Polish gentleman . . . highly intelligent, dignified, handsome with a sensitive pale face lit by a lovely smile. He also had that sense of fun that children recognize at once.'[30] Malinowski dedicated the Polish edition of *The Sexual Life of Savages* to him, and Feliks Gross recounts how, in the late 1930s, Malinowski begged him to approach Estreicher, as rector of the Jagiellonian, for financial help for Tadzio.[31] The Szymberskis died tragically, committing suicide by the roadside near Vichy during the German occupation of France. Stanisław Estreicher himself was to die in Sachsenhausen concentration camp (along with many of his professorial colleagues) after having refused the Gestapo's invidious invitation to take over the presidency of the province.[32]

A somewhat older friend with whom Malinowski and Staś climbed and skied in the Tatras was Jerzy Żuławski. A modernist poet and dramatist, Jerzy was the first Polish science-fiction writer and is best remembered for a dystopian trilogy set on the dark side of the moon. In 1907 he married Kazimiera Hanicka, another of Malinowski's friends who would recollect that, in order to develop his strength of will and body, a frail Malinowski would climb 'dangerous rocks and chimneys' and practise 'yoga habits'.[33] The Żuławskis were an affluent couple who ran a salon in Zakopane and later in Paris. Jerzy's younger brother Zygmunt was also an occasional Zakopane companion. A passionate socialist and student activist, Zygmunt became a trade-union leader and parliamentary deputy. Later still he distinguished himself as a leader of the Polish underground during the Nazi occupation.

An older friend was Tadeusz Miciński, a leading Symbolist poet, playwright and novelist, who was venerated by Staś as 'the only great Polish poet before and after the war'.[34] Miciński's byzantine novel *Nietota*, published in 1910, features a refined yet 'cold and wise' scientist who was a caricature of the ambitious young Malinowski:

> There was also a scholar, Sir Xerxes Jakszma, who at the age of twenty-two had discovered the component elements of sunspots, at twenty-three had written a splendid treatise about the sexual degeneration of Countess Wawiłonska, and now at twenty-four returned full of fame after a discovery of Siamese tombs.[35]

Malinowski as a soulful Xerxes, wearing a large coloured scarf and a huge white mitten, was commemorated by Staś Witkiewicz in a striking oil portrait.[36]

In 1904 Staś befriended Karol Szymanowski, a musician who used Tatra folk airs in his monumental orchestral pieces; he would become Poland's greatest twentieth-century composer. In the same year, Szymanowski introduced Staś to the visiting pianist Artur Rubinstein, whose portrait Staś wanted to draw.[37] Malinowski came to know both these musicians, too, though he did not enjoy Szymanowski's music.

The Russian revolution of 1905–07 put a dampening effect on the neo-Romantic movement (it was said that 'Young Poland grew old overnight'), at least as it was being played out in Zakopane. Socialism was suddenly in the bracing air. Neither Malinowski nor Witkiewicz was particularly interested, though Leon Chwistek certainly was, having been influenced by Feliks Dzierzynski, the Bolshevik leader who became the reviled head of the Cheka, Moscow's murderous secret police. A 'People's University' opened in Zakopane and a 'Workers' Tourist Association' was formed.[38] The closest brush with revolutionary doctrines Malinowski ever experienced came straight from the horse's mouth a few years later. Feliks Gross tells how the poet Jan Kasprowicz invited Malinowski to tea to meet an 'interesting' Russian revolutionary who was living in exile in Poronin, a village near Zakopane. His name was Vladimir Lenin. Malinowski was reluctant to go: 'Listen, they tell the same stories, they always lecture you about Karl Marx, they are a dull crowd.' But Kasprowicz insisted and Malinowski enjoyed a long conversation with Lenin, whom he found 'sympathetic and pleasant'.[39]

Malinowski also made friends for reasons other than ones of personal affinity, as he confessed to Elsie Masson when telling her how well he had known Henryk Sienkiewicz's son.

> [We] sat on the same bench in Cracow University for two years and spent ab. 3 hours daily together. He is a very nice, perfectly gentlemanly character with a distinct pose to be English, but perfectly anaemic mentally and absolutely uninteresting. My friendship with him is one of the saddest pages in my mental history, because I stuck on to him out of pure snobbishness.[40]

The snobbery was occasioned by the Nobel Prize that Sienkiewicz had been awarded in 1905, an honour that greatly enhanced the international literary reputation of Cracow and Zakopane. But Sienkiewicz was not greatly esteemed by the younger generation, and Malinowski told Elsie that he 'belonged to that clique in Poland, who simply will not mention the name of Sienkiewicz except to revile him and sneer at him'.[41] By 'that clique', he was probably referring to the modernist movement known to cultural historians as 'Młoda Polska', or Young Poland.

'Rut and debauch' in Cracow

For one who devoted much of his professional life to thinking about the formative influence of culture on the human individual, it is curious that Malinowski neglected to acknowledge in any of his writings (including his autobiographical notes and sketches) the cultural movement that animated Cracow and its satellite, Zakopane, during the most impressionable years of his youth. As an acute observer extremely sensitive to his social environment, Malinowski could not have been immune to the manners and mores, and the attitudes and postures of Young Poland's intelligentsia. By 1902, the year in which he matriculated, Cracow had become a hothouse for artistic and literary experimentation.

Self-styled after modernist movements in other European countries (there was also a Young Czech movement), the Młoda Polska epoch spanned the two and a half decades between 1890 and 1915. It lacked the coherence of a school, being more an amalgam of neo-Romantic artistic fashions and literary trends reacting against the stodgy positivism and dull realism of the preceding generation. Fired by French Symbolism, German modernism and a pan-European *fin-de-siècle* Decadentism, it was abruptly extinguished by the Great War. Among its other ideological elements were nature romanticism, eroticism, individualism, Nietzsche's philosophy of the *Übermensch* and the cult of genius, humanism and (as always) Polish patriotism. Clearly, these strands were not all mutually compatible. Any cultural movement that is in part a reaction and which develops imported ideas and fashions according to local exigencies, and, not least, any movement that engages a significant proportion of a nation's intelligentsia and persists for an entire generation, must contain many contradictions. Young Poland was no exception.[42]

According to one scornful critic, the fashion was for

decadence, melancholy, discouragement, and pessimism, as well as for long hair, wild beards, capes, wide-brimmed hats, a grimace of disdain and contempt for everything, and a certain looseness of behaviour. This was accompanied by strange, pretentious poems and extravagant, frequently 'indecent' paintings.[43]

Cracovian youth wore the whole bohemian drag, so to speak, common to many other European cities during the *fin-de-siècle*. The older generation was naturally dismayed by the extravagance and the posturing, though much of it was probably motivated by a simple desire to *épater le bourgeois*. Sienkiewicz was one of those who, purporting to be shocked, defended older values and attacked the new literature as 'rut and debauch'.[44]

As first home to Young Poland, Cracow regained some of its ancient cachet as the cultural capital of the imaginary nation, though by 1902 the movement had spread to Warsaw and other Polish cities. Historical accounts of the period refer to several salient cultural events occurring in Cracow around the turn of the century that nicely epitomized the movement. These were the founding of an influential literary journal, the opening of a satirical cabaret and the staging of Stanisław Wyspiański's play *The Wedding*.

Founded in 1897, the literary periodical *Życie* ('Life') was for the brief period of its existence the militant organ of Young Poland. It came under the editorship of the *enfant terrible* Stanisław Przybyszewski, who preached an exalted view of the artist – a message that sounded a responsive chord in Staś Witkiewicz. 'Art has no other aim than itself, it cannot serve any idea, and cannot be checked by any aesthetic rule; it is the highest source from which life itself flows.'[45] *Życie* published the most distinguished contemporary poets – Kazimierz Tetmajer (the melancholy poet of the Tatras), Wyspiański, Miciński and Jan Kasprowicz – each of whom Malinowski knew personally, if not intimately. In addition to being a charismatic literary prophet, Przybyszewski was a notorious drunkard and womanizer, a Nietzschean 'satanist' who exemplified *fin-de-siècle* decadence. His dictum 'In the beginning was lust' would doubtless have appealed to the adolescent 'eroto-mania' of Bronio and Staś.

In 1902 another Young Poland writer whom Malinowski came to admire took up residence in Cracow. This was Wacław Berent, one of the first Poles to publish essays on Nietzsche.[46] His translation of *Thus Spake Zarathustra* appeared in 1905, though it is likely that Malinowski first read it in the original German. Berent's novel *Próchno* ('Rotten Wood'), published in 1901, depicts a cosmopolitan, nihilistic group of artists in *fin-de-siècle* Berlin and would have been mandatory reading for young Cracovians. Its existential theme is 'art as a hunger of the soul' and the inability of decadent, world-weary artists to satisfy it. Berent's view was Nietzschean: modern man is a flawed, unfinished being who must make way for the *Übermensch*. The characters in *Rotten Wood* are given to interminable soul-searching, ultimate despair, alcoholism or suicide.[47] While not exactly a popular writer, Berent appealed to his own elite constituency. Some of the literary idioms in *Rotten Wood* have a distinct echo in Malinowski's first (1908) diary: 'If the hunger of the spirit has conquered the hunger of life, then he [the artist] will plunge ever deeper into new depths of dark riddles and into a new abyss of more powerful passions. There he will also flounder, sink and disappear.'[48] Of course, it could be that both Berent and Malinowski independently expressed themselves through the inflated rhetorical tropes made fashionable by Nietzsche.

Cracow was not all angst and high seriousness. In 1905 the Zielony Balonik ('Little Green Balloon') cabaret opened in an artists' café called Michalik's Cave. It became celebrated as 'the spiritual synthesis of Cracow', 'a re-vindication of the right of laughter' and 'an anticipation of [Poland's] freedom'.[49] The Little Green Balloon's literary notoriety began with the involvement of Tadeusz Boy-Żeleński and from 1906 he was its moving spirit. Boy (his pen name) was a gifted satirical poet and songwriter who had become enamoured of the French *chanson* while studying medicine in Paris. His songs satirized everything – from Cracow's self-important traditionalism and 'monument mania' to the pseudo-Romantic pretensions and capitalized sentiments of Young Poland's poets, for whom 'Everything lives only with Spirit/ Everything breathes only of Beauty'. A particular target of Boy's satire was Stanisław Tarnowski, professor of Polish literature at the Jagiellonian and one of the old guard who scorned modernism. Another tempting target was the 'peasant-mania' of Young Poland, and Boy mercilessly parodied Lucjan Rydel, the Cracovian poet whose marriage to a peasant woman had provided Wyspiański with the plot for *The Wedding*. Boy's satire played on Rydel's difficulties in adapting to village life, but his larger target was Young Poland's sometimes ludicrous flirtation with peasant culture. As well as the satire and the *chansons*, Malinowski would have enjoyed the irreverent bohemian company of the Little Green Balloon – though not, one fancies, the all-night carousing. His health was scarcely up to such excesses.

The revival of the Cracow theatre at the turn of the century provided an enormous boost to Young Poland. As well as the work of Polish play-wrights, it staged plays by Gorky, Maeterlinck, Hauptmann and Ibsen, so it was before an already sophisticated audience that Wyspiański's *The Wedding* opened in 1901. The play was an immediate sensation and is still regarded as one of Poland's greatest dramas. An intensely literary work, rich in allusions to Polish mythology, history and literature, it is also a comedy of manners that offers 'a bitter vision of Polish society' as represented by the microcosm of Cracow.[50]

An important feature of the Young Poland movement as Malinowski must have experienced it during his late teens was the companionable dimensions of the stage upon which it was enacted. The leading figures were not only well acquainted with one another but lived practically cheek by jowl. Central Cracow, where the literati, the intelligentsia and the gentry clustered, could be crossed on foot in minutes. Wyspiański's house, for example, was just behind the academic dormitory in Mały Rynek, which was two streets away from Floriańska where Michalik's Cave could be found. A stone's throw from the cabaret-café was the Academy of Fine Arts, while the Academy of Sciences and Arts (to which Malinowski would one day belong) was in the very next street.

Leon Chwistek wrote sardonically of the pretentious public response to this inbred studio culture: 'Conversations were full of quotations from Nietzsche, Ruskin or Bergson, even Kant was invoked. . . . Writers and artists were idolized. Every ambitious young man wanted to be a poet, and

Polish literature and philosophy were the chief subjects of study at the university.'[51] To the degree that Malinowski moved in these circles, the impact of the movement upon him was direct and unmediated, and as an ambitious young man himself he most certainly wanted to be a poet and to- study philosophy. Insofar as he was a youthful bystander rather than a participant, he absorbed its influence by intellectual osmosis. His closest friends were demonstrably engaged by the movement, and his personal acquaintances included older men, such as Miciński, Kasprowicz, Boy-Żeleński and Żuławski, who were among its most articulate exponents. So too would he have been susceptible to the all-pervasive ideas of Nietzsche, the chief philosophical inspiration of Young Poland. Indubitably the modernist milieu helped to shape his aesthetic tastes and literary style. We can most easily detect traces of this heady epoch in the content and expressive style of his personal diaries, and perhaps even in the neo-Romanticism of his ethnographic masterpiece, *Argonauts of the Western Pacific*.

But Malinowski always thought for himself. He was ever his own man, as his wayward friend Staś clearly recognized. Despite the fast and furious lifestyle of the Cracovian bohemians, one glimpses Malinowski keeping a disdainful distance from their follies. By means of a certain inner reserve (marked as aloofness or coldness by some of his friends) Malinowski allowed the excesses of the movement to wash over him. In the eyes of his contemporaries, Malinowski was not a modernist in the strictest sense of the term. To this extent he probably felt himself to be an outsider, self-consciously uneasy in the debauched atmosphere of Michalik's Cave.

What was the reason for his diffidence? He was not without artistic impulses and for a time fancied himself a poet. Beginning about the turn of the century he intermittently versified for almost twenty years. None of his poems saw print, however, and what has survived in manuscript, back-of-envelope form, is scrappy, unpolished and of no particular merit. But he was obviously inspired by contemporary Symbolist poets such as Tetmajer and Kasprowicz, and his satirical verse probably owed something to Boy-Żeleński. In other artistic realms Malinowski was even less talented. He sketched in a perfunctory manner but never painted. He experimented with photography, but in a timidly realist fashion, not in the boldly imaginative manner that characterized Staś Witkiewicz's efforts. Although a music lover, as a player Malinowski was limited to a few years' study of the violin. In 1912, a year of some fervent versifying, he also toyed with the idea of writing a drama, but, distracted by other projects, he did not even begin. Nor did he ever attempt to write a novel. In the early 1920s he drafted a few Conradian short stories but his literary agent failed to interest a publisher. By then, of course, he was an accomplished essayist in his chosen field of anthropology, but he did not regard this as an artistic endeavour.

Some of Malinowski's immunity to Young Poland, then, could have resulted from his ineligibility to pursue an artistic vocation. Invidious comparison with the many budding artists and writers who surrounded him would have only underscored his limitations. Having decided that his talents lay elsewhere, he could turn his back on the bohemian affectations of Cracow and Zakopane. His closest friend, who became Witkacy the prolific artist and 'graphomanic' writer, alias Vitcatius, Witkatze, Witrejus, Mahatma Witkac, Witkós, etc, brilliantly symbolized his epoch in a manner impossible for Malinowski, the sober scientist.

Chapter 5

University Student

Entering the Jagiellonian

As the son of a professor, there was every expectation that Malinowski would go on to university. But there were other options and, unusual though it might have been, the case of Staś Witkiewicz shows that views opposed to university education could prevail. In September 1903, when Malinowski had already completed his first year at the Jagiellonian, Staś Witkiewicz received this advice from his father:

> I believe that you should not go to the university this year, that you should work for a while independently and think the whole matter over so that your choice of subject is already a result of fully conscious aims and a complete cleansing of the school attitude to learning. . . . Do not think, my dear boy, that I want to cramp you. I want you to take the most independent and individual way – I advise you to do so because, as you know, what I care for is the *essence of life* and not a formal negotiation of the external order. I am concerned not about a university diploma but about the complete development of your kind soul.[1]

Although he was not directly affected by such arguments, Malinowski must have heard and weighed them, coming as they did from a man whom he appears to have admired. Witkiewicz senior probably did not realize what a tremendous burden of choice he was placing upon his son. Young men who are uncertain of their footing do need to enter into 'a formal negotiation with the external order' before they can reasonably begin to contemplate 'the *essence of life*' and develop their souls. It is perhaps as well that Malinowski did not to have to confront such a choice. There were, however, other choices to be made: which of the four faculties to enter – law, philosophy, theology or medicine – and, the philosophy faculty having been selected, what subjects to study within it. Malinowski does not appear to have been unduly sullied by 'the school attitude to learning', and he obviously derived satisfaction from the intellectual mastery of difficult subjects. But Witkiewicz senior's letter to his son does give pause to wonder how far Malinowski's choices were 'the result of fully conscious aims'.

He was in his eighteenth year when he registered, on 6 October 1902, in the faculty of philosophy. As the son of a Jagiellonian professor he was entitled to a special stipend, and for the four years of his formal courses he was exempted from university fees.[2] Originally founded as an academy in 1364 by King Kazimierz the Great, the university was refounded in 1400 by the Lithuanian king Władysław Jagiełło, allegedly to fulfil the dying wish of his wife. King Jagiełło, whose dynasty gave its name to the university, guaranteed funding and donated the graceful medieval building that became the Collegium Maius, the architectural treasure situated at its very heart.

Malinowski studied for only four years before reaching the level of *absolutorium*, which permitted him to sit written exams and defend a thesis. The four-year course would be equivalent to a modern honours course in some Western universities, or to a general degree course with a master's year in others. As in many continental systems, however, the doctorate had to be confirmed at a later date by another examination (the habilitation) following a further year or two of study. It was a gentlemanly form of higher education, and the Jagiellonian, like other reputable European universities, was not primarily a qualification-awarding institution (a degree factory in today's contemptuous parlance), but a community of scholars and a traditional seat of learning. Even so, for conscientious students the schedules were demanding: lectures began as early as 7 a.m., the last ones as late as 8 p.m. Explaining this elite system of university education at the turn of the century, Borowska notes that 'students were not required to sit examinations . . . the regulations required regular attendance at lectures, the reading of papers at seminars, participation in laboratory work and oral examinations (*colloquia*).'[3] After completing their studies, students could leave without taking a degree, but those who intended to pursue professional careers were required to submit a doctoral thesis and sit two major examinations, comprising written papers and an oral, known as *rygoroza* (the *Rigorosum* of German-speaking universities). This latter course was the one followed by Malinowski and his friend Leon Chwistek in 1906.

'*A bias towards laws and regularities*'

According to Malinowski's student record, during his first year he attended lecture courses and seminars on geometry, mathematical analysis and experimental physics. He also joined laboratory classes on physics and inorganic chemistry. The only concession he made to the humanities was a second-semester course in the history of modern philosophy from Bacon to Kant. The study of mathematics clearly dominated this first year (eleven hours a week), followed by physics (nine hours) and philosophy (four hours). Considering that this was Malinowski's first opportunity to sample the intellectual wares of 'the Polish Athens' (as the Jagiellonian was proud to be called during this period of Galician autonomy), it seems a rather narrow set of options to tackle. Most likely, he had decided to master ways of thinking that would provide him with a secure foundation for later studies. The fact that he continued to study mathematics for several more years is proof enough that he had a natural aptitude for it and was content to submit to its rigour.

The significance of this early devotion to mathematics for his subsequent career in anthropology is not immediately obvious (though in 1932 the linguist Alfred Korzybski, himself a mathematician, believed that it explained why Malinowski had done such 'remarkable work').[4] Other than the routine gathering of statistical data in the field, Malinowski did not develop quantitative methods. Indeed, he taught that the calculus of everyday life eluded measurement, a keynote of his ethnography being that people evaded rules almost as often as they obeyed them. But the paradigmatic concept of function that he developed owed its initial inspiration to the concept of 'symbolic function' in mathematical logic. There was also a conceivable mathematical input into his anthropology in his respect for numerical data, perhaps even more so in his systematizing approach that listed and correlated ethnographic information in synoptic tables. In short, it was a passion for theoretical order and clarity rather than any hope of mathematical systematization that inspired his ethnographic methods. Unlike the young Bertrand Russell, Malinowski held no faith 'that in time there would be a mathematics of human behaviour as precise as the mathematics of machines'.[5]

The question remains why Malinowski was attracted to mathematics and physics. It is tempting to appeal to the notion of compensatory interest, given the conspicuous artistic talents of his closest friends and the promise of intellectual refuge that sensitive natures seek when confronted by their own inadequacies. Pushing this argument, one might imagine that the sheer beauty of crystallized truth that mathematics and physics offers to the initiated would be immensely comforting to one whose existence is otherwise insecure. Mathematics offers not only demonstrable intellectual truths, but also a measure of emotional security in its assurance of certain knowledge (as a child, an unhappy Bertrand Russell found geometry 'delightful' and 'intoxicating' for precisely these reasons).[6] But such speculations fall short in Malinowski's case. Compensation for his artistic deficiencies can probably be ruled out, for Witkiewicz and Chwistek were also adept at mathematics (the latter eventually good enough, in fact, to earn Russell's commendation). Moreover, the evidence does not allow the claim that Malinowski's childhood and youth were so unhappy as to drive him to seek consolation in the virtual world of numbers and formal proofs.

There is more to be said, however, if not on mathematics itself then on the kind of mind that relishes abstractions and general propositions. Here we can take into account Malinowski's own insight into his proclivity for a certain kind of anthropological theorizing. In the autobiographical notes he sketched for his unwritten textbook, he referred to 'a general bias towards' and 'a greater interest' in 'laws and regularities' and a complementary aversion ('repugnance' was his more emotive word) to the 'historical, [the] concrete, [the] unique'. He offered no psychological explanation for this bias, but in circular fashion attributed it rather to his scientific training. He also invoked 'personal experiences, limited as they were', in being exposed to different cultures and languages, and his notes continue on the subject of 'samenesses' versus 'differences' between cultures, and how his theory of functionalism stressed the former by digging beneath 'what appears on the surface'. Functionalism, in short, satisfied his need to find 'laws and regularities' in widely differing societies.'I speak about my "bias" as [a] scientific preference. I saw [in anthropology] a greater interest [in] diversities & I recognised their study as important, but underlying sameness I thought of greater importance & rather neglected. . . . I still believe that [the] fundamental [is] more important than [the] freakish.' Malinowski's predilection for finding similarity in diversity and the general in the particular is one of the grounds of his achievement as an anthropologist.[7]

Professors and mentors

Since the time of Copernicus mathematics had been a particular strength of the Jagiellonian. In Malinowski's day physics was also in a dynamic stage of development, and within a few years the discoveries of Albert Einstein and Max Planck would revolutionize the subject. The exact sciences (which came within the faculty of philosophy) were represented by an impressive array of professors. The university as a whole was stocked with relatively young Poles who, 'after wandering through continental Europe and Great Britain in search of advanced learning, returned to teach in their native language'.[8]

Malinowski's mathematics teachers, with whom he spent so much class time in 1902 and the following years, were Stanisław Zaremba and Kazimierz Żorawski. Zaremba had studied in St Petersburg and at the Sorbonne and his main interest was in mathematical physics, especially the theory of differential equations. Malinowski attended his courses and seminars in every one of his four years at the university. Zaremba's junior colleague Żorawski, whose research interests lay in differential geometry, had studied in Leipzig.

The senior professor of physics was August Witkowski, one of Bronio's godfathers. Matlakowski remembered Witkowski as a brilliant orator whose lectures on mechanics were 'crowded to capacity by students from several faculties'. Malinowski took lectures and seminars from him throughout his four years. Władysław Natanson was another eminent theoretical physicist, an expert in thermodynamics who later worked on radiation and quantum mechanics. One of his pupils recalled that his lectures were 'so beautiful that the difficulties disappeared'.[9] For three years Natanson taught Malinowski theoretical mechanics, elasticity, hydrodynamics, electricity and magnetism, and the dynamics of electrons.

The professor with whom Malinowski developed the most affectionate and enduring relationship was his philosophy teacher, the Rev. Stefan Pawlicki. Over the years Pawlicki became his principal academic advisor and moral tutor, and Malinowski corresponded with him for several years after leaving Cracow. 'Bronek was very much his favourite,' according to Matlakowski. 'Pawlicki used to invite him to dinners which were of a very high standard because the Reverend was such a connoisseur of the culinary art.' There is always a sting in the tail of Matlakowski's recollections, and he added: 'Uncharitably, Bronek would poke fun at the philosophy of his benefactor.'[10] Leon Chwistek was another of Pawlicki's favourites. Other than a passing mention of Witkowski, Pawlicki is the only one of his Jagiellonian teachers whom Malinowski referred to in later years, and whenever he did so it was in tones of veneration. Pawlicki must therefore be ranked as a personal influence on the young Malinowski, equal to any of his mentors in England.

Among the Cracovian intelligentsia, Pawlicki was something of a Renaissance figure: 'a scientist-eccentric and priest-monk, having unusual interests and strange habits.'[11] The bohemians also claimed him, and Boy-Żeleński wrote warmly of Pawlicki as a 'Man of the Palaces', one equally at home in the university, the street café, the Academy of Science and the Papal Academy: 'an Epicurean, glutton and charming fop.'[12] Pawlicki began his career as a philosophy teacher at the Main School in Warsaw, but it was as a priest – a member of the Community of the Resurrection, a doctor of theology and a member of the Papal Academy – that he arrived in Cracow in 1882 to take up a chair in theology. A decade later Pawlicki performed another intellectual somersault and was appointed professor of philosophy. As Andrzej Flis notes drily: 'His unparalleled turn from assistant professorship to a monastic cell, from positivism to theology and from theology to Greco-Latin philosophy, remains an inscrutable riddle to this day.'[13] Pawlicki published books on Schopenhauer and Darwinism, two volumes on the history of Greek philosophy, a biography of Ernest Renan, and a study of Spinoza and monism. His discovery of Schopenhauer in 1865 (the year in which he wrote a dissertation on him in Latin) was a decade before the philospher became fashionable in his native Germany, and almost a full generation before the avant-garde intellectuals of Young Poland made him one of their icons.

As befitted a polymath, Pawlicki's lectures covered an enormous range of topics. In addition to the history of modern philosophy, he taught courses on logic and dialectics, Aristotle's politics, critical positivism, Nietzsche, socialism and the philosophy of the state, and, not least, psychology. His seminars brought together a handful of select students, including Malinowski and Chwistek. It was this somewhat bizarre and contradictory figure who captivated Malinowski, as much by his manner, no doubt, as by his intellect and learning. Pawlicki's influence increased year by year, culminating in 1905–06 when Malinowski was working towards his doctorate. A letter to Pawlicki, dated 1 November in what could only be 1905, gives some indication of the intellectual intimacy Malinowski enjoyed with his mentor:

I am looking forward with great impatience to the moment when you, Father, return to us for good and when I can satiate my philosophical doubts and perplexities at the source. For the time being I am devoting myself to causality, reading Lange's *Kasualproblem* [1904] and the last work

of Mach [probably *Erkenntnis und Irrtum*, 1905] of which I want to give
you a thorough account. Several colleagues have divided among themselves the first few chapters of Hume . . . so that our first meeting is
settled.[14]

In a forthrightly flirtatious manner Malinowski went on to say: 'If you do
not give me authority to see you by special arrangement, I shall be so importunate as to – having found the time and place – surreptitiously waylay you,
especially since I want to beg of you, Father, a small favour, but do not dare
bore you with it in a letter.'

The seduction of philosophy

In addition to his staples of mathematics and physics, Malinowski broad-
ened his studies in his second year to include at least three courses in
humanities. From Pawlicki – the man whose personal motivations no one
understood – he took a course in psychology, which had only recently
become an experimental science and was still regarded by many as a branch
of philosophy. From Leon Kulczyński he took an introductory course on
pedagogics and another on the formation and training of 'volition and
character' (suggestive in view of Malinowski's youthful obsession with
self-control). Kulczyński was an adherent of Johann Herbart's views on
apperception and 'the mechanics of representations' which Malinowski
criticized in his doctoral dissertation.[15]

The following year, Malinowski balanced his devotion to mathematics
and physics with an even greater weighting of humanities subjects. Class
hours increased to a formidable total of twenty-eight or twenty-nine a
week, and if he attended every class for which he was enrolled it would
have left little time for private study. In addition to mathematics and physics,
Malinowski took two philosophy seminars, Kulczyński's lecture course on
the application of psychology to education, Maurycy Straszewski's 'Introduction to Philosophy' and another on ethics, a 'Slavonic Seminar', and a
weekly lecture on 'Polish Lyrical Poetry since Mickiewicz'. Last but not
least in view of Malinowski's introspective habits, there was a weekly lecture
on 'The Psychology of Emotions' by Władysław Heinrich. The second
semester gave even greater weight to philosophy, taught principally by
Straszewski and Pawlicki. In addition to his philosophy seminar, Pawlicki

gave lecture courses on 'Logic and Dialectics' and 'The Philosophy of Friedrich Nietzsche'.

Władysław Heinrich had been trained as a physicist, but his main work was in psychology and his first task at the Jagiellonian was to organize a laboratory for conducting research into the psychology of optical sensations. Some years later he gave up experimental psychology and was appointed to a professorship in the department of the history of philosophy.[16] It was in this capacity that he taught Malinowski, though later still he was to resume his experimental work on the psychology of perception. He published at least a dozen works: on the psychology of sensation and perception, on the philosophy and methodology of science, and on the history of philosophy. In his psychological research he explored the connection between physiological responses and introspection – a clue to one of Malinowski's enduring preoccupations in his diaries.

Maurycy Straszewski had the 'best lineage' of the trio of Cracow philosophers – in Andrzej Flis's judgment Pawlicki was 'the most peculiar' and Heinrich 'the most original'.[17] Straszewski had studied under Albert Lange of Zurich and the monist Hermann Lotze of Göttingen before being appointed to the chair at the Jagiellonian, a post he filled for more than thirty years. Like his two younger colleagues, he worked in several disciplines, though his focus was more narrowly philosophical and he was a pedantic lecturer.[18] Straszewski produced a shelf-full of works on his four main specialities: the history of philosophy, epistemology, metaphysics and the philosophy of science, and the philosphical thought of the ancient East.[19]

With no end-of-year examinations to sit, no annual tests of comprehension and aptitude, no assessments of dedication to learning, Malinowski took courses not to obtain credits or certificates, but from a desire to learn. Here was a liberating philosophy of education that encouraged knowledge to be pursued for its own sake – an important principle when universities were genuine, if elitist, seats of learning. According to Ewa Borowska's reading of the Jagiellonian record, in his final year of university studies Malinowski concentrated during the first semester on differential geometry, integral calculus, electricity and magnetism, and took an additional course on physical chemistry. In the second semester he gave equal time to philosophy, notably ethics and metaphysics. According to B. Średniawa (and Grażyna Kubica who follows him), Malinowski's student album lists his philosophy courses first, most of which are not mentioned by Borowska. These were psychology taught by Straszewski and Pawlicki's courses on ethics, Aristotle's philosophy, the history of modern socialism and the philosophy of the state. Średniawa rightly warns that we cannot be sure Malinowski took all of the courses recorded in his album. In view of his extracurricular activities during the first half of 1906, it would be astonishing were he to have spent as long in the lecture hall, seminar room and laboratory as his album indicates. Not only did he take an Italian holiday with his mother during April and conduct a surreptitious love affair during May, but he also worked on his dissertation in time to submit it in late July.

The subjects Malinowski tackled during his four years of study at the Jagiellonian can be summarized under four categories. 1. Mathematics: including geometry, analytical functions, integral calculus, differential geometry and differential equations. 2. Physics: including experimental physics, heat theory, theoretical mechanics, electricity and magnetism, theory of elasticity, electronics, electromagnetic waves and light waves. A course or two of physical chemistry might also be included here. 3. Philosophy: comprising the history of philosophy, ethics, psychology, pedagogics, logic and dialectics. 4. 'Humanities': including Polish poetry and literature, Slavonic studies and modern history.

A simple calculation shows that Malinowski spent most time, and presumably most effort, on philosophy. To this he devoted more than one-third of his total lecture and class time. This was followed by physics at just under a third, and mathematics at about one-quarter. Other subjects account for only about five percent of the total. According to this crude measure, then, about ninety-five percent of Malinowski's university training was in philosophy, physics and mathematics. There has been some disagreement among Polish scholars about this balance of subjects, and even concerning what Malinowski actually studied. Andrzej Paluch, for instance, writes that Malinowski 'studied physics and mathematics, but not chemistry', while Kubica finds that he took a course in inorganic chemistry taught by Professor Olszewski in his first year, and Borowska that he took physical chemistry taught by Professor Bruner in his last year.[20] Paluch is incorrect in stating that Malinowski 'switched to philosophy as a main subject' in the last years of his studies, for it is clear that he had pursued philosophy (broadly defined here to include psychology and pedagogics) in all four years, and most intensively in his third. Since Malinowski took up neither mathematics nor physics as a career, it is reasonable to suggest that it was his training in philosophy that most significantly shaped his future thinking.

Andrzej Flis has given a succinct account of the complex currents of philosophical thinking in Cracow that formed an essential part of the background to Malinowski's studies.[21] The reigning intellectual principles were scientific ('all reliable knowledge is scientific knowledge'); minimalistic ('avoiding speculations and going beyond facts'); nominalistic ('recognising individual entities only'); empirical ('everything from experience'); naturalistic (the natural sciences provide the model for all sciences); and positive (serving the improvement of human existence). To a quite remarkable extent, these principles were imbibed by Malinowski in his youth and guided his thinking for the rest of his life.

By the end of the century, however, some of these tenets had come under attack, and within a few years the philosophical scene was brilliantly illuminated by stars such as Husserl, Bergson, James, Freud, Croce, Moore, Dewey, Einstein and Russell. Yet despite the appearance of so many diverse and stimulating new trends of thought, when Malinowski studied in the Jagiellonian's faculty of philosophy it was still a bastion of late nineteenth-century positivism. This was the so-called 'second positivism' or 'neo-positivism' of Ernst Mach (1838–1916) and Richard Avenarius (1843–96), a more sophisticated version of the mid-century positivism propounded by August Comte. Marburg neo-Kantianism reached Malinowski (only faintly perhaps) through Heinrich, but Flis is surely correct in claiming that Malinowski could not have been acquainted with German phenomenology, nor yet aware of British analytical philosophy, both of which were still in their infancy when he was studying at Cracow. It was only later, too, that he read Bergson, Dilthey and William James.

We must therefore attend closely to Ernst Mach, the Moravian-born physicist, psychologist and philosopher of science whose name is popularly associated with jet aircraft and the speed of sound. Mach was a resourceful experimenter and brilliant thinker who had achieved international fame by the turn of the century. First as professor of experimental physics at Prague, then as professor of the history of science at Vienna, Mach investigated an astonishing range of subjects which nowadays constitute separate branches of physics and human physiology. To list but a few: acoustics, ballistics, electricity, hydrodynamics, microphotography, motor sensations, optics, shock waves and thermodynamics. Mach invented a device to measure blood pressure and discovered the balance-maintaining functions of the canals of the inner ear; he published major works on the conservation of energy, the history of mechanics, the analysis of sensations, the principles of physical optics, as well as his magnum opus on epistemology, *Knowledge and Error.* 'I don't think anyone ever gave me so strong an impression of pure intellectual genius,' said William James on meeting Mach in 1882. Among others he influenced were Nietzsche, Einstein, Karl Pearson, the poet Hugo von Hofmannsthal and the novelist Robert Musil – not to mention the entire Jagiellonian philosophy faculty who taught Malinowski. Mach's psychology of perception helped shape the modernist aesthetics and architecture of Young Vienna, while his version of Marxism impressed Austrian socialists and drew hostile fire from Lenin. Mach was godfather to Gestalt theory and to the logical positivism of the Vienna Circle, which ultimately rejected Wittgenstein's philosophy in favour of Mach's. Despite his high standing among philosophers, however, it was the esteem of his fellow natural scientists that he sought. As a committed positivist he believed that without science philosophy had no proper warrant; indeed, science provided the only kind of knowledge of practical value to humanity.

Mach's own chief debt was to Berkeley and Hume. He reduced all knowledge to sense data: 'the world consists only of our sensations.'[22] The only way to study the external physical world, therefore, was through the study of the 'sensations' (or 'elements', as Mach preferred to call them) of man's perceptual and ideational world. As an ardent empiricist, Mach was resolutely opposed to metaphysics. The Newtonian absolutes of space and time (no less than the ego and the atom) he regarded as metaphysical conceptions – provisional theories that one day would be made redundant by mathematical formulae. Quite literally, it took an Einstein to persuade Mach that atoms might exist in reality. The task of science, in Mach's view, was to describe sense data as economically as possible with the goal of uniting physics and psychology into a psychophysics. Physical theories were economical descriptions of sense data, that is, simplifications of experience. Mathematical functions simplified most usefully and were to be preferred for their economy.

Mach was opposed to 'armchair psychology' since it perpetuated the belief in pernicious metaphysical entities, just as Malinowski would later oppose 'armchair anthropology' because it perpetuated speculative theories. And just as Mach led his generation of psychologists into the laboratory, so did Malinowski – with his exhortation to 'come down off the verandah' – exemplify the movement to take anthropology into the village.

Malinowski also found congenial the Darwinian strain in Mach's theorizing. The ultimate goal of science (as of all cognitive activity) is the survival of the species: knowledge serves biological ends by facilitating adaptation to the environment. From a reading of Edward B. Tylor, Britain's leading anthropologist in the late nineteeth century, Mach recruited 'savage mentality' to his speculative understanding of the origins of science. Mankind's initial knowledge of his natural surroundings was 'a product of the economy of self-preservation'.[23] In *Knowledge and Error* (which Malinowski appears to have read in 1905), Mach discoursed on the psychology of enquiry, but always from a psycho-physiological baseline: 'Ideas gradually adapt to facts by picturing them with sufficient accuracy to meet biological needs.'[24] The starting point of Malinowski's own thinking about science was fundamentally Machian.

Since Nietzsche as well as Mach was an influence on the young Malinowski, it is as well to mention what the two German-speaking thinkers had in common. Although Nietzsche approached philosophy from philology and not, like Mach, from physics, both can be described as epistemological phenomenalists. Both were hostile to metaphysics and agreed that the ultimate objective of science was the satisfaction of human needs. But whereas Mach situated the satisfaction of needs in a social and moral context, Nietzsche urged that each 'superior' individual should attend to his own biological imperatives and disregard existing Judeo-Christian values. Mach took a stand against Nietzschean ethics on this point and was scornfully dismissive of 'the ideal of an overweening Nietzschean "superman", who cannot and I hope will not be tolerated by his fellow-men'.[25]

There were of course other neo-positivist philosophers whom Malinowski read during his university years, among them Richard Avenarius, Hans Cornelius and Joseph Petzoldt. The jargon-ridden variety of positivism developed by Avenarius was called 'empiro-criticism', a label adopted by the Cracow School. Although a monist and phenomenalist like Mach, Avenarius was an even more radical empiricist; likewise Cornelius, who restricted science to the study of the 'immediately given'. All these thinkers were taught to Malinowski by Straszewski, Heinrich and Pawlicki, each of whom presumably added his own philosophical spin. Malinowski also read that Machian bible, Karl Pearson's *Grammar of Science* (1900), and was still recommending it to his own pupils twenty years later.

Indisputably, then, it was Ernst Mach's thought that had the most enduring effect on Malinowski's theorizing, and although he flirted with many other philosophical ideas in later years they were acceptable to him only insofar as they were compatible with the bedrock principles of Mach. The allure of William James's pragmatism, for example, was that of a beloved mistress adorned in new clothes. James's influence on Malinowski has been confused with Mach's, but the latter's was prior and more fundamental.[26]

The economy of Malinowski's thinking

The surest guide to Malinowski's philosophical views at this time is his doctoral dissertation. Predating his first diary, it is the earliest of his writings to have survived.[27] It is worth considering for this reason alone, but even more so because the philosophical stance he adopted in it remained substantially unchanged for the rest of his life. His general approach to science and scientific method, the lineaments of his methodological functionalism and its role in his 'scientific theory of culture', can be discerned in this dissertation, written over a period of weeks when he was twenty-two years old.

The thesis is brief by modern standards. It comprises a seventy-two-page manuscript of about ten thousand words in English translation.[28] The handwriting is doubtless that of his mother, who copied it for him in her elegant script. The main topic of the essay is succinctly captured by the title: 'On the Principle of the Economy of Thought'. This would have immediately identified its concern with the positivist epistemology of Ernst Mach. In this respect it was neither an unconventional nor intellectually adventurous thesis, but one whose subject matter would have been dear to his philosophy teachers – especially Straszewski, who had published a book on the same topic a few years earlier.[29]

Mach's philosophy of science was no longer very new. As early as 1868, in a lecture to a Prague audience, he had asked whether science was 'anything more than a business' based on the 'miserly mercantile principle' of economy. 'Is not its task to acquire with the least possible work, in the least possible time, with the least possible thought, the greatest possible part of eternal truth?'[30] And in 1882, two years before Malinowski was born, Mach addressed the Academy of Sciences in Vienna on the topic of 'The Economical Nature of Physical Inquiry': 'When the human mind, with its limited powers, attempts to mirror in itself the rich life of the world, of which it is itself only a small part, and which it can never hope to exhaust, it has every reason for proceeding economically.'[31]

In essence, Malinowski's essay is a critical evaluation of the epistemology of Mach and Avenarius: its philosophical sufficiency and scientific application, and the degree to which the principle of 'economy of thought' (or 'least effort' in Avenarius's formulation) contained metaphysical assumptions. The compressed nature of Malinowski's argument – admirably deploying an economy of words – defies précis, though its central thesis can be stated simply. The principle is valid, he claimed, insofar as the mimimum expenditure of work (measured in terms of psycho-physiological resources) achieves a maximum result (measured by the practical value of a scientific proposition or law). In Malinowski's own words, the principle 'is absolutely suited to express the role played by the functions of the human brain in relation to its mastery of the outside world'.[32] He agreed with Mach that science is an objective mode of knowledge that most efficiently serves human needs; but in insisting that its purpose is *social*, and therefore relative, he contested Mach's view that it is objectively valid in terms of individual psychology.

Malinowski concluded his essay, as he began, by reflecting on the 'stubborn war on metaphysics' being waged by scientists and philosophers. But he is equivocal about their weapons of empiricism, positivism and especially of monism (which succumbs to its own metaphysics of unity), and he questions whether they have sufficient fire power to vanquish metaphysics altogether. He had shown throughout his argument how metaphysical assumptions lurked in every corner of the philosophy of science. He concluded, then, that empiricism is a necessary though not sufficent basis for philosophy, which cannot as yet dispense with 'uneconomical' metaphysical thinking. An uncharacteristic restraint shadows his closing passages, and one suspects he would have made a more forthright defence of metaphysics had it not been for the need to keep a wary eye on the anti-metaphysical convictions of his examiners.

In sum, Malinowski's essay generally endorses Mach's methodological refinement of Occam's razor, arguing the superiority of Western science in its rigorous application of this principle. The dissertation amply demonstrated Malinowski's own philosophical acumen within a fairly narrow field of late nineteenth-century epistemology. Although not based on any great erudition – he had scarcely had time to acquire it – and without extensive reference to more than a handful of philosophers, the thesis is clearly and consistently argued. It obviously delighted his examiners, Pawlicki and Straszewski (whose own broadly Machian views it doubtless reflected and endorsed), and they praised it as an 'an excellent work, endowed with quite exceptional qualities'.[33]

What did Malinowski derive from this philosophical exercise in terms of his own economy of thought? Mach had declared that functional relations between things, not phenomena in themselves, constituted the proper study of science. Crucially, Malinowski seized upon this notion of mathematical function as 'the main tool of science'. The mathematical conception of function is less anthropomorphic than the notion of biological function, although Malinowski exploited (and sometimes confused) both senses of the term in his later work.

Mach's operational view of science as the investigation of functional relations between elements of a given system provided the inspiration for Malinowski's treatment of culture as a functionally integrated system. In practice, the task of the anthropologist was to investigate the functional relations between the elements – 'institutions', as Malinowski would call them – of a given culture viewed as 'an integral whole'. This approach was to revolutionize the discipline and form the basis of a unique school of anthropology. But Malinowski also adopted Mach's naturalistic and instrumental view of science as serving biological ends and he transposed it to culture at large. Culture could then be regarded as a vast 'instrumental apparatus', the function of which was to satisfy human needs, both primary and derived. This view, however, is scientistic rather than scientific, for the questions it poses are predicated on the answers. (Q: What is the function of horticulture in satisfying human needs? A: The provision of food.) In embryonic form, both functional approaches are evident in Malinowski's dissertation.

A similar bifurcation is to be found in Mach's thinking. He developed the idea of an 'internal' purpose of science as the description and functional relation of sensations ('the adaptation of thoughts to facts is the aim of all scientific research'), and the Darwinian idea of an 'external' purpose of science defined by its biological function in providing man with the most efficient means of adapting to his environment. This is clearly analogous to Malinowski's twofold deployment of functionalism.

Another lesson he learned while writing his thesis was the indispensability of metaphysics. Later, he would need a quantum of metaphysics to give coherence to his own anthropological vision. Mach's approach to what science studies, based on a puritanical empiricism (sensory experience is everything, all we can possibly know), Malinowski found deficient and stultifying. As Paluch puts it, the 'positivist spectacles' that Malinowski wore were 'not very strong'.[34] The empiricism he settled for was of a more permissive kind ('nothing without experience'). This allowed him to accept the reality of certain things that Mach could not: intangible 'entities' such as the ego, the unconscious mind, society and culture, none of which is accessible to the 'pure experience' of the senses. Malinowski would need such epistemological latitude to address theoretical problems of anthropology such as the meaning of magic, the role of totemism, the sociology of fatherhood and the function of primitive exchange. He had decided as early as 1911 that theory (and not experience, narrowly defined) must precede description: 'every precise description of facts requires precise concepts, and these can be provided only by theory.'[35] But if Malinowski departed from Mach on the subject of what was knowable, he followed him closely in his overall view of science as an instrumental social activity, the task of which was to describe the given world in the most exact, economical way. Explanations were secondary to descriptions which, if sufficiently accurate, would be predictive and therefore of practical utility.

Flis rightly cautions against the attempt to trace a philosophical 'lineage' for Malinowski. Not only did he take up a different discipline with different problems than those usually addressed by philosophy; not only did he have 'an open and lively mind' that was inclined to be eclectic; he was also 'too creative' to adopt any one philosophical view in its entirety. To play on the 'miserly mercantile' metaphor, it is obvious that Malinowski borrowed heavily from Mach and profited handsomely from the loan during the years to come. All his major statements on fieldwork method, on functionalism and on culture theory owed something to Mach's original seed-capital, so it is fair to say that Ernst Mach funded Bronislaw Malinowski's theoretical development as an anthropologist. It was an intellectual legacy he never repudiated nor entirely squandered, and at the end of his life he was still spending it, economically as before. There were, of course, other borrowings and Malinowski's intellectual solvency owed much to his willingness 'to accept all the risks which eclecticism carries'.[36] As we shall see, Frazer and Freud, Wundt and Westermarck, Rivers and Durkheim, among others, also contributed to his theoretical working capital.

A naïve realist

While in Melbourne in early 1919, Malinowski made several pages of notes towards a *systema philosophiae*, prepared for an informal seminar composed of his circle of friends.[37] In the absence of any coherent, published statements of his 'philosophy', these jottings are instructive for what they say about Malinowski's basic tenets of belief. By 1919 he had completed his Trobriand fieldwork and recently re-read William James. (By a curious coincidence, in that same year Staś Witkiewicz wrote a play called *The Pragmatists*, which has been called a Wildean satire on James's book *Pragmatism*. Philosophies are like people, James had observed, and Witkiewicz took him literally, creating characters out of philosophies.)[38]

Malinowski began his notes with a list of eight principles of belief: '1. No God; 2. Mind only in Man; 3. No Immortality; 4. Parallelism; 5. Determinism & No Free Will; 6. Reality exists independently of observer; 7. Truth means correlation to reality; 8. Natural law based on real regularities.' Thus, Malinowski declared himself to be at once an atheist, a determinist, a phenomenalist, a positivist, an empiricist, a monist and a pragmatist (of sorts).

His notes are neither wholly consistent nor entirely comprehensible, but the gist of them is plain enough. He now advocated a 'naïve empiricism' for 'assessing the existence of the World "as we find it"'. The standpoint of 'naïve realism' persists after we leave 'the armchair, university chair, pulpit or any other intellectual shelter'. Not that it is 'best or most pragmatic to believe and accept as real what naïve realist empiricism dictates, but if we deny it, we *lie* to ourselves'. Philosophy 'should formulate Truth as we live it and not as we think (or more often misapprehend) it at the end of an armchair nap in a metaphysical mood'. Yet metaphysics remains ineradicable, and 'our naïve empiricism contains not only *objective* elements of reality, but also subjective ones. They are not watertight, and they interact with the intellectual elements of our consciousness.' On the necessity of monism, he observed: 'The content of my inner life is the Objective World. It is not something apart from my cognitive faculties. The World . . . is in me.' Concerning knowledge, he still appeared to follow Mach:

Knowledge is not a *mirror of Reality*, only a set of rules of conduct for Man, leading him to a definite result & indicating this result in a manner avowedly symbolic, i.e. indirect. Truth of a proposition means *not* that it portrays reality, but only that it indicates the quality of an Experience, which must be known to the subject from life. . . . If *general* and *abstract* and *functional relations* exist in Fundamental Experience, then *truth* means quality of perception. Exactly as acuteness or correctness of sight or hearing is a *quality* of the subject's sensations, in the same manner truth is the quality of his perceptions.

By 1919, then, Malinowski had considerably diluted Mach's austere epistemology and was calling himself a naïve empiricist: 'My system of scientific method would simply give an honest, straightforward statement of how things *are*.' Clearly, he preferred a 'commonsense' view of reality. He had been impressed by the way Melanesian villagers coped with a reality that was similar to the one presenting itself to his own senses. Discounting the refractions and distortions produced by language, he could assume that they perceived the world much as he did – a world consisting of the same physical (if not psychical) entities. Attempting to view reality any differently – as 'at the end of an armchair nap in a metaphysical mood' – would add immeasurably to the already difficult task of trying to see through native eyes. After all, there was quite enough to describe and interpret that was strange in their world, so he fell back upon the sensible expedient of making 'honest, straightforward statement[s] of how things *are*' without troubling himself too much about the epistemological status of the sensations he experienced. That he was alert to the difficulties, however, is revealed by his comments on the 'recording apparatus' constituted by his senses – principally sight and hearing – while occasional asides in his diaries attest to nagging epistemological doubts during his fieldwork. At the very least, if 'truth means quality of perception' then one should double-check everything one hears and sees. These notes testify to a recognition that the quality of his own perceptions was an essential ingredient of his success as an ethnographer.

Chapter 6

Decadents

Parallel lives

The first half of 1906 was a particularly busy period for Malinowski. As well as writing his doctoral thesis, he visited Italy with his mother in April, and during May and June found time for a brief love affair. Staś boarded with the Malinowskis again that spring while he attended the Cracow Academy of Fine Arts. His father had been dismayed by his decision to enter the academy, and their relations had become strained. 'You intend to join the herd of piglets,' he scolded. 'You, who as a child had pride and the independence of a free spirit, are to transfer today the responsibility for your art onto some wretched school?'[1] By May 1906, however, he was reconciled to his son's defiance and writing to him as before with pontificating paternal pride: 'Try to wrench yourself free from the commonplace, vulgarity. Aspire to great things, powerful feelings, people and women – naturally wonderful, exceedingly beautiful, heroic, noble – and not "dolts", not "dolts". . . . Your announcement that you are going to write a theory of art has made me very happy.'[2]

Malinowski, meanwhile, was conducting a correspondence with his own 'father': the Rev. Stefan Pawlicki. They exchanged letters or postcards once or twice a month, most of them of simple bread-and-butter communcia-tions. On 10 March, for example, Pawlicki wrote to instruct his pupil to prepare a discussion for the next philosophy seminar; on 20 April Malinowski sent his teacher greetings from Pisa; on 24 May Pawlicki invited him to tea to help instruct a fellow pupil. Malinowski joined Staś in Zakopane for a couple of weeks immediately after submitting his dissertation on 26 July. He then returned to Cracow where he spent the rest of August preparing for his *rigorosa* examination.

'Ego sum nunc Cracoviae et multum doceor ad Doctoratum [I am now in Cracow and studying a lot for the Doctorate],' Malinowski wrote to Father Pawlicki at the beginning of September, complaining that he was 'suffering from all the horrors of a summer spent in town'.

> At the moment I am diligently studying the history of philosophy. About Aristotle I am reading from Piat's book which you recommended and lent me. I am also looking through Zeller. But I am waiting for you to help me elucidate some doubtful points which I can find nowhere clearly formulated. Apart from that I am reading Schopenhauer in the original which gives me much joy, and with difficulty I am forcing my way through Ueberweg's *Grundriss*. The learned German can indeed make every subject so dull, sterile and insipid! The only solace, then, in my toils, is the thought that before long I shall see you, Dear Father; for I am quite alone since my Mother has gone to Nauheim.[3]

Two letters to Malinowski from his mother survive from this period. As well as revealing some of the domestic details of their life in Cracow, they show how Józefa Malinowska, with brisk affection, continued to treat her twenty-two-year-old son as if he were a teenager. She was aware of the need to counter Bronio's impractical side by constant reminders. The contrast between Witkiewicz senior's grandiose bombast and Madame Malinowska's down-to-earth instructions could hardly be more vivid. Her first letter, dated 27 August 1906, was written from Nauheim spa, where she and her brother Bronisław were taking the waters. She had received a letter from Bronio telling her of his return to their old apartment in Cracow; now she gives him precise, motherly instructions:

> The mattresses and pillows lie right on the piano. You hid your books yourself in the washing room, wrapped in a towel, if I remember correctly. Your suit is in the valise, the underwear on top of the bed and some more in the basket . . . all the keys are in the little punnet. Take as few things out as possible, and try not to scatter things around, as they can get damaged and dusty. In the valise you'll also find my pension book and receipts signed by the owner of the house. All we need is the signature of the parish priest of St Nikolaus, who doesn't need to know that we don't live there any more.

She enters into considerable detail concerning the renewal of her passport and is not above implicating her son in a little deceit regarding the authorities:

The passport will probably take a week. If you want it sooner you'll have to go to the police in person, through the gate, deeper in, next to the stairs, it says 'Inspection', from that room further to the left to the senior officer. I'm staying in the country or in Zakopane (that's what you must say), I have to go to the Congress Kingdom [Russian Poland] on family business, hence the urgency.[4]

Three weeks later she wrote from Warsaw concerning their travel plans for the coming autumn. 'Firstly, it's unthinkable to set off for Genoa before 1 October. The professors are never back so early; even if they were and if you passed your doctorate by then, we still couldn't go.' She was right – as mothers usually are – and Malinowski took his *Rigorosa* on 5 and 10 October. Although Józefa does not specify their destination, they had probably already decided on the Canary Islands.

I hate the idea of going through Hamburg, I'd rather go slowly through Genoa, even if we were to wait until 1 November. Personally, I'd rather go via Lisbon than Hamburg, or via Marseilles, if possible. . . . You must always remember, dear boy, that your mother is in poor health and is afraid of this journey.

She raises the matter of the Index, for it appears that some of the books Bronio wishes to read were proscribed: 'I want to be in agreement with the Church, and I want to be able to read to you all the books that you need. Apparently, priest Bandurski is still in Cracow, so please, go to him and ask if I should write some application for permission to the bishop.' The Church charged for such dispensations and Józefa proposes to sell an item of furniture. This devoted, fussily concerned mother ends her letter with 'a million hugs' for her 'dearest son'.[5]

Earlier that summer Staś had written to Malinowski: 'Will you let me come to the defence of your thesis for the doctorate? After the exam you can treat me to dinner at the Grand Hotel.'[6] But the main topic of Staś's letter is a 'diabolical dirty trick' he has played on him. To understand what it was, we must meet the fictional alter egos of Witkiewicz and Malinowski which deepen insight into their parallel lives.

Bungo and the Duke of Nevermore

Between 1909 and 1911, about the same time that James Joyce was working on *A Portrait of the Artist as a Young Man*, Staś Witkiewicz wrote an autobiographical novel with the picaresque title *622 upadki Bunga, czyli Demoniczna Kobieta* (The 622 Downfalls of Bungo; or, The Demonic Woman). Although he added a preface and an epilogue in 1919, the manuscript was not published during his lifetime.[7] His father had strongly advised against publication. Not only was its treatment of sex too forthright for Catholic Poland, but the characters in the novel (a genuine *roman-à-clef*) were thinly disguised versions of the author's friends. Life and art are intricately interwoven in all Witkiewicz's novels and dramas, but *The 622 Downfalls of Bungo* is the most blatantly autobiographical. The eponymous hero is, of course, Stanisław Ignacy Witkiewicz himself, and Bungo's best friends are Edgar, Duke of Nevermore (Malinowski) and Baron Brummel de Buffadero Bluff (Leon Chwistek). Other significant characters are Akne Montecalfi (Irena Solska, the actress with whom Staś began a scandalous affair in 1909), Angelika (Helena Czerwijowska, to whom Staś was briefly engaged in 1912), Magus Childeryk (Tadeusz Miciński, the Young Poland poet) and Teodor Buhaj (Tadeusz Nalepiński, a poet and aspiring dramatist who was a close friend of both Staś and Malinowski).

Like other novels in the genre, *The 622 Downfalls of Bungo* is about the hero's struggle to become an artist. It grappled with Staś's real-life indecisions, for by 1910 even his indulgent father was becoming impatient with his failure to earn a living. The loosely structured plot concerns the sentimental education of a naïve young artist in search of an identity. The prolonged tussle Bungo/Witkiewicz depicts is almost entirely with his own unruly impulses; there are no political or religious ideologies to combat, only existential ones. Many of his father's views are put into the mouths of Nevermore and Magus. The setting of the novel is a peaceful, bucolic world – the forests of Bukowina and the mountains of Zakopane – and pathetic fallacies abound. Nature is almost a character, benign and forgiving, and only man is vile.

The refrain from Edgar Allan Poe's poem 'The Raven' clearly provided Edgar, Duke of Nevermore's name. That Malinowski was complicit in this fictional identity is suggested by an uncompleted poem called 'Nevermore' which he drafted in 1912, about the time he was reading Staś's novel. There is a convergence of symbolism in the works of Poe and Witkiewicz. Staś's preoccupation with the image of the 'demonic woman' can be traced to the misogynists Schopenhauer, Nietzsche, Strindberg and perhaps also Otto Weininger; it had much in common with the *fin-de-siècle* notion of the *femme fatale*.[8] But the most obvious influence is Poe, whose women of 'monstrous will and intellect' turn into vampires, and whose tortured men are 'undead'.[9] (Vampirish women and walking corpses would become stock characters in Witkacy's dramas.) Poe's morbidity and Gothic gloom seem to permeate Witkacy's plays and novels, as does his moral indifference and vision of a dehumanized mankind. On a more particular level, the eye is a potent symbol in the work of both writers. The Raven's eye was 'luminous beyond comparison'; the mutilated cat's 'solitary eye of fire' glares at the doomed narrator in Poe's story 'The Black Cat'. Witkiewicz describes his characters' eyes with extravagant relish, while his portrait subjects – whether in photographs, paintings or drawings – often have eyes of terrifying intensity.

The 622 Downfalls of Bungo also owes some of its inspiration to Oscar Wilde's *The Picture of Dorian Gray* ('Dorian Fidious-Ugenta' was yet another of Staś's fanciful self-appellations). One can imagine the appeal of this allegorical tale of a beautiful young man whose painted visage accrues the loathsome marks of his 'unspeakable' vices while his real face remains unblemished until the moment of his death. The novel ambiguously celebrates the aestheticism and decadent hedonism of its characters while hinting at their moral depravity (assumed by most readers to refer to sodomy), and it was principally this work that confirmed Wilde's guilt in the narrowed eyes of British justice and sent him to jail in 1895. It is tempting to cast Lord Henry as Duke of Nevermore and Dorian Gray as Bungo – especially in the light of Staś's earlier nickname for Malinowski: Lord Douglas, Wilde's lover and nemesis.

As in life, Nevermore/Malinowski is complementary to Bungo/Witkiewicz:

> Their friendship, strengthened by conflict, demanded more enduring, more perfect bonds. Nevermore, besides being the friend who complemented Bungo's nature the way the color red complements the corresponding green, exerted a fundamental influence on his views about life. . . . Bungo, despite constant quarrels with Edgar . . . knew how to take from Edgar the best that was in him, because he truly loved him.[10]

Discount the touches of surreal caricature and a persuasive portrait of the young Malinowski emerges from the novel:

> Every year Nevermore underwent treatment for his nerves. . . . Blasé about salon perversions, for which he used to dress up in special black

tights, and bored with fanatical work (he was an incomparable chemist and a dilettante in mechanics and mathematics), the Duke had given himself up to total rest and all kinds of country diversions.

On Malinowski's purposeful walk and fragile health:

Nevermore, taut as a bow-string, barefoot (he had feet like those of Greek statues), and in khaki pants and leggings, strode ahead with a sure, steady step and looked off into the distance, overcoming his astigmatism by cocking his head slightly, and his face, charged with frightful will power, expressed a longing to satisfy every appetite for life – a desire thwarted by the sickly Nevermore constitution progressively enfeebled over thirty-six generations.

On Malinowski's penchant for swearing in foreign languages and his poor eyesight:

'*Me cago en la barba de Dios!*' the Duke swore in Spanish, stumbling over a protruding stone. 'Give me your hand, I cannot see anything at all.' The Duke suffered from a chronic eye ailment, one of the truly monstrous specters against which he had to battle.

On his bizarre, decadent appearance:

His head was closely shaved; he insisted that this hairstyle had all the ladies falling for him, particularly those of the South. His green eyes, cold as a reptile's, piercing through seventeen-power glasses, made an uneasy contrast with the childish smile on his huge, red, beautifully painted lips.[11]

Nevermore has a young student read mathematics to him:

The Duke was drinking buttermilk on the porch while a pimply-faced young man read one of Goursat's works on mathematics aloud to him in an atrocious French accent. . . . [Nevermore's] eyes were dilated, almost black, and the look on his face was one of concentrated will power forcibly self-imposed.

In contrast to the vacillating, unfocused Bungo, Nevermore is a 'conquerer of life', fully formed, decisive, powerful and self-controlled. In one of their 'essential conversations' about life and art (which seem to parody the didactic duologues of Oscar Wilde), the Duke advises Bungo:

'If you do not have any spiritual underpinning, if you cannot forge within yourself a single steel axis around which the whole complex of the life machine is able to turn, you will become an intellectual Harlequin, patched together out of old scraps. . . . Now I no longer know what the centre of your being is, because art alone cannot resolve those problems for you. . . . Life is either a masterpiece or a farce, which we create out of the raw material of our ego.'

Conversation with the Duke acted on Bungo 'the way a platinum sponge does on a mixture of oxygen and hydrogen – it served as a catalyst'. But his reply is defiant:

'Your principles for the acquisition of strength and the conscious creation of life are good for people who have lost the capacity to live. . . . When you finally decide to live, you won't have anything to experience or anything to create. . . . For me you are like the miser who has hoarded money all his life, and after he has grown impotent and crippled with arthritis, developed a liking for wine and women. I cannot live in that fashion. I have too spontaneous a desire to live to think of storing up capital for the future.'

In turn, Nevermore muses on Bungo's chaotic life, contrasting it with his own aloof and self-sufficient existence:

'Your life is a series of accidents, from which you happily extricate yourself, quite by accident too. In your creative work you do not have what I would call a coherent conception of yourself, not even as an artist. . . . I know that the anecdotal side of your life is seemingly rich, but your experiences do not constitute a whole bound together by a single will, just as your "works" do not bear the mark of any single style. You must learn to be solitary, the way you must know how to draw. Now I am absolutely alone regardless of whether I am at a ball at the Duchess of Norfolk's or on the summit of Pic de Teyde.'

Bungo responds:

'You are all of one piece, but why? Because you never had any inborn natural gift for diversity. . . . I must live out everything I have in me. And if some day I become all of one piece, it will mean that I have taken hold of the flying sparks I consist of. . . . Nietzsche said, "To give birth to a dancing star, one must have chaos in one's heart".'

To this the Duke tartly replies, 'True enough, provided the star is not a Roman candle you can buy at any corner store.'

Allowing for literary hyperbole, there is every reason to suppose that such dialogues between Nevermore and Bungo distil the countless conversations Malinowski and Witkiewicz had exchanged since their adolescence.

From time to time, beyond their shared erotic experiences, beyond their reciprocal outsmarting each other by means of plotting, gossip, and atrocious pranks, at which the Duke excelled, as well as by carrying on a rivalry in all possible and impossible fields, they felt the need to disclose their inmost thoughts on 'essential' matters.

Although these 'essential conversations' on life and art form the core of the first chapter of *Downfalls*, they are bracketed by conversations of a more 'diabolical' nature.

Triangles

A remarkable photograph of Staś and Malinowski taken in 1911 on the verandah of Mrs Witkiewicz's pension in Zakopane shows the two young men standing on either side of an extraordinarily slender young woman whom they are holding aloft by her elbows so that she appears to be levitating. The image is unsettlingly ambiguous. The girl whose head forms the apex of the human triangle is looking directly at the camera, smiling faintly. Should we read triumph or submission into her smile? Has she commanded the men to lift up her seemingly weightless body into some ethereal realm, or is she the helpless victim of their masculine playfulness? Staś and Bronio are both looking intently at their hands cupping the girl's elbows, as if concentrating solely on their task. It is impossible to judge whether they are symbolically elevating Helena Biedrzycka (for that is her name) or symbolically dominating her, for nothing is known of the particular relationship that she had with either man. This photograph, however, visually evokes another triangle involving a different young woman named Zofia Dembowska.

Curiously, this triangular relationship was itself an inversion of one that Zofia's aunt formed with Staś's father and mother. It had been evolving in the Witkiewicz household with the intrusion of Maria Dembowska, an unctuous wealthy admirer of Stanisław. The growing estrangement between his parents had been a factor in Staś's defiance of his father in 1905 when he enrolled at the academy. The issue was partly resolved in 1908 when

Witkiewicz senior went to live at Lovran on the Istrian coast, ostensibly for the sake of his tuberculosis but accompanied by Madame Dembowska.[12] Ambiguously abandoned, Maria Witkiewicz remained in Zakopane to manage her boarding house at Bystre.

The bare facts of the younger triangle are as follows. Staś and Zofia Dembowska had known one another since childhood, but it was not until early 1906 – when they were both attending the Academy of Fine Arts – that they embarked upon a brief affair. Zofia appears to have been smitten, but Staś soon wearied of her attentions and invited Malinowski to 'befriend' her. Bronio did so in Cracow on 16 May, though he too must have known her for quite some time beforehand. Still distressed over Staś's rejection, Zofia then returned to her home in Lithuania. From Vilnius (Polish Wilno) she bombarded Malinowski with rambling letters, to which he intermittently replied with soothing advice – to the effect that she should forget Staś and the 'sensual madness' that he incited. At some stage during the summer Staś attempted to win back her affections, but by late September a wiser Zofia had cut herself free from both friends. What Malinowski felt for Zofia one can only guess, though he would hint in his diary of 1912 that it was to 'compensate' his loss of her that he had sought another affair of the heart later the same year. The very fact that he kept Zofia's letters until the end of his life suggests that he retained fond memories of her.[13]

Zofia Dembowska was the only daughter of Tadeusz Dembowski, an eminent surgeon and physician with a practice in Vilnius. It was a family with aristocratic connections, and in her letters Zofia refers to herself as a 'high-society girl'. She studied painting in Vilnius, Munich and Paris, as well as in Cracow. To Staś and Malinowski, on paltry incomes, Zofia must have seemed extremely well-off, but a deep frustration at her dependence on her parents surfaces in the letters ('if I refuse to comply with their wishes, I'll be deprived of the chance to go abroad next year'), and her bitterness strikes some dramatic poses ('I shall drown myself in the Seine'). Her parents' surveillance was oppressive. On one occasion she was scolded for reading Nietzsche, judged to be an inappropriate author for a young noblewoman. She was also expected to report to them concerning her correspondence with the likes of Malinowski, and for this reason she instructed him to send his letters to clandestine addresses.

Despite what an ungallant Staś said about her plain looks, Zofia was an amorous young woman and, although only twenty-two (a year younger than Bronio), her list of suitors was impressive and included at least one aristocrat. Her letters betray a rebellious nature. To modern ears there is a tone of whining, exaggerated complaint, not unlike the one to be heard in Malinowski's diaries – a note that grates on the stoic nerves of the British reader. But this is in large measure the mannered voice of Young Poland. Zofia's correspondence conforms, in that it beseeches and supplicates, gripes and protests in what can be mistaken for adolescent pique. But she was no callow maiden. She had read widely and intelligently. In addition to Nietzsche she refers to Cornelius, Emerson, Nordau, Lombroso, Gorky and Oscar Wilde – many of them read in the original – and her letters are sprinkled with foreign phrases and literary quotations. She was perhaps trying to prove to Malinowski (and doubtless also to Witkiewicz) that she was not the intellectual stooge these arrogant young men took her to be, but a spirited young woman with a mind of her own. Indeed, Zofia eventually succeeded as a prolific painter and portraitist in the classical style.[14]

On his reading of the one-sided correspondence, Daniel Gerould concludes that Zofia was by no means blind to the game that Staś and Malinowski were trying to play with her. 'She dissects the nature of the triangular relationship with precision and intelligence, considering that the truth is not to her liking. And once she fully realizes that she was just a pawn . . . she summons up her pride and calls it quits.'[15]

We are now in a position to understand the letter Staś wrote to Bronio concerning a 'diabolical dirty trick' he had played on him. Malinowski had discovered some unpalatable facts about Staś's treatment of Zofia, though his letter of rebuke to Staś has not survived.

I'm answering right away to explain that I wrote a letter to Zofia Dembowska saying I told you about the debauchery she and I engaged in. . . . Well, then I had such sharp pangs of conscience with regard to Z.D. that I wanted somehow to set things right, even if it meant playing a dirty trick on you. . . . She is so fabulously magnanimous that she wrote you everything, I offer you my sincere apologies for doing that, but a person who has played so many diabolical dirty tricks as I have can somehow find reasons for just one more. . . . I can see your demonic smile as you read this. I'm sending you her letter, from which you will perhaps draw interesting conclusions. As for your reproach that I am 'low', I forgive you thinking so with all my heart. . . . Evidently you haven't worked on mathematics hard enough to find the equation for the curved line drawn by my artistic hand.[16]

As Malinowski's *Rigorosa* loomed he had every reason for neglecting his correspondence. On 19 September Zofia began what was perhaps her last letter to him.

> Dear Loving Sir, I am writing to you again, but only a few words, to give you my new address in the country. . . . I would like to apologize for my last letter reproaching you for not writing to me for so long. I have no right to do so, and it might discourage your friendship with me. Please write whenever you feel like talking to me.

A day or two later she continued the letter:

> I just received your letter written while you were reading *Dorian Gray*. I am glad you like it. I was very interested in the character of Lord Henry as the prototype of his kind. . . . I will not reply to the gossip passed on by Staś. When are you coming? You must be very tired and irritated. . . . Lovingly, Zofia D.[17]

Zofia Dembowska soon disappears from the young men's correspondence. To pursue the story further we must return to Staś's autobiographical novel, into which he projected a fictionalized version of the triangle.

At the very beginning of *Downfalls* the reader is forewarned that some 'depravity' will ensue. Edgar, Duke of Nevermore appears in the first sentence in 'a huge black automobile', chauffeured by a man whose face 'bore the marks of homosexual deviation'. Bungo joins his friend, 'followed by the uneasy gaze of Bungo's mother, who without any justification regarded the Duke as her son's evil genius'. The first conversation between Bungo and Nevermore concerns their rivalry over Donna Querpia, an effective way of introducing the protagonists' 'essential' friendship as well as of parodying Donna's epistolomania, for Donna is, of course, Zofia Dembowska. There is authorial ambivalence in this first description of Nevermore: the 'lascivious smile of complicity' with which the Duke asks to see Donna's latest letter, 'while his eyes retained a tinge of jealousy mixed with admiration and disdain'.

Bungo tells Nevermore:

> 'Donna writes that she loves me again and longs for my lips. She also writes that your friendship cannot satisfy her entirely. The letter is, however, unmistakably in your style. The word "essentially" is used at

least ten times. So you obviously have an "essential" influence on her. . . . Evidently your perfect tutelage of her soul . . . is not in her opinion the most essential thing in her life and she would like to fall a second time through my efforts, sinking lower this time so you could raise her even higher. You should establish a home for fallen women, and appoint me as inspector general of bedrooms.'

Nevermore trumps Bungo's card by saying he had also received a letter from Donna, 'identical as to the date, and only slightly different as to the contents'.

Bungo read out loud. 'I went to the theatre yesterday. Dear, beloved Edgar, forgive me. There was an actor so like Bungo, who so reminded me of his lips, that I could not resist writing a letter to him. I know that it is not essential and that is why I am writing. Forgive me. Tomorrow I shall begin to concentrate anew and then I'll write to you again. It is two in the morning (I am writing in bed). Dear, beloved Edgar. I am already concentrated. Tomorrow I am going to paint a still life with fruit and I shall try to get control of myself, even in such trifling matters. I squeeze your hand very, very hard. Your friend, Querpia.'

The tone and trivia of this fictional letter exquisitely parodies Zofia Dembowska's letters to Malinowski, so many of which were concerned with her relationship to Staś. Nevermore's view of Donna is patronizing ('a nice, decent little girl who has a certain English chic'), but Bungo demonizes her as 'a perfect example of the spiritual prostitute, the hysterical liar, and the fundamentally perverse woman'.

At the end of the chapter the two friends bring their 'essential conversation' back to the subject of Donna. Nevermore says:

'You see, my Bungo, the difference is I can say of each moment of my life that I have created it myself. From the most to the least important things. Even including my relationship with Donna Querpia. I wanted to free her from your influence and I have succeeded in doing so. Her vacillations stem from a negligible instability of character and a lack of thorough self-analysis. That will pass. I wanted to take her soul in hand and I did not take her body, although I could have. She was never yours, but part of her life unconditionally belongs to me.'

But Bungo has his own trump card to play, and he shows Nevermore the first of Donna's letters:

'The letter in which she begged you to get her away from my influence, in which she all but declared her sublime feelings for you. She wrote that letter at my dictation. . . . I never possessed her because I never loved her even for a moment; her stupid perversities simply amused me. I grew bored with her and decided to make a fool of you, with her help. You were so ridiculous with your frenzied concentration after your return from Africa. You, the conscious creator of life, were as lovesick as a school-boy for two whole months over a silly, perverse little girl.'

It is with 'a feeling of triumph not devoid of a kind of pity' that Bungo punctures Nevermore's pride. While a certain fondness for tricks lingered in Malinowski's mature personality (as many of his colleagues and pupils would later testify), he was no match for his diabolical friend Witkiewicz.

A decadent affair

The 622 Downfalls of Bungo also commemorates a particularly sensational 'fall' that almost certainly occurred in real life. Although there is no sound corroborative evidence, the veiled remonstrations of Witkiewicz senior point unmistakably to a homoerotic ingredient in the relationship between his son and Malinowski. Karol Estreicher wrote that the 'symbolically tainted' eroticism and 'sensual folly' that Young Poland encouraged as part of its celebration of decadence found expression in the early literary exercises of these young men, but he had nothing to say about their active sexuality.[18] It was surely this, however, that allowed them to entertain, complicitly, the notion that they were 'perverse', 'degenerate', 'depraved', 'low' and 'brutal'. What else but erotic 'perversions' would have led Staś to boast covertly in his letters (and in his novel) about their demonic decadence? They enjoyed feeling wicked, but for the most part it was a histrionic pose, doubtless nurtured by a desire to shock their elders. The 'unspeakable' crimes of Dorian Gray stretched their lurid imaginations, but the peccadillos of the young Malinowski and Staś are 'unspeakable' only in the sense that we are ignorant of what they were. We know nothing, for instance, about these young men's first sexual encounters. It is quite likely that they were independently initiated into sex by girls older than them-selves, perhaps such 'village broads' as Staś refers to in his novel. There was almost certainly, too, some homosexual experimentation between them, the most likely cause of Witkiewicz senior's alarm. Their mutual enjoyment of one another's intellects seems to have generated a charged erotic relationship in which the sharing of objects of desire – such as Zofia – was a natural expression of their combined narcissism. In short, there was a covert homoerotic element in their triangles. But neither man was homosexual in the accepted sense of the word and their mature sexual preference was unerringly for women.

Chapter Three of Staś's *Bildungsroman* begins by dwelling on the Duke of Nevermore's decadence:

> He had become involved in a complicated and abnormal affair with a former classmate of his at the university, Miss Saphir, who was a sadist at an embryonic stage of development. She confined herself to clipping the blasé Duke's nails till his fingertips bled, while he writhed in exquisite pain and used his tongue to lick her convex and, as he himself said, repulsive belly button.

Meanwhile, Bungo 'tagged after the Duke like his shadow, observing the degenerate faces of his friends and immortalizing them in his paintings and drawings'. (Staś's antic portraits of his friends do indeed provide a vivid record of the era.) One night, 'unnerved by the sadism of his girlfriend Saphir', the Duke begged Bungo to come home with him to Birnam Palace (an allusion to *Macbeth* that cannot be inadvertent). The description of the contents of Edgar's salon captures something of Malinowski's untidy personal habits, and in a shrewd aspersion the narrator observes that a 'striking characteristic of the salon was the total absence of any work of art'. Although Malinowski appreciated fine architecture, he never cultivated a taste for painting.

Edgar gives up his bed for Bungo and lays a mattress for himself on the floor. It is he who makes the first seductive gesture. He looks 'grotesque', resembling the demonic figures in Bungo's own drawings: 'his eyes, without his glasses, were hazy and had a confused look of criminal desire, mute supplication, and repulsive sorrow.' Bungo is 'paralysed with fear', but then falls prey to the same temptation. Next morning Bungo is appalled: 'It all came back to him in a flash and the pain of the loathsome act that once done could never be undone crushed him beneath its monstrous weight.' Then he is ambivalently reconciled. 'No matter what,' he thinks, 'it was an experience.' Edgar and Bungo part without a word about what had happened.

'Shortly thereafter Nevermore left for England with his mother to take possession of the lordly estates inherited from the last scion – recently deceased – of the English dukes and he settled there permanently.'

As Witkiewicz represents it, the homosexual experiment with Malinowski had tested their friendship to the limit. It was a one-night stand not to be repeated. In Poe's words: 'Quoth the Raven, "Nevermore".' Whether Malinowski felt the same way, we do not know, for his diaries make no reference to this episode. His relationship with Staś seems to have lurched on its uneven way, with increasingly lengthy separations. In 1910, while Staś was writing his novel, Malinowski did indeed travel to England, though not with his mother, and certainly not – unless we allow an extravagant anthropological metaphor – in order to come into possession of a lordly inheritance.

Staś's novel describes many more 'falls' – most dramatically into the arms of the 'demonic' opera singer Akne – before concluding with a mountaintop epiphany worthy of his father. Bungo discovers his true self, feels the call of destiny and realizes that his art has its sources in 'the deepest essence of his being'. He renounces Akne, and the novel ends on a note of triumphant optimism: 'Never had he felt so strong, alone, and absolutely free.'

But life went on for Staś Witkiewicz, and in 1919 he returned to the manuscript and added an ironic epilogue. By then, having suffered the suicide of his fiancée, and having toured Ceylon and Australia with Malinowski, fought with the tsar's army and witnessed the bloody Russian Revolution, he had matured precipitately. Wearying of Bungo's prolonged adolescence, Staś casually killed him off, thereby 'cutting the Gordian knot of his own youthful problems'.[19] Significantly, he also struck out of his text all references to his father.

The manner of Bungo's demise is eerily prophetic. In an absurd accident he loses an eye while walking in the forest. Staś was perhaps recalling Malinowski's youthful ordeal when he wrote: 'His head and eye wrapped in bandages, alone in a single room, Bungo used his remaining eye to cast melancholy glances at the world . . . and he understood for the first time what the essential problems really were.' (Clearly, for Staś, the horror of blindness fuelled an admiration for Malinowski's courage in overcoming this adversity.) But Bungo's second eye becomes afflicted, and in a 'final, decisive show of will power' he cuts his throat with a Gillette razor blade. Staś Witkiewicz's own gruesome death imitated his art. On 18 September 1939, trapped in a Ukraine forest between the advancing German and Russian armies, he slit his wrists and bled to death.

Edgar, Duke of Nevermore is disposed of rather more kindly in the final, wickedly satirical paragraph of the novel's epilogue. Presciently, this was written before Malinowski's return to Europe and ten years before the publication of *The Sexual Life of Savages*:

> Of the entire band that once wandered in the enchanted land of the mountains discussing essential things, there remained only the Duke of Nevermore and Brummel. . . . The Duke was deported to New Guinea for certain unheard-of crimes he committed in the byways of Whitechapel with a pair of lords and while he was there wrote such a brilliant work about the perversions of those supposedly savage people contemptuously called Papuans [*The Golden Bough of Pleasure*, Cambridge University Press] that he returned to England as a Member of the British Association for the Advancement of Science and a Fellow of the Royal Society. The rest of his life was nothing but a series of wild and improbable triumphs.[20]

Chapter 7

An Ascetic in the Canaries

To the islands

Immediately after sitting his *Rigorosa* examinations in philosophy and physics early in October 1906, Malinowski and his mother left Cracow, bound for the Canary Islands. They were surely keen to escape the Polish winter, but why did they decide to go so far? Perhaps they wished to find an island as well as a warm climate; islands appealed powerfully to Malinowski's romantic imagination and would be important in his career. Whatever their reason for choosing the Canaries, mother and son found them so restful and salubrious that they stayed for eighteen months. Bronio had finished his formal studies at the Jagiellonian so there was no pressing need to return to Cracow. The completion of his doctorate gave him the status of a scholar, but in order to obtain paid employment as a *docent* in a university he needed another qualification – the habilitation. He was supposedly preparing himself for this final hurdle.

From Hamburg, Malinowski and his mother sailed for Gibraltar, Madeira and Tenerife aboard the S.S. *Hamburg*. On 8 December he sent Father Pawlicki a postcard from the island of La Palma, telling him that there was a plague epidemic in Tenerife and that all ships were being quarantined – not an auspicious beginning to an extended health-cure holiday. While not as popular in 1907 as they would later become, as a tourist destination the Canaries had gained a reputation among the more adventurous members of the sun-starved bourgeoisie of northern Europe. The western islands (Tenerife, Gran Canaria, La Palma, Gomera and Hiero) are renowned for their balmy oceanic climate and their spectacular volcanic peaks. The mainly Spanish population of the islands numbered several hundred thousand; they grew grapes for wine, sugar cane and bananas, and the fishing was bountiful.

The new year saw mother and son settled on the heart-shaped island of La Palma, which is dominated by a barren volcanic cone some 7,000 feet high. From its only town, Santa Cruz, Malinowski wrote a long and affectionate letter to his 'Reverend and Dear Father'. He had been meaning to write for a while, but 'as is well known, lazy people have least time when they are doing nothing and this is exactly what happened to me'. He continued cheerfully:

> For I have given myself totally to the health-resort routine: first of all, I eat a lot and sleep besides; I bathe in the sea and in the sun, all day long I sit on the seashore, in a word I am peaceful, happy and idle. . . . Mother and I are staying in a small villa, prettily situated on the sea, outside the town. We have found perfect conditions here: excellent climate, incomparably warmer and more stable than on the Mediterranean coast, great peace – because there are no other foreigners on the whole island but us.

Concerning the 'natives', his observations are those of a complacent tourist from the heart of empire rather than those of a budding anthropologist. 'The local people, while on the one hand a hundred years behind in respect of culture, on the other hand are distinguished by a complete absence of liveliness and temperament; therefore not an irritating environment.' With the same air of superiority he continued:

> A few weeks ago some epidemic broke out in . . . Tenerife, as everybody says privately it is bubonic plague though very mild. Well, first of all the authorities have not made any formal announcements . . . in order not to ruin the island's reputation. . . . In consequence a war broke out between the islands. The inhabitants of Tenerife wanted to run away to other islands. The quarantine was set up and those subjected to it are being mercilessly robbed. Here, on Palma, where there are no appropriate facilities, neither passengers nor goods are received at all. The Governor's delegate and escorting carabinieri were welcomed with lead shot. The gendarmes on the shore took up arms against the gendarmes in the boat. 'Cosas de Espana'! I saw it all with my own eyes! Now we are cut off from the world and only the post reaches us.[1]

Appropriately enough, amid this Spanish fiasco Malinowski had begun to read *Don Quixote*. He had 'picked up some Castilian' and almost forgotten Italian: 'They say the two languages cannot exist simultaneously in one head.' This exuberant letter from the Canaries is the only one to have survived. Malinowski's life left no further trace in 1907 and we can only surmise that he continued to enjoy speaking Spanish and sunbathing and that he persevered with his studies for habilitation.

The following year is also bereft of correspondence, but there is ample biographical compensation in the personal diary that Malinowski intermittently kept for four months during early 1908. With this journal, indeed, a more intimate biography is possible, for it opens a window onto the inner self of a terrifyingly earnest young man embarked upon a punishing regime of self-transformation. The agreeably relaxed hedonist ('peaceful, happy and idle') who wrote to Pawlicki has gone. The Malinowski who penned that cheerily ingratiating letter on 4 January 1907 is scarcely the same person as the one who writes in his diary a year later: 'I know that it is possible to reach a state in which the creative powers develop in such a way that they answer to the needs of my individuality. I wish to reach such a point. Then I shall really begin to live.' The contrast between the blandly easy-going self he presented to his father-figure, and the overwrought, self-absorbed person he reveals in the diary is stark indeed. Many have gone to the Canaries in search of Lotus-land, but Malinowski's higher purpose was to combat Lotus-living and to banish any desire for it. Through the lens of the diary, the long sojourn in the sun appears not so much a recuperative holiday as a sustained exercise in self-examination and self-experimentation.

The diary of an ascetic

Staś's portrait of Malinowski as the iron-willed Duke of Nevermore was exquisitely drawn, and with this first of many diaries we find ourselves on similar psychological terrain. We can now detect, from the inside, those traits of ambition and 'coldness' remarked upon by his friends. We find some of the posturing and self-dramatization of youth, certainly, but there is also something more conspicuous: a striving to see himself clearly and honestly, a naked soul under the scrutiny of his own relentless self-judgment. Peeling away pretensions and false attitudes like the skins of an onion, he seeks a rock-solid centre to his being which he might pound into better shape.

Self-analysis can lead to self-disgust, and the reader's first impression is the uneasy spectacle of a young man at war with himself, fighting his battle in virtual isolation. Mother is mentioned only once. The outside world scarcely impinges on the diarist; it exists only as a daily challenge by which to measure the strength of his will-to-change. Even more so than the dairies of 1914–18, published as *A Diary in the Strict Sense of the Term*, this ledger of a striving soul is a 'rubrication' of a moral, ascetic, almost monastic kind. An image T. E. Lawrence conjured of himself seems apt: Malinowski was a monk in his own body's cell.

He frequently fails to live up to his own icy ideals, and there is both pathos and bathos in the way he is forced to lower his sights and readjust his values. An obsessive concern with self-control characterizes the diary and, as so often, physical penance is the price of spiritual struggle. To parody some of his own tropes, he is striving to hammer out a philosophy on the anvil of his own body, to forge his soul in the purifying fires of self-inflicted suffering, aspiring to 'the smile of the Buddha' and the *amor fati* of Zarathustra's *Übermensch*. Malinowski's first diary, then, is rotten with perfection and reeks of Nietzsche. Almost ten years later, he wrote:

> In my younger days, especially in what I call my Nietzschean period (though seriously speaking, N's influence on me was only an insignificant ingredient in my mental 'chemism' of that time) I was very strong on the value of diaries. I was quite right in it, too. There is, on the other hand, a certain danger in writing them, because they necessarily must transform life. They naturally tend to interfere with the normal technique of life: to develop autoanalysis, constant criticism of oneself, constant shifting of values.[2]

The chief clue to this diary is Malinowski's quest for health. It was 'owing to illness', after all, that he and his mother were living in the Canary Islands and benefiting from a prolonged sun cure. The similarities to Nietzsche's physical state are striking: both men suffered from poor eyesight and weak health, including headaches, stomach troubles and insomnia. It was for reasons of broken health that Nietzsche began, in 1879, his restless traversal of Europe as an 'eternal fugitive'. Both men despised their physical weakness and fought against the tempting 'line of least resistance' induced by invalidism. Malinowski was following, if not emulating, Nietzsche in believing that he could *will* physical health through the rigorous exercise of his mental faculties. For this, self-discipline was essential. Although Nietzsche condemned the life-denying, moral asceticism of the priest he endorsed the yea-saying ascetic ideal of the philosopher. As his diary reveals, Malinowski fervently embraced the ascetic ideal, too, not as a moral virtue but as a means of conserving energy and economizing on scarce psychic resources. 'I ascertain deep inside myself a dormant, unbridled [desire] to fufil a "*will to power*",' Malinowski wrote, and the following passage from Nietzsche, with its Machian ring, could well have served as an epigraph for his diary: 'Not merely conservation of energy, but maximal economy of use, so the only reality is the will to grow stronger of every centre of force – not self-preservation, but the will to appropriate, dominate, increase, grow stronger.'[3]

While Malinowski may have found spiritual encouragement in Nietzsche's writings (though he refers only to *Thus Spake Zarathustra*), the impulse to self-mastery sprang from a profound source within himself; it was not a mere literary affectation borrowed from the scions of Young Poland. The proof of this is his keen alertness to self-posturing (even that lurking in 'literary ardour'), and whenever he detects it he squashes it firmly. To the extent that the urge to transform himself into a healthy 'free spirit' welled from within, Malinowski could claim that Nietzsche was 'an insignificant ingredient' in his mental chemistry. It was a constituent of his character, noted by others, that he nurtured fierce ambition, and in order to achieve what he wanted to do (as yet inchoate and undefined) he had to create a self that was tough yet resilient. Nietzsche provided a metaphoric language for the struggle. The impulse went beyond a desire for self-betterment – a ubiquitous feature of individualism in the West – for Malinowski's was an 'unbridled' passion for self-transformation. The desire was not to be a 'better' person in order to store credits towards a future life, or to be loved and esteemed by others, but to become a more efficient, exhalted and 'purer' person in order, as he put it, to 'intensify' his 'capacity for life'. It was therefore necessary to shed the weak, vacillating self so prone to ill-health, mundane distractions and petty temptations. 'The snake that cannot cast its skin perishes.' Thus spake Zarathustra.[4]

'Towards a concentration of forces'

The narrative force of the diary is weak; it was not Malinowski's intention to record daily events. What it documents instead is a series of injunctions, a programme of self-development and a commentary on its author's faltering progress.[5]

He began the diary on 9 January 1908 while sitting by the sea at Breña Baja, a coastal village a couple of miles to the south of Santa Cruz de la

Palma. Like a spiritual manifesto, the first entry sets the tone for the remainder of the diary.

> New values. The need for talent, for the possibility of creating, emerges. Things acquired are, first and foremost, means. Strong muscles, a strong heart, strong nerves, a physiological mastery of the organism. . . . The two-sidedness of my present work: To put the accent on a work minimum, on acquiring minute, technical details. To remember that my ultimate aim is an overall intensification of my capacity for life, an increase in my individual value in my own eyes. . . . Minimum programme: strengthening of the will (physiologically). Ergo: asceticism, control over associations, control over the sensations. This state of continuous watchfulness, struggle, discipline is already in itself a higher form of life. . . . The elimination of the commonplace from life; of small-mindedness. . . . I distinguish two totally incommensurable sides of life: Life within the framework of one's own individuality and life for others.

It was 'life for others' that he so conspicuously omitted from the diary. Later that day he senses ennui and self-doubt, but then boosts himself with a spiritual pep talk. Such counterpoints occur throughout the diary.

> My asceticism excludes in advance any souring, obscuring, distortion of life whatsoever; it is a form of the joy of life, a certain form of experiencing. Above all it is a means. Towards a concentration of forces. Towards making independent the highest and most profound instincts of the personality. It is a dam, not for destroying the power of the stream and fixing its course, but for making it deeper and increasing the efficiency of its fall. My virtues ought to be: wisdom, strength and courage, beauty, nobility. I have my own evaluation. These are virtues only in relation to each other – they contain nothing moral, that means they do not submit my individuality to any external laws. I am interested only in eradicating within myself everything that I see within me of cowardice, stupidity, sordidness, ugliness. . . . The chief slogan of the present moment: *May my words become the language of destiny.*

After a month's silence Malinowski resumed his diary with further exhortations to asceticism: 'To live in a world of entirely different values; after all, life is only a quest for values. Asceticism is also, as I saw at the moment of sowing, an indispensable condition of any productive work whatsoever.' He is pursuing his studies in mathematics ('I do geometry in bed') and chemistry ('rather indifferently'), though he does so as part of his general training regime. They are no more, indeed rather less, important than the gymnastics or other exercises he does to strengthen his will and sharpen his concentration. At times he regards them as the easier part of his programme: things he can do conscientiously when he is emotionally unfit (through 'boredom, longing') for the more demanding exercises of self-control.

Malinowski kept his diary fairly consistently for the rest of the month, summarizing his thoughts, monitoring inner states and progress in what he sees as an experimental period of 'work' upon himself. He warns himself against the dispersal of thoughts and the dissipation of energy, and he registers the cost of petty distractions: 'Reading newspapers, later controlled by enormous effort. Result: Tiredness of the heart linked with an excess of physical energy.'[6]

A 'résumé' on 13 February includes an account of the precise nature of his physical exercises, the 'physiological side of work' he undertakes towards a 'fortification' of the will. 'I begin a pulsation of the biceps (with a chair) making extremely light innervations. I do the same with squatting.' A few days later he defines an ideal gymnastics, one that would command reserves of energy: 'To train and oppress the body in the most varied ways. To sleep on the floor, out of doors etc.'

> The higher asceticism, leaving the entire burden to the heart, the nerves work terribly powerfully; e.g. I get up in the morning, exaggerate the unpleasantness of the mood. 'I look it straight in the eyes', i.e. I seduce it with total awareness. The nerves accustom themselves at the expense of the work of the heart, which must work v. powerfully.

Apart from the absurdly trivial acts he intends to 'work upon' (getting up in the morning, sunbathing, walking), one wonders why he sets such store by those physiological entities 'heart' and 'nerves'. What complex processes do they signify for him? They are clearly central to his understanding of the workings of his body. By the 'higher asceticism' Malinowski appears to mean a deliberate filtering out of extraneous impressions, thoughts and feelings, the better to concentrate on a particular task – be it ever so simple or mechanical. He aspires to 'inner purity', to a perfect control of 'associations'. To achieve even the first stage of control he needs to 'close the door' on the world in order that he may conserve mental energy. It also involves cultivating a state of consciousness that maintains 'contact with one's whole life'.[7]

Since the basis of normal procedure is a certain quality of temper: calmness, equilibrium etc, [I should] try to enter into it, for without it –
nothing! . . . If I desire to overcome resistance, approach it slowly, feeling
the resistance increasing. . . . What is important is to develop the powers
within oneself in the direction of things which one desires to achieve.
. . . The emphasis must always remain on self-control.

He realizes that 'introspective physiology' will not be enough. He needs
to 'take into account the social, pedagog[ical] side, its significance for psychology'. Although he does not use the word, he appears to be trying to
integrate the workings of his mind ('psychology') and his body ('physiology') through acts of willed self-consciousness. This is presumably the 'continuity' and 'equilibrium' to which he frequently refers. He instructs himself
on 18 February 'to place the chief emphasis on improving efficiency. . . .
To reckon with my infirmities.' This is the first candid admission in the
journal that his health might still be a problem. But if his hypochondria is
muted it finds expression in a minute attention to the workings of his body:
'the dependence of the heart, lungs, muscles, nerves.' While apparently in
good physical health, he adopts a kind of spiritual hypochondria.

There is a bleak philosophical dimension to this 'higher asceticism', a
scarcely human ethical prescription for the self-mastery of the Superman.
He exhorts himself: 'To shed immediately all the leaven of joy, complacency,
triumph – as a grimy, turbid residue. To reduce every achievement straight
away to the level of everyday commonplaceness. And to live not by what
has been acquired as something already possessed but as a guarantee of new
achievements.' He has a fresh insight into what might be called the everyday constitution of individuality: self-affirmation through minor acts of
consciousness – 'innumerable minute associations, impressions, emotional
reactions' – which make one day different from another, one's own day different from someone else's. He glimpses that this means rejection of the
strictures and standards of others. He must be self-sufficient, and he ponders
'methods of defence against the crowd, the prostitution of the spirit'.

A few days later he calls himself to account again. He detects an increase
in energy, but notes some flaws, some insufficiency in the programme. He is
not sure whether the cause lies in himself or in the system. But there is protest
beneath his rationalizing: the demands are too great, he yearns for 'life', for
'happiness'. His frail health is also at fault, making him vulnerable: 'I am dis-
sipating my energies; I am forgetting about myself, I am immersed in garbage.'

. . . Overwork, overtiredness, which followed very easily on account of my morbid weakness of heart, muscles and nerves. All manner of weaknesses and temptations beset my weakened organism, like filthy vermin on a corpse.' In another flush of ascetic virtue he cautions himself against being carried away by 'literary ardour'. He does not wish to be seduced by fine words, not least his own: 'I negate all literary ideas; i.e. those which like a swarm of trouble-some insects assail our souls. . . . These ideas deplete without creating; they feed on each other with no further aim – without results.'

Malinowski suspects that his 'supreme virtue' is an 'instinct' for evalua-tion, for knowing what is worthwhile in whatever he takes up. In a prac-tical self-assessment:

> I assign myself as a general task getting accustomed to research work. As for my basic attitude to scholarship, for the time being I do not know what to say except: It is my chief talent (an instrument of creativity); I possess scientific curiosity to a high degree; at present learning gives me pleasure (as an increase of general analytical capabilities).

The confident tone signals his lack of concern about the future direction of his career in science. He has the measure of his own talents for research and original thought; why then should he worry? What matters for the moment is the consistency of mental application and 'continuity of the higher states' of consciousness.

The torpor of Breña Baja is 'very good as a form of self-hypnosis', and he resolves to 'increase training in fortitude and efficiency' with a tightened schedule that is unusually specific in its details:

> 1. *Punctuality.* 2. Abstention from narcotics and fads. (To be careful not to overload my stomach.) Further to 1. It is a matter of spending two morning hours solely in training the nerves and body. Generally gymn. and bathing. If not the former, an air-bath with a rub-down. In addition one hour in the morning on philosophy (without fail!). After lunch two hours of geometry (or chemistry). One hour of general thinking. 6–7 gymn. 8–9 a walk (to develop my courage). 9–10 to go to bed, self-examination.

Testing the will

One day Malinowski challenged himself to an arduous climb up a steep gorge. Neglecting his own advice to avoid 'literary ardour' he wrote: 'I am

going in order to bathe in solitude so as to wash away, with fresh and beautiful impressions, a certain patina with which I have lately become covered.'
As an exercise in the application of willpower the walk was a failure. His
body betrayed him and he almost fell down a cliff. He blamed his frailty
on lapses of concentration and was disconcerted by the 'juxtaposition of
what I had expected and what was realized'. What he had expected was the
impossible: 'power and tirelessness; proficiency . . . the certainty of each
movement and each step and total tranquillity as a consequence of this.'
What he actually experienced as he wheezed nervously up the slope was
dismal anticlimax. It was as if, he thought contemptuously, he had been
'walking through *town*'.

If this exercise was a failure, a far more important challenge looms. He is
to attend an Easter carnival. After weeks of solitude and the steady application of his 'minimal system' he is about to expose himself to the excitement
of a colourful public event. There will be crowds; there will be acquaintances (he mentions no friends in this diary); there will be an abundance of
pretty young women dressed in their finest; there will be dancing and drinking. In short there will be temptations aplenty. This worries him and he
resolves: 'To remain myself at all times. To use this exclusively as a test; subtle
participation of the appetite and of vanity.' He warns himself against 'intoxication' of various kinds. This does not entail simple stoical repudiations, but
the more difficult and treacherous path of accepting intoxicants (whether of
the narcotic, alcoholic or merely social kind) and remembering his 'individuality' though 'inner concentration', reducing the temptations to 'a mere
pittance'. The easier option would be simply to stay at home.

On the day before carnival, Malinowski is nervous. Ideas are only means
to an end, he thinks. An idea only has value when 'given substance', transformed 'into a vital empirical truth' and realized 'in the conduct of a fuller
life'. To achieve this he needs to maintain his self-awareness, to be in the
world but not of the world, to remember always the virtue of solitude when
being swamped by 'the herd'.

> I shall not 'forget myself' in the flirtation of conversation with ladies,
> with clowns; appetites: gluttony, erotica, vanity. Motifs of surrender to
> them: 'I ought not to curtail [them] artifically, to shorten the way; this
> gives me pleasure, so go ahead; I myself shall get control of myself by
> myself, etc.' In point of fact as necessary as Pilate in the Creed. The main
> principle: to reduce to a minimum.

During carnival, he tells himself, he should take walks outside the town and go to bed early. But he lamely admits that, beneath the tough-minded resolve, 'I do not feel equal to checking my inclination to carnival; I would best prefer to stay at home.' He will go, however. He genuinely *wants* to go: 'To relax and enter the mud . . . the loss of a couple of weeks. After this I want to be as fresh and eager for work as I am now.' He delivers a final boost to his morale by reminding himself of his present progress:

The enormous *certainty* of the norms that guide my conduct. . . . To destroy within myself even this reaction: "Something is going to be happening around me, I am happy about it!" What is happening is only what you mould with your own hands, only what you surmount concretely within yourself, what you learn in the realm of experience. And so: towards a theory of self-control and will!

That afternoon, after writing, he was taken by motor car ('sitting on the dicky-seat for two hours') to the unnamed carnival town. His account of the event is retrospective, for the next entry in his journal is dated 18 March, almost three weeks later. He had gambled and lost: carnival had overwhelmed him and the herd had won. Whatever happened?

It is almost with relief that one reads, between the reprimands and self-reproaches, of Malinowski's evident attempt to enjoy himself in ways befitting a twenty-four-year-old. Even so, on the first day he was assailed by boredom, 'looking for things with which I can drug myself'.

Instead of analysing and looking for things *imperceptible*, interesting or profound, I am looking for narcotics. Sleepiness, boredom, tiredness propel me to bed. . . . I do not go to bed, however, and it is this which is fatal. I dance with Amparita; she bores me. . . . I drink vermouth. Latin with Don Antonio – this is my main expenditure of energy.

On the second day: 'In the morning I come to grips with myself. A late breakfast. *Jota* with Casanova and Sorrella. A spree with Juan Enriques Paranda. . . . I sing *La Pilar* in the Pharmacy. I go to the Club. . . . At Morrero's I dance with Nievita.' His diary entry fades into barely legible phrases and abbreviations as the effort of recollection wearies him. Despite his disdain for 'boring amusements', Malinowski had been caught up in a whirl of social diversions. He talked, sang and danced with *señoritas*; he promenaded from one café and nightclub to another; he 'caroused' on wine and sherry, and smoked a cigar or two. He even allowed himself a moment's doubt that all this 'social froth' was really harmful: 'Is that which is gilded, soft, enchanting, seductive poetry – that which from afar calls and entices like dance music on a beautiful moonlit night – is that evil . . . that stands in the way of the crock of gold – is that only and solely the voice of the body, minor appetites?'

'The whip raised'

Malinowski resumed his diary with a postmortem. What can he do but start all over again?

> An enormous dissipation of energy during carnival. An interruption of impetus, a drying-up of the supreme goals – a weakening of the body, an awakening of the appetites. For a long time I did absolutely nothing. Then a little mathematics. Now I wish to get down to organic work once again. . . . To strengthen the muscles, to strengthen the nerves. To enter absolutely into solitude.

Despite the disastrous result of the 'experiment', once he has recovered his equilibrium and moral stamina Malinowski seems cheerfully unrepentant. Following his own precept of putting all experience to use, he decides to 'analyse and write down the time wasted; to fortify myself for future work'. He renews the aphoristic onslaught on his appetites: 'To keep the fires burning under the pots – never to appease the appetites; to keep them continually taut. A hungry body, thirsty and greedy, is strong and capable of work, like a tense bow.' He chides himself now for aestheticizing his longings and finds a new target for his scorn:

> It is impossible to criticize or strip the appetites of the poetry with which I depict hunger, thirst, longing. I ought to criticize what appears to me in an equally strong light – hob-nobbing with riffraff. Why? Because this fritters away my energy, renders shallow, sucks dry and gives *nothing*.

He acknowledges that 'criticizing the crowd' implies criticizing also the despicable behaviour the crowd elicits from him: 'sham brilliance, renown, boasting and all the other chief sins.'

On 23 March he redefines his goals: 'Physio[logical] proficiency and fortitude (the negative formulation of this: asceticism, the capacity of assuming burdens). . . . Especially: control over associations; control over internal narcotics (music, poetry, fear and other superstitions), control over the appetites, independence of superstitions and herd instincts.' Almost as an afterthought he wonders what will be left for him if he banishes 'all these stimulants'. What then would be 'the material of experience'? With appetites eliminated must he forfeit love, friendship and 'new worlds in the hearts of people encountered'? But this is surely 'what most of all draws us to the earth', and in a concession to sentiment he notes: 'I know of nothing more worthy of recognition and love than the heart of a friend.'

After neglecting his diary for almost three weeks, on 13 April he announces another New Plan. One senses that he is tiptoeing around his life, wondering ineffectually where best to seize it. Although the New Plan contains many of the same precepts as earlier ones ('control over associations', 'inner purity', 'philosophical buoyancy and calmness'), it is notable for its appeal to 'concrete' work. This consists of three aspects: 'Gymnastics, Studies, and Philosophy of Living, over which asceticism still reigns'. He accepts, however, that he cannot 'overcome inborn physiological things' like eroticism: 'On the whole I shall not overcome the sexual drive but I can suppress it within myself for some length of time and in some circumstances. And therefore to overcome this completely inwardly!'

He is still having difficulty eliminating distractions and channelling 'associations'. Among other distractions, he registers 'the May holidays, excursions, letters, newspapers, books' – a list that indicates that he is living at least partly in an everyday world. Following the lessons in introspection he learned from studying Johann Herbart, Mach and others, he observes that associations run in 'appetitive series' along 'a certain directional line'. The art of controlling these 'guests from the past' lies in ambushing them and analysing what it is that triggers them: 'either certain impressions or certain memories making their appearance unexpectedly.'

He contemplates his study methods:

Motto: 'If one wishes to push ahead as quickly as possible in the control of material, one must move at a snail's pace in basic and concrete preparation and the mnemonic assimilation of details.' While smoothing out ideas one must create for oneself the most favourable conditions possible: complete inner calm, in order to give the nerves a maximum of ebullience.

He poses again the 'fundamental question of life: What to do?' He now has, he thinks, a clear knowledge of the quantum of energy available to him and therefore to what extent he is 'in a position to work in a certain specified direction'. But if this appears to presage a choice of scholarly career, it proves to be yet another false premonition. 'Life wants work, actions. At present I *want* to work hard. General instructions: to examine whether I shall be in a condition to accustom myself to research, exact thinking.'

A few days later, poised above 'another abyss', Malinowski begins to wonder whether all the work of previous months had been pointed in the right direction, concluding that 'an "inner life" is beyond my powers' and that 'mathematics has become simply unbearable for me'. His entire 'system' now begins to seem shaky, and he questions what drives him along this dubious course of self-improvement. His answer, as before, lies in intro-spective self-assessment. 'Analysis of my attitude to work and of obstacles to work,' he announces briskly, but the resulting diagnosis is by now pre-dictable. The prescription amounts to more of the same medicine. 'I do not have sufficient asceticism, a basis of sufficient indifference with regard to unpleasant periods in my work.'

When he resumes his diary on 8 May after two weeks' neglect there is a modulation of tone. Despite 'certain desperate negative states' caused by 'not following a system', he finds that he has accomplished some things without conscious monitoring: 'My motto was even: actions exclusively. I worked tolerably well, I did gym and was fairly free.' One day, after some 'light intellectual work', he takes a brisk walk uphill and in a palm grove he experiences utter calmness, 'a profound sense of the moment': 'I should direct the course of my life in such a way that it runs in a calm, even flow. So that the power of the fall is not wasted in whirlpools and currents. . . . One should choose one's work in such a way that it answers one's *natural* inclinations.'

In the same questing mood, infused with Zarathustrian images and romantic hyperbole, he declaims:

I am entirely alone. There is nowhere for me to find help and incentive – nowhere to draw from except a single source. I myself should be the initiator of the struggle, a witness of the defeats and triumphs. . . . I simply must summon up the strength once again for the capacity of calm suffering – of giving myself nerve. The whip raised.

On a mundane level, he appears to have reconciled himself to mathe-matics. At any rate, he is still studying it as the best way to discipline his thinking and to prepare himself for whatever may follow. He warns himself as before, however, that it is merely a means to an end and that 'success' in scholarship is no assurance of success in the larger struggle. 'To build as a foundation within myself: a capacity for carrying out orders in the face of momentary whims – a capacity for inflicting suffering on myself.' A surprising afterthought follows, illustrative of the way Malinowski's mind shifts easily from hairshirts to cosy beds: 'Do I perhaps very badly need erotic, emotional elements in my life?'

> I wish to give an entirely different character to my whole way of thinking, to my inner attitude to the world. To develop what seems beautiful to me: tranquillity, strength, aiming straight at the goal, self-control, continuity. To root out vanity, indulging the appetites in daydreams, false values, cowardice.

To give him his full due, Malinowski did, it appears, try to uphold these ethical ideals, to pursue these classical (Hellenic rather than Christian) goals throughout the rest of his diary-writing career, and probably throughout the rest of his life. His 'inner attitude' is invisible for long periods, for after July 1918 he kept no more personal diaries. But during the decade in which he did, he consistently sought an inner 'tranquillity, strength, aiming straight at the goal, self-control, continuity'. His later diaries also bear witness to the persistent, if low-level, struggle he waged to eliminate in himself vanity, cowardice, indulgence of appetites (usually libidinous) and false values such as those attending snobbery and the desire for material wealth.

Oscillations

In the last dated entry of the Breña Baja diary, 21 May, Malinowski argues the need to 'sign a pact' with himself concerning his future. Although he does not refer to his departure from the Canaries, it is imminent. He has been re-reading his diary and is compelled to assess once again his inner life, his general capabilities, his prospects for a career, his evaluation of what kind of 'success' is worth striving for. 'There is no sense in making excessively far-reaching plans, proposals for myself. I know my strength. . . . I know that in my previous intentions and hopes there was more than anything simply too much daydreaming . . . not in the least reckoning with what the conditions of success were.' Towards the end of this entry

Malinowski makes further resolutions. They are more indulgent than those with which the diary began. 'Ist resolution: Joyful, calm, full experience. Suggestion: not to wear myself out with excessive work and work [which is] contrary to my natural inclinations. 2nd resolution: Aiming straight for development in the direction of increased endurance, will as well as a rise in intellectual *productivity*.'

He wonders whether 'it isn't precisely this changing of my very self, this inner transformation, which is the essence of my creativity'. But this is surely an unwarranted presumption, for the internal evidence of the diary is that he had not been notably successful in transforming himself. His 'system' continually broke down; it was too rigid and unforgiving. His path as trodden through the diary is littered with false starts and abrupt endings. The fiasco of carnival – when he 'forgot' himself for a week and took a further two weeks to collect himself – was replayed on a minor scale twice more during May. There were nonetheless perceptible benefits to his strenuous attempts at self-transcendence. If it was a time of testing himself, his health as well as his will, his physical as well as his psychological endurance, he learned much about his own limitations.

This early diary reveals, as do the later ones, a temporal pattern of oscillations of mood and attitudes familiar to anyone who has kept a personal diary. If the peaks and troughs seem exaggerated in Malinowski's case, one cannot yet be sure how much this was due to literary embellishment and the hyperbole of his Young Poland rhetoric. Certainly, he 'romanticizes' himself and often reaches for the most lurid colours to describe his moods. But there is in addition a detectable swing between elation and depression, optimism and pessimism, joy and depair, strength and weakness, asceticism and indulgence, self-congratulation and self-castigation, creative longing for 'life' and abject apathy. On the upswings and downswings alike, he formulates new resolutions in the attempt to keep on course, to inject new energy into his psycho-physical 'system'. It is another such rhetorically rich entry that concludes the diary, and it is especially interesting because Malinowski defines an 'oscillation' for himself. 'In lapping up the slops of life from the hand of chance I feel unremitting nausea. With a violent movement I wrench myself free and go on my way. After a while I begin to feel the cold; an uncontrollable longing for life arises. I fling myself into the slops etc.'

George Stocking has referred to Malinowski's sojourn in the Canary Islands as 'the central site of those early ventures with his mother into extra-

European otherness'.[8] Without the evidence of this diary it is a plausible conjecture, but the truth was surely otherwise. Apart from his occasional references to walks into 'town' and his account of the Easter carnival, there is nothing whatever in his diary about the 'extra-European otherness' of his situation. He might just as well have been back at home in Cracow for all the observations he makes about his surroundings. He valued La Palma, it seems, not for its exoticism but for its lack of distractions. His hermetic soul embraced what appears to have been a virtual social vacuum ('still too much fraternizing with the tradespeople,' he chided himself after one walk through the town). At any rate, whatever social intercourse he indulged in did not greatly distract him from his preoccupation with himself, and 1907–08 must rate as one of the most friendless, narcissistic periods of his life.

Only at the very end of the diary, and only by reading between the lines of his disjointed jottings, does one find any indication of the existence he had shared with his mother. The brief entries have a certain poignancy, for the moment of departure from La Palma deflects him from his self-absorption. He sees and experiences things unmediated by that authoritarian, ascetic self who is his witness. Although still clinging to a petulant, self-critical view, while sailing away from the island he indulges in some of the commonplace sentiments he had been busily denying himself in previous months.

> The last day, a *dance*. Apathy; becoming shallow. Looking for cheap amusement, without even the basic passion of life. . . . In the morning I walk to the sea, a few photographs, giving presents. . . . Brief flirtation with a *señorita*. . . . Journey to town by boat. . . . With great love and emotion I look for the last time at . . . the deepening of the *calerdeta*, the highway, the work of the port. Aboard ship I look at Breña. . . . Regret for the life that I spent there. Tears well up. . . . The coast passes by. . . . The salt works, the high crag. The steep shore beyond Maro; volcanic cones above the seashore, hidden by the clouds beyond a certain height. . . . I go down.

There is an elegiac air of something coming to an end: 'My gaze flies above the sparkle of the still sea and draws to the heart of Palma.'

The island world of reflection

Malinowski's Canary Islands diary says a great deal about his character. It is plainly an immature version of the complex personality inscribed in the final diaries from the distant islands of New Guinea. His deeply dualistic nature is evident on every page: a romantically divided self of erotically charged inclinations and steely intellectual purpose who yearns for their integration, as if this would release a healing burst of energy. One detects also an invented, literary self that closely echoes (and sometimes gauchely imitates) the heroic introspections of Nietzsche. He is committed to self-improvement by the most rigorous means, yet his asceticism is too youthful to forgo any experience, rant as he may against the distraction of 'impure' impulses. Contemptuous of emotional comfort and intellectual complacency, he has defined himself as a seeker for the subjective Truth of his own individual being. A true *moderne*, he believes passionately in his unique individuality, and he believes with equal sincerity that it is his life's mission to strengthen and realize it. To that end he is prepared to endure, and bitterly enjoy, solitude and a degree of self-imposed misery. He is not without a desire for happiness (it is only later that he seizes upon Stendhal's axiom that 'happiness is the promise of bliss'), but he is thoroughly monastic in his capacity to deny himself present satisfaction for future spiritual gain. It is plausible that his earlier Catholic upbringing instilled and amplified some of these traits, but Malinowski was already a secularist and a freethinker, a prospective rationalist and humanist.

In 1908 he was also a proto-Freudian. Although Sigmund Freud was practising his new science of the unconscious in Vienna at this time, there is only the most dubious evidence that Malinowski knew anything about him.[9] But the modernist *Zeitgeist* of individuality and the cult of genius – exemplified by Nietzsche a generation earlier – had been joined by a more complex idea of human sexuality. Through Freud and his disciples, sex would soon come to be regarded as an expression of unhappiness. It promised no bliss. Without repression and its attendant miseries there could be no human culture. Based on this ascetic imperative, Freudianism became a secular religion to which Malinowski was set to be converted. For his part, had Freud read this diary of an ascetic he would surely have diagnosed Malinowski as an obsessional neurotic – if not in quite the same league as Rat Man, whom Freud was treating at precisely this time.

In his 1912 diary Malinowski asked himself what had gone wrong with his programme for self-improvement in the Canaries: 'Why did I suffer defeat there? And to this I reply, chiefly owing to the excessive negativity of my work. I was locked in some sort of fetters. I dug wells – but I was not looking for their sources at the same time.' This suggests that he came to believe his ascetic imperative had denied him the freedom necessary to know himself. The demands he placed upon himself were too constraining; he tapped the wellspring of his libido, as it were, without comprehending its source. As for the future, his mistrust of the body would remain, together with his readiness to exact penance from it, but he would never deny its needs to the same extent again. One might even say that he knowingly left open the door to concupiscence.

The diary is entirely devoid of humour. Once or twice Malinowski smiles grimly at himself, but he seems to find nothing funny in the world he inhabits. It is perhaps unfair to judge him by the unrelenting high seriousness of these pages. They represent, after all, the raised whip, just as his nagging self-assessments are his hairshirt. Through this and later diaries he attempted to control his wayward emotions and bend them to his will as a hopeful aspiration to virtue; but he seems to be unaware of any element of absurdity in his frailties.

In the last analysis, Malinowski *did* enjoy La Palma and was sorry to leave. That he also found something amusing in the Canaries is illustrated by his early letter to Father Pawlicki, even if it is the condescending humour of one who finds the antics of the natives funny. The Canary Islands in 1907–08 became for Malinowski a touchstone of what it meant to self-commune in comparative solitude, and they were probably in his mind in 1917 when he wrote to Elsie Masson about the value of a diary devoted to 'autoanalysis': 'I used to maintain . . . that a man ought to have regular times of seclusion a few weeks yearly or half-yearly, say. During that time one would have an absolute taboo on outward life and live only in the world of reflexion.'[10]

The emperor's ring

At some point during his stay in the Canaries Malinowski composed a careful letter, in German and in the third person, to the aged Hapsburg emperor Franz Josef, then in his fifty-ninth year on the Austrian throne. Encouraged by his Jagiellonian mentors, Malinowski sought approval for his doctorate to be granted under the royal seal, *sub auspiciis Imperatoris*. It was an understandably obsequious letter (protocol demanded a combination of lofty salutation and fawning phrases of the Most-Gracious-Emperor-and-Sovereign-Lord kind). He mentioned first his 'Roman Catholic persuasion', his 'outstanding results' in his entrance examination to 'the third

Imperial and Royal Gymnasium in Cracow' (he tactfully avoided its Polish name), and the 'grave illness and an eye operation' for which he was 'forced to break off his Gymnasium education and take the final school examination as an external pupil'. Appealing thus to the emperor's sympathy, Malinowski emphasized his academic success in the teeth of the impediments of illness, and towards the end of the letter he mentioned the other handicap under which he had suffered: 'As the son of a university professor, drawn early into the realm of learning despite a vexatiously sickly constitution and an unfortunate fate whose decree brought about his father's death when the boy was 14 years of age, Your most humble servant persevered in his studies.'[11]

It must have been with a persistent flutter of doubt that Malinowski begged the imperial system to recognize him. The so-called *Promocja* (Promotion) was a rare honour for any young scholar of the day, for the senate of the Jagiellonian could propose only one candidate a year. The candidacy had to be approved by the emperor himself, since all expenses were borne by the Crown. The tangible token of the honour was an inscribed gold ring, in which a diamond was set.

Malinowski's application to the emperor for the doctorate summa cum laude took time to work its way through the bureaucratic labyrinths, and it was almost a year later, in July 1908, that the rector of the university was informed that His Imperial and Royal Apostolic Majesty had 'kindly deigned to permit' Bronisław Kasper Malinowski his request. The formal act of promotion was to be mediated by the imperial delegate in Cracow, the Royal Councillor Adam Fedorowicz. Fittingly, the promoter for the occasion was Malinowski's surrogate father, the Rev. Stefan Pawlicki.

At twelve o'clock on 7 November 1908, the solemn award ceremony was duly held in the Aula (main auditorium) of the Collegium Novum of the Jagiellonian University.[12] The medieval hall was filled with prominent Cracovians. Preceded by two mace-bearers, the academic procession was led by Councillor Fedorowicz, followed by the rector, members of the academic senate and professors of the four faculties. The choir sang 'Gaude Mater Polonia' and the imperial Austrian anthem. Having been led into the assembly, the doctorant, Bronislaw Malinowski, made a formal request to the rector for the *Promocja*. The rector granted it and instructed the promoter to read out the academic oath of allegiance, during which the audience stood and the beadles crossed their maces. After Pawlicki had handed Malinowski his diploma and delivered 'a suitable speech', there was a fanfare of trumpets. Then the imperial delegate presented the new doctor of philosophy with the emperor's keepsake, the bejewelled gold ring. Malinowski received the formal congratulations of the dignitaries, deans and professors, and the ceremony was concluded by the signing of his diploma by the delegate, the rector, the dean of philosophy and the promoter. The assembly filed out of the Aula in the same order in which they had entered, and Dr Bronisław Malinowski walked immediately behind the mace-bearers of his faculty.

The ceremonious pomp lent a fairytale quality to the event. It impressed Malinowski enormously and gave him a lifelong taste for dignified rites of passage that enhanced his self-esteem. A portrait photograph, taken the same day, shows a studiously solemn Malinowski, a hint of moustache smudging his upper lip, in voluminous academic robe and four-peaked cap, clutching the scrolled diploma in his right hand. He stares into the camera enigmatically.[13] Many maternal aunts, uncles and cousins were present at the induction. According to one eyewitness, 'Malinowski stood very close to his mother,' and after the presentation of the ring turned to her and kissed her hands and cheeks. 'It was really his mother's work.'[14] That evening, following the celebratory dinner held in his honour, Bronio took his uncle Edward Landié to the Little Green Balloon cabaret. In an appropriately Polish way, the day that began with such regal solemnity ended with satirical farce.

Chapter 8

The Music of Love in Leipzig

A travelling affair

After some visits by a young philosopher, I realized that the real point of him helping me in my work was a young and beautiful musician's wife, whom he had met in my flat. . . . Fortunately the beautiful lady had to leave for Warsaw and the philosopher went to Leipzig for further study.

Thus Helena Czerwijowska on Malinowski's entanglement with Felicja ('Fela') Ciszewska.[1] Bronio was captivated, but unhappily so, and he cursed the sorry affair as 'a physiological excrescence' on his life. Cryptically, he summed up his grudging attitude to Fela: 'I feel [she] is nothing to me, and that I desire her; I regret this.'[2]

Grażyna Kubica suggests that Malinowski 'escaped' to Leipzig immediately after his graduation ceremony not only to study but 'perhaps also to avoid his romantic problems'.[3] While Malinowski's retrospective diary hints that he was under some moral pressure to leave Cracow, he would almost certainly have gone to Leipzig University whatever the circumstances. The fact that his father had studied there a generation earlier was probably one inducement. Malinowski was still intent on studying physics and chemistry, in particular the thermodynamics of liquids and gases, for which Leipzig was the renowned centre in Europe. He was also keen to pursue his interest in the physiology and psychology of perception, and the university's rector was Wilhelm Wundt, the venerable experimental psychologist. The romantic appeal of this ancient seat of learning, founded a mere sixty years after the Jagiellonian, might also have been a factor. Among other luminaries, Goethe, Novalis and Wagner had studied there, and it was at Leipzig that Nietzsche discovered Schopenhauer. A city of markets like Cracow,

Leipzig was above all a unique centre of musical culture, the home of J. S. Bach.

On 21 November 1908, Malinowski officially enrolled in the faculty of philosophy.[4] His departure from Cracow may have been precipitated by an aborted affair (or two); he certainly appears to have carried a bitter aftertaste away with him and his first days in Leipzig were miserable. He looked at the city 'through eyes of indifferent hatred, as if it were something utterly dead'. Soon after his arrival, however, he became romantically involved with an older woman, one who came to play an important part in his life during the next four years. In his epistolary essay to Aniela Zagórska, Malinowski wrote that if it hadn't been for 'Mrs N., an Englishwoman from the colonies (New Zealand [sic])', he would 'never have taken up sociology', nor would he have gone to London and 'become to a certain extent Anglicized'. These are strong claims. His departure for London in the spring of 1910 was one of the crucial turning points in his life, so it is important to learn something about Mrs N.

In reality, she was Annie Jane Brunton, an aspiring concert pianist from South Africa. Malinowski first met her on 23 October 1908 during a preliminary visit to Leipzig. Their friendship grew rapidly, though they appear to have spent an uncomfortable Christmas together (she later reminded him it had been 'horrid').[5] Annie Brunton was a widow and at least ten years older than Bronio. In his diaries he usually indicated her by a circled 'N', which stood for 'Noosie', the nickname he bestowed upon her. She addressed him as 'Niusiu', an affectionate diminutive of Bronius. Annie was born of English stock in Cape Province; her father was a surgeon from Essex, her mother was from Cape Town.[6] Annie was genteel middle-class, owned a few shares and drew a small widow's pension. In Leipzig she had casual employment as companion to an older woman known only as Flöhchen. Annie was married on 24 April 1900, but in hundreds of pages of correspondence she does not once refer to her husband. A death notice of Andrew Brunton reveals that he was a Scottish banker who died of consumption aged forty-two in Bloemfontein in 1902. There were no children. After her husband's death, Annie trained as a concert pianist in Berlin, but her public engagements seem to have been infrequent. On her return to South Africa in 1914 she taught piano privately, but by 1920 was teaching in a girls' school.

Annie's letters to Malinowski – most of them written in the period 1914–16 – are those of a woman who did not expect to see her beloved again. She loved him steadfastly and hopelessly, and every letter reveals an unselfish concern for his welfare and happiness. She clung to his 'friendship' – a word she imbued with selfless love – as token of a rosy, happier past. For his part, Malinowski's early infatuation with Annie matured into an affectionate friendship. He was still thinking fondly of her unwavering loyalty in 1918 during his last visit to the Trobriand Islands.[7]

With hindsight, Malinowski would have seen the period he spent in Leipzig as crucial for his future development. It was there that he set himself on the course that would one day bring him fame as an anthropologist. Yet Leipzig was liminal. It represented a step westwards, away from Poland towards England, but it was not a city in which he ever felt at home. Leipzig represented the best of German science, but in the very guises that he was about to relinquish. Leipzig was also the theatre of one of his major internal battles, one waged with his own future as hostage. What he imperceptibly decided during his time in this German city was that his true vocation lay in ethnology rather than physics, in primitive sociology rather than physical chemistry. In terms of the dualities he so often conjured, he chose art over science.

Behind this decision lay an irresistible inclination to follow his emotions in the shape of Annie rather than to follow Mind's unconsoling mistress. If it was Staś Witkiewicz who inadvertently pushed Malinowski away from art, it was Annie Brunton who fortuitously brought him back. It was a compromised return, however. For the practice of social anthropology, falling uneasily as it does between art and science, reliant on intuition as much as on reason, did not require him to renounce science entirely. Indeed, his fame came to rest on the success with which he blended the two or, more precisely, with which he injected scientific principles into an anthropology grounded in fieldwork-based ethnography. To the end of his life his watchwords were a *scientific* anthropology, a *scientific* theory of culture, a *scientific* method for the study of man. But if he did not entirely abandon science, neither did he fully embrace art – at least, not in any of the forms that his friend and rival Witkiewicz practised with such astonishing flair.

The change of direction Malinowski took towards the end of his stay in Leipzig is starkly indicated in the only surviving record of his enrolment at the university. It states that although he had registered for three semesters, he was suspended for non-attendance in the summer of 1910. He had departed for London in March, having completed only two semesters. He was struck off the roll altogether in February 1911.

'Keep a diary!'

The two diaries that Malinowski kept intermittently during his stay in Leipzig are the only source from which to reconstruct his life there.[8] Ironically, the first time he mentioned Annie Brunton – on 7 January 1909 – it was to declare that the affair with her was 'simply history'. He had broken it off to 'begin an inner life' and once more take the ascetic path of Breña Baja. Annie had made it easier for him by leaving Leipzig for a time, but another factor probably lay behind Malinowski's decision: his mother had joined him.

There were no other romantic distractions during the first half of 1909 and, encouraged by his mother, Malinowski devoted himself to his studies. He was not without his usual angst, however, and the first diary charts a course of oscillating moods similar to that of the previous year. No clear picture of his daily life emerges, though certain themes recur: the monitoring of subjective states and the attempt to impose order on his university work; musings about Annie; observations on music; a wary battle against masturbation and other unseemly indulgences.

On 20 February he exhorted himself: 'Keep a diary! Everything that passes through me must leave a lasting trace.' It was not until 12 March, however, that he began a more sustained journal, one which opened with a list of deceptively simple (and inadvertently comical) resolutions: '1. Anchoritism: [desist] from eating, smoking and drinking (not absolute: to get drunk only on worthwhile things). 2. Putting my life in order. 3. Diary (inner order). 4. A mood of calmness and equilibrium.' His new regime demanded 'gymnastics and subjective considerations until breakfast', then he would study mechanics and thermodynamics. He sought to develop 'a high sense of obligation' towards his work. Aided by two hours' walking each day, he resolved to place 'the accent' of his life 'on a solitary investigation' into himself. While striding through Albert Park, however, his thoughts soon turned to love and a longing for 'physical sensations'. The oscillations between 'solitude' and 'life' had begun.

A month later, a letter from Annie reminded him again of 'the stormy side of life'.[9] In a feat of prescience based on self-analysis, Malinowski foretold the course of his liaison with her, predicting that it would follow the same emotional trajectory as previous love affairs. There would be 'a sad beginning, full of apprehensions', then rapture and a qualified happiness, with 'perhaps a little boredom and repletion'.

Then the impossibility of tearing myself away from her, cowardice; the final moments; mute dejection, the real pain leading from the realm of fiction to life: collapse. The wounds slowly heal; intelligent analysis begins to distil an intoxicating narcotic from wormwood; life recedes; once again only the stage and the spectator.

Despite this astute self-knowledge and a suspicion that he would be a 'spider falling into its own web', he allowed himself a delusory degree of freedom. The temptation Annie represented was not yet irresistible. He also doubted her capacity to meet his spiritual needs. 'Does she lend herself to greater depth?' he asked himself. 'Are there any prospects of spiritual development for me?' Some days later he formulated his quintessential problem: 'I want to place the burden of my "I" on some woman of value.'

Far from seeing himself as selfishly narcissistic, however, Malinowski believed that he suffered from an acute sensitivity to people and a slavish dependence upon their opinion of him. Some weeks earlier he had written: 'I still do not have enough brute resistance and lordly nonchalance to ignore the mood of others.' While he would not concede anyone else's *intellectual* superiority, how should he behave towards those with greater physical or social presence? His answer shows to what extent he was unsure of himself. An affectation of 'lordly nonchalance' masked the doubt at the core of his self-regard; his arrogant exterior concealed a flinching, defensive ego. He lamented his impressionability, his vulnerability to the gravitational pull of another's personality which sometimes threatened to obliterate his own. 'I experience feelings as if something were enticing me. . . . Then I look around: Who is watching me? In front of whom am I playing the comedy? Is this a feeling of some sort of direct, natural thrust? Why does it always come from the outside?' Nine years later, Malinowski rephrased the question as an ethical one: 'why must you always behave as if God were watching you?'[10]

At the beginning of the Easter vacation Malinowski took a train to Berlin, using the journey to ponder the latest of Annie's letters and evaluate his inner state. Despite earlier resolutions, he was living largely in the realm of sentiment. Music pushed him 'straight into life', he wrote, and it was surely one of Mrs Brunton's attractions that she brought so much music into his life. As he described for himself the oscillations he had recently experienced concerning Annie, the triangular amatory pattern emerged. Just as his liaison with Zofia Dembowska had been erotically and intellectually complicated by Staś Witkiewicz, so his budding affair with Annie was complicated by a third party. Her letter appears to have dwelt on her uneasiness about the betrayal of a fellow musician called Schneider. 'The "smelly" side of this affair emerges,' as Malinowski noted. Such love triangles posed delicate ethical problems, and the presence of another male was to him both a challenge and a reproach. On a Freudian interpretation, of course, the rival male was a projection of Malinowski's father. The father who died as the son reached puberty had broken the Oedipal triangle. It was as if the son persisted in a doomed quest to restore its integrity, and then prevailed in ejecting the father again.

Malinowski's introspections on this train journey are revealing of the way he perceived his own character. He found the effort to hold fast to a unified personality immensely burdensome, and edged towards moral panic.

> My conduct must be in agreement with my ideals. If I am unable to attain something [I should] forgo it. Constant vigilance and control of myself, linking up the slightest stirring of my mind and instinct with the great organic whole, its subordination to the most profoundly acquired features of personality; a continual sense of what one is and on which rung of one's personal scale of values one is standing; this is all madly exhausting; it imposes an unbearable burden. . . . I am falling into a bottomless abyss. I am out of breath; I am standing on the very edge: better to cross over, better – a little while longer and I shall not be able to carry the burden; madness?

The threatening mental crisis is reminiscent of the 'abyss' he experienced in the Canaries. Insofar as it recalls Zarathustra's existential agonizing over the burden of consciousness it appears to be self-induced. (Malinowski seems to be cursing himself with the terrible knowledge of Nietzsche's prophet: 'Man is a rope stretched betwixt beast and Superman – a rope over an abyss.') The breathless, vertiginous spell he describes here recurs elsewhere in his diaries.

The vertigo of the previous entry yielded to cooler introspection and a more measured set of psychological ideas as he gazed vacantly out of the train window at the passing woods and pastures of central Germany. He began to scribble again:

The inner self – an unenclosed, unlimited space; we experience what goes on inside it in the form of amorphous, dynamic blocks of reality. . . . The point is to know how to record, in the simplest possible way, that which has passed and not to simplify it excessively. It is plainly dangerous to subsume one's experiences under hackneyed categories; to express them in conventional commonplaces. . . . The individuality of a given moment is precisely what gives it intrinsic value.

Despite its idiosyncratic view of the relationship between language, thought and reality, Malinowski's observation offers a clue to his later success as an ethnographer. His ability to observe human conduct in an alien setting in a fresh yet meticulous manner, joined with a stylistic capacity to write unhackneyed sentences: these are as much a part of his originality as his passion to explain himself to himself. Although he would contest the view later, he appears to suggest here that it is the task of language to articulate thought as precisely as possible – and not simply in the default mode of conventional clichés – in order to stabilize and fix the flux of reality as, moment by moment, it impinges upon consciousness. Malinowski did indeed take considerable pains in his diaries to render his experiences faithfully, as if no one had ever recorded such things before. This *ab initio* approach also suffused his ethnography. 'It is I who will describe them or "create" them,' he famously announced in the Amphlett Islands.[11]

Arriving in Berlin on Saturday 26 March, Malinowski met some unidentified cousins (probably visiting from Warsaw) and they toured the city together. Berlin's 'vast, massive stone-lined landscapes' had an oppressive effect upon him. Always sensitive to moods induced by architecture, he loved Venice but disliked Vienna, probably for much the same reason he felt uneasy in Berlin. Blatant evidence of the power of the state 'that dazzles the mob with its grandeur' was perturbing. But balmy spring days followed and he fell under the 'evil charm' of Berlin. One evening he felt a need to be sociable and showed off his command of foreign languages. Later he criticized himself for dropping 'into a blustering, buffoonish tone'. He also disapproved of his own snobbish pride. At a concert given by the Berlin Philharmonic Orchestra he sat with a score on his lap, showing off his musical literacy. The ostentation cost him all enjoyment of the Brahms being performed. Before returning to Leipzig he mused that travelling in this way did not broaden one's horizons. But he forgave himself: 'it could have been worse.'

Dualities

In reviewing his mental state before he went to Berlin, Malinowski had detected 'clear symptoms of overwork'. Folk idioms of diagnosis recur throughout the diaries: for instance, 'congestion', 'atrophy of the brain' and 'violent exhaustion of the heart' caused by 'intellectual excitement'. More seriously incapacitating, perhaps, were diffuse bleak moods resembling acute depression. He described one such attack which recapitulated 'the black weight' familiar to him from Breña Baja. The passage recalls the desolate existential musings of Dostoevsky in *Notes from Underground* and Kierkegaard in *Either/Or*. The sense of unreality is suffocating.

> 'Reality used to be vivid for me, or rather, it had a third dimension. . . . Today I have only a dull, grey rag before me. I hurl myself against what is happening around me as if against hard, impervious prison walls . . . on this side – I, on the other – the void. Void inside me and soundless nothingness outside me. Reality is only an infinitely fine barrier separating void from nothingness. Thus spoke to me the murmur of the waves and the odour of rotting seaweed.'

The quotation marks betray a literary affectation. It was not, then, a clinical depression that prompted such alienated reflections.

Music engendered other intimations of duality in Malinowski. Never had he listened to so much as in Leipzig, and much later he would fondly remember his musical education there, claiming to Elsie Masson that he had 'hardly ever missed a concert'. To save money he usually attended the afternoon dress rehearsals.[12] In his diary he wondered how he might intensify his enjoyment of music. He well knew that the degree of sensual surrender he experienced (what he called 'musical hedonism') depended upon his mood. Full receptivity required 'a cataleptic hypnotic state'; but what was the relation of this receptive state to an understanding of music? Intellectual understanding, he suspected, inhibited 'the deep imbibing of music' – just as in Berlin he had failed to savour Brahms by doggedly following the score.

On Good Friday he hedonistically enjoyed a performance of the Bach *St Matthew Passion*. It 'penetrated' him and corresponded to his ideal of an art that enriched life by energizing it. 'After listening to music I must control myself with a great effort in order to be able to work. I feel full of energy.

And so to concentrate enormously . . . to mark it out with strong resolve like a weir collecting and discharging vital energy, and to direct it towards productive work.' He described a psycho-physiological reaction to a surfeit of Bach as 'a characteristic "insane itch" in the back part of the brain and in the nerves'. On another occasion, a Bach mass sent him into an ecstasy of 'religious exultation'. This, he imagined, was how the trumpets of the Last Judgment would sound.

On 14 April, Malinowski worried about the problem of ultimate values. With yet more hydraulic imagery he set out for himself the metaphysical constraints that shape destiny, concluding: 'Perhaps through a consciousness of hidden springs and subterranean sources we can increase their yield.' He appears to have been toying with a notion reminiscent of Freud's theory of libido and the role of repression in channelling it. He had similar concerns about the debilitation that can occur when motives are continually subjected to introspective scrutiny.

> Sometimes I have the impression that such a thing, when brought out into the open from underground and examined in the light of day, has lost its power, which sprang from its mysterious, undefined position – while at times it seems to me that if I were to become entirely clearly aware of this whole nexus then sooner or later I should have to become all of a piece and live only this life.

His quest for integrity, a harmonious self of undivided steely purpose, seems precocious. He was just twenty-five. There remained, too, a seed of doubt that the kind of commitment to a single, dedicated mode of life that a powerfully unified self would demand was not what he really wanted. A case of hedging his bets, perhaps, like St Augustine's 'God make me good, but not yet'. Still, the prospect elicited a more practical wish list: 'I wish to collect [scientific] material. I wish to go on acquiring a capacity for [literary] expression. A complete loss of mastery of the word would be simply fatal for me.'

> And yet it is only when I am living in this fire, when I feel a lawgiving power within myself, when I myself direct the course of my work and life, that I feel happy, that I have a sense of my own worth. I am fated to go against the current. . . . I shall always be split in two, to go in and out of life. But work, tranquillity and cool buoyancy will always be a sure haven for me.

He was caught in an unresolvable tension between the fire of life and the cool buoyancy of mind. Although he acknowledged that he would always 'be split in two', he refused to capitulate to duality, and he would continue his quest for the integrity of an undivided will in full control of mind and body.

Since the beginning of the year, Malinowski had been studying mechanics, thermodynamics, mathematics and physical chemistry. He referred to 'lecture work, lab, library and the like' as the formal framework of his days, so he was evidently attending the university. It is also clear that he did much of his studying at his lodgings, some of it in bed in the mornings. He mentioned neither ethnology nor psychology during this period, though he alluded briefly to Wilhelm Wundt and the philosopher of history Karl Lamprecht. His theoretical studies in physics and chemistry during this first term prepared him for practical laboratory work, which he began on Monday 19 April. It is hard to judge from his scrappy notebooks how much of this work was standard training – replicating experiments and testing the hypotheses of others – and how much was original research. In any event, he became sufficiently engrossed in it to neglect his diary for a month. When he resumed it on 20 May it was to record neutrally that he had worked 'fairly well'.

Following the tempo of the academic year, the diary draws to a close. Among the last sporadic entries are some sharp self-observations on his struggle with duality: 'I am looking for personal values (possibly in a woman). You ought, for the sake of this, to work on yourself, so as to be able to pay value for value. . . . Deep inside, there remains a suspicion about the existence of such value. A fear of taking life seriously, of Woman.' Casually he mentions that 'N' has returned to Leipzig and that 'something' will soon be happening. Meanwhile he is aloof, willing to wait for her to re-enchant him. The last date in the diary is Sunday 20 June, under which he wrote his final coherent entry: 'I pose the problem clearly: to work properly on theoretical chemistry; to work aggressively in the laboratory, to lead a v. structured life. Utterly to avoid daydreams, sentimentalities, slovenliness.'

'Intellectual dilettantism'

Malinowski's second Leipzig diary opens with several pages of impressionistic notes concerning the August which he had spent with Annie in Switzerland.[13] Five years later she recalled how they had been in Lucerne just before she left for Zurich to join her music director, Professor Franio Stern. 'Do you remember . . . how you begged me to give you just another day because of your *Namenstag* [saint's day]? And on 1st September we went down to the lake of Lucerne together, and on the morning of the 2nd we parted. . . . Then we looked upon a parting of a few weeks almost as a tragedy.'[14]

Under the heading 'Historical', Malinowski attempted to reconstruct a sequential account of what he and Annie had done together. They met in Zurich on 1 August, walked along the quay and drank beer in a café. He felt 'a catlike wariness and sensitivity'. While in Buchillon, a village on Lake Geneva, he wrote a page or two in English, as if wishing to practise his skill. Notably, he described their sleeping arrangements:

> A few evenings we began the night in my small room. There was also this 'most beautiful' time. I think we also slept there one or two nights. As a rule we went each evening to her room, I went in my [sic], arranged the window, the bed & came back. She was then ready. Of course I was rather exhausted all this time . . . that I hardly did enjoy it anywhen [sic] as well as those 2 nights in Leipzig. I often have been irritated.

Separate rooms but shared beds. The passage offers a fair summary of Malinowski's pre-marital love life: the secrecy and subterfuge, the eroticized 'beauty' eclipsed by satiety, self-disgust and nostalgia for some more perfect occasion; the frequent irritation with the one who evokes such feelings.

There is an abrupt transition in the diary as Malinowski abandons his attempt to reconstruct the events of August and, resuming Polish, turns to 'Current Problems'. Under this heading he presents an unusually precise – and patriotic – statement of his plans for the immediate future.

> It is my intention (from a social point of view) to work in my country and for my country. . . . Because of my previous specialization, I am now continuing in the mathematical and natural sciences, while not neglect-ing other fields. A more precise field: the science of heat, particularly the second law of thermodynamics. . . . In Leipzig [I ought] to concentrate, too, on the proper use of a laboratory without getting flustered, without chattering, without looking for inspiration from the outside; to strive above all else for *proficiency*.

Clearly, he was intent on pursuing research in physics and physical chem-istry for his habilitation; the culture history and *Völkerpsychologie* he was reading under Wundt were secondary interests.

Biographical sketches of Malinowski's career invoke just two names in connection with his studies at Leipzig – those of Wilhelm Wundt and Karl Bücher.[15] Yet it would overstate the case to call either of these men his intellectual mentor. Unlike that of, say, Pawlicki, their influence on him appears to have been of an impersonal and entirely formal kind: that of lecturer to student. There was a considerable age difference, of course, Wundt being fifty-two and Bücher thirty-seven years older than Malinowski. Indeed, Wundt was then in his seventy-seventh year and still teaching as well as presiding as rector.

Karl Bücher (1847–1930) was an economic historian, already well known for his theory of the economic stages through which Europe had passed from antiquity to the present. Malinowski was critical of this scheme. In particular he objected to Bücher's argument that primitive peoples lacked economies and therefore represented a pre-economic stage in human history. Bücher's key work, *Arbeit und Rhythmus* (1896), however, had a perceptible influence on Malinowski's thinking. This is nowhere more apparent than in his essay on the Australian *intichiuma* ceremony, written in 1911, in which he showed how magical and religious conceptions could provide economic incentives. Later still, his Trobriands work demonstrates how assiduously he pursued the comparatively novel problem of the relationship of magic to economics, particularly in the organization of labour.

Wilhelm Wundt (1832–1920) achieved international fame as the father of modern experimental psychology. His teaching was mainly in physiological psychology, to which Malinowski's diaries and notebooks of his Leipzig period frequently, if cryptically, refer. Wundt regarded psychology as the common basis for all scientific and cultural knowledge; it was the science that must precede philosophy.[16] University records indicate that in 1909–10 Wundt gave a lecture course on the history of philosophy as well as the psychology course that Malinowski doubtless attended.[17] Wundt's psychology dealt with unmediated subjective experience. Introspection detects 'mental elements' that are always in flux, sensations with specific qualities and intensities; it also reveals how mental processes are compounded into 'perceptual wholes'. In addition to sensations there are 'elements of feeling'. Such concepts informed many of the introspective passages in Malinowski's personal diaries.

During his later decades Wundt turned to 'the natural history of man' and became a historian of culture or, as he saw himself, a special kind of social psychologist. In the ten volumes of *Völkerpsychologie* (1900–09), he produced a systematic exposition of the nature of the human mind as manifested in culture and society – in language, law, myth, religion and art. Still, there was an unbridgeable methodological gap between Wundt's empirical, scientific psychology and his speculative social psychology geared to a progressive evolutionary scheme, and while Malinowski accepted much from Wundt he firmly rejected the latter. But the fact that he set at least one of Wundt's works for his own pupils during the late 1920s suggests that Malinowski acknowledged the general truth of what Wundt had called 'starting principles'.[18] Among these were: all human institutions and cultural products are 'essentially mental processes or the expression of psychical activities'; 'folk psychology' is explicable in terms of general psychology; certain mental phenomena cannot be understood by reference to individual psychology alone; and, therefore, a collective psychology is necessary to study the products of the group. Malinowski baulked at the last principle. He also rejected the evolutionary edifice that was the result of Wundt's encyclopaedic attempt to apply these principles to various stages of human development. Although Malinowski himself would speculate on the individual psychological motivations and dispositions that animated social institutions, he rejected those theorists – such as Wundt, Le Bon and Durkheim – who invoked supra-individual psychology.

There are some clues in Malinowski's Leipzig notebooks to his thinking along Wundtian lines. Thus: 'Psychol. plays too much at basic philosophizing; it is too little concerned with the introsp. cataloguing of facts; e.g. the facts of feeling in connection with physiological processes.' Again: 'As long as we examine sense impressions we move in a world bordering on physical objectivity.' Significantly, there are also hints in these notebooks that he had begun to study the literature on Aboriginal Australia. But then, his fragmentary notes indicate a smorgasbord of topics from musical notation to the freezing point of benzine, from colorimetry to the evolution of human thought, from the American Civil War to Aboriginal totemism. This does not mean that he was squandering his finite energies by trying to advance on a broad front of learning, for he had no particular wish to be a polymath like Wundt or Pawlicki. 'Concentrate on one thing,' he urged himself in his diary, and a few years later he would declare that it was his 'intellectual dilettantism' that had finally pushed him into the social sciences.[19] By then his commitment to anthropology (sociology as he called it at the time) was irreversible. It was on the same occasion that he made the curious claim that he 'probably' would not have taken up sociology if it had not been for

Annie Brunton – by which he presumably meant that he would not have taken it up *seriously* if he had remained on the Continent. He clinched the matter by saying that he had already begun work on a dissertation in *Völkerpsychologie* while at Leipzig, and that one of the reasons he went to London was to complete it. Eventually, the dissertation would transmogrify into his first book, *The Family among the Australian Aborigines*, and traces of Wundt's teaching would be erased.

Annie in Weimar

On 13 October, Malinowski was in Weimar pretending to be an old 'bald-headed gentleman' while nervously hunting for a flat to rent. When he met an elegant Annie at the station, they seemed 'foreign to one another'. He conducted her to the apartment he had found and they sat together on a sofa. He gazed at her adoringly and asked if she loved him. Then, as he put it: 'She wants to go to bed already. We lie down. A violent blaze of passion; such dear memories come alive in the senses.' But Annie confesses that she loves 'the other one' more. 'I put out the light and burst into torrents of weeping. . . . She does not react. A loss of friendship, a new coldness. I feel unhappy all night long. At daybreak, tired, wanting to get some more sleep, I go to the other bed.'

During their first night together since Lucerne, Malinowski had both rediscovered Annie and lost her. She was attached to another, the shadowy concert performer Herr Schneider. While Annie was happy to engage in this tryst in Weimar, she was unwilling to renounce her tie to the other man. It appears that on their previous romantic excursions Malinowksi had not greatly minded that she had another, perhaps more official, lover. Now, however, he wants to love her possessively. But the very fact that she demurs, diminishes his love for her: he now suspects she does not love him as much as he believed, and therefore he cannot love her as much as he had wanted.

They spent the following day sightseeing, visiting the Gartenhauschen where Goethe used to work. Malinowski was fascinated by the study with its simple desk and a view from the window of a green rampart of trees across the meadow. They went into the tiny garden where Goethe used to sit with Madame von Stein. While they strolled, Malinowski explained to Annie his need of her friendship. She told him of 'her *guilt*, of the impossibility of happiness in her present position'. He responded by relating details of his unhappy affairs in Cracow. They arrived at 'redoubled love; the need for expiation', and that night the pleasure flowed marvellously.

Next day they visited the Goethehaus and Malinowski reverently observed Goethe's drawings on the walls, the garden room and the bedroom, including the armchair in which the great man died. He was impressed by the simplicity of the furniture as well as by the Romantic associations of Germanic genius. Goethe, after all, was a man who had embodied the reconciliation of art and science, heart and mind, as Malinowski longed to do.

A mysterious quarrel enveloped Annie and Malinowski as they walked through the woods. She reproached him; he felt misunderstood. Thwarted and self-pitying, his reflex was always to retreat into thoughts of work and a cocoon of emotional detachment, withdrawing 'from all the needs of the herd' into solitude, 'quiet, cold, without happiness or worry'. But by the evening Bronio had recovered his good temper. It was his last night in Weimar. 'One should forgive a great deal in consideration of the morrow,' he thought. Annie looked lovely in the café and he gazed at her 'with undivided love'. He kissed her and sought her forgiveness. But something went wrong again. 'She asks whether I love her. This question arouses in me a whole series of associations about that which was. . . . Passion continually checked by deeper doubts. "I can love her only with my senses; in a woman who gives me pleasure I should also see the soul."' Malinowski needed to clothe naked passion in spiritual garb; but he simultaneously realized that his unspoken reproaches were unfair. It was as close as he came to admitting that it was Annie's body he wanted more than her soul. In truth, though, he wanted both. 'I am playing a dirty trick,' he wrote, justifying himself in the callous manner of Staś Witkiewicz, '"and what *the devil*, should I not play around with a woman because of scruples?"'

'Decorative loneliness'

Malinowski left for Jena while Annie remained in Weimar. He soon tried to put some emotional distance between them. 'I think about Leipzig and about my hard, active, energetic, methodical regime.' But he still had hopes of winning her. 'If my relationship with N shapes up, if she will be my friend and satisfy my longing for the *Eternal Feminine*, then this thing will have value.'

From Jena he took a train to Rudolstadt and climbed to one of the castles to take in the view. He recalled that his romantic rival, Schneider, had given a concert there the previous year. Walking back to Jena along the broad valley of the Saale, he mentally conversed with Schneider and an unpleasant realization intruded as he contemplated their triangle:

> My love arose from the sight of their happiness, from the base instinct of jealousy, imitation, and the desire to take [the spoils?] . . . base rapacity. It is shameful, too, that he, the weaker, must now regard me as a thief. I decide to give up and to allow her to return unconditionally.

He intuited the role of imitation in triangular desire. His love for Annie was mediated by Schneider, whose own love for her enhanced her value. The only honourable course for Malinowski now would be to renounce her.[20]

Back in Leipzig a few days later Malinowski found new lodgings at Windmülemoy 3.[21] He was thinking obsessively about Annie and Schneider with 'a direct altruistic pain since because of me they cannot now be happy'. He felt that he had 'shamefully destroyed a beautiful thing'. Despite this spasm of selflessness, he was soon moping for Annie and wishing Schneider out of her life. Unable to read one evening, he went to where he believed they were staying and stood miserably beneath their windows. With contorted mouth he wept until he was exhausted. 'I groan endlessly about the impossibility of scholarly work,' he wrote next day. 'It is devouring me, decidedly.'

During the days that followed, he oscillated between 'the happiness of a man cured' and the despair of a jilted lover. In a burst of energy he 'whacked away' at Max Planck and went to the institute 'full of titanic zeal' and the desire to work aggressively. Despite 'the spectre of melancholy' he retained a bemused detachment. 'I wallow in decorative loneliness: how pleasant to be able to be with oneself as with an old, understanding, devoted friend. To be a friend to oneself.'

He urged himself to reach a decision concerning Annie. Should he renounce her and, if not, on what terms should he try to keep her? He considered all possible options, their emotional correlatives and temptations, experiencing day-by-day swings between renunciation and desire. Marriage was the only option he did not consider. He wrote her an ultimatum, though honest introspection obliged him to record a certain discrepancy in his diary:

When I discuss the whole matter with myself, I do so in quite a different tone, calmly, firmly, with determination; when speaking in a letter to her, I write with uncertainty, preyed on by my emotions – this is not lying, but rather a proof of this complete emotional dualism. And so, to be by myself.

Happiness regained

On Saturday 23 October, Malinowski bought some chocolates and went to an afternoon concert in the hope of seeing Annie. During the music he could stand his misery no longer. Shaking as from a fever, he bought flowers and paid a visit to Flöhchen, the woman whom Annie attended as a companion. Flöhchen gave him hope by telling him that Annie had left Schneider and that Malinowski could now have her love. He delivered another letter to Annie that evening. 'I am in love up to my ears, like a schoolboy,' he told his diary.

Next day, on receiving her reply, he felt 'joyful intoxication, a complete interior transformation'. He read her letter several times, then replied, adding to his own letter transcriptions from his diary. He would do the same for other women in years to come. As a device for gaining access to the beloved's heart it was a Trojan Horse, a strategy of captivation, tantamount to saying: 'I am entrusting you with my innermost thoughts, offering you the most precious gift of myself. You must repay with secrets of your own, and you must love me faithfully for the intimate knowledge with which I burden you.'

Malinowski was madly happy when he visited Annie that afternoon: 'She seems marvellously beautiful to me. A kiss like a soft juicy fruit which has ripened. The marvellous touch of her low-cut pink wool blouse. At first I look in her eyes, unconscious under the impact of the impression – then pleasure and happiness begin to penetrate me.' So he was restored to Annie Brunton's favour, though it is unclear on what basis their relationship now stood. They did not live together, though for her part she no longer lived with Schneider. The emotional crisis of the previous week had been resolved, however, and as if the compulsion to keep a diary had been weakened, the entries that follow are brief. Yet as Malinowski admitted two weeks later, his 'centre of gravity' still lay in his emotional life.

He visited the laboratory almost daily throughout November, working with colleagues on problems of thermodynamics such as the freezing point of water and the boiling point of benzine. He referred also to electrolysis experiments involving camphor and copper. He continued to study optics and botany, and to attend lectures and classes in culture history and *Völkerpsychologie*, presumably given by Wundt. For the first time, perhaps, he read Durkheim. He continued to keep himself in check, too, and on Sunday 7 November he resolved to 'eliminate all encumbering factors' that marred his laboratory work: 'conversations, quarrels, jealousies, friendships. . . . To ignore external things just as today I ignored the streets of Leipzig.'

Annie once wrote to him that 'music is our strongest link', and during these few wintery weeks they listened to a great deal, mostly at the Gewandhaus concert hall.[22] They heard pieces by Bach, Beethoven, Brahms, Tchaikovsky, Mendelssohn, Handel and Wagner. It was his affair with Annie that was of greatest interest to Malinowski as a diarist, however, and later he recalled that he 'was sustained by the hope of those rare days when I saw her'.[23] But there seem to have been few days when they did not meet for a couple of hours at least. Whether or not it was to observe the proprieties that they lived apart, the nature of their 'friendship' was tacitly acknowledged by their acquaintances – though the widowed South African pianist in her mid-thirties and the bachelor Polish scientist in his mid-twenties might have seemed an unlikely couple. While rather more attentive to his social surroundings in these diaries than he was in the Canaries, Malinowski gives little space to anyone but Annie. He appears to have had many acquaintances but no close friends. One might fancifully interpret his Leipzig diaries as an attempt to reconstruct that elusive triangle – comprising Annie the beloved, Bronio the lover or observed ego, and Malinowski the observer or alter ego. Splitting himself in this fashion was a natural consequence of the self-analytical 'function' of his diaries. There is little room for anyone else outside the charmed triangle of Double Self and Female Other.

Annie's letters offer some clues to the identities of their acquaintances. 'Our Leipzig circle', as she referred to it later, consisted mainly of musicians.[24] There was the hapless Schneider whom Malinowski had upstaged; Ethel Cooper, an Australian pianist who would become trapped in Leipzig during the war; Franio Brzeziński, a Polish lawyer and music scholar, and Anna, his German opera-singer wife; Emchen, the violinist daughter of Professor Franio Stern; Lambrino, an Italian pianist who married an Australian woman; Sandor Vas, a Hungarian music teacher. There were also a few non-musicians in their circle, such as Annie's benefactor, Flöhchen, and Willie Blossfeld, a university teacher. Many of these men and women were Jewish, and to escape Nazi persecution in the 1930s some of them fled to America.

Stepping Westward

On Saturday 13 November, Malinowski took stock. Annie was now relegated to a secondary place in his preoccupations; he was more concerned about his lax working habits, his 'grey and unfruitful despondency'. He rebuked himself for staying in bed too long in the morning and for neglecting his gymnastics: 'I am losing whole days in desultory loafing,' he wrote. 'I cannot go on like this!'

In another echo of his Breña Baja diary, Malinowski urged upon himself fresh resolutions: 'Once again to kill inside myself the miserable creature that keeps on raising its head over and over again.' The miserable creature happened to be the one that was deeply attached to Annie (and Mama); the spineless, gregarious fool who wept when thwarted. But this creature was peripheral to his core, wherein lay the solitude ('the crystalline ether of loneliness') in which he must nurture his genius. To forget this was to sink to the level of the herd.

He formulated prescriptions for his future conduct:

> I. At home: activity; efficiency; to deal with business (letters that have to be answered by a certain time, purchases, books); to work consistently on the right theories. II. In the laboratory: not to 'sham'; not to chat; to listen sometimes; to be absolutely independent of personal relations . . . ; not to want factitiously to 'show' anyone what I am and what I can do; but to work intensively, to do everything with an almost exaggerated calmness and slowness and with absolute concentration.

His strongest strictures concerned the turmoil caused by his erotic, yet incomplete liaison with Annie: 'III. In my emotional relationship with N and my line of work to eliminate hysteria and fussiness, over-meticulousness in my feelings. . . . At the same time undue hypersensitivity and unsatisfied urges. A certain fasting helps me and also an abstention from pornographic reading.' Finally, a resolution for everyday conduct: 'Every morning – to make a brief plan and write it down.'

Saturday's morale-boosting exercise was challenged on Sunday when he 'got up rather late' and had an 'unnecessary' conversation with a colleague. On Monday and Tuesday his laboratory work was 'poor', and on Wednesday he recorded 'dejection; a lack of drive forward'. On Thursday, he could not even remember what he had done in the laboratory ('I probably wasted time for the most part').

Perhaps Malinowski abandoned his diary at this point through sheer discouragement, though he bestowed on it a symmetry of sorts by ending it on 22 November, the anniverary of his arrival in Leipzig. The pendulum swing of his self-discipline and relapse, the ebb and flow of his good intentions, is by now familiar. Dissatisfied with himself and with his progress, Malinowski screws himself up to a pitch of high moral resolution, but within days he has breached his own rules and dashed his own hopes.

With the sudden ending of his diary, little more can be deduced about his life in Leipzig and his curiously discontinuous love affair with Annie. We must imagine him working in the chemistry laboratory – with that characteristic blend of passion and impatience – and studying a range of other subjects in the library. At some stage during the autumn he began a dissertation on *Völkerpsychologie*, though it is not clear whether this was a requirement for his habilitation, or whether he was writing it out of pure scholarly interest.

Annie departed for England at the beginning of December and Malinowski saw her off from Hamburg. He was already planning to follow her: 'I am happy about the trip to London,' he wrote later, 'as if it should somehow bring me a very full life.'[25] But first he returned to Leipzig for the remainder of the semester and a miserable, flu-stricken Christmas. In the New Year he wrote Pawlicki a letter that offers the clearest statement as to his practical intentions. [26] His Jagiellonian mentor had urged him to complete his habilitation speedily so that he could secure a schoolteaching post. This was the accepted way of embarking upon an academic career and was the path Pawlicki, as well as his own father, had taken. But Malinowski had other ideas, and offered two reasons for delaying this course of action.

> Undoubtedly, I am intending to do so and I will in the future but I admit frankly that I would like it to be only an initial stage of my career, my reasons being that the teaching vocation is physically taxing and my voice is very weak and it is hard for me to speak much.

This is the first (and only) time he ever complained about his vocal capacity. It was almost certainly a fabrication, and it is odd that he tried to pass it off on one who knew him so well. But he also offered a better excuse: 'Besides, in order to exert positive influence on young people one ought to be well educated and know more than an average Galician teacher. . . . I am very keen on going to England for at least a year, for there, it seems to me, culture has reached its highest standard.' He requested Pawlicki's support in his application for a Barczewski Scholarship from the Jagiellonian. This was worth 600 crowns a year – almost twice the amount of his earlier Potocki studentship, though still less than one-tenth the salary of a junior Jagiellonian professor.[27] Malinowski's plan to go to England largely depended on receiving this grant. Fortunately, it was duly awarded him and appears to have been his principal source of funding until 1913.

In a later diary, Malinowski summarized his last week in Leipzig thus: 'microscopy; lots of unfinished calculations from the laboratory. The journey to Oberhof, Aachen, then Liege, Ghent, Bruges and London.'[28] If he had left some of his laboratory work undone, it was apparently without regret. His journey across Germany and Belgium was the most direct route, taking him to Ostend where he caught the ferry to Dover – 'the classic approach to England', he called it. Of that journey in early March, 1910, Malinowski himself had much to say, excited as he was about the prospect of a very full life in London. Under a misty sky lit by an opal sun, he was borne across the pale-green waves of the English Channel. It was his Rubicon; once it had been crossed, the dice of his career were cast.

Part II

1910—1914

Chapter 9

A London Spring

'A highly developed Anglomania'

Approaching an island-nation permitted Malinowski an imaginative dis-junction with the European continent where his ill-defined homeland lay. His fascination with islands had begun in the Mediterranean when he was a youth – or perhaps even earlier in the Frisians – and was renewed during his sojourn in the Canaries. Although of a vastly different scale, England's sea-girt land exercised a similarly romantic enticement. An island, he wrote, was 'a definite, integrated whole' that could be imaginatively encompassed. The lure of islands is evident, too, from his choice of fieldwork locations in Papua – Mailu, the Trobriands, the Amphletts. If, as he wrote, the 'great-est charm of travel is the instantiation of a dream', then Malinowski's recur-rent dream was of islands.

In the epistolary essay he composed for Aniela Zagórska, Malinowski described his fateful crossing of the English Channel.[1] He indulged his fas-cination for seascapes, displaying the 'quality of perception' that is attentive to both external reality and sensual apperception. His description of the port of Ostend – with its fishing boats, its markets, its old town of narrow tenements and its fashionable esplanade of villas and elegant hotels – is cursory compared to the passages he devoted to the open sea, into whose vacancy he could project his own moods.

> The view which one has constantly before one's eyes is not very complex in its general outlines: a vast expanse of water, intersected by a ship's side, and a piece of sky. . . . But within this broad, but extre-mely simple frame, there is room for how many infinitely subtle and rich changes in the character of the sea and sky, in the light, in the

condition of the sea particularly, depending on whether it is more or less rough.

Another typical passage, adverting to the mysterious power of the sea, is distinctly Conradian in tone, sentiment and elusiveness (though, as he wrote this in early 1913, he was mindful of the awesome tragedy of the *Titanic*).

The open sea is a huge prison, the most open and beautiful emptiness – one's gaze runs uneasily to its farthest limits, rounds them, returns; behind it a thought, and behind that, longing; such is the wide world – the widest, the road that leads everywhere, promises everything, and in its empty vastness already seemingly contains a perfidious smile of warning. We are initially seized with a strange restlessness, flavoured with boredom; we look for a kind of prop in what the ship offers us. The contrast between this [shipboard] life, carved out of the most luxurious and technically perfect cultural reality, a reality created by man, and the breath of the inexorable and incomprehensible, essentially ungrasped reality of the open sea – this contrast is something that always produces an infinitely powerful effect.

Although the narrative ends abruptly before Malinowski reached his London destination, it records his early infatuation with England. It is also the only document in which he explains his abandonment of the exact sciences and his turn towards anthropology. There is a confessional tone to the essay, and it is unlikely that he would have admitted such craven adulation of the English to anyone but an intimate Polish friend. Given Aniela's relationship to Joseph Conrad, he was perhaps also offering her a covert justification for the novelist's defection to England and adoption of the English language.

Malinowski's fascination with British culture and the English character had a lasting effect upon him, though like all infatuations it faded with time. It was not until 1931 that he acquired British citizenship, but by 1913 he was already calling England his 'second spiritual home'. His 'highly developed Anglomania', he told Aniela, was almost 'a mystic cult of British culture'. The English way of life was a model of 'the highest elegance and refinement'. He had met many English people on his travels abroad and had been 'overwhelmingly' impressed by their 'style and superiority'. He set them 'on a pedestal' and surrounded them 'with a halo of that elusive attribute that we designate by the term "breeding"'. In short, the English were 'the aristocracy of the nations'. Beneath his profound admiration for the English, however, lay an uneasy incomprehension. Could he ever be inducted into the mysteries of their superior culture and be accepted by them? The aloof reserve of the English presented a formidable obstacle. 'They are undoubtedly very stiff,' he wrote, 'especially towards people who do not speak their language well.' He had yearned for a close friendship with an Englishman or, better, with 'a beautiful Miss' with whom he could flirt, and he admitted that this longing had inflected and intensified his affection for 'Mrs N' (Annie Brunton). 'She was the first Englishwoman whom I got to know better, and who treated me with distinct fondness.'

Ostensibly, he offered his paean to the English in an attempt to explain why, in his twenty-sixth year, he had embarked for London and a 'totally new course of scholarly activity', and why, at this comparatively late age, had begun writing in English as a means of assimilating English culture. Acknowledging the fortuitous opportunity provided by 'Mrs N' in leading him to 'take up Sociology' in England, he wondered how he could have permitted himself, irrationally and perhaps irresponsibly, to follow his heart when his 'occupation, career or calling' was at issue. But then, the direction his future might take remained uncertain:

I cannot regard myself as an exceptionally impressionable man of fantasy who despises the sober and practical management of his life. After all I am undoubtedly not very spontaneous: the disproportion between my intellectual substance and the energy required for its full exploitation makes me a man forever standing at the crossroads.

'Trembling uncertainty'

The dominant note of Malinowski's epistolary version of his arrival in England is exhilaration and optimism. His retrospective diary version, by contrast, is distinctly gloomy.[2] According to this account he felt tired and unhappy on the journey and arrived in London 'full of anxiety' and with a 'trembling uncertainty'. He had no money and there was no one to meet him at Victoria Station.

He soon found Annie, however, and together they located a small flat on the edge of Bloomsbury at 16 Fitzroy Street. This was to be Malinowski's official address, where he collected his mail and kept his belongings. It was a front, however, for he lived with Annie in nearby Saville Street. As the advertisement might have said, Fitzroy Street is situated conveniently close to the British Museum.[3] Although Malinowski was probably unaware of it at the time, 'Fitzrovia' was home to London's literary and artistic avant-garde. Henry Lamb had recently taken over Augustus John's studio at 8 Fitzroy Street. Adrian Stephen and his sister Virginia (later Woolf) lived at 29 Fitzroy Square, George Bernard Shaw's previous abode; the painter Walter Sickert lived at number 19, while at number 21 John Maynard Keynes stayed with Duncan Grant on his visits from Cambridge.[4]

Malinowski was 'proud' to be in London and keen to assume a new scholarly identity. His retrospective diary dwells upon the 'newness' of this phase in his life: the new surroundings, the new people and even 'a new way of working in the library' that involved 'independent research with the concrete idea of publication'.

Above all, there was a radical change in his home life. 'For the first time,' he wrote, 'I was living . . . in conditions corresponding to married life. Every evening I came home, I was expected, we slept together and the like.' Saville Street, where he stayed with Annie, was a narrow, filthy little street. It was 'emphatically Jewish', and in the mornings it reeked of smoke and fried fat. During the day, 'if it wasn't children making an unmerciful racket in the street, it was the sound of a hurdy-gurdy or some other deadly instrument of torture'. The flat consisted of a tiny vestibule, a kitchen and toilet, a dining and a sitting room. For breakfast they drank tea and ate porridge, bread and jam; for supper there were salads and cold cuts of meat, occasionally a roast and a bottle of Australian burgundy. It could only be because he wanted to be with Annie – who was presumably teaching piano – that Malinowski chose to live in a cramped and noisy house in what he claimed was the dirtiest street in the district.[5] Given her fastidiousness and middle-class prejudices, it is all the more surprising that Annie herself chose to live there, though later that year she moved to a more salubrious abode at 36 Upper Marylebone Street.[6]

Their domesticated affair was being conducted with a token decorum. He slept only twice at Fitzroy Street that spring, once when Annie was sick and a second time when returning late from a night on the town. But each morning, after doing his exercises and eating breakfast, he would return to Fitzroy Street, climb the stairs 'almost anxiously' to his room, change his shoes and collect his mail. At 9 a.m. he would take his black leather briefcase and stroll down Tottenham Court Road to Bedford Square and thence to the British Museum.

He wrote of this period: 'At first I look upon London as the acme of elegance, of culture and tranquil beauty. But this slowly passes.' His diary notes made no reference to the stirring political issues and events of the day – Home Rule for Ireland, widespread industrial unrest, the marches and hunger strikes of the Suffragettes – though he could scarcely have been oblivious to them. His arrival in London coincided with the demise of the Edwardian era, which had begun in 1901 with the accession of Queen Victoria's son to the British throne. (Malinowski happened to be at Midhurst in Kent the day King Edward VII died – a public event that did warrant a mention in his diary.) 'A hinge between two centuries,' this era has been called; an intermission between 'the age of reason and the age of anxiety'.

> Standards of propriety were still observed, not because they were believed in, as they had been under Victoria, but because a façade had to be kept up. Victoria had lived her moral righteousness. King Edward was a model for the double standard. . . . [His] affairs were numerous, but his standards of public morality were severe.[7]

Even before the era's end a reaction was under way against Edwardian hypocrisy. In 1906, Arnold Bennett had written a novel about divorce, and Havelock Ellis was openly discussing sex. In 1910, H. G. Wells's *The History of Mr Polly* and E. M. Forster's *Howards End* were published. Cheered on by George Bernard Shaw, Henrik Ibsen's plays were being staged. All these works promoted the subversive notion that self-fulfilment was more important than duty to society or the state. To Malinowski, no doubt, such challenging attitudes were already commonplace, for the tail end of the Young Poland movement had been steeped in them.

Even so, although somewhat diluted by the filtration of the British class system, Edwardian proprieties continued to be observed in Malinowski's middle- to upper-middle-class milieu and it was still the case that 'smartness was crucial – in dress, in manner, in conversation'.[8] Malinowski brought with him a code of social conduct and formal etiquette influenced by, if not derived from, the Hapsburg Empire. (As his eldest daughter put it, his personal style was not bourgeois but *ancien régime*.) Initially at least, the niceties of English class behaviour would have been lost on him, but as a foreigner – and by his manners a well-born if not an aristocractic one – he was entitled to ignore some rules with impunity. The English style to which he referred approvingly was the cultivated, gentlemanly ethos which, despite its reserve, permitted provisional membership of the British upper-middle class, subspecies intelligentsia.

'On or about December 1910 human nature changed,' Virginia Woolf declaimed grandly, referring to Roger Fry's Post-Impressionist exhibition in London. Although never a member of the charmed circle of 'Bloomsberries' himself, Malinowski literally lived in their midst, and his own circle of acquaintances intersected theirs through the likes of John Maynard Keynes and the Fry sisters. In addition to high intelligence, an elitist worldview and a leaning towards sexual radicalism, Malinowski possessed another of the qualifications for entry to Bloomsbury – a needle-sharp wit. ('One is tolerated as long as one is *amusing*.') The 'trembling uncertainty' with which he entered the 'superior' world of the English gave way to a more confident attitude once he realized he could hold his own among them. By December 1910, his human nature, if not changed, was more at ease in its social environment. It helped greatly that, within a few months of his arrival in England, he had made himself known to most of the leading British anthropologists.

The Cambridge School

At the time Malinowski was completing his schooling in Cracow, a significant event in British anthropology was taking place: the Cambridge University Expedition to the Torres Strait. Although their names meant nothing to him then, three members of this expedition would become influential in directing the course of his career. The Torres Strait expedition may truly be said to mark the beginning of modern, fieldwork-based anthropology in Britain. Not only did it demonstrate the value of expert fieldwork, but also conferred upon it an institutional, professional respectability such that it could be funded as might any other scientific activity. After the turn of the century anthropology ceased to be the preserve of amateurs, and the days of the armchair anthropologist became numbered.

The expedition was the inspiration of one man, Alfred Cort Haddon (1855–1940), a figure who bridged the old anthropology and the new. Haddon's significance for Malinowski's biography lies in his role as a founder of the institutional framework into which Malinowski was inducted in 1910 and within which he remained until his departure for America in

1938. Another innovative figure, W. H. R. Rivers (1864–1922), had developed methods that Malinowski was to adopt and ultimately claim as his own. A third significant figure was C. G. Seligmann (1873–1940), who would provide the personal, financial and institutional support Malinowski needed to establish himself in British anthropology. Notwithstanding the importance of these three veterans of the Torres Strait expedition, in one way or another Malinowski would in time repudiate the kinds of anthropology they had practised and preached, kicking away the ladders by which he had climbed to eminence.

An introduction to the triumvirate of Haddon, Rivers and Seligmann is a necessary digression, for it will help set the anthropological scene into which Malinowski sailed in 1910. The careers of the three men were each in their own way exemplary, by which Malinowski might have measured his own, though each was separated in age by a decade or two from the others, such that Malinowski was almost thirty years younger than Haddon, exactly twenty years younger than Rivers, and a little more than ten years younger than Seligmann.

Haddon's generation had come of age when 'the ebbing tide of mid-Victorian liberal optimism was overtaken by the cresting wave of empire' and 'when the universities were open to dissenters, evolution was a scientific orthodoxy, and careers in scientific fields neighbouring to anthropology were a possibility'.[9] Haddon trained as a zoologist at Cambridge, where he imbibed an almost religious belief in science. At the tender age of twenty-six, he was appointed to the chair of zoology at the Royal College of Science in Dublin. In 1886, anxious to move on, he applied for a newly established chair at the University of Melbourne, but a Mancunian named Baldwin Spencer beat him to the post. With the encouragement of Thomas Huxley and a grant of £300, Haddon sailed in 1888 for the Torres Strait, the island-strewn passage that separates Australia from New Guinea. There he intended to study the structure and fauna of coral reefs.

In Haddon's baggage was a copy of *Notes and Queries on Anthropology* and James Frazer's questionnaire on savage 'customs, beliefs and languages'. As well as corals and marine animals he collected native 'curios', sketched and photographed traditional dances and, guided by *Notes and Queries*, recorded local folklore. In short, Haddon became converted to the moral as well as scientific cause of anthropology. He saw it as both an imperial and a scientific responsibility to record primitive cultures before their inevitable disappearance under the corrupting onslaught of Western civilization. The

notion of 'salvage' anthropology by field naturalists such as himself, recording the customs of exotic peoples before their demise, gave to Haddon and
his generation a particular urgency. Indeed, it also stirred successors like
Malinowski, whose first monograph on the Trobrianders opens with the
lament that just as scientific ethnology was achieving methodological maturity the 'material of its study' was melting away.[10] Haddon's argument for
an imperial responsibility was no less cogent, and he was among the first
to press for the anthropological training of colonial officers.

Haddon did not immediately abandon zoology for anthropology. Huxley
reminded him of the need for 'an irreducible minimum of bread and butter',
and could not 'see any way by which a devotee of anthropology is to come
at the bread – let alone the butter'.[11] It was not until 1901, when he was
elected to a fellowship at Christ's College, that Haddon felt secure enough
to resign his Dublin professorship and bring his family to Cambridge.
Although broadly speaking an evolutionist, Haddon was more interested in
the distribution of forms within a defined geographical area than in universal sequences of development. Specifically, he was interested in variant
forms of material culture such as house-types, art motifs, string figures,
tobacco pipes and canoes. Haddon's was an evolutionary ethnology that
stressed the spatial rather than the temporal aspect, not only because
explanatory theories based on the former were easier to confirm or falsify
than those based on the latter (lacking, as preliterate cultures did, any control
from historical evidence), but also because generic relationships between
adjacent cultures could more readily be assumed than between those separated by great distances. Hence, the distributional aspect of Haddon's evolutionism was arguably more scientific than the temporal and unilinear
aspect common to the evolutionism of Edward B. Tylor, James Frazer and
others of the previous generation. There was another corollary to Haddon's
interest in the distribution of cultural traits, and this was the need for field
surveys: the collection of information by the peripatetic ethnography of the
naturalist.

In 1898 Haddon became *the* leading field anthropologist in Britain by
organizing and leading the Torres Strait expedition. He was motivated not
only by scientific curiosity and the urgency of 'salvage' ethnography, but
also by political instinct, for he was convinced that the best way to found
a school of anthropology at Cambridge was to promote field research of
this kind. The story of Haddon's selection of the six members of his team
has been told many times, most recently in a volume of essays celebrating

the centennial of the expedition. [12] In addition to himself as ethnologist and physical anthropologist, Haddon took the Oceanic linguist Sidney H. Ray, the psychologists Charles S. Myers and William McDougall (both pupils of Rivers) and a graduate student, Anthony Wilkin, who was to study material culture and serve as photographer. Haddon's obvious choice for an experimental psychologist was William Halse Rivers Rivers.

It had been Haddon's own mentor, the physiologist Sir Michael Foster, who invited Rivers to Cambridge in 1893 to teach the physiology of the senses. Initially trained in medicine, Rivers established the first laboratory for experimental psychology in Britain (he had earlier studied under Wundt in Leipzig). Haddon put Rivers in charge of all psychological experimentation on the expedition, and he could later boast that 'for the first time psychological observations were made on a backward people in their own country by trained psychologists with adequate equipment'.[13] The results were equivocal, however, as the methodological problems of testing in the field – as distinct from in the controlled conditions of the laboratory – were almost insuperable.[14] Rivers's contribution to anthropology on the expedition provided a more positive and lasting legacy, for it was the occasion of his invention of the so-called 'genealogical method'. This became a standard field technique for gathering information on kinship. Rivers's relatively late serendipitous initiation into anthropology (he was already thirty-six) was to change both his own life and the course of the discipline.

At the last moment, a friend of Myers named Charles Gabriel Seligmann begged to be allowed to join the expedition at his own expense. Seligmann was a medical pathologist, and just as Haddon's conversion to anthropology had occurred in the Torres Strait, so too did Seligmann's. Many of the specialities he developed – including physical anthropology, race, a distributional approach to evolution, and an ethnological focus on New Guinea – were shared with Haddon. In a sense, Seligmann did for anthropology in London what Haddon did for the discipline at Cambridge, including the teaching of missionaries and colonial officers. But one of the factors that made their otherwise comparable careers distinct was the unpredictable person of Malinowski himself. While Haddon nurtured many academic progeny, none had the disruptive potential and paradigm-shifting genius of Malinowski, Seligmann's protégé. The fundamental English decency of both men was often taxed by the volatile Pole, and Haddon was doubtless relieved that Malinowski remained at arm's length in London.

Seligmann, like Malinowski, was an only child; his father died when the boy was sixteen, his invalid mother shortly afterwards. 'Sligs' was a lonely, studious boy who found consolation in reading and natural history. After studying medicine at St Thomas's Hospital in London, he specialized in pathology and gained several honours in this field before turning to anthropology. For some years after his return from the Torres Strait he continued research in pathology, but the lure of ethnological 'salvage' fieldwork was strong and in 1904 he led a three-man expedition to British New Guinea. Thereafter he became increasingly committed to anthropology. In 1907–08, accompanied by his intrepid wife, Brenda, he did fieldwork among the aboriginal Veddas of Ceylon, and on two winter trips to Egypt and the Sudan he extended his anthropological horizons even further. Seligmann's anthropological interests were of the widest scope conceivable, embracing prehistory and archaeology, physical (or biological) anthropology, material culture, psychology and, of course, ethnology. He once demurred that he left 'the social stuff' to Brenda, and his wife's anthropological interests were indeed more narrowly inclined to wards kinship and kin terminologies. In this she was a devout follower of Rivers, until Malinowski converted her to his own viewpoint. Independently wealthy, the Seligmanns collected Chinese porcelain and Sligs developed a passionate interest in oriental glass.

In 1910 the publication of Seligmann's huge synoptic work *The Melanesians of British New Guinea* coincided with his appointment to a lectureship in ethnology at the University of London, and three years later he became the foundation professor of ethnology at the London School of Economics. By the time of his retirement in the early 1930s, Seligman (as he had become in 1914) had done fieldwork in more locations – Queensland, Torres Strait, British New Guinea, Ceylon, Eygpt and the Sudan – than any other anthropologist of his generation, and his status as *primus inter pares* among fieldworkers was acknowledged by Haddon. As a scientist, Seligman was uncomfortable with lofty theorizing; he preferred raw facts and things that could be handled and measured. But his zeal, persistence and indefatigable gathering of data, joined to a passion for classifying, carried him to the highest rank of his profession.[15]

Blunt, gruff and sometimes awkward in social gatherings, Sligs never quite outgrew his childhood reticence. But as his letters to Malinowski reveal, behind the reserve was a thoroughly honourable man, generous to a fault, who cared deeply for the wellbeing of his pupils. He was not without a dry sense of humour. Raymond Firth once heard him say of McDougall's controversial theory of the instincts: 'I know there's an acquisitive instinct because I've got it!' Malinowski sometimes poked fun at his ponderous mentor. When Seligmann dropped the last letter of his surname in a mild attempt to deflect attention from his German-Jewish origins, it provoked the brilliant barb: 'How typical of Sligs to do things by halves!'[16]

Only eleven years older than Malinowski, Seligman was more a supportive elder brother than a father-figure. Plagued by ill-health, the two men formed a collegial bond of suffering which they nourished by the exchange of bulletins on their latest symptoms. From the earliest years of their association they corresponded frequently and their letters (of which over three hundred survive) document the ups and downs of a personal and professional relationship spanning almost thirty years. They quarrelled occasionally, sometimes seriously enough for their missives to seethe with exasperation or radiate a wintery chill, but until the very end there remained a deep undercurrent of mutual affection. Malinowski never forgot his debt to Seligman. It was, after all, Seligman who urged upon him the crucial importance of field research ('what the blood of martyrs is to the Church'); it was Seligman who found the funding for his research in New Guinea; it was Seligman's bureaucratic persistence that gained him his doctor of science degree; and it was largely thanks to Seligman that he secured his appointment to and promotions at the London School of Economics.

Reading Rivers

Malinowski's reverential wonder at finding himself in the British Museum echoed that of William Makepeace Thackeray: 'It seems to me one cannot sit down in that place without a heart full of grateful reverence.' Malinowski was awed by the Reading Room, with its great dome and respectful silence: 'I regard it with piety,' he wrote. 'The special quality of the research that emanates from it.' He sat at desk D2. (Karl Marx wrote *Das Capital* seated at O7.) The first English acquaintance Malinowski made in the museum was a man called Spearman, who told him about Rivers. Malinowski duly called for *The Todas* (1906), Rivers's monograph on people of the Nilgiri Hills in southwestern India. He also read Leo Frobenius, Hutton Webster, Lewis Henry Morgan and Lucien Lévy-Bruhl. Clearly, he was broadening the studies he had begun at Leipzig, but it was almost certainly Rivers's book that made the most profound impression. Methodologically self-conscious as he was, he had discovered an ethnographer after his own heart.

Rivers began *The Todas* by stating that he intended it to be 'not merely a record of the customs and beliefs of a people, but also a demonstration of anthropological method':

> The great need of anthropology at the present time is for more exact method, not only in collecting material, but also in recording it, so that readers may be able to assign its proper value to each fact, and may be provided with definite evidence which will enable them to estimate the probable veraciousness and thoroughness of the record.[17]

He took pains to describe how his information was collected – the first principle of which was 'to obtain independent accounts from different people'. He assessed the relative trustworthiness of his informants; he compared the independent accounts and questioned discrepancies. In addition to the 'direct corroboration' of cross-checking, he used 'indirect corroboration' by 'obtaining the same information in different ways', for example, by eliciting abstract formulations of some social norm followed by concrete instances. Another scrupulous point of method Rivers used was to make a clear distinction between his ethnographic descriptions and the theoretical constructions that he placed upon them. Fact and theory should be kept separate.

Malinowski applauded such moves, and his own introduction to *The Family among the Australian Aborigines* – although referring to Rivers only once – shows how anxious he was to scrutinize his sources with the methodological rigour demanded by Rivers. Later, in his '*Baloma*' essay of 1916, and later still in his Introduction to *Argonauts of the Western Pacific*, Malinowski would echo Rivers's strictures. By that time he had also absorbed Rivers's important contribution to the 1912 edition of *Notes and Queries on Anthropology*.

Rivers had conducted his Todas fieldwork during a period of 'several months' in the latter half of 1902. It was one of the very first attempts by a British anthropologist to apply the – as yet unformulated – principle of 'the intensive study of a restricted area'. Yet it was serendipity that led Rivers to remain in the villages of the Todas for the duration of his fieldwork. As his biographer Richard Slobodin writes: 'Judged by the survey model, Rivers' work on the Todas was intensive; judged by any standard it was extensive.'[18] There is a curious echo in Malinowski's experience of the Tro-briands, a place and a people already adequately 'described' by the standards of the day. Rivers noted that the literature on the Todas was 'so extensive' that he was 'reproached by more than one anthropologist for going to people about whom we already knew so much'. But Rivers was puzzled by existing accounts of the social organization:

> I had not worked long among the Todas before I discovered the existence of many customs and ceremonies previously undescribed, and I was able to obtain much more detailed accounts of others which had already been repeatedly recorded. I found that there was so much to be done that I gave up the intention of working with several different tribes, and devoted the whole of my time to the Todas.[19]

Replace 'Todas' by 'Trobrianders' and Malinowski could well have written this paragraph in 1916.

In prose as transparent as glass, Rivers gave an exhaustive account of the lives of eight hundred polyandrous pastoralists who led an isolated existence in symbiotic relationship with three other tribes. Renowned for their religious ceremonies surrounding the cult of the buffalo, the Todas were also a byword for sexual laxity – as Malinowski's Trobrianders would become a generation later. Indeed, earlier observers held that the Todas represented a primitive stage of 'group marriage', something that Rivers politely contradicted. But his major methodological innovation was a demonstration of 'the genealogical method', the technique he had devised during the Torres Strait expedition while investigating the hereditary transmission of colour blindness.[20] Among the Todas it became Rivers's most valuable instrument of inquiry. By drawing up family pedigrees for the entire community he could locate every individual Toda in terms of his or her affiliation by kinship and marriage.

> Whenever the name of a man was mentioned in connection with a ceremony or social custom, his name was found in the genealogical record and the relation was ascertained in which he stood towards others participating in the custom or ceremony. By this means a concrete element was brought into the work which greatly facilitated inquiry. Customs and rites were investigated by means of concrete examples in which the people taking part were real people to me as well as to my informants.[21]

The genealogies helped him work out the kinship system and the regulations governing marriage. Rivers also drew attention to a more general use of pedigrees:

> The savage mind is almost wholly occupied with the concrete. Discuss his laws of inheritance with him, and you will probably soon become hopelessly entangled in misunderstanding. Take a number of concrete cases, and his memory will enable him to heap instance upon instance showing how property was inherited in given cases.[22]

The operative word is 'concrete', which was echoed like a watchword by the next generation of anthropologists. In its simple fashion, the 'personalizing' of ethnographic recording was a breakthrough, one that Malinowski would exploit to a far greater degree in the Trobriands.

Rivers's book was hailed as an exemplar of the new anthropology. It demonstrated that fieldworking anthropologists were 'engaged in a science rather than in a literary exercise'.[23] This too would have appealed to Malinowski's conscientious concern with scientific method, though he would try to have it both ways by presenting his own ethnological science in a literary manner. On some crucial matters of method, however, Rivers was slipshod by the standards later set by Malinowski. He failed to state how long he had spent in the field, and he made no serious attempt to learn the vernacular (he used Toda nouns in a setting of English verbs, adverbs and pronouns – a 'smattering' technique familiar to every neophyte ethnographer). Rivers's chief interpreter, moreover, was a Christian catechist, and it was against the initial objections of some Todas that Rivers employed him. On another dubious point of method, Rivers admitted that because the Todas were 'inveterate beggars' accustomed to being paid for every service demanded by Europeans, he was obliged to pay for information, though he was careful to pay a stipulated sum for the time spent with him, and not for the type or quality of information – a distinction that might well have been lost on his informants.

During his honeymoon period in the British Museum, Malinowski also read the Rev. J. Matthew's *Two Representative Tribes of Queensland*. His two-page review appeared in the September issue of the Royal Anthropological Institute journal, *Man*. It was Malinowski's first published piece and the review is notable for at least two other reasons: his endorsement of Rivers's principle that facts and opinions must be strictly kept apart, and his call for more concrete information on quotidian Aboriginal life. The following might almost have been a statement – in rather clumsy English – of his nascent methodological credo:

Every side and feature of native life should be described in as concrete terms as possible. Even details, insignificant and superfluous as they appear, may in the light of a new method of investigation prove of the greatest importance. On the other hand, it is always good if the observer refrains from mixing his own theories with the related facts as much as possible. The book on the Todas, by Dr. Rivers, stands as a model in both these methodological respects.[24]

Meeting mentors

Soon after his arrival in England, Malinowski made a special trip to Cambridge to introduce himself to Rivers and Haddon. He referred to the visit in his retrospective diary as 'the honeymoon of my ardour for England'. It was a moonlit night when he entered the 'fabulous' courtyard of St John's, one of the oldest, largest and wealthiest of the colleges. Conducted to Rivers's rooms, he found 'a tall, thin gentleman'. After paying Rivers compliments about *The Todas*, Malinowski began to talk about 'magic & economy'. It is not hard to imagine that Rivers's first impression of Malinowski was of a brilliantly intense young man who spoke forcefully in a melodious Polish accent, urging the virtue of his theoretical spin on Karl Bücher – for the reference to 'magic & economy' doubtless relates to Malinowski's reading in Leipzig. The next day he met Haddon, who introduced him to Barbara Freire-Marecco, later to become a friend and colleague at the London School of Economics. At this time she was studying under Haddon in preparation for fieldwork among the Pueblo Indians of New Mexico.

Malinowski's first surviving letter to Haddon, dated 20 March 1910, was written soon after his visit to Cambridge. He had promised to show Haddon what he was currently writing: 'As usually [sic] my work goes much slower than I expected and I think it will not be until another fortnight that I shall be able to go to Cambridge with a clean typescript of my work.' He mentioned that he had 'visited Dr Seligmann & had dinner with him. He was very nice & I had much profit from his conversation.' Haddon had lent Malinowski his copy of *The Melanesians of British New Guinea*, so it was probably he who effected the introduction to Sligs. In his awkward English, Malinowski betrayed something of his 'Anglomania':

I also hope that your son will be not yet away, as I would have so much pleasure to meet him again. I find him awfully charming and he symbolizes for me quite a new, unknown type of man: the english colonial pioneer – a type for whom I always had so much admiration & respect.[25]

Three months later Malinowski again wrote to Haddon to say he had still not finished his 'article' and would postpone his visit to Cambridge until July.[26] It was probably on this occasion that he first met James Frazer. 'Dr Frazer was very kind and gave me an excellent bibliography for Slavish [sic] folk-lore studies,' he wrote to Haddon in August from Warsaw.[27]

Supposing he made himself known at the London School of Economics soon after his arrival in England, Malinowski would have met Rivers's pupil, A. R. Brown, who was teaching ethnology during the Lent term.[28] Among the recommended reading for his course was *The Todas*. Malinowski's diary notes refer to other meetings: 'Westermarck; introduces me to Wheeler, seminar.' Professor Edward Westermarck's sociology seminar for advanced students began on 25 April, so it was presumably around this time that Malinowski made the acquaintance of someone who would do as much as Rivers to direct his anthropological thinking during 1910–11.

For the Whitsun holiday Malinowski and Annie went to the Isle of Wight, where they stayed at Ventnor in 'a lovely cottage right above the sea'. The dramatic chalk cliffs with their tumbled terraces and layered, wind-buffeted vegetation impressed Malinowski greatly, and he would be reminded of them by similar limestone cliffs in Papua. After a few days Annie returned to London while Malinowski stayed in Ventnor for the rest of the week, drafting a talk he was to give to Westermarck's seminar. Under the influence of what Rivers had told him and what he had learned from reading Lévy-Bruhl, he had begun to think about age-classes and their relationship to the Australian Aboriginal family. But he was dissatisfied with his manner of working and his retrospective diary contains a familiar tirade of self-criticism. He chided himself for working unsystematically and 'according to the whim of the moment'.

Fifteen years later Malinowski nominated 1910 as marking a turning point in the development of anthropology.[29] 'At or about that date,' he wrote, 'a number of important anthropological events occurred.' He listed the publication of James Frazer's *Totemism and Exogamy*, which began a 'lively and vigorous discussion'; the publication of Charles Seligmann's *Melanesians of British New Guinea* and *The Veddas*; T. A. Joyce and Emil Torday's *Les Bushongo*; Arnold Van Gennep's *Rites de Passage*; Lucien Lévy-Bruhl's controversial ideas on 'primitive mentality', and Rivers's discussion of diffusionism. During the next few years, major works were published by Emile Durkheim, Richard Thurnwald, Baldwin Spencer and Francis James Gillen, Rivers and Edvard Alexander Westermarck. Modesty forbade Malinowski to mention that 1910 was also the year of his own advent on the British anthropological scene.

Chapter 10

Finnish Connections

Starting sociology

It was probably Haddon who suggested to Malinowski that his 'sociological' interests might better be served at the London School of Economics than at Cambridge, where anthropology had a more 'antiquarian' flavour. Malinowski's earliest student record at the LSE has not survived, but the timing of his arrival in England suggests that he first registered, as an external student, for the summer term of 1910. It appears that his Jagiellonian doctorate was not recognized by the University of London authorities. His matriculation was granted only in January 1914 – almost four years after he came to London – and it was not until 26 March 1914 that the university senate approved his application to register as an internal student in the faculty of science. This was made retrospective from October 1913. As an internal student he could 'proceed to a higher Degree', that is, to the DSc in anthropology. Seligman was appointed his academic supervisor.

The London School of Economics and Political Science was one of several schools and colleges which, from 1900, constituted the newly federated university. The LSE itself was founded in 1895 by the Fabian couple Beatrice and Sidney Webb, aided by the playwright and critic George Bernard Shaw. Another Fabian co-founder was Graham Wallas, a high-principled political scientist whom Malinowski came to know well, though his relations with the Webbs remained distant and it is uncertain whether he ever met Shaw.[1]

Sociology had been introduced into the curriculum in 1903. Following the Fabian socialist agenda, the School authorities believed sociology would be likely to interest 'Borough Councillors, Poor Law Guardians, Trade Union Officials, Members of Committees of Philanthropic Institutions and

Societies, Scripture Readers and Rent Collectors', a list that G.B.S., tongue firmly in cheek, might well have penned.

In 1907, a Scottish philanthropist named Martin White endowed a five-year lectureship in sociology which was offered to Edward Alexander Westermarck (1862–1939), a Finnish-born anthropologist and moral philosopher. Westermarck was already renowned for his remarkable synoptic work *The History of Human Marriage* (1891). White's endowment was made permanent in 1911 for the part-time professorship Westermarck held until his retirement, a post he combined with one at the University of Helsingfors (now Helsinki). The student body at the LSE, Westermarck claimed, was 'the most international' and 'the most varied in colour of any university in the world'.[2]

White also endowed a permanent chair of sociology. Leonard Trelawny Hobhouse (1864–1929), a lecturer at the LSE since 1904, was its first incumbent.[3] Like Westermarck, Hobhouse had been captivated by Edward Tylor's lectures on evolutionary anthropology at Oxford, and he too wrote voluminously on the evolution of morals, though he eschewed the neo-Darwinian stance favoured by Westermarck. Politically, Hobhouse was an anti-imperialist and a believer in the Common Good. Liberty was 'not so much a right of the individual as a necessity of society' – an argument that Malinowski would replay in *Freedom and Civilization*. Hobhouse's biographer doubts whether he was really a sociologist at all as distinct from a rather woolly-minded political thinker, and it was with 'a conspicuous lack of enthusiasm' that he had accepted the Martin White Chair as Britain's first professor of sociology. His only true disciple, Morris Ginsberg, was also his successor, and it was through him that Hobhouse's social philosophy lived on.[4] While Malinowski was much closer to his contemporary Ginsberg, he occasionally socialized with Hobhouse and his wife. He also acknowledged Hobhouse for reading the proofs of *Argonauts* and offering 'valuable advice'.[5]

The professionalization of anthropology in Britain began during the first decade of the century. The difficulties Malinowski encountered in starting his career in anthropology were as nothing compared to those faced by aspirants of the previous generation. His arrival was timely, in that academic anthropology in Britain had only recently gained institutional status and a measure of funding. He therefore entered an expansive, optimistic milieu in which those who had won the battles for recognition smiled benignly on their pupils and urged them to go forth and conquer. There was every expectation that Malinowski's generation of anthropologists would reap rich harvests in the field (the agricultural trope was an infectious one), and there was no question that if one wanted to do anthropology, one did fieldwork. The distinction between those who collected ethnographic material in the field and those who analysed it in the study was about to be abolished. 'Now is the time to garner, the elaboration of the sport can be done at any time – but in order to observe intelligently it is necessary to be instructed properly. . . . Hence the endowment of teaching should accompany that of field work.'[6] Thus spoke Haddon, mixing his metaphors in 1901, the year he was elected to a Christ's College fellowship and could at last devote himself full time to anthropology. It was Haddon who then did most to gain a precarious toe-hold for anthropology at Cambridge. With the support of James Frazer and other university senate luminaries, he was instrumental in establishing a board of anthropological studies in 1904. Lecture courses were soon being offered by Haddon, Rivers, William Ridgeway and Charles Myers, and in 1908 a diploma programme was introduced with an emphasis on fieldwork. The following year Haddon was appointed reader in ethnology. After years of making ends meet by juggling part-time jobs, Haddon must have seen his satisfactory salary as a sign that anthropology had finally 'arrived' in Cambridge. He was now belatedly able 'to enjoy the relatively comfortable life of an Edwardian academic gentleman'.[7]

Anthropology also found a niche at Oxford University in 1905 with the formation of a committee on anthropology by Robert R. Marett (1866–1943). Despite Sir Edward B. Tylor's reputation as Britain's foremost anthropologist – the founding father indeed – he had failed to establish anthropology as a discipline at Oxford owing to its tainted association with Darwinism. In a university still dominated by clerics, Marett the classicist and genial Jerseyman won over the opposition by realigning anthropology with classics and archaeology.[8] He held similar views to Haddon about the urgent need for fieldwork, though as an armchair anthropologist himself he continued to endorse the division of labour between fieldworkers and theoreticians. With a typical flourish, he wrote: 'Whilst the weather lasts and the crop is still left standing, garnering rather than threshing must remain the order of the day.'[9] By the time Malinowski was setting off to the field, Marett had already despatched three of his own pupils, two of them to Melanesia.

At the LSE, representing the third corner of the dominant university triangle in England, ethnology was first taught in the academic year of 1904–05 as part of a sociology honours degree. Haddon was appointed lecturer, and for five years he travelled down from Cambridge to give a weekly course on 'Tropical and Sub-Tropical Peoples of Africa, Asia and Australasia'. In 1909–10 another Cambridge man took Haddon's place. This was Alfred Reginald Brown, who also taught a special area course on Australia. Radcliffe-Brown, as he would rename himself, had already completed almost two years of fieldwork in the Andaman Islands and was now keen to investigate Aborginal societies at first hand.

The first full session at the LSE attended by Malinowski was that of 1910–11. The *Calendar* for that year proclaimed:

> The importance at the present moment of the study of such a subject as Sociology scarcely needs to be emphasised. Special attention is drawn to the lectures on Ethnology. Everyone who proposes to carry out administrative or missionary work in outlying parts of the British Empire should make a special study of this essential subject.[10]

Thus, from his very first exposure to ethnology in London, Malinowski was made aware of the British intent to give the academic discipline a practical rationale. Ethnology in Leipzig (subsumed under *Völkerpsychologie*) had no such pretensions to being useful. Malinowski's later turn to 'practical anthropology' (his term for applied anthropology) was therefore not without precedent in England and owed nothing to his Continental roots. If the *Calendar*'s explanation was intended to appeal to the Colonial Office, however, it fell on deaf ears and it was left to Martin White to provide an annual sum of £120 to finance thirty lectures.[11] Having been appointed to the lectureship in 1910, it was Seligman who thereafter taught the course in ethnology. His syllabus was concise: 'The varieties of man; their social and cultural characteristics. The migrations and present geographical distribution of the more important races and peoples. The antiquity of man; the physical characteristics of the most ancient types. The prehistoric cultures.' Equally brief, Seligman's reading list in 1910–11 comprised only four titles: Keane's *Ethnology*, Deniker's *Races of Man*, Haddon's *Races of Man* and Tylor's *Primitive Culture*. In 1911–12 he added Parkinson's *Dreissig Jahre in der Südsee*, and his own synoptic volume *The Melanesians of British New Guinea*.[12]

With anthropology now seeded in three universities, the training of professionals could begin; up to this time there had been no anthropologists who had not converted from some other discipline. The cult of fieldwork was accordingly in full swing, and by 1912 Seligman (like Haddon in Cambridge and Marett in Oxford) was busily promoting it as the key to future developments. He approached the LSE director, William Pember Reeves, for an annual sum of £150 to be set aside so that fieldwork might be undertaken every other year by 'a promising student'. He also tried to impress upon Sidney Webb 'the absolute necessity of providing for field work if anthropology is to flourish at the School'.[13] Webb may have agreed in principle, but the director was unmoved. Resources were scarce, and paying for graduate students' fieldwork in exotic places was a luxury the School could not afford.

The courses Malinowski took during 1910–11 can be surmised from the lecture list in the *Calendar* for that year. Those given by Hobhouse, Westermarck and Seligman would have interested him most. Hobhouse taught a course on social evolution that included social psychology; he also held a seminar in sociology for advanced students that Malinowski probably attended. Many other courses were offered under the banner of sociology, though there is no evidence that he took them. He refers in his retrospective diary only to Westermarck's lectures and seminars, and they would have been more to his taste than anything Hobhouse had to offer. Westermarck's fifteen lectures on social institutions (each followed by a class) were given on two evenings a week in the summer term. The syllabus was extraordinarily comprehensive and indicative of the scope of Westermarck's interests. A brief sample:

> The characteristics of social phenomena as distinguished from biological and psychological phenomena. The systems of paternal and maternal descent. The family, joint family, clan, tribe, nation. The biological and psychological facts on which the formation, scope, and coherence of a society depend. Customs and laws as rules of conduct. Moral approval and disapproval. The origin and function of marriage.[14]

Several of Malinowski's abiding anthropological interests are here – marriage, the family and primitive law. The syllabus of Westermarck's second lecture course, on social rights and duties, refers to additional topics such as warfare, magic and religion that Malinowski subsequently made his own. Westermarck's reading list for his two major courses included, in addition to his own multi-volume works *The History of Human Marriage* and *The Origin and Development of the Moral Ideas*, classic texts by Herbert Spencer,

Emile Durkheim, Adam Smith, Carveth Read, Ernest Crawley and James Frazer. A bundle of Malinowski's notes on Westermarck's seminar have survived and they confirm that, in addition to Crawley and Durkheim, he was reading Marett, Andrew Lang, Hutton Webster and Van Gennep.[15]

By far the most important academic friendship that Malinowski made during his first year at the School was with Edward Westermarck. A large and colourful personality, Westermarck was 'a worldly man with a great sense of fun', addicted to travel, good food and fine wines. He has been characterized in paradoxical terms as 'a bachelor who studied marriage, a proper European who studied Morocco, a relativist who studied morality, and a disbeliever who studied religion'.[16] His keen ethnographer's eye probed British mores as entertainingly as it did those of his beloved Moroccans. Westermarck and Martin White were good friends and birds of a feather; they drank brandy in London clubs and celebrated the end of each acadmic year with champagne dinners.[17]

Malinowski developed an enormous liking for Westermarck, and the affection was mutual. They had much in common, despite the age difference of twenty-two years and Westermarck's sexual preference for Moorish boys. Malinowski felt a rare intellectual kinship with this Swede–Finn, who not only shared his veneration for the British Museum and a fascination with exotic forms of marriage, but also the Anglophilia that tempered his cosmopolitanism. 'I have never felt myself as a foreigner in this country,' declared Westermarck who, like Malinowski, had grown up amid linguistic and cultural diversity.[18] 'The sociologist,' Westermarck said in his 1907 inaugural lecture, 'must cut himself off in thought from his relationships of race, country, and citizenship.' In 1910 Malinowski would have agreed; he was already preparing to distance himself from his Polish origins.

After he had accomplished his own unique Trobriands fieldwork, Malinowski paid sincere tribute to Westermarck's achievement in Morocco:

> No better field-work exists. . . . It was done with a greater expenditure of care and time than any other specialized anthropological research; it has brought to fruition Westermarck's comprehensive learning and special grasp of sociology; it revealed his exceptional linguistic talents and his ability to mix with people of other race and culture.[19]

When Westermarck retired in 1930 Malinowski was delighted to inherit his office armchair; and several years later he acknowledged this mentor as one 'to whose work I owe more than to any other scientific influence'.[20]

Wheeler, Czaplicka, Borenius

Westermarck's other pupils included two Finns who had followed him to London: Gunnar Landtman and Rafael Karsten, both soon to do fieldwork after further training under Haddon. Landtman went to the Papua, where he spent two years doing intensive fieldwork on Kiwai Island in the estuary of the Fly River. Karsten went to South America and worked among several tribes of the Bolivian Chaco. Another Finn joined Westermarck's seminar a couple of years later: Rudolph Holsti, who would become a cabinet minister in Helsinki. His pioneering study *The Relation of War to the Origin of the State* (1914) probably influenced Malinowski's own thinking on the anthropology of war.

Malinowski struck up a more intimate friendship with a somewhat older protégé of Westermarck named Gerald Camden Wheeler (1872–1943), who had recently completed a library thesis on the political organization of Australian Aborigines. He was already a seasoned fieldworker, however, having accompanied Rivers and Arthur Maurice Hocart (an Oxford-trained student the same age as Malinowski) on an expedition to Melanesia in 1908. After a two-month training spell with Rivers and Hocart on Eddystone (Simbo) Island in the Western Solomons, Wheeler spent ten months alone in Bougainville Strait. Hocart had remained on Eddystone for more intensive research, while Rivers island-hopped aboard the flagship of the Anglican mission, gathering the material that would result in *The History of Melanesian Society* (1914). Wheeler appears to have become competent, if not fluent, in the Mono vernacular and belatedly published a book on Mono-Alu mythology.[21] He hung around the LSE for a number of years, teaching part-time and collaborating with Hobhouse and Morris Ginsberg on a Tylorian comparative study, *The Material Culture and Social Institutions of the Simpler Peoples* (1915), but he failed to secure a university position after the Great War and dropped from sight. Haddon passed sad judgment on Wheeler many years later when he applied for a civil-list pension: 'I regard him as one of those men of ability in their own subject who somehow has not succeeded in life.'[22] Nevertheless, Malinowski valued his friendship during his early years in London and Wheeler helped him to get his first book through the press.

Maria Antonina Czaplicka was another member of Westermarck's seminar. She was a Warsaw-born compatriot of Malinowski, exactly his own age, and for a time they followed parallel career paths. She had studied natural science and geography in Russian Poland before coming to Britain at about the same time as Malinowski. Although enrolled at Bedford Women's College, she studied with Westermarck and Seligman at the LSE before going on to Oxford where she took the diploma in anthropology under Marett's tutelege. While Malinowski was completing his Aboriginal Australian studies, Czaplicka was serving her own armchair apprenticeship and using her knowledge of Russian to good effect by writing a monograph on aboriginal Siberia; and on the eve of the Great War, when Malinowski left for Australia and New Guinea, Czaplicka departed for Russia and northwest Siberia.[23] They would never meet again. Maria Czaplicka, 'a pure flame too intense for mortal body to support', committed suicide in 1921.[24]

It was through Westermarck that Malinowski met yet another Finn, Tancred Borenius (1885–1948), who became one of his closest friends. There was a political affinity, so to speak, for Finland was also ruled by Russia. Like Malinowski and Czaplicka, Borenius and his wife (and Westermarck, too, of course) belonged to nations under foreign domination. Tancred, who was whimsically named after a storybook Crusader, had studied the history of art in Helsingfors, Berlin and Rome and written a PhD thesis in English on the Vicenza School. An Anglophile years before Malinowski, Borenius had also studied under the hallowed dome of the British Museum. Roger Fry, whom Borenius had met in Venice, helped him to publish the thesis that established his reputation in the London art world. Handsome editing commissions followed, and he felt secure enough to marry his childhood sweetheart and second cousin, Anna-Mi Runeberg, the granddaughter of Finland's national poet. The couple rented a flat in Mecklenburg Square. Borenius's friendship with Fry was an entrée to the Bloomsbury set, and the young couple were often to be seen at Lady Ottoline Morrell's 'evenings' in Bedford Square. In her diary, Virginia Woolf mocked Tancred's heavy accent and long-winded Continental manner of telling stories. He was gregarious, an expansive host and raconteur, and spoke at least as many languages as Malinowski. In 1913 he was appointed lecturer in fine art at the University of London, and in 1922 professor of the history of art – then a little-studied subject in Britain.[25]

    Anna-Mi remembered how Tancred first met Mali (as they called him) at a dinner given by Westermarck's pupils.[26] It was a cosmopolitan occasion and Malinowski delivered a mock speech 'in a made-up language' complete

with appropriate gestures. 'He could imitate perfectly the sounds and into-
nation of a language, such as Swedish, even though he didn't understand it.'
That night Borenius enthused to his wife that he had met 'the most marvellous, amusing, witty and intelligent man', and they had Mali to supper
the very next evening. He was then still officially living at Fitzroy Street –
he did not tell the Boreniuses about Annie – but in 1913 he rented a
furnished room above theirs at 29 Mecklenburg Square.

Anna-Mi remembered Mali as a prankster. Once when they were enter-
taining some high-born visitors, an imperious Malinowski appeared with
the Hapsburg emperor's gold ring prominently clasping his tie. 'I knew you'd
be feeling awkward with your grand guests,' he told his friends afterwards,
'so I thought I'd impress them.' A more elaborate prank involved Maria
Czaplicka. Anna-Mi recalled her as a gifted, ambitious, thin-lipped, highly
strung young woman who 'used to throw her weight about in discussions'.

> As we had this picture of Czaplicka, Tancred and I were flabbergasted
> when Mali and she came one day and said they were engaged and sat
> holding each other's hands and demonstratively calling each other
> Darling in a very unconvincing way. Tancred was upset and very for-
> mally congratulated them. Then they said that it was all a hoax and they
> only wanted to see how we would take it.[27]

Malinowski liked to pun: 'I supply the polish and Borenius the finish.'

Aborigines and the family

During the nineteenth century Aboriginal Australia was the locus for
intense argument about the nature of early human society. Isolated for mil-
lennia from cultural developments elsewhere, Australia was the only continent occupied exclusively by hunters and gatherers. They were defined as
much by what they appeared to lack as by what they possessed. Most conspicuously, they lacked agriculture, domesticated animals (except the dingo),
permanent houses and settlements. The view that Aborigines were 'man's
living ancestors' was entrenched, and many scholars (Durkheim and Freud
among them) based their studies on the premise that Australian Aborigines
were at the lower end of the evolutionary sequence, that they were the
living representatives of the universal primeval culture from which all other
cultures had evolved.

Late in 1910 Malinowski wrote a substantial review of his friend Wheeler's recent book *The Tribal and Inter-Tribal Relations in Australia*.[28] This provided him with an opportunity to state his theoretical position and covertly to announce that he was working on a major study of the Australian Aboriginal family. His extensive reading of Australian ethnography had taught him that much of the material was 'ambiguous, contradictory, and confused'. As he saw it then, his scholarly task was to evaluate and compare the sources as they pertained to particular ethnographic problems: age-grades, initiation, marriage-classes, totemism and the family. Finding reliable, unvarnished descriptions of these institutions was not easy. Malinowksi was discovering that in ethnology the same 'facts' could be presented in many different ways, according to the status or occupation of the observer, and according to his (very occasionally, her) preconceptions. Such reports were not 'scientific' enough; they were contaminated at the source by observer bias. Even professional ethnographers had their own theoretical axes to grind and presented their 'facts' to demonstrate pet hypotheses. The review allowed Malinowski to air these complaints of an armchair anthropologist and it was little short of a broadside against prevailing methods – or the lack of them. Theories can only be as good as the ethnography they are based upon, and the latter was decidedly deficient. It became a familiar strategy for Malinowski to mount the vehicle of another's book in order to drive home his own messages. Much later, not only would he make homiletic use of book reviews but also of the prefaces to his pupils' monographs.

Westermarck's prefatory note to Wheeler's book claimed it as exemplifying

> the kind of research which is encouraged at the University of London so far as the lower stages of civilization are concerned. . . . next to sociological field-work . . . there are, within this branch of study, no other investigations so urgently needed as monographs on some definite class of social phenomena or institutions among a certain group of related tribes.[29]

This was a green light to Malinowski. The book he was preparing dealt with the family, not on a global scale as Westermarck and Crawley had done, but within a defined geographical and culture area. The deficiencies of universal comparisons were becoming obvious, and the idea was rapidly gaining ground that the comparative method would be more effective if its use was circumscribed.

The theoretical context in which Malinowski's first book, *The Family among the Australian Aborigines*, was written can best be understood by citing from his own intellectual tribute to Westermarck. This was published in *Nature* in 1922, in a congratulatory review of the fifth edition of *The History of Human Marriage*.[30] The history of anthropological discourse on the family began, Malinowski wrote, with 'the uncritical assumption that the family was the nucleus of human society':

> that monogamous marriage has been the prototype of all varieties of sex union; that law, authority and government are all derived from patriarchal power; that the State, the Tribe, economic co-operation and all other forms of social association have gradually grown out of the small group of blood relatives, issued from one married couple, and governed by the father. This theory satisfied common sense, supplied an easily imaginable course of natural development, and was in agreement with all the unquestioned authorities, from the Bible to Aristotle.

But during the latter half of the nineteenth century the family theory of the origin of human society was challenged. Johann Bachofen's *Das Mutterrecht* (1861), John McLennan's *Primitive Marriage* (1865), Lewis Henry Morgan's *Ancient Society* (1877), and Friedrich Engels's *Origin of the Family, Private Property and the State* (1884) all proposed alternative (though convergent) theories on the basis of comparative studies of 'survivals' and 'antiquarian reconstruction'. The conception of primeval monogamous marriage and the nuclear family was jettisoned as a myth.

> Primitive humanity, they said, lived in loosely organised hordes, in which an almost complete lack of sexual regulation, a state of promiscuity, was the usage and law. . . . Thus, instead of the primitive family we have a horde; instead of marriage, promiscuity; instead of paternal right, the sole influence of the mother and her relatives over the children.

The leaders of this school of thought constructed several 'successive stages of sexual evolution through which humanity was supposed to have passed'. Mankind began with promiscuity, passed through a stage characterized by group marriage dominated by matriarchy, then a stage of polygamy, until the higher civilizations achieved monogamous marriage as the final product of development. 'Under this scheme of speculations,' Malinowski noted drily: 'the history of human marriage reads like a sensational and somewhat scandalous novel, starting from a confused but interesting initial triangle, redeeming its unseemly course by a moral *dénouement*, and leading, as all proper novels should, to marriage, in which "they lived happily ever after".'

Then there was a reaction. As a student of anthropology in Helsingfors, Edward Westermarck had begun to add his contribution to the work of Bachofen and Morgan; but as he accumulated evidence the arguments for their fashionable theories 'began to crumble in his hands'. In 1891 he published the first, one-volume edition of *The History of Human Marriage* in which he argued:

> that monogamous marriage is a primeval human institution, and that it is rooted in the individual family; that matriarchate has not been a universal stage of human development; that group marriage never existed, still less promiscuity, and that the whole problem must be approached from the biological and psychological point of view . . . through an exhaustive . . . application of ethnological evidence.

Westermarck's views gained ground, and over the course of thirty years the book went into several editions. Scholars no longer accepted the naïve theory of the family 'as a kind of universal germ of all social evolution', nor did they take seriously the umpteen stages of marriage traced from promiscuity to monogamy: 'A union between man and wife, based on personal affection springing out of sexual attachment, based on economic conditions, on mutual services, but above all on a common relation to the children, such a union is the origin of the human family.' In short, 'marriage is rooted in the family, rather than the family in marriage'. This, in essence, is what Malinowski had learned by writing *The Family among the Australian Aborigines* under the sway of Westermarck's views.

In addition to its methodological rigour, what most distinguishes Malinowski's first book is its insistence on empirical observation and its dismissal of evolutionary assumptions. His opening paragraph set the tone:

> The problem of the social forms of family life still presents some obscurities. What appears to be most urgently needed is a careful investigation of facts in all the different ethnographical areas. I propose in this study to undertake this task for Australia. I shall avoid making any hypothetical assumptions, or discussing general problems which refer to the origin or evolution of the family. I wish only to describe in correct terms and as thoroughly as possible all that refers to actual family life in Australia.[31]

He subjected the most respected authorities to testing scrutiny, showing how even A.W. Howitt and Baldwin Spencer had distorted the evidence of their senses by forcing their observations to conform with the expectations of evolutionary theory.

Malinowski showed conclusively that the individual family was the basic unit of social organization throughout Australia. He applied Westermarck's definition of marriage to demonstrate that 'group marriage' was a misnomer for varieties of sexual licence and wife-sharing, which in no observed instances gave rise to 'group families'. He defined the family in terms of its membership, activities and responsibilities, and he made a clear distinction between sex and marriage. On the subject of sexual licence (which had preoccupied so many of his precursors), he made the firm point that such 'licence' during initiation ceremonies was constrained by rules prescribing who may copulate with whom. Likewise, there were rules governing the notorious institution of wife-lending, *pirrauru*. These discussions foreshadowed Malinowski's later contribution to the topic of 'primitive law' and social control. Thus, wife-lending and ceremonial licence were not evidence of lawless savagery, as previous writers had argued, but were institutions that, like marriage, obeyed the proscriptions of incest and exogamy.

Reviewing Aboriginal beliefs about conception, Malinowski concluded that throughout the continent the role of the father in procreation was unknown. (Three years later his own conviction that such ignorance was universal among 'primitive' peoples was fortuitously confirmed by the Trobriand Islanders.) Variously referred to as the 'ignorance of physiological paternity', 'procrative nescience' or, more generally, 'doctrines of virgin birth', the issue has provided one of the hoariest debates in social anthropology, one that was still being aired at the end of the twentieth century. A recent authority concludes: 'For those who like their facts cut and dried ("Were the Aborigines ignorant of the connection between sex and reproduction? Answer yes or no"), the outcome of a hundred years of research must seem singularly disappointing.'[32] Such knowledge for Aborigines was clearly not 'adaptively significant in the prehistoric past'. In other words, 'men did not need to understand the role of semen in order to copulate frequently; nor was male sexual jealousy dependent upon a knowledge of fertilization'. On the contrary, mystical theories of conception could serve a variety of ideological purposes. Malinowski might well have seen them as illustrative of the Machian principle of 'economy of thought'.

In an introduction to a reprint of the book, John Barnes correctly assessed its value in foreshadowing the way social anthropology would develop – largely through Malinowski's inspiration – a decade or two later:

> We can see here the insistence on real behaviour rather than on the bald statement of 'customs', the interest in breaches of custom as well as in conformity to them, and a clear indication of the thesis that items of social behaviour cannot be studied in isolation but only in their total cultural context.[33]

Malinowski also showed how 'kinship is not the automatic consequence of genetic connection, but is a set of relationships that arise, at least in part, as a consequence of beliefs about the processes of human reproduction'.[34] Although there is truth in L. R. Hiatt's sweeping claim that in this book 'Malinowski sealed the fate of evolutionism in British social anthropology and simultaneously established the foundation for a new paradigm preoccupied with empirical description and the sociological function of contemporary institutions', it would be some time before anthropology came to acknowledge as much.[35]

Malinowski had begun work in the British Museum with 'the concrete idea of publication'. Although it would not appear in print for another three years, *The Family among the Australian Aborigines* was a modest but significant milestone in his career. It was finally completed and ready for submission in April or May 1911, and by then he had shown all or parts of it to Westermarck, Seligman, Haddon, Rivers and Wheeler. On 19 June, showing all the impatience of a first-time author, Malinowski wrote to Haddon begging him to find out what had happened to his typescript, which he had sent to Cambridge University Press weeks earlier.[36]

In the event, CUP rejected the book. Instead, the University of London Press accepted it on condition of a subvention being offered to defray the costs. Nudged by Westermarck, Martin White came to the rescue with £60 and Malinowski was suitably grateful, though it meant that White was now disinclined to grant him any further money for fieldwork. Seligman thought it 'sad' that Martin White did not rise to this 'great opportunity', and found it 'queer that people will find money to publish books which are only extracts from other books & yet jib at providing for fieldwork'.[37] There were more difficulties and further delays, giving Malinowski a foretaste of the problems he would encounter with the publication of most of his other books.

Radcliffe-Brown reviewed *The Family among the Australian Aborigines* for the leading anthropological journal *Man*.[38]

> [I]t is by far the best example in English of scientific method in dealing with descriptions of the customs and institutions of a savage people. . . . [I]t may well serve for some time to come as a model of method, and for this reason alone should be in the hands of every student of ethnology.

High praise indeed, for Radcliffe-Brown was surely not overlooking *The Todas*. As one of the leading experts on Australian social organization (soon to become *the* leading expert), he was in a better position than most to evaluate the significance of Malinowski's book which, he claimed, 'affords an overwhelming argument against hypotheses of group-marriage'. He registered a few disagreements, however. Malinowski's attempt 'to throw light on the the native notion of kinship by an examination of mythological beliefs' was misguided, for indigenous notions of kinship 'cannot be studied without reference to what the author calls "group relationships"'. Because Malinowski had confined himself to individual family relationships 'this part of his work remains imperfect'.

Implicit in this criticism is an appeal to a theoretical stance radically different from Malinowski's, a glimmer of the difference that would eventually typify the approaches of the two anthropologists. Crudely put, one would come to see society from a point of view outside society, the other from the vantage point of the individual within it. Their different understandings of 'functionalism' may be said to have begun here.

Polish visitors

On 16 June 1911, Malinowski invited Staś Witkiewicz to visit him in London.

> I can always find something cheap and comfortable for you. I have already got a big, pretty and clean room for 8/- (=10 francs) per week and if you come immediately you may count on this. . . . At present I am not so busy and scholarship does not obtrude; as to 'women': this would not be a problem, anyway there is no one, unfortunately![39]

Malinowski gave as his address an LSE hostel in Tavistock Place. Annie Brunton, it seems, was travelling in Europe.

Staś duly arrived with Józefa Malinowska and their friend from Zakopane, Tadeusz Nalepiński.[40] Staś stayed for about two weeks, the others much longer. The Boreniuses appear to have met Józefa at this time. Anna-Mi recalled her self-possession and fine intellect: 'a great personality; in the way she moved one could see a person of consequence who knew it.' They conversed in French and there were intense political discussions between Józefa, Malinowski, Tancred and Isabel Fry. The Poles and the Finns were fiercely anti-Russian; the Quaker Englishwoman pro-Russian, believing as late as 1914 that there would be no war. Józefa was prophetic: 'If that is the attitude here,' she declared, 'then God help England.' The Boreniuses finally broke with Isabel Fry over her sympathetic attitude towards Russia and they remained estranged despite Malinowski's efforts to reconcile them.

The other Polish visitor, Nalepiński, was a minor poet and dramatist who had taken his doctorate in Prague. He inspired Malinowski to write poetry and the flavour of their relationship can be surmised from verses they dedicated to one another. A sonnet Nalepiński drafted in Kew Gardens in December 1911 says in the frankest terms what he thought of his friend:

> To Bronislaw Malinowski, a gentleman *in partibus defloratorum.*
> It isn't hard to win a bet but it's bad to stay stubborn
> And flaunt your navel proudly to the mob.
> Sometimes what shines like gold is only copper.
> In the stable we don't know God by his top hat.
> It's bad when one locks onself alone within a chamber
> And lets one's wings of action be covered with stinking mould.
> Yes, it's tough to be a moth, still worse a herring
> Or any creature that can't manage much. . . .
> You who have never sinned by showing too much courage
> But have measured your pace in life with care
> So as to get ahead when the others tire
> Rejoice! For it isn't failure but a weak reflection
> Of deeper things that make you count out five coins today
> And makes me, among woods and meadows, write this way.[41]

If Nalepiński was flippantly reproaching Malinowski for arrogance, stubbornness, cowardice, meanness and cunning, Malinowski would return the favour by clipping Nalepiński's pretentious poetic wings:

> Do you remember once in Bedford Square
> While digesting a Lyons lunch

> I plucked some feathers from your Pegasus
> And talked about the poet's living truths?
> If he proclaims his faith, then he must live it
> Or else he shouldn't dress in prophet's clothes
> But if he's to create art for art's sake
> He must impress us with its brilliance.[42]

In mid-August, Malinowski wrote to Staś from Ilfracombe in north Devon. As in all their correspondence there is a teasing exaggeration of mood; it would be difficult otherwise to reconcile the sentiments of this letter with Malinowski's diffuse satisfaction with life in England:

> Today I am suffering from a fit of deep nostalgia, which I never knew before but which now occurs frequently. . . . Finally I have escaped from London and for a few days I have been resting at the seaside . . . I am completely alone here and especially on account of the great stiffness of the Englishmen I feel lonely, and rather abandoned. . . . I long to be in the mountains in Zakopane. It is the only place where I feel really well.[43]

In Zakopane, meanwhile, Staś was furiously writing *The 622 Downfalls of Bungo*.

Work and magic in Portsmouth

In early 1911 Malinowski was invited to contribute to a *Festschrift* for Westermarck. He chose a topic that had preoccupied him since reading Karl Bücher in Leipzig: the economic function of ritual acts and religious beliefs.[44] A recent reading of Frazer's *Totemism and Exogamy* (1910) crystallized his ideas. Although the essay was not published until late in 1912, he had completed it by August of the previous year – just before taking that lonely holiday in Ilfracombe – and he seized the opportunity to present an early condensed version in a public forum. In early September, the British Association held its congress in Portsmouth, and Malinowski went there directly from Devon to deliver his paper to Anthropology's Section H. It was probably the first time he had addressed a scientific conference – certainly one so distinguished – and it would have gratified him to see that *The Times* of London, in reporting the proceedings of the day's session, had devoted two column inches to his paper, about the same coverage that Seligman received for his address on 'The Divine Kings of the Shilluk'.[45]

Malinowski took as his starting point Frazer's insight that totemism in central Australia had an economic aspect. Frazer had proposed that since each Arunta clan possessed magical control of its totem there was an implicit division of labour between several clans; but although their magical powers were exercised for the good of the whole community, the 'sound economic principle' of the division of labour must be 'misapplied' since it was based upon irrational magical assumptions. Therefore, argued Frazer, totemism cannot have had any influence on the economic progress of mankind, and consequently was of little scientific interest. Malinowski disagreed.

The *intichiuma* ceremonies . . . may be shown to possess quite a special theoretical interest for ethnological economics if viewed not as primitive forms of division of labour, but from a slightly different aspect, that is as an attempt by means of the totemic ideas to organize the community and to impose upon it a collective and regular form of labour.[46]

In short, one must look *behind* the ostensible and self-evident meaning of ceremonies.

Drawing largely on the work of Spencer and Gillen on the Arunta of central Australia, Malinowski surveyed the literature on *intichiuma*: the 'most important' and 'most solemn' of all the ceremonies whose aim was to promote the increase or fertility of totemic animals and plants. Malinowski proceeded to demonstrate that these ceremonies involved the organized, collective labour of local groups, and that the work done during them, 'involving hardships and privations', was of a 'higher, more economic, type' than work performed at other times. The intricate nexus between magic and science, between religion and economic ends, or more generally between the mystical and the practical, was one that fascinated Malinowski, and he would make fruitful use of it throughout his anthropological career. Reflecting on this nexus in the *intichiuma*, he wrote: 'If magic is a form of primitive technique and if it be assumed that in the course of evolution it develops, at least to a certain extent, into rational technical methods, then all enterprises performed by means of magic may develop into economic enterprises.'[47] Here Malinowski began a train of thought – though subsequently without the evolutionary underpinnings – which he was to complete more than twenty years later in his last monograph on the Trobriand Islanders.

In the final section of the paper he wrote:

> [T]he most important aim of science remains the correct and exact description of facts. Like the theoretical branches of physics and chemistry, theoretical ethnology has for its express aim the interpretation and exact description of the results of field research and observation. In the present case an attempt has been made to show that the magical rites of the *intichiuma* present an economic aspect, or, in other words, to find a connection between 'economic' and 'magic'.[48]

This is admirably clear, though from what followed it is no less clear that Malinowski had capitulated to some evolutionary assumptions. He stated that work performed at 'a low level of culture *differs essentially* from economically productive labour' characteristic of industrial society; it is not so much the amount as the nature of the work that differs. In 'civilized' economic enterprises, labour must be systematic, continuous, repeated, done according to some rational plan – all requiring forethought, volition and self-restraint. 'The savage is not yet capable of such labour', and his attitude is closer to that of ours 'at play or sport'. He referred here to Bücher's *Arbeit und Rhythmus* to show how 'play, excitement, ecstasy, intoxication, rhythm' can obviate 'free volitional effort'. The *intichiuma* ceremonies provide such stimuli, and 'totemic traditions and ideas' possess 'a powerful ascendancy over the mind of the natives' and the 'advanced form of labour' found in *intichiuma* is borne along by them.[49]

The essay, closely argued and brilliant as it is in its way, concluded by taking a step backwards in insisting that the *intichiuma* example shed light on the evolution of 'economic labour'; that magical and religious ideas are 'coercive mental forces' that 'train' man in economic activity; and that the *intichiuma* ceremonies 'and similar rites were of great importance in the development of economics'.[50] Here Malinowski appeared to endorse the evolutionists' belief that modern institutions were the teleological goal of earlier, more 'primitive' societies, such that the latter can best be defined by what they lack. Another unexamined assumption of his paper is that work is both unpleasant and to be undertaken reluctantly, perhaps only under compulsion. But these negative connotations clearly spring from the 'developed' notion of work, which by definition Malinowski's 'savages' did not possess. Moreover, the Australian Aborigines cannot be positioned simultaneously as both Western man's ancestors and his primitive contemporaries, as illustrative of both 'a low stage of culture' (ancestral to ourselves) and a 'primitive race' (our contemporaries) that had failed to evolve to our culturally superior level.

At bottom Malinowski's argument is an acceptance – almost a demonstration – of Frazer's view that mankind's intellectual liberation from superstition was the principal plot of human history. But, as Raymond Firth has pointed out, the essay is 'contra-Frazer' for all that superficially it appears as 'a gloss on his proposition' concerning the economic (or quasi-economic) functions of totemism.[51] During 1911 Malinowski was already, quietly and in his native Polish, mounting a devastating attack on other positions held by Frazer.

The Portsmouth conference would be remembered for a far more dramatic event than a young Pole's public début in British academe. Rivers chose the venue to announce his conversion to what would come to be known as diffusionism. His presidential address, 'The Ethnological Analysis of Society', was in the words of his biographer 'a major theoretical statement, one of the most significant, certainly in British anthropology, between 1890 and the early 1920s'.[52] To many in his audience it must have seemed a betrayal of their cherished beliefs, though Grafton Elliot Smith – the arch-diffusionist – would have been gleeful at gaining such a distinguished adherent to his own cause.

Rivers lamented the fact that there was 'no general agreement about the fundamental principles upon which the theoretical work of our science is to be conducted'. In Britain, anthropology was 'inspired primarily by the idea of evolution founded on a psychology common to mankind as a whole'. Where similarities of custom and institution are found in different parts of the world, 'it is assumed, almost as an axiom, that they are due to independent origin and development, and that this in its turn is ascribed to the fundamental similarity of the workings of the human mind'.[53] In France, however, there was a rooted objection to the psychological assumptions used by British anthropologists, which were perceived to be reductionist, and Durkheim and his school urged that 'the study of sociology requires the application of principles and methods of investigation peculiar to itself'. In America, anthropologists were so busy recording what was left of native American cultures that they devoted little attention to general evolutionary questions. Finally, in Germany there was the most fundamental difference in viewpoint and method. Adolf Bastian's evolutionism based on 'elementary ideas' of mankind was being replaced by Friedrich Ratzel's *Anthropogeographie*, the *Ethnologie* approach of Fritz Graebner and, to a lesser extent, the *Kulterkreise* of Pater Wilhelm Schmidt. To this modern German school the key to ethnological understanding was 'the blending of cultures'.

Where British anthropologists saw the evolution of material objects or social institutions, German anthropologists saw 'the mixing of cultures, either with or with-out an accompanying mixture of the races to which these cultures belonged'.[54]

Rivers then explained why he had abandoned the evolutionary school. He claimed to have been led quite independently by his recent researches in Melanesia to a similar position to that of the Germans. He found that he could only satisfactorily explain the similarities and differences in social structure between island communities of Melanesia by postulating several migrations of peoples. The basic methodological principle, however, was that 'the analysis of culture must precede speculations concerning the evolution of institutions'.[55]

But ethnological analysis was not the only task of anthropology. Rivers was a psychologist first and an ethnologist second, for whom 'every problem in ethnology was essentially psychological'.[56]

> Side by side with ethnological analysis, there must go the attempt to fathom the modes of thought of different peoples, to understand their ways of regarding and classifying the facts of the universe. It is only by the combination of ethnological and psychological analysis that we shall make any real advance.[57]

Malinowski could hardly have agreed more.

Rivers began his final paragraph with an observation that Malinowski was to repeat, in almost identical terms, at the very outset of the ethnological voyage he conducted in *Argonauts of the Western Pacific*. Thus Rivers:

> It is a cruel irony that just as the importance of the facts and conclusions of ethnological research is thus becoming recognized, and just as we are beginning to learn sound principles and methods for use both in the field and in the study, the material of our science is vanishing.

A decade later, in the same rueful tone, Malinowski echoed rhetorically:

> Ethnology is in the sadly ludicrous, not to say tragic, position, that at the very moment when it begins to put its workshop in order, to forge its proper tools, to start ready for work on its appointed task, the material of its study melts away with hopeless rapidity. Just now, when the methods and aims of scientific field ethnology have taken shape, when men fully trained for the work have begun to travel into savage countries and study their inhabitants – these die away under our very eyes.[58]

Stocktaking in Zakopane

'I feel very tired now and I am going to Poland for a holiday,' Malinowski wrote to Westermarck after the British Association meeting, adding:'I wish I could be with you in Finland!'[59] He resumed his diary for two of the several weeks he spent in Poland. A 'London Retrospect' began with an assessment.

> Only after a lapse of two years have I once again found myself in seclusion and am I able to take stock of the past and gather new strength for the future. At present my main problems lie in my work technique and husbanding my physical energy; my energy is very limited, while cravings of every possible kind [are] immeasurably rampant. I have managed to restrain them in many respects and thereby to reduce my outlays of unnecessary energy. Nevertheless, although I know my own resources, I do not know how to harmonize them with my intentions, and therefore both my work technique and the ratio of plans to things accomplished are very poor. . . . The main thing . . . is to raise the level of my creativity . . . to look for paths which answer to my personal interests, rather than to certain external needs. Such work will shelter me from the temptations of trivial things – it will be . . . a fortified castle in which I shall feel comfortable.[60]

Malinowski is being unduly self-critical. Immeasurably rampant cravings and inefficient work techniques notwithstanding, his husbanded energy had yielded much during the previous eighteen months. Although only two of his book reviews had appeared by this date, a couple more were in press and several essays were almost ready for publication. He had finished *The Family among the Australian Aborigines*, and the *intichiuma* essay in honour of Westermarck was close to completion. He had begun a paper on Aboriginal male associations or age-classes, and what was to become a trilogy of essays on Frazer's *Totemism and Exogamy*, the four volumes of which he had begun to study after their appearance in 1910. Finally, as a by-product of his Australian book, he was beginning to prepare, in German, a lengthy literature review on the sociology of the family. To accomplish this degree of scholarly output he had saturated himself in the Australian ethnographic literature, the literature on marriage and the family, and the literature on age-classes. With the utmost critical attention he was reading the latest works by Lucien Lévy-Bruhl and the writings of the Année Sociologique school of Emile Durkheim. Soon, having temporarily exhausted his inter-est in marriage and the family, he would return with renewed zeal to the study of magic and religion – the stuff of *The Golden Bough*. He had also been attending lectures and seminars at the LSE, cultivating his relations with senior anthropologists and, with the encouragement of Seligman, begun to learn Arabic.

So why such vexed dissatisfaction with himself? At bottom it reflected a habitual discontent focused on his frail health. He felt his physical and mental energies to be finite; they were not to be squandered on 'triviali-ties' but channelled into productive work. The 'system' to which he had devoted so much attention in the Canaries, and which he tried hard to revive during periods in Leipzig, had become moribund. His cohabitation with Annie the previous year had bred enough domestic contentment, perhaps, to enfeeble his ascetic impulse. Still, he maintained a residual self-discipline: monitoring his diet, doing his gymnastics and generally keeping a watchful eye on those 'cravings' that threatened to debilitate him.

His main hope was 'to raise the level of creativity', suggesting some dis-content with the style and content of his recent scholarly efforts. He wanted 'more creative work' in which he could express his own thinking. Criti-cism of the work of others was ultimately a derivative exercise that failed to gratify him. As in an earlier diary, he urged himself to follow his own deepest interests and not be distracted by the 'external needs' of earning a living as a scientist or scholar. He would despise that particular path as the one of 'least resistance', and the 'fortified castle' in which he would feel 'for-midable' could only mean the redoubt of self-confidence that a man inhab-its once he has learned to heed his calling and ply his own particular talent. Precisely what this might entail in Malinowski's instance was still not fully clear to him, and indeed would not be for another two or three years. Even then, nervously embarking on his first field trip with all its uncer-tainties, he was far from feeling formidable in the fortified castle of his self-knowledge.

To follow Malinowski to Zakopane in the autumn of 1911 is to enter a rustic scene of solitary walks and mushroom-picking.[61] 'I am here to recu-perate and to concentrate,' he wrote; 'to equip myself for the future; to create a superior type of work.' Olcza is a scattered hamlet of farmhouses and chalets set amid undulating meadows a couple of miles to the east of Zakopane. Late September was harvest time, and the constant racket of the peasant farmers disturbed his morning study of Arabic. It was also the season for *rydze* mushrooms (*Lactarius deliciosus*), and he devoted hours each day to gathering, cooking and eating them.

He spent much time with Staś Witkiewicz, who had begun to sketch and paint him, and also with Tadzio Nalepiński, who goaded him with his puerile versifying. They dined together frequently and argued about 'creativity in relation to life'. Malinowski saw something of Aniela Zagórska, too, and reached a new understanding of their sub-erotic friendship. Mrs Irena Solska was another addition to his circle, for it appears that he had never met her before ('I feel ill at ease . . . a brunette, rather elegant and handsome'). The flame-haired actress, recently divorced, was conducting a scandalous affair with Staś. She was his 'demon woman', the Akne who caused Bungo's principal fall. Malinowski was more than simply curious about her: could this be another triangle in the offing? Throughout this diary he refers to her formally as Mrs Solska, though a year later 'Irenka' had become a more intimate friend. With her striking, haughty looks, she attracted him as she attracted so many men, and after writing to Annie Brunton one night he lay in bed and thought about 'dirty tricks with Mrs Solska'. He visited her regularly with a solicitous capful of mushrooms.

Józefa Malinowska came to spend a week with her son, and by 5 October he was feeling 'significantly better; stronger and healthier'. He belatedly resolved to 'establish stricter living conditions' by clearing all 'excremental channels' – such as visits to Mrs Solska, walks into town and inane conversations. 'Always to go to bed at ten and to rise punctually at six. Not to over-eat at night. This is the essential framework for my stay here. A framework that I shall absolutely not transgress. Besides this, I must go further towards defining sociological creativity and writing a retrospective diary.' During the next few days, although suffering from a surfeit of company and mushrooms, his resolution crumbled. On Sunday 8 October he bade farewell to his friends and left for Cracow, and then for London a week or two later. Summarizing his Zakopane holiday he wrote: 'It was impossible to accomplish anything.'

Chapter 11

Żenia

Sligs of the Sudan

'I possess an immense displaceability [sic] of projects,' Malinowski had rebuked himself in Leipzig three years earlier. It remained true in 1912, another year of indecision and uncertainty concerning his future. At the end of January, Annie sailed for South Africa with Flöhchen, and soon afterwards Malinowski left London for Poland, where he remained until the following January. His only academic engagement that year was in March, when he presented a paper on 'Tribal Male Associations in Australia' to the Academy of Sciences and Arts in Cracow.[1] The main reason for this lengthy sojourn in Poland was a family crisis in Warsaw. He and his mother were in grave financial difficulty owing to the failure of her brother's factory, and there were bitter squabbles as the Łąckis tried to decide what to do. Malinowski naturally took his mother's side, though without much practical effect, and by the end of the year they had lost 12,000 roubles (about £1,200). He had intended to return to London in October but, paralysed by a love affair, he changed his mind.[2]

Seligman and his wife were doing fieldwork among nomadic Arabs of the Sudan. In February, Malinowski wrote to say that he was still interested in working with him – a possibility mooted the previous year – and would consider it 'a piece of enormous good luck if I could go out with you and Mrs Seligmann next winter to the Sudan'. He would soon return to London to help them sort their notes and 'to work strenuously' at learning Arabic.[3] It was late April before Seligman replied, having just returned to England with an ailing Brenda. He was encouraging, though there seemed little chance of getting his protégé a grant from the Sudan Government.[4] Before taking further steps, however, Seligman wanted to know Malinowski's private plans and how committed he was to their working together. Malinowski took some months to reply, and when he did so it was with profuse apologies. He was living in 'quite unsettled and most unpleasant conditions' in Warsaw, engaged in 'highly distasteful' business matters. He and his mother had suffered considerable 'pecuniary losses' and the worry had affected her health. Concerning the Sudan he had not changed his mind, though his study of Arabic had stalled. He hoped to resume work and return to England in the autumn, 'and you could judge, or rather Mrs Seligmann could judge, whether I am sufficiently prepared with the language to go out'.[5] Quaintly, he added: 'in this case I shall certainly feel bound to put myself to your disposal for next winter in the character of an interpreter and assistant', and he ended the letter, 'trusting that in spite of all the adversities I shall be able to see the fulfilment of all my hopes, that is to work with you'.[6]

Seligman wrote promptly to William Pember Reeves, the LSE director, outlining a fieldwork proposal for Malinowski in support of which he invoked the names of Haddon, Rivers and Westermarck.

> Dr Malinowski would reach the Red Sea Province of the Sudan some time during the coming winter. . . . After a few weeks spent at Suakin and the immediate neighbourhood he will in the first place study the sociology of the Rasheida (Zebediya) tribe. . . . Should time and funds allow . . . I think I could arrange for him to be given special facilities to study the Bisharin.

Seligman concluded that 'an investigation of the Rasheida would . . . constitute a base line for past and future work on the mixed "Arab" populations of the Sudan'. He requested a modest £125, hoping that the Sudan Government would treat Malinowski 'in some ways as if he were in government service' and allow him free travel. He would personally lend him a camera, a phonograph and all his 'camp and camel gear'.[7]

A week later, a brusque memorandum informed Seligman that the council of management had decided not to award Malinowski a grant. 'They felt that they had rather exhausted themselves over Ethnology,' the School secretary had written in pencil at the bottom of the page. The remark referred to a recent decision by the university to make ethnology a bachelor-degree subject. If Seligman was delighted at the imminent expansion of his subject, he did not admit it to Malinowski, though he too would benefit in the long run. An expanded syllabus gave leverage for the appointment of new staff and eventually the demand for an autonomous department. This is what ultimately happened at the LSE, as the single appointment in ethnology evolved into a department of anthropology.

Seligman wrote to Malinowski to explain the circumstances of the School's refusal of a grant, concluding: 'I don't think that the situation is at all hopeless for the future, and I know you are well thought of . . . by Westermarck and Martin White.'[8] Malinowski replied from Zakopane, saying how grateful he was for 'all the kind care you take in my fate':

> [Y]ou have tried now again to direct the favourable winds towards my sails! At any rate the increasing zeal for ethnology promises better hopes for the future, and if there will be no possibility for me to go out this winter I shall try to prepare myself for field work under your guidance.[9]

He did not renew his promise to return to London in the autumn, however, and abandoned the study of Arabic. Although he would not follow in Sligs's footsteps in the Sudan, he would eventually retrace them in New Guinea.

A diary of love, work and dreams

The year 1912 marked a further stage of Malinowski's psychosexual development. He was twenty-eight years old and coming to terms with a Freudian-informed understanding of himself, abetted by consultation with a Zakopane psychoanalyst to whom he confided his dreams. He knew that the pattern of his love affairs was repeating itself. His abrupt oscillations of mood – from romantic infatuation to cool indifference to crippling jealousy to bleak despair and back again to intoxicated love – were causing him to squander a good deal of time that might otherwise have been devoted to productive thinking and writing. While his surrender to such moods was sanctioned by the ethos of the circles he moved in, it is diffi-cult to believe that all young Cracovian men of the time were tossed by such tempestuous currents of anguished love. There was a *characteristic* aspect to his wayward emotional storms. Sentimental to a fault and hostage to his own need of love, he could never turn away from any source of it as long as it flowed in his direction. According to a simplistic Freudian reading (of which he was quite aware), his emotional disturbances and temperamental instabilty were rooted in his early relationship with his parents: the 'wooden', absent father for whom he had felt a profound ambivalence, and the passionately devoted mother whom he deeply loved. But these traces were partly covered over, and for all his dabbling in Oedipal theory he did not blame his parents for his emotional predicaments. He squarely laid the blame on his own imperfections and made sincere, if generally ineffective, efforts to change himself. The leitmotif of his struggles, as ever, was a yearning for psychic integration.

His 1912 diary – the longest of any he kept in Poland – is dominated by his energizing and debilitating desire for Żenia Zielińska. It is a nakedly honest document of his attempts to reconcile love and ambition, sex and work. A summary of the course of this affair would simply plot its doomed trajectory in banal terms: love gambled, love won and love lost. But in the detailed telling there is enough poetry and passion for any messy modernist novel, and as an intuitively gifted psychologist of love, Malinowski was the equal of Stendhal.

So how did Malinowski reconcile the opposing impulses? How did he solve the persistent, nagging problem of answering the call of his genius (assuming this was not entirely imaginary) and obeying the urge of his biological nature, his powerful sex drive? Like the majority of men, he compromised. But it is in the nature of his compromise that much of the fascination of his biography lies. He compromised eventually by taking a wife and fathering children, as do most men. The imagined alternative of the 'cold' life of solitude and celibacy, which he fancied would best satisfy the inchoate urges of his genius, tempted him until he resolved finally to marry Elsie Masson. There was a moment in the Trobriand Islands when, anticipating T. S. Eliot's Mr Sweeney, Malinowski acknowledged a 'concrete formula of life' that incorporated the life of the mind: '*Mate with her, beget children, write books, die.*'[10] Other twists he gave to the compromise involved sexual promiscuity. What makes Malinowski's attitudes to, and struggle with, his own sexual impulses particularly fascinating is his later reputation as an authority on sex, marriage and the family. The love life of the author of *The Sexual Life of Savages* must engage our interest.

Love's drama

Malinowski began his diary on Sunday 4 August, the day after his arrival in Zakopane.[11] He took lodgings in a pension in Olcza that he and his friends jokingly referred to as 'The Brothel'. The first few pages of the diary indulge an introspective flight of metaphysical fancy as Malinowski ruminated about the bridge of time and 'the hopeless periodicity of life' that had brought him once again to Olcza. To combat the stagnation he feared, he listed the tasks that faced him: to train and fortify his nerves for intellectual work; to develop better techniques for reading books, taking notes and writing articles; to look inside himself and seek 'the mainspring of activity — a spiritual *perpetuum mobile*'.

He pondered again how the life of the unfettered mind seemed always to lie just beyond his reach. It was a practical problem of 'the economy of thought', a matter of liberating the intellect from daily distractions, and he deplored the amount of energy he expended on simply breaking through the superficial crust of mundane thought. The topic of totemism and exogamy on which he was then working was central to the theoretical anthropology of the day. That most venerable of anthropologists, James Frazer, had recently devoted four large volumes to it and Malinowski had embarked upon a laborious critique of them. But he felt that this kind of work was derivative. The raw materials, the scientific 'facts', were second- or third-hand; they were not of his own making, and all he could do was subject them to critical scrutiny and reassemble them in fresh patterns of interpretation. In his view, this did not measure up to creating 'something important in sociology' that he was anxious to achieve. The nagging dissatisfaction with the main object of his intellectual exploration was to last throughout the year, though he distracted himself by turning to philosophical problems of art, myth and drama.

Although his current mood precluded the warmth of women, Malinowski was excited at the prospect of Żenia's imminent arrival in Zakopane. Eugenia Zielińska née Bentkowska was a young woman of obvious charm and sound education, a painter who had studied at the Academy of Fine Arts in Warsaw in 1904–05. She was married, not contentedly it seems, but not so unhappily that she was willing to leave her husband. Although she must be counted among the most significant loves of Malinowski's life, very little is known about her and even less about her husband Stanisław, a lawyer of Jewish-Christian descent whom Żenia had married in 1904. Precisely when she and Malinowski first met is uncertain, but his diary suggests that their affair began in March or April of 1912 at the wedding of his cousin, Maria ('Mania') Łącka.

Malinowski had been in Zakopane for a only a few days when a post-card from Żenia upset his equilibrium and reduced him to 'the helplessness of a disabled man'. Later in the day he regained his balance and entertained the hope that he could keep Żenia in her place. After all, he did not really *need* her: 'My personal relations with Staś entirely satisfy my emotional requirements – and in any case I am full of material. A woman is entirely superfluous to me now. . . . And yet I become spontaneously happy at the thought that she will be here.' It was on the Feast of the Assumption – he noted wryly – that Żenia arrived. As her train pulled into the station a crowd gathered and Malinowski felt exposed: he had 'an abhorrence of these veiled acts of life's drama [taking place] *in public*'. He contorted inwardly as Żenia approached him and they kissed formally. Jerzy Żuławski had also come to meet her, and a pang of jealousy created a liberating moment. After lunch they repaired to Staś's place, where other friends had gathered and, 'stiff as a board', Bronio scrutinized Żenia coldly. Later that afternoon they walked up the ridge of Antałowka to Olcza, and he warmed to her again. He remembered how, in Warsaw, he had struggled for her sake 'with the prostitution of the spirit and the whoring of the emotions', but now he was unsure what she felt for him, or even whether she wanted to see him. If she did, he fancied wildly that he might have her to himself in Olcza while yet keeping her at a self-protective distance (according to 'the harem system', he jested). But he suspected that this ideal compromise would not work: the proximity of a desirable woman was incompatible with the detachment and solitude he needed for study.

Malinowski was jealous of his solitude. He would have agreed with Gibbon: 'Conversation enriches the understanding, but solitude is the school of genius.' He repeatedly rebuked himself for surrendering to his gregarious impulse; he frequently resolved to shun company so that he might commune with his depths. Yet what must strike the dispassionate reader of his diaries is the *relative* nature of his solitude during these months in Zakopane. In truth he was satisfied with comparatively little. For Malinowski, a day during which he talked to three or four people for three or four hours was a day spent in solitude. On a typical day he would rise at leisure (never before 8 a.m. and often much later), do some gymnastics, eat breakfast, sunbathe if the weather was fine, write or read and take notes for a few hours, then visit Staś, Tadzio Nalepiński or others before lunch. His friends' routines were similar. They were artists, dramatists, writers – regular consumers of solitude. After lunch he would work for a while or take a solitary walk, though this might be delayed until the evening. He would read before and after tea, or someone would call and they would drift into town for the evening. In Zakopane he would sit in a café or visit one or more houses and enjoy, or endure, several hours of mixed company. Unless he was feeling very poorly, he would not think of staying home at night. Perhaps, despite his frequent complaints, he had the balance of solitude and social intercourse exactly right – as long, that is, as Żenia was not in the vicinity.

Allaying his fear that she would avoid him, Żenia called on him in Olcza and they climbed a nearby ridge together. She told him she was going away for a week. He reacted like an abandoned child. A tragic mask settled on his face and he felt the prick of tears. Żenia seemed oblivious to his distress, and later he reflected that he had suffered a personal defeat. 'She attracts me madly by her incomprehensibility,' he noted, 'and simultaneously terrifies me to such an extent that I want to flee.' At supper that night she talked about her husband, and in a revealing insight Malinowski observed how, with 'a shallow egotistical disregard' for those things that did not immediately concern him, he had constructed a false picture of his future with her. He candidly confessed his resentment: 'After taking a stand on this imaginary outpost of rights acquired through daydreams, I felt hatred towards her, rancour and anger about all her "offences" against me.'

While moping over her during the days that followed, Malinowski tried to compose verses ('unsuccessful of course') and toyed with the possibility of writing a play like Nalepiński. Not for the first time, he compared himself unfavourably with Staś: 'On the one hand he fascinates me, and [on the other] he disconcerts. I am unable to resist his influence . . . but I have a sense of my own sterile inferiority, which is unpleasant. For this reason I follow the ostrich's practice – to bury my head.' Yet when he pondered his individuality in relation to others he realized that he needed people of Staś's calibre. He constructed a stronger and more definite identity for himself in his company. Rivalry with Staś kept him on his toes.

Again, when 'creative possibilities' inspired by magnificent scenery came to mind, he inevitably thought of Staś. Malinowski's self-doubt in this domain seems unjustified, however. Although not an artist in the flamboyantly brilliant way affected by Witkiewicz, passages in Malinowski's journal reveal an ability to pen poetic prose to which English translation cannot do full justice. A fine example occurs when he interrupted his self-interrogation to record an epiphany. It is sketched in lush nature-writing worthy of the Romantics. If there are rough edges we must recall that it was not edited and not ostensibly written for others to read.

> I trip lightly uphill. . . . The crystal-clear sky lays the gentle benediction of its azure depths on the smiling earth with the last warm kisses of the day. . . . Around me everything breathes forth promise. I come to a place where a deep gorge in a hill reveals a broad view of the valley of Zakopane. In the sky the tousled cirrus heralds a change of weather – hanging in the west above Gubałowka. The air saturated with vapour – the mountains enveloped in violet shadow, above them a golden half-moon over Giewont. Silence, crickets with their monotonous chirping break up mercilessly the rhythm of time. From the valleys comes a warm, gentle breeze, something like a memory, swollen with longing, of southern seas. . . . I am alone, I yearn for life – I wish this moment could last for ever – that life might be transformed into such a moment and be something homogeneous and definite.

The passage is bracketed by despairing thoughts about Żenia. He whispered her name as he began his walk, pondering the problem of strength: 'I must not be so weak as to allow myself to be dragged along by the cart, to tumble downhill, enveloped in the pleasurable folds of the fleeting moment. . . . Thus let my love have value and depth. Either I shall renounce her, or let her be my – wife.' The conclusion is startling, perhaps even to Malinowski (was the hesitation before the last word a gulp?). Yet it was no slip of the pen, and a few days later he cried: 'If I could only have children with her!'

Rather than succumb to the transient sensuality of the moment he thought they should consolidate their love for the future:

> It is a matter of not submitting to every strong gust of passion, but of creating something great and beautiful. So that it will not cast us both into the mire, but create in us a firm base for further development . . . so that it may transform the instincts of a prostitute into the purity of an unblemished maiden.

Such idealism was, to say the least, unrealistic. It took no account of Żenia's own wishes or of her compromised situation as a married woman.

About this time there is clear evidence that he had begun to study Nietzsche's *The Birth of Tragedy*. The tangled metaphysical tirades and allusions from Greek mythology that punctuate his diary were probably inspired by this source.

> The right of surrender – of submitting to a woman – of assuming subjective value for her through an objective form of creativity – her spiritual impregnation before she is impregnated physically – this is the voice of Moloch – of a life which, in order to receive from us the supreme sacrifice on its altar through bribery of the highest longing and the deepest sufferings, wants to draw us into its snares by means of pleasure. . . . *The Eternal Feminine* draws us down – into *the Eternal Boggy*.

Henri Bergson and Otto Weininger, perhaps, as well as Nietzsche are comically reflected here. To counter the misogyny there is a romantic notion that he will develop later: he must be worthy of the woman he idealizes and offer her spiritual gifts that will fertilize her and enable her to flower. Malinowski decided to write an article on tragedy and dedicate it to Żenia. Such gifts of himself would lay the foundations of his future happiness:

> I should like to be with her – to think and write for her. To give her what I am able to give her, in a simple and unpretentious form. My literary and poetical conceptions; to offer and dedicate to her the substance of my reflections. . . . And once again that image comes to mind – to grow wise alongside her.

The idea (or ideal) of renunciation soon gripped him and he derived a wintery satisfaction from the prospect. The obstacles in this love affair were by no means only social and emotional; they were created in part by the spiritual wariness that Malinowski cultivated. On one level, he knew perfectly well that his love was illusory, a creature of his own imagination. In a revealing passage he wrote about a conflation of longing for the loved one and a 'metaphysical longing' for the aesthetic ideal she could inspire him to achieve. If he gave her up it would therefore entail a double renunciation. Malinowski's overwrought sensibility conjured a kind of paradox: it was not love of the flesh-and-blood Żenia that obsessed him but an ethereal ideal of her. 'I lose myself completely and become merely a painful reflection of her,' he wrote, 'like an image cast onto the black sheet of a mountain lake.' He recalled her arrival in Zakopane, just two weeks earlier, when he was able to greet her with a 'diamond sharpness of gaze' before falling into the abyss of hopeless love. Next time, he told himself, 'I would receive her with less spiritual fanfare – and I would try not to squander myself utterly in her.'

The seduction of study

A new phase in Malinowski's equivocal relationship with Żenia began with her return to Zakopane on 26 August. His hardening decision to break with her was instantly subverted. He greeted her as a puppy greets its master ('I lose my head at first. Excitement'). He kissed her hands, removed her chamois hat – observing that she was prettier without it – and rested his head upon her shoulder.

Next morning he was intensely happy, his inner self 'expressed in melodies'. It was the music of love. But that evening Żenia told him she was unable to give him as much as he gave to her. By confining him in an incomplete relationship she suspected that she was doing him harm. He was quietly stunned, and when he looked in the mirror he saw 'buffoonish dualism . . . One who feels and suffers and the other who looks on quietly and enjoys the fact that something has brought him out of his temporary boredom and greyness.'

His relationship with Żenia during the last two weeks of August was one of social and sexual restraint. In addition to the pity and contempt he felt for himself, the longings he described were principally those of the spirit and only once did he refer to frustrated physical desire. His various solutions seemed to preclude sexual satisfaction; it was 'purity of spirit' he wanted. For her part, Żenia granted him kisses but otherwise kept him at arm's length. If Malinowski was planning her seduction he did not say so, but on Sunday 1 September he made a move that brought them closer. He decided to involve her in his studies.

When he visited Żenia the next day he persuaded her to go home with him. Typically, he noticed what she was wearing: 'a navy-blue jacket with a white collar and a blouse with coloured embroidery'. They read together for part of the afternoon and he began to draft an essay on Nietzsche.[12] Studying alongside Żenia promised its own kind of gratification as intellectual activity became suffused with desire. It was in this manner that he had studied with his mother.

The next afternoon, they read William James's *Principles of Psychology*. They sat side by side and Malinowski inclined his head towards her and kissed her hair. Perversely, after a time he wearied of her company. 'I should like to amuse myself, to refresh myself, to go to see Solska, where there is uninterrupted light and a life of ease.' He left her and accordingly spent a few hours with Irena Solska and friends, enjoying 'a good supper, a liqueur, ribaldry, sweets and plums'. Refreshed, he rushed back to Żenia, who now took the initiative. Perhaps the afternoon's intimate study had aroused her – or Bronio's flight to Irena had tipped the balance of longing – for she was ready to seduce him. Ambivalently, he described what happened:

> She takes hold of me gently; this disconcerts me. I stand aloof. . . . She hums French, Ukrainian and Russian songs. I sit, a bit lonely, a bit serious, at 11 I want to go, she keeps me until 12. I lie down on the bed. She sits besides me; she lurches and then reclines on me. . . . She acts fabulously. I go home.

Malinowski dreamed vividly that night: 'A theatrical performance in a kind of hippodrome; the action on stage has its parallel in the audience. Then I go off with Mama on some sort of vehicle. . . . The carriage turns into a wheelbarrow, in which Mama carries me around a marketplace.'

A few days later he walked with Żenia in the lower mountain forests. Gazing at the silhouettes of trees against the yellow sky, he wanted to lose himself, 'to enter into the landscape'. On the way home Żenia hummed 'Non, tu ne sauras jamais,' a tune that would haunt him for years to come. She wanted to read after supper, but Malinowski reached to kiss her. Earlier they had discussed erotic techniques and she told him that she had a name for each one. They retired to the 'sleeping car' – Malinowski's euphemism for the box-like wooden bed – and talked about the future. 'We ought to belong to each other,' he thought recklessly. 'I should marry her.' But Żenia spoke only of being satisfied with friendship. She then developed a headache and gently turned him out.

Żenia subjected Malinowski to an examination. He had read parts of his diary to her, pretending it belonged to a 'Mme Mal'. Now he tried to explain to her the mainspring of his journal. 'I attempt to formulate my affairs; my normative experiences; a general act of assessment; non-discrimination – artistic pulp; then a concrete life programme. The tragic essence of this form of creativity; I recall Nietzsche and his tragic sense

... of the incommensurability of realization and conception.' This did not satisfy Żenia, so he read her more from his diary and she listened with a faintly unpleasant expression on her face. Her criticism turned on its 'schematization' and lack of lifelike touches; she objected that such diaries could not evoke past feelings. Malinowski would remember this uncomprehending response five years later and tell Elsie Masson, who made similar objections to keeping a diary: 'It is funny that Żenia shared your views and expressed them almost in the same terms. . . . "Why draw a hard, rigid contour around each happy, fleeting moment of our lives?" '[13] But, as he well knew, that was only a small part of what it meant to keep a diary.

Żenia asked him to explain the 'normative things' he recorded. 'I speak of a life of experience, of encompassing life; but she drives me into a corner. I have the impression that I am once again being cross-examined by someone who understands these things better than I.' Malinowski's formidably sharp intelligence and debater's wit – with which he would later awe and intimidate his pupils – was challenged and even vanquished by this young Polish woman. On this evening, he admitted to feeling 'a bit crushed' and 'abject in her presence'. Intellectual defeat dampened eroticism. Even so, they were in the sleeping car for 'rather a long time' and afterwards he thought that he 'must have been terribly happy'.

On Friday 13 September, they spent the morning in a flurry of activity. Then, bade farewell by Jerzy Żuławski and other friends, Żenia took the train to Nowy Targ. She must have got off at Poronin, however, for that was where she joined Malinowski on a later train for Cracow. They sat in the corridor, amusing themselves by reading passages from Staś's manuscript of *The 622 Downfalls of Bungo*.

It was already evening when they arrived at the Hotel Royal beneath the towering walls of Wawel Castle. After checking into separate rooms, they strolled to a café in the market square. As they glanced at newspapers Malinowski thought, 'I feel I would be happy with her in all life's situations.' They walked back to the hotel and he sensed the poetry of a sleeping city. In Żenia's room, with the electric lamp on the floor, they sat and talked before going to bed. Of that night, Malinowski recorded: 'At times fatigue and dropping off to sleep. Then strong waves of emotion. Like this until morning. I go to my own room to sleep. . . . Żenia is somewhat negatively disposed towards me. A weary and sadly smiling "madonna".' Seeing her off on the train to Warsaw the next day Malinowski suffered an attack of sentimentality. The honeymoon-like night spent in one of Cracow's best hotels made a lasting impression upon him, and he would recall it as he was packing up to leave the Trobriands: 'Friday the 13th! and the sixth anniversary of a memorable day I spent with Żenia Zielinska in Cracow.'[14]

'Sex really is dangerous'

Back in Zakopane, a forlorn Malinowski tried to cope with his loss by urging himself to 'work like the devil'. His study of Georg Simmel progressed 'shamefully', however, through 'a complete lack of interest and concentration'. He had also begun to read *La cité antique* by Fustel de Coulanges, a work that impressed and enthused him. Nevertheless, it is odd that despite the months he spent studying Georg Simmel and Fustel de Coulanges (many pages of neatly written notes survive), his writings of this period contain nothing that can be directly attributed to their influence.[15]

He penned some poems for Żenia and was pleased with them, enjoying an inner sense of 'expanded power'. In this creative mood, he began an essay on Wacław Berent's recent novel *Ozimina* (Winter Wheat). It was a kind of intellectual vacation; even so, he found the writing difficult and was continually distracted by thoughts of Żenia. 'The world of emotions is hopelessly entwined with the world of pure thought,' he wrote in the introduction to his essay on *The Birth of Tragedy*.[16]

On Sunday 29 September, Staś sketched his friend. It was probably one of several charcoal drawings of Bronio, of which the best known is entitled 'Fear of Life in Malinowski', Witkiewicz's little joke.[17] In this full-faced portrait Malinowski, dressed in a jacket, collar and tie, gazes woodenly at the artist. His dark eyes stare from behind the oval lenses of his spectacles. His hair recedes drastically to leave an insular tuft in the centre of his high forehead, and a thin moustache shades his unsmiling lips. This, surely, is Staś's vision of Edgar, Duke of Nevermore.

During September and October, Malinowski proofread *The Family among the Australian Aborigines*, and to this period must be attributed the five-page Addenda, notable for the enthusiasm with which he referred to Ernest Crawley's classic study of sex and marriage *The Mystic Rose* (1902).[18] He was struck by how 'Mr Crawley analyzes the psychology underlying human relations (those of sex in particular) from their religious side'. Given that

The Mystic Rose 'brought into focus the repressed sexual themes running beneath the surface of intellectualist anthropology',[19] Malinowski appears to have found ethnographic resonances with respect to his own constrained situation. Crawley's thesis was that primitive man believed the sex act to be dangerous and therefore hedged it with taboos. Marriage was a religiously sanctioned rite for the breaking of these taboos and nullifying the peril of sexual contact. Not the least of Crawley's appeal was his exposition of views similar to Malinowski's concerning 'physiological thought' – that is, non-rational, quasi-mystical thinking infused with emotion. The pre-Freudian overtones in *The Mystic Rose* were evident only later, and it is ironic that the editor of the second edition (published in 1928) incorporated references to Malinowski's own writings on Trobriand sexuality. In a review of this edition, Malinowski heaped praise upon Crawley, even granting him posthumous recognition as a founder of 'the functional method of modern anthropology'.[20]

He surely found in Crawley's account of physiological thought an echo of his own irrational anxieties: 'a strong apprehension of danger arising from contact with other human beings'. (One is reminded of 'Fear of Life in Malinowski'.) The 'aura of supernatural fear' that surrounds strangers, the sick, the marginalized and, 'above all, people of the opposite sex' is 'checked by two devices: the taboo and the ritual breaking of it'. As Malinowski would do, Crawley made the strange familiar, rendering primitive superstitions into 'a comprehensible scheme of essentially human behaviour'. Above all, Malinowski was impressed by Crawley's account of the 'mixed attraction and fear, of distrust undermining love', which dominates the relations between the sexes. He could well ponder this theory of sex antagonism at the very time he was being tormented by thoughts of Żenia. As he would write: 'I maintain that sex is regarded as dangerous by the savage, that it is tabooed and ritualized, surrounded by moral and legal norms – not because of any superstition of primitive man, or emotional view of or instinct about strangeness, but for the simple reason that sex really is dangerous.'[21] In the rules that regulate relations between the sexes in any society,

> we find all those ideas which express the danger of sex – the ideas of evil and sin – at the very core of love and passion; the conviction that the highest happiness in erotic union can only be obtained at the cost of infinite pains and precautions; belief, in short, that sex is religiously sacred, *sacer*, that is, at the same time holy and polluting.[22]

In an apt image he noted of Żenia in his diary: 'She is already becoming a symbol of longing for me. Something akin to a religious cult.' When he kissed her on one occasion he confessed to 'a feeling of sacrilege'.

'I guard against dreams as lies'

Staś had recently begun a course of psychoanalysis with Dr Karol de Beaurain, and he persuaded Malinowski to record his dreams so that they might compare them. Not to be outdone, Malinowski consulted another Zakopane psychoanalyst, Dr Borowiecki. How often he saw him is uncertain, but Malinowski recorded many dreams during this period and presumably related them to Borowiecki as well as to Staś. Although he rarely bothered to comment on them himself, Malinowski believed vaguely in 'the value of dreams in understanding life', and his do indeed offer privileged glimpses into his troubled psyche. He was not impressed by his psychoanalyst's professional insights, however, and after one session of dream-talk he wrote dismissively: 'Borowiecki, who studied all this from his arm-chair for an hour and understands nothing, is supposed to explain it to me.' Meanwhile, Dr de Beaurain informed a hapless Staś that he was suffering from an 'embryo complex'.[23]

Malinowski had been staying at Irena Solska's villa for a few days. His relationship to Staś's 'demonic' ex-mistress is ambiguous, though we might surmise that it was haunted by imitative, triangular desire. His diary drops a clear hint that, while he was staying with her, Irena invited him to spend the night in her bed, an invitation that produced 'a tumult in the soul'. Some weeks later he dreamed erotically about her, their contortions reminding him of his night with Żenia in Room 69 at the Hotel Royal.

> I am lying on her; conscious that I do not love her . . . she says, never mind, I know that I am not attractive to you, but that will make it better. . . . I have a feeling that this is unethical, disloyal. . . . I do not even feel that artificially imposed lust which comes from repugnance and perversion.

Later he dreamed of Irena again. He is aboard a train with her together with her estranged husband. Two Austrian officers are cutting cards. He opens a tin of English sweets. 'I treat Irenka and surreptiously take something better for myself. I ask her to kiss me; I kiss her on the mouth and rub my bare stomach against her breasts very erotically.' In another episode of the dream, the train has become the Ivanhoe Hotel. There is a breakfast room with an English maid and the hotel is full of top-hatted Englishmen. He noted about this sequence of dreams: 'Eroticism for Irenka – but somehow false, imposed; she is continually returning in my sleep, whereas when awake I do not give her even half a thought . . . in tonight's dream a kind of (half-muted, fabricated?) regret for Irenka.' His erotic response to Irena clearly indicates that, subconsciously at any rate, he did desire her. Although he had dismissed this possibility, after the second dream he was half-willing to admit that there was some muted attraction which he had 'fabricated' himself. It is noteworthy that the erotically charged backdrops to his dreams are railway carriages and an English hotel where he had stayed with Annie Brunton.

He related these dreams to Staś, who suggested that Irena was 'a substitute', presumably for Żenia. Staś was unwilling to believe that Irena did not appeal to Malinowski and reminded him that in dreams 'unpleasant, suppressed complexes' appear. The 'Mother Complex', for instance. Like Annie, Irena Solska was nine or ten years older than Bronio and Staś. We should recall, too, that the latter's impossible infatuation with the actress, which had scandalized even bohemian Zakopane, formed the principal plot of *The 622 Downfalls of Bungo*. What the long-suffering Maria Witkiewicz, abandoned by Staś's father, thought of her son's sexual experiments with a woman he believed to be his 'mother-substitute' beggars the imagination.

A few weeks later Malinowski had another dream which incorporated many of the familiar themes and cast his mother in a starring role. He is in a hotel with her and Tadzio Nalepiński. He has to discourage his friend (who displays characteristic 'tactlessness and indelicacy') from following Mama to the toilet. Later, the dream takes an erotic turn as Malinowski lies on top of 'a nice old German woman stripped to her chemise'. A less appetizing love object could scarcely be imagined: 'Her skin is something like tree bark, broken and stratified, or rather pancake batter, full of blisters, coarse and shiny, her stomach and breasts a single flabby, shapeless protruberance. Her nipples lost amidst her coarse, grubby and hairy skin.' She is a widow from Latvia who had 'lived through so much': 'A scoundrel ruined her; he did nothing but sit and write; she had a daughter (undoubtedly just like her!) and often she was so cold that her father (the scoundrel) had to lie on her for hours at a time.' The repulsive widow then turns into her daughter and the dreamer ejaculates. Later still in the dream another woman whom Staś is courting 'makes eyes' at Malinowski, while outside there is a group of military policemen and an English officer is giving orders to recruits.

This is the second dream Malinowski recorded in which the daughter of an erotic object substitutes for the mother, collapses the triangle and commandeers, as it were, the action. Once again there are images of travel or transport associated with his own mother, and menacing authority figures in the guise of soldiers. There is also the recurrent motif of an erotic triangle with Staś and a shared woman. On another occasion he dreamed erotically about Jadwiga Janczewska who was soon to become Staś's fiancée.

He also dreamed of Annie and a little daughter, sired by a Jew. 'I look at her intently; and she looks pretty and very young, a bit Jewish. I kissed her and thought of Żenia. Then I could feel how Żenia kisses him [her husband] and I began to feel unwell.' In another dream about Żenia: 'She was playing a piano, leaning over a bit like Emchen Stern [Annie's friend in Leipzig]. Her husband is sitting beside me on a sofa and praising her, raving about her playing. Then the three of us at table; supper. . . . Certain complications; he knows something.' Malinowski does not comment, but the dream is plainly about his relationship to Żenia's husband, whose complicity he seeks. Ambivalence also seeped into his dreams about Żenia: 'I am walking with her along the Planty. . . . I think to myself: Aha, how she has changed: she has really put on weight; she has acquired the Jewish type . . . she is wearing a Rembrandt hat; I think to myself: Aha, what an awful hat!' He asked himself: 'Is this dream a reflection of certain doubts which I have had while awake: "is this really *it*?" ' But he distrusted his dreams and at another point in his diary he wrote: 'I guard against dreams as lies.'

He often dreamed about his maternal relatives. 'Mama and and I are at the Łącka's and she [his aunt] says she is going to sever relations with us for a year; I say "all right"; then a fire; I rush out pompously from the gateway into the street.' This dream evolved into another one set in Staś's house:

> Staś is courting a certain young lady who is making eyes at him. I keep off, but it disconcerts me a bit; Staś is doing something, developing negatives . . . in Andalusian costume, he is courting this lady on a sofa with a guitar; I move (like *Pierrot*), we dance, mutually kicking each other in the arse (secret rivalry). Staś and I in bed, Mrs Witkiewicz speaks of difficulties (these difficulties identical with the difficulties in the factory!)

About this dream Malinowski commented briefly: 'The return of the complex of Łącki and the factory is characteristic.' His worry concerning his mother's financial losses understandably intruded into his dreams; but it is intriguing that Malinowski saw – or dreamed that he saw – a parallel between the 'difficulties' of his mother's problems and the 'difficulties' of being found in bed with Staś by the latter's mother. Yet another dream alluded to homoeroticism and mimetic triangles: 'With Staś in London in a big hotel room; something homosexual; a chambermaid, thin, red-headed – I lick my lips. I kiss her with remorse.'

Believing as he did in the Oedipal source of some of his conflicts (the prime example being an inordinate emotional dependence on the women with whom he fell in love), such knowledge was bound to infiltrate his dreams and overdetermine their imagery. In this light the recurrent images of travel surely have a maternal source. The association of eroticism with travel is an obvious one to make, especially in the simplistic terms that if *all* sexually attractive women are refractions of his mother, then *all* journeys have erotic potential. In an even more reductionist manner, it might be said that Malinowski's life was a search for achievement through restless wandering – an analogue of the Trobriand Islander's interminable quest for eroticized wealth objects: the symbolically gendered shell valuables of Kula. The mythopoeic Malinowski became entangled with the fate of the skin-shedding Kula hero Tokosikuna, whose magic flute enabled him to win all the valuables and marry all the women.

Working for Żenia in absentia

Although his mental associations still led inexorably to Żenia, the intensity of his love was diminishing. 'I no longer have that frank, garrulous communicativeness,' he noted. 'She has already ceased to be my inner companion. I think of her and for her; but I am alone.' They exchanged letters frequently, and although none have survived, one can deduce from his diary that Żenia continued to torment him by waxing hot and cold, alternately offering her love and withdrawing it. Although out of phase, her oscillations seemed to mirror his own. Their relationship was fundamentally unstable, as changeable as their moods and the autumn weather.

Characteristically, whenever Żenia rebuffed him, Malinowski beat an ascetic retreat into his intellectual citadel, his imaginary monastic option.

But he suspected total renunciation was an 'inward suicidal gesture' that would impoverish his mind: 'would my psychological states lose their metaphysical tails?' he wondered. If only she were free, he wrote, 'I would give myself to her unhesitatingly, totally; stronger than any considerations whatsoever. As things stand – I cannot see a concrete method of getting her. By threatening suicide? But in the first place I do not feel so dead certain that this would be justified, and later – how would it help me?'

Despite the misery, these October days were full of poetry. Besides his own 'wretched versifying' and 'worthless rhymes', he read the poetry of his friends Nalepiński, Miciński and Żuławski, as well as that of Poe, Słowacki and Richepin. Occasionally he jotted down aphoristic insights. 'History studied thoroughly turns into sociology,' he pronounced. Lurking within this statement is the germ of his theory of myth-as-charter. He was well into the essay on *The Birth of Tragedy*, enjoying the challenge despite himself. He was working well on Wundt, too, and his mood of confidence coincided with the first snow of winter ('the sky like a dirty rag, brown, suspended'). A letter from Żenia evoked a joyful response: '*It's all right.*' She had offered him renewed hope.

> I feel it is possible to remain completely alone with my thoughts, and yet utterly faithful and devoted to Żenia. I hope – I am sure that she will leave with me. I am resolved to marry her; I long to have children with her and am drunk with happiness at the thought.

One day while working 'splendidly' on *The Birth of Tragedy* he fell into 'a genuine intellectual trance'. In his essay on Nietzsche he wrote:

> the essence of art, that which distinguishes it from other forms of self-expression, is the direct action of certain sensory elements (musical sound, colour, line, rhythm, the sound of human speech) through which the recipient is put into a specific state of trance or ecstasy. . . . In such a psychic state reality appears before us in a new form. . . . Thus, art, metaphysics, and myth are genetically related.[24]

He criticized Nietzsche's Apollonian–Dionysian distinction, not because it was metaphysically invalid, but because it was not properly grounded in psychological (or physiological) realities. Malinowski saw 'a distinct difference introspectively between an ecstatic or narcotic experience of music, for example, and its orgiastic enjoyment'.[25] In the ecstatic workings of art it is as if 'a new world opens up within us', whereas in the orgiastic experience 'we externalize ourselves' as if our bodies were obeying a force outside us. Malinowski often referred in his diaries to his ecstatic experiences of music, and in a year or two he would discover a talent for the tango and tap into, as it were, the orgiastic roots of dance.

It would be surprising if Malinowski's philosophical essay on *The Birth of Tragedy* were not saturated with ambient emotion. It was a continuation of his diary by other means. In dedicating it to Żenia he was acknowledging her role as muse. Inadvertently or not, she had inspired in him a 'tragic sense of life' which he introspectively explored in the essay. To adopt one of his own images, his suffering transmuted base emotion into crystalline thought; or (to borrow another of his tropes) his painful love gave birth to a prose poem, a philosophical meditation on life, art and death. Nietzsche had provided the inspiration, Staś the intellectual stimulus, and Żenia the emotional spur. But if he expected praise from his muse he was disappointed. Sadly – or tragically, as Malinowski experienced it – she did not appreciate his attempt to impregnate her spiritually. Her indifference to his gift was a rejection of him.

'Goodbye to happiness'

Malinowski spent the middle of November in Cracow, staying at Mrs Borońska's pension at 22 Karmelicka.[26] He visited the academy and the Jagiellonian library, saw Kazimierz Nitsch and Stanisław Estreicher at the university, and 'wasted a lot of time' with friends. The 'Cracovian merry-go-round' was bad for him, he complained, though superficially he appeared to have enjoyed himself. He had been faithful to Żenia, if not entirely to himself. 'I experienced many temptations of the eye and mind,' he wrote later, 'but I struggled and emerged completely victorious in her name.' Work had 'saved' him, as he busily made notes on Frazer and came to a fresh understanding of totemism.

In this diary, Malinowski made fleeting references to the rumours of war that had swept Europe since the Kaiser began to flex Germany's military muscles. Otherwise talk of war barely registered on the diarist's consciousness. He had apparently discussed the threat of war in one of his letters to Annie, however, for in late November she responded:

Would you have been exempt from military service and are you an
Austrian or a Russian subject? If the latter and there had really been a
war . . . you would have been on our side, as England and Russia are
allies. I suppose though that you would be an Austrian subject. Would
you in Austrian Poland really have to fight against your own country in
Russian Poland if it ever came to war? I think there would be a revolution in Poland first.[27]

Since she had known him for four years and lived with him for almost two,
it is curious that Annie could be so unsure of Malinowski's nationality. She
guesses correctly, but her very uncertainty is indicative of the silence her
lover must have kept on the matter. Whether this was owing to indifference or to a presumption that Annie, being British, would have little interest in the complexity of his nationality is another question. It is nonetheless
testimony to the open, cosmopolitan nature of educated European society
in the years before the Great War. Meanwhile, Annie was homesick for 'the
only home life' she had ever known – with Malinowski in London. Her
existence in South Africa was 'just a dull ache'. Sadly, his own dull ache was
not for her but for Żenia.

On 19 November Malinowski took the train to Warsaw. When Żenia met
him at the station he was embarrassed by his swollen face, caused by a tooth
extraction the day before. She looked so 'marvellously beautiful' in her heavy
fur coat that he could not take his eyes off her. But considering his earlier
anguished longing the meeting was an anticlimax. Their conversation was
stilted and Żenia seemed to be avoiding his gaze.

He went to Uncle Kazimierz's house at 32 Belwederska (today a shabby
concrete building, pockmarked with bullet holes) and slept till noon the
next day. His uncle was depressed, though the atmosphere lifted immediately his mother arrived from the country. The following afternoon he
visited Żenia at her studio in a smiling, hopeful mood. It was the moment
he had waited for, but he was bitterly disappointed. He found her almost a
stranger, untidy, embarrassed and absent-minded. She declared categorically
that she was not going to get a divorce. Malinowski's options had suddenly
narrowed. He could not tolerate for long the uncertainty of not being loved
as he believed he deserved. As they walked together in Castle Square, he
seethed with resentment. On leaving her he walked along the bank of the
Vistula suffering 'a horrible childish attack'.

I think about my work, which is becoming unproductive; about life; an impression that I am saying goodbye to happiness, and terrible self-pity; I hardly think about her at all – only about myself. Rancour towards her and perhaps hatred; but suppressed in my mind; only the clairvoyance of her femininity; the intensity of my irresponsibility.

His world has turned into 'an enormous grey pulp'.

I have lost a lot of faith in her. . . . I have experienced a couple of moments outside the dogma 'I cannot live without her'. . . . I have lost the belief that she is as saturated with me as I am with her; the problem of giving and the necessity of its being counterbalanced.

He was discovering in his own heart the cast-iron rule that unequal exchange in love confers power on the one who loves least. All was not yet lost, however, and although he admitted to the feeling of a 'dogma' being shaken, there was a residuum of religious adoration for the inaccessible, 'sadly smiling madonna'.

'I take everything emotionally'

Malinowski observed that his reading of Frazer was having a subjective effect, shaping his daydreams and lending mythic form to some of his most intimate reveries. He was alluding to *The Golden Bough*:

I play a role in mythological matters, strong emotional apperceptions; points touching erotica and metaphysical pain emerge clearly; I take everything emotionally. Castration, as a mad leap into the abyss of liberation; the myth of the ravaged and slaughtered god – all this takes hold of me with the force of emotion. It is a fact that I have applied a great deal from my work and preoccupations to the outside, to her.

He will approach many anthropological issues with similar mimetic projections and subjective touchstones, apprehending them emotionally. In observing how 'the affects are crystallized in magic ideas' he wrote: 'passion leads us to automatic mimetic acts; if we hate someone, we are capable, in our rage, of tearing, biting, and mutilating him through whatever is within our reach; these facts must be taken into account insofar as we wish to recreate a critical, psychological synthesis of magic.'[28]

It was during these despondent, Żenia-tormented weeks in wintery Warsaw that Malinowski sketched a critique of Frazer's theories of religion and magic. His main quarrel was with Frazer's use of associationist psychology which, in its Herbartian guise as the workings of an 'apperceptive mass', he had already rejected in his doctoral thesis. This psychology led Frazer to the conclusion that magic was a primitive form of science since both appealed to man's own natural powers, and that both were opposed to religion, the chief characteristic of which was an appeal to deities. Rejecting the intellectualist assumption that savages organized their institutions in the way academic committees might do, Malinowski cut the cake a different way. Psychologically, magic was different from science because 'it does not perceive in the world of objective things but relates emotionally, subjectively'. Religion sprang from the same psychic source, from emotional stress and life crises, though as a social institution it 'fulfils a basic organizing function, creating a common cult and a common system of norms'. Magic, on the other hand, 'is only the efflorescence of certain sundry wants'. Shadowing Malinowski's argument against Frazer is Mach's distinction between the domain of sense impressions, belonging to science, and the domain of emotions, about which science has little to say.[29] The difference between magic and science, therefore, is not one of 'false' versus 'true' assumptions about the working of the world, but one of goals and means. The aims and methods of magic, unlike those of empirically guided science, refer chiefly to the realm of the emotions. Malinowski would take up these issues and the tripartite distinction between magic, science and religion at far greater length during the 1920s. The fact that he continued to ponder them for the rest of his life is an implicit tribute to Frazer.

On Sunday 24 November Malinowski and Żenia met again, and in Ujazdowski Park they managed an abortive kiss. He told her of her purifying effect on his sexual ethics and of her rendering of his work fertile. But it was with an almost masochistic hopelessness that he continued to see her. He documents rebuffs, slights, apprehension, sadness, self-disgust, fury, resentment and 'severe, unrelenting pain'. There were moments of 'beatitude', but fleeting happiness was 'a dream in which a rude awakening already lurks'. He was tortured by indecision and self-doubt, though for a while he grudgingly accepted the status quo. He had flashes of resolve to be alone, though he knew it to be an illusory option for he lacked the moral strength to repudiate the Eternal Feminine. 'Femininity,' he mused, 'automatically phosphoresces on the surface.' It was something he would never be able to resist.

Bronio took supper with his mother some evenings and read his essay to her. It is unlikely that he confided in her concerning Żenia, though she could not have failed to notice her son's vexed, erratic moods. At 32 Belwederska there were heated arguments about the family's worsening financial crisis. 'Mama talks of suicide,' he noted with alarm. 'I have very pessimistic apprehensions about the future.' The spectre of the bailiff loomed.

Despite these domestic worries, Żenia continued to preoccupy him. He wondered about her true feelings for him: did she really love her husband more? Adept as he was at conscionable two-timing, he understood her dissimulation perfectly. After supper one evening, Żenia agreed to accompany him to a symphony concert. Nervously flirtatious, she nestled close to him in her seat, while Malinowski relaxed and listened to the music with studied concentration and 'something of a pose'. The evening nurtured his hopes, and when he visited her the next day he found her 'excited and radiant'. They spent the afternoon talking and reading together, and he told her that his work on *The Golden Bough* had become 'permeated' with her. When he left her studio he was ecstatic.

The end of the affair

Malinowski still believed in the possibility of a miracle; Żenia did not. All too soon her teasing ambivalence precipitated another crisis. His own fretful outbursts aggravated the situation; his demands had become tedious if not intolerable. Although his male pride was at stake, he felt compassion for her complaisant husband who seemed to be doing his best to behave with decorum. Żenia was making it difficult for both of them. 'Attendance at conjugal scenes is something ghastly,' Malinowski noted disingenuously. He would simply have to give her up, but what would life hold for him without her?

> I know perfectly well that this has been the most intense thing in my life. It has changed a lot in me; I now feel total sexual purity within me; it is only through the prism of love that I am able to view sexual matters; for me, only one woman exists – and now I am losing her.

It is curious how willingly Malinowski prolonged the relationship without any prospect of physical intimacy. How could he have accepted so much less in Warsaw than had been granted him in Zakopane? His desire for Żenia's spiritual seduction was now uppermost, but she did not reciprocate his spiritual gifts, did not even appear to appreciate them. 'She barely reads the things I write for her,' he protested. Her rejection made him feel unworthy: 'I believe in her for me, but I do not believe in myself for her.'

For a few days he felt suicidal. *The Golden Bough* obliged him with its ornate descriptions of noble contempt for death. To unburden himself, he visited his sympathetic friend August Zaleski (elected leader of the Polish community in Britain and later Poland's foreign minister), who was also suffering from a broken heart. Malinowski then submitted himself to the solace of a symphony concert, only to be assailed by 'terrible pain and despair' during the *Symphonie Pathétique* – surely among the most harrowing musical offerings for a grieving lover. Happening upon Ethel Eaton ('a pretty but stupid Englishwoman'), he wondered, without much hope, whether a flirtation would ease his pain. Experimentally, he took her to a concert next day but discovered that he did not desire her in the least. He then reproached himself for thinking, however fleetingly, that 'Eatonka' could possibly replace Żenia.

Remarkably, his work had not gone too badly at this time. Despite the irritating distraction of another domestic row over his mother's finances he had found time to write something on totemism. It was characteristic of the man. Despite his tiredness and heartache, despite the family ructions, despite the doleful daily socializing and, above all, despite his forlorn complaints concerning his own inability, Malinowski demonstrated an extraordinary capacity for sustained intellectual effort. For the rest of his life he would, for one reason or another, deplore his unsatisfactory or impossible working conditions, yet his output remained undiminished. While never ceasing to lament the obstacles to his work, he somehow overcame them.

An abject Malinowski tried to grasp the nettle and deliver an ultimatum to Żenia: 'If she says no, or else wants to draw me in once again – then I shall persevere. No, I shall not see her any more; perhaps never. – I shall live, knowing that there exists someone with whom I could have been happy.' A few days later she telephoned to offer him the compromise of a platonic friendship. He protested that, after such intimacy, friendship between them was impossible. But he was still desperate to keep her and considered her offer. He revisited all the arguments and ended up where he began, in hopeless vacillation. 'I need a woman of talent, in order to feel through her,' he thought. This was his justification for the superficial scab of compromise. That night he dreamed of 'an excursion *en trois*' with Żenia and her husband.

Monday 23 December was a day of rapprochement. He visited Żenia, and in recounting what happened adopted an ironic tone: 'I agree to friendship; harmony, *shaking hands*. From our conversation it turns out that this is to be a friendship of a very sentimental character.' Żenia's husband appeared and Malinowski stayed to supper, which he could do more comfortably as a friend than as a lover. 'I behave as if it is *all right*,' he explained.

The pact of friendship proved hollow within days. On Christmas Eve Malinowski did much socializing, though he lectured himself on the need to be careful of squandering his inwardness on 'this threepenny experience'. Christmas Day provided another excuse for hectic social calls. He visited relatives with Mama, then went off on his own to see Maria Czaplicka, home from London with news of the Seligmans. The following night he went to a party. Ignoring the dancing and the parlour games, he roamed restlessly through the rooms. Finally, Żenia arrived and they were alone for a few moments. But she said nothing to him – 'her little mouth like a cat's' – and he left the party in disgust. The next day he went to her studio and waited for her. She came late, and he detonated his anger in his diary: '*Resentment*. A brief altercation. She can't even turn up for our last talk – can't give me more than five minutes and even complains that I see something in this. I have had enough!'

His cousin Zygmunt Staszewski had died, and on the afternoon of Malinowski's departure from Warsaw he attended the funeral. 'I still feel bound to Żenia by a thousand threads,' he thought as he glimpsed her, smartly dressed alongside her elegant husband. He spoke to others in the social stir following the burial, but not to Żenia. They exchanged a quick glance on the way out of the cemetery, then she was gone from his life. Although he would think of her often for months and years to come, the 'friendship', like the affair, was over.

On the train to Cracow late that afternoon, an old Jew taught him how to read a Yiddish newspaper and praised his quick intelligence. Then a woman with whom he discussed the Jewish question gave him two flowers. These encounters comforted him. The strangers' spontaneous interest in him filled his emptiness.

The consolation of Karola

As so often when he moved from one city or country to another, Malinowski interrupted his diary. On this occasion he resumed it in Zakopane ten days after leaving Warsaw. They were eventful days, however, for he made a lightning trip to London to consult various people – Wheeler and Hobhouse among them – about the publication of his book on the Aboriginal family. The managing editor of the University of London Press now wanted it to appear in a sociological series. Fearing further delays, Malinowski emphatically did not, and wrote at length to Westermarck for advice.[30]

He then hastened back to Warsaw and within a few days was in Zakopane, seeking the comfort of Staś's company. They talked about Staś's entanglement with Jadwiga Janczewska and Malinowski confided his bruising experiences with Żenia. He now bore her a mighty grudge, and this enabled him to cope. The friends lunched with the novelist Stefan Żeromski and that night there was a large gathering at the Zagórskas' villa. Malinowski had re-entered the social whirl of Zakopane.

He did no work during these first weeks of the new year. His diary is a confusing roster of names and places as he shuttled on foot or by sleigh between 'Nosal', the Pharmacy, the Crab Apple Café, Solska's place and the Zagórskas' villa. The mixed company of friends played parlour games, held obstacle races, tobogganed on the slopes, went to the theatre and sat for poetry readings at long café tables. 'I feel perfect emptiness in relation to people,' Malinowski recorded sourly. At least he was less preoccupied with Żenia.

By 7 January something was afoot with Karola Zagórska, Aniela's sister. 'We talk about love,' his diary hinted. She asked him if had been thinking about her. 'No,' he replied. 'That's good,' she said; but she had 'suffered'. The next evening Karola explicitly confessed her love. Later the same evening he had an intimate, if guarded, conversation with Aniela. 'The day before she would have said a great deal to me. Now, no longer so.' Her wariness doubtless had to do with her sister's sudden play for him. It was only a few months since Malinowski's intellectual friendship with Aniela had acquired an erotic charge. This attraction seems to have been mutual: 'She tells me about going through a very intense period on account of me. . . . I talk to her a lot about myself . . . about my relationship to her; about her raptures; about using her as a cataplasm; about cleansing my feelings for her. About my sonnets and the "essentiality" of my writing.' How she responded to this pompous self-revelation, he did not record, but it was presumably during such conversations that Aniela urged him to write about his Conradian defection to England.

In later years, the Zagórska sisters wrote memoirs of their cousin Joseph Conrad. The penumbra of the novelist's fame faintly illuminates Karola. When, in 1920, she spent several months at 'Oswalds', the Conrads' home in Kent, the novelist enjoyed hearing stories of her childhood on her mother's estate in central Poland.[31] She told him about the liberated atmosphere she had enjoyed:

> 'You see, Konradek, it may seem strange to you but I did not grow up in the gloom of captivity. . . . And in spite of everything that was happening I felt free. . . . After all everything depends only on our inner attitude towards life.' And then I added, 'But a great many did not want to wait. Their belief in freedom was a creative force – so they fought and perished. And about the majority of them no one will ever hear anything.'

This upset Conrad, whose father had died for Polish freedom. He stood up abruptly and glared at her, his lips twitching.

On Saturday 11 January, Malinowski returned to Cracow with Karola. They had cunningly co-ordinated their departure. The private compartment on the train was hot and Karola took off her coat. Malinowski noted that it was of black velvet and lined with pink silk. His own cheeks became flushed. She told him that she loved him too, and spoke of her 'duality', her suitor Mark (loyal but deceived), her homelessness, her unhappiness. He felt 'a strong sympathy for her, of the sort one always has for a heart which is throwing itself wide open'.

Arriving in Cracow, they strolled up to Wawel Castle, then to Kazimierz, pausing in a romantic mood at Corpus Christi Church. They took rooms at Mrs Borońska's pension and after supper sat in Michalik's Cave and gossiped with acquaintances. The next afternoon Malinowski went to Karola's room. 'She unbinds her hair; she is marvellously beautiful. We lie down on the bed and kiss; my lips get bitten.'

Karola left for Warsaw that night, and for the rest of week Malinowski dealt with family matters and impatiently scribbled away on 'lousy totemism'. As for Żenia, he hardly thought of her at all, and without batting a fickle eyelid admitted to himself that he missed Karola more. His feelings for her were ambivalent, and he was uncharacteristically reticent about what those hours spent on (or in) her bed had meant to him. A postcard from his mother begged him to come through Warsaw on his way to England. 'At first I decide *no*; I think of meeting with Karola, of seeing her room and *no*.' Then he thought of his poor mother and her problems and decided that he would go to Warsaw after all.

He was thinking intensely of Żenia as his train clattered into the city. Up to this point in his diary an air of caution enveloped all mention of Karola, as if he did not wish to acknowledge his infidelity. Had the self-deception been too painful, of course, he could simply have interrupted his diary and stopped confronting himself with the unpleasant truth that he was, at the very least, a faithless sexual opportunist. Instead, he almost relished the self-castigation that the affair afforded him. Żenia's 'purifying effect' on his sexual ethics of which he had boasted a few weeks before seems to have been nullified. He might even have consoled himself that Karola, too, exhibited a kindred duality as a faithless sexual opportunist. There was, however, no comparison to be made between the 'inexorable' feeling he had for Żenia and the shallowness of his attraction to Karola. He thought: 'I feel that I ought not to go on.'

But go on he did, and after spending some time with his mother, he collected Karola one fine, frosty afternoon and they went to hear the Philharmonic play Mozart and Beethoven. He gazed at her approvingly; she was 'exceedingly subtle and beautiful' in her velvet coat. At first she would not look him in the eye – an evasiveness he had resented in Annie and Żenia. That evening, after taking supper with Mama, he thought about Żenia and resolved 'to be *firm*' and not to kiss Karola again.

But he was teasing himself, for he wrote this entry in his diary *after* he had already broken his resolve. He not only visited Karola later that night, but made energetic love to her and recorded what had happened in unusually explicit terms. Yet he presented the episode innocently, as if he had every good intention of persuading Karola that he did not want to 'soil' two love affairs. 'I clearly tell her this and why I want it this way; nevertheless our talking together, our closeness leads us down that path once again. . . . We lie on the ottoman, which shakes terribly.' He left her in the early hours to find Mama waiting up 'in the greatest anxiety'.

As he was now captivated by Karola's charms, his desperation mounted with the imminence of his departure for England. Another separation loomed, but sexual surfeit could dull the impending pain of loss. The next afternoon he returned to Karola's rooms, where they made love again, and yet again later in the evening.

> She is infinitely beautiful and has a fabulous temperament. . . . She always talks to me about Mark . . . about how she is his only love; I have certain doubts. I should like to meet him, to be sure. Marvellous drowsiness alongside her. . . . I tell her I love her, that I am sorry it has worked out this way; otherwise, if it weren't for him, we might have fallen in love.

In Karola he had again found a woman ostensibly committed to another. He would even endorse the triangle by meeting her steadfast suitor. While Malinowski declared his love for her, he also declared it a pity that they could not 'fall' in love, a distinction he had also made with respect to Żenia. The evidence of his diary, however, is that it was invalid: he both loved Żenia and was in love with her. We may surmise, however, that he did not love Karola — it is easy, and not untruthful at that moment of drowsy satisfaction, for a man to say he loves the woman to whom he has just made love.

Despite the passionate intimacy of their encounters, the emotional distance Malinowski maintained was evident the next day, his last in Warsaw.

> At 12 we meet again. She shocks me by her [piano] playing and her singing; she isn't musical! We sit on the sofa. A flea on her collar. This gives me a psychopathic [sic] shock. I catch it and kill it. I feel ill at ease. On the other hand, I look at this room which I have so frequently returned to in my thoughts . . . and tears come to my eyes.

Emotional distance did not preclude sentimentality. 'She grows numb but does not cry, she is unable to kiss me. . . . I say goodbye to her. She walks away, stiff, sad, shrunken. Her lips were cold when I pressed them for the last time.' He who leaves, parts most lightly. His mother saw him off at the station, where a big moon was rising over the platform.

Settled in the train and ignoring a garrulous Frenchwoman, he thought only of Karola, in his mind's eye pale-featured and dressed in black. He thought of her too as he strolled in Berlin, 'the great city awakening from its unsound sleep'. The Channel crossing was exhilarating and optimism flooded him. 'So many memories press upon my heart! Since the time when I first left to begin a new life, to meet Annie and to begin to work on new things — how many times have I crossed the Channel! A special mood; a change of inner atmosphere. England!' On the train to Victoria he thought with pleasure of the Boreniuses. He took a taxi to their apartment where Anna-Mi welcomed him.

'Landed on an unknown shore'

The diary draws to a close. In a page of 'supplementary notes' Malinowski summarizes his recent experiences in an attempt to grasp their moral significance.

> During the course of these events my life has passed through a profound crisis; I have the impression . . . that I am landed on an unknown shore. . . . On [Żenia's] behalf I moved ahead; I started to write poetry; independent things . . . for her. This era, full of longings and pain in Zakopane, was nevertheless one of the most productive in my life. All this was destroyed in Warsaw. Then I wanted only to forget, to disengage myself, to heal my wounds. Towards the end in Warsaw I did little work – and 'amused' myself; at the same time I hadn't completely finished with Żenia. . . . Only after my departure – in Zakopane I shed her almost entirely. Then came the affair with Karola and it soiled, and at the same time inflamed the thing. – It turned out disastrously!

So much for the events in Poland, the drawn-out trajectory of his affair with Żenia and the parabola of his fling with Karola. He does not mention his dedicated reading of Simmel, Wundt, Frazer and Fustel de Coulanges, or the essays on totemism and exogamy, magic and religion that he had disciplined himself to write. He commends rather the 'independent things' on Wacław Berent and Nietzsche that he had written for Żenia. If this was 'one of the most productive' periods of his life, then he might be forgiven for drawing the conclusion that the love of a woman – however hopeless, perhaps even *because* it was hopeless – was a necessary stimulus and adjunct to achievement. It would confirm his suspicion, fostered by Nietzsche, that from the tempering fires of suffering is born a creative self. At the very least, he would have learned that tranquillity of mind was not necessarily a state most conducive to intellectual work.

Malinowski's euphoria soon evaporated. If he had expected 'an end to life's storms and tempests' in London he was disappointed. The Boreniuses appeared to lose interest in him, and he felt 'a certain disillusionment' with them. Even when Anna-Mi fell ill and was admitted to hospital, he was 'almost bitter' about the amount of time the diversion cost him (though she would recall later that Mali's bedside visits cheered her). His room was so cold and uncomfortable that he was unable to work in the evenings. Not least, he was homesick for Poland and he paced the streets of Bloomsbury unable to connect with his past. His life with Annie Brunton was a distant memory. As an antidote to London's alienating effect he renewed his acquaintance with the Polish Circle, a group of expatriates who congregated at premises in St Martin's Lane. Yet at the core of his malaise were his recent 'disastrous' experiences in Warsaw. The penultimate entry of his diary, written on Tuesday 28 January, confessed that his emotional state was almost out of control. As for his fading Polish lovers: 'I experience a negative reaction to Karola and intense longing for Żenia – which ultimately offers a foundation of absolute hopelessness. . . . I keep on thinking of them both and of Aniela; I long for my country.'

The final entry in this diary is dated 30 January. Malinowski bewailed his tiredness, his toothache and his 'damp, nasty, repellent room'. While working in the British Museum, Żenia continued to haunt him: 'At times I am seized with a profound, but undifferentiated lust. At times, when looking at the Eygptian women, at the sacred symbols of marriage and motherhood, a hopeless longing for Żenia sweeps over me.' There had been more bad news from Mama and he had heard nothing from Karola. He feared 'the worst' – a hint that he was concerned she might be pregnant. In short, there was nothing on which he could peacefully rest his thoughts. Yet there is a curious finality about his last, emphatic sentences: 'Today my feelings towards Karola have much improved. . . . But always in comparison with what I feel for Żenia and what I am trying to *kill* – that is *a negligible quantity*.' Malinowski's diary ends with the abruptness of a crashed computer screen, shutting down this privileged view into his inner life.

Karola Zagórska's name does not appear in subsequent diaries and it is quite possible that Malinowski never saw her again. She nevertheless deserves a postscript. Karola made her first visit to England in 1916. Cousin Joseph begged her to stay with him. 'Do you realize,' he said, 'that you are our first visitor from my family?' There was a photograph of her father, Karol Zagórski, on the mantelpiece of Conrad's bedroom. Karola stayed with the Conrads at Oswalds for a longer period in 1920. There is photograph of her with Conrad in the garden; her downturned head rests lightly on his shoulder as she clasps his arm. Her short dark hair frames a plump, pretty face. John Conrad, aged fourteen, befriended Karola and recalled her daily singing practice and his attempts to prevent the dog from joining in.[32] Conrad had aged by then and Karola's description is of a moody old man sunk in reverie. About this time he wrote to Aniela, giving her authority to translate his works into Polish. We learn from these letters that Karola had tuberculosis and had been sent to Italy for a cure. For three years Conrad made her an annual allowance of £120.[33] Subsequent letters do not refer to her illness, so she presumably made a complete recovery. According to John Conrad she became an opera singer and went to America, returning to Poland after World War II.[34] She died in 1955.

Chapter 12

Totems, Teachers and Patron Saints

'Something is happening'

By 1913 the debate on totemism had engaged a generation of anthropologists. Properly understood, they believed, totemism would provide a key to the origin of human society. Adam Kuper has nominated it as 'arguably the most pervasive and enduring anthropological contribution to the European conception of primitive society'. It provided:

> a foundation myth of rationalism; yet at the same time it offered a symbolic idiom in which a poet could celebrate a more natural time, when man's spirit was at one with the plants and birds and beasts, and mythical, poetic thought was commonplace, and sexual instincts uninhibited. It was the anthropologists' Garden of Eden.[1]

While Malinowski did not subscribe to such an Arcadian view, he too became engrossed by the problem of totemism and its relation to primitive religion. He knew that anything he wrote about it would be heeded. The trouble was that most of what he did write on this subject was in Polish, a language inaccessible to the British anthropologists he most wanted to impress. Although he recorded his intention to translate these works into English he failed to do so.

Malinowski had written to Aniela Zagórska at the end of February that the 'intellectual dilettantism' from which he 'would never escape' had finally led him into the field of social sciences: 'I have the impression that I shall now stop switching, especially since I have already begun a series of papers which I shall want to finish, and as I push ahead with them new problems will undoubtedly arise and thus I shall no longer be able to get away from this field.'[2] There is no hint here of the passionate calling to serve Frazerian anthropology that he was to recount (or retrospectively invent) in 1926. Rather, it is as if he had stumbled into anthropology by accident and now proposed to follow it along the line of least resistance. His dilettantism had been evident during the previous year in Poland. Although he continued his disciplined reading in anthropology and sociology, his diary testifies (allowing for characteristic exaggeration) to a frequent lack of enthusiasm. But even though it was negatively phrased, there is in his confession to Aniela evidence of a growing commitment, and indeed the year 1913 saw Malinowski consolidate his intellectual and institutional position with respect to British anthropology. Thus far this had been marginal: that of a research student living on a meagre Polish stipend, grateful for whatever notice the anthropological establishment might bestow upon him. His book reviews for the leading journals of *Man* and *Folk-lore* earned him a measure of attention, as did his well-received conference papers, and he knew he would attract even more notice when his book on the Aboriginal family finally appeared. In the meantime, there were a couple of other ways of reducing his marginality and making a small splash. Teaching was one. Joining battle with eminent seniors was another, and it was impossible to aim higher than the disparate triumvirate of Frazer, Rivers and Durkheim.

'I am in London at last,' Malinowski wrote to Westermarck early in February 1913, 'and would be very glad, if I could be allowed to deliver a few lectures on a subject which I would dare to submit to your approval in the form of a short syllabus.'[3] He asked if his lectures might be arranged for the spring term, but it was not until November that the LSE appointed him as a special lecturer. Nevertheless, the spring brought other gratifications. 'Something is happening', as he characteristically said of exciting movements in his life. (Conversely, as he wrote in Zakopane, 'where nothing is happening there can be no drama'.) The new year brought excitement and drama aplenty in a new love affair, this time with a young woman he met through the Polish Circle.

The greatest influence on his domestic life was once again Annie Brunton. In late March she returned to England with her elder brother's twenty-year-old son, Brian. 'What a happy moment it was when you walked into the Ivanhoe Hotel,' Annie recalled of her reunion with Malinowski in Southampton.[4] They spent Easter together at the Devonshire resort of

Torquay. Then, as Annie remembered, they began a 'happy life in London, when we three were such good pals'.[5] They rented a flat in Compton Street in Clerkenwell, where, according to Brian, 'Auntie Annie used to boss us both.' The young man's 'affection and gratitude' towards Malinowski was 'as deep as a brother's' and it was with unfeigned nostalgia that he wrote from Cape Town the following year: 'I missed you most acutely when you left with your mother for Poland and especially so when Auntie and I returned to London and the dear old flat in Compton St . . . The few months we spent together will always be treasured in my memory as the happiest time of my life.'[6]

Bearding Frazer

The 'series of papers' that Malinowski told Aniela he wanted to complete included, most importantly, a three-part essay for *Lud*, a scholarly journal of folklore published in Warsaw. What had begun in 1911 as an extended review of Frazer's *Totemism and Exogamy* eventually became a full-length book. He wrote to Adam Fischer, the editor of *Lud*, on 28 January 1913, belatedly enclosing the second part of his essay, and saying that he would also be unable to meet the agreed deadline for the third part. This he promised to complete within a few weeks, but at the end of May he wrote again to say that the third part had now expanded to about 120 pages. He believed this part to be 'of incomparably greater theoretical importance' than the other two as it was 'an attempt at expounding and solving the problem of totemism through a totally different approach'.[7]

By July, however, he had still not finished the third instalment. Fischer presumably demanded an abridged version, for when it finally appeared towards the end of the year it proved to be the shortest of the three parts. The reason for Malinowski's delay in completing it was neither procrastination nor the difficulty of formulating criticisms of Frazer. It seems that his mother had been urging him to write something even more substantial. His letters to Kazimierz Nitsch explain.

Malinowski wrote to his old tutor at the end of June to say that a copy of his book on the Aboriginal family would soon reach him, and that he would inscribe it with a 'flowery dedication' when he came to Cracow. But the main point of his letter was to ask whether it would be permissible to submit work for his habilitation in typescript form.

My mother is most anxious that I should proceed with my habilitation as soon as possible. It so happens that I already have a completed Polish manuscript. . . . It is something which has grown from an endless expansion of the third part of the article for *Lud*. In the end, I decided to slash through the thread connecting these two unco-ordinated, twin embryos of my spirit to the mutual advantage of both. To a certain degree I am satisfied with this bit of work and consider it as fit for publication; later on I hope to translate it into English.[8]

Wierzenia pierwotne i formy ustroju społecznego is usually translated as 'Primitive Beliefs and Forms of Social Organisation', though Malinowski told Nitsch that he first conceived of the title in English as 'Primitive Religion and Social Differentiation: A Study of Totemic Beliefs and Social Organization', but he suspected this might not 'sound good' in Polish. The final subtitle better indicates the book's topic: 'The Problem of the Genesis of Religion with Particular Reference to Totemism'. Understandably perhaps, the work was never translated into English. Not only did Malinowski lack the time to undertake the task himself, but he must have judged that his career in Britain would not be served by the publication, several years delayed, of a monograph on what by 1920 had become a somewhat stale and fruitless topic. In 1913, however, it was a rewarding exercise that doubtless strengthened his commitment to anthropology by boosting his self-confidence. He could count himself among the handful of ethnologists who had throroughly mastered the entire literature on primitive religion as well as on Aboriginal Australia.

Since it was an outgrowth of his *Lud* essay on Frazer, 'Primitive Beliefs and Forms of Social Organisation' must be approached through it. It is important also to bear in mind Malinowski's quasi-filial relationship to James George Frazer (1854–1941). After their first meeting in 1910 Malinowski appears to have seen very little of the reclusive Scot. Although they corresponded once or twice during the period Malinowski spent in Australia it was not until his return to England in 1920 that their friendship can be said to have ripened – insofar as friendship was possible with such a self-effacing man thirty years his senior. On meeting Frazer in 1900, William James noted: 'he of the "Golden Bough" . . . a suckling babe of humility, unworldliness and molelike sightlessness to everything but *print*'. It was William James who asked Frazer whether he had ever met any of the savages he wrote about at such length, eliciting the famous reply, 'God Forbid!' James was no less astute about Lilly Frazer: 'a deaf and *lebenslustig* cosmopolitan Frenchwoman, clever in all sorts of directions, a widow with a motherly heart, who has adopted him and nurses him.'[9] During 1941–42, the year that separated their respective deaths, Malinowski wrote a biographical appreciation of his Scottish mentor who, paradoxically for one whose works were so enormously influential, 'could never brook personal contradiction or even engage in an argument'. With tactful understatement, he added that Frazer was 'easily put out in meeting a stranger, and had great difficulty in adjusting to unusual personal contacts'.[10]

> He is not a dialectician, nor even perhaps an analytical thinker. He is, on the other hand, endowed with two great qualities: the artist's power to create a visionary world of his own; and the true scientist's intuitive discrimination between what is relevant and what is adventitious, what fundamental and what secondary.[11]

This 'great humanist' was the most famous anthropologist in the world. To adopt Ernest Gellner's fanciful analogy, within British anthropology Frazer was King Harold, 'the last king of the old regime' whose destiny it was to be slain by the foreign Conqueror, Bronislaw Malinowski.[12]

Although Malinowski appears to have seen nothing of Frazer during 1911–13, the author of *Totemism and Exogamy* was often in his thoughts. He probably spent more time and effort studying this work than any other in his lifetime, and his eighty-page review is by far the longest of his forty-odd book reviews. Malinowski's immediate intention was to exercise his own critical muscle, and *Lud* offered him the opportunity to mount a devastating attack on the evolutionist position held by Frazer without compromising his future relationship with the sovereign figure of British anthropology. His three-part essay revealed an emperor with only the scantiest of methodological clothing. It was an acute and scholarly critique mounted on several fronts, but because Frazer did not read Polish it was a campaign conducted behind his back and probably without his knowledge. It was the literary equivalent of the mocking faces Malinowski would pull, much later, in the presence of the aged, near-blind Frazer.[13]

Malinowski wrote for *Lud* to bury Frazer not to praise him, though he began the first part of his essay with the statement that the four-volume treatise on totemism and exogamy was 'undoubtedly the most important publication which has appeared in English in recent years', and he complimented its author on his 'unusual erudition' and 'beautiful' style.[14] But while the assemblage of ethnographic facts would be 'an invaluable treasury and mine of facts for a host of scholars', the theories that informed their arrangement 'cannot stand up to serious criticism'. First, there was the 'lack of a clearly formulated, purposeful method, the lack of posing a problem and tracing the course of research'; consequently, Frazer's survey was 'very chaotic'. Second, he failed to separate fact from theory and made no distinction between facts and inferences from facts. Another basic flaw of Frazer's work was his 'complete arbitrariness': he gave equal weight to all his sources, however unreliable, yet ignored those that did not support his theories.

Frazer's basic hypotheses and implicit assumptions were evolutionary and he arranged the ethnographic facts concerning totemism in a developmental series. Malinowski pulled these assumptions to pieces. Data were uneven and incomplete, therefore uniform comparison between totemic tribes was impossible. Different authors advanced different theories and different stages of development. The cornerstone of Frazer's argument was that the tribes of central Australia (the so-called Arunta) were the most primitive, whereas Durkheim and Andrew Lang, reading the same sources, had reached the opposite conclusion, regarding them as among the most developed. Howitt had placed the Arunta in the middle of another evolutionary series. If the experts could not agree, then we have speculation, not science.

Malinowski would have concurred with Haddon's private view that Frazer was 'a literary man, not a man of science'.[15] To be fair to Frazer, however, he came to anthropology from classics and not from physics or zoology. Malinowski stated his own positivist position thus:

> The interest of an exact scientist should focus on understanding and pen-
> etrating the mechanism and essence of social phenomena as they exist at
> present and are accessible to observation, and not in order that these phe-
> nomena should serve as a key to solving the riddle of a prehistoric past
> about which we cannot know anything empirically.

Admitting this to be a 'banal truth' for natural scientists, he would reiterate it for many years until the evolutionists were fully vanquished.

'Totemism is both a religious conception and a social institution,' observed Malinowski, and there is a nascent functionalism in the idea of their interconnection: 'As is every social institution, totemism is also linked with a number of social phenomena, and keeping track of these connections and dependencies . . . makes it possible for us to expand our ideas about these phenomena and even to discover new sociological laws.' Frazer had largely ignored sociological criteria, though 'religion is just as much a form of social organization as it is a collection of beliefs'.

Malinowski devoted several pages to the criticism of Frazer's views on the difference between religion and magic as propounded in *The Golden Bough*, concluding that they were 'entirely in error'. He argued that 'the psychic processes from which magic draws its juices' are 'emotional factors' that cannot be reduced to an association of ideas or to purely mental processes. 'Psychological concepts cannot serve to define religion and its relationship to magic.' He offered his own ponderous definition of religion in which the concepts of system, cult, beliefs, practices, public, tradition, norms, dogmas and supernatural sanctions were thown into the pot and stirred. But importantly, he added: 'The criteria for defining religion in this manner lie in social, objective facts, and therefore they are easily accessible to close observation, even among savage peoples.' Just how accessible to close observation they were (though he would want to qualify 'easily'), he demonstrated a few years later in '*Baloma*', his lengthy essay on Trobriand religion.

In the third part of his essay Malinowski tightened the critical screw and presented another litany of objections to Frazer's methods. His theories concerning the origins of totemism and exogamy Malinowski showed to be 'false', 'naive' and 'untenable'. He found 'quite unacceptable' Frazer's thesis that exogamy was the result of deliberate social reform to avoid incest. In short, Malinowski concluded, *Totemism and Exogamy* was not, 'in the proper sense of the word, a scientific work'; it was 'simply a compilation, accomplished with great erudition . . . but not digested and not grasped within a theoretical framework'. The only tenet that Malinowski managed to rescue from Frazer's fumbling theoretical grasp was the supposedly universal ignorance among primitive peoples of the father's role in procreation – though what Frazer did with this 'justified hypothesis' was silly. Totemism arose, according to Frazer's third and last theory of its origin, from 'the ignorance of the fact of paternity and of the faith in the incarnation of animals, plants [etc] in women'. But the notion that totemism began with the fantasies or 'fixations' of pregnant women struck Malinowski as absurd. It did 'not merit discussion', though discuss it he did, relentlessly exposing its inadequacy to explain such a complex form of social organization as totemism. He deduced that Frazer did not really know what he wanted to explain.

Finally, Malinowski questioned the essential conception — common to most scholars of the time — that totemism was 'an integral whole, a cultural unity, as if it [everywhere] came from a single casting', such that what one finds today are 'vestiges', 'rudiments' and 'faded' forms of an imagined 'pure and full totemism' that Frazer and others supposed to represent an 'organic phase in human evolution'. Malinowski effectively demolished this assumption, and in challenging the 'totemic illusion' he foreshadowed Claude Lévi-Strauss's attempt to dissolve the problem half a century later.[16] Malinowski concluded his essay with the sceptical question: 'Does totemism exist at all?' In reaching this point he had made it clear that his attack on Frazer's theories and methods was *ipso facto* an assault on all speculative evolutionary theories. 'It is hard to believe that the same set of circumstances has always appeared in all of humanity at a certain stage of development or that such an extremely complicated collection of conditions could appear in the same way which could identically form such a specialized and complicated product as totemism.'

Notwithstanding the severity of Malinowski's youthful challenge, when he revisited Frazer's theories a quarter of a century later in a review of *Totemica: A Supplement to Totemism and Exogamy* in 1938, the only note of criticism was a muted one: 'Frazer himself keeps aloof in this book from controversy; nor does he work out his earlier theories any further.'[17] In considering them again himself, Malinowski cleverly rescued something from each of the three discredited theories of the origin of totemism. It was as if he sought to recruit Frazer, anachronistically and *ex post facto*, to his own school of Functionalism. Some sleight of hand was needed, but he pulled it off. On Frazer's behalf he constructed a functional definition:

> totemism expresses ritually and mythologically man's selective interest in a number of animal or plant species; it discloses the primitive's profound conviction that he is in body and mind akin to the relevant factors of his environment. These he is able to control magically in virtue of the kinship; and towards them he has to observe a religious attitude of reverence and consideration.[18]

In a remarkable reversal of his 1913 conclusion, Malinowski declared: 'Frazer's theories explain not only the origins of totemism but also its functions.'

Wading into Rivers

While criticisms of Frazer were simmering in his mind, Malinowski also turned on Rivers. Although never very close, his personal relations with this reticent but sympathetic man remained cordial. 'Rivers is awfully nice to me,' Malinowski wrote to his wife in 1920, 'he showed much more real understanding than all the other chaps taken together.'[19] It is curious that with the single exception of a letter that Malinowski wrote to Rivers in 1915, no correspondence between them has survived. While there can be no doubt that he continued to admire him, after Rivers's defection to diffusionism Malinowski seems to have regarded him as a lost cause. His later published utterances on Rivers remained respectful (though they were sometimes barbed: 'a truly brilliant thinker [who] advanced Socialism in England because he thought that Melanesian savages were communists'), and he properly claimed that most of his own generation of anthropologists were pupils of Rivers 'by direct teaching or from the reading of his works'.[20] But he found himself in fundamental disagreement with Rivers over issues such as the priority of monogamy and the individual family over group marriage and the clan. Rivers derived his views on these matters from Lewis Henry Morgan's 'communistic' view of early humanity.

In early May 1913, Malinowski had an opportunity to confront Rivers in a public forum when the latter delivered a trilogy of lectures on 'Social Organization and Kinship' at the LSE. The lectures were probably inspired by Alfred Kroeber's 1909 paper on 'Classificatory Systems of Relationship', which had argued that kinship terminologies reflect psychology, not sociology. This assertion challenged a major premise of Rivers's forthcoming work *The History of Melanesian Society*, and it was perhaps to launch a pre-emptive strike at potential critics that Rivers argued the case for the historical and sociological interpretation of kin terminologies.[21] Ironically, British anthropology eventually turned its back on *The History of Melanesian Society* (which was never reprinted), and instead accorded classic, landmark status to the booklet *Kinship and Social Organization* (reprinted in 1968). In his preface, Rivers acknowledged 'suggestions' made by Malinowski 'in the discussions which followed the lectures', though he does not indicate what they were.

It was another methodological issue that drew Malinowski's sharpest criticism of Rivers. This was the validity of the evolutionist's concept of 'survivals' which Rivers sought to defend in a paper delivered to the Sociological Society on the evening of 20 May.[22] If his copious notes are any guide, Malinowski was a vociferous discussant and we can only imagine what the quietly spoken, sometimes stuttering Rivers thought of this passionate young Pole who spoke so vehemently. It seems likely, however, that Malinowski's attack was overshadowed by a weightier one delivered by Westermarck, for it was the latter's critique to which Rivers responded in print some years later.[23]

Rivers defined 'the doctrine of survivals' as 'the persistence of a custom inexplicable by its present utility and only intelligible through past history'. His field research in Melanesia in 1909 had convinced him that the avunculate (the special kinship significance of the maternal uncle) was 'a true social survival', a 'vestigial' form of a previous 'social condition' of which it is the 'living relic'. Survivals illustrated 'the intense conservatism of mankind', but Rivers believed that psychological explanations of such customs were misguided and invalid. Sociology was a historical science, the task of which was 'to determine the correlations and sequences of social institutions and processes'. Only when sociology had advanced, Rivers said, 'will it be profitable to call upon psychology in the explanation of social phenomena'.

Malinowski thought the paper addressed 'burning questions' but otherwise he had nothing kind to say about it. He disagreed first with Rivers's definition of survival, for 'every custom, however out of fashion or out of use it might be, does perform some social function'. Second, he disagreed with Rivers's rejection of the validity of psychological explanations, for a sharp distinction cannot be maintained between the psychological and the sociological: 'The bonds holding together human groups consist of ideas and feelings; sociology deals with the grouping of human beings and with the function of such groups. And it cannot possibly reject in a wholesale manner the help of psychology.' This could be illustrated by 'the very example of survival'.

> Any given custom is handed on as an outward form which persists; it is the meaning, the psychological contexts of this form that change. Survival is not the custom, which animated by its present meaning is a living social being – to speak metaphorically. Survival is the ancient meaning given to it before.

He illustrated this by the Christian sacrament of communion:

It would seem simply absurd to any believer. . . . that this is a survival of crude and barbarous superstitions. And yet it [emerges]. . . . from Robertson Smith to *The Golden Bough* that communion is a survival of very inferior rites and beliefs. . . . the crude embodiment of . . . eating the God. Communion is not a survival if we explain it by the high *mysterium* of Christianity.

In a more homely example:

If we see in Piccadilly or Regent Street a lady wearing a hat of last season's fashion, then certainly we have in front of us a survival. Nonetheless, the hat does perform a function and we can understand it entirely without having recourse to its history. Last year's fashion is not a survival as far as its secondary function goes, namely the protection of the head.

It is a survival only in terms of its function as fashion. But we would be 'entirely at a loss if we neglected the psychology of fashion', and he thought the ladies of London would agree with him that 'the psychology of fashion is essential in understanding anything'. Malinowski's opposition to the mischievous idea of survival was uncompromising, and he was still attacking it just as vigorously towards the end of his life: 'The real harm done by the concept of survivals in anthropology consists in that it functions on the one hand as a spurious methodological device in the reconstruction of evolutionary series; and worse than that, it is an effective means of short-circuiting observation in fieldwork.'[24]

Rivers had advised in his paper that psychology should wait in the wings until sociology had put its house in order, to which Malinowski responded that the two disciplines must develop 'simultaneously and not piecemeal'. Moreover, it was impossible to take 'a step in sociology without using psychological terms'. To be fair to Rivers's extraordinary versatility, he changed his position a number of times on the role of psychological explanation in anthropology, having previously announced in 1911 that 'the final aim of the study of society is the explanation of social behaviour in terms of psychology'.[25] He also smuggled psychology into *The History of Melanesian Society*. Echoing Malinowski, in 1920 Robert Marett would say of Rivers: 'for a long time he cried "to-morrow" to his poor handmaid, eager to serve. She must sit in the cold and wait. But somehow she has slipped in and got to work; and it is plainly not in his heart to wish it otherwise.'[26] But by then Rivers had demonstrated the value of Freudian therapy in his famous work among shell-shocked soldiers at Craiglockhart.[27] As an anthropologist, neurologist, psychologist and psychiatrist Rivers was a scientist whom it was impossible to pigeonhole.

It was also in 1913 that Rivers published an exacting statement of 'intensive' fieldwork. It was nothing less than a charter for the kind of fieldwork Malinowski would soon embark upon in New Guinea. Rivers argued that British anthropology had been content for too long with 'survey work' and the 'superficial knowledge' it produced.

> A typical piece of intensive work is one in which the worker lives for a year or more among a community of perhaps four or five hundred people and studies every detail of their life and culture; in which he comes to know every member of the community personally; in which he is not content with generalized information, but studies every feature of life and custom in concrete detail and by means of the vernacular language. It is only by such work that one can fully realize the immense extent of the knowledge which is now awaiting the inquirer, even in places where the culture has already suffered much change.[28]

In the light of this proclamation it is scarcely surprising that Malinowski adulated Rivers as his 'patron sain[t] in fieldwork'.[29] Less certain, however, is what inspired him to nominate Rivers as 'the Rider Haggard of anthropology' – if indeed, he ever said such a thing. The apocryphal remark, attributed by Raymond Firth to Brenda Seligman's recollection of what Malinowski said to her, has nonetheless passed into legend: 'Rivers is the Rider Haggard of anthropology; I shall be the Conrad.'[30] Author of colonial adventure stories, notably *King Solomon's Mines* and *She*, Henry Rider Haggard achieved neither the psychological penetration nor the literary power of Joseph Conrad's novels. George Stocking has perceptively interpreted the claim in the light of Malinowski's belief that, thanks to his intensive fieldwork, he had probed more deeply into 'the cultural dynamics of the human psyche' than Rivers was able to do.[31]

While it is possible that Malinowski did verbally express his ambition thus to Mrs Seligman, what he wrote to her from the Trobriands in 1918 concerning Rivers, Rider Haggard and Conrad is rather less facile and somewhat more modest.

> I have been re-reading Rivers' 'Melanesians' just a couple of weeks ago, and I quite agree with you that it is a wonderful work. Indeed, since I

have been doing field work, I have come to appreciate Rivers considerably more than I did before. None the less, I see very clearly his limitations, and his mind is not really congenial to me. To draw a parallel: it reads like Rider Haggard rather than Joseph Conrad. It is rather a pursuit of fact than of the philosophical importance of fact.[32]

Sir Arthur Keith would later ask Malinowski if 'many people suspected a relationship between Conrad & you – especially concerning the ease with which you handle the English tongue?'[33] While perhaps not explicitly stating his ambition to be 'the Conrad of anthropology' the thought had probably occurred to him, perhaps as early as 1913, for it was in that year that he first met the illustrious novelist. They were introduced by a young Polish woman whose identity is disguised as Tośka in Malinowski's diary. They took the train one frosty morning to Ashford in Kent, and thence to Capel House, where Conrad conversed with them in French and Malinowski presented him with an inscribed copy of *The Family among the Australian Aborigines*.[34]

Pricking Durkheim's bubble

Frazer and Rivers were not the only leading anthropologists lambasted by Malinowski that year for their methodological shortcomings; he also set his sights on Emile Durkheim (1858–1917), the pre-eminent French sociologist. He approached Durkheim through William Robertson Smith (1846–94), the Scottish biblical scholar who had greatly influenced Frazer as well as Durkheim. Malinowski always acknowledged *The Religion of the Semites* (1889) as *the* foundation text of the sociology of religion. The novelty of Robertson Smith's work was to give priority to the study of rites rather than to creeds or dogmas. Finding ritual more accessible to observation than beliefs, ethnologists sensibly followed suit. Malinowski naturally approved of Durkheim's mission to establish sociology as a distinct field of inquiry and took to heart many of the prescriptions set out in *Les règles de la méthode sociologique* (1895), agreeing that 'culture was a reality *sui generis* and must be studied as such'.[35] When it came to a choice between the British intellectualists (Tylor, Frazer, Lang and Hartland) and Durkheim's school, Malinowski aligned himself decisively with the latter. Marett had rejected Frazer's intellectualist psychology of religion a few years earlier, replacing it with a social psychology better attuned to collective belief and behaviour. Malinowski frequently acknowledged Marett in a general way, and clearly thought of himself as in the same camp, along with Durkheim, William McDougall, Lucien Lévy-Bruhl and Arnold Van Gennep.[36] Membership of this wider intellectual fraternity, however, did not inhibit Malinowski from finding fault with his bretheren.

He acknowledged his indebtedness to Durkheim in *The Family among the Australian Aborigines*, which has been called his 'most Durkheimian work'.[37] Yet when, in late 1913, he reviewed *Les formes élémentaires de la vie religieuse: le système totémique en Australie* (1912), he was sharply critical of its methods and conclusions.[38] His cavils are indicative of his thinking while he was writing his own Polish book on the origin of religion and the sociology of totemism. Fashionable as the topic then was, it is no great coincidence that Durkheim and Malinowski were independently engaged in a similar enterprise. (To compound the coincidence, it was in 1913 that Freud published *Totem and Taboo*.) There is otherwise little to compare between the French classic, regarded by many as the greatest of Durkheim's works, and Malinowski's Polish habilitation thesis which has remained untranslated and read by few outside Poland.[39]

Unmoved by Durkheim's precept that it was sufficient to examine 'one well-conducted experiment', Malinowski objected to the restriction of his ethnographic focus to a single Australian group (Spencer and Gillen's Arunta again), as if these people were the world's most primitive. Further, on the basis of this sole ethnographic example, Durkheim generalized a universal distinction between the Sacred and the Profane. Malinowski was unconvinced that all primitive peoples recognized such a categorical distinction, and he cited a number of exceptions. He was also uneasy about Durkheim's assumption that totemism was *the* elementary form of religious life (its *ab origine* principle, as it were). Next, Malinowski took issue with Durkheim's main argument that the totemic 'principle' or 'force' represented not only the deity but also the collectivity of the clan ('society is to its members what a god is to his faithful'). Such metaphysical conceptions were anathema to Malinowski as they were to other British anthropologists, including Frazer. While they could accept Durkheim's fertile notions of 'collective consciousness' and 'collective representations' (or 'social ideas' as Malinowski preferred to call them), they baulked at the conception of society as 'a collective being, endowed with all the properties of individual consciousness'. (Here Malinowski was reminded of Hegel's Absolute, 'thinking itself'.) He later pithily characterized Durkheim's view as '*Vox populi, vox dei*'.[40]

Malinowski also rejected the 'disappointing' argument that the origin of 'collective consciousness', and hence of religious conceptions, lay in crowd phenomena (the 'exaltation' or 'effervescence' of an assembly or congregation), though he accepted that this might provide 'the only scientifically admissible interpretation' of Durkheim's theory, since it allowed 'an atmosphere in which *individuals* create religious ideas'. 'These ideas are collective only insofar as they are general, i.e. common in all members of the crowd. Nonetheless, we arrive at understanding their nature by individual analysis, by psychological introspection, and not by treating those phenomena as "things".' The ultimate appeal to individual psychological explanation violated a principal tenet of Durkheim's own rules of sociological method: it was reductionist. Moreover, Malinowski pointed out, 'mental effervescence in large gatherings can hardly be accepted as the only source of religion'. Many other critics – among them A. A. Goldenweiser, E. S. Hartland, Pater Schmidt and Arnold Van Gennep – challenged Durkheim in similar terms; his overem-phasis on the social eclipsed the religious experience of individuals. While Malinowski accepted the crucially formative and mediating role of society in religion, he always gave full weight to private, individual experience. He declared that 'the strongest religious moments come in solitude, in turning away from the world, in concentration and mental detachment'.[41] Here he might have had in mind his own soul-searching in the Canaries or the Tatras, recalling as well, perhaps, his reading of William James's *The Varieties of Religious Experience* (1902).

Although Durkheim regarded the Arunta's *intichiuma* ceremonies as a key illustration of his theory of collective consciousness, Malinowski did not refer in his review to his own pragmatic, materialist interpretation of their significance. A more curious omission is any reference to Durkheim's functional, utilitarian and instrumental interpretation of religion, though Malinowski would certainly have broadly agreed with it. For Durkheim, function meant the contribution that an element or component of society made to the whole. The system of collective representations and ritual behaviour that constitutes any religion has both a cognitive (intellectual) and active (ritual) function, in that it renders the world intelligible and guides action towards morally ennobling ends. (The *moral* was always an important feature of Durkheim's sociology.) Thus the primary function of religion, according to Durkheim, was to provide 'a system of ideas with which the individuals represent to themselves the society of which they are members, and the obscure but intimate relations which they have with it'.[42] But again, the notion of reified society worshipping itself was for many anthropologists, in France as well as in Britain, too hard to swallow. Malinowski repeatedly attacked this aspect of Durkheim's sociology of religion in the years to come. 'Durkheim's theory is itself a somewhat mystical act of faith,' he wrote in 1935. 'He personified society himself, and he attributed this personification to primitive man.'[43]

Malinowski was unable to stomach the idea that all of *his* thoughts and feelings were implanted in him by Society. In the last footnote of his essay on Trobriand religion he announced that he was 'entirely out of touch with Professor Durkheim's philosophical basis of sociology' which invoked the untenable 'metaphysical postulate of a "collective soul"'. Since fieldwork involved the study of 'the whole aggregate of individual souls' he confidently dismissed the postulate of a collective consciousness as 'barren and absolutely useless for an ethnographical observer'.[44] This broadside against Durkheim won him favour with Frazer: 'I am pleased to see that you prick the bubble of the "collective consciousness" which has been blown to such a height by some French writers.'[45]

As 'a naïve realist', a pragmatist and – to borrow Max Weber's term – a methodological individualist, Malinowski quite understandably parted ways with Durkheim over the metaphysical character of the collective consciousness and the diminished role of individual psychology in sociology. Yet he continued, ambivalently perhaps, to acknowledge Durkheim's inspiration. In 1935 he made a somewhat self-contradictory claim that his own theory of culture 'consisted in reducing Durkheimian theory to terms of Behavioristic psychology'.[46] And in his very last statement on him, he attributed to Durkheim 'one of the fullest and most inspiring systems of sociology'.[47]

Durkheim's influence on Malinowski was most pertinent to the 'dilettante' stage of his anthropological career, from mid-1909 to early 1914, when he completed 'Primitive Beliefs and Forms of Social Organisation'. He then ceased to be an anthropologist of the armchair and everything he published thereafter bore the stamp of his New Guinea fieldwork. This four-year period of his library-based apprenticeship, it should be stressed, was continental-European as much as it was British. Although he spent longer in

England than in Poland during these years, he actually published more in Polish than in English.[48]

Autumn in Poland

In July 1913 Malinowski wrote again to Kazimierz Nitsch with a copy of Marett's review of his book on the Aboriginal family. It had appeared in *The Athenaeum*, 'one of the most reputable English publications', and Malinowski took care to mention that Robert Marett was Sir Edward B. Tylor's successor at Oxford. He was flippant about Marett's enthusiasm for his book, 'but yesterday, while I was in Oxford, he showed me the book all marked up – obviously he had read it!' He begged Nitsch 'for a little indulgence', for, 'of course, the book is quite unreadable – it's so utterly boring!' He also betrayed his diffidence by asking Nitsch to circulate Marett's review 'discreetly' within 'competent circles', before adding, 'maybe better not'. Malinowski then asked whether 'there is a shadow of hope' that the academy might publish his treatise on primitive religion. 'I am not so afraid of censorship, but (so my mother says) they are terribly slow to print.'[49] Nitsch's reply is lost, but it appears that the Jagiellonian University would not grant Malinowski's habilitation on the basis of unpublished works. Despite what he had told Nitsch in June, Malinowski had not yet completed his treatise and he worked on it intermittently for the rest of the year. The preface to 'Primitive Beliefs' was written in April 1914, the month that he delivered the work personally to the academy in Cracow.

Malinowski and his mother returned to Poland in August. He had invited the Boreniuses to visit them in Cracow and they duly arrived there after holidaying in Italy. Anna-Mi remembered that they stayed, at Malinowski's expense, in a pension where the guests, gentry and intellectuals, were served by a barefooted maid. 'Mali' showed them the sights of Wawel Castle and the Jewish ghetto of Kazimierz, where he teased children by pulling their plaits. Anna-Mi admonished him but he replied, 'They know I'm a friend of theirs.' Although he was not anti-Semitic, Anna-Mi thought he had that 'characteristic Polish consciousness of Jewishness'. She also recalled how, in the Sukiennice cloth market, he bargained jokingly with the Jewish women in their cumbersome cow-hair wigs until their husbands protested that he had no intention of buying anything and chased him away.[50]

It was also during August that Staś Witkiewicz held his first one-man exhibition in Cracow, presenting some eighty landscapes and other compositions.[51] The portraits he had done of Malinowski the previous year would have been among them. Staś now signed himself Witkacy, a contraction of his second and last names. He had recently become engaged to Jadwiga Janczewska, the daughter of a Minsk lawyer; she was 'pretty and attractive, intelligent and well-read', but 'hypersensitive and neurotic'.[52] Although 'he loved her deeply and sincerely', Staś toyed with her. In his biographer's view: 'The demanding and rapacious Witkacy harassed his fiancée with scenes of jealousy (for example about Karol Szymanowski), rapid changes of mood and the "strangeness of surroundings" in which, according to eyewitness accounts, the sensitive though provincial girl "could not differentiate between truth and mystification".'[53]

Wilful mystification was a stock-in-trade of Staś, and his reading of Frazer ran against the grain of Malinowski's. He studied his friend's essay for *Lud* and read his manuscript of 'Primitive Beliefs'. They would have discussed Frazer's theories, as they discussed everything in their 'essential conversations', sometimes with boisterous good humour, sometimes heatedly to the point of quarrelling. Staś felt an affinity for Frazer's theories of magic and religion – *The Golden Bough* provided ideas for several of his plays – and his take on totemism was wildly at variance with Malinowski's. For Staś the source of religion lay in 'metaphysical feelings'. Religion being moribund in the twentieth century, it was the function of art to transmit intimations of 'the mystery of existence'.[54] The 'primitive' beliefs that Frazer and later Malinowski tried to comprehend in scientific terms were for Witkiewicz to be understood symbolically as an attempt to grasp 'the strangeness of life and of existence in general'.

In his play *The Metaphysics of a Two-Headed Calf* (1921), Witkiewicz wove together a number of themes from Frazer and Malinowski and transmuted them into a bizarre fantasy. He dramatized totemism as the religious principle, a conduit for the mysterious forces of life and death, and used the concept to pose fundamental questions of identity: 'Who am I?' (or, as an illegitimate character in the play was anxious to discover, 'Who is my father?'). When another character asks what is the cause of the 'atrocious mess' that is the contemporary family, the clan chief Aparura replies (with a distant echo of Freud): 'If it weren't for our totems. . . . your so-called civilization wouldn't exist. . . . It does not matter that Malinowski, this damned

Anglicized, uncontrollable dreamer, has investigated us. Totems are true. No matter what scientists write about them.'[55]

Witkiewicz profoundly disagreed with his friend's understanding of religion. He maintained that the 'pragmatic fallacy' undercut living belief, as demonstrated in his play *The Pragmatists* with its parody of the spiritually destitute empiricism of the scientific mind as personified by Malinowski. The 'cash value' of religious beliefs regarded as pragmatically rewarding was for Witkiewicz a false coin. And he would have been contemptuous of the Platonic noble lie with which Malinowski concluded his Riddell Lectures in 1935: 'The rationalist and agnostic must admit that even if he himself cannot accept these [eternal truths which have guided mankind out of barbarism to culture], he must at least recognise them as indispensable pragmatic figments without which civilization cannot exist.'[56]

During this visit to Cracow, Malinowski took another tilt at evolutionism when, in late October, he read a paper to an academy audience on the topic of his still-uncompleted book.[57] He picked up two problems at the precise point he had left them in the third part of his *Lud* essay: first, how to define the essence of totemism; second, what is its genesis? The questions were linked, such that one had to be answered in the light of the other. Totemism, he showed, is not a discrete institution but 'a set of heterogeneous and loosely connected' religious and social phenomena. Sociologically, it is a system of beliefs that differentiates a tribe into a number of smaller groups, or totemic clans, and simultaneously integrates them into a whole. On the genesis of totemism, Malinowski offered an essentially psychological explanation: 'religious ideas arise everywhere that man acts and thinks under the influence of strong emotional factors.' The appeal to higher powers is a response to man's perception that he is unable to control reality unaided. 'Animals and plants play a more or less equivalent role as food objects' which 'acquire a religious significance as a result of the economic activities aimed at obtaining them.' Generalized as species, animals 'become the subject of strong emotional experiences, and as a consequence of this the subject of religious ideas'. From these assertions, Malinowski slipped easily towards the conclusion that totemism is a type of zoolatry, a 'special form of man's attitude towards his environment'. What distinguishes totemism from other kinds of zoolatry is a particular kind of social organization comprising clans that independently celebrate, and separately taboo, different totems. The unity of the system, 'the coordination of the separate beliefs into a whole, lies only in its social aspect', that is, in the functional relationship between the component clans of a tribe. Thus, he concluded, it is necessary to investigate primitive beliefs and social differentiation 'in parallel', for only 'by juxtaposing the two aspects can we comprehend the essence of primitive religion'.

This, in brief, is the subject of the book he wrote in Polish during 1913, bringing to bear everything he had read and already written on the subject of totemism and the genesis of religion. He disavowed the fruitless search for origins and refused to answer the question: which came first, the totem or the clan? He concluded with a Machian allusion to a scientific method 'which will take on the task of achieving maximum results with a minimum of effort and risk': 'The passing of ethnology to a phase where speculation must reckon more and more with the toilsome collecting and comparing of facts and be satisfied with partial and modest, yet certain, results, seems to be a necessary result of the development of this science.' One can almost hear in this prophetic statement the faint call of his own destiny as a methodologically disciplined fieldworker. One may reflect, too, that this was the last occasion he would address his Cracovian teachers and colleagues before embarking on a scientific venture that was so far beyond their own experience that they would scarcely be able to comprehend his achievement.

By the end of October Malinowski was in Dresden 'admiring the paintings and enjoying the beer'.[58] There he met up with Annie Brunton, who had been travelling in Germany.[59] He read his lectures to her, practising for the course he was soon to give at the LSE. 'I think it is wonderful that you should be able to give those lectures in English after so short a time in England,' Annie wrote later.[60] By the beginning of November they were back in London, where Malinowski resumed his official address of 16 Fitzroy Street.

Commencing on Tuesday 11 November 1913, at 5 p.m., Dr Bronislaw Malinowski delivered a course of six weekly lectures on 'Primitive Religion and Social Differentiation'. The synopsis in the *L.S.E. Calendar* promised an exploration of the 'connection between the forms of creed and the forms of social organisation' by examining the 'social functions and features of the totemic clan'.[61] It was 'the essence of totemism' that Malinowski would seek to define. 'My lectures went on quite all right,' he told Westermarck. 'I had in the average twelve hearers.'[62] 'Twelve is a good number,' replied Westermarck encouragingly, 'especially when disciples are concerned.'[63] Transcripts or drafts of these lectures have not survived, but it is clear that they were based on his Polish work-in-progress and on his essay for *Lud*. It is possible that Frazer and his wife were in the audience.

Fieldwork prospects

Meanwhile, Malinowski's academic patrons had been lobbying behind the scenes to find him funding for fieldwork. His own role in this delicate process appears to have been that of a bemused bystander, for nothing resembling a research proposal has survived. Haddon, Seligman and Marett each played a significant part and, together with Rivers, they seem to have persuaded Malinowski that he should work in Melanesia. Rivers would have favoured the Solomons or the New Hebrides; Haddon and Seligman, New Guinea. The main initiative in the search for funding was Seligman's. He conceived of Malinowski's fieldwork as a follow-up study to fill some of the gaps left by his own 1903–04 expedition to British New Guinea. This in turn had been a geographical extension of the Torres Strait expedition of 1898–99. Thus, according to Seligman's plan, Malinowski would follow in a direct line of recent British anthropological tradition. To Haddon, the doyen of Melanesian anthropology, Malinowski expressed great enthusiasm for the idea of working in New Guinea (just as, eighteen months earlier, he had expressed great enthusiasm to Seligman concerning fieldwork in the Sudan). To an impartial Westermarck, who had no stake in Melanesia, he betrayed some diffidence.

On 17 November Malinowski wrote to Haddon in his usual unctuous manner, thanking him for his help in securing a travel grant of £100 from the British Association.

> I know quite well that . . . it is exclusively through your recommendation and you can measure my feelings of gratitude by the keenness with which I wanted to go out [to Australia]. . . . I spoke already with Rivers and Seligmann about my prospects, but I hope I shall be happy enough to get your advices [sic] on the subject and I hope still more – namely that I shall make my first steps on New Guinea in the field of ethnographic research under your personal patronage.[64]

Seligman, 'pleased with all that is being done for Malinowski', wrote to Haddon a week later. He had 'just managed to extract a promise of £250' for Malinowski from a philanthropic industrialist, Robert Mond, who sat on one of the LSE committees and took a keen interest in ethnology. Seligman had also sounded the possibility of a Constance Hutchinson Scholarship, worth £200. As he told Haddon: 'I think this [£450] ought to last him for very nearly two years work. He told me he was prepared to spend that amount of time in the field if I could raise the money.'[65]

Marett, too, would later claim credit for getting Malinowski to Australia. Remembering him as 'a close friend, even if he was in no sense my pupil', Marett recalled how, as recorder of Section H of the British Association, he needed a secretary for the 1914 congress. The Australian government would find his travelling expenses. With the relish of a raconteur, Marett explained: 'Thereupon that brilliant pupil of mine, Miss M. A. Czaplicka . . . besought me to assist her compatriot that he might see with his own eyes those of the Antipodes about whom he had hitherto known from books alone.'[66] Yet it was with muted enthusiasm that Malinowski wrote to Westermarck just before Christmas: 'If I get some more money I'll go afterwards some-where to Melanesia (probably New Guinea) & do some fieldwork. I'll start in June – so I'll still see you, to which I am very much looking forward. I see Wheeler very often & he seems to be much better-spirited this year.'[67]

Malinowski, too, was better-spirited at the end of the year than he had been in January. He had made a mark with his book, his reviews and his lectures, thereby strengthening his position in British anthropology. He was now less marginal. His patrons and mentors had rallied round and he had been deemed worthy of British funding for fieldwork. Although it would have had no impact in England, his demolition of Frazer's theories and methods in *Lud* represented a subtle psychological victory, an Oedipal con-quest of a powerful patriarch – the very one (if Malinowski is to be believed) who had fathered his anthropological vocation. Things even looked more hopeful on the home front. He had gratified his mother and almost com-pleted his habilitation thesis, and he had met his compatriot hero Joseph Conrad. Across this rosy picture, however, fell the shadow of another drain-ing love affair with a married woman.

Chapter 13

Tośka

'An incomparable mistress'

The beautiful, twenty-four-year-old Polish woman who took Malinowski
to visit Conrad one morning in late 1913 meant a great deal more to him
than simply a literary go-between. They met in the spring of that year,
pursued a clandestine affair in London, Cracow and Zakopane, broke it off
at least twice and finally parted in June 1914. They do not appear to have
met again, though for several years after their separation she haunted Malinowski's dreams as his erotic ideal. Memories of this 'incomparable mistress'
were evoked whenever he opened a novel by Conrad.[1] On reading *Romance*,
for example, during his first anxious and unsettled days on Mailu Island in
November 1914, he wrote in his diary:

> The subtle spirit of Conrad comes through in some passages. . . . I still
> think about and am in love with T. It is not a desperate love; the feeling
> that I had lost creative value, the basic element of the self, as happened
> with Ż[enia]. It is the magic of her body that still fills me, and the poetry
> of her presence.[2]

On scrutinizing a photograph he had taken of her in London:

> The sight of the sadness in her face – perhaps still in love? – filled me with
> painful dejection. It reminds me of the mood in the black-papered room,
> that dark afternoon, when the husband found us in the end and she could
> not go out with me. . . . I see in her face the embodiment of the femi-
> nine ideal. Once again she is immensely, indescribably close to me.[3]

Identified as 'T' in the early part of his 1914 diary, Malinowski slips gradually into the use of 'Tośka'. Just once, he offers a clue with 'Retingerka',

another with 'T. R.'.[4] But never does he commit to his diary her full name. As it was she who introduced Malinowski to Joseph Conrad, it is fitting to allow the novelist to introduce Tośka. He knew her as Madame Otolia ('Tola') Retinger, née Zubrzycka. Her mother owned a country estate to the north of Cracow in Russian Poland, and it was she who invited the Conrads to stay there in July 1914. Conrad had been introduced to Tola's husband, Józef Hieronim Retinger, in November 1912 by the novelist Arnold Bennett. Soon after meeting them, Conrad described Tola as 'the very type of Polish country girl' and Józef as 'a young literary man with brains'; by that time they had been married for ten months.[5] Tola's portrait photograph (paired with Józef's in Najder's biography of Conrad) shows a wanly pretty young woman with hair worn fashionably short at the neck. Her dark brows are slightly raised above soulful eyes.

Józef Retinger was born in Cracow four years after Malinowski. The son of a lawyer, Retinger trained in law at the Jagiellonian before taking a doctorate in French literature at the Sorbonne. He had come to London with his wife to open an information bureau dedicated to the Polish Question, and it was Retinger who revived Conrad's dormant passion for his homeland. Like Malinowski, he was a brilliant talker, a man of great intelligence and personal charm. Subsequently, he led a colourful career as a wartime diplomat, spy and military adventurer.[6]

The American writer Katherine Anne Porter (best known for her 1931 novel *Ship of Fools*) had an affair with Retinger in Mexico in 1923. She thought he was the most attractive man she had ever met, despite 'a gaunt physique' and 'somewhat simian face'.[7] Porter's biographer suspected Retinger of being 'a less than passionate lover' who 'preferred intrigue and complicated situations'.[8] This might explain his seemingly complaisant attitude towards Malinowski in 1913–14. With his affinity for amatory triangles, Malinowski would have provided enough intrigue and passion for any couple.

Retinger was himself a victim and purveyor of mediated desire, and at the time he was Porter's lover he was miserably in love with her rival, the 'vivacious and reckless' journalist Jane Anderson. This beautiful American woman had stayed with the Conrads in 1916 while recovering from an illness. Joseph Conrad was captivated, and he used her as his principal model for the seductive heroine of *Arrow of Gold* (1919).[9] Conrad's son Borys, ten years younger than Anderson, also succumbed in Paris the following year, when Retinger, too, fell for her, irreparably damaging his friendship with the infuriated novelist. Although the Conrads' marriage survived Jane Anderson, the Retingers' did not. According to Retinger's biographer, the marriage had broken down by the end of 1917, despite Tola having given birth to a daughter that summer.[10] It is perhaps nothing more than a coincidence that the infant was named Malina Wanda. Divorce followed a few years later. In view of these overlapping and replicating triangles it is diverting to learn more about the love affair that Malinowski had with Retinger's wife.

Conceivably, he derived the name Tośka from Tola, though it is likely that it was also consciously borrowed from the tragic heroine of Puccini's opera, for the first time he used it in his diary he spelt it the Italian way, 'Tosca'. She worked regularly in the British Museum – probably as a research assistant for her husband – where Malinowski frequently sought her out. The early stages of their relationship can only be surmised from Malinowski's remorseful reminiscences, and the hopeless affair was bordering on disintegration by the time he recommenced his diary in mid-April 1914. Tośka had tried to end it, but, in a manner reminiscent of his affair with Żenia, Malinowski was loathe to let her go. The die was cast with regard to Australia; he would leave in June to be there in time for the British Association meetings in August. He thought, or rather hoped, that he could keep Tośka until his departure. Yet with characteristic ambivalence he also wanted to break with her, and his inability to do so engendered resentment towards the cause of his suffering.

As much can be learned about Tola alias Tośka through her friendship with the Conrads as through her fraught affair with Malinowski. In letters to her husband, Conrad expressed tender concern for her pregnancy.[11] While Retinger devoted an entire book – lively but factually unreliable – to his reminisences of Conrad, Tola's memoir is a brief article, published under her maiden name.[12] A straightforward, even ingenuous piece of reportage, it adds a few touches to the heroic myth of Conrad. Tola does not mention her then husband, though her occasional use of 'we' indicates his presence. She describes Capel House, Conrad's rambling, moated farmhouse at Orlestone, as 'small' and 'very modest' – inappropriate adjectives that betray the exalted standards of Polish gentry. Concerning Conrad himself, she was struck by his 'Polish looks, eyes, voice, borderland accent'. Her own English was so poor, she admits, that she found it difficult to follow Jessie Conrad's 'soft and indistinct pronunciation'. (She would have conversed with Malinowski mainly in Polish, though interestingly he mentions that they spoke English when they were together in Poland.) On one occasion – Malinowski's diary suggests it was during May 1914 – the Conrads accepted Tola's invitation to visit the Retingers' home in London. The reclusive Conrad visited London as little as possible, so it was a small victory. What she describes as their 'apartment' appears to have been a two-storey maisonette. On the evidence of Malinowski's diary it was located in England's Lane in the affluent suburb of Belsize Park.[13]

A few minutes' walk away is Primrose Hill, where Malinowski liked to stroll and cogitate. There was 'always a sort of casting off of the yoke there', he noted on one occasion. His diary recalls how he went there on the last Saturday of January after he and Tośka had broken up for the second time. Alone that chilly night on Primrose Hill, he was happy to be released, 'overflowing with strength and joy, with a feeling of freedom and creativity', absolutely determined that he would not go back to her.

Farewell to Annie

The previous spring, as he walked through the squares of Bloomsbury to Annie's rooms, he had 'felt the vernal mood of awakening love'. Annie suspected something, but Malinowski kept his secret from her. When he returned to Poland with his mother in August, Tośka was already there, probably without her husband. It was with painful remorse that Malinowski remembered that summer in Cracow and 'how with crude sensuality' he had treated her 'like a cocotte' . He had made love to her in Olcza, too, on 10 September 1913 – a night he would recall from the lonely distance of Papua.[14] 'I took her, as one takes an easy and cheap conquest. I did not then have a sense of wrong-doing.' There was a penalty for this soulless seduction. As he moralized in his diary: 'I was unblushingly and criminally insouciant. I am paying for it now; one may not be a greater swine than one has a right to be. Intellectual depravity is not a passport. Ethics answer certain needs of the emotional life which one may not libertinize.'[15] When he returned to London that November after meeting Annie in Dresden, he felt remorse for her too, and also for Żenia: 'a deep despondency' about his ' "ill-spent" life'.

On 31 January 1914, however, Malinowski was glad to have broken with Tośka, and it was precisely one week later that Annie sailed for South Africa.

Annie was dutifully returning to be with her ailing mother, but she felt profoundly unhappy at leaving Malinowski, a parting that she knew might be definitive. Her first shipboard letter is filled with poignant memories of their final moments on the lower deck, where they had stolen their last kiss. Annie watched the Isle of Wight fall astern in the gathering darkness:

> I felt that all that made my life worth living was going with it . . . I watched you to the last too . . . & long after I was lost to your view, I could still recognize you, standing there with your attache [sic] case in one hand & your handkerchief in the other. . . . with your turned down hat, your green overcoat hunched up around your neck. . . . You have come to me so often like that sweetheart − it is quite your most typical outdoor appearance − & I love it.[16]

Crossing the Bay of Biscay the next day, Annie played the piano for an hour, thinking of Malinowski all the while. She now regretted her hasty departure. By overriding her sense of duty, she might have stayed a few months longer. But she was uncertain whether he would have really wanted her to stay. She ended the letter as her ship approached Tenerife. From there she sent a box of grapes to his new London address at 6 Mecklenburgh Street.

In the Lent Term, beginning on 17 February, Malinowski delivered a course of six lectures on social psychology. The syllabus in the L.S.E. *Calendar* promised an analysis of 'psychological explanations in sociology'.[17] He would have presented his critiques of Frazer, Rivers and Durkheim, and doubtless have elaborated his own ideas on introspective psychology as he had recently argued them in his Polish monograph. Annie's sympathetic glosses on his self-criticisms are the only surviving comments on his course:

> I am delighted that your second lecture was such a success & that in spite of the former one being less good your number of listeners had not decreased. It must have been very embarrassing not to be able to give the examples asked for of Hegel's ideas on Philosophy of History.[18]

Immediately after his last lecture on Tuesday 17 March, Malinowski took the train to Windsor, where he spent the night with Tośka. There followed a period of passionate intensity which he would dwell upon ruefully in the future: 'In my mind's eye, I go over and over the moments at Windsor and after my return, my complete certainty and feeling of security. My serious plans, made several times, for living with her permanently.'[19] But soon enough they quarrelled and another gulf opened between them. Five months later, when he was in Port Moresby, this break still seemed extremely painful, 'a sudden transition from bright sunlight to deep shadow'.[20] The emotionally charged sites of their bitter rows are recorded in his diary: Primrose Hill, St Pancras Station, Earl's Court skating rink. He took a portion of the blame, recalling his 'growling, contemptuous mood' at a Beethoven concert, and his 'stupid, malicious' remarks to her in his mother's presence.[21]

As she sailed on, Annie complained of the dullness of the voyage. Whenever dances were held on board she wondered how Malinowski was getting on with his tango lessons. This raunchy dance from the bordellos of Buenos Aires had reached London in 1913, and he had been eager to learn it. 'Who is the most graceful dancer – after you?' Annie asked. 'You seemed to me to pick it up much quicker than those other men.'[22] Malinowski did have the knack of mastering dances, displaying a sinuous physical grace that women found appealing. Anna-Mi Borenius remembered how 'madly fond' of dancing he was. He told her: 'The tango is so wonderful, you can dance it on all fours.'[23]

By the beginning of March Annie was back at home in East London in South Africa. Malinowski had written to her from Ventnor, where he had gone immediately after bidding her farewell. She recalled how he had once terrified her in Ventnor by scrambling recklessly across a crumbling cliff-face: 'As long as I live darling there will be someone who will care for & be anxious for you – & who would scold you if necessary for doing careless risky things. . . . Parting has its compensations, it shows one the depth of one's affections.'[24] His letter referred to a concert he had been to after her departure, and she commented with a hint of reproach: 'We had no opportunity this time when I was in London of hearing music together – & it always brought us so much into touch with each other.' As if mindful of his suspected infidelities, she continued:

> Niusiu darling, don't conceal anything from me for fear of hurting me.
> . . . There is nothing else you can write about to interest me more, even
> if it is of your dancing (or flirting) or both with someone else. . . . when
> I am parted from you like this, my love is much more unselfish than
> when I am nearer or with you. For then I feel I have certain rights &
> privileges & I want to kill anyone who I feel is wresting these from me.

Malinowski wrote to Annie twice during the latter part of February, and her replies indicate that his letters were in the form of a diary and far from perfunctory. Being enamoured of someone else did not prevent him from missing Annie's consoling presence, and he appears to have written from a genuine desire to keep alive the flame of friendship. Their use of this word raised its meaning to a higher power. As Annie wrote: 'friendship is not a trifle to promise anyone – it has obligations as well as love – don't forget that my friend. I shall always be proud of your friendship, & grateful too – & need hardly tell you that you can count on me for always.'[25] Annie's friendship for Malinowski ('love' is certainly more fitting in her case) was that of a woman who had turned forty. It was a mature and unwavering love that extended to thoughtful gestures like writing to his mother and being concerned about whether he was eating properly. She wanted to give her own letters the form of a diary too, but her days were too mindlessly dull to document. She offered him a sample:

> The whole day today it has rained. . . . I started to do some mending & I found that all my clothes were needing it so badly. So I just sat the whole live-long day & sewed on buttons, & darned. In the evening I helped Mother with some business papers. . . . And this is the sum total of what I have to record.[26]

Malinowski would have smiled on reading this. Annie clearly didn't get the point, and later, in similar circumstances, he would reproach Elsie Masson for recording mere 'externals'. Subjective states provided the only grist for an intimate correspondence or an intimate journal.

Annie responded to a mention of Rivers with a brief disquisition on Malinowski's health and a sly dig at his hypochondria.

> I am so glad that Dr Rivers . . . doesn't think the climate of Melanesia will be dangerous to your health. – And I think you will take the reasonable precautions necessary to guard against severe attacks of malaria. You are not quite sane on the subject of food, [but] if it be necessary to take quinine or to dose yourself in any way, it will be entirely to your taste, for you love that kind of thing, don't you sweetheart.[27]

Although she had been home for several weeks, Annie had not yet opened her piano. Her mother was still grieving for Annie's brother, who had died the previous year. Discouraged from exercising her only talent, Annie was pathetically bored:

I wish I had the education to enjoy some sort of deep reading that would make me concentrate on something. . . . I would like to understand something about astronomy for instance but it is such a difficult thing to take up . . . when you are in Australia we can be looking at the same stars and perhaps I will learn to recognize them.

There was nothing artful in Annie's candour. She was simply stating a dismal truth about herself:

Don't laugh at me about this – I am frightfully ignorant & I know it, & the 'bigness' of every subject always makes me afraid to tackle it, & then I am so ashamed of my stupidity that I don't like to ask for help so as not to betray myself. . . . I dread getting older & older and having no real interest except my music to occupy me – & perhaps not being able to play any more & then spending my life reading novels.[28]

It says something about Malinowski that he had cherished this self-confessedly 'ignorant' and 'stupid' woman to the degree that he did. He thrived on intellectual challenge and thrilled to women, such as Żenia, whose minds he could regard as the equal of his own. He was also an elitist, inclined to be dismissive of inferior, uncultivated intellects. Yet he seems to have overlooked such deficiencies in Annie, the woman with whom he had shared an intimate domesticity for a longer period than with any other except his mother.

Easter in Ventnor

'The sky clear, the sea calm; a happy, peaceful mood. . . . On the whole in recent days a strong tide [of energy], after a long period of floundering on the shoal.'[29] On this sunny seaside note Malinowski resumed his diary on Easter Sunday, 12 April 1914, a few days after his thirtieth birthday. He was writing in Ventnor, the small resort town improbably situated in a shallow fold of the terraced chalk cliffs that form the southern coast of the Isle of Wight. A winter retreat for the tubercular and weak-chested (Karl Marx had regained his health there), Ventnor boasts the sunniest aspect in the British Isles. The town rises in tiers like a theatre auditorium, its stage the sea. Its sunshine and scenery, its reputation as the English Madeira, its seascaped island character, appealed strongly to Malinowski. He had visited the place at least twice before, with Annie in 1910, then after she had left for South Africa. This time he had for company his mother and one or two other Polish women. 'I can't fancy you going on holiday with a party of people like that,' Annie wrote. 'I can imagine there would be much that would be trying to you – but it was nice of you to go for your Mother's sake especially as it would be the last holiday you will spend with her for some time to come.'[30]

By a happy coincidence, Malinowski's review of Hutton Webster's *Rest Days* had just been published.[31] He had read it in the light of Karl Bücher's ideas and augmented Webster's thesis – that among primitive peoples rest days were periods of abstinence sanctioned by 'superstitions' – by pointing out the function of holidays in 'shaping, regulating, and framing' economic activities. He alluded to his own pet theme: the significant part ('hitherto almost entirely ignored') that magic and religion have played in man's economic evolution.

Malinowski began his diary not to commemorate Annie but rather to explore the complications of his affair with Tośka. The proximity of the sea was perhaps an unconscious stimulus (he also began 'island' diaries in Breña Baja and Samarai). But whatever the unarticulated incentive to examine his life in this fashion, once begun, the diary continued for a time under its own internal momentum.[32]

The optimism with which he began was soon dispelled by some introspective scratching, and he revisited his unresolved dilemma of the antinomy between work and love. Although he does not name her at this point, it is Tośka who lurks beneath his ruminations concerning 'the problem of a genuine relationship with a woman'.

> Physical love produces a strain of the emotions and a longing of the soul, which leads to awful conflicts, to the extent that the egos are internally impermeable. Constant struggle, concealed explosions of hatred and artificial attempts at creating something from the void. . . . The conscious renunciation of higher things, reassuring oneself that one cannot find anything ideal in life. Searching for 'a woman and child'. And then the silent sorrow, ressentment [sic] and the axiom that 'one expects a miracle in love'.

Returning to consider his present limbo in Ventnor, he found himself floundering again. Walking to Sheephill Cove he marvelled at the colours of the ebb-tide, how 'the brown stones wallow in the blue sea and take on warm, violet hues'. 'I sense the emptiness of the present; I am neither by myself nor with anyone. Life appears to me as shallow water, though which I work my way with difficulty, unable either to submerge or to extricate myself.' His peevish mood sat oddly with his appreciation of the seascape. 'A peculiar seaside despondency takes hold of me; I know it well from the islands. The sea breathes a void filled with promises; the inexorability of its vastness attracts and disenchants.' While on another undercliff walk he became one with the scene. Sensations of 'merging with the landscape' were for Malinowski a form of religious experience. 'I stand on a big mossy rock and experience a metaphysical fusion with my surroundings. . . . My elation evokes the strong need of ascertaining the reality of that which I have in front of me.' He was reminded of the Buddhist concept of nirvana 'as the killing of oneself though a spiritual fusion with nature', the only form of 'rational suicide'.

One warm spring evening in London a few weeks later, after tiring himself with gymnastics, he experienced another epiphany: a 'metaphysical vision', a submission to fate, a dissolution of self. 'Such moments are genuinely religious,' he wrote, recalling how his friend Tadzio Szymberski had likened them to 'a conversation with God'.

He was putting the finishing touches to his Polish book on primitive religion. Only now did he see to what extent it was 'a document of ignorance', but he was utterly convinced that (contra Frazer and other intellectualists) magico-religious phenomena had an emotional, ultimately biological, source.

> Man, especially primitive man who lives in a constant struggle for survival, cannot be and is not a reasonable and reasoning being. . . . His life is mainly emotional and active, full of emotions and passions, and it is these elements that shape his whole behaviour, and not philosophical reflection. . . . Primitive man has urgent strong needs, constant, sometimes dangerous, vital pursuits, and it is easy to show that these very elements lead him to the performance of such acts and activities which constitute a germ of religion.[33]

Under the pressure of emotion, primitive man crosses the boundaries of logic and empirical knowledge and enters 'the realm of faith'. Thus do magic and religion help to resolve the uncertainty of achieving desired practical ends. Here, playing through Malinowski's mind in Ventnor, was the essence of his mature theory of magic and religion, only fully developed after he had completed his Trobriands fieldwork.

He derived 'a certain constructional enjoyment' from making the final corrections to his manuscript and the work filled some of the emptiness that troubled his stay in Ventnor. He was baffled by the sheer difficulty of self-improvement. His 'theoretical interventions' in life had not been notably successful, and the goal seemed as distant as ever. Yet he believed he was right to continue the 'permanent, pertinacious, systematic' supervision of himself. Now, for example, he should distance himself from his feelings for Tośka to allow them to 'burn out completely'. But there were times when he wished she would return to him − if only so that he could 'leave handsomely'. This betrayed a wounded pride, for she had rejected him. The pattern of his response to the loss of Żenia was being repeated with respect to Tośka.

'You fool about too much'

A distraught letter from Staś Witkiewicz awaited Malinowski on his return to London. Indeed, his own aggravations and anxieties at this time were as nothing compared to those of his friend in Zakopane, whose fiancée had committed suicide. On 21 February, Jadwiga Janczewska had gone to the foot of a cliff in Koscielisko, laid a bouquet of flowers at her side, and had then shot herself. Her theatrical death, apparently the result of some triangular intrigue involving Karol Szymanowski, plunged Staś into remorseful despair.[34] He had written to Malinowski with the news at the end of February:

> Much that has taken place since the beginning of the year is my fault. I was deeply troubled, she thought it was her doing, and as a result things occurred that, given the fatal web of circumstances, led her to such a step. If it weren't for Mother, I would long since have ceased to be amongst the living.[35]

For months he would remain inconsolable, feeling that everything had 'come to an absolute dead end'. He told Malinowski: 'For me you are the sole bright point in the world other than my parents.' Annie commiserated from South Africa, and suggested Malinowski persuade Staś to accompany him to Australia. 'A complete change of scene & surroundings would be the best thing for him.'[36] The idea had already occurred to Malinowski.

In an undated letter in March, Staś wrote again in even deeper despair. By then Malinowski had written to him with his rescue plan. Staś clutched at it, offering his services on the expedition as a 'photographer and draftsman'.

> Only the thought of traveling with you to some savage country offers any hope. A change so radical that everything would be turned upside down. . . . But these are only ways of dulling the pain. Death is within me wherever I am, and it's not dependent any more on memories or on places. Only death can cure me.[37]

Malinowski was not too hopeful, noting in his diary on 19 April: 'I realized that this was already, perhaps, the end of him.'

He was soon complaining again that London did not agree with him. Trying to keep thoughts of Tośka at bay, he was beset by an 'undifferentiated concupiscence'. He now suspected that she was not such a fine person to love after all, and that she was therefore unworthy of him. Such saving doubts had helped to cure him of Żenia. Was she worth pursuing more resolutely, or should he continue to accept her rejection and call it quits? He sought her in the Reading Room, sometimes speaking lightly to her, sometimes simply watching her from a distance. When she wasn't there, he fell into 'a state of wild collapse'. His pride was also damaged. He had 'begged for mercy' when she broke off their affair, and still hoped that she would return. It was 'a hope fed chiefly by self-love'. Yet it bitterly amused him that he was engaged in this struggle with a woman who was more of an absence than a presence in his life, but one who was also paralysing his capabilities. 'Now I understand clearly why woman is a symbol of evil, of destruction, of man's undermining. This is a struggle for independence; a struggle between a truly creative man and a quiet member of the herd.' One might easily suppose that Malinowski was a raving misogynist.

In an outburst of unselfish love, Annie wrote to him about her concern for his gloomy moods.

> I would much rather you were in a whirl of gaiety . . . I wish that a deep tender love for some worthy woman would come into your heart. . . . I

1. Lucjan Malinowski.

2. Józefa Łącka.

3. Józefa Malinowska and baby Bronio, *c.* 1885.

4. Schoolboy Bronio in gymnasium uniform, *c.* 1895.

5. Józefa Malinowska and Bronio in a Bedouin camp. North Africa, *c.* 1904.

6. Malinowski in Algeria, *c.* 1904.

7. Malinowski and his mother, c. 1906.

8. Bronislaw Kasper Malinowski following the award of his doctorate. Cracow, 7 November 1908.

9. Stanisław Witkiewicz with his son Stanisław Ignacy Witkiewicz. Lovran, 1913.

10. Staś Witkiewicz, Helena Biedrzycka and Bronisław Malinowski. Zakopane, 1911.

11. Zofia Dembowska.

12. A. C. Haddon (*seated*) with (*left to right*) W. H. R. Rivers, C. G. Seligmann, S. Ray and A. Wilkin. Mabuiag, Torres Strait, 1898.

13. Seligmann taking notes in Hula, Central Division. British New Guinea, 1898.

(*left*) 14. Edward Westermarck.

15. Sir James Frazer, *c.* 1914.

16. Otolia Retinger, née Zubrzycka.

17. Joseph Conrad and
Karola Zagórska.
'Oswalds', Kent,
summer 1920.

18. 'The fear of life in
Malinowski', 1912.
Charcoal drawing (lost)
by Staś Witkiewicz.

19. David Orme Masson at his lecture bench. University of Melbourne, 1913.

20. Baldwin Spencer, *c.* 1913.

21. Elsie Masson, Marnie Masson and Mim Weigall (*seated*). Melbourne, *c.* 1908.

22. The Mission house on Mailu Island, 1916.

23. Mailu dancers.

24. Resting dancers at a *soi* feast in Suau.

wish you could marry, & marry the right woman, darling – but you fool about too much. . . . Of course, now you are going out into the wilds of Australia it is doubtless out of the question, but you will have many new interests there I hope & will come through bravely.

Infected by Staś's despair, suicide had been a topic in his last letter to her. Annie admonished him soundly.

To talk of suicide & to express an admiration for it is ridiculous – it requires great courage certainly but for a gifted being like you with his whole life in front of him it is wicked. . . . Whilst alive you may yet rise to great heights. . . . Of course I know that because of your greater intellectuality you feel more keenly, whereas it takes very much less to satisfy and please me – but nevertheless I do feel how much I have missed all along the line. There is nothing that could give me keener joy than to know that you were really happy, & I shouldn't feel a spark of jealousy for the woman who brought you happiness. But I do feel jealous about some of your frivolous pretences at love, especially if you are perhaps thereby causing unhappiness to others – the Tacha (is that the way to spell it?) type of flirtation I mean.[38]

Annie obviously had Tośka in mind, though unless she was being extremely tactful she seems to have been unaware that it was more than a flirtation. She was worried, too, about the prospect of Malinowski's letters becoming infrequent after his departure from England. Like all lovers, she feared that she would be unable to imagine his life once his journey had begun.

Unhappy returns

Helped by his mother, Malinowski made the final revisions to his manuscript and on 22 April he left London for Poland, ostensibly to deliver his book to the academy in Cracow, but also to visit his suicidal friend in Zakopane. The journey to Folkestone reminded him of the time he and Tośka had visited Joseph Conrad. Train journeys seemed to increase the operatic intensity of his suffering.

I look out of the window at the Thames. . . . I shut my eyes . . . I see her more and more clearly as she comes with reproach in her face and stands before me; a vision born of pain and longing; I feel her presence physically. In my ears the motif of hopeless pain from Parsival [sic] rings continually. . . . Tearful regret. I do not even have the clear certainty that I shall not return [to her].

At Ashford, the station where they would have alighted for Orlestone and Capel House, he remembered her, 'a little sparrow – in that hat with a feather', and the resonance of Conrad's voice in French.

The hallucinatory memories of Tośka eclipsed anything he may have wished to recall about conversing with his literary hero. It seems all the more theatrical, then, that he was reading a Conrad story during this ride through Kent. 'The Return' (1897) is an intense psychological drama about the abrupt collapse of a hypocritical bourgeois marriage. The estranged wife of the tale tries, but fails, to leave her husband for another man; the incredulous husband, unable to bear the betrayal of his belief in her 'idealized perfection', leaves her instead. Malinowski pronounced the story 'a prodigious thing'. Ruminating bitterly as he was on his broken affair with Tośka, he could scarcely have failed to notice a complicitous echo of Conrad's plot.

The smiling spring landscape of Holland was discordant with his dark mood, though he captured both in his diary: 'The fruit trees in flower, the forests, meadows – everything so marvellously green, everything raging and rigid in the supreme rapture of full bloom and promise – with its delicate, transparent, intermittently tousled veil, all this conceals the black, bottomless, uniform void.' Tośka the unattainable, or rather the lost, tormented him, and not least the fact that he was the rejected one.

> I bear a grudge against her that she left first. . . . I should have wanted her to suffer, too, and to be able to hurl all the blame in her face. Then moments of coming to my senses. I am curious how she feels. A feeling of my own littleness. Indeed, perhaps this duality is worst of all.

His words echo those of the disillusioned husband in 'The Return' who blames his indecisive, possibly unfaithful and utterly inscrutable wife for destroying his peace of mind and inflicting upon him an 'excess of feeling'. In this respect the husband, a boorish paragon of upper-middle-class English reserve, was the very antithesis of Malinowski: 'it was part of his creed that any excess of feeling was unhealthy – morally unprofitable; a taint on practical manhood,' wrote Conrad.[39] Directly referring in his diary to the enigmatic wife of the tale ('She had no gift! What was she? Who was she?'),[40]

Malinowski unkindly suspects Tośka of a similar incapacity to bestow conjugal contentment – that most precious 'gift' of women. 'Thus, she too did not have the 'gift' and she too would be forever something dangerous, something that might lead to suicide, to a corruption of life. Thus she would have corrupted my life – how can I tell?'

Berlin at night was a 'ghastly castle'. Malinowski indulged in a national comparison. Now he felt a 'clear sympathy' for the Germans, 'a fabulously versatile and artistic nation'. In comparison with the English, they impressed him 'by their particular, fundamental efficiency; but not by their smartness or style'.

Almost three months later, Tośka was passing through Berlin with her husband and the Conrad family. Then on the verge of war, the city was already dramatically different from Malinowski's Berlin of late April. She recalled: 'A strange atmosphere prevailed there: agitated people stood in groups in front of the latest news-sheets pinned to the walls, and snatched the latest editions of newspapers from each other. . . . And we were heading towards the middle of that volcano which was about to erupt.'[41]

Exhausted by sleeplessness, Malinowski went about his business in Berlin. He visited an optician and a dentist, purchased some medical supplies and hunted for anthropological equipment. Professor Felix von Luschan, director of the Berlin Museum, took a friendly interest in him and gave him colour scales with which to measure the dusky skins of Papuans. In the afternoon he attended a performance of *Tristan and Isolde*, determined, it seems, to salt the wound of his misery. Sure enough, in the second act, he felt 'an intense pain, like red-hot pincers'. His masochistic inclination was disappointed next day, however, when he failed to get into a performance of *Parsifal*. Instead, he walked in the Tiergarten, where amorous couples embraced on the benches. He wrote, 'I must go on repeating to myself that I shall absolutely not return to her.'

In Warsaw the next day he called on Uncle Szpotański who gave him 300 roubles, and on Uncle Kazimierz who gave him 480 ('a thousand shillings,' as his uncle put it).[42] He also called on Żenia Zielińska, but there is scarcely a hint in his diary of the turmoil she had caused him eighteen months earlier. Her conversation disappointed him and he was momentarily disconcerted to find that she was pregnant. He tried to tell her that he was sincerely pleased for her happiness, but it was with relief that he took his leave and freed himself 'from her artless charms'.

That evening he fancied going to the opera with Ethel Eaton – the dull but pretty Englishwoman of previous Warsaw visits. Fragmented images of his three days in Warsaw give the impression that between his more formal engagements Malinowski prowled the streets like an amorous alley cat, craving 'something interesting'. Failing to seduce a certain Wandzia, for whom he felt 'the inspiration of love', he 'fooled about' (as Annie would have said) with Ethel Eaton instead. As he wrote from the safe distance of Zakopane: 'Strong impressions at parting with Eatonka – her despair and the awful remorse that I could do such a thing completely coldly and gratuitously.' While mourning the loss of one woman, he had teetered on the brink of love with another, and made an easy conquest of a third. For the first time in many months, however, he was free of sexual agitation, and for the moment he felt calm and almost contented.

On 28 April, Malinowski spent a busy day in Cracow. He delivered his manuscript to the secretary of the academy, Bolesław Ulanowski, and visited his godmother, Mrs Witkowska, whose husband had recently died. 'I have tears in my eyes,' he wrote. 'I loved August like a father.' Then he caught the train to Zakopane, reminded of Tośka by every station along the way. 'She never understood me inwardly,' he consoled himself.

Although his friends in Warsaw and Cracow had forewarned him, Malinowski was shocked by Staś's appearance when they greeted each other at the station. During the next few days Staś told and retold the tragic tale of the betrayal and destruction of the woman he loved. But Malinowski achieved one small victory on this visit to Zakopane: Staś wanted to go with him to New Guinea. On Monday 4 May, Malinowski left for Cracow. Despite the festive spring weather, he had been depressed by the wretched state of his friend, whose ruin had shaken his own faith in the alliance of art and genius. 'I believe in Staś,' he wrote. 'He is for me the incarnation of the spiritual superiority and separateness of the Polish spirit.' But in this tragic affair he saw that Staś was 'also the incarnation of its worst sides and weaknesses'. As Annie had warned in one of her letters, he was afraid that Staś's longing for death would infect him too. The arguments he had used in urging his friend to live seemed shallow and flimsy to his own ears. But among the broken phrases of his diary there lay a straw of hope that Staś would recover. 'I shall not go into the depths of his condition. . . . I am not able to – have no obligation to – go on, to follow my friend as far as the very gates of Hades, as likely as not, in order to accompany him back, on his return.'

As usual when passing through Cracow, Malinowski stayed at Mrs Borońska's pension. One of the objects of this visit was to approach potential benefactors for funding. He called on Count Zamoyski, fruitlessly it seems, then on the Count de Strassburg, who granted him some money – though in none of his publications did Malinowski acknowledge this particular source. Another appointment he kept in Cracow was with his dentist for a tooth extraction. He felt so unwell afterwards that he decided to spend another night at Mrs Borońska's, quietly reading Conrad's *Nostromo*.

As he approached London on the evening of 9 May, Malinowski felt joy to be back in England. He expected to return to Poland in two years at most, but it would be eight before he saw his homeland again. By then the ramshackle empire of which he had been a complaisant if not contented citizen would have finally collapsed. When he finally did return, it was to an independent Poland in a Europe irrevocably changed by war.

Return to Tośka

The three weeks leading up to his departure for Australia were hectic. There were arrangements to be made, people to see, equipment and supplies to be purchased and despatched. There were also the delicate, painful crises of Staś and Tośka to be managed. Staś would come with him, that seemed certain now. Malinowski had promised to lend him 500 roubles, and the British Association would contribute to his fare to Australia. But Tośka would be left behind – probably forever – and, despite all his earlier resolutions, Malinowski was not yet reconciled to the loss of her. He made no attempt to resist the temptation to see her on his return to London, and soon enough went actively in search of her. He tried to pull himself together, to see her 'objectively' so as to break her captivating spell. 'I am very clearly "idealizing" her,' he told himself, reminded perhaps of the husband's intolerable predicament in 'The Return'.

Malinowski's obsession with Tośka threatened to complicate his departure by distracting him, not only from essential tasks but also from the attention he wanted to devote to his soon-to-be-bereft mother. As it was, he spent too little time at home with her in Mecklenburgh Street. He was often at the Seligmans' and spent many hours with Tancred Borenius, Isabel Fry, and various members of the Polish Circle. The summer term was well under way at the LSE and he attended Westermarck's sociology seminar on

Monday evenings. When he wasn't visiting friends, shopping for anthropological instruments and dropping into the British Museum looking for Tośka, he was practising photography.

On 15 May he went to a performance of *Parsifal*, but it was such ghastly torture that he walked out after the second act. 'I have her continually before my soul's eyes,' he wrote of the elusive Tośka, who at that time was hosting the Conrads. London was 'steeped in her presence'. For Malinowski, sentimentality would always be an addictive by-product of love, and during these busy days he became increasingly aware of its unhealthy grip on him.

> Terrible longing for that which was. . . . I recall with clarity moments of hallucination, when she would drop in on me, in a dark violet velvet suit and a little straw hat with bright flowers. She used to lift up her veil and let me kiss her lips. We were so terribly familiar, so terribly close to each other. Things were going so well for us. Her presence acted on me like the sea.

At the Seligmans' for supper one evening Malinowski met Dr William Mersh Strong of Port Moresby. Strong had assisted Seligman in Papua in 1904 and was the only fully qualified medical officer in the colony. He had also served as a part-time government anthropologist, though he was a reluctant fieldworker and made no ethnographic discoveries of any significance. Concerning the evening's discussion, Malinowski noted privately for the first time that New Guinea was really beginning to interest him.

Staś Witkiewicz arrived in London on Sunday 24 May. It lifted Malinowski's spirits to see his friend again, though on that day he apparently neglected him: he lunched with Westermarck and the Hungarian anthropologist Emil Torday, and in the evening he had supper with the political scientist Graham Wallas.

Equipping the colonial explorer

Sometimes accompanied by his mother and Staś, Malinowski went on extended buying sprees to equip himself for fieldwork. With Seligman's guidance he had already purchased some photographic equipment and drawn up lists of pieces of tropical camping gear and essential provisions. Malinowski's inventories are of particular interest to anyone who has done fieldwork in remote places. Like the proverbial laundry list, a shipping invoice is a metaphor for biographical trivia; but Malinowski's invoices are historical documents of extraordinary richness.[43] They record not only the types and brands of commodities he chose, but also their cost and quantity. They therefore provide insight into the style of living he envisaged for himself in that liminal cultural space, 'the field' – expectations that were shaped by conversations with veterans such as Seligman, Haddon, Wester-marck, Rivers, Wheeler and, latterly, William Strong. The invoices also offer intriguing clues to Malinowski's personal tastes.

In 1914, the cutting-edge technology of tinning permitted an exuberant range of foodstuffs. Everything edible was experimentally stuffed or poured into cans and hermetically sealed. The results were not always what the manufacturers, or the consumers, expected. Labels were largely irrelevant, as Arthur Grimble recalled of tinned food in the Gilbert Islands in 1916; 'the taste of one and all . . . was the taste of iron filings boiled in dishwater'.[44]

Malinowski's orders reflected the technology, as can be seen from the supplies he purchased from those worthy purveyors to the empire, the Army and Navy Co-Operative Society in Victoria Street.[45] On 1 July 1914, the Army & Navy (as it is better known) shipped twenty-four 'packages' to Sydney per S.S. *Euripides*, whence they were to be trans-shipped to Port Moresby by a Burns Philp steamer on which Malinowski also expected to travel. Passenger and goods were due to arrive in Papua on 23 September. The initials of the 'exporter' were C.G.S. At the point of sale, it seems, Seligman paid for the goods consigned to Malinowski.

The twenty-four packing cases reveal how colonial purveyors took into account the logistics of expeditions. The supplies were packed in batches, rather like food hampers. There were six cases marked 'A' and eleven marked 'B', so that the gentleman explorer might take one of each on, say, a month's expedition without needing to open them to check their contents, secure in the knowledge that they would contain all that was required in the way of delicacies. Each stout case was secured with a padlock.

The lists of victuals packed into these cases are reminiscent of Rabelais's sumptuary recitals. The cases marked 'A' contained bottles of Heinz tomato ketchup, lemonade crystals, jars of French mustard and Dutch beetroot, packets of dried peas and Brussels sprouts, together with a smorgasbord of tinned treats: sliced bacon, Irish stew, lobster, mackerel, oysters, sardines, Swiss cheese, Suchard's vanilla chocolate, Peter's milk chocolate, Heinz baked beans, Lyle's cocoa, Spanish olives, spinach, *petits pois*, Dutch beans, and Moir's cod roes. In the cases marked 'B' there were tins of condensed milk and morning tea and six different jams, tins of kippered herrings, various dried fruits and mixed dried vegetables including split peas, Keiller's marmalade, a jar of extract of beef, candles and a bottle of Camp coffee. In these cases there was a large tin within which there were many smaller tins containing a variety of biscuits, rusks and crackers. Obviously, Malinowski did not intend to risk living off the land.

In addition to these luxury 'staples' replicated in their marked cases, there were several cases of toothsome tinned foods that he would have selected personally: essence of chicken, jugged hare, roast turkey, half-hams, fresh herrings, Van Houten's cocoa and Bourneville cocoa, arrowroot, sprouts, carrots and French beans. There were two whole cases of Nestle's milk and Ideal milk, and another case containing two bottles of French brandy, three bottles of ink (two black, one red), four 2lb tins of Epsom Salts, 2lbs of precipitated sulphur, 6lbs of boric acid, bottles of tincture of iodine, assorted packs of lint, bandages and cotton wool, and one (only one) toothbrush.

Malinowski also shipped cases from other suppliers. There was a chest of medical supplies from Burroughs Wellcome which fully catered for his hypochondria. Among more esoteric preparations, this box contained almost five thousand tablets and capsules of quinine, phenacetin, aspirin, Dover powder, cascara, cathartic compound, bromide, iron and arsenic.

Then there was the camping equipment, which showed how much careful consideration he had given to his material comfort in the field. On 16 May, Seligman had accompanied him to Lawn & Alder ('Home and Colonial Outfitters'), where they drew up a long list of items. These were duly delivered to Mecklenburgh Street. The list of equipment is as intriguing as the lists of provisions. It includes a screw-face tropical wristwatch (conspicuous in a photograph taken in the Trobriands in 1915), a combination tool knife (with can-opener), a travelling rug, a box of fifty .455 cartridges, an oil-painted bedding bag, a camp bed with metal rods, a hair pillow in ticking, a hair mattress, a kapok pillow, an army blanket and a camel hair blanket, camp-bed sheets and pillowcases, a canvas tent (9×7 feet) with groundsheet, a tent pole strap with lantern arm, a yard of spare canvas and assorted canvas bags and buckets, a canvas bath and washstand, one large and one small roll-up table, a high-backed canvas chair, two mosquito curtains, a galvanized canteen, a five-pint iron kettle, a mechanical lamp with spare wick, a water bottle, a haversack, a 'furnifold' chair and a sun umbrella lined in green. Malinowski was taking no chances with the tropical environment. At six guineas, the most expensive item by far was the tent; when he finally came to use it in the Trobriands, however, he found it was too small.

And what did the well-equipped explorer wear in 1914? From Lawn & Adler he purchased an oil-cotton coat with special collar and sou'wester, a Cawnpore sunhelmet complete with oilskin cover, two pairs of light-coloured puttees, a pair of red rubber tennis shoes, a pair of canvas gaiters, a pair of mosquito boots, two pairs of size-eight colonial boots (hobnailed) and a dozen pairs of brown laces. At F. W. Green, a civil and military tailor in Chancery Lane, Malinowski was fitted for two Norfolk jackets and breeches, and a spare pair of trousers and 'knickers' (presumably shorts). From the sports and general outfitters Gamage of Holborn, Malinowski (helped on this occasion by his mother and Staś) chose socks, collars, pyjamas, shirts, belts, more trousers and yet another jacket.

The most indispensable tools of the anthropologist's trade are to be found at stationers. Having given some thought to the kind of notebooks he wanted, Malinowski went to Ryman of Great Portland Street, where he placed an order for two dozen custom-made notebooks (a quantity, alas, that would prove to be insufficient). These sturdy notebooks were octavo pads of a hundred pages each, of plain cream bank paper. In addition he bought nine writing pads, three foolscap sketch books and three hundred envelopes; but there is no mention of writing implements. The cost of this stationery was a very reasonable £1.8.4 (cheaper than his wristwatch or his Norfolk jacket).

Six dozen wax cylinder records were also shipped. The legacy of Malinowski's field materials includes only six cylinders of sound recordings (each of four tinny minutes' duration), so the technology probably failed him. At £4.10 the cylinders were costly – almost equivalent to the amount he spent on medical supplies, though still far short of the £18.11 he expended on photographic equipment, of which the most expensive single item was a quarter-plate Klimax camera.[46] Malinowski later calculated that he had spent £146 on kitting himself out in London.[47]

Farewell to Tośka

On Tuesday 26 May, Malinowski met Tośka near Waterloo Bridge. They strolled along the Embankment and, after lunching at a Lyons tea shop, went into Westminster Abbey. He questioned her about her love. 'Why do you torture me?' she asked. Impulsively, he proposed marriage to her. She said nothing, and they parted. It was an afternoon he would recall with anguish in a Sinhalese temple several weeks later.

Even more poignant was their conversation the following day while they walked in St James's Park. Tośka told him about her financial difficulties and her desire to work for a living. She spoke of her 'suicidal mania; of her aversion to life, of the impossibility of enjoying it'. Malinowski was hurt and dismayed, as much for himself as for her.

> The terrible pain of realising that this woman, who is a symbol of the beauty and pleasure of life for me, sees nothing in me, that I can give her nothing, that she cannot lean on me. A blow equally to my deepest self-love as well as to my basic love for her.

During the next few days he rushed about on business, resisting the temptation to telephone her. He attended Westermarck's annual luncheon party and talked to Martin White and the psychologist Alexander Shand. He met Seligman and Robert Mond, his chief benefactor. His bedroom at 6 Mecklenburgh Street was transformed into a storehouse of tropical gear, as he and Staś packed things and tried on their new clothes. 'What will come of all this?' Malinowski wondered.

Late in the afternoon of Monday 1 June, he called on Tośka. She seemed light-headed and he could smell alcohol on her breath. They strolled on Hampstead Heath, then nestled together on a bench. 'I tell her that she does not love me; she does not contradict.' Near the ponds he took her in his arms for what they agreed would be the last time. Tośka wept. She told him that she was sinking 'to the bottom', that she was going to leave her husband. Unkindly, Malinowski took her confession as 'the affirmation of wicked fears that she is *au fond* simply a whore'. It was with relief that he parted from her in the shady streets of Belsize Park. But they met again a few days later, this time in the Natural History Museum in South Kensington, and yet again at her house, where he took her photograph. Then there was a moment of 'abashment' when her husband suddenly came home.

Monday 8 June was the eve of Malinowski's departure. In the morning he went with Staś to the Royal Anthropological Institute and the British Museum. He worried about his aching teeth and had his eyes and spectacles checked by an occulist. At home he practised using the new Klimax camera. In the afternoon he met Tośka at the museum and they took yet another farewell stroll in Hyde Park. 'Once again she tells me of her pow-erlessness, of her hopeless passive relationship with her husband. . . . She tells me that the question of a child depends on the mercy of fate – this disconcerts me terribly.'

He returned to Mecklenburgh Street to find Mama alone – only to abandon her again when Tośka appeared. After a final kiss he escorted Tośka to her tram. 'I tell her that she will always be my ideal, and that that should oblige her to struggle with herself, to take on strength. We walk once again around the little square near King's Cross. . . . I see her for the last time as she boards the tram.' Four years later, Malinowski will end his last diary with remorseful recollections of this occasion. But it is concerning his mother that he will feel 'furious regrets and guilt feelings' about their last evening together, an evening 'spoiled by that whore!'[48]

Chapter 14

A Passage to Ceylon

Ship of fools

The long voyage to the Antipodes began inauspiciously. Waking in Meck-lenburgh Street on the morning of departure, 9 June, Malinowski suffered a violent toothache which gave him a 'gloomy prospect for the future'. He was suddenly struck by the 'senselessness' of the trip. The immediate itin-erary was via Paris and Toulon, where Malinowski and Staś would board their oceanliner. They saved several days, and probably a few pounds, by embarking in southern France rather than at Tilbury. By avoiding the Bay of Biscay they were also spared certain seasickness.

Mama and Westermarck saw them off at Fenchurch Street Station. It was another painful train journey for Malinowski, and from the Folkestone ferry he glimpsed the cottages of Sandgate as the shores of England receded. 'There she and I walked together, there on a snowy evening we sat in the moonlight on the shore of the murmuring sea,' he remembered. Jerzy Żuławski met them at the Gare du Nord and Malinowski's spirits lifted. Fifteen years had passed since his first visit to Paris with his mother; now he was enthralled by its vitality. 'Everything is continually ming-ling, seething, brushing against itself; human glances, bad tempers and quarrels, street flirts . . . the houses, trams, trees and lanterns create the impression of a single compact kaleidoscopic mass, in which it is simply impossible to orient oneself.' The métro, too, was a riot of colour and move-ment, like 'a masquerade in a brothel'. After supper with the Żuławskis, Malinowski and Staś visited the poet Andrzej Strug and his wife. Later they strolled along the dark and silent Seine. Shadowed by thoughts of Tośka and his mother, Malinowski's moody reflections have a Conradian cadence:

Strange calm and forlornness; as if we were walking alone, as if the enormous city were only an artistic accessory for augmenting the immeasurable convergence of time and place. Old memories; the whole charm of Paris reflected in so many works of art, in so many historical memories. I continually walk with her, with her shadow, with her ideal.

Guided like tourists by the Żuławskis, Malinowski and Staś saw the sights next day. They gazed at the *Mona Lisa* and Egyptian antiquities in the Louvre. After visiting Notre Dame and the Left Bank bookstalls, they caught the evening train to Marseilles. With its air of southern decay, the city delighted them and they penetrated the back streets where slovenly Italian women were hurrying to their factories. In Toulon they loitered wearily, awaiting embarkation. Finally, at 2 p.m. on 11 June 1914, they boarded the Royal Mail Steamer *Orsova*, an Orient Line two-stack liner of 12,000 tons. Large and comfortable by the standards of the day, it accommodated four hundred passengers in first and second class, seven hundred in third.[1] Malinowski and Witkiewicz travelled second class.

The next day they awoke to see the northern tip of Corsica, then Elba, Montecristo and Giglio:'the entire sea strewn with islands' – a foretaste for Malinowski of eastern New Guinea. That morning he wrote a long letter to his mother, describing the bright, drifting islands and the calm sea. The main business of the letter was to reassure her that he was financially solvent and would not need any more of their savings; Seligman would transfer £100 to Sydney as soon as the university authorized payment of Robert Mond's grant. As for the company travelling on the *Orsova*, it was mostly English and 'savage' Australians. 'But we keep our distance,' he added.

Józefa Malinowska received the letter within days and replied immediately, grateful for his vivid descriptions ('if you carry on like this, you'll have an interesting diary of your journey'). She reported her attempts to complete the bibliography for his Polish book, and to obtain reviews of his English book as required by Stanisław Estreicher in Cracow. She explained that she would go to Tilbury next day to see the captain of the *Orontes*; she wanted to give to him a package for her son when he joined the ship at Colombo. It would contain some chocolates she had forgotten to pack in his travelling bag, a spare key to his green bag, various receipts and several letters, including one from Tośka. Józefa's letter was replete with motherly advice, reminding him what keys open which cases, begging him to rinse his hair with sulphur at least once a week, and giving him instructions (complete with a little diagram) about how to set his alarm clock. She advised him to buy another oilcloth purse for his money, but that meanwhile he should wrap it in waxed paper.

> Mrs Retinger . . . has come often, helped a lot, cried a lot. We hugged a lot and I tried to calm her down. You must write to her sometimes, but mind what I am saying to you and act honestly, and when you've read this letter a couple of times, throw it in the sea.[2]

His mother now knew that Bronio and Tola Retinger, aka Tośka, had been more than just good friends.

The first port of call was Naples, where the two friends spent the day sightseeing. Malinowski's last visit had been with his mother in 1904. His diary records:

> Wild rapture over Naples; over its picturesqueness, the marvellous types of people, the life of the streets. Overwhelming liking for the Italians. . . . Vineyards where small and old houses nestle, so primitive and artistic that one senses in them a refinement of ancient culture unchanged from thousands of years ago.

Reboarding the *Orsova* they crossed the Bay of Naples and, next day, as they sailed along the wild shores of Calabria, Malinowski was thrilled to recall that these were places where Pythagoras taught and the cities of Magna Graecia flourished. At Taranto they were immediately surrounded by a band of children, and as they walked down broken alleyways women peered at them from behind iron grilles. Malinowski was pleased to discover that his Italian was understood. That evening they sailed for Port Said.

During two days without landfall Malinowski took stock of his physical and emotional health:

> Only the 6th day on ship . . . but I have already had completely enough of this. . . . I do not see clearly where I am going; I do not feel within myself a goal or direction. Physically I feel rather low. I have a sort of head cold, sore throat and coughs [sic], despite the furious heat. . . . Nor do I see in my view of the future how I shall feel in the climate of New Guinea.

As for his psychosexual condition:

I have extremely frequent attacks of sentimentality, centring around T. Looking today at a little girl sitting in front of me, I had tears in my eyes. The paternal instinct is beginning to awaken. I nip my prostitutional instincts in the bud, even if they are only day-dreams. I want to attain total sexual purity during this period. Otherwise I would have no right to marriage or to happiness in marriage.

He was concerned about Staś, who remained deeply despondent. Staś had written to him in April, begging him to fetch some potassium cyanide from his old laboratory in Leipzig. 'With your contacts it will be easy for you to get (on account of the trip, being roasted alive by savages or something of the sort). If you love me even just a little, you'll be doing me a big favour.'[3] It is unlikely that Malinowski had complied with this request.

After leaving Taranto, Staś wrote a formal suicide note, addressing it to Malinowski with the instruction 'Send it to my family'.

I am writing for the last time. The terrible wrongs for which I am to blame prevent my living any longer. Forgive me, dearest parents. I cannot go on. I am frightfully guilty. . . . Forgive me, Broneczek, for abandoning you, but you don't know how frightfully I'm suffering. I kiss you and bid you farewell. Don't be angry with me. You alone know the entire ghastliness of my suffering. Your Staś.

Attached to the letter was a last will and testament, dividing his paintings, drawings, photographs and other things among his friends, including Irena Solska, Jadwiga Janczewska's parents and Aniela Zagórska (to whom he left all his literary works). To Malinowski he bequeathed his camera, adding, 'If he returns from the expedition, he may choose any painting he wants *à discretion.*' There was a codicil requesting the burial of all Jadwiga's 'letters and mementos with her under the stone which is to be erected for me at the spot where she took her own life'. And there was another, vengeful one: 'God forbid that that ultra-ham Miciński should write a single word about me. This is my most ardent wish. I would rather be completely forgotten.' In a lugubrious postscript he willed a composition called 'The Kiss of Death', one of the last he had painted, to Eugenia Borkowska 'on the understanding that she will never try to take her own life'.[4] This must rank among Witkacy's most morbid jokes.

Presumably, Staś did not hand his letter to his travelling companion until much later, for it was with cautious optimism that Malinowski wrote to his mother: 'Staś stopped having those attacks of dejection, sighing and despairing, that he used to have in London and all the time in Zakopane. He looks better, occasionally cracks jokes, and is generally a very pleasant and easy companion.'[5] Either he was telling her white lies, or Staś was somehow managing to conceal his suicidal state.

Although slightly seasick, Malinowski amused himself by reading ethnography. A ship voyage, he complained to Mama, was like being in prison and the cramped conditions induced disgust for one's fellow passengers. He had to keep reminding himself why he was on this seemingly meaningless voyage. Port Said brought welcome distractions, however, and he recorded a flood of impressions in his diary:

> Attack on the boat by wild men. . . . Trip ashore. Purchase of cards and stamps. Street bazaar, illuminated; wonderful smell of trees and ghastly stink of the streets; large, dark houses with circular balconies. From far away Arabic music can be heard. . . . Cafés, fruit-sellers. A cortege with music comes along; a huge Negro, a Shilluk perhaps?

For his mother he elaborated: 'The streets were unpaved, of course, terribly dirty, with a stench reminiscent of Tunis, Tangier etc. The typical "oriental aroma": a mixture of ammonia, burnt olive oil, and cheap perfume.'[6] The sound of clarinets and drums attracted them to the Arab quarter where they watched a wedding procession with torches, carriages and musicians, followed by a crowd of spectators.

Passing through the Suez Canal the heat began to take its toll. 'The worst are the nights in the cabin,' he told Mama. 'It's like descending from the burning deck into a steam bath.'

> In the morning I feel terrible weakness and the thought of going for a bath and then putting on my sticky sweaty clothes fills me with disgust. Of course I wear the khaki suit, with no underwear, and often take off the jacket, sitting in my shirt, which is perfectly acceptable here.

In his diary he observed:

> On the right-hand side, Egypt; evidently artificially irrigated; from time to time tamarisk groves; palm oases; above this, violet mountain ranges. On the left-hand side, pure desert drift sand completely bare; or else covered with straggly dwarf shrubs. . . . The huge ship barely has room; it is strange how this naval colossus cuts through the very heart of the desert.

Meanwhile, in paroxysms of self-pity, Staś wrote his own melodramatic diary.

> The night in Port Said allowed me an insight into what things will be like in the future. . . . All the things I can see, beautiful, strange or unusual, turn into a terrible torment. I would have liked so much to admire all this with Her. . . . There is nothing inside me now except a frightful love for her. The more frightful because revealed too late.[7]

He railed against his false friends Karol Szymanowski ('a born scoundrel') and Tadeusz Miciński ('an obscene ham') for their part in the imbroglio that led Jadwiga to kill herself. 'But the worst guilt is mine,' he added.[8]

Although the monotony of the voyage continued to oppress him, Malinowski gradually became involved in shipboard society. He strolled, chatted and played deck sports with some French passengers and conversed at length with Henry Newton, the Anglican Bishop of New Guinea. He nevertheless complained to his diary: 'I live too little with the sea, with astronomical and thermal phenomena; I work too little. . . . At night I sleep rather poorly and last night I had nightmares, which indicate a weakening of the heart.'

The letter his mother sent to Taranto with news of Toška had not reached him in time, and he would not receive it until he was about to leave Colombo. He still longed for her and with increasing distance his love became purified. What he called his 'monogamous instinct' was asserting itself.

> I have a sort of idealized Tosca [sic], good, intelligent, loving, genuinely and deeply feminine, towards whom all my erotic and, now significantly stronger, family instincts impel me. I feel that she is my perfect complement, that she is the sole incarnation of my longings for a steady relationship with a woman.

'Unfortunately,' he added, 'analysis does not confirm this intuited image.' He realized that he no longer trusted her, and that there could be neither happiness nor genuine love between them. It was as well that he had escaped her by leaving London when he did. 'I felt ever more strongly that if she did not love me, then by this very fact she lost her value to me.' Writing these words reminded him of his mother:

I think too little of the one person who possesses genuine and lasting value for me and who really cares about me. Mama surely experiences my absence strongly now. . . . It is a terrible thing, this one-sidedness of the relationship of parents to their children. Now when feelings of the paternal are awakening in me, I already begin to feel this tragedy at first hand somehow.

On this same day, 20 June, Malinowski noted that Staś was particularly gloomy, though his friend confounded him that evening by composing a pretty melody. It was perhaps only concern for his parents that prevented Staś from killing himself. 'Do you realize what it means to suffer because of your parents?' he wrote with emphasis at the top of the first page of his memorandum of pain, and further down: 'I would like to die in peace but I cannot do it because of my parents who would not survive it.' To his psychoanalyst Karol de Beaurain, he wrote:

> It's either death or New Guinea now. But easier said than done. Death and my thoughts which lead to it are the same here, on the Red Sea, as they were in Zakopane. I shall try, however, to reach Colombo. . . . It is only Her that I love and only myself that I hate.[9]

During their three-day traversal of the Red Sea, the humid heat distressed Malinowski. He found breathing difficult and had moments of panic. Cold baths helped, and some afternoons, between fitful sleeps, he was even able to begin work on Motu grammar. He also read Stevenson's *The Master of Ballantrae* and dipped into *Notes and Queries on Anthropology*. Keeping to his cabin, Staś tortured himself by reading *Lord Jim*, Conrad's story of betrayal, guilt, remorse and expiation.[10]

'I've been feeling rather rotten,' Malinowski admitted to his mother on 26 June. He had overindulged in cold baths, food and drink, resulting in lassitude and a migraine. Sleep was almost impossible in the suffocatingly stuffy cabin. They were a day out from Colombo, and he was relieved that this leg of the voyage was almost over.[11] Józefa wrote to her son on about the same date. She was alarmed that he hadn't got her letters in Taranto and was now worried that he wouldn't receive them in Colombo either, or the packages she had sent him. She cabled Orient Line for them to be redirected to Perth. 'It's the last thing I can do for you. The further you go the more difficult it is for me to do anything for you and my influence diminishes to zero!' She had assembled all the reviews she could trace of his book on the Aboriginal family and sent them to Estreicher, who had 'almost promised' to do the second proofreading of the Polish book, though he wanted Józefa to do the first and Ulanowski the third. She encouraged her son to write more diary-letters: 'The conditions you are in aren't those of grey, everyday life. All the time new stimulations, new feelings, new thoughts perhaps.' Motherly instructions followed: 'Look after your eyes, don't read in a draught, use the sulphur on your hair at least twice a week, massage your head two or three times a day . . . this may stop your baldness from progressing. A thousand hugs.'[12]

From South Africa, Annie Brunton replied to Malinowski's plaintive letter from Port Said. She was surprised to learn he was travelling second class. Colonial life in Australia couldn't be as bad as he feared and he would surely meet the most cultured people there. She supposed 'everybody will be putting themselves out to do you honour, & entertain & amuse you, so it must be pleasanter than being a 2nd class passenger at sea'. Annie was also sceptical about his declaration of chastity:

> I rather smiled at your protests about your Don Giovanni career. I don't think it is really over – perhaps it is just a reaction you are suffering from – and at any rate you won't have much opportunity I suppose in Papua for launching on a new career of that sort – & perhaps for your health it will be just as well to live chastely – as you propose for the next two years. It is so sweet of you Bronio to say that I am the only English speaking person you really feel in touch with & that you would have liked me to be with you on the boat. I should have loved it too.[13]

'The tropics are beyond all my imagining'

The *Orsova* docked in Colombo in the early hours of 28 June. 'We spent our last days at sea in frightful heat, apathy and lethargy,' Staś wrote to his father.[14] The second-class passengers had been permitted to sleep on the first-class deck, but 'Bronio preferred to choke in his cabin'. Sweating profusely, they packed and put on their tropical outfits and pith helmets.

On landing in the sprawling colonial capital, Malinowski sought out Ronald Fergusson, editor of *The Ceylon Observer*, for whom he carried a letter of introduction from Haddon. The son of an author of guidebooks, Fergusson recommended what sights the travellers should see. First they took rickshaws to Victoria Park. Staś wrote: 'I had thought a ride in a rickshaw would be something unpleasant because of having a guilty conscience. That's not the case at all. They give the impression of being animals. Wonderful people. In colour ranging from red chocolate to black bronze.' Malinowski's staccato account was impressionistic:

> We ride through the open fields; large English buildings. The Sinhalese half-naked in white and red rags; dark eyes fixed on the unknown distance. There are almost no whites to be seen. Sinhalese boys [playing] football. Humpbacked cattle. Little houses covered with tiles; little shops opened to their full breadth. A broad street, the houses shaded by matting or wooden grilles. Types in turbans. A Muslim burial. Victoria Park. Huge bamboos; tall trees with purple flowers; strange grass, red earth; a feeling of the distinctive character of the tropical flora. Return along the lake, palms. Small and miserable Buddhist shrine.

They took a tram to the Cinnamon Gardens where Malinowski saw 'women with flat noses pierced by gold ear-rings. Buddhist priests in yellow duds, holy whores in red dresses.' He looked mainly at the women, 'with curiosity, but without erotomania'. The friends spent the night sweating under mosquito nets in a cheap Sinhalese hotel. 'Mysterious bronze monkeys wait on us half-naked,' Staś told his father, and in the port 'instead of seagulls, red-bronze vultures with jagged wings fly about'.

They caught the 7 a.m. train to Kandy, a twisting, chugging four-hour journey into the mountains, dominated by Allagalla Peak. Staś saw 'diabolical vistas', the vegetation became 'madder and madder', and the people 'more and more gaudily but wonderfully dressed'. In the ancient capital of Kandy, Malinowski was intrigued by the artificial lake built by the last feudal king: 'Created and designed for rest, for oblivion, for a life of the moment, of that which is and passes – a locality full of promises of happiness.' Staś wrote to his father from the Hôtel Suisse, 'on the slope of the mountains covered with palms, lianas and the devil knows what, on the edge of a lake full of fish and turtles'.

The companions seem overwhelmed by their impressions; but inside they suffered, each in his own way. Malinowski complained: 'I am considerably befuddled; I get tired terribly easily. . . . I give over my moments of energy to the reception of impressions, at times I feel [them] more strongly; usually I feel them apathetically. . . . I try to write to Mama, to describe my impressions; it comes very hard. 'Dearest Mama,' he began. 'I've been here for a day and a half. I feel so stupefied and enchanted by all this that I don't know how to begin. . . . The tropics are beyond all my imagining.'

Staś returned to his grief at the end of his own letter: 'She won't see this [beauty]. . . . I wouldn't wish my worse enemy to go through what I've been living through mentally. . . . Will this inhuman suffering ever come to an end! I kiss you, Dad, my dearest Dad.'[15]

That day they had circled the lake in rickshaws, past gardens and palaces, along broad, bright streets with 'awful smells', seeing sluggish Sinhalese and 'Afghans with magnificent rich clothes and busy, open mouths'. In the evening they took a tour of the Temple of the Holy Tooth with its bell-shaped shrine. The inner courtyard swarmed with people: 'vendors of flowers, betel, incense; dark, half-naked figures shuffling along softly and lazily. They have something deceitful and beggarly about them.' Malinowski was irritated by the persistent begging.

Respectful of the Eastern philosophy he had read under Maurycy Straszewski at the Jagiellonian, he was now disillusioned by the manifestations of popular Buddhism: the statuettes of all sizes, the trinketry and devotional articles wrapped in rags. The image came to him of a 'nursery of children playing at sacred mysteries'. With a surprisingly narrow-minded sourness for an aspiring anthropologist, he regarded the scene as an affront to his aesthetic sensibility: 'In its crude, common form Buddhism appeared to me as something sterile; something that I already know from the shoddy Catholicism of southern Italy; something that does not have the charm of strange artistic effects related to and based on age-old traditions.' He reflected on his disappointment:

> First contacts with an entirely new culture . . . first impressions of an entirely unknown country, religion, landscape are always full of such anti-climaxes. Only at times, very rarely a happy coincidence . . . a happy arrangement of circumstances in a given place allows one to grasp immediately the substance of a new world, the quality of beauty in new surroundings.

Grumpily, he admitted that on this trip the happy coincidence was missing, 'if only because of my worries about the future, about acclimatization in the tropics and the great tiredness brought on by the heat'. For the first time, he acknowledged that the main purpose of the fortnight's sojourn in Ceylon was to test his tolerance for the tropics. So far, the response of his delicate constitution had not been encouraging, and he had every reason to be alarmed about what awaited him in New Guinea.

That night in the Hôtel Suisse, Malinowski's surly mood persisted, though their rooms were cool and comfortable and the dinner copious. He was irritated by the silent, fawning staff and the stuffy English guests who dressed for dinner and had nothing of interest to say. Next morning they visited the botanical gardens at Peradeniya. Malinowski's enthusiasm for the flora contrasted with his evident contempt, verging on disgust, for local humanity. From the darkness of the streets, he wrote, 'emerges some brown, half-naked figure, some red or white rags; a head, a pair of big, vacant, moist eyes'. In the afternoon, he paid a visit to the government commissioner of archaeology, Henry Bell, whom he described to Mama as 'quite old, fat and grey, as if the climate had drawn all the energy out of him'. Bell recommended visits to the ancient sites of Matale and Anuradhapura.

As he gazed over Kandy's lake in the humid darkness that evening, Malinowski was aroused by the erotic landscape. 'The little island evokes tantalizing thoughts of a marvellous pavilion of love, where a stout, pot-bellied king possesses beautiful women in his huge, voluptuary embrace; on a stifling night, when the sky seems to lean over the earth and enfold it in the warmth of its embrace.' Alone, he prowled the streets, 'drawn by some undefined impure, confused hope of glimpsing something that will incite me to evil. I control myself; I have already struggled a couple of times against unclean thoughts.'

Before leaving for Matale next day, Bronio and Staś took Lady Horton's Walk, relishing its exuberant jungle and splendid views of Kandy. With 'the worthy apperception of an ignoramus', Malinowski passed summary judgment on Ceylon:

> I have the strange impression that this marvellous country is devoid of something, that it is beautiful decoration which lacks drama. A country with historical importance or a country totally wild each has a charm of its own. But a country whose history is . . . a collection of petty, senseless moves on the chess-board of the mean politics of petty rajas and the disgusting politics of the colonizing powers, a country whose purpose in today's times is the enrichment of planters and speculators – such a country has no charm at all.

In Matale, however, his excited first impression was of being at last in 'primitive Ceylon'. Here, there were no Europeans, only languid figures and 'the same woe-begone empty faces; red-white rags; pigtails, shawls, turbans'. They took a cart to a tiny shrine with a carved cupola, observed an aristocratic wedding party and, entering the jungle, discovered some ruins. The day in Matale was the most interesting so far, he told his mother, and he described for her the chiselled hills, the bizarre vegetation, the colourful but curiously uneventful streets. The people continued to disappoint him. They were 'barely alive', sitting limply and looking about with glassy eyes: 'they don't evoke your sympathy or interest; they're too slow, heavy, lifeless.'[16]

Unable to find accommodation in Matale they returned to Kandy, ambling by bullock cart for three enchanted moonlit hours. In cheap lodgings that night their sleep was disturbed by fleas and the vomiting of a drunk next door. In the morning they travelled by train to Anuradhapura, a city of ruins. Leaving behind the 'stiff extravagance of the palms' and 'the wildness of lianas and creepers', they entered a dry zone of thorn bushes, burnt grasses and leafless trees. They booked into the only hotel, hired a guide and went sightseeing in a cart. For over a millennium Anuradhapura had been Ceylon's capital, and the pair poked about among its abandoned shrines and ruined temples. That night, exhausted by the stifling heat, Malinowski slept heavily for twelve hours.

Meanwhile, Staś was plumbing fresh depths of despair. That night he penned a letter of 'Explications' in shaky English to the Ceylonese authorities, exculpating Malinowski in the event of his suicide:

He was so kind that he has lent me fifty pounds . . . and has taken me in a very bad psychical state with him and on account of it has had many troubles. He was so good as a best brother. And I am sorry that I must do him an injustice and leave him in his dangerous tripes [trip]. . . . I am writing it in scope [hope] that my dearest Friend Dr Malinowski has no troubles on account of my death to make him avoid any formalities and inquiry, that can make him late for his ship . . . because he must be in Australia for the Congress of British Association. It would be for me a very great pain that I instead to be grateful to him have made him any trouble. Excuse me my horrible English.[17]

In a Polish postscript he wrote: 'Dear Bronio, You'll think this is ham acting. I don't wish you ever to suffer even a part of what I've been through.' The envelope was marked 'B. Malinowski: Open in case of my death'. But two Australian addresses also appear on the envelope, and the single word 'humorous' beneath 'Explications'. This was obviously added later, as probably were the Australian addresses; Staś apparently kept the letter until this particular crisis had passed.

Despite their intimate friendship, they appear not to have shared their innermost thoughts and feelings on this trip. A sleeping Malinowski was unaware that his friend was still awaiting the moment to kill himself, though next day he noted in his diary: 'Staś had an awful day; he doesn't look; he despairs; talks of strength. He was supposed to write an article.' Incredibly (for even Malinowski admitted that he could not have written an article under such conditions), Staś was forcing himself to keep the commitment he had made to a Polish journal.

From Anuradhapura they travelled by bullock cart to Maradankadawala. That night they stayed in a British government rest-house where Staś tenaciously wrote his article. Malinowski felt better the next day, even happy, as they trundled again by cart through monotonous green walls of parched jungle. Sometimes he went on foot and took photographs; sometimes he sat lazily in the cart marvelling at the trees. 'Speading mimosas, like open parasols; cultivated rubber plants with tangled branches and shoots like groups occupied in lively and familiar conversation; they link arms, hold out their hands, gesticulate.' At times he glimpsed rice fields and views of distant mountains. Fields of stubble and sheaves of yellow grain 'standing like bouquets' reminded Malinowski nostalgically of Galicia.

They found a roomy rest-house in Dambulla, and that evening walked to a nearby village. There they chanced upon an event that had enormous significance for Malinowski. His diary records:

> On the road, beneath scaffolding of four upright sticks and four split pieces of bamboo supporting them horizontally, we see a man sitting above a small table covered with flowers, incense and candles, and performing a magic ceremony. We help him with our umbrella as he lights a candle. He reads out prayers and burns incense on coals. This, the first magic ceremony which I have seen, conducted in the light of the moon, beneath the twisted roots of a cultivated rubber plant, by a black devil, surrounded only by the same kind of wild men as himself, makes a serious and deep impression.

He wrote excitedly about this to his mother:

> For the first time ever I had a chance to see a magic ceremony conducted by people of another culture . . . the first, completely puzzling

and inexplicable example of 'magic'. I wished, for the nth time, that I
knew the local language, otherwise I cannot get anything out of such
events.

Later they came upon a group of pilgrims camped in the forest. They
had come for the Full Moon festival at a local temple. Malinowski was
reminded of Częstochowa, the centre for Catholic pilgrimage in Poland.
They wandered up a granite path to the rock temple that glittered in the
moonlight, to a series of caves surrounded by squatting Buddhas. Inside the
caves were altars and chapels overflowing with sculptures. The terrace was
full of chattering people garbed in white. Each group uttered a shout on
entering the temple, then paraded, murmuring prayers and pausing before
each altar to light candles and lay floral offerings. It made a 'profound
impression' upon him, he wrote to his mother:

> Popular Buddhism presented itself to me through this service in a very
> pleasant way. The offerings are pretty, simple and attainable for everyone,
> and the service had nothing of a mysterium about it, nothing of a rehearsed
> spectacle, performed in front of the people as a form of esoteric revela-
> tion. Everything had a strangely natural and democratic character.[18]

The only jarring aesthetic note was that of the ubiquitous white rags, hung
everywhere as offerings: 'The sacred Bo tree looks as if Lilliputians were
doing their washing in front of it.' Malinowski's tempered enthusiasm for
popular Buddhism was inspired by his observation that it lacked a 'caste of
priests'. It was therefore less authoritarian and hierarchical than the Catholicism that provided his native model for Christianity.

He slept miserably in the rest-house that night, unaware that Staś sat
trembling in his room with a Browning revolver pressed against his temple.[19]

Next morning they climbed a rock-hewn stairway to the top of the giant
granite dome that dominates the plain surrounding Dambulla. Its stark silhouette against the forest reminded Malinowski of the black fields of lava
that cut into the green gardens of the Canaries.

> Dark grey, with a subtle hint of chocolate, it recalls the shape of an enor-
> mous elephant. Everywhere I see what look like huge hindquarters, the
> drooping ears, the rounded expanse of hide. The character of the rock,
> languor, passivity, immobility – something like the expression on the face
> of a huge image of the Buddha staring into the distance.

Malinowski studied the magnificent panorama intently, eager to understand its geological composition. He noted the volcanic cones, dolomite peaks, towers and crowns, the broad tablelands, ranges and rolling hills.

> All this in miniature, assembled in a single panorama, as if displayed under an enormous bell-jar – and in addition everything covered by a monotonous green mantle, painted with a thick varnish – which gives to everything a kind of blandness, placidity and delicacy – removes the awe and wild majesty from the sternest and most fantastic forms.

Typically, Malinowski demystified his romantic appreciation of landscape by bringing to bear a scientific understanding. In New Guinea, too, no matter how entranced he was by its scenic beauty, he would seek a rational comprehension of the land's secret.

On 8 July, the travellers went to the village of Nalande, stopping on the way to inspect more shrines and ruined temples which Malinowski described in lavish detail for his mother. His letters to her from Ceylon were frequently more detailed than the entries in his diary. That night he dreamed of Annie and Leipzig: 'images of the town imbued with terrible longing, speaking in the language of sentiment.' Although Tośka also appeared in the dream, it was Annie for whom he longed. 'Staś was very unwell in Nalande,' Malinowski wrote to his mother, 'he had attacks of crying; despair.' Indeed, that night Staś had again contemplated shooting himself. 'I could not do it,' he admitted a month later, 'thoughts about my Parents kept me from it at the last minute.'[20]

Crossing the line

They returned to Colombo via Matale and Kandy, arriving on 10 July. In two weeks they had seen and experienced a great deal. Malinowski had taken many photographs – all of them, alas, now lost – and, despite his acute mental suffering, Staś had written an article and perhaps painted a few pictures.[21] After taking their luggage to the *Orontes*, they went to the Tamil district. As the sun was setting, they sat on the verandah of a hotel with glasses of lemonade. Malinowski observed:

> Black figures in white clothes, rickshaws carrying often half-naked natives, carts pulled by mules – all these Ceylon types were moving before

us for the last time. For a moment I wished we didn't have to leave, and I thought without enthusiasm about the long journey awaiting us.[22]

Despite his qualms about the journey, the ten-day voyage across the Indian Ocean proved more enjoyable than the one to Ceylon. Although smaller and older than the *Orsova*, the *Orontes* was a friendlier ship and carried fewer passengers. Other members of the British Association were aboard, Haddon and his daughter Kathleen among them – but the latter were presumably travelling first class for Malinowski does not mention them in his diary.

On boarding, Malinowski had at last received his mother's letters and the packages she had sent from England. He wrote to thank her for the chocolates and the cotton bag she had made to hang around his neck to hold his notebook. Tactfully, he referred to Tośka:

> As for the lady you mention as 'often visiting, helping and crying', her letter is very temperate. . . . At some point I too was charmed by her, I even felt attached and had some far-fetched plans for the future. . . . But I came to the conclusion that it would be impossible. I feel a lot of friendship for her, however, and would like it if Mama stayed in touch with her.

'Travelling alone is the saddest of pleasures,' he sententiously wrote to his mother, not forgetting that Staś was a companion of sorts. 'Staś isn't much better yet,' he told her:

> He keeps having attacks of sheer despair and hopelessness. It's very painful and of course doesn't contribute to the pleasure of the journey. But I don't have any problems with him, for he fully cooperates with the journey's technicalities, is very helpful, sweet and easy. . . . I try to be as helpful as I can to Staś, and remain calm, trying not to lose my balance and spirits. We must hope for the best.[23]

For Staś the trip was still 'unmitigated torture', though he managed to complete his article.[24]

Approaching the equator it grew cooler and, Malinowski told his mother, 'if it wasn't for the rocking, life on the ship would be quite pleasant'. He found the second-class passengers 'incomparably nicer' than those on the *Orsova*. Four were bound for the British Association meetings: a pair of museum curators and a married couple, the Goldings, who dressed for dinner each night and arranged dancing sessions in which he took part. Flora Golding was a thin woman 'with a completely male face and sharp, rough movements', but kind and pleasant in manner. She felt sorry for Staś and tried to befriend him.

Malinowski described the crossing-of-the-equator ceremony as 'comic sports . . . a fight of fellows tied to a pole, a race with potatoes etc.' During the mornings he pored over Sidney Ray's Melanesian grammar and studied astronomy with Staś. Thus did the voyage become unexpectedly pleasant and he stopped counting the hours to landfall.[25] Two days out from Australia the weather turned cold and showery. The darkening ocean, covered in a grey metallic sheen, reminded him of the North Sea and he remembered the sea voyages he had made with his mother.[26] The days were already short, the shadows long and the sun low in the north. 'At night we observe new southern stars,' he told Mama. 'The Cross itself is nothing special, but together with the two stars of the Centaur lying right next to it, it's very nice.'[27] In Cape Town, Annie was also looking at the southern constellations and thinking forlornly of him.

Part III

1914—1920

Chapter 15

An Alien in Australia

First contact

Like a travelling circus, the eighty-fourth meeting of the British Association was scheduled to be held sequentially in the state capitals of Perth, Adelaide, Melbourne, Sydney and Brisbane between 28 July and 31 August 1914. The congress had been mooted as early as 1909. A committee was formed at Melbourne University, chaired by the president-elect of the Australian Association for the Advancement of Science, Professor David Orme Masson – who, as fate would have it, became Malinowski's father-in-law. The Commonwealth government granted £15,000 to help meet travel and accommodation expenses for the three hundred-odd visiting scientists who were expected. The Overseas Party, as it came to be known, consisted overwhelmingly of British scientists, though there was a sprinkling of Americans, Germans and other nationalities. Malinowski was the only Pole.[1] The president of the B.A. that year was the Cambridge geneticist William Bateson, and the president of Anthropology Section H (founded in 1884, the year of Malinowski's birth) was Sir Everard im Thurn, ex-governor of Fiji. The meeting set a new attendance record; in addition to the three hundred overseas members, almost five thousand registered in Australia.[2]

The main contingent of visitors travelled on the *Euripides*, an Aberdeen Line ship on its maiden voyage. Rivers and his twenty-two-year-old Cambridge pupil John Layard were aboard, together with Marett, Grafton Elliot Smith (then professor of anatomy at Manchester), Felix von Luschan of the Berlin Museum and, among many others, the Nobel laureate physicist Sir Ernest Rutherford, and the physicist and spiritualist Sir Oliver Lodge. The Blue Funnel Line steamer *Ascanius* and the Royal Mail Steamer *Orvieto* were due in Fremantle on 28 July, each bringing about seventy members of the Advance Party. This party, including Staś and Malinowski, would board the *Orvieto* for the final leg of their sea voyage to Adelaide. Having arrived in Perth first, they, along with the Goldings and a few others, were in advance of the official Advance Party.

As the *Orontes* entered Fremantle harbour on 21 July 1914, Malinowski glimpsed the distant skyline of Perth, rising gently on two hills. His first impression of Australia – the most remote continent from Europe – was one of colonial freedom, of great possibilities, of astonishment at 'things of whose existence I did not even have an inkling'.[3] With the arrogant presumption of a European newcomer, he saw a land unspoiled by the cultural appropriations of earlier generations. As he enthused in his diary: 'Completely fresh, new views, not comprehended either in actual fact or in any artistic imagination.'

Malinowski was treated regally by his Western Australian hosts. Ernest Le Souef was a zoo director, 'a big, untidy solid fellow', who met him and Staś off the boat and drove them to south Perth in a horse-drawn wagonette. During the ride Le Souef lectured them on local botany. The Australian 'bush', Malinowski told his mother, 'looks more or less the same wherever we come across it', but he was fascinated by the myriad varieties of eucalyptus. The Le Soeufs' wooden house squatted on a knoll and its wide verandahs overlooked Perth Water. The extensive gardens incorporated the city zoo. Ellen Le Souef, a pastor's daughter, was a thin, oval-faced woman whom Malinowski judged to be 'the strongest invididual in the family [with] typical Protestant narrowness of views and stubbornness of character'. But she was kindly and provided her guests with excellent fare. To the delectation of Malinowski's sweet tooth, there was fig jam and cream for lunch.

After inspecting the zoo, they drove Staś to a hostel in the town. (He was obliged to find his own accommodation in Australia, Malinowski's being provided by local hospitality committees of the British Association.) After supper Malinowski sat with the Le Souef children and told them about Ceylon. He was amused to be treated with evident 'adoration and "pedestalization"' by Mrs Le Souef and Miss Reymont, a guest from South Australia. Doubtless he had alluded to his Polish nobility and impressed them with his cultivation. From his bedroom that evening he could hear animal noises and the squeaking of the windmill, and when he swam in the ornamental lake the following morning it was in the exciting proximity of lions and tigers.

At noon he walked into Perth where he was joined by Staś for a visit to the university ('where nobody knows anything'). Then, led by Le Souef, they rode on horseback past 'unkempt houses of sheet metal or wood' to the outskirts of the town. On this afternoon, Wednesday 22 July, Malinowski encountered his first Aborigines. He wrote to his mother about this first contact with representatives of the people to whom, sight unseen, he had devoted an entire book. 'I saw a black man from the tribe called (by Spencer) Lurija that inhabits the area next to Arunta. The conversation was very difficult because we could hardly understand each other.' Neither in his diary nor in any of his letters does Malinowski mention the degradation of the Aborigines by the white colonists who had occupied their lands.

Next day they took a long railway excursion to the legendary gold-mining town of Kalgoorlie. They travelled through interminable bush sprinkled with exotic 'blackboy' plants, then through broad fields of grain amid the wilderness, on through endless expanses of low bushland and red earth. Kalgoorlie was cold and clear beneath a yellow-green sky. They took a tram to Boulder, where they inspected the gold-diggings: 'Hammers breaking up the greenstone; then balls crushing it; moist grinding-mills,' Malinowski observed. Staś helped himself to some sodium cyanide crystals at the mining site – and on his last day in Perth went so far as to lick one, though, as he confessed later, he 'didn't have the courage' to swallow it.[4]

Back in Perth on 26 July they rode out to Guildford, where a mounted policeman conducted them to an Aborigine camp. They were treated to a demonstration of boomerang-throwing, though Malinowski admitted to his diary that he was unable to gather 'any definite information'. He was presented with a *woomera* (spearthrower) and a *churinga* (engraved sacred object). He wrote proudly to his mother next day: 'I've already seen a few Aborigines, dressed in the European way, of course, and quite "civilized" – but I think I could get a lot of information out of them, after long research.'[5] His visit to Guildford was noticed in the local Perth newspaper: 'Yesterday morning, Dr Malinowski and A. E. Le Souef paid a visit to the aboriginal encampment at Guildford and subsquently proceeded to the residence of Mr Cusack at Middle Swan.'[6] There is no mention of Staś.

A family anecdote survives concerning Malinowski's meeting with Aborigines in Western Australia. He had wandered off into the bush, and when Staś went in search of him he was alarmed to see, in the near distance, his friend being 'roasted' over a fire by a small group of Aborigines. Arms flailing, Staś ran to his aid, but Malinowski explained that they were helpfully driving away the ants that had swarmed over him when he had inadvertently sat on their nest.

On Tuesday 28 July, Malinowski visited the so-called Protector of Aborigines. They discussed boomerangs and initiation ceremonies, and he was shown 'an interesting penis of wood and stone, which they show to boys during initiation'. That evening he and Staś attended a state reception for the Advance Party which had arrived on the *Ascanius*. At this event Malinowski impressed Ellie Le Soeuf with his *savoir faire*. She wrote to him later: 'In my memory portfolio is a picture of you standing chatting to Lady Barron at Govt. House looking so delightfully happy & at ease & so born to it, that one felt glad you had the gift of adaptability when the buggy & the zooman's family & home loomed in the background!'[7]

The Empire at war

Alfred Haddon, Henry Balfour (of the Pitt Rivers Museum) and doubtless other members of the Anthropology Section were among the Advance Party, and Malinowski mingled with them next day on a visit to the Perth Museum. That evening there was a graduation ceremony at which Haddon was conferred with an honorary degree by the University of Western Australia. There were more local excursions, but Malinowski interrupted his journal on 30 July and left no record of them. They were in any case completely overshadowed by sudden, shattering news from Europe. The British Empire was at war with Germany.

Malinowski's letter to his mother from Albany, on the south coast of Western Australia, contained the first note of alarm: 'I'm very worried about the war news. . . . In Melbourne I'll have to find out at the consulate if there are any special requirements for Austrian subjects – in the worst event I'd probably be asked to return.'[8] From the same hotel address, Staś wrote an even more distressed letter to his parents:

> Today the terrible news about the war reached us in Albany. If it turns out to be true, then I'm coming back on the first steamer from Fremantle. This is the only way I can be useful and do something. Otherwise there's nothing left but the frightful prospect of going mad without being able to do creative work, the sole justification for my existence. Perhaps in this fashion I'll end my life more worthily than by suicide or painting landscapes in New Guinea or catching yellow fever.

The war gave him a reason to live and he now regretted having come to Australia. 'The absurdity of this trip is dreadful. Bronio is increasingly distant from me. Looking at specimens of Australian flora while back home such terrible things are happening makes no sense whatsoever.'[9]

On the same day, from Oderberg in Germany, Józefa Malinowska wrote to her son:

> It's indescribable what's happening in Europe. The telegraphs aren't working, the post office doesn't take responsibility for letters. . . . Nobody accepts paper money and prices are soaring. I've lost my suit-case and it's impossible to do anything about it. The suitcase contained the complete bibliography [of his Polish book] and your films. . . . Innumerable crowds of people are everywhere, here at the station and in the streets of Oderberg. . . . Tonight the last civilian train to Cracow is leaving.[10]

Others too were losing their suitcases in these tumultuous days. Although Malinowski seems to have been unaware of the fact, Tośka was simultane-ously travelling to Poland with her husband and the Conrad family. On 25 July – the day Malinowski and Staś were in Kalgoorlie – the four Conrads and the Retingers left London for Harwich and thence to Hamburg.[11] It was just three days before the war between Austria-Hungary and Serbia began, the curtain-raiser to World War I. By an extraordinary coincidence, Tancred and Anna-Mi Borenius, on their way to Finland for the summer, encountered the Retingers at Hamburg railway station, where each couple was frantically searching for lost suitcases. Anna-Mi recalled later that Malinowski had introduced them to Józef Retinger in London, though she had 'a very definite feeling that he did not like him'. Mrs Retinger, however, was 'very pretty' and Tancred had teased his friend about her. But Malinowski had responded: '"Oh no, she's a goose" with such conviction that there seemed to be a long row of o's in the "goose".'[12]

The Conrads never reached Tośka's mother's estate. It was just over the border in Russian Poland, which was now at war with Austrian Galicia. By the time their party reached Cracow the mobilization had begun. Tośka recalled: 'Our arrival at the station in Cracow in the evening of 28 July was quite a shock. What a terrible turmoil and confusion: trains full of men in uniform; soldiers everywhere – farewells, women weeping. War!'[13] The Retingers conducted the Conrads to Zakopane, where they stayed for several weeks with the Zagórska sisters in 'Konstantynówka' (the villa so familiar to Malinowski). Thanks to Józef Retinger's diplomatic efforts, the Conrads then made their way back to England, which they reached on 2 November. By then, Malinowski had begun his fieldwork in Mailu.

Adelaide

Ellie Le Souef was sorry to see Malinowski leave. She gave him some fig jam as a parting gift and wrote to him some weeks later:

> Please do not thank us for any little thing we were able to do for you, we consider that we were very privileged in having you as our guest . . . you fitted into our home life so happily and comfortably, I think you must have the gift of adapting yourself to all circumstances & surroundings, even to the old buggy!

She remembered Staś's desolation:

> I shall try to write to our 'mournful friend'. . . . Please give him our very kindest regards & sympathy both in the war troubles & in his own troubles, & we do trust that we did not ever inadvertently cause him pain thro' our joking & light conversations. . . . Time is a wonderful healer tho' the individual day & hour is most dreary.[14]

This would have given little consolation to Staś, who continued to pour out his despair in a rambling, hysterical letter to his parents. Aboard the *Orvieto* on 5 August, he bewailed his tragic fate: 'The time has come to set aside personal matters, renounce suicidal thoughts, which are utterly trivial compared to what is actually happening, and make something of one's life and of what is left of one's strength.' The trip had become a charade. He was reduced to contemptible inactivity by his distance from Europe. 'Now the sole possibility of saving one's honour and at last accomplishing something by dying in the ranks of the combatants has been taken away from me. . . . Not to be there with everyone else when the fate of Poland hangs in the balance, and to travel through Australia sightseeing.'[15]

Malinowski's predicament was no less acute, though his anxiety was as much to do with his mother's situation as it was with his own. Annie Brunton intuitively grasped his dilemma:

> How terrible it will be for her to be cut off from communication with you. . . . You are out of the fighting for which I am inwardly thankful,

but my heart bleeds for your Mother & you will feel it terribly too knowing that she is in a country where war is being waged.[16]

Despite the outbreak of war, the meetings of the British Association proceeded as scheduled: honorary degrees were solemnly conferred, speeches and toasts graciously given and received, edifying lectures entertainingly delivered, and scientifically informed excursions undertaken by motor car, train and tram.[17] Having spent years on elaborate preparations to host this 'Parliament of Savants', the Australian organizers decided to conduct the congress as if nothing untoward had happened, and after the first few days of anxious deliberations it was a case of 'don't mention the war'. Especially delicate was the situation of those foreign guests who, according to their national allegiances, suddenly found themselves to be enemy subjects. As an Austrian Pole, Malinowski was among these; as a citizen of the Russian Kingdom of Poland, Staś was not. There was some initial unease among the Australian authorities concerning how to treat the German scientists in particular. But when the *Orvieto* docked at Adelaide on the morning of Saturday 8 August, Professor David Orme Masson came aboard to greet the Germans with cordial messages from the prime minister. The Commonwealth's obligation of hospitality would be honoured and there would be no question of imprisonment.[18] Even so, a few wanted to return to Germany as soon as possible, and they were given letters of safe conduct to London.

It is likely that Malinowski made his first acquaintance with his future father-in-law under these distressing circumstances, nervously listening to reassurances from the distinguished Scottish chemist. Another fateful acquaintance he made during these few days in Adelaide was that of Sir Edward Charles Stirling (1848–1919), chairman of the South Australian British Association organizing committee and the father of five daughters. Stirling's family manifested what has been politely referred to as 'hybrid vigour', for his father was born in Jamaica of a Scottish father and a mulatto mother. [19] Stirling himself was a Cambridge man of many parts – surgeon, physical anthropologist, professor of physiology at the University of Adelaide, director of the state museum, and South Australia's first F.R.S. Having been elected to the local House of Assembly in 1884, he staunchly supported the legislation that enabled South Australian women to be the first in the world to win the franchise. Stirling accompanied the 1894 Horn expedition to central Australia, during which Baldwin Spencer's meeting with Frank Gillen, postmaster of Alice Springs, resulted in the most famous anthropological partnership of the era. In an age of armchair anthropology, Stirling discovered: 'It is only those who have made the attempt to investigate the modes of thought and mainsprings of action of the lower races of mankind who can fully appreciate the difficulties of the task.'[20] Although he subsequently published little on Aboriginal anthropology, he acquired for the South Australia Museum the largest collection of Aboriginal artifacts in the world. He was a generous-hearted man and, despite a betrayal of his trust, he did as much as anyone in Australia to steady Malinowski's shaky career.

On 10 August (the day the Commonwealth government issued a proclamation calling on all German subjects to report themselves to the police), Stirling led an excursion to Lake Alexandrina, 'for members of the Anthropology Section to study natives of the Narrinyeri tribe'. The event was reported in the local press. The party included Malinowski, Everard im Thurn, Balfour, Haddon, Marett, Rivers, Felix von Luschan, Fritz Graebner and one of Stirling's daughters. She was Nina, the youngest.[21]

Meanwhile, Staś Witkiewicz kept to his room in Clark's Botanic Hotel, penning more lines of paranoid recrimination. The longest of his writings from Australia to survive, it documents his superstitious belief in the inauspicious personal significance of the time 'twenty minutes before ten' and the number seventeen. It is an essay in what Jung would call synchronicity. For example: 'When I received the letter from Bronislaw Malinowski which decided everything about the whole trip . . . [the] clock was pointing to that hour.'[22] Despite many such 'warnings', he had embarked upon the trip, which happened to be the seventeenth voyage of the *Orsova*. When they boarded the *Orontes* in Colombo the hour was twenty to ten. After receiving news of the war, he had intended to wait in Perth for a boat back to Europe, but Malinowski had persuaded him to go on to Adelaide. It was a mistake, for he missed the last steamer. ('Bronio's advice, seemingly good, always turns out to be bad'.) Between fruitless visits to the Russian and the Austrian consuls in Adelaide that morning he noticed a clock at twenty minutes to ten. He admitted to being half-deranged and concluded with a note to his parents, begging their forgiveness. In another note to Malinowski he wrote: 'don't laugh at what I'm writing. Some day you'll understand it all.'[23] More conventionally, Malinowski's superstition concerned Friday the thirteenth.

Melbourne

On the afternoon of 12 August – the day the British Empire declared war on Austria-Hungary – the Overseas Party and accompanying local members packed into three special trains and travelled through the night, arriving in Melbourne the next day. The capital city of the state of Victoria, Melbourne was also the provisional seat of federal government pending its transfer to Canberra, the as yet unbuilt capital of the Commonwealth of Australia. Malinowski's arrival in Melbourne coincided with the extension of surveillance to citizens of Austria-Hungary. He kept no diary during these days, so his impressions of two of the most influential men in Melbourne, Baldwin Spencer and Atlee Hunt, are unknown, but his future in Australia and Papua lay firmly in their hands. Their combined patronage laid the very foundation of his future work.

Manchester-born Walter Baldwin Spencer (1860–1929) was foundation professor of zoology at the University of Melbourne (to which post he had pipped Haddon in 1886) and director of the National Museum of Victoria. He was also secretary of the organizing committee of the British Association; he and Chairman Masson were not only colleagues but the closest of friends. Internationally, Spencer was renowned as Australia's most distinguished anthropologist. Almost certainly, he had met Malinowski during a fleeting visit to London in January of that year. He would have known him as the young Polish author who had favourably reviewed his last book, *Across Australia*, and who had questioned some of his ethnography in *The Family among the Australian Aborigines*.[24] Spencer had gone to Britain to collect various honours and to present George Macmillan with the manuscript of *Native Tribes of the Northern Territory of Australia*. He had also visited his old friend James Frazer – whose evolutionary assumptions underpinned Spencer's own work – and had found time to lecture in Manchester, Oxford, Cambridge and London. It was probably on the occasion of the last of these lectures, held at the Royal Geographical Society, that Malinowski had first met him. Annie Brunton remembered the man and the occasion, especially 'those interesting records we heard', referring to Spencer's sensational multimedia lecture in which he deployed phonograph, lantern slides and cinematography.[25] 'He spoke badly though,' Annie thought, and she couldn't follow what he said.[26] In another letter she referred to him as 'quite an insignificant looking man'. True, he was slight and thin-faced with drooping melancholy eyes, but his impressive Nietzschean moustache would have surely belied her epithet.[27]

As chief host to the visiting anthropologists, Spencer presided over a cosy coterie of senior British colleagues whom he entertained at the gentlemanly Melbourne Club. From this distinctly English professional cabal Malinowski and Staś would have been excluded. Balfour stayed with Spencer, his classmate at Oxford. Marett was rector of Spencer's former college, and was lodged nearby with Haddon and Rivers. Where Malinowski stayed is uncertain, and of the association's meetings he recorded nothing, though he would have attended a large reception at the National Museum and inspected the major exhibition of stone artifacts mounted by Spencer. He would also have attended the Section H session, in which Rivers read a paper on the complexity of Australian culture, and Grafton Elliot Smith one on the spread of 'certain customs and inventions' (including megalithic monuments). This paper represented the latest chapter in the development of Elliot Smith's extravagant diffusionist theory which Malinowski would attack scornfully in years to come. There were other social events. On Friday evening, Sir Oliver Lodge surrendered the presidency of the British Association to William Bateson – with such reluctance, it seems, that he was promptly nicknamed Sir Oliver Hard-to-Dislodge.

Among the local members of the British Association were Miss Elsie Rosaline Masson and Miss Marianne Weigall, who wore white roses as badges and acted as campus guides. They perhaps went unnoticed by Malinowski, though he did meet Elsie's elder sister Marnie, who was acting as secretary to her father and handling the visitors' mail. John Layard, in a 'mental fog' at the time, remembered meeting Malinowski and Radcliffe-Brown (then still A. R. Brown) and of 'feeling most inferior' when their conversation went completely over his head.[28] They would have had much to talk about – the varieties of Australian totemism for one thing, which was the subject of the paper Radcliffe-Brown delivered in Sydney.[29]

Malinowski carried with him a letter of introduction from Pember Reeves, the director of the LSE, to no less a personage than Joseph Cook, the Australian prime minister, though it was to the permanent secretary of the Department of External Affairs that he presented himself. Arthur Atlee Hunt (1864–1935), an efficient, impeccably attired lawyer and senior public servant, was the gatekeeper to Papua. He had done much to steer through the federal parliament the bill, enacted in 1906, that brought British New Guinea under Australian control. Hunt, moreover, had an enlightened belief in the practical value of anthropological research for colonial administration. A 'responsive, congenial and decisive friend' of Baldwin Spencer and Alfred Haddon, Hunt consulted them on issues concerning Australia's territories (Spencer on the Northern Territory, Haddon on Papua) and they kept him privately informed of matters that the more formal communications of the administrators were inclined to ignore or obfuscate.[30] It was probably on the personal recommendation of Spencer and Haddon that Malinowski was granted urgent access to Hunt within a day of his arrival in Melbourne.

Pember Reeves's letter opened the official file on Malinowski, a file that thickened inexorably during the years that followed until it was closed with Malinowski's departure from Australia on 25 February 1920.[31] He was, wrote Reeves, 'an investigator of exceptional promise and ability' who 'proposes to spend from a year to eighteen months doing Anthropological research work in New Guinea'.[32] Atlee Hunt, in turn, provided Malinowski with several letters of introduction to managers of the Sydney-based trading company Burns Philp, to administration officers in Papua and, of course, to Hubert Murray, lieutenant-governor of the Colony of Papua. These letters, all dated 14 August 1914, are clear evidence that, despite Malinowski's status as an 'enemy alien', Hunt had no hesitation in endorsing his plans for fieldwork and facilitating his travel to Port Moresby.[33] The letter to Murray was explicit about Malinowski's intention 'to begin in Mailu' and, in case Murray was in any doubt: 'The Minister has taken a personal interest in his mission and desires that everything the Government can properly do to help him should be done but I am sure one has only to mention his mission to you for you to give the fullest possible instructions on his behalf.'[34] Hunt's relationship with Murray was abrasive and often strained, and each was wont to spell things out with excessive politeness for the other's benefit.

Malinowski was heavily armed with a number of other letters of introduction, most of them dated late June, so they had most probably been solicited by Seligman after Malinowski's departure and forwarded to Perth by his mother. Dr William Mersh Strong wrote severally to the London Missionary Society missionaries Holmes, Dauncey and Riley at their stations in the Papuan Gulf, saying that Malinowski was 'particularly anxious to learn all he can in the short time at his disposal about the Purari tribes'. Hedging his bets, Strong wrote also to Mrs Elizabeth Mahony, 'the Queen of Sudest', in the Louisiade Archipelago of eastern Papua, as well as to the Anglican missionary Copland King in the Mambare region of northern Papua.[35] Sidney Ray, veteran of the Torres Strait expedition, also wrote to

Holmes in the Gulf, indicating that Malinowski's inquiries would be 'in the Sociology of the Gulf peoples or in the Folklore', adding, 'I think also you will find him interested in the languages.'[36] The most informative of these letters, however, was that of Seligman to the Rev. Dauncey, a missionary whom he had met while conducting his survey of British New Guinea in 1904. Seligman expected Malinowski to 'work among some of the people between Hood Point and Mullins Harbour, especially in the neighbourhood of Mailu'. He added: 'but I dare say he will also be down your way, and I shall be very grateful for any help or kindness you may be able to give him.'[37] Few neophyte anthropologists can have entered a foreign field with support from so many well-connected sponsors calling upon the assistance of so many influential local figures. Yet at this very juncture Malinowski was having second thoughts about going to New Guinea.

Sydney

The newspapers were dominated by despatches from the Western theatre and gave almost no coverage to events in Eastern Europe. On 23 August, Malinowski wrote to his mother:

> I'm extremely upset by the present situation, how you will be able to cope in this state of affairs. After a lot of thought I decided against going back to Europe. . . . Most certainly you are in Cracow now, where, I believe, you'll get as much help and provisions as one can get during a war. It's terrible sitting here doing nothing while such horrible and momentous things are happening at home.

He had been talking to Haddon and Rivers, and they suggested that he might usefully accompany the latter on his survey of another part of Melanesia:

> As for myself, I still have enough money and I'm going with Rivers and another young man [Layard] to the New Hebrides. I decided not to go to New Guinea directly. The New Hebrides have a much better climate, so I can adapt myself to the climate gradually. Also the training I can get from Rivers is extremely important. So please don't worry about me.[38]

Haddon and his daughter Kathleen, who was collecting string figures, had originally planned for Layard to accompany them up the Fly river, but Haddon was forced to make other arrangements as the Papuan government boat was stranded and all other vessels were being requisitioned for war service. Haddon gave Layard the £50 that he would have spent in Papua and committed him to Rivers's tender care 'as he would thus have the invaluable opportunity of practical tuition and supervision by the greatest field investigator of primitive sociology that there has ever been'.[39] It was fortunate for Malinowski, however, that the plan to accompany Rivers to the New Hebrides fell through. After only two weeks, Rivers abandoned Layard on an offshore island of Malekula and continued with his own style of itinerant anthropology aboard the flagship of the Anglican mission.

With some exaggeration (though it is testimony to the reassurances Atlee Hunt had given him), Malinowski told his mother that the Australian government had 'guaranteed' him some sort of 'temporary job'. He did not think this would be necessary, however, as Mond's advance had come through and he now had £220. The next day he wrote again, summarizing his reasons for not returning to Poland: '1. It would be impossible for me to get from here to Austria; 2. I don't think I could be of much use; I'd more likely cause some difficulties, because I doubt if I'd be able to bring in the money in gold, and paper money would be worthless there.'[40] These were sound enough reasons. Unlike Staś, Malinowski was unfit for military service owing to his poor eyesight, and unlike Staś, who was born in Warsaw and could travel with Russian papers through allied territories to Russian Poland, Malinowski would have been prevented from returning to Austrian Galicia. Staś was returning to Poland, Malinowski now told Mama: 'The news of the war shocked him tremendously and transformed him; he wants to be at home at any cost.'

Malinowski was already uncertain whether his letters would get through and, like many people similarly separated, he and his mother wrote repetitive letters and posted them in scatter-gun fashion, in the hope that one at least might reach its destination. Later they would also send their letters through various third parties in different countries, by this device crossing enemy lines. Seligman was one such conduit, Miss Halina Nusbaum in Warsaw another, and soon more distant aquaintances – Poles, Australians, Italians, Swiss and Americans – kindly passed on their letters. Many months elapsed before they were delivered, however. Personal news was invariably out of date when it arrived and the more unsettling for that.

The British Association arrived in Sydney on 20 August, having travelled overnight from Victoria. Malinowski had banking arrangements to make, and business with Burns Philp concerning his supplies. Through Haddon he met Charles Hedley, a zoologist and ethnologist at the Sydney Museum. They became friends and subsequently Malinowski looked him up whenever he passed through Sydney.

Section H held its meetings in the University of Sydney. In his presidential address, Sir Everard im Thurn held forth on the 'primitive character' of Melanesians and Polynesians, taking the benevolent view that 'the reception by "savages" of the first white men they saw . . . was apparently kindly, though this kindness may really have been due to fear and not to charity'.[41] Malinowski was perhaps reassured by this. In his own paper ('A Fundamental Problem of Religious Sociology'), delivered on Tuesday 25 August, Malinowski revisited the Durkheimian categories of sacred and profane. As in his review of *The Elementary Forms of Religious Life*, he argued that there was no warrant for claiming universality for the distinction, and that it was therefore not an 'essential and fundamental feature of religion', but an 'accidental' one dependent upon 'the social part played by religion' in any given society.[42] The session that day was opened by Haddon with a discussion of the practical uses of anthropology for colonial administration.

Brisbane: 'Finis amicitiae'

The lumbering caravan of the British Association came to a final halt in humid Brisbane, the state capital of Queensland. A celebratory lunch was provided by the government, and the following day there was a civic reception hosted by the mayor. Next day Malinowski and Staś joined a rail excursion to Nambour and the Blackall Ranges, winding past the inselbergs of the Glasshouse Mountains.[43] On Monday 31 August, they took a steamer down the Brisbane river, and that evening, the last one of the congress, Haddon gave a public lecture on 'Decorative Art in Papua'.

The resoundingly successful meeting ended, according to schedule, on 1 September. The war, however, had disrupted the travel arrangements of many of the visitors. About forty of them remained in Brisbane to await the *Montoro*, which would take them to Cairns, Java and Singapore. The majority, numbering about ninety, were returned by train to Sydney, where they embarked for Europe aboard the *Morea*.[44] Staś Witkiewicz was among them.

Malinowski had accompanied him to Toowoomba. There they had chatted with Sir Oliver and Lady Lodge and Staś tactlessly 'corrected' his friend in their presence. Whatever he said, it infuriated Malinowski and almost destroyed their friendship. They parted on the worst of terms. Reflecting on the event in his diary two months later, the incident still rankled and Staś's subsequent letters of rebuke had made it worse. '*Finis amicitiae*', lamented Malinowski. 'Nietzsche breaking with Wagner. I respect his art and admire his intelligence and worship his individuality, but I cannot stand his character.'[45]

It was an unhappy but not entirely unpredictable development. Their friendship had been under enormous strain throughout the journey. Apart from petty disagreements over money, there had been Malinowski's failure to cope adequately with Staś's despair. A European war now placed them on opposing sides. As Poles first and foremost, though not fiercely patrotic ones, it might have been different had they been in Cracow or Zakopane when the war broke out. Malinowski would not have fought in any case, and had Staś been at home in Zakopane he might have thought twice about joining the Russian army, considering how many of his friends were fighting for Galicia. But so far from home both men were hostages to distance. Staś was now passionately committed to joining the battle, to sacrifice his life in order to save it. Malinowski was ambivalent about returning, despite the plight he imagined his mother to be in, and he presented arguments for remaining detached, not simply to reassure his Australian hosts, but out of a genuine desire to begin his fieldwork with the least fuss. Under the circumstances, the two friends had few grounds for agreement.

There was also something deeper, something in the personalities of both young men that had stitched a persistently antagonistic strain into their friendship. Years ago Staś had charged Malinowski with a cold 'scientific' detachment that he found distasteful and even repellent; while Malinowski (alias Edgar, Duke of Nevermore) had charged Staś with a lack of integrity, an undisciplined squandering of vital energy. So the essence of their quarrel lay in Staś's disgust with Bronio's detachment, in his placing personal career above everything, and Malinowski's disgust with Staś's personalizing of the war, such that he would sacrifice himself to assuage his guilt over the suicide of his fiancée. It was a poignant quarrel: that of two greatly talented men whose complementarity forged a unique and passionate comradeship that was suddenly dashed on the rocks of a terrible circumstance – a world war no less. Mutual recriminations continued for months, and their frayed friendship never fully recovered, though this was in part owing to the radical divergence of their subsequent careers, and to the fact that henceforth they lived in different countries and saw very little of one another.

On 5 September, Staś boarded the *Morea* and sailed for Europe. Among his fellow passengers were the Goldings, companions of the voyage from Ceylon. Florence Golding wrote to Malinowski concerning Staś while their ship was rolling in the Great Bight: 'The silent artist has found the boat too unsteady for work so far but hopes for better luck after Fremantle. He talks more than he did but doesn't look any happier.'[46]

Staś, too, wrote to Malinowski from Fremantle. 'I wish you'd devote some thought to your character. Not for my sake, but for your own. You may have some very serious regrets later on.' Without being specific about the nature of his friend's offence, he continued:

> A person can make mistakes and try to atone for them. But one cannot regard oneself cynically. Because that closes the door on any hopes of improvement. I must confess that as it stands now I don't believe in you. . . . And I bear no grudge against you on my own account, only on your account.[47]

This was probably the letter that Malinowski received in Mailu on 29 October. It upset him deeply, as his diary records:

> I see almost no possibility of reconciliation. I also know that however many faults I have committed, he acted very ruthlessly toward me; all the time having gestures and airs of persecuted greatness and moralizing in accents of deep, mature, objective wisdom. . . . I am terribly dejected and dispirited by the bankruptcy of my most essential friendship. The first reaction of holding myself responsible for everything predominates, and I feel *capitis diminutio* – a worthless man, of diminished value.[48]

Staś's mood lifted during his voyage to Europe, and something of his old jocularity animated his letter to Malinowski written a day out from Aden:

> The *Morea* is very appealing, far better than the Orient liners. . . . Mrs Golding is a marvelous woman. Too bad she's old. . . . I seduced a Portuguese whore from Brazil, but without any great pleasure. . . . I've been flirting with various foreign broads. I hardly recognize myself. I've gone completely soft in the head. I'm sketching quite a few portraits. Social life quite diabolical. . . . I try to stupefy myself so as to endure this trip. . . . I squeeze your crooked claws. Sometimes I'm fearful about your health.[49]

About the same time, Malinowski wrote in his diary in Port Moresby: 'Occasionally I think of Staś, with increasing bitterness, missing his company. But I am glad he is not here.'[50]

A fragment survives of a letter from Florence Golding to Malinowski, offering her version of Staś's improved spirits:

> [He] 'came out' tremendously on the homeward voyage – did charcoal sketches of various passengers, fell in love temporarily with a professor's wife, and became quite an intimate chum of mine and my husband's. . . . He certainly has the most lurid personality of anyone I have ever met and we got very fond of him in spite of his peculiarities and difficult temperament.[51]

In Alexandria, Staś was arrested by the British and held briefly on suspicion of being a German professor named Penck (a mistaken identification he would have found hilarious). He then made his way to Petrograd (St Petersburg) and despite the loss of his papers managed – not without some agonizing – to enter the training school for elite officer corps. He wrote to Malinowski with news of events in Poland.[52] Many of their friends had taken up arms against Austria, but 'now the skirmishing in Galicia has completely collapsed and every Pole can with a clean conscience go against our only true enemy, the Germans'. Stefan Żeromski had been wounded, Strug killed, and Tetmajer shot himself. To Staś's father, however, the Russians were the only true enemy and it distressed him to learn that Staś had opted to fight on their side. Kept apart by the war, father and son never met again. Stanisław Witkiewicz died in Lovran in September 1915 and was given a celebrity's burial in Zakopane.

Staś was now feeling some 'pangs of conscience', fearing his friend might 'die of a tropical fever or something worse'. Despite these expressions of friendship, Staś was still bitter about the moral defection of 'Malinowski':

> I'm writing to your former spirit. Malinowski has ceased to exist for me and I must admit that I haven't felt any nostalgia for him. In your company I felt nostalgic for Bronio, and now I think about the good old days when the dialectic of the void and the spouting of quintessential lies concealed the poverty of our deeds.

He accused Malinowski of teaching him cynicism: 'to have a total lack of faith in any noble impulses whatsoever . . . and the conviction that at bottom human motives are always petty and mean.'[53] By splitting Malinowski into a good and a bad, a past and a present, self, Staś could forgive him: 'Don't think I hate you. . . . I'm writing to Bronio about Malinowski and about the person who has stopped being Staś, but has not yet become anyone else.'[54]

Malinowski's letters to Staś have not survived, but his diary reveals the depth of his hurt and indignation, even to the very last page, dated 18 July 1918, where he refers simply to 'Staś's betrayal'.[55]

'An expedition all on my own to the tropics'

Malinowski felt deserted when the cosseting crowd of the British Association had departed Brisbane. He opened his retrospective diary of the period: '1st September began a new epoch in my life: an expedition all on my own to the tropics.' Beneath the bravado was a wistfully sad statement of fact. He had not expected to be alone, and 1 September was the day he had parted so bitterly from Staś.

He stayed at the Hotel Daniel and visited the Queensland Museum with anthropologists Peter Pringsheim and Fritz Graebner, both of whom were anxious to return to Berlin. A far more important contact in Brisbane was Adelaide-born Elton Mayo (1880–1949), foundation lecturer in mental and moral philosophy at the University of Queensland. Mayo was a Left-leaning social theorist with a passionate interest in workers' education who would become one of the most influential industrial psychologists in the United States. Elton and his wife, Dorothea, invited Malinowski to dinner the night before he sailed. They impressed him as 'immensely charming people' and he always contrived to stay with them on subsequent visits to Brisbane.

Malinowski bought more medicines: cocaine, morphine and emetics. He was taking no chances. 'Strong fear of the tropics,' he noted in his diary, 'abhorrence of heat and sultriness – a kind of panic fear of encountering heat as terrible as last June and July.' On 5 September he boarded the *Matunga*, the Burns Philp boat that carried his transshipped cargo from Europe. Despite the war, some things still ran smoothly. He waved the Mayos out of sight and felt he was taking leave of civilization, 'afraid I might not feel equal to the task before me'. He soon cheered up, however, and began to enjoy the trip along the Great Barrier Reef, with a self-important awareness that he was 'one of the more notable passengers aboard'. He studied Motu grammar, played cards and in the evenings danced on deck with Mrs MacGrath, the landlady of a boarding house in Port Moresby.

On 9 September, the ship docked at Cairns in a lovely bay flanked by forested mountains. Malinowski soon dismissed the town as 'small, uninteresting, its people marked with tropical self-conceit'. Ashore, he talked with an Aborigine ('from whom no information whatever could be obtained') and met 'a drunken Russkie' who smuggled birds of paradise. The *Montoro* entered port bringing the Haddons and Balfour; the latter was bound for Singapore, the Haddons for Thursday Island in Torres Strait.

Malinowski chided himself for reading a Rider Haggard novel during the voyage. But he was also reading Rivers who, meanwhile, was steaming from Sydney for the New Hebrides with his hero-worshipping but soon to be disillusioned pupil, John Layard.[56] Malinowski reboarded the *Matunga*. Queasy on a rough sea, and unable to do anything except sing English songs on the deck with the ship's company, he finally approached the humid shores of New Guinea.

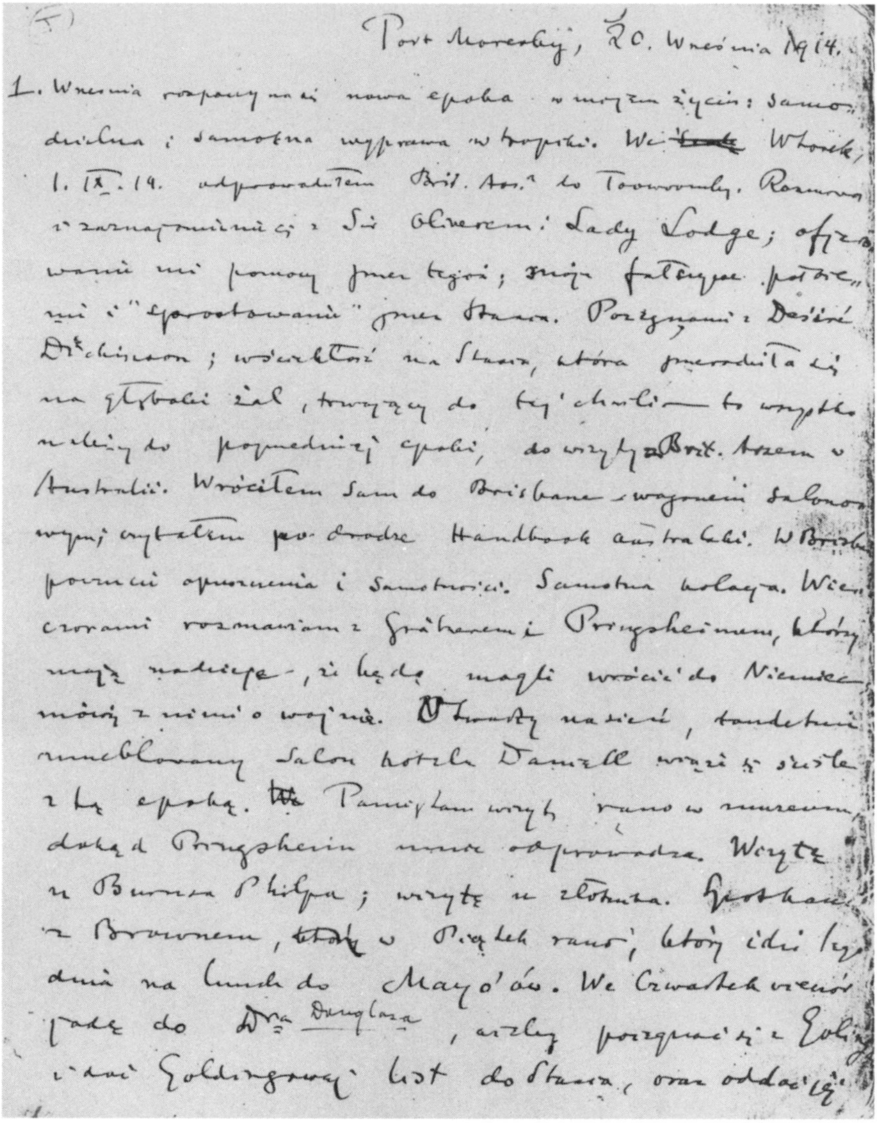
Port Moresby, 20. Września 1914.

1. Września rozpoczyna się nowa epoka w moim życiu: samodzielna i samotna wyprawa w tropiki. We wtorek, 1. IX. 14. odprowadziłem Brit. Ass.n do Toowoomby.

Fig. 1 Facsimile of the first page of Malinowski's New Guinea diary. Port Moresby, 20 September 1914.

Chapter 16

'The Promised Land'

A view from the verandah

Landed on New Guinea soil on the morning of Saturday, 12 September 1914, it took Malinowski only a day to realize that, for him at least, the 'quintessence' of Port Moresby lay in the axis connecting its native villages with Government House. Hanuabada, the 'Great Village' of local Motu people, represented the very purpose that had brought him to Papua; it comprised several streets of ramshackle huts on stilts which straggled into the harbour from the refuse-littered shore. Government House was the locus of imperial power which could help or hinder him; it overlooked Hanuabada and more distant Motu villages from its position on the hillside.

Malinowski visited neither site on the day of his arrival. Tired and rather depressed, he remained in the sprawling, shabby township, supervising his cargo, checking into the Moresby Hotel, presenting his credentials to Herbert Champion, the government secretary and Miles Staniforth Smith, the administrator. He then dragged himself up the hill to visit Mrs Ashton, a widowed planter, from whose verandah he surveyed the calm blue harbour in its splendid setting of sun-seared hills.[1]

From the larger verandah of Government House, a mile distant around the harbour, Lieutenant-Governor Murray enjoyed magnificent sunsets. Compared to the solid splendour of the governor's residence in German New Guinea, Murray's cheaply constructed house was shoddy. The local climate could be trying, and in Murray's words the site was 'swept for eight months of the year by the full force of the south-east trades, and scorched by the almost vertical rays of the sun'.[2] The surrounding hills were usually biscuit-brown, but there were visual compensations in the seaward views of islets and coral reefs, and of course the brilliant sunsets. Malinowski's

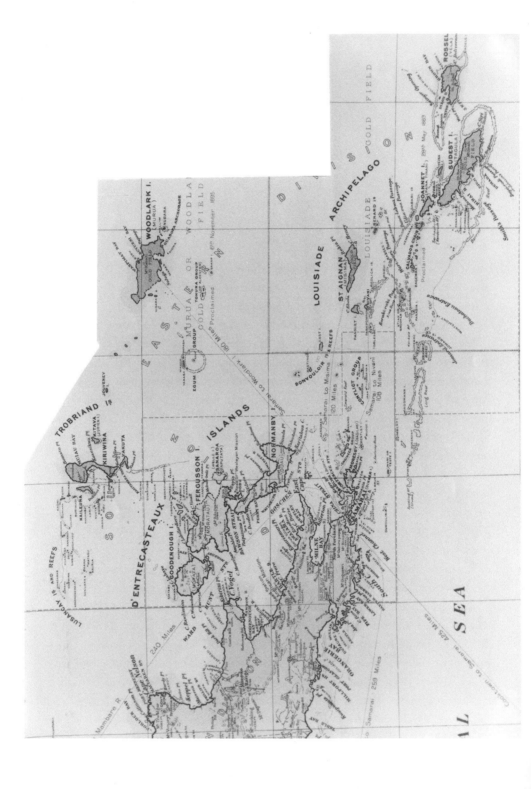

descriptions, more extravagant than Murray's, deployed a painterly palette that included milky-pink shadows, turquoise vegetation, rich purple stones, deep-sapphire sea, azure-blue sky, 'a mad orgy of the most intense colours.'

Malinowski was also impressed by the trappings of colonial power that surrounded Murray in this otherwise threadbare town. On his first visit to Government House he was rowed around the harbour by whaleboat. Its crew 'of fuzzy-headed savages in government uniform' gave him 'very much the "sahib" feeling'. He was greeted and conducted to the residence by Leonard Murray, the governor's nephew and private secretary.[3]

Larger than Britain in area, Papua is the southeastern quarter of the vast, thickly forested and inconceivably rugged island of New Guinea which perches like a great bird above the Australian continent. The western half had been claimed by the Dutch, the northeastern sector by the Germans, and in 1884 – the year of Malinowski's birth – the southeastern portion had become a British Protectorate. In 1906 the Commonwealth of Australia took over responsibility for British New Guinea and renamed it Papua. The colony, or Territory of Papua (as Australians preferred to call it), was therefore only eight years old when Malinowski arrived, though it had been thinly settled by Europeans for more than thirty. Intentionally or carelessly, Malinowski usually referred to Papua in his publications by the anachronism 'British New Guinea'.

The man who did more than anyone to shape the destiny of Papua was John Hubert Plunket Murray (1861–1940). At the time of his death in Samarai he had achieved international renown as a colonial administrator; he was still in office then, having served an unprecedented thirty-three years as lieutenant-governor. Born in Sydney of Irish descent, Murray was a commanding six feet and three inches in height and weighed a muscular fourteen stone. He was a fine swordsman, had rowed for his Oxford college, and once won the amateur British heavyweight boxing championship. At Oxford, where he had been a contemporary of Baldwin Spencer, he took a first in classics before studying law. Every year he reread Pindar's *Epinicia*, Milton's *Paradise Lost* and Goethe's *Faust*. He had served in the Boer War with distinction, attaining the rank of lieutenant-colonel. After practising law in Sydney for a number of disappointing years, he came to Port Moresby as chief judicial officer and served under the administrator of British New Guinea, Captain R. F. Barton, an amateur ethnographer who had assisted Seligman.

In 1906, a royal commission of inquiry gave Murray his chance. His testimony of maladministration, incompetence and sundry wrong-doing in the colony brought about the dismissal or resignation of several officers, including Barton. Amid much ill-feeling, Murray replaced him as administrator, and after the passage of the Papua Act he was appointed lieutenant-governor. Still, his authority remained circumscribed by Atlee Hunt and his minister who held the purse strings in Melbourne. Hunt had actually favoured Staniforth Smith for the top job but Murray outmanoeuvred them and Smith had to be content with the lesser post of administrator. Their antagonism became legendary.

Murray favoured a spartan existence in this raw and uncultured frontier society. He had sworn off drink years before and, although married, he was a grass widower: his wife could not abide the climate and spent most of the year in Sydney. To female admirers like the Irish-Australian writer Beatrice Grimshaw, Murray was shy and modest; to his enemies like Staniforth Smith, he was coldly calculating and malicious. For his part, Murray regarded Smith as 'a large ex-politician who discourses on all subjects with equal facility and ignorance'. Murray's opinion of Atlee Hunt was even more unkind: 'a commonplace bounder, fat of both body and brain'.[4] By comparison, what he said about Malinowski was only mildly offensive.

Murray's mask of indifference and his cultivation of stoic virtues disguised an emotional nature that sometimes erupted in spasms of temper.[5] His physical presence could inspire awe and he looked every inch an imperial governor out of Rudyard Kipling. On first meeting Murray, twenty-two years his senior, Malinowski was reminded of his Uncle Staszewski. He found him to be 'pleasant, calm, and a bit stiff'.[6] Although Malinowski's relations with the most powerful man in Papua were initially cordial, it was not long before Murray felt antipathy towards him. 'He is a very clever man, I think,' he wrote to his brother George soon after Malinowski's arrival, 'but I do not like him. It is not merely that he treats me with that strange mixture of patronage and intolerance which is the inseparable heritage of men of science: there is something wrong about him though I do not know what it is.'[7] Better known as Gilbert Murray – later Regius professor of classics at Oxford – George would form a more agreeable opinion of the anthropologist and by the late 1920s they had become good friends. Hubert Murray's view betrayed a more general prejudice against scientists, especially those who were not British, and he came to suspect Malinowski of pro-German sympathies and moral turpitude. For the moment, however, the Polish ethnologist was entertained at Government House, where he met Murray's senior officers and the thin cream of Port Moresby society.

Murray's Papua

Pro-consul Hubert Murray pursued a dual policy with somewhat incompatible goals: to encourage the economic development of Papua and to raise the Papuan, as he put it, 'to the highest level of civilization of which he is capable'. Although he did not subscribe to the common belief that Papuans were 'a childlike race', like most imperial officers he did believe in the innate inferiority of the colonized. The native was not so much lazy as 'lacking in determination and perserverance', and he sought to promote 'an industrial ideal' – which meant, in the main, wage labour for whites on their plantations and in their mines. To protect Papuans from exploitation, Murray developed one of the most complex bodies of labour legislation in the colonial world. Inevitably, its strict application made him enemies among settlers who depended upon a ready supply of native labour. Under Murray, Papua would never pay for itself and he governed on the shoestring budget grudgingly granted by the Commonwealth. Lord Hailey (with whom Malinowski collaborated concerning Africa in the 1930s) probably got it right when he pronounced that the legendary 'Murray System' of administration amounted 'to no more than a well-regulated and benevolent type of police rule'.[8]

In 1912 Murray had estimated that half the Territory remained unexplored. There were no roads worthy of the name, and all travel had to be done on foot or by boat. There was only the most general idea of the size of Papua's native population, and estimates varied wildly from one-quarter to three-quarters of a million. Murray's goal was peaceful penetration. His broad scheme was first to pacify the whole of the Territory and then to tax the natives in order to fund their own development through the provision of education, health and other amenities. Bringing areas under government control involved the creation of 'islands of influence' through an 'oil-stain policy'. A government station was like a drop of oil which spread out from where it fell; a number of such spots would eventually merge to cover the entire surface.[9] Strenuous patrolling was the key to maintaining links between centres and peripheral areas, and Murray happily set an athletic example by his own arduous treks. He abjured punitive expeditions and held his officers to account for any loss of life that occurred during exploratory patrols; by 1914 spears hurled in one's direction were no excuse to open fire on nervous natives.

The suppression of tribal fighting was a necessary preliminary to full government control. By this Murray meant the implementation of 'Native Regulations' concerning clean and sanitary villages, coconut plantings and the reporting of offences to government-appointed village constables. These were empowered to take culprits to the nearest government station to be dealt with by the resident magistrate, as district officers were called.

By 1914, except for a few isolated pockets of resistance, all the coastal areas from the Dutch border in the west to the German border in the northeast were under government control. But much of the interior remained uncontrolled and some areas awaited exploration. Increased pacification required the establishment of more government stations and the recruitment of more field officers and armed native police to man them. Native administration at remote outstations largely depended on the calibre of the resident magistrates in charge and Murray was chronically short of 'good men'. The war reduced his staff by a third, and many of his best officers volunteered for active service.

Murray's administration was criticized by white settlers for pampering and coddling the natives, but to the villagers whose lives were shadowed by government intervention it must have seemed very different. Beginning in 1890, the list of 'forbidden acts' proscribed by Native Regulations grew by the year. To mention only those enacted in the few years before Malinowski's arrival: Papuans with dysentery were forbidden to enter Port Moresby (they were already forbidden to live there unless employed by whites); drumming and dancing in the town and nearby villages were forbidden after 9 p.m. Already proscribed were abortion, gambling and the consumption of alcohol; regulations concerning health and sanitation were legion. In short, the colonial government, allied with the missions, sought to control the very bodies of the natives 'for their own good'. Papuans had to be protected from themselves as well as from Europeans. Adultery and sorcery were, after homicide, among the most serious offences; both were punishable by six months' imprisonment.

In the villages, resident magistrates were empowered to prosecute and punish offenders against the regulations – including the offence of disobeying orders issued by the magistrate himself. The scope for local tyranny was considerable, and the wonder perhaps is that more officers did not take despotic advantage of their position. But Murray's own oversight was keen, and his handpicked 'outside men' were bound by tight rules of conduct, infractions of which he punished without favour.

The relationship most white settlers had with Papuans was one-dimensional and based on a perception of racial caste. Papuans were regarded primarily as workers or servants, and stereotyping followed accordingly. At their worst, they were characterized as intractable, lazy, slothful, indigent, excitable, mendacious, untrustworthy, stubborn and licentious. There was a strategic necessity as well as a cultural preference for the social distance that separated whites from blacks, for if hundreds of thousands of Papuans were to be ruled by a few hundred European officers the latter had to cultivate an attitude of aloof superiority to maintain white prestige. Murray called it 'administration by bluff'. Keeping up standards was therefore an imperial duty ('discarding one's socks leads to the beach and the loin cloth'), and fear of polluting their caste meant that it was only proper to dismiss officers who consorted with native women.[10] Directly exposed as he was to these colonial values and protocols, Malinowski did not seriously challenge them.

The broader colonial society within which Malinowski pursued his fieldwork between 1914 and 1918 was loosely organized. It was governed from Australia and consisted predominantly of British-Australian officers, missionaries, traders, miners, planters, pearlers, service personnel and an assortment of other settlers, altogether numbering barely twelve hundred in 1914. There were marginal people, too – half-castes, a few Chinese, Malays and Filipinos – though Malinowski had little to do with any of these. In his ethnographic accounts of Papuans he largely ignored members of the colonial scene. When he did refer in his texts to the Government Officer, the Missionary, and the Trader, he presented them as stereotypes. In his diaries, however, they loom large, impacting as they did on his daily life. His character sketches of certain figures are acute and they appear in all their idiosyncratic variety. If read with an alertness to their historical detail, his diaries permit a better view of the colonial context of his fieldwork than do any of his monographs.

Before moving to Mrs McGrath's less rowdy boarding house, Malinowski spent a few nights at Tom McCrann's Moresby Hotel. This was a typical Australian country-style hotel with wide, trellised verandahs; it had gas lighting, running water, a billard room and fresh food brought by the regular Burns Philp Line steamers. Tom Ryan's more upmarket Papua Hotel could boast electric lighting, ceiling fans and a freezing plant that supplied the town with ice and frozen meat. Next door was an open-air cinema which screened silent films twice weekly.

Port Moresby was the exclusive preserve of whites; unless they worked in the town, Papuans were assumed to have no business there. Considerably smaller than, say, Ventnor or Cairns, Port Moresby's population was under four hundred. But Papua was booming in 1914 and the town had begun to acquire modern amenities. Recent discoveries of gold, copper and oil had raised expectations. A light railway was even planned and there was every hope that it would enable the white residents to settle in the cool, healthier heights of the hinterland. War halted work on the railway, however, and it was never resumed.

The Royal Commission of 1906 reported that the climate of Papua had been much maligned. Like northern Queensland, it was 'comparatively healthy', though (and Murray concurred) 'Papua will never be a white working-man's country'.[11] Staniforth Smith's *Handbook* to the Territory gave advice on clothing: best was a drill or duck suit with a military collar and a flannel shirt, while the most suitable headgear was a pith helmet.[12] Dr William Mersh Strong, the chief medical officer and occasional ethnographer whom Malinowski had met in London, contributed several pages of 'Hints on Medical Treatment' to Smith's *Handbook*. Malinowski had studied it carefully.

By 1914, Port Moresby had a school for European children, swimming baths (for whites only), a telephone service, a wireless-telegraph link with Australia and a town water supply. There was a hospital, a couple of banks, two butchers and two bakers, as well as the general stores of four trading companies, chief of which was Burns Philp, which Malinowski patronized during his time in Papua. There were also several churches for the various denominations, and a community hall that housed a modest library and served as a venue for operettas, balls and other public entertainments. Had he wished, Malinowski could have played cricket, badminton or tennis with the white residents; it is equally unlikely that he was ever tempted to join the Aquatic Club, the Rifle Club or the Racing Club.

The town was served by a weekly newspaper, *The Papuan Times and Tropical Advertiser*, run by a confirmed enemy of Murray. The paper was unashamedly racist and sneered at every development for which Murray might conceivably have been responsible. The new government vessel, the

Elevala, looked 'like a floating dromedary' and was a waste of public money, while Murray's austere new house was 'a jerry-built villa'.[13] Malinowski dismissed the rag as a stupid publication.

On his second day ashore Malinowski got down to work by reading the *Papua Annual Reports*. Murray's lengthy, sardonic prefaces were an important source of knowledge about the colony. The reports also contained appendices of linguistic and ethnographic notes submitted by resident magistrates. From a reading of past reports and Seligman's monograph, Malinowski would have been able to bring himself up to date on the gradually unfolding ethnographic map of Papua. He would also have read Murray's stocktaking book *Papua or British New Guinea* (1912), which contained a descriptive survey of the native population, or what was known of it, in the various districts of the colony. It was larded with anecdotes and settlers' gossip as well as a wealth of anthropological factoids culled from his officers' reports. Although he referred only once to Seligman, and to Haddon not at all, Murray belied his modest claim to be ignorant of ethnology. Later, indeed, he would take pride in his election to the presidency of the ethnology section of the Australian Association for the Advancement of Science. Following Seligman, he classified the colony's peoples as either 'Papuans' (original stocks speaking Papuan languages) or 'Papuo-Melanesians' (immigrants who speak Austronesian languages and generally occupy coastal areas). As determined by Seligman, the Papuo-Melanesians were divided into eastern and western branches. The Motu, for instance, belonged to the latter, the Trobrianders to the former. The Koita and the Mailu, on the other hand, were of 'Papuan' stock and their languages were quite unrelated to those of the 'Melanesians'.[14]

Murray's was an administrator's view, of course, in that he discussed each district with respect to its degree of pacification, the problems it posed for control, the reputations of the local tribes – whether as warriors, sailors or cannibals – and the district's natural resources and potential for exploitation. His comment on the Mailu is typical of his style. They have 'remarkable skill in carving the floor-boards of their houses – an art of which they are particularly vain, and which, in their opinion, is conclusive evidence of their superiority to Europeans'.[15] The waspish humour, with its hint of Oxonian condescension, is characteristic of his writing style.

Murray wrote of the islander of the Eastern Division as 'commonly a mild-mannered, law-abiding citizen, often industrious, and not infrequently a regular attendant at Church; but at first these people were particularly wild and intractable'.[16] Had Malinowski been persuaded that Trobrianders were quite so civilized he would surely have been inclined to slake his thirst for the exotic in a more 'savage' corner of the Territory.

Beginning fieldwork

Without much ado, Malinowski tried his hand at fieldwork among the Motu and Koita people living in the immediate vicinity of Port Moresby. His study of Motu had not advanced very far, but within a matter of days he had a smattering of Police Motu, the creole language of coastal Papua which was beginning to compete with pidgin English. In Murray's opinion, the Motu were 'a quick and intelligent people, pleasant and easy-going in disposition', though he found them 'averse to discipline and hard work – except at sea'. The Motu were indeed practiced sailors who made annual trading trips, called *hiri*, to the Gulf of Papua in sturdy, multi-hulled canoes with crab-claw sails.[17]

For two weeks Malinowski dabbled in the kind of ethnography his supervisor had conducted a decade earlier. Seligman had arrived just after Murray took up his post as chief judicial officer, and Murray's diary records a visit to Hanuabada with him to investigate 'sympathetic magic'.[18] Malinowski not only covered much of the same ground as Seligman, but also used his principal informant, Ahuia Ova, who was Murray's interpreter for the Central Court. Whenever he was free of official duties he conducted Malinowski around his home territory. Ahuia became something of a legend as a professional informant. Haddon had photographed him in 1899, Captain Barton had used his services, and Seligman, who based his entire 140-page account of the Koita on his information, described him as a man of 'quite unusual intelligence'.[19] Ahuia was a local 'big man' who wielded considerable influence by brokering government relations in his capacity as village constable, and later councillor, of the village of Poreporena. Not least, his people feared him as a sorcerer. According to F. E. Williams, who recorded his life story in the late 1930s, Ahuia spoke English 'relatively well, gravely and deliberately picking his words'.[20] Ahuia recalled how Seligman had unwittingly amused villagers by asking a man to imitate the posture of a woman giving birth: 'Dr Seligman was very wild because they laughed.' But his reminiscences of Malinowski are tediously factual and concern only what they did and where they went; they concede nothing personal and are in this respect, as Williams said of Ahuia's account as a whole, 'disappointing'.

Malinowski's first visit to Hanuabada, soon to become Papua's first urban village, was on Sunday 13 September. Together with Murray and Mrs de Righi ('a kindhearted, horsy Australian woman'), he was conducted around the village by Ahuia. The first impression Malinowski recorded was of women wearing grass skirts. The visitors examined gourds filled with lime for betel chewing, and as they walked the length of the village Malinowski noted that some of the houses were built of 'tin' (corrugated iron).[21] Later he expressed his disappointment to Seligman: 'The villages are beastly corrupted and polluted: there are a couple of iron bungalows stuck right into the middle of the old houses.'[22] His disapproval echoed that of Seligman, who had referred scornfully in his field diary to the emergence of 'a calico-clothed, hymn-singing generation'. Eleven years earlier he had made a similar tour of Hanuabada in the company of Administrator Barton and noted: 'Burns Philp's Motu clerk appeared, a portent of what the Motuan may be like in 20 years. Khaki trousers, white vest, braces, scarf round throat, straw hat many sizes too small perched on his stiff mop of hair.'[23] Anthropologists, like other Europeans of the time, viewed with derision those natives who aped the ways of the white man. In his autobiography Ahuia Ova recalled Murray's advice: 'You must do everything from your old customs, so that they will fit you. You may try to copy us, but you cannot be the same.'[24]

Malinowski made his second visit to Hanuabada the following day, this time alone:

> There, in Ahuia's house, the old men had gathered to give me information. They squatted in a row along the wall, fuzzy heads on dark torsos, dressed in torn old shirts, patched-up jaegers, and pieces of khaki uniform, while under these civilized clothes peeped out *sihis*, a kind of belt that covers the thighs and adjacent parts of the body. The bamboo pipe circulated rapidly. A little intimidated by this conclave, I sat down at the table and opened a book. Got information concerning *iduhu*, genealogy, asked about the village chief, etc.[25]

His notes on this first foray into the 'field' begin:

> Every *iduhu* [patrilineal clan occupying a village section] has got a common ground. The whole piece was fenced round with a wooden

fence made of mangrove sticks or other sticks. In this land there was
planted bananas, yams, taros, sweet potatoes, no cocoanuts [*sic*]. Every man
had a plot of land in the ground.[26]

Such piled-up generalizations are typical of his first fumbling attempts.
There are no 'concrete' data in these early pages of his notebook, though
later he got Ahuia to draw a sketch-map of his village section's land hold-
ings. He also took sample genealogies (mainly from Ahuia, it seems) to
check statements (presumably Ahuia's) concerning land tenure.

On this first working day 'in the field' Malinowski was introduced to
Motu and Koita sex taboos. 'Connection' as a euphemism for coitus was
probably Ahuia's court jargon:

> From March till July people start making new gardens, no man has con-
> nection. A man who would like to have connection would have to tell
> it to father who would not allow him to go to the garden. . . . After con-
> nection banana garden not allowed to be entered, unless fruit formed.
> Not allowed to eat bananas in garden because flying fox comes in.[27]

Representing his first exercise in the genre, Malinowski's Motu-Koita
fieldnotes are of considerable interest. They exist in both original notebook
form and as a lightly edited and typed transcription of about forty quarto
pages.[28] They are in English and interspersed with Motu words and phrases;
the syntax often follows that of his informant, so one can sometimes hear
Ahuia's halting English in the text. Malinowski paid particular attention to
gardening, land tenure in relation to the *iduhu*, the seasons, marriage, bride-
price, sex and eating taboos, food categories, garden magic, the large *tabu*
feast, sorcery, pig- and wallaby-hunting, dog magic, fighting and war. There
are also notes on the distribution of the catch following a hunt he had
observed first-hand, on smoking game, sago-making, yam-growing and the
hiri expedition to the Gulf. He enquired about the sexual division of labour,
names of the stars, fire-making and fire taboos, and took notes on Motu
migrations, childbirth, dreams, ancestral and other spirits, and sickness and
its treatment. He did not neglect technology, and there are descriptions of
wooden dishes, net bags, shell ornaments, twines, spoons, nets and weapons.
Many of the stories he took down from Ahuia were 'concrete instances'. If
they stretched his credulity, he nonetheless recorded them dispassionately
and without comment. Intuitively, he grasped the importance of representing 'the native's point of view'. 'Doriga Yago, a Kila-Kila sorcerer was

swallowed by a snake and carried by it far away into the bush. Then the snake allowed him to get out by the same way as he entered him and Doriga saw lots of devase [spirits] and learned how to puri-puri [bespell] gardens, etc.'[29]

Malinowski also gathered information on Motu religion from the Rev. William Lawrence, a Scotsman who headed the local London Missionary Society. Lawrence had spent much of his missionary career in eastern Polynesia and was able to enlighten Malinowski concerning comparative conceptions of *mana* and *tapu*.[30]

'I'm working with these natives mainly for practice,' Malinowski wrote to his mother, 'besides I'm trying to collect lots of things that Seligman didn't touch at all, and which are very important.'[31] On the other hand, he deliberately neglected anthropometry and somatic observations. A decade earlier Seligman had measured the 'pulse tension, pigment spots etc.' of the inhabitants of fifteen households in Ahuia's village section.[32]

A week after his arrival Malinowski joined Ahuia on a wallaby hunt in the hills beyond the town. Although he frequently remarked on the parched landscape, he did not seem to be aware that it had been a particularly dry year throughout the Australasian region. According to Murray, it was 'one of the worst droughts we have had – everything parched up and the bush on fire in many places'.[33] The drought persisted into 1915 throughout most of the Territory and in subtle ways affected Malinowski's fieldwork.

Accompanied by a Motu guide, he rode on horseback through 'a narrow little valley covered with burnt grass and thinly scattered pandanus and small trees of the Cycas species'. Soon, amid dry grass that arched above his head, he came upon Ahuia and 'saw women with netlike bags; a few naked savages with spears'. The men had kindled several fires which 'crawled up the hillside in narrow ribbons . . . eating at the tall strong grasses' with purple tongues of flame. Suddenly the fire roared towards them, and an exhilarated Malinowski walked directly into the flames, 'a completely mad catastrophe rushing straight at me with furious speed'.

After such excitement the hunt itself was an anticlimax. Despite Ahuia's skill as a champion pig-catcher (he would claim a tally of 136 during his hunting career),[34] not a single animal found the nets that day. On the way back to town Malinowski inspected Ahuia's garden and was invited into some houses, sorry that he had brought no 'tobacco and candy, for it made it harder to make contacts with the people'. At Government House later that afternoon he drank beer and watched a game of tennis. Such were Malinowski's first days of fieldwork.

'Here I am at last in the Promised Land,' Malinowski wrote to Seligman the day following the abortive hunt.[35] His letter exuded optimism. Characteristically, he began with an account of his health. The climate was 'simply delightful', not as hot as he had feared, and he was 'bearing the tropics considerably better' than he had thought possible. He mentioned 'the very kind reception' extended to him by the governor and his officers, and he reassured Seligman: 'I am so far entirely conforming with your orders and waiting for the first opportunity for going East to Mailu, where I propose to settle for my first period of work.' In the meantime, he was 'studying the Motu language & collecting Motu texts & also dealing with Motu & Koita Sociology . . . as a sort of training'. He was consulting 'that fat, green covered book' (*The Melanesians of British New Guinea*), and so far he had not, Seligman would be pleased to learn, 'hit upon any detail of importance' that had escaped the master. All in all, he was 'much more eager' now to extend his stay.

> Of course I have not yet really tried my forces & worked on my own; here I am still guided by you & undergoing a kind of practical training in your School. But I have a concrete idea of what the difficulties will look like & I have lost my original diffidence.

In the earthy, fledgling town of Port Moresby that night he waltzed to 'The Blue Danube' and tangoed 'not too well' with Mrs McGrath on her spacious verandah.

A week later Malinowski wrote in his diary a more cautious assessment of his work and physical wellbeing than he had given to Seligman: 'I cannot say that I have felt really fit physically. . . . Insomnia (not too marked), overtaxed heart, and nervousness (especially) seem so far the symptoms.' In addition to the fatigue induced by riding, he blamed lack of exercise combined with intensive intellectual work. Arsenic solution was an 'indispensible' (sic) tonic, and a measured amount of quinine was essential. As for work, he was absorbed by his 'ethnological explorations'.

> But they suffer from two basic defects: (1) I have rather little to do with the savages on the spot, do not observe them enough, and (2) I do not

speak their language [alternative translation: They speak their own language]. This second defect will be hard enough to overcome although I am trying to learn Motu.[36]

These important points of method were brought home to him with renewed force in Mailu.

Expedition to the Laloki

Malinowski settled into a brief routine, monotonous compared to previous days. He hired a Motuan 'cookboy', Igua Pipi, from the offshore village of Elevala, who would also serve as his interpreter in Mailu. He talked to Ahuia on the days the latter was not busy at the courthouse, and he extracted information from senior government officials. He also gleaned bits of Papuan lore from the Rev. Lawrence and Captain Robert Hunter, a trader and explorer married to a local woman. He met 'the beautiful Kori' who awoke his 'admiration and desire for *das ewig Weibliche* [the eternal feminine] framed in a bronze skin'.[37] He indulged in escapist novel-reading until disgust set in. He invited himself to lunch at Government House. He walked up Paga Hill above the town, where Judge Herbert and Dr Simpson lived. He often went to bed early. He was trying not to think too much about Poland's fate, and the twinges of homesickness he felt were 'egotistical'. He often thought of his mother, though his body longed for Tośka.

In total ignorance of his whereabouts, Józefa Malinowska wrote to him from Cracow that week. It would be months before he received her letter.

My Dearest, Beloved Little Boy!

Every other day I send a card to you, but nearly all of them are returned. . . . Of course, I'm always thinking about you and for some reasons I'm sorry and for some I'm happy you are not here. On the whole I think it is lucky your journey happened this year, because with your strength and your eyes you would be no soldier, and your scientific work wouldn't be possible either. . . . I'm only terribly sad that I've had no news, even an empty addressed envelope, but written by your hand. . . . All our friends have left Cracow, even Prof. Nitsch. . . . Perhaps I too would've left by now, but I have no money. I haven't had my pension since June because I'm unable to meet all the official requirements. . . . Your work, as I wrote you many times, is in press. Prof. Estreicher . . . is very hopeful both about the printing and the value of your book, also about your future, but he's a bit of an optimist. . . . Józef Retinger was interned in France. . . . Tola was staying with her mother. . . . If you write before the truce, remember that all the letters are censored. I hug you a million times, give Staś my love, my dearest beloved little Son![38]

The most important event of Malinowski's week was an expedition to the Laloki, a river that runs parallel to the coast behind a range of low hills. Murray sent a horse for him and, accompanied by Igua and a Hanuabada man, he rode through gardens and down a valley sprinkled with pandanus trees. He saw 'fields of tall bronze grass that kept turning crimson and violet, waving and shimmering in the sun like velvet caressed by an invisible hand'. They were joined by the ubiquitous Ahuia, who pointed out land boundaries which Malinowski plotted on a sketched map. At a 'murky little river dragging on sluggishly between the trees' he saw his first sago palms. Ahuia said a prayer, warning him not to drink the water for this was a domain of ancestor spirits. They finally approached the Laloki through a forest of monumental, buttressed *ficus* trees. Malinowski glimpsed gardens, and then they were in a small settlement on the riverbank: 'four little houses around a clearing of smoothed, dried earth.' There were a few Koita people with their children and pigs. Malinowski spent the night with them, presumably in one of the huts, talking into the evening with Goaba and Igua.

He overslept next morning and missed the beginning of the hunt. Crossing the river with Ahuia, he saw wallabies being smoked on a platform and women boiling food in petroleum cans. He took photographs of hunters with their nets and spears, and sat with them at the edge of the forest while others fired the grass. It was a less exhilarating fire than previously, and he could see little for the thick smoke. A wallaby crashed into the stretched net, overturned it and fled back into the bush; another was trapped and speared nearby, and Ahuia killed a pig. They returned to the settlement through charred grass, the heat and smoke battering his face. Incongruously, Malinowski then took lunch with Governor Murray and Mrs de Righi who had ridden from the town that morning.

During his last week in the town, Malinowski had moments of moral collapse and fits of dejection. He attempted to cure them by reading, but was beset by a longing for his life with Annie in London. He thought obsessively of Tośka, too. The war, by contrast, seemed utterly remote. There was a 'sense of incommensurability' between his life in Papua and what was happening in Poland. 'I am completely cut off from Mama when terrible things must be happening at home, things that I can't and don't want to imagine, with a totally unpredictable outcome.'[39] Occasionally he thought of Staś, missing his company.

On a pleasanter note, he enjoyed beautiful moonlit evenings on the McGraths' verandah, surrendering himself to choreography and 'trying to instill the tango into Miss Ashton's mind and heart'. Such flirtations apart, he kept the Australian working folk of Moresby at a distance. Superciliously, he wrote: 'I am filled with dislike for these ordinary people who are incapable of finding a glimmer of poetry and style in certain things which fill me with exaltation.'[40]

'A burden to the Commonwealth'

Hubert Murray, of course, was anything but an ordinary person; not only a powerful figure and a social equal, but also a cultivated man of considerable intellect. He was perhaps the only person in Papua to whom Malinowski felt it necessary to show deference. For his part, Murray was still going out of his way to be helpful to the foreign scientist of insecure status and dubious national loyalty. The day before Malinowski boarded the *Wakefield* – the boat he had been awaiting – he lunched at Government House and discussed with Murray a 'letter to be written to Atlee Hunt'.

This letter proved to be consequential. 'When I was starting on my expedition,' he reminded Hunt, 'I intended to stay for at least two years in Papua. To carry out this plan I had a reserve of £400, besides the funds I was carrying with me.' Half of the £400 'reserve' was the LSE scholarship he had been promised for 1915 and 1916; the other half was his own money, now 'absolutely inaccessible' in Russian Poland. Alas, the university scholarship was also in serious doubt, as British awards would not be granted to citizens of countries with which Britain was at war: thus his financial embarrassment.

I have not lost all hope yet, but if this Scholarship fails me I shall find myself in a rather difficult position. . . . And as I am here as a prisoner of war (Austrian Subject, member of the *Landsturm*, or second reserve) I am afraid I shall be in any case a burden to the Commonwealth Government.

He then made a bold request for £120, which he judged would allow him to work in Papua for a year. In return he would make himself useful as best he could, suggesting that he might 'publish some fairly complete account of one or two districts'. He concluded the letter with another appeal to economic good sense: considering that he would soon become a liability to Australia, the small sum would allow him to complete his investigations 'on which so much public money has been spent already'.[41]

Malinowski would perhaps not have dared to approach the Australian government with such an audacious request if Murray had not offered his support. In a memorandum to Hunt, the lieutenant-governor wrote:

> I think he knows his work, and the Government might dispose of him cheaply by keeping him here during the war, and letting him study ethnology. I confess that personally I do not like him – there is I think something crooked about him, tho' of course this is perhaps imagination – but as you would have to feed him it is as well to let him work and it will probably be as cheap to keep him here as anywhere else.[42]

While perhaps deploring Murray's cynical tone, Hunt agreed and pencilled at the bottom of the memo: 'Will be glad to discuss this with the Minister. I think we should give the poor chap a chance to go on. We shall have to keep him anyhow.'

The poor chap eventually came out of it rather well, and his cheeky request paid off to the tune of £250 (equivalent to the annual salary of an assistant resident magistrate), which he received in several instalments during 1915. Hunt and Murray (the latter to a more cautious extent) believed they would get value for money by paying for the services of an unofficial – if somewhat maverick – government anthropologist. Malinowski encouraged them in this belief. Later, however, Murray was disgusted to discover that Atlee Hunt had tricked him by charging Malinowski's 'salary' against the Papuan budget.

When he wrote to tell Seligman about his submission to Hunt – dramatizing his enemy status in Papua as 'a prisoner of war' – Malinowski suggested that the LSE director might also support him by appealing to the Australian high commissioner in London.[43] It was not until January 1915 that Seligman replied (having by this time dropped the second 'n' from his name). He was alarmed by Malinowski's effrontery and chided him for bringing himself to official notice 'not as a working anthropologist, but as an enemy alien with a definite request which might easily be considered impudent'. It seemed to Seligman that as long as his fieldwork remained undisturbed Malinowski should keep his head well down. If he did find himself in trouble he should get an occulist to certify that 'no country in this world would have you as a soldier at any price'. Meanwhile, the less said the better and he proposed to say nothing at the LSE about Malinowski's 'imprudence'.[44]

By the time this dire warning reached Malinowski the matter had been settled in his favour. Seligman had argued from general principles without knowledge of the local situation, the political nuances of which Malinowski had accurately judged and risked acting upon. Still, this exchange of letters illustrates the differing personal styles of the two men and their divergent attitudes towards administrative authority and bureaucratic protocol. They would clash frequently in the future over many such matters of procedure. Malinowski's bold expediency, brash opportunism and preparedness to tackle obstacles by charm or wheedling contrasted starkly with Seligman's conventional caution and distinctly English concern for propriety and due process.

Sailing to Mailu

The shipping traffic along the south coast of Papua, linking the two principal ports of Port Moresby and Samarai, was more frequent in 1914 than it is today. Difficulty of terrain ensured that Papua was a maritime colony; today it is part of a nation largely dependent on aviation. Wherever he happened to be on this coast, Malinowski could not complain of being too isolated.

The captain of the *Wakefield* was a brutal German with a big belly who abused and bullied the Papuan crew; the engineer was a vulgar, arrogant Scotsman. Among the fellow passengers were a tall, handsome, squint-eyed Englishman who cursed the Australians for their lack of culture; an elderly planter and good-natured Quaker named Alfred Greenaway; and the son of an Irish Lord, the Hon. Richard De Moleyns, 'a drunk and a rogue' but 'certainly a thoroughbred'. Another ship of fools, in short, and by the time the three-day voyage was over Malinowski was fed up with all of them.

He felt unsure of himself throughout the trip, burying his nose in Maupassant's short stories, though he keenly observed the changing panorama and the different character of each of the coastal villages. The dry belt that characterizes the Port Moresby region yields to a wetter zone beyond Aroma, and the coastline, indented here and there with deep bays, was a lush, bright green. He was reminded of cruising on Lake Geneva: 'shores lined with luxuriant vegetation, saturated with blue, leaning against a high wall of mountains.' But to European eyes there was something sinister and unfriendly about this tropical landscape: 'Not at all like our Tatras at Olcza, where you'd like to lie down and embrace the landscape physically. . . . Out here the marvellous abysses of verdure are inaccessible, hostile, alien to man.'[45] What appears to be 'a beautiful mangrove jungle is at close quarters an infernal, stinking, slippery swamp' of tangled roots and soft mud 'where you cannot touch anything'. The jungle itself is 'full of all kinds of filth and reptiles; sultry, damp, tiring – swarming with mosquitoes and other loathsome insects'.

At Abau, a government station magnificently situated on a rocky islet, he met Resident Magistrate Armit – 'genial, casual, not too refined, a bit *homo rusticus*' – who invited him to sleep ashore. Next morning Malinowski boarded the boat for the last leg of his trip. Sailing into Amazon Bay on Friday 16 October he was violently seasick, but by the time he disembarked on Mailu Island he pronounced himself 'happy to be in such a marvellous place'. The steep, grass covered island was encircled by palms and casurinas. The mainland beyond rose in serried green and purple ranks to the lofty summits of the Owen Stanley Range.

In what would become a familiar trope for generations of anthropologists to come (if it was not already familiar to previous generations of readers of travel literature), Malinowski famously wrote of his arrival in the Trobriand Islands: 'Imagine yourself suddenly set down surrounded by all your gear, alone on a tropical beach close to a native village, while the launch or dinghy that has brought you sails away out of sight.'[46] The heroic figure of the lone ethnographer – or 'the image of the old-fashioned castaway'[47] – was a literary device, but close enough to the truth of Malinowski's experience to serve as the opening image of the myth that he would spin of the archetypal Ethnographer. He transposed this arrival scene to the Trobriands, but it properly belongs to Mailu.

Stepping ashore on the island, unloading his gear from the *Wakefield's* dinghy, the first person to welcome him was Omaga, the village constable. Then, to Malinowski's relief, the missionaries appeared. The Rev. William Saville and his wife, Frances, greeted him and he happily accepted their invitation to stay with them. He was soon to learn that just as Governor Murray dominated Port Moresby, so Missionary Saville presided over Mailu.

Chapter 17

Mailu

In the realm of the missionary

Malinowski could feel, at last, that he was 'in the field' where no anthropologist had worked before; though as he already knew, William Saville was
an amateur ethnographer. Seligman had met and worked briefly with him
in Port Moresby in late 1904, and his presence at Mailu was presumably a
factor in Seligman's choice of field-site for Malinowski. The missionary
could ease him gently into the local culture. At any rate, by settling at Mailu,
Malinowski placed himself at the centre of a relatively unknown area
deemed to be important because it bordered the better-known ethnographic province of the Massim to the east.

Saville's domain extended along the sheltered side of the island. His sturdy
'English'-style mission house – with its walnut study and varnished hard-
wood fittings, its spacious verandahs commanding sweeping views of the
turquoise sea and the purple mountains of the mainland, its orange groves,
tree-shaded croquet lawn and cricket field – altogether put Murray's austere
Moresby residence to shame. Discreetly out of sight of the mission house
was the comparatively tiny teachers' house and a boarding school for fifty
children (the village school had a further 123 children on its register). Saville
wrote textbooks and taught English, 'but we cannot get the children to
speak it to us,' he lamented.[1]

Malinowski recorded none of these facts about the Mailu mission, or
the full extent to which his fieldwork was conducted in its shadow. The
village, of between four and five hundred people, was ten minutes' walk
away on the seaward side of the island. As he described it to his mother,
there were 'two long rows of houses, parallel to the sea, creating a wide

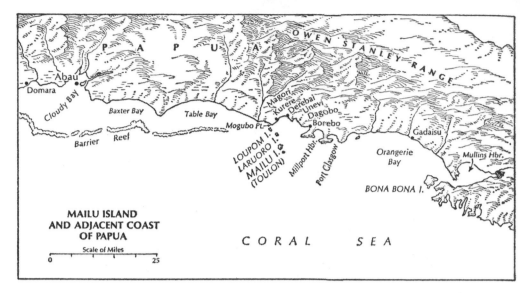

Map 2   Mailu Island and the adjacent coast of Papua.

street. . . . From the sea the village looks like a sandy beach, with children playing all the time and women making pots, men repairing boats.' The islanders were not self-sufficient in food, which had to be imported from the mainland, 'so their main occupation is trade'.[2] On his first evening, Malinowski felt obliged to attend the service conducted by Saville in the little church by the mission house. He was entertained by 'the comical effect of the Psalms being roared out in a savage language' and 'managed to feel well disposed to the farcical humbug of it all'. This patronizing attitude did not augur well for congenial relations with the missionary.

William James Viritahitemauvai Saville was born in Surrey in 1873, the son of a missionary. He came to New Guinea in 1900, immediately after being ordained by the London Missionary Society, and spent most of the next thirty-five years on Mailu. Saville never seriously doubted his vocation, though initially he despaired of his 'proud, ungrateful, selfish' flock. Papuans, he believed, were 'awfully low in the scale of mankind' and he formulated ten 'laws' for dealing with the Mailu that reveal an aloof paternalism and a horror of white caste pollution. 'Never play the fool with a native'; 'Never speak to a native for the sake of speaking'; 'Never *touch* a native, unless to shake hands or thrash him'; 'Warn once, afterwards proceed to action.'[3] Saville's bigotry extended to every race, creed or nation not his own. Australian crudity scandalized him; so too did English trade union-ism, French greed, Roman Catholic perfidy and Papuan ribaldry. Little wonder that cosmopolitan Malinowski found him small-minded and parochial: 'a petty greengrocer blown up by his own sense of importance into a caricature of a petty sovereign,' as he wrote (in English) in his diary.[4] Saville mellowed with time, however, and grew more forgiving of his ungrateful flock. He taught them to play cricket and had the boys in his school drill with toy rifles. The book he published about the Mailu, *In Unknown New Guinea* (1926), conveys an affectionate respect for them, even a paternal love.

Malinowski's first impressions of Mailu from the *Wakefield* had been of a reef-fringed volcanic island set in a sapphire sea. An orderly line of Gothic-gabled houses crouched behind the canoe-strewn shore. The scene evoked joy and a sense of freedom. 'I would imagine life amid palm groves as a perpetual holiday,' he wrote. The euphoria of his arrival quickly evaporated, however, and within a few days he was 'escaping from it to the company of Thackeray's London snobs' in *Vanity Fair* and vicariously enjoying the advertisements in Saville's outdated London newspapers. He rebuked himself: 'I am incapable of burying myself in my work, of accepting my voluntary captivity and making the most of it.'[5]

The cause of this sudden collapse of morale was the missionary, who promised to help him but then found more important things to do. It had begun well enough, with Saville conducting the visitor on a tour of his domain, 'to the flagpole, to the village, then to the gardens'. But the fol-lowing days were wasted in waiting for help that was not forthcoming. Impatience triggered ill-feelings and it irritated Malinowski, too, that the missionary had not offered him free bed and board. He tried to work in the village alone but it was with great difficulty, though Saville convened 'a conclave' of elders at the mission house for the anthropologist to talk to in the evenings. For the remainder of the week he took notes on dancing – the visual spectacle impressed him greatly – and escaped into novel-reading, now Conrad's *Romance*: 'I couldn't tear myself away; it was as though I was drugged.' His sudden addiction to fiction was a salve to insecurity and what would now be called 'culture shock'. He escaped, too, into memories of Tośka and the lost opportunities of loving her. Thoughts of Tośka triggered thoughts of Mama, for whom he now felt 'a deep, strong longing' in his soul.[6]

He managed to do some work that first week, however. While Saville disgusted him with his attitudes of racial superiority, he conceded that the English missionary treated the people 'with a fair amount of decency and liberality' (he had noted the popularity of cricket) and did not appear to push them around too much; he supposed that if Saville were a German 'he would doubtless be downright loathsome'.[7] It is only fair to record that several of Saville's rules for keeping Papuans at arm's length were unwittingly observed by Malinowski during moments of his infuriation with Mailu recalcitrance. He was guilty of sudden rage when they thwarted his intentions, answered back or were otherwise rude to him; but he did not dare to 'thrash' them, and had not yet learned to refer to them as 'niggers' or 'niggs'.

It was not so much an ideological antipathy that ill-disposed Malinowski to Saville, more a personal dislike, though during this period he tended to rationalize the latter by means of the former. He could tolerate missionaries of various denominations in small doses. He had got on fairly well, it seems, with the London Missionary Society's William Lawrence and the Anglican Arthur Chignell in Port Moresby, and he would soon take favourably to Charles Rich in Suau and Frederick Ramsey at Samarai, also to the old Oxonian Anglican Henry Newton, whose aquaintance he had made on the *Orontes* and whom he would meet again early in 1915. Later still, he would maintain cordial relations with the Methodists Matthew Gilmour at Ubuia and Ernest Johns in Kiriwina. And much later, in London in the 1930s, he would form close friendships with Edwin Smith and Joe Oldham of the International African Institute. Indeed, some of his bread-and-butter information came indirectly from such missionaries. With the exception of Saville, it seems, Malinowski's earliest tirades against missionaries were ideological rather than personal; and later, too, when their roles were reversed and Saville sat at the feet of the anthropology professor at the London School of Economics, he was not only prepared to forgive Saville his faults, but even to praise him as a 'modern type of missionary who has been able to fashion himself into an anthropologist'.[8]

Malinowski was galled by his dependence on Saville. It wasn't simply that he was paying for his own keep (25 shillings a week, he told his mother) and having to be civil to a man he detested – though that was bad enough for someone with such a volatile temperament – but he also depended on Saville for introductions to local informants and guidance in local ways. After fourteen years on the island the missionary spoke the Magi language tolerably well and had even published a grammar. By the standards of the day he was a competent ethnographer in his own right, the kind of 'man on the spot' that armchair anthropologists in Britain relied upon.

The first generation of fieldworkers routinely consulted Christian missionaries, and ever since the Torres Strait expedition Haddon had encouraged missionaries to become more anthropologically minded, the better to serve ethnology as well as their own cause. What missionaries needed, he held, was 'a good grounding in anthropology, carpentry and medicine', and at Cambridge he taught vacation courses expressly for them. While not uncritical of their insensitive methods of proselytizing and the destructive effects of their work, he judged them worth cultivating for the information they could gather about the religious cults they had dedicated themselves to abolishing. It was prudent, then, for itinerant ethnographers to cultivate missionaries in order to tap their knowledge of local customs, and although missionary-anthropologists of the stature of R. H. Codrington and Maurice Leenhardt were exceptional in Melanesia, in many areas missionaries were thicker on the ground than government officers.[9] Malinowki's other mentors, Rivers and Seligman, had also made considerable use of missionaries, and it was understood that he would do likewise.

'The whole question of working with a missionary depends on the personal equation of that missionary,' Seligman advised him the following year.

> [T]here are some parts you will in any case have to do yourself; it would not do to trust an outsider, whether he worshipped the bon Dieu or the devil, in working out the social relationship system. On the other hand, once you have got an outline a good missionary can be very helpful and save an enormous amount of time . . . but you must teach any man you work with to use his technical terms aright. . . . And you must intellectually have the upper hand of your missionary.[10]

By the time he received this advice, however, Malinowski had almost entirely dispensed with the assistance of missionaries. He effectively brought the historical partnership between British anthropologists and missionaries to an end, and the gradual process of professional disengagement may be said to have begun in Mailu. For the moment, however, he was stuck with the petty sovereign.

Alienation

Malinowski engaged the services of Omaga, the village policeman, who conducted him around the village with Igua in train as interpreter. He also worked with a number of men – Kavaka, Papari, Velavi, and Dimdim are names that crop up frequently in his fieldnotes and diary – and doled out sticks of black twist tobacco, taking notes from them on dances, on the seasons, on burial rites and on technology. Some days started badly. He got up late, dispirited, and read old newspapers and back issues of *Punch*. His informants likewise were sometimes 'lazy and unwilling'. *Notes and Queries* was his standby and he referred to it frequently, questioning directly on topics suggested by the manual. He also worked with Alf Greenaway, who ran a nearby coconut plantation in Baxter Bay. Of Kentish working-class origin, Alf was an 'extremely decent and sympathetic boor; it's "bloody" all the time, and he drops his h's and is married to a native woman and feels miserable in respectable company, particularly feminine'. He was nevertheless a fund of curious information: on cleanliness, for example, upon which – taking his cue from *Notes and Queries* – Malinowski questioned him on 12 November. 'An old coconut is scraped. Then fold the scraped stuff in their hand put a drop of water over it then squeeze it all over their heads and rub it well. That kills the lice. Then they rub the remainder over the body.'[11] This might well have reminded Malinowski of his mother's sulphur treatment for baldness.

On the last day of October he visited the mainland with Saville, and at Derebai that night he reflected in his diary on the strange enhancement of his surroundings caused by the moonlight: 'The exoticism breaks through lightly, through the veil of familiar things.' But he still felt discouraged. 'The work I am doing is a kind of opiate rather than a creative expression. I am not trying to link it to deeper sources. . . . Reading novels is simply disastrous.'[12] His dissatisfaction with the uninspired nature of his work echoes that of earlier diaries. Yet here he was, finally, in a blank spot on the map, a place previously unvisited by questing ethnologists. How quickly he learned that fieldwork can be tedious; that its very strangeness as a daily occupation can induce boredom and alienation, precipitating that curious amalgam of 'culture shock' and ennui, as a defence against which the ethnographer retreats into memory or into reading fiction – novels being comforting reminders of more interesting lives lived elsewhere. Few have documented better than Malinowski this shock of the new and the bewildered mind's response of detachment. The best respite is sleep, perchance to dream, to avoid confronting the daily reality of one's existentially absurd situation – for to the extent that we are creatures of our cultural and social milieu, our lives come to seem absurd without those frequent affirmations of who we think we are. An academic training in anthropology does not prepare one adequately for such experiences, and the phlegmatic British – born to rule as they believed – were especially vulnerable to estrangement if they were not treated with the respect they had been taught to believe was their birthright. Malinowski's position was even more tentative. Being Polish and having spent a childhood among shepherds and peasants did not necessarily equip him for life in a Melanesian village.

On the mainland opposite Mailu he visited gardens. 'I asked about the division of land. It would have been useful to find out about the old system of division and to study today's as a form of adaptation.'[13] This suggests that he was thinking imaginatively, and not always mechanically following the instructions of *Notes and Queries*. He thought, too, about government regulations: the 'irrationality of prohibiting pigs and the injunction to concentrate the villages; about the suggestions I'd like to make to the Governor' – not that Murray would have taken kindly to them. Some of the villages he visited on this short trip yielded little information, and in one he was met with laughter for his trouble. But others yielded much: in Borebo there were 'very intelligent natives' and the information 'bubbled out' as fast as he could take it down. He was learning that the success of this kind of peripatetic fieldwork was entirely contingent upon the availability of a handful of patient and articulate men willing to answer questions – also, of course, upon his own energy and sense of wellbeing.

It proved to be a bad week. He felt poorly much of the time and tended to stay at home in the mission house, reading newspapers. When he did go to the village he could find few informants. He began to read Dumas's *The Count of Monte Cristo*, compulsively burying himself in the tale of inexorable revenge as he sailed once again on a trip to the east with Saville. At Port Glasgow, 'out came an old man with a pleasant expression and clear gaze full of calm and wisdom' and the information flowed. But all too soon Malinowski became enraged when 'the old man began to lie about burials' – presumably suspecting the inquisitive ethnographer to be an agent of a government that forbade burial within village confines. A walk in the gardens did not soothe him, or the marvellous fragrance of exotic blossoms.

He enjoyed the walk only in retrospect, 'as an experience sealed in my memory rather than directly'.[14] Capturing such retrospective experiences precisely was one of the main functions of his diary.

On 29 October mail arrived. Besides friendly letters from the Mayos in Brisbane, Ellie Le Soeuf in Perth and Florence Golding aboard the *Morea*, there was the hurtful, reproachful letter from Staś which rankled for days. The best of the batch were five letters from Annie in South Africa ('the only thread linking me with the past,' he mused). The following week he decided it was time to despatch a progress report to Seligman.

Despite his dependence on Saville, he believed he had done a creditable amount of work and already 'gathered a nice store of information'. He had 'picked up a certain amount of Motu' in Moresby and was now improving it. The men of the village were busy making sago for the upcoming 'great feast', called *govi maduna*, which he hoped to see in December or January, though it promised to be a modest one this year. This could well have been owing to the drought, though Malinowski blamed the war scare, 'which has upset even pig-trading in New Guinea'. The Mailu had not yet made their customary trip up the coast to Aroma for pigs, which they exchanged for sago and locally manufactured pots and armshell ornaments. In summarizing his observations for Seligman, he covered house structure, family life, kin terms, clans, gardens, men's houses and canoe-trading, as well as the 'great feast'. He concluded: 'I have got some notes on the disposal of the dead . . . on the division of seasons and on some technical points (potmaking, house-building, canoes). But I feel I have not got yet into the "heart of the people".'[15] Considering that he had put in no more than fourteen full days' work by this time, he was surely expecting too much (after fourteen years Saville would have admitted to a similar failure). Still, Malinowski demonstrated that he had already grasped the essential outlines of Mailu culture. Now, he told Seligman, he intended to make 'some excursions, both East & West of Mailu'.

A couple of days later he wrote to Mama, anxious to tell her news that would make her proud of him. '[I] started my ethnographic work – for the first time all by myself, on completely new territory, so far there's been nothing published on these natives.' He explained to her how he interrogated them.

The only way I can work is through a double interpreter. My 'boy' or servant, born in Port Moresby (his name is Igua and he has a striking resemblance to a chimpanzee), speaks . . . the Motu language, which is the lingua franca of New Guinea. . . . He translates my English into Motu, another native translates his Motu into Mailu, then the elders answer my question, which travels by reverse post via the educated Mailu native and Igua back to me. This procedure is slowly being simplified by the fact that I can now understand quite a bit of Motu and I'm beginning to speak it, so Igua serves me mainly as a 'pocket dictionary'.[16]

Malinowski would repeat this explanation – including the phrase 'pocket dictionary' – in the introduction to his monograph on the Mailu.

'Haddon & Co.'

In his letter to Seligman, Malinowski mentioned that Haddon was still in the Papuan Gulf region. It therefore 'unnerved' him when, on 8 November, the itinerant Cambridge don and his daughter landed on the beach of Mailu. The visit must have been pre-arranged, otherwise Malinowski's diary entry would surely have been richer in fulminating expletives. Ostensibly, Haddon's purpose was to gather material on canoe-building as part of his comprehensive survey of canoes in Oceania, while his quietly intrepid daughter Kathleen was collecting 'cat's cradles' (she subsequently published a book on string figures).

Malinowski had journeyed for several months to the far ends of the earth, so it must have been disconcerting to be visited by the greatest living authority on Melanesian ethnology. Alfred Cort Haddon, after all, was the most influential figure in British anthropology, mentor and patron of Malinowski's own mentor and patron, Charles Seligman. Secure in his professional seniority and invulnerable British status in a British colony, Haddon by his very presence would have been an uncomfortable reminder of the insecurity of Malinowski's own somewhat precarious position. Although 'Haddon & Co.' remained in Mailu only a few days, it was long enough to antagonize him. He probably felt that his fieldwork domain had been encroached upon even before he had had a chance to lay claim to it. He confessed to his diary his 'hatred for Haddon, for annoying me, for conspiring with the missionary'.[17]

Still, tangible benefits flowed from Haddon's visit, and from a historical point of view the event was an epiphany, an imponderable yet defining moment for British social anthropology. The world was beginning to fight a terrible war and the era is faithfully if idiosyncratically evoked by the miscellaneous artifacts and activities of Western civilization that Malinowski mentions in his diary: the phonograph, barrel organ, billiards, hymn-singing and injection of arsenic as a nerve tonic. In this remote coast on the very edge of empire were gathered 'a petty greengrocer' missionary, a 'drunk as a sponge' son of an Irish peer, a working-class English planter who dropped his aitches, a half-caste who had killed his own mother, and several hundred anonymous 'savages' who were the only reason for the two anthropologists being there. There was a fortuitous juxtaposition of old and new anthropology in the perfect exemplars of Haddon and Malinowski: cat's cradles versus household censuses, canoe technology versus the economics of trade – in a nutshell, Haddon's peripatetic prospecting surveys versus Malinowski's methodological impulse to stay in one place and excavate deeply.[18]

Malinowski wrote to his mother on 24 November. 'Every day I go to the village . . . I work systematically but don't overwork – so far I've been feeling quite well in every respect, except for some sluggishness.' Although the work itself was not particularly hard it required great patience. 'The "savages" are quite suspicious here – because of the mission and government regulations. Slowly I obtain all the information, but in the area of funerals, after-life beliefs, etc they are incredibly reticent.'[19]

He wrote to Seligman the same day, and it is clear from this progress report that he was blithely engaged in survey anthropology *à la* Seligman himself.

> I am going on not at a tremendous pace, but steadfastly. . . . I think I have now got a fairly complete all round picture of the Mailu – but it is a rough sketch in black and white so far and the touches of colour are much more difficult to get. I am trying to *see* as many things done, as I can.

He outlined his immediate plans:

> I am going East – there is the Mission launch going to Samarai – and I shall, on the way back, stop in one or two places, especially at the very point where the Mailu & the Suau touch. This will only be a rough sounding, but it will be very helpful in discovering the touches of Eastern [i.e. Massim] culture here.

His weakest points, he confessed, were photography and phonographic recording. 'I have taken very few photos so far – but I have ambitious schemes of recording much of their dances, children's plays & economic activities (fishing, making gardens etc.) & technology. But whenever skill comes into play, I am not much good.'[20]

Nor would he ever be very good at photography, and the sheer bother of its technical demands frequently frustrated and infuriated him. Always something of an impractical person (he baulked at mending a fuse or changing a light bulb), he managed photography in a bumbling fashion. Although he came to regard it as a secondary occupation of fieldwork, he nevertheless spent much time and money on it out of a dutiful regard for its methodological value. As for the phonograph, it appears to have failed him altogether in Mailu.

Seligman's reply, of 4 February 1915, was encouraging despite the long delay. Haddon was back in Cambridge and had written favourably of Malinowski's 'good work' at Port Moresby and Mailu. 'I think he will make an excellent field worker,' was Haddon's judgment. This was high praise from Britain's premier fieldworker, who had introduced the very term into anthropology, communicated through the man whom Haddon later eulogized as the most indefatigable fieldworker in the empire. In time, however, Malinowski's reputation as a fieldworker would totally eclipse theirs.

'Touches of colour'

Despite his complaint to Seligman, there are many colourful touches in Malinowski's Mailu fieldnotes (his diary, of course, scintillates with colour). On 13 November 1914, he worked with Dimdim on questions of marriage, seeking 'concrete' instances. His notes on the interview record in part:

> D. represents it a little bit queerly. Every year one pig to be given for wife. This called AVEISA & VOEVOE. Part of this pig returns to giver, his wife cooks it. If pig not given, wife he cries [sic: The conversation was obviously being conducted in pidgin English]. Dimdim married to UDAMA of BOILADUBU. . . . If neither Boiladubu [clan] nor Maradudu have got [*maduna*] feasts D. does not give any pigs.

Clearly, in a fairly common New Guinea pattern, bridewealth pigs were transacted on the occasion of the great annual feast. Malinowski sketched

Dimdim's wife's genealogy in his notebook, together with a list of men and their clan affiliations to whom Dimdim had given pigs at previous *maduna* feasts. His notes then refer to the *tselo* dance, which he was about to witness that evening at Kurere: 'Tselo – the prettiest of the melodies I have heard here. My scientific and artistic curiosity both gratified. Despite everything there is a great deal of primitive man in this, going back to the age of polished stone.' But the interview somehow went wrong and Malinowski became impatient and 'closed the notebook'.[21]

Dimdim, 'a half-caste and modern Orestes', had killed his own mother in a state of possession called *o'o* which resembled amok. What he had recorded about *o'o* from Puana and Alf Greenaway a few days earlier is another touch of colour. Concrete instances illustrate his ethnographic exploration of the concept:

> Shooting stars called in Mailu KARAVENI enter the man or woman and make them o-o. There need not be any cause; no angry [sic], no sorry [sic]. They simply get seized by this spirit. In olden days they used to kill a man or a woman, destroy property, chop up a canoe; throw spears at a house . . . LAURUOLO woman, Vaila by name, used to have such fits regularly; she used to dress up with weeds on her head and round her waist; she used to take a spear or drum and perform some of the customary dances.[22]

With Haddon still in the vicinity it was perhaps a relief to stay with 'Dirty Dick' – the Hon. Richard De Moleyns – the aristocratic remittance man who worked at Mogubu plantation. Malinowski sailed there by canoe on 14 November with Charlie and Dimdim, recording the trip in staccato, poetic images: 'Under a yellow sail, spreading its wings. . . . On the green water – turquoise, only transparent – the violet silhouettes of the mountains . . . . The water laps between the boards of the raft – the sea peeps through the holes and the spray smashing against the edges of the boat.' Mailu was visible in the distance, 'a misty silhouette with a noble profile of volcanic rock'. The weekend at Mogubu offered a welcome change from the mission house. Life with the unshaven, pyjama-clad De Moleyns was uncivilized. In this house without walls Malinowski tasted squalid colonial comfort: 'Having a crowd of boys to serve you is very pleasant,' he noted. His host was as 'drunk as a sponge' so long as there was any whisky to be had. Fortunately, he finished his last bottle shortly after Malinowski arrived, so conversation became possible. When sober, Dirty Dick had strikingly good manners, though Malinowski judged him to be poorly educated with 'little intellectual culture'. Two years later, this thoroughbred figure would cut his own throat in the Samarai hospital.

A week of illness followed for Malinowski. As he described it: 'tiredness and mental fog, felt miserable and couldn't work, felt sick, lonely, in despair.' Dosed with quinine and arsenic, he read newspapers and Kipling stories. He fell under the spell of *Kim* – appropriate reading given his ambiguous situation, for it is the most ethnographically descriptive of Kipling's novels and its eponymous orphan hero is in search of a racial and linguistic identity.[23] The atmosphere of the mission house had relaxed during Saville's brief absence and Malinowski found Mrs Saville 'much more lively' than her husband. The latter's return provoked angry ruminations.

> Mentally I collect arguments against missions and ponder a really effective anti-mission campaign. The arguments: these people destroy the natives' joy in life; they destroy their psychological *raison d'être*. And what they give in return is completely beyond the savages. They struggle consistently and ruthlessly against everything old and create new needs, both material and moral. No question but that they do harm.[24]

Yet he was about to rely on Saville again as they prepared for the trip to Samarai.

Among the letters Malinowski wrote on 24 November was one to Atlee Hunt. After only five weeks in the field he was already looking forward to leaving it.

> Dr Haddon has been here and has given me some hints and encouragement. Acting under his advice, which confirmed my former plans, I decided to go South for February and March in order to write up my results, digest my experiences and – metaphorically – to look at my work from a distance; and then of course to go again over the same material, as I return to Papua.

An additional reason for wanting to return to Australia, he said, was to study the Papuan collections in the Australian museums. He had perhaps been advised by Haddon about what to say next:

> There are many specimens rapidly disappearing or entirely disappeared from the field. I would like to see them and subsequently to gather as

much information concerning them, as I can. There are lots of specimens which are not even identified and satisfactory technological and socio-logical description is exceptional.[25]

Hunt was sympathetic to this request and even tried to get Malinowski a free rail pass from Brisbane to Adelaide. 'So far as I am aware,' Hunt wrote to the secretary of the Department of Defence, 'there is no reason to suspect this gentleman of any improper practices but of course I am not recom-mending that permission be given him to leave the area over which the Australian Government exercises control.'[26]

To Samarai and Suau

Stricken by seasickness, Malinowski lay in the mission boat as it sailed east-ward. In the sheltered waters of Isulele Bay – which reminded him of Lago di Garda in northern Italy – Malinowski met Saville's colleague, the Rev. Charles Rich. A shoemaker by trade, Rich was 'a friendly, frank, jovial fellow'. Like Saville, he had come to New Guinea in 1900 and would stay for nearly forty years.

Malinowski immediately noticed a different feeling about the villages. He was now in the Massim, the term Haddon had adopted for the insular ethnographic province at the tail end of Papua. Malinowski had come to view the Massim from the perspective of the Mailu, to whom it was the source of superior goods (baskets, decorated carvings, weapons and orna-ments), the most melodious songs and the finest dances. It was also the home of cannibals and the most virulent sorcery.[27] Going ashore in Isulele Bay, he opened himself to aesthetic impressions of 'the new *Kulturkreis*'.[28] He noted that houses with saddle-backed roofs were 'prettier' than those in Mailu, and it was in Arcadian terms that he came to describe these villages of the southern Massim in *Argonauts*.

> When, on a hot day, we enter the deep shadow of fruit trees and palms, and find ourselves in the midst of the wonderfully designed and orna-mented houses hiding here and there in irregular groups among the green, surrounded by little decorative gardens of shells and flowers, with pebble-bordered paths and stone-paved sitting circles, it seems as if the visions of a primeval, happy, savage life were suddenly realized, even if only in a fleeting impression.[29]

The English missionaries had much to do with the flower gardens and bordered paths, but, as Malinowski reminded himself, the attractive stone circles were associated with unspeakable deeds. For these 'pleasant, apparently effete people' used to be 'inveterate cannibals and head-hunters' who conducted 'treacherous, cruel raids, falling upon sleeping villages, killing man, woman and child and feasting on their bodies'. Physically, he found the Massim people shorter and less robust in appearance than their true Papuan neighbours to the west; their hair was less woolly, their skins lighter, their noses 'squashed' and their eyes 'oblique'. In manner, they were 'shy and diffident, but not unfriendly — rather smiling and almost servile, in very great contrast to the morose Papuan, or the unfriendly, reserved South Coast Mailu'. At first blush, the people of the southern Massim gave 'not so much the impression of wild savages as of smug and self-satisfied bourgeois'. They were, indeed, 'efficient and industrious manufacturers and great traders'.[30]

Sailing on around the gentle bulge of the spectacularly mountainous Suau coast, Malinowski 'drank in the pleasure of the landscape'.[31] As they approached the end of the mainland, the silhouettes of drifting islands ahead of them, he experienced the thrill of discovery. The mountainous spine of New Guinea terminates here, popping up like a series of afterthoughts in a chain of coral-fringed archipelagos. As you round the last Suau cape, the Solomon Sea opens up: a panorama of melting islets, shimmering seascapes and abrupt volcanic islands. The colonial capital of this insular realm of rock and coral was tiny Samarai, gateway to the Massim, to the ports of German New Guinea and (so the earliest explorers believed) far beyond to China. Samarai was an international port, the hub of commerce in eastern Papua, rivalling Port Moresby in importance. As well as copra, the main commercial crop, gold, pearls, bêche-de-mer and turtle-shell flowed through the tiny maritime capital. From here the colonial government reached out to the numerous inhabited islands, and from here Burns Philp would ship supplies to Malinowski when he was ensconced in the Trobriands. Seligman had referred in his diary to 'the spurious attractions' of Samarai, likening it to a 'section of Thursday Island [in the Torres Strait] removed and dumped in a more pleasing environment'.[32] It was certainly prettier than Port Moresby, 'a mystic island, a toy domain . . . all palms and crotons set in a crystal sea'.[33] Malinowski would visit the island many times during the years to come. It invariably evoked ambivalence in him: 'The contradiction between the picturesque landscape, the poetic quality of the island set on the ocean, and the wretchedness of life here.'[34]

The Savilles and their passenger did not stay in Samarai, however, but at the mission station on Kwato, another little island in China Strait. Since 1890 this had been home to Charles Abel and his large family. Malinowski sat on the verandah of the mission house and while a game of cricket was being played below, he leafed through a book by James Chalmers, the pioneer missionary who met his end at the hands of Fly River cannibals. The Abel family, like the Riches, made a favourable impression on him, though he would later disparage Abel's *Savage Life in New Guinea* as an 'amusingly written though superficial and often unreliable booklet' that inadvertently parodied the missionary view of 'lawless, inhuman' savages.[35]

Malinowski endured a Sunday service at Kwato conducted by Abel. 'We sat in the rectangular chapel or lodge that looked like a rotunda. Very distinct stench. The service was long, with hymns repeated several times.' After lunch, he borrowed Saville's dinghy and Igua ferried him across the strait 'in the calm languor of a beautiful Sunday afternoon'. At Samarai he reported to the resident magistrate, C. B. Higginson, who received him curtly. He then called on another missionary, the hearty, sports-loving Anglican Frederick Ramsay, who had served as rector on Samarai since 1906. Malinowski helped him to classify his collection of stone tools. The next day, the resident magistrate gave Malinowski access to the jail, where Papuan prisoners were lined up and he 'picked out a few for the afternoon' – captive informants, so to speak. Seligman had also interrogated and measured prisoners at the Samarai jail in 1904.

During the following week Malinowski developed a routine. In the mornings he worked on Mailu texts with Saville at Kwato ('I try to be polite and to avoid friction, which is not easy'), and in the afternoons he worked in Samarai with men from the jail. Some days he lunched with the local medico, Dr Shaw; other days he munched on bars of chocolate while strolling around the island. Despite a surfeit of missionaries, at Samarai he 'felt *at home, en pays de connaissance*'.[36]

Two British destroyers came into port and Malinowski glimpsed the Union Jack. Another reminder of the war was the arrival in the jail of six native prisoners, arrested in German New Guinea for beating up a missionary. The *Morinda* had brought them from Rabaul. There were 'brutish German faces' aboard, presumably prisoners of war. The Savilles were departing by the same boat for six months' furlough. Malinowski's farewell was cool, and to the very last his dealings with the missionary were unpleasant; this time they argued over the hire of the launch that was to take him back to Mailu.

On Monday 7 December, Malinowski began the return journey. He planned to take a couple of weeks, calling at several Suau villages along the coast. Here, as at Mailu, the annual feasting season was under way, and he was keen to witness the food distributions and pig exchanges that Suau people called *so'i*. At Nauabu in Baxter Harbour he found a native missionary teacher and a simulacrum of civilization as created by Abel's Kwato mission: 'A scrawny emaciated Samoan woman treated me to a coconut; the table was covered with a cloth, there were flowers on the table.' But just outside, he noted that all the stone sitting circles had been destroyed by the missionaries. A *so'i* festival was in preparation, and that evening there were intimations of Conrad's *Heart of Darkness*:

> For the first time I heard the protracted, piercing sound of a sea shell being blown . . . and with it a monstrous squealing of pigs and roar of men. In the silence of the night it gave the impression of some mysterious atrocity being perpetrated and threw a sudden light − a somber light − on forgotten cannibal ceremonies.[37]

He spent three days in the next village, Isuisu in Farm Bay, where he witnessed and photographed another stage of the *so'i*. The people wore their festive dress and were so preoccupied they scarcely noticed the white man who strolled about the village in his pyjamas early next morning. He waited in vain that day for a ceremonial slaughtering of the pigs, only to discover the pigs were exchanged live. Next he crossed the bay to Rich's mission station on its tiny offshore island. Gliding over the smooth waters in the calm of a fine afternoon induced a festive mood and he decided to give himself a holiday. Charles and Caroline Rich received him well, and he spent a couple of pleasant evenings with them discussing *so'i*. Watching a rosy sunset one evening, he was overcome by sadness and 'bellowed out themes from *Tristan and Isolde*'. He was homesick and missed his mother.[38]

Sailing westwards again, he visited Silosilo, another small Suau-speaking village in an all but landlocked bay. It reminded him of a mountain lake in

the Tatras. Silosilo was also caught up in its *so'i* festival and he watched as
men carried pigs into the village slung on poles. He persuaded Sixpence, a
local informant, to organize a dance – presumably paying the dancers with
tobacco – and noted down the song and the choreography. Then he spent
an uncomfortable night in the *dubu* (men's house) and awoke 'feeling as
if just taken down from a cross'. He was beginning to sicken again. He
returned to reading Conrad but was gripped by a terrible grey melancholy
that swirled around the edges of his consciousness. 'I tore my eyes from the
book and I could hardly believe that here I was among neolithic savages,
and that I was sitting here peacefully while terrible things were going on
back there.'[39]

That day he moved into another house at Kalokalo, where he spent three
nights, none of them pleasant. In his feverish state, the stench, the smoke,
the noise of people, dogs and pigs, unnerved him. He dragged himself
around to watch the *so'i* events, but was unable to concentrate. A fruitful
ethnographic opportunity was slipping away, lost to his physical weakness.
Processions of men carrying pigs came and went, each greeted by gor-
geously decorated dancers. Quarrels erupted which almost became brawls
('a gang of fellows who looked really savage broke into the midst of an
obviously frightened and nervous crowd') and Malinowski was not surprised that disputes had formerly led to fighting. The leader of one group
aggressively presented him with a pig. He tried to give it back but the givers
refused to accept it. This so unsettled him that he went off to bed, thereby
missing one of the pig ceremonies.

At Dahuni in Mullins Harbour the next day he bought some household
objects. He had been collecting ethnographic specimens (or 'curios' in the
idiom of the day) since his arrival in Mailu, and had been notably 'envious'
of Haddon's expertise in so quickly securing a haul of artifacts there. One
of the enduring mysteries of Malinowski's fieldwork on the south coast of
Papua in 1914–15 is the fate of all the artifacts he collected. They have disappeared without trace.[40]

Leaving the Massim behind at this point, they sailed on to Gadaisu in
Orangerie Bay, where he dropped in on a local planter. Malinowski was
having trouble with his 'boys', who were becoming rebellious. A clash with
one of the boat's crew provoked his rage. Next day he visited a cemetery
within a lagoon, where bundles of bones and whitened skulls lay among
the rocks. They sailed on through a sea fog, reaching Mailu that afternoon.
'I suddenly felt empty,' he wrote. 'The future was a question mark.'[41]

Mailu revisited

Malinowski was at something of a loss. 'I came to a deserted place with the feeling that soon I'll have to finish, but in the meantime I must begin a new existence.'[42] In fact, it proved to be his most productive period in Mailu. He moved into the old mission house on the station. The Savilles had left instructions for it to be tidied up for him (which mitigated his annoyance with them), and he tasted true independence on the island for the first time. But that evening, as if to remind him that he could not escape the supervising eye of government for long, Hubert Murray and his nephew anchored off the island. Malinowski invited himself aboard the *Elevala* for supper. 'I was on the same footing with them as before; free friendly conversation, and it was I who gave it colour, without feeling obtrusive.'[43] Murray probably did not see it the same way.

The boat had brought his mail. There were two letters from Annie, 'the first fairly dry and short, peeved by my silence', the second more loving. She was overjoyed to have heard from him. His letters from Cairns and Port Moresby had finally reached her, including some photographs taken on the voyage out. On some of these she detected down on his upper lip. 'Are you cultivating a moustache again?' she asked. 'It won't be as soft & silky as the one you had when first I knew you!' She presumed Staś had taken the photographs. One of them made him look 'most horribly ill'. The one she liked best was 'the one without any visible clothes – your neck & shoulders bare. I have seen you so often looking just like that, coming towards me – only very slightly "dressed" & it just sent a warm glow through me!'[44]

Wistfully, Malinowski felt that Annie was his only contact with a friendly world, but immediately recognized the unfairness of this perception. He admitted to his diary that 'the people I meet here are on the whole very well disposed and seem hospitable, so that I have a feeling that I am among friends'. The Europeans he had met during the previous weeks had all treated him kindly. He did not refer to the Papuans who had also shown him hospitality – or at least had tolerated him.

For Christmas he went to Campbell Cowley's plantation at Mogubu Point. Cowley was open and expansive, 'a typical Australian' who told tales of elephant-hunting in Africa. They gossiped about missionaries and neither of them had a good word to say for Saville. Malinowski then buried himself in another Dumas novel until Puana collected him on Boxing night and they sailed back to Mailu. The following days were lost to the world of Dumas as Malinowski battled fever and a violent toothache.

In Cracow, meanwhile, his mother had received another of his letters via Dutch Indonesia. 'I'm sending you no political news,' she wrote, 'though I'm sure you know nothing from your English newspapers . . . all newspapers write lies in wartime.' She still had no news of her sister Eleonora at the 'Janiszów' estate on the Russian side of the border. 'At the moment we can't leave Cracow, because they would let us out but wouldn't let us back in again.' She was sceptical about her son's claim to have sufficient funds:

> My dearest is bluffing a little in his letter when he writes that he's got £220 and a <u>guarantee</u> from the government about a temporary engagement. . . . It was wishful thinking invented to reassure your mother. I think that my guarantee is more secure and I'm saving up every penny for you, though at the moment everything is so expensive, sometimes you can't even buy basic things (milk, bread), it's hard to save.[45]

Early in the new year she wrote again via Portofino in Italy.

> It's become very quiet in Cracow after several weeks of anxiety. It seems like the siege is not going to happen, though in time of war nothing can be ruled out. Anyway, our heroic army is defending us magnificently. . . . The countries that have been most ruined in Europe are Belgium, part of France, but worst of all our poor country! The only consolation is that our armies are fighting so well.

Having offered these sops to the censor, Józefa Malinowska turned to more intimate matters. 'And what about your hair,' she concluded her letter, 'are you taking care of it?'[46] Her motherly obsession with his encroaching baldness exceeded his own concern.

The first week of the new year went well. He questioned Puana, Papari and Pikana about kinship and taboos. The village was now vibrant with people and there was dancing every night in festive dress of feathers, ornaments and body paint. With a sudden shift of the wind to the east, however, the men left Mailu to sail to Domara in the west to obtain pigs for the annual feast. Malinowski wanted to go with them but baulked at paying the £2 they demanded. It was a serious misjudgment, and on realizing he had missed a unique opportunity he was infuriated and despondent. He immersed himself in Dumas's *Vicomte de Bragelonne* for several days, reading without interruption from morning till midnight. 'My head was humming, my eyes and brain were bloodshot – and yet I read, read and kept on reading without letup as though I were reading myself to death.'[47] He resolved never to touch another novel while he remained New Guinea.

Dog days of idleness continued during which the only productive work he did was to take photographs and desultory notes from Igua. For the rest, he leafed through works by Shakespeare, Renan and Norman Angell (presumably *The Great Illusion* on the futility of war). He also re-read Annie's letters and contemplated his past. 'At moments I feel like writing the story of my life,' he noted, but he was already finding entire epochs remote and alien. His years of schooling, his years of doctoral study with Leon Chwistek, seemed almost to have nothing to do with him. He grew feverish and exhausted again. Typically, his temperature rose each afternoon, a sure sign of malaria. Unable to work properly, he was bored and had moments of wild longing for music. Beethoven's Ninth Symphony played insistently in his head.

Tośka's photographs reminded him that he was he still in love with her, though compared to Żenia 'psychically we had nothing in common'. Even so, he daydreamed that if either of them could be with him now, he would choose Tośka. Despite his erotic imaginings about Ethel Eaton and several other women, he somehow fancied that his monogamous instincts were stronger. While he still loved Tośka, she was simply 'a provisional substitute for the *only one*'.[48] But a few nights later he had a dream that suggested that his unconscious was far from ready to embrace monogamy. Three of his erstwhile mistresses – Żenia, Tośka and Annie – all of them in one room, were sleeping 'separated by *corrugated iron* partitions'.[49] He awoke with a feeling of wasted happiness. A few days later he devoted pages of his diary to the recollection of his quarrels with Tośka in March, concluding again that he 'had a strong attack of monogamy, with an aversion to impure thoughts and lusts'. He wondered rhetorically: 'Is this because of loneliness and an actual purification of the soul or just tropical madness?'

Reading Rivers gave him the impulse to work and enabled him to profit from his observations 'in an entirely different way'. He did not explain what this was, nor did he specify what he meant by 'problems of the Rivers type' to which he admitted he had previously paid insufficient attention. They presumably concerned kinship as Rivers had addressed them in *Notes and Queries*. Implausibly, he was also thinking about the possibility of a government post in what was now ex-German New Guinea, though he suspected that Haddon favoured John Layard for the job. He was right, for Haddon had written to Atlee Hunt in early September (just after Australia had seized New Guinea), saying that he hoped Hunt 'would not forget Layard when the time comes to make a move'. He was referring to discussions they had had in Melbourne, which Haddon later crystallized in a formal memo-randum to Hunt, recommending the appointment of two ethnologists to Papua and ex-German New Guinea at a salary of £200 with expenses.[50] Presumably with Papua in mind he told Hunt: 'A. R. Brown is already at work in Queensland & I am perfectly convinced he is the very best man for the job.'[51] In the event, Layard suffered a mental breakdown following his fieldwork in the New Hebrides and it was another of Haddon's pupils, the Australian Ernest Chinnery, who was appointed to the New Guinea position in 1924.[52] The job in Papua went briefly to yet another of Haddon's Cambridge pupils, W. E. Armstrong, then in 1922 to F. E. Williams, an Australian who had studied under Marett at Oxford. Given Malinowski's enemy-alien status in 1915, it is almost inconceivable that he would have been considered for either position had they existed then.

A flotilla of canoes returned to Mailu on 16 January, and despite his fever and a period of depressing rain, Malinowski went to the village frequently during the week that followed. They were days of conscientious photography as the villagers prepared for their *govi maduna* feast. He photographed the cooking of sago, the scraping of coconuts and the interminable dance rehearsals. His fever ebbed and flowed like the tide, and his temper snapped more than once while taking photographs with his cumbersome equipment. Despite 'frightful sluggishness' – he was getting up between 9 and 10 a.m. and collapsing into bed again during the afternoons – he managed to do some work with Omaga, Koupa and Pikana. He said little about these Mailu men in his diary, except when they enraged him by not turning up after he had hired them for a session, or when they failed to grasp his meaning as the ethnographer moved pawns around on the ground to represent dancers. Then he became angry and the situation grew tense. Exactly what the Mailu thought of this querulous white man with tinted eyeglasses and less hair on his head than he should have, we shall never know, but they appeared to forgive his outbursts as readily as he forgave their obtuseness.

He was, after all, an inexhaustible supply of stick tobacco and the persistently inquisitive stranger would be gone soon enough.

His last few days in Mailu were dulled by weariness, and he oscillated, typically, between fiercely determined hard work and regretful sloth. There were moments of poetic appreciation of the light-patterned landscape, and of freedom and happiness when sailing over the translucent waters of the bay. He doled out tobacco and people rehearsed their intricate circling dances for his camera, but despite his instructions they would not pose long enough for his exposures. One such incident ignited his fury – after accepting his tobacco they simply walked away. On recording this he gave vent to the most discreditable statement of his Mailu diary. Quoting Conrad's Kurtz in *Heart of Darkness*, he wrote: 'On the whole my feelings toward the natives are decidedly tending to "Exterminate the brutes".'[53] It is perhaps significant that during these days he was reading William Prescott's *The Conquest of Mexico*, that other classic text of imperial savagery.

Awaiting a boat that would whisk him off the island, he was in limbo. He gave presents to children at the mission, he hummed Żenia's Ukrainian tunes and he walked along the shore in the starlight, at moments with a nervous dread of what the future might hold. He dreamed of travel, of a honeymoon with Tośka, of staying in a palace with Ethel Eaton. 'I am *"covering the ground"* of my territory more and more completely,' he noted. 'Without doubt, if I could stay here for several months more – or years – I would get to know these people far better. But for a superficial short stay I have done as much as can be done.'[54]

Why he did not remain longer in Mailu is unclear – the *maduna* was building to its climax and his ethnographic material would have been greatly enriched had he stayed to observe it. He probably felt he and the Mailu had exhausted each other's patience, that he had done quite enough fieldwork under what he kept referring to as 'poor circumstances'. The missionary was on leave and would not return for some months, though Malinowski doubtless believed that he had squeezed that particular source of information dry. In any case, he could make no further headway unless he learned the Magi language of Mailu; and that he seemed unprepared to do. His health was another factor. He was monitoring it with his usual close attention, and in recent weeks had been suffering what he called his 'characteristic lack of energy', a dullness and weariness that made even the most trifling of activities (such as changing the plates of his camera) 'a monstrous cross on the Golgotha of life'. Injections of arsenic and iron enlivened him, as did occasional body massages by Igua, but the relief they afforded was temporary.

It was early in the morning of Sunday 24 January when the *Elevala*, sailing from Samarai, called at Mailu. Malinowski hastily gathered his things, paddled out in a canoe and was greeted by the governor 'with a distinct blunt, cold reserve'. He nonetheless invited himself and Igua aboard for passage to Port Moresby. He said goodbye to his Mailu hosts, to 'the whole crowd of savages and the blubberers of the mission'. He was happy to be leaving and experienced 'a sense of freedom – as if I were starting a vacation'.[55] It was the same happiness he had described on his arrival three months earlier.

Chapter 18

Sinaugolo

Moresby interlude

Two events on the trip back to Port Moresby tested Malinowski's trepidation regarding the sea. A poor sailor, he was frequently seasick. Occasionally he claimed to have found his sea legs – until the next time proved him wrong. With boyish aplomb he climbed the main mast of the *Elevala*. It was 'a delightful feeling of freedom mixed with fear' until he lost his nerve. A little later he steeled himself to climb it again. But then, beyond Domara, the boat ran aground on a patch of coral. Dismayed, he scurried down the mast to join the rescue operation. He thought about the possibility of losing his fieldwork materials – an anthropologist's worst nightmare – and he felt a curious sympathy for Governor Murray as well as a loss of faith in the ship itself. He felt, too, for the hapless captain as the ship 'wriggled and twisted' on the reef. There was joyful relief when they finally managed to pull the ship free, but the experience left Malinowski with 'a hysterical fear' of shipwreck.[1]

Back in Port Moresby, Malinowski shared a room with a Finnish sailor at Tom McCrann's hotel. There were 'monstrous roars during the night' from a gang of drunks. Letters awaited him from Staś and from Halina Nusbaum in Warsaw; he was deeply moved by the sheer uncertainty of their predicament. He wrote to Seligman, saying how relieved he was to have indirect news of his mother and how grateful he was to him for helping to keep them in touch. He then brought his supervisor up to date on the completion of his work in Mailu, disparaging the help he had received from Saville. 'In fact the missionary has done his best to interfere with my work in his . . . subterranean ways, and after he left I got on with the natives infinitely better than before.' He had taken some fairly good photographs and

– as Seligman was probably by now resigned to him doing – neglected only anthropometry, 'the measuring side of the business'.[2]

In the hot and humid town Malinowski rummaged for stores in Burns Philp and made his dutiful social rounds, reporting first, as a government proclamation required, to the resident magistrate, then seeing Herbert Champion, Leslie Bell, Judge Herbert, and Seligman's old friend and collaborator William Mersh Strong. He spent an evening with Strong but was no longer impressed by his knowledge and found 'inadequate' his views on magic and the 'Papuan soul'. Despite more than a decade in the Territory as a medical officer and unofficial government ethnologist Strong had failed even to master Motu.

During the following days Malinowski visited local villages with Igua and Ahuia. In the evenings he socialized with European residents, talked about the war, and listened to music on the gramophone. He drank sherry and rather more beer than he was accustomed to. Although icy beer was 'pure bliss' in the humid climate he did not enjoy being drunk, even less the hangover that invariably followed. Throughout his life Malinowski preferred wine to beer and remained a very moderate drinker.

On 1 February he was interviewed again by Government Secretary Champion, who hinted that financial support would be forthcoming. On the strength of this, Malinowski took the afternoon off and read *The New Machiavelli*, H. G. Wells's most autobiographical novel. It impressed him deeply. 'He is very like me in many respects,' he noted of Wells's fictional alter ego: 'An Englishman with an entirely European mentality and European problems.' Moreover, the love affair between the hero and Isabel strongly reminded him of his affair with Żenia, a 'love permeated and interwoven with intellectual understanding'. The character of the protagonist's wife Margaret, on the other hand, 'with her eternal passivity, all affirmation, anticipation, and "second sight"', vividly reminded him of Tośka.[3]

The English domain at Rigo

Late in the afternoon of 2 February 1915, Malinowski boarded the *Puliuli*, a small vessel put at his service by Staniforth Smith. He was eastward-bound again, this time for Rigo, a government station forty miles to the southeast of Port Moresby. He had plotted the geographical extent of Mailu culture to the east where it bordered Suau, and now, again following Seligman's suggestion, he was intent on investigating the Sinaugolo, eastern neighbours of the Koita and the Motu. According to Seligman, they were 'a powerful and influential tribe whose villages extend from the edge of the hilly country some three miles from the coast behind Kapakapa', the last village of the Eastern Motu.[4] Seligman had collected only sketchy information on the Sinaugolo, though he considered them remarkable for their claim to have originated *dubu,* the large, ceremonial men's houses with carved posts so characteristic of this part of the Papuan coast.

Malinowski had about a week to spare. As well as Igua, this time he took along Ahuia, trusting that the work could be done more expeditiously with his assistance. He felt a renewed sense of his own importance as the cutter made sail: 'I was on "my ship" – strong feeling that the ship is for my exclusive benefit.' He was happy – until he went below deck and his head began to spin. After nightfall they sailed on in the moonlight and his fears of scraping reefs and worse mishaps were revived. He slept badly and the sound of the boom scraping the mast sent him scurrying anxiously up to the deck.[5]

Safely ashore at Rigo next morning, he was inspecting the ruined *dubu* with their superbly carved columns when Albert English approached on a bicycle. English was an ex-resident magistrate turned planter, one of the very first in British New Guinea. His were the first rubber and sisal plantations in the colony, though like other planters his most secure investment was in coconuts. Malinowski observed that the road was lined with coconut palms, frangipani and mimosas; lovely scents commingled with the stench of drying copra. There were hedges and arbors, as in a park, and fragrant white flowers that reminded him of Żenia's perfume. Having lived in the area for the last thirty years, English had transformed the landscape with his exotic plantings. He had another obsession: the collection of stone clubs and axes, of which he had amassed a great number from all over Papua. English had a reputation for being crusty, and Strong had advised Malinowski to humour him. So Malinowski helped him to classify his collection of stone implements and English became positively amiable. Malinowski noted: 'a typical man (like me) – he won't do anything disinterestedly, he recognizes and appreciates people only to the extent he needs them at the moment.' Enjoying the plantation atmosphere of English's civilized domain, he felt at ease 'in the shadow of government protection; in my relations with the friendly Rigo people, in the lovely surroundings; in my relatively good health'.[6]

During the following days Malinowski worked in nearby villages with Ahuia in attendance and a young interpreter, Diko, loaned to him by the resident magistrate. Malinowski took to Diko immediately ('a very nice though probably not a very honest boy'), and admitted to his diary that he felt a distinct homosexual attraction to him.[7] He found the Sinaugolo much pleasanter than the Mailu people and easier to deal with. 'They tell every-thing without embarrassment and speak good Motu,' he noted. Among other topics, they discussed 'sexual matters', though his fieldnotes suggest their discussions remained at a very general level.[8]

His fieldnotes also indicate how much he relied on Ahuia as both an infor-mant and translator while in Rigo. Adding to his notes on Koita and Koiari ethnography, he now tackled the Eastern Motu (his earlier work in Port Moresby had been concerned with the Western Motu). He noted mourn-ing and burial customs, naming protocols, *hiri* trade, myths and mythical heroes, beliefs in spirits and the afterlife, and the several kinds of mortuary feasts. Again, he bounced many of his inquiries off Seligman's earlier mate-rial. He had begun the admirable practice of taking down descriptions in Motu verbatim, and they appear with increasing frequency in his notebooks.

The main purpose of his visit to Rigo, however, was to collect material on the Sinaugolo. As he wrote later, he was aided in this by 'a number of well-informed, intelligent and outspoken natives'.[9] His notes on Sinaugolo amounted to about seventy pages and, in addition to the above-mentioned topics, he covered land tenure, gardening, hunting, forms of property, social organization, various systems of magic, courtship, betrothal, sex and mar-riage. He later claimed to have got 'exceptionally good information' on courtship practices in Sinaugolo, as he 'was admitted into the confidence of a smart and fast set of Rigo young men, who discussed matters among themselves in my presence in Motu, which they all speak as a second mother-tongue'.[10] He never published the materials in these early note-books, though he referred to them later (often in extended footnotes) when making comparisons with the Mailu and Trobrianders. He told Seligman he believed that his 'scraps' on the Sinaugolo, Koiari and Woodlark were 'much better quality though small in quantity' than his 'stuff on the Mailu'.[11] But in truth, there was scarcely enough information in his notes for more than an article or two.

On the planter's verandah one evening, Malinowski experienced what he called 'violent surges of sexual instinct for native girls, for English's servants'.

These interrupted 'moments of concentration and spiritual elevation' during which he 'dissolved in the landscape'. He then ruminated on the aesthetic connection between sexual desire and the sensuality of the sunset: 'in the beauty of the landscape I rediscover women's beauty.' Conversely, a beautiful woman could symbolize the beauty of nature.

Later that evening he had what appears to have been some sort of homoerotic encounter with Diko. They were discussing courtship and Diko spoke approvingly of 'good' sex, showing the ethnographer with graphic gestures how Motu and Sinaugolo boys customarily approached a girl for intercourse by first sitting upon her knees. Aroused, Malinowski followed Diko into the kitchen. 'I asked him whether they knew about homosex. here. He said no, "*kara dika*" [bad custom].' Ambiguously, Malinowski recorded that Diko added: 'I'll say no more. Soon we'll go to sleep.'[12]

Among Haddon's papers there is an undated, unsigned typed note that was almost certainly written by William Saville.

You ask me about Malinowsky (I forget how you write his name). I have only heard hints, probably the same that you have heard, about not having got on too well, in some quarters, with Government Officials. And hints are not worth noticing. But I must candidly confess that I hope we shall never have to entertain that gentleman again. I suppose that being a foreigner, we do not understand him well enough. I admired his enthusiasm for his work, but he spoiled that altogether by not being intelligently able to understand that other people also might have a right to interests in which they are as much justified and just as likely to be quite as enthusiastic as he was about his. And that we, being only servants, had duties to think of as due to our masters. Dr Malinowsky seemed unfortunately to think that our time and that of our people should be given up to him. He very likely did not mean this, but his experience of men seemed to be of the smallest and he was pretty much like a child with a new toy. The problems he was trying to work out were of the keenest interest to me, but the minds of some of us must have relaxations from one subject, by the tackling of others. Had he been a man, who would enter into the position and minds of another, whether native or white, he could have got twice as much information in one twelfth of the time. A native is not a class room student, and a native likes a bit of fun and a game, Dr M. seems to understand neither, nor could he understand anybody who did. Perhaps it was our fault, perhaps it was that we are so unfortunately very english [sic].[13]

Although he doubtless never read them, Malinowski would have been aggrieved and infuriated by the injustice of these remarks. That he was misunderstood by the British officials and missionaries he dealt with cannot be disputed, but that he was importunate in his demands seems equally certain. Another indiscretion came to light much later. Recollecting a conversation with Malinowski in Port Moresby, Herbert Champion was struck by the anthropologist's remark that 'the standard of living of the Papuan was superior to that of the peasants of eastern Europe'. This was innocent enough, but Champion also wrote that 'Malinowski must have been hetero [sic] sexual since he told Leonard Murray who told me that for sexual satisfaction a boy was to be preferred to a female or words to that effect.' 'Hetero' is surely the slip of an old man's pen for 'homo' – Champion was ninety-one when he wrote these words – but it was an injudicious comment for Malinowski to make to the governor's nephew, however jocular.[14]

It was with some regret that Malinowski prepared to leave Rigo. After watching dance rehearsals in the nearby village, he walked to Kapakapa (or Gabagaba) with Diko, 'a little fed up with the savages, eager to renew contact with nature'. The smell of the jungle, he noted, 'penetrates and drenches you like music'. At Kapakapa he was ferried though house pilings into a kind of village stockade. Direct sensual contact with this Papuan version of a 'lake-dwelling culture' filled him with bliss.

Early next morning the *Puliuli* picked them up and, rolling from side to side as the boat tacked into a furious wind, he observed the tiers of mountain ranges from the boathouse roof. Despite imminent seasickness, he had the hedonistic feeling that he was having the time of his life. They were unable to make Port Moresby that day and anchored at Tupuseleia. Like Kapakapa it was built on piles over the sea, the gold and grey thatched houses looking like 'a lot of haystacks set over the blue lagoon'. He was determined to spend the night in this remarkable village which from the outside seemed to have 'something of the melancholy of the Venetian lagoon – a mood of exile or imprisonment'; indeed, in the sketch map he drew in his diary, he named two of the 'canals' after the principal canals of Venice. On the inside, however, the village was swarming with life; there were crowded verandahs, 'gondolas', squealing children and dogs. It was low tide that evening and he urinated from a height of twelve feet. Next morning at high tide the haystack houses stood directly upon the sea, 'dipping their long thatch beards in the water'. On the short trip back to Port Moresby, comfortably seated astern on pillows like a pasha, he interrogated a Koiari man about the inland tribes.

During the next few days in Moresby, he did only a little work with Ahuia. Their association was practically at an end, for on subsequent visits to the town Malinowski did not pursue his investigations into the Motu and Koita. He talked, rather, with Miles Staniforth Smith, Dr Simpson, Mrs Ashton and the Duboises (local planters who plied him with icy beer), with Strong and Champion (with whom he appeared to be getting on rather well during at this time), with Brammell at the local 'museum' and with H. A. Symons, the resident magistrate at Woodlark Island in the South Eastern Division.

Woodlark Island

He sailed eastwards from Moresby on Tuesday 16 February. This time he was alone (no Igua, no Ahuia), though Brammell and Symons were also aboard. On the first day of the trip he outlined an article on Motu and Sinaugolo (which he never completed), read Seligman and watched the coast slip by. By the following morning they were plying along the Suau coast again, which inspired a flood of sensuous poetic images: 'Shoals of rain alternately embrace and forsake the mountains. Moist velvety sheen of verdure . . . freshness of the stones dark from the rain. The silhouette of the mountains through a curtain of rain – like reality's shadows cast on the screen of appearances.'[15]

At Samarai he dutifully reported himself to Higginson, and talked at length to Henry Newton, the Anglican bishop, who presented him with a copy of his recent book, *In Far New Guinea*. He took an immediate fancy to Dr Shaw's beautiful wife, and almost fell in love with her over dinner that evening. About noon next day they sailed for Woodlark Island – called Muyuw or Murua before Europeans turned it into a goldmine. Malinowski was on deck, enthusing about the seascape in China Strait: volcanic pyramids and coral islets everywhere, 'phantom forests floating in melting blue space'. Typically, he chided himself for having a book in his hands (Kipling's *Plain Tales*), blaming 'the uncreative demon of escape from reality'.

The heavily forested island was already in view when he awoke next morning. Seligman had been on Woodlark, too, and had already written about its ancient trade in finely polished axes of a locally quarried green-stone. Symons conducted Malinowski ashore in a whaleboat, to the dismal mining settlement and administrative centre of Kulumadau. The heat was hideous and Symons unfriendly. Malinowski met missionaries and miners, a drunken Englishman and 'two little Jews'. He got tipsy on beer in the seedy hotel – an unpleasant 'male brothel'.[16]

The next day, despite his utter weariness, he trekked through the forest, half-carried at times by his porters ('I simply hung myself on two boys'). The dark, gloomy forest delighted him (reminding him of Lady Horton's drive in Kandy), and he inspected the 'candelabra of ferns' and the trunks of gigantic trees. He was happy to be alone again with Papuans. They were crossing the island to Dikoyas, an important village on the north coast, where he slept in a makeshift hut of palm leaves erected over a shaky stick floor. Charged up by arsenic, he was feeling much better. His malaise of previous days had included an interesting transient phobia: a nervous 'aversion for protruding objects' ('pointophobia' or 'stickophopia' he had jested).

In retrospect, Tuesday 23 February 1915 was a significant day. While working in Dikoyas that morning he heard the bellow of conch-shell trumpets followed by 'a general commotion'. Without understanding what he was seeing, he observed his guide Aus give a *bagi* shell necklace to another man, whom Aus referred to as 'a friend'. Malinowski was in fact witness-ing his first Kula transaction.[17] But without pursuing the matter, he con-tinued to take notes on spirits and funeral rites. Things were going so well at Dikoyas that he decided to stay for another day before making his way back to Kulumadau (half-carried by two 'boys' again). They arrived in the nick of time, and it was with sheepish relief that he boarded the *Marsina* for the trip back to Samarai.

'I have decidedly won a victory'

Malinowski awoke as they were gliding over the porcelain blue waters of China Strait. He noted how 'the pink body of the naked earth steeped in the dawn light showed through the tropical forest'. The sensuous imagery was motivated perhaps by an amorous desire for Mrs Nevitt, a female passenger. The sea surrounding Samarai was at its Sunday best, and he strolled around the island, 'the shore perfectly elegant, surf breaking, depositing a silvery foam at the foot of gentle palms'. He longed to write to Annie – and did so in his head – to tell her of his experiences. He hosted a lunch for the Shaws and the Newtons, and late that afternoon he boarded the *Marsina* again as it sailed for Port Moresby.

He was blessed with female company again: pretty Miss Craig, the daughter of an Australian planter from the island of Sudest. During the short voyage up the coast he discussed the collection and housing of artifacts with Brammell and made friends with the assistant resident magistrate from Samarai, Burrows, to whom he proposed 'possible expeditions and eventual collaboration'. It was the first of several attempts Malinowski made during the year to involve others in his ethnographic research. Not that he doubted his ability to work alone, but rather that it took a while to rid himself of the assumption of his mentors that fieldwork done in conjunction with 'men on the spot' was more fruitful than work conducted without their assistance. (In 1904, for instance, Seligman had coopted, among others, Francis Barton, R. L. Bellamy, E. L. Giblin, Henry Newton and William Strong.)

Before reaching Port Moresby, Malinowski wrote a letter of effusive thanks to Atlee Hunt, promising to call upon him soon.[18] He spent only one night in Moresby, drinking beer with the Duboises, and in the morning he paid calls on Murray, Champion, Ahuia and Mrs Ashton before reboarding the *Marsina*. Gazing at the Coral Sea next day he felt happy – tired but exalted. The first phase of his field research was over. He had accomplished a great deal, his health had withstood the tropics and he was able to cope better with seasickness. 'True, it's not all over yet; but in the light of old fears and uncertainties I have decidedly won a victory,' he congratulated himself.[19]

He felt moved to write to Staś Witkiewicz, and in the unfinished letter (perhaps a fair copy) that survives among his papers there is something of his old bravado, something too of the histrionic hyperbole with which the two friends used to swap their experiences. An unforeseen benefit of his recent Papuan adventure had been an initiation into self-sufficiency. For the first time in his life he had been thrown entirely upon his own resources, and he had found himself equal to the challenge. He wrote:

Unexpectedly – considering how pessimistic I was about the prospects for any success and you know only too well that I had many reasons to think that way – I'm coming back rather healthier and stronger than I was before the trip, and, I think, with totally gratifying results. The work and the stay in the 'savage' parts of N.G. was fabulously fascinating. I had no inkling whatsoever that it could be so rich in possibilities. Of course, there were some rough moments as well. Especially being sick – I was sick several times, and sickness is no fun. But the work at the very source – and not just digesting received ideas, or simply polishing commonplace formulations – is very hard work indeed that requires constant mental alertness and initiative, total subjugation of the natives, organization of transport, food supplies etc., and is something that completely changes a man. Coupled with dreadful loneliness, independence and the feeling that one has to rely completely and exclusively on oneself – all that has had a most beneficial effect. Up to now I have experienced true life in the jungle on a rather small scale. But by the end I realized that I am capable of traversing the most difficult terrain with the help of 2–4 natives who drag and push me along. So for the next year I am planning more ambitious expeditions to the heart of the jungle. The Australian government has promised me financial help for the duration of the war, and the local (N.G.) government helps me a lot too. So much about myself. Forgive me for writing so much, but I suppose that, despite everything, you did not lose interest in me.[20]

Coincidentally, on the very day that Malinowski wrote to Staś, Józefa Malinowska was writing from Cracow to her 'Dearest Sweetest Little Son':

Yesterday I got a letter from Halinka [Nusbaum]. . . . She writes that you were well on October 15, in good spirits and pleased with your work. I'm very glad if it's true, but I know that you wouldn't write if it were otherwise. . . . Janiszów has been looted by the Cossacks, but it looks as though the manor is still there because both Auntie [Eleonora], Uncle [Kazimierz] and the Wolski family [Cousin Stefania, husband and child] are in Janiszów. I also found out that Staś is in Petersburg, where he must have gone as a Russian subject. Apparently he's very depressed again, and of course he can't go back to his mother.[21]

It is remarkable that six months after the war began Józefa was still ignorant of the exact whereabouts of her son. 'Have you been to Tasmania, the New Hebrides, and are you indeed in New Guinea already?' she asked. 'I'd rather you were in the New Hebrides with Rivers, because it's healthier there and you wouldn't be alone.' In fact, having long since deserted the hapless Layard on an offshore island of Malekula, Dr Rivers would soon be back in the relative safety of England, ready to play his famous role in the psychiatric treatment of shell-shocked soldiers.

Chapter 19

Autumn in Adelaide

An arresting welcome

As the *Marsina* was nearing Cairns on the first day of March 1915, Malinowski resumed his diary. 'The most important thing now,' he urged himself,
'is not to waste my stay in Australia but to use it carefully in the most
productive way. I must write an article about Mailu. . . . I must check the
museums insofar as possible. So there won't be time for nonsense! I must
give a detailed account to Mr Atlee Hunt and try to impress him.' He was
as good as his word. The 'article' he wrote on the Mailu burgeoned into a
substantial monograph of 212 pages which he dashed off in six weeks. He
visited several museums, and – not least – he did manage to impress his
benefactor and protector, Atlee Hunt. But he also found time for some
'nonsense'. He fell in love.

During the voyage to Brisbane he worked on his Mailu notes. He also
read Newton's *In Far New Guinea* and took pages of notes from the veteran
resident magistrate Arthur Lyons, on furlough from the Western Division.
There were more importunate distractions. 'The fact that I am lusting after
Miss Craig and Mrs Nevitt is not to my credit,' he wrote sourly. He especially fancied the latter, but she was 'boundlessly stupid' and would leave
the ship at Cairns. There were fleas in his bunk, the ship rocked interminably
and he was seasick. He took quinine and surrendered to a novel. On 4
March, while watching raft-like coral islands glide into view, he began to
compose a synthesis of the voyage, but abandoned the attempt after two
paragraphs and the diary ends abruptly. The meshing of mood and seascape
recalls the travelogue he had written for Aniela Zagórska two years earlier:

> As I gazed, everything echoed inside me, as when listening to music. . . .
> The sea is blue, absorbing everything, fused with the sky. At moments,

the pink silhouettes of the mountains appear through the mist, like phantoms of reality in the flood of blue, like the unfinished ideas of some youthful creative force.[1]

Malinowski reported to the military commander's office in Brisbane. From there he took a train to Sydney and again presented his papers for inspection. He stayed at the University Club for several days, writing letters and visiting Charles Hedley at the Australian Museum. On 14 March he wrote a long letter to his mother, delighted to have received hers of 8 November, but only too aware that her news was considerably out of date. There were letters, too, from Aunt Staszewska and cousin Mancia with depressing news of the pillage of Janiszów, though the Lisów estate had so far survived. It was reassuring that his mother was with friends in Cracow, though he knew that she would never tell him the worst. 'Through the optimism of your letter I can see all kinds of terrible things,' he wrote to her. He relayed his latest news from Staś in St Petersburg and from 'Mrs Brunton' in Cape Town. Then, glossing his own optimism, he told her about his good health, his successful work in New Guinea and how, thanks largely to the promise of money from the Australian government, his 'future prospects exceeded all expectations'. The administration in Papua had been 'fabulously helpful, very decent and honourable' and he was 'on good terms with the Governor and all the mandarins'. Or so he believed.

> As for the natives, one could without the slightest hesitation walk all over the continent (except in the west) alone, with a stick in one's hand, equipped with just 4 pounds of tobacco. There is malaria everywhere, but if one doesn't drink oneself dead drunk (95 percent of the white population is normally semi-drunk), it's less annoying than 'flu in Europe.[2]

If only he could be sure, he added, that Mama had 'at least 10 percent of the comfort and security' that he had, then he would be at peace, 'as much as one can be during such a brawl as this'. Throughout his letter he referred to the war in euphemisms: 'storm', 'row', or 'brawl', and for the benefit of the censor, he added in English: 'Written in Polish, does not contain any mention of Public Matters, nor any reference to recent happenings.' He was learning the rules. But his most intimidating brush with the military was about to come.

Foolishly, he failed to report to the authorities in Melbourne when he travelled from Sydney on 18 March, and soon after his arrival in Adelaide he was arrested. In an apologetic letter to Atlee Hunt he explained what had gone wrong. When he arrived in Melbourne he was suffering a bad attack of malarial fever. On learning that Hunt was not in town, he booked himself a sleeping berth to Adelaide that very afternoon, 'simply forgetting' to report himself and get a new travel pass. He was held by the district military commander and told that he would be interned in a concentration camp. His recurrent dreams of soldiery two years earlier suddenly became a waking nightmare. Providentially, he was rescued by his hosts, the Stirlings, who telephoned the district commander and pleaded for his release. In this abject letter, Malinowski reminded Hunt not merely of his technical neutrality as a Pole, but of his pro-British and anti-German sentiments:

> During my residence in England I always preferred to be a Pole and everybody knows that this means that I cannot be an 'Austrian' in the national sense of the word, though I happen to live in a part of Poland annexed by Austria and to be an Austrian subject. . . . I have lived for over four years in Great Britain and worked in an English University as a student and lecturer and I hardly need to say that independently of my Polish nationality I am deeply grateful for all I experienced in Great Britain. If I were not with all my sympathies on the side of the Allies as a Pole, I would be as a man who owes everything to British culture and British science.[3]

'I don't think that I can be considered as dangerous,' he concluded hopefully, and begged Hunt to intercede with the Defence Department. Without its permission he would be unable to leave Adelaide, let alone return to Papua.

Hunt duly obliged ('he will not do anything prejudicial to the interests of Great Britain') and, in a sardonic reply, trusted that Malinowski would experience no further inconvenience. The Secretary of Defence issued the mildest of rebukes: 'No doubt he will be more careful in future.'[4] If this was the closest that Malinowski ever came to being imprisoned, other enemy aliens in Australia were less fortunate. By the end of the war, 6,739 men had been interned, 200 of whom died, 50 became insane and only 59 escaped.[5]

The Australian talent for bureaucratic efficiency had yet to flower, and it was partly administrative ineptitude that allowed Malinowski to remain at large. Several prisoner-of-war forms were completed and filed on his behalf by different officials between 1914 and 1917. According to these, his height hovered between 6 feet and 5 feet 7 inches (in fact it was 5 feet 10 inches). From grey-green, the colour of his eyes turned brown then hazel, while his hair ('going bald' or 'thin on top') was described as fair or brown. His build went from medium to slight, his complexion from fair to sallow. His illness during 1916 could well account for changes in build and complexion, but scarcely in height or eye colour. The documents got the facts wrong in other respects. In one he is named Branistau Malinawski and identified as 'an Australian Pole'; in another, his Melbourne address is incorrect. Officials did not bother to check his actual whereabouts when their letters were returned 'addressee unknown'. One officer testified that Malinowski left Sydney for Woodlark Island on the S.S. *Mindini* at 4 p.m. on 23 October 1917. In truth, he left Sydney for Port Moresby aboard the *Makambo*. The date at least was correct.

It emerges from the dossier on Malinowski (Alien No. 11612) compiled by Military Intelligence that they had only the haziest idea of who he was, what he looked like, and where he lived. Had he really been a spy, as Hubert Murray idly suspected, it would not have been very difficult to evade such casual surveillance by such incompetent officers. For his part, Malinowski treated the officers with exaggerated politeness, and appeared to parody them by signing himself 'Your Obedient Servant'.[6]

Writing Mailu

It was doubtless an invitation from Sir Edward Stirling that brought Malinowski to Adelaide. He had met Stirling's youngest daughter when the good professor conducted the visiting British Association anthropologists to Lake Alexandrina in August 1914, though on that occasion he 'found little music in her company'.[7] Still, it is likely that she was one of the reasons he made directly for Adelaide.

The well-connected Stirling family lived in rustic splendour at St Vigeans, an estate at Mt Lofty to the north of the city. Edward Stirling had built the house in 1882, naming it after his father's Scottish birthplace.[8] The family also had a town house with easy access to North Terrace, where the city architects had conveniently placed the South Australian parliament, museum, library, art gallery and university in a stately row. Four of the five Stirling daughters – two sons had died young – were already settled in

careers by the time Malinowski met them. Three were involved in chari-
ties. Harriet and Mary remained unmarried; Jane had married a professor
of physiology at the university, while Anna had married a Sydney lawyer.
Nina, the youngest, was in delicate health and led a more sheltered life than
her sisters. Malinowski grew fond of the parents. Sir Edward, 'although stiff
and patriarchal at times', always behaved as a perfect gentleman towards
him, while Lady Stirling treated him kindly.

Despite feeling seedy, he settled down to work immediately, immersing
himself in that desk-bound mode of ethnographic experience called 'writing up'. This was the second stage of the ethnographic process: the discursive re-creation of Mailu culture in written form. He saved himself a
great deal of time by adopting for his report the most convenient model at
hand. *Notes and Queries*, the fieldworker's manual that had served him well
during the first phase, also came to his aid during the second. It enabled
him to group his topics under conventional headings and write without
too much concern for structure. Hence, his 'fairly systematic division' of
chapters into Geography, Social Divisions, Tribal Life, Economics. Magico-
Religious Activities and Beliefs, and Art and Knowledge bears a close
resemblance to the topical organization of *Notes and Queries*.[9] The technical
monograph that resulted had no institutional focus, no unifying topical
theme, no functional plan, no narrative form. These literary and theoretical
strategies he developed only later with respect to his Trobriand ethnography. If *Argonauts* is a window on the future of ethnographic writing, *The
Natives of Mailu* was a door closing on the recent past, recalling the kind of
reportage typical of Haddon and Seligman. (Indeed, Malinowski states in
his introduction that he used Seligman's 'masterly outline' on the Koita as
a model.) Understandably then, the self-consciously heroic ethnographic
persona that Malinowski presented in his later monographs is lacking in
Mailu.

A good proportion of the text of *Mailu* is technical description of
customary practices and techniques. Never again would he devote so much
space to technology. But he was less sure of himself when reporting things
that he could not witness at first hand, or that were by nature inaccessible
to observation. He cites local authorities, white or indigenous, when he
senses the possibility of dispute over his findings. But he is frequently tentative and diffident, honestly admitting to the reader whenever his information is deficient. This is one of the most striking characteristics of the

monograph: its candidness and openness to correction. Here he was putting into practice what he had most admired in Rivers's work, the principled separation of fact and opinion. He knew that the ethnographer who confesses his ignorance can be trusted when he states what he claims to know; at least, it was a rhetorical device that he cultivated. He is also scrupulous in telling the reader what events he had or had not witnessed, appealing to the 'seeing eye' as the hallmark of his authority as an ethnographic witness.

When he departs from the Procrustean format of *Notes and Queries*, his ethnography becomes more creative and characteristically 'Malinowskian' in its rhetorical confection of vivid observation, native commentary, reflexive anecdote and theoretical aside. The most original sections of the monograph are precisely those – notably on legal institutions and on the great feast – that were unconstrained by the prescriptions of *Notes and Queries,* and he presented his material on them in a thoughtful and challenging way, opening up possibilities for further research. In this connection it is interesting to note that in August 1914 he had talked with Sidney Hartland – the British folklorist and a fellow British Association delegate to Australia – who had lent him a draft manuscript on primitive law. Malinowski had written to Hartland from Port Moresby, telling him that he would 'pay special attention' to points that Hartland had raised concerning exactly what constituted law in primitive societies, and the need to avoid projecting Western notions of law onto their regulative institutions. 'Nevertheless,' Malinowski added, 'I think that a classification of the sanctions a certain rule enjoys is very important & that the nature of the sanctions throws much light upon the social importance of a rule.' He would develop this idea a decade later on the basis of his Trobriand material, but his discussion of sanctions in *Mailu* – including the tricky concept of taboo – foreshadows the more sophisticated treatment of the subject in *Crime and Custom in Savage Society*.[10]

If the adoption of a conventional format facilitated 'writing-up', so too did his practice of adhering quite faithfully to many of the entries in his field notebooks. In short, there is a remarkable congruence between the first-order ethnography of his notebooks and the second-order ethnography of his monograph. This, too, was a function of the constraint he was under to write up as quickly as possible. He gave himself little time to digest and rethink his material. Later he would write that 'the distance is often enormous between the brute material of information . . . and the final authoritative presentation of the results', but in respect of his Mailu ethnography that distance was very small indeed.[11] This has its advantages, of course, in that the immediacy of notes taken in the field enlivens the formal text of the monograph; it also allows his personal style to flavour otherwise dry observations. Put another way, there is a continuum of forms of representation in the three kinds of document Malinowski produced as an ethnographer. At one end is the personal diary (itself continuous with other diaries he kept before going to the field), which, however self-indulgently experimental as a literary artifact, must be privileged as the most 'authentic' and iconic expression of his fieldwork experience. At the other end is the formal, guarded, polished and relatively impersonal published document, be it an article or a monograph. Between these poles are the field notebooks, whose authorial imprint is less subjective than that of the diary, but more colloquial and unfettered than that of the official publication. In *The Natives of Mailu* the stuff of his notebooks bubbles to the surface of the text; the English is smoothed and shifted to a more respectable register, but there is often a close congruence between what he jotted in his notebook and what he published in his report.

Interesting exceptions occur when he felt obliged to censor his notes to meet prevailing standards of decorum. He did not publish his detailed notes on delousing, for example, presumably out of respect for British squeamishness. And despite his promise 'to give a full account of the erotic life of the Mailu', he did not reproduce the salacious details he had recorded.[12] A story related by Alf Greenaway, for instance, told of 'a father holding his daughter in order to be humped by a man to whom she was married and whom she did not like'. Again: 'During the Maduna general licence prevails. It is usually during the dances. The two agree & sneak away. Sometimes twelve boys hump one girl.' In his monograph Malinowski suppressed such spicy details, stating flatly that he did not see 'any sign of quickening sexual life' at the feasts he witnessed in Suau.[13]

Insofar as his report was composed as a compendium of ethnographic facts copied more or less directly from his notebooks, the writing was easy. He could transcribe entire pages with little pause for thought. For certain topics, however, the facts had to yield to interpretation. Kinship, land tenure, law, taboo and feasting, for instance, had to be treated within a discursive and theoretical frame, and the intellectual task of writing about them was more demanding. His sections on the more complex institutions are the longest and most theoretically informed, and the most 'distant' from the facts as recorded piecemeal in his notebooks. That they had 'worried' him a good deal while in the field is evident from the way he returned to them again and again as opportunity offered.

Many of the pet topics that he later pursued in the Trobriands appear in *The Natives of Mailu*. These interests point directly to fascinations and fixations of his own in his non-professional life. He seemed determined to find the Mailu ignorant of physiological paternity – as, with better evidence, he later found the Trobrianders to be. It was doubtless his own superstitious fear of darkness, confronted repeatedly in Zakopane in 1912, that prompted him to investigate it – and even spuriously calibrate it by means of measured amounts of tobacco – in both Mailu and Kiriwina and to write about it at inordinate length. In *Mailu* he justifies this by making what appears to be a reasonable methodological claim: 'It is important to study not only the ideas of the natives concerning ghosts and spirits, but also their emotional reactions towards those ideas.' He found the Mailu to have 'an intense dread of darkness' because of their belief in sorcerers, but his explanation is less convincing than his graphic depiction of that dread.[14]

The rhetorics of Malinowski's ethnographic writing appear in embryonic form in this monograph. Within the constraints of the borrowed template and the limited time he had for reflection, there was scope only for the occasional anecdote and apt illustration, but these do enliven the pages and allow him to exercise his literary talent in brilliant flashes of colour. He embellishes certain ethnographic points with stories about his field experiences, showing how his interactions with Mailu informants had generated additional – and often unexpected – information. Some of the experimental interventions he describes seem ethically questionable today (bribing youngsters with sticks of tobacco to gauge their fear of the darkness); others are surprisingly scrupulous for the period (forbearing to publish the texts of magic spells in case they fell into the wrong hands). Such anecdotes say as much about Malinowski's status as a member of the colonizing race as they do about the colonized people he was studying. It was no slip of the pen that allowed him to refer to his 'cook-boy' Igua Pipi as his 'personified personal dictionary' and also as his 'valet'; as we have seen, Malinowski found it just as gratifying as other whites to have 'a crowd of boys to serve you'. He took the colonial culture largely for granted; it was the unarticulated background of his ethnography that can be glimpsed only through his anecdotes.

There is a guileless quality to Malinowski's self-representation in *The Natives of Mailu*, though here and there he parades the persona he will deploy to great effect in later works. The probing Ethnographer who extracts valuable information from 'intelligent' natives is one version. Another is the urbane gentleman traveller, equally at home in a Papuan village as in a Parisian salon. In order to illustrate the coercive power of convention in Mailu, he makes rhetorically effective use of distancing by referring to Europeans' slavish obedience to absurd dress codes.[15] Yet another characteristic rhetorical device is his Aunt Sally trick by which he overturns an overstated argument, such as 'the universally reported native's dread of darkness'. The rhetoric in such instances is disproportionate to its end.

Another guileless persona is the linguistic adept who dominates – for sound methodological reasons – the latter portion of the Introduction. He had found Police Motu 'a completely satisfactory instrument of investigation' and by the end of his stay in Mailu was able to speak it almost fluently. It is with evident pride that he refers to his linguistic abilities. 'I am afraid I must explicitly boast of my facility for acquiring a conversational command of foreign languages, since I understand that the time in which I learned to speak Motu would have been normally too short a period for acquiring a foreign, and especially a native, tongue.' The boast is more memorable than the methodological point he seeks to make concerning the value of being able to eavesdrop: 'Over and over again I was led on to the track of some extremely important item in native sociology or folklore by listening to the conversations of my boy Igua with his Mailu friends.'[16]

He used another section of the Introduction to describe the 'conditions of work', a principle of ethnographic method he exhibited famously in *Argonauts*. Characteristically, he exaggerated the length of time he spent in the field, and it was patently untrue (his own diary providing the best record) that he 'was living quite alone with the natives, except for short periods of about two or three days', during 'the best part of December, January, and February'. In fact, of the seventy-odd days he spent among the Mailu, only half of them could be counted as untainted by social contact with Europeans and, even had he wished, it would have been impossible to escape them altogether. Still, it was with the force of a personal discovery that he 'found that work done under such circumstances [i.e. living quite alone with the natives] is incomparably more intensive than work done from white men's settlements, or even in any white man's company'.[17]

If he had not yet lived up to the principle of total immersion, he had nevertheless gone one better than his mentors Haddon, Rivers and

Seligman, none of whom had made a particular virtue of avoiding fellow Europeans. He had learned (as the veterans of Torres Strait might have told him) that close proximity to village life yielded unexpected ethnographic benefits. 'Participant observation' would become the catchphrase to describe his later ethnographic style, although he had done little of it among the Mailu. He had also learned that direct questioning was not the most effective means of extracting information from informants; indeed, he generalized that 'it never discloses their attitude of mind as thoroughly as the discussion of facts connected with the direct observation of a custom, or with a concrete occurrence in which both parties are materially concerned'.[18] (There is a parallel here with the teaching method he later favoured: because they enjoined personal interaction, seminars were more effective than lectures.) Mindful of Rivers's first rule that 'the abstract should always be approached through the concrete', Malinowski would make the recording of 'concrete occurrences' and 'actual cases' another cornerstone of his ethnographic method. In the only surviving letter that he wrote to Rivers, from Kiriwina in October 1915, he told him that he was following his advice 'of getting everything through concrete facts'. He mentioned *Mailu* in a dismissive postscript: 'As it is my first attempt, it is of course very weak, and if it ever comes into your hands, please don't condemn me on its account.'[19] Obviously, he had no intention of sending his patron saint of fieldwork a copy. That same day he wrote to Haddon, too, referring to his fieldwork in Mailu as 'a time of trial and learning of method and I made of course lots of blunders and wasted half my time'.[20]

Looking back some twenty years later, Malinowski reviewed his apprentice fieldwork in sketchy notes towards the introduction to the textbook he never completed: 'What were my experience[s] as [a] professional worker in the field?' he asked himself at the beginning of a section provisionally called 'Cultural Reality of Fieldwork'. He selected some apparently random memories of this period of 'raptures, shivers, triumphs & disappointments'. In Mailu, it was '6 [sic] months of striking stone and no water. Rely on Miss[ionary] – picking his brains – brains he had, and good mat[erial], [but] no time!' Concerning his monograph, it was composed of 'ordinary stock in trade: kin terms (worthless!), technology, taboos, totemism, ornamentation, bits of folklore'. He had 'failed' with regard to economic institutions 'because not enough freedom in language & observation, also lack of theoretical scaffolding'. He 'failed', too, in dealing with law for lack of a theoretical focus.[21]

While it certainly falls far short of later standards of ethnography (standards largely set by Malinowski himself), when judged in the light of other Papuan monographs of the period, *The Natives of Mailu* loses little in comparison. Williamson's *The Mafulu* (1912), Jenness and Ballantyne's *The Northern D'Entrecasteaux* (1920) and Landtman's *The Kiwai* (1927) were all based on at least one year of fieldwork conducted a few years before Malinowski's meagre months spent among the Mailu. The remarkable thing is that Malinowski's ethnography is as richly detailed as it is, given the time devoted to its execution. Although he belittled and disparaged his monograph, variously referring to it as a 'paper', 'article', 'pamphlet', 'essay' and even 'booklet', it helped to earn him a doctor of science degree from the University of London.

Partly because of its modest location in the annals of a colonial scientific society, it went unnoticed by anthropology journals in metropolitan Britain, though *Nature* granted it a belated review. The linguist Sidney Ray was blandly approving: *Mailu* was a 'credit' to the Royal Society, which published it, 'a fine piece of work, and an extremely valuable and interesting contribution to the ethnography of New Guinea'.[22] It received no reviews at all in its birthplace, Australia.

The politics of publishing

Malinowski had finished his report before the end of April. Perhaps to oversee the preparation of his manuscript, he moved into Adelaide for a few days, boarding at 58 Melbourne Street, a squat bungalow with an ugly portico. From there it was a fifteen-minute walk to the South Australian Museum. A couple of museum employees were recruited to help him. Miss Clarke redrew his figures and diagrams and a stenographer typed the handwritten text, incidentally producing several carbon copies which Malinowski used as scrap paper for several years to come. The text of *The Natives of Mailu* is about 80,000 words long; there are also thirty-four photographs and over fifty figures. If we allow that Malinowski spent a maximum of forty days in Adelaide, his written output could not have been less than two thousand words a day – a considerable achievement for one who claimed to be 'seedy' for much of the time. The typescript reveals, however, that much effort went into the task of editing it for publication, and that Malinowski's own hand was not the most conspicuous of those that worked it over. He owed to Edward Stirling the most conscientious and drastic editing. 'It is a thorough & conscientious piece of work & honestly done,' Stirling told Haddon in August. 'On abstract questions he writes quite well, but there is some trouble with his technical descriptions which however I hope to put right.'[23] Despite Malinowski's evident lack of enthusiasm for recording technology, his monograph has been, more recently, commended by a museum anthropologist as 'a veritable treasure-trove of data on objects, their manufacture and function'.[24] Another admiring critic has suggested that Malinowski's drawings and instructions 'would enable an ardent reconstructionist to build a house, a canoe and go fishing with a high degree of cultural specificity'.[25]

It was Edward Stirling, South Australia's first Fellow of the Royal Society, who suggested to Malinowski that his report be published locally in *The Transactions and Proceedings of the Royal Society of South Australia*. This might have seemed an unlikely venue for an anthropological monograph of such length (and it would certainly ensure that few people in Britain would ever see it), but Malinowski was quickly persuaded of the advantages to be gained by doing so. As he wrote to Seligman, with a jocular mixture of apology and defiance, he judged that 'there would not be the remotest chance of it [his monograph] seeing the light under the grey skies of England, in the present troubled times'. But the Royal Society of South Australia 'had opened its arms to receive the new born Papuan infant'. Stirling 'has been as kind to me here – nearly as you have been over there. He read my M.S. and corrected the English and the stile [sic] in its logical aspect and took great interest in the stuff.'[26]

The advantages of publishing it in Australia were several. In addition to there being a local editor willing to smooth his English, there was speed of publication – no need for the messy business of sending the typescript overseas and waiting interminably for a response. But most important was the diplomatic factor: 'as I am pumping money from this soil, it is only fair (and what is more, it's wise for the future) to let my sweat manure the same soil.' He pointed out, too, that the LSE, 'which stipulated first option on publication of my results, has no claim on this lot, as I did it without their assistance'; but he would acknowledge the benefaction of Robert Mond in the subtitle of the report. Even so, he suggested deferentially, the 'final decision' would rest with Seligman.[27]

Malinowski did not mention that he had already committed himself to publishing with the Royal Society of South Australia, and if his supervisor had indeed exercised a veto it would have caused great embarrassment. He had travelled to Melbourne and been interviewed by Atlee Hunt on 27 April, and the very next day submitted a formal, written report on his Mailu research, shrewdly pitching his account for government approval. He had 'paid special attention', he said, 'to the economic and sociological aspects of native life, as well as to their beliefs and general psychological features'. He had also addressed problems arising from social changes wrought by European contact and had 'studied the extremely interesting . . . process of adaptation' to new conditions. In other words, he stressed his interest in problems of direct concern to the colonial administration of Papua.[28]

Atlee Hunt acted promptly and forwarded the report to his minister with a memorandum making it clear that the proposal to publish Malinowski's results in Australia was a clinching argument for granting him money for further research. It was as if Malinowski had 'sold' his Mailu monograph, sight unseen, to the Commonwealth government for the promise of a year's salary. Atlee Hunt's memo also implied that his advocacy would have been less forceful if Malinowski had been engaged only in the kind of ethnological investigations that Seligman and Haddon had expected him to carry out. 'He has not concerned himself with the more technical branches of the science such as are involved in the measurement of bodies, etc., but deals with the mental attitudes and particular customs of the people.' Crucially, Malinowski had investigated matters 'likely to be of much use to the Government in our dealings with the natives', for instance, 'the native ownership of land, ignorance in regard to which has frequently caused considerable trouble'. Hunt then recommended that Malinowski's 'extremely moderate' request for £200 be granted 'for the current year'.[29] Within days the minister had given his approval, though Hunt made it plain to Malinowski that his investigations must include 'the system of native ownership of lands' and that his writings should be published in Australia or Papua.[30]

On receiving his first instalment of £50 Malinowski acknowledged in writing his obligation to do 'practical' work. 'I shall pay special attention to the sociological, legal and economic problems of native life, which might be useful for practical purposes of administration and legislation, and I shall make a report on the results I obtain.'[31] The generality of this pledge left him ample room to pursue his own researches. He also gave himself a loophole by warning that there might be 'technical difficulties' in publishing 'a large volume' in Australia, which would in any case require financial subsidy.

During his few days in Melbourne at the beginning of May, Malinowski stayed at 'Darley', Baldwin Spencer's spacious house near the university, and they went over his Mailu manuscript together. 'He struck me as being an exceptionally able man. . . . I could see that he was doing good work,' Spencer told Haddon later that year.[32] And by a remarkable coincidence, Malinowski was sitting in Hunt's office when a letter from Haddon, enquiring after him, was delivered to Hunt's desk. 'I had a glance over the MSS,' Hunt replied reassuringly to Haddon, 'and I am sure it will be a valuable contribution to our knowledge of the sociology of the South Coast Tribes. The poor fellow is rather strained financially, but I am glad to see I got the Government to give him £150 for this year. That will enable him to go on & may be a useful precedent for enlarging our anthropological inquiries at a later date.'[33]

Malinowski, it seems, was part of Hunt and Haddon's larger game plan for government-sponsored anthropology in both Papua and New Guinea. Significantly, in the same letter that Haddon inquired about Malinowski, he delightedly congratulated Hunt on his rumoured appointment as governor of ex-German New Guinea ('I do not know of anyone better for the post'). Although the rumour was false, it indicated where Hunt's ambitions and Haddon's hopes lay.

The political significance of the Mailu monograph can be judged from Hubert Murray's indignation at not being sent a copy – though Malinowski had sent one 'as an act of personal courtesy' to the government secretary Herbert Champion.[34] Although *The Natives of Mailu* was published in December 1915, it was not until the following August that Murray complained to Hunt and forthrightly asked for a dozen copies. Baldwin Spencer replied to Hunt on Malinowski's behalf, saying that he had received only twenty-five copies, of which more than twenty had been distributed among 'various Scientists and Scientific Bodies'. Malinowski could therefore spare no more than one copy. Murray would not be placated, however, and he sent a stinging reply to Hunt.

> I have the honour to suggest that as this Government paid Dr Malinowski's salary more than one copy of his book should be supplied to us. I do not think this gentleman ever realized that it was the Papuan Govt. that was paying him, and I feel certain that if this is pointed out to him he will readily admit that he owes us some return.[35]

Murray's suspicions concerning Malinowski's pro-German sympathies had not been allayed by the interview he gave to the Sydney *Daily Telegraph* just before he embarked again for Papua; yet he could not have been more forthright in his support of the Allies. Speaking as a Pole, he believed 'the Polish spirit' was 'entirely on the side of the Allies and of freedom for small and oppressed nations'. In referring to 'the special link of sympathy' between Poland and Australia, Malinowski invoked the names of Count Strzelecki, who explored the Australian Alps and named the continent's highest peak after Kosciusko, the patriot who fought for Polish liberty and American independence. Then he listed the Polish legions fighting for the Allies. Without voicing his distrust of the Russians, he welcomed the zsar's promise to grant Poland self-government after the war. The interests of Great Britain and Poland in crushing Prussian militarism were convergent, for the existence of oppressed nations precluded 'peaceful development' and the liberty of twenty million Poles would have to be 'one of the conditions of a peaceful future'.[36]

'One of the most beautiful young women'

During his last weeks in Adelaide, Malinowski had begun an ill-advised and ultimately doomed love affair with Nina Stirling. It would cause them both a great deal of misery, and the scandal would damage hitherto cordial relations between three eminent academic families in two cities, between, indeed, those knights of the realm who were Malinowski's Australian patrons. It almost cost him his career.

Nina Eliza Emmeline Stirling was twenty-six years old. Although Malinowski spent barely four weeks in her presence (plus a fifth, awkward week in 1917) he dreamed and agonized about her for over four years. They exchanged a substantial correspondence, but none of it survives (it was deliberately destroyed in 1919) save for a single, pathetic missive: Nina's final reproach to Malinowski. Unlike his previous loves, she was neither married nor committed to another when he met her. She was a candid, ingenuous soul, young for her years, and there was doubtless a pedagogic aspect to their relationship: a mutual friend perceptively referred to Nina as Galatea to Malinowski's Pygmalion.

Malinowski mentioned this budding friendship to Annie Brunton. Encouraging as always, she replied:

> I am extremely interested to hear about Miss Nina S. & hope that there will be further developments. You know my wishes about your future, &

a Colonial girl of the best type is not to be despised. . . . She was not quite indifferent to you I am sure – I don't think any girl could be that if you 'spread yourself out' to her.[37]

What Nina saw in him we can only conjecture. She would have agreed with Anna-Mi Borenius, perhaps, that 'he was incredibly charming, amusing, high-spirited; he was a real Pole, tremendously up and then down'. Somehow he induced Nina to fall in love with him, and through his letters he opened her mind to new horizons. She had a keen interest in photography and many of her striking images of eucalyptus landscapes found their way into Malinowski's own collection.[38] A photograph caught her in the garden at St Vigeans – famous for its magnificent rhododendrons – holding a parasol and a bunch of Michaelmas daisies in the crook of her arm. She is wearing a full cotton skirt and a white blouse with ballooning sleeves. A collar and dark tie lend her a somewhat formal air. She has a strong nose, full cheeks and lips, and heavily lidded eyes. Her gently curling hair is fair-to-light brown and gathered in a loose bun. Her expression is slightly pouting, her demeanour pensive. Nina Stirling, as a smitten Bronio told his mother, 'is one of the most beautiful young women I've ever met'.[39]

It was in the luxuriant gardens of St Vigeans that his love blossomed. As he would tell Lady Stirling three years later (stiffly, for he was on the defensive), he had been 'very strongly impressed' by Nina from the first, though it was 'only during the last few days a personal and subjective note entered our relations'. When they parted, it was 'knowing only that we liked each other & that we would like to correspond', and it was during their correspondence 'that we found more serious elements pervading our friendship'. Even so, 'we both were aware of almost insurmountable difficulties arising from differences in outlook, upbringing, temperament and manner of living'. His own doubts arose, he wrote, 'because I always felt that I was & am destined to lead an unsettled, roving, homeless life & I hardly thought I was justified in even dreaming of more definite plans'.[40]

On 1 August 1915, the only diary entry Malinowski made during his first stint of fieldwork in Kiriwina, he made a portentous announcement. 'Today is an important day. . . . I have clearly realized an idea that had long been dimly present, wandering through the welter of wishes, dreams, and uncertainties – it has now clearly emerged – I am thinking seriously of marrying N. . . . If in the end I marry N. March and April 1915 will be the most important months in my emotional life.'[41]

'Gate to the field'

'Early next week I am starting for the N.E. Coast,' Malinowski wrote to
Seligman on 13 June. He had been in Samarai for two weeks, awaiting a
boat and putting the finishing touches to his Mailu manuscript ('I am eager
to resume fieldwork as soon as possible,' he had concluded his Preface, dating
it 9 June 1915). He told Seligman of his latest plans.

> Possibly I shall go by the Trobriands. Bellamy is leaving for the front, and
> I would like to get out of him as much as possible and get his help in
> securing some of the Trobriand stuff (specimens). The Trobriand people
> are the leaders of the whole material and artistic culture of this end, and
> it is quite essential to get an idea of what is going on among them. I
> should stop there for ab. one month, and then go by the B.P. small
> steamer 'Misima' to the Mambare River, which will be the main theatre
> of my operations this season.[42]

Baldwin Spencer had asked him to collect artifacts for the Melbourne
Museum. This was reason enough to visit the Trobriands – named by the
French explorer Bruni d'Entrecasteaux after one of his officers – but Malinowski did not mention to Seligman his desire to see for himself the islands
that boasted such an exotic reputation. Everyone, from Administrator
Sir William MacGregor and Royal Commissioner Mackay to Governor
Murray himself, had observed that Kiriwina in particular was 'different', and
the travel writer Beatrice Grimshaw had nominated it 'among the most
civilized' places in Papua. All agreed that the gardens were more fertile, the
yams bigger, the chiefs more dignified, the dances more colourful, the decorative art more pleasing, and the girls prettier – flouncing in shorter skirts
than were to be found elsewhere in Papua – and more sexually alluring.
('Chastity is an unknown virtue,' as Malinowski would put it later.)[43]
The siren call of Kiriwina was irresistible to a curious ethnographer, and
Malinowski sailed north from Samarai with high expectations.

Armed with an introduction to the Rev. Matthew Gilmour, he passed
through his 'gate to the field' (as he captioned the back of a photograph of
China Strait) between the mainland and the island of Sariba. At Ubuia, an
islet off the northwest corner of Normanby Island where the Wesleyan
Methodist mission had its headquarters, John Wesley Booth, a man of Malinowski's own age, was repairing a launch when the anthropologist, dressed

in 'tunic, trousers and boots', stepped onto the jetty.[44] Booth escorted him
up the steep winding track to the top of the hill, where Gilmour and his
wife lived in a spacious house open to the cool sea breezes.

A Scotsman who had emigrated to New Zealand, Gilmour came to
Papua in 1901 and served under the autocratic William Bromilow before
succeeding him as chairman of the New Guinea Mission. Unlike Bromilow,
Gilmour was a practical man who loved tinkering with engines and believed
in the educative value of an industrial mission.[45] His native pupils built
launches in a well-equipped workshop. Less bigoted than Bromilow, whose
uncompromising view of primitive Papuans was that they were a degenerate
child-race, he astonished Murray in 1905 by telling him that he thought
the children of Kiriwina were 'quicker at learning' than white children.[46]
A humanitarian of sorts, after a year's acquaintance with Kiriwinans,
Gilmour described them as 'bright, clever, industrious, dear people'. They
were 'excitable, brave and revengeful' yet 'deeply emotional and loving'.[47]
In 1903 he introduced them to the gentlemanly game of cricket, partly as
a ploy to divert their sexual energies. Alas, the muscular missionary's intention was gloriously subverted by the Trobrianders, who turned the game
into a colourful ceremonial competition, enhanced by erotic display in
dances as salacious as any the mission had tried to ban. It is curious that
Malinowski's Polish prejudice against the English game prevented him from
seeing it as a cultural innovation rather than as a simple 'borrowing'. He
seemed not to notice that cricket in Kiriwina was different from the cricket
played at Kwato under the stern paternal eye of Charles Abel. But then, as
he would write much later in a droll aside, 'to another type of savage, a
Pole', cricket was 'pointless – a tedious manner of time-wasting'.[48]

Malinowski stayed a few days with the amiable Gilmour, extracting
from him information on death and burial, belief in witches, and a lengthy
version of the Tudava myth – which, in his later challenge to Freud,
Malinowski would deploy with an inverted Oedipal message.[49] Gilmour
had spent several years at Oiabia – the mission station on Kiriwina founded
by the Rev. S. B. Fellowes in 1896 – so his knowledge of the Massim and
of the Trobrianders in particular was not to be lightly dismissed. Seligman
had quoted him extensively in his monograph, and Malinowski was already
familiar with Gilmour's published notes on canoe-borne trading expeditions from the village of Kavataria. Later he would acknowledge that
Gilmour 'was fully acquainted with the facts of the Kula'.[50] In early 1918,
indeed, Malinowski discussed with Gilmour the possibility of collaboration,

presumably on the publication of a Trobriand grammar.[51] With a sympathy untypical of Malinowski when writing about missionaries, he later described Gilmour ('the Grand Inquisitor of the Methodist Mission here') to Elsie Masson:

> Intelligent, energetic, keen, with a mentally broad outlook and a certain amount of culture, he has got many points on which I can think and feel with him in common. . . . He has also a really good understanding of the native mind (limited by Missionarism) and he knows more about the Kiriwinians than anyone (not excepting even the humble ethnographer, in some matters at least).[52]

So it was by no means onto *terra incognita* that Malinowski set his booted foot, but onto the missionized and well-patrolled domain of Assistant Resident Magistrate 'Doctor' Bellamy, who did more than anyone to set the colonial scene and establish the conditions of Malinowski's fieldwork there.

Chapter 20

Kiriwina

The government officer's Trobriands

The missionary schooner *Saragigi* – the Dobu name commemorated William Bromilow's astonishing trick of removing his teeth – brought Malinowski finally to Losuia, the government station on the placid lagoon of western Kiriwina. On 27 June 1915, the anthropologist was set down with all his gear on the timbered landing stage of a broad coral jetty, completed by prison labour only the year before. Prison labour, too, carried his sixty boxes and cases to the house of the resident magistrate. With its sweeping verandahs and vaulted corrugated iron roof freshly painted in red oxide, this was the largest, most imposing building in the Trobriands.[1] It overlooked pearl-oyster beds, the focus of European commercial interest in the islands. Beyond the reefs were the dark outlines, like cardboard cutouts, of the mountains of the D'Entrecasteaux islands – the fabled Koya – home of cannibals and witches. In the months to come a homesick Malinowski would sometimes walk along the jetty feeling 'so empty, so unhappy, looking to the south'.[2]

He now found himself in a grassy compound of twenty-six acres, enclosed by a massive coral wall. Besides the magistrate's house, where he stowed his luggage, there were police barracks, a gaol and prison warder's quarters, a hospital with male and female wards, a dispensary and several food storehouses. Tidy rows of coconut palms marched across half the compound. There was an orchard of citrus trees as well as several vegetable gardens. Crotons, hibiscus and other ornamental shrubs pleased the eye.

The jack of all trades who had created this tropical settlement was ten years older than Malinowski. A fair-haired, blue-eyed Englishman of sound Staffordshire stock, Raynor Bellamy was likeably boyish and 'absolutely imperturbable'. He had studied medicine at Cambridge and Edinburgh (though he did not take his final examinations until 1917), before sailing to New Zealand to try his luck at goldmining. When that failed he came to British New Guinea and travelled throughout the colony, scratching unsuccessfully for gold, treating sick miners and penning whimsical despatches for *The Grey River Argus*. Seligman met him in Samarai and was impressed. In 1905, Administrator Captain Barton offered Bellamy the joint post of assistant resident magistrate and medical officer in the Trobriands, where a special hospital was being built to combat the alarming spread of venereal diseases. They had been introduced in the previous century, it was supposed, by American whalers and by Malays and Manilamen fishing for bêche-de-mer. Bellamy postponed his plan to return to England and sailed for Losuia to become a pioneer of public health. By the time Malinowski arrived, Kiriwina was one of the most efficiently governed and healthiest places in all Papua.

'I fancy my district shall show its heels to the rest,' Bellamy claimed, and it was with extraordinary energy and determination that he transformed the new government station into a well-regulated, fortified settlement.[3] His magisterial authority, and the prison labour at his disposal, gave him the powers of a satrap, though one with an English passion for landscaping. This was done on an impressive scale. He ordered a wall of coral debris, six feet high and wide at its base, to be constructed around the station. Its ostensible purpose was to keep out maurauding pigs, but the villagers were mystified.

Bellamy was two-finger typing his annual report when Malinowski entered his domain. It would be the last of his despatches from the Trobriands. Drought, he wrote, had been 'the most important event of the year from the native standpoint'. It had lasted from June 1914 to mid-December, so the crops had been planted much later than usual. Sixty miles of 'track improvement' were accomplished that year. The pearling industry was 'practically dead' owing to a fall in prices in Paris because of the war. Low prices meant low wages and reluctant divers, and there were now only eight licensed buyers; but Bellamy saw some benefit to the depleted oyster beds which would have a chance to recover. Bêche-de-mer fishing was taking up some of the slack. One hundred and eighty-six prisoners had passed through the gaol in 1914–15 – down from 346 the previous year – and Bellamy had used them to extend the wharf, level the coral frontage of the station and plant several more acres of coconuts. There were thirteen Europeans in the Trobriands. In addition to the nine traders, there were four white missionaries: the Rev. Johns and his wife, and two teaching sisters.

There were also three Fijian teachers and one Rotuman; fifteen Kiriwinian teachers were in charge of other village schools. Nicholas Minster, an infamous Greek trader, had died during the year (though tales of his legendary exploits and insatiable whoring were still fresh), and the Rev. Andrew Ballantyne (brother-in-law of the anthropologist Diamond Jenness) succumbed to blackwater fever while on a visit from Goodenough Island. Bellamy judged his native population to have remained steady at 8,500, despite a dysentery epidemic.[4]

As for Bellamy's view of the Trobriander:

> A keen trader, kindly and affectionate in his domestic relations, an indulgent parent, accustomed by tradition to recognize the authority of his village chief, he accepts the overlordship of the Government pretty much as a matter of course, and obeys its orders. . . . His mentality is vigorous, but undeveloped. He can be taught quickly. Latterly he has shown an appreciation of some of the minor comforts, such as kerosine and hurricane lamps, corrugated iron for roofing purposes, billy-cans etc.[5]

A paragon of administrative virtue, Bellamy had served ten years at Losuia and was pleased with the changes he had brought about: 'cleaner villages, greater freedom from disease, better houses, cleaner habits, [and] a growing recognition that behind the white man's gaol lies the white man's justice.' This, then, was the Trobriands District at the time of Malinowski's arrival.

In a modest way, Kiriwina was the breadbasket of the Massim. In addition to the main staple of taitu (or lesser yam), it yielded an abundance of yams, taro, sugar cane, bananas and sweet potatoes. In good years it exported the surplus: up to 300 tons a year were bought by the government, the mission and by traders for sale to other islands. Bellamy's station was itself a miniature breadbasket, and during the severe drought of 1911 he boasted of gardens that yielded enough to feed the eighty-five occupants of the station and hospital for a period of six weeks.

Without being fully aware of it, perhaps, Bellamy acted in the manner of a Trobriand chief – as a banker of food wealth which he could use to pay for services or dole out as charity in times of need. However he dispensed them, such donations enhanced his prestige. The difference was in the manner of accumulation, for the polygynous Trobriand chief derived his food surpluses from numerous in-laws in the form of annual 'tribute', whereas Bellamy derived his from the work of his prisoners. The economy of the government station turned upon his statutory powers to incarcerate villagers who breached Native Regulations, enabling him to command their labour. Nevertheless, Doctor Bellamy was no Kurtz, and the principled *raison d'être* of his labour force was public works – however eccentrically construed. He exercised 'indirect rule' through seventeen village constables who reported to him weekly. These men he hired or fired at his own discretion. A detachment of two armed constables, appointed and trained in Port Moresby, provided the only physical sanction at his disposal. Losuia's minuscule police force was illustrative of Murray's 'government by bluff'.

Bellamy was fanatical about village cleanliness. He ordered people to devote one day a week to tidying their hamlets. 'A moderate amount of compulsion', he admitted, was needed to get them to comply, and fully half of the convictions in some years were for breaches of the Village Cleaning Regulation. Another civilizing project was road-building, and Bellamy got villagers to create tracks for non-existent horse-drawn buggies. His greatest enterprise, however, was coconut-planting. Access to coconuts was traditionally a prerogative of chiefly rank – a privilege that Bellamy abrogated. In 1912, he set a blanket taboo on the consumption of coconuts; he then initiated competitive planting, within and between villages, and awarded prizes of trade tobacco to those who excelled. Those who did no plantings were gaoled – two hundred in 1913–14. By this carrot-and-stick method Bellamy oversaw the planting of 120,694 coconut trees along 241 miles of track throughout the several inhabited islands. Bellamy's well-executed scheme for local 'development' was far ahead of its time. Coconuts ceased to be a scarce resource monopolized by chiefs and became a cash crop. An unintended consequence of this project was its contribution to the democratization of Trobriand society.[6]

Bellamy's other signal achievement was to bring venereal diseases under control. In 1906 Colonel Mackay, chairman of the Royal Commission on Papua, called at Losuia and found Bellamy 'pink as a new chum just landed'. The medico was doing 'great work' as one of the two most 'practically useful men in Papua' – the other being the doctor at Samarai. They were 'the natives' best friends and possible saviours'. Mackay was referring to the 'festering plague' of VD.[7] Estimates put the infection rate at between 6 and 10 percent of the population.

Bellamy's treatment was at first punitive. He had to overcome 'native prejudice and superstition'. Patients were rounded up and incarcerated in the hospital until they were either cured or dead. Eventually, having learned the language and the exercise of 'tact and perseverance', he induced patients to come forward voluntarily. Among his difficulties was that of persuading the incredulous islanders that venereal diseases were transmitted by sexual contact. He had discovered what Malinowski was later to confirm: that Trobrianders denied any link between male insemination and female conception. Bellamy diagnosed at least five clinical varieties of venereal disease, though he probably exaggerated the incidence of syphilis, so easily confused with yaws. His treatment by injection was commemorated by Trobrianders in a burlesque song-and-dance routine.

Bellamy had begun regular medical patrolling in 1908, his aim being to examine every man, woman and child in each of the 156 named villages, not once, but every year until venereal disease had been vanquished. It was a task verging on the heroic, and by 1915 he had brought the rate of infection down to 1 percent. As he registered the name of every person he examined, his records took the form of a census. In 1913 he ordered village constables to record all births and deaths in their districts and, collating these, began to compile a central register. For many years Bellamy's were the only reliable census figures from anywhere in the Territory, and his were the first calculations of birth and death rates. He also recorded the incidence of epidemic diseases such as dysentery, and endemic diseases such as malaria. (Up to half the population suffered malaria attacks during prolonged wet seasons.) While making his census, Bellamy recorded people's totemic affliations and a good deal of additional ethnographic information, much of which was published by Seligman. He also wrote an article on Trobriand 'customs'.[8]

Anthropology, then, joined demography and epidemiology in the spectrum of Bellamy's scientific purview, and within a month of their first meeting Malinowski had invited him to co-author a book on the 'sociology' of the Trobrianders. Although this was probably an impulsive, ingratiating offer (recalling similar suggestions made by Malinowski to Seligman and Strong and to the missionaries Newton and Copland King), Bellamy took it seriously enough to tell his sister: 'I suppose I know more about [Trobrianders] than any other living white man, but compared to the war sociology seems very small "beer" and I'm turning the offer down.'[9]

Trouble with magistrates

'He is a Pole from Cracow originally but quite a nice chap. Very clever and all that,' Bellamy wrote to his sister soon after Malinowski's arrival. When the trader Cyril Cameron visited from Kitava Island he found the anthropologist following Bellamy around with a notebook and pencil, jotting down Kiriwinian words. Malinowski slept in Bellamy's room, Cameron on the verandah and Bellamy under the table.[10] During these early days Malinowski also took notes from Cameron and Sam Brudo – another trader who lived at Kavataria – and Corporal Bunuwagola, one of the armed constables. He prevailed upon the two missionary sisters, Ethel Prisk and Margaret Jamieson, to translate some vernacular texts for him, hoping that 'there was nothing obscene in them'.[11] He even invited Cameron and Bellamy to write directly into his notebook. Cameron – a young Scotsman who was reputed to keep a veritable harem on his plantation – discoursed on Kitavan theories of reincarnation. He duly provided Malinowski with an eighteen-page account of the 'origin of *Milamala*', the annual harvest festival that was the main inspiration for Malinowski's essay on *baloma* that he completed the following year. There he acknowledged Cameron in a curiously defensive fashion, as one who 'has in no way lost the "caste" and dignity of the white man, in fact he is an extremely kind, hospitable gentleman; nevertheless he has assumed certain native peculiarities and habits such as the chewing of areca nut, a habit seldom adopted by white men.' He was also 'married to a Kiriwinian' and regularly hired the local garden magician to bespell his gardens: which was the reason, Malinowski's informants told him, that Cameron's gardens were better than those of other white men.[12]

Bellamy obligingly wrote several pages about the chief's authority, which extended 'as far as he would send pigs to', and added notes on chiefly polygamy. At some later date Malinowski jotted in purple pencil in the margin of these pages: 'R. L. Bellamy does not know much!'[13] He told Seligman so in his first letter from the Trobriands.

> I came here first to sound the terrain – I was told as a matter of fact that Bellamy is a cash [sic] of information only to be tapped and I thought it would be a pity to let him get killed by the bloody Germans (he's going to the front) before draining him. He knows more than the average R[esident] M[agistrate] but nothing amazing. . . . I found again that it is quite futile to reckon on anyone but oneself, though there is a trader here, a Turkish Jew, who helped me a great deal.[14]

The 'Turkish Jew' was Sam Brudo from Paris, and Trobrianders immediately perceived an affinity between them: 'People wonder whether I and Brudo belong to the same *dala*, as we both talk the same language [French] and both have beards.' (*Dala*, as he was learning, was a matrilineal sub-clan, the principal unit of social identity in the Trobriands.) On his next field trip to the Trobriands Malinowski would discover an even greater affinity for Sam's younger brother Raphael. Another trader companion was Billy Hancock, who leased an acre of land at Gusaweta. It was in Hancock's 'compound' that Malinowski sought refuge when suffering from a 'surfeit of native'. Although they became close friends, Hancock never lost the habit of addressing Malinowski as 'Doctor'.

According to his biographer, Bellamy 'developed a profound dislike for Malinowski . . . based on a fundamental difference in their attitude towards sexual matters'. In 1926, indeed, Bellamy told a colleague 'that Malinowski had undone much of the work he had done during the ten years he spent in the Trobriand Islands'.[15] This astonishing charge probably referred not to the increased incidence of venereal disease Bellamy discovered when he returned to the islands, but to the anthropologist's subversive views on matters such as village burial and the exhumation of bodies for divination, the practice of sorcery, the traditional powers of the chiefs and their polygamy – all 'customs' that Bellamy had tried to suppress or modify. Malinowski took the liberal view that government intervention was unwarranted and essentially destructive of native institutions. As in Mailu, he could not fail to notice that people tried to conceal from him certain practices, and he correctly deduced that fear of the government was the reason. He would have quickly learned, too, how the power of the chiefs had been curtailed by Bellamy in a series of administrative measures, and how he had flagrantly undermined the paramount chief's prestige when, in 1912, he imprisoned Chief Touluwa on a sorcery charge and forbade the other prisoners to observe customary obesiance. For Bellamy it was a matter of opposing intimidation and 'the malevolent power of the chiefs based on sorcery and fear'; for Malinowski it was arrogant colonial interference, 'short-sighted' in that it undermined 'native tribal law' and introduced 'a spirit of anarchy'.[16]

If Malinowski reciprocated the 'profound dislike' Bellamy conceived for him, it might explain why he never acknowledged the magistrate's help and hospitality, why he never cited Bellamy's article on Trobriand customs, and most importantly why he never mentioned Bellamy's role in creating the largely favourable conditions – administrative and medical – under which he conducted his fieldwork. Almost certainly, Kiriwina would have been a less accommodating place if, instead of this energetic and exacting man with the patience of an accountant, it had been under the desultory control of the usual run of hardy but unimaginative officers. Years later, however, Malinowski did formally acknowledge at least some of Bellamy's virtues in a letter to Hubert Murray: 'I regard him as one of the finest officials I met during my stay – a lover of natives and of native culture, and a man of the highest intelligence.'[17] Bellamy joined the war in October, survived the front line in France, and went on to Edinburgh to complete his medical degree. Fully qualified, he resigned his commission and returned to Papua in November 1918 – missing Malinowski by a matter of weeks. Thereafter he returned only intermittently to the Trobriands. Called to a higher station, he served as William Strong's deputy in Port Moresby, eventually succeeding him as chief medical officer of the Territory in 1929.

John Norman Douglas Campbell, Bellamy's successor at Losuia, was less dedicated, less diligent and less affectionately remembered. He had come to Port Moresby as a clerk in 1907. The war gave such men the opportunity for promotion. Taking the measure of Campbell's mediocrity, Malinowski and Billy Hancock nicknamed him 'Thirty Percent'. Malinowski's relations with him were initially cordial. On taking up his post Campbell wrote politely to Omarakana to tell Malinowski that his personal documents could remain in the Losuia office safe, and that he could continue to use as an informant the prisoner who had accompanied him.[18] On his second trip to the Trobriands, however, Malinowski wrote of 'that odious official' Campbell in the most uncomplimentary terms. 'He is a low brute,' he told Elsie Masson in 1918, 'but apparently his bark is worse than his bite and so far he has not given me any trouble, so I am keeping aloof.'[19] Malinowski was probably unaware that Campbell had already given him 'trouble' by reporting to Murray some of his unguarded statements concerning the war.

The capital of Kiriwina

Within days of his arrival Malinowski was drawn as by a magnet to Omarakana, home of the highest-ranking sub-clan and of Touluwa, the paramount chief. All the early European visitors to the Trobriands remarked on the Omarakana chieftainship which appeared to be unique in Papua (though by Polynesian standards Touluwa was a petty chief indeed). The protocols and privileges of the various local chiefs formed part of a complex system of hereditary rank. Their authority was backed by henchmen and coercive sorcery, but the power of the Omarakana chief was sanctioned ultimately by his control of sun magic – the ability to bring and banish drought and famine. Touluwa had sixteen wives in 1915 – down from twenty-four at the beginning of his 'reign' – and his wealth derived both from the customary harvest gifts of yams provided by their relatives and from his pivotal position in the ceremonial exchange system of Kula. Despite the attrition of his authority, Touluwa's 'name, prestige, and renown' was 'carried far and wide over the Archipelagoes', though his political power did not extend beyond the district of northern Kiriwina.[20] Before the advent of the white man, it was claimed, the supreme chief had more than sixty wives, one from each of the 'tributary communities'.[21]

With his aristocratic pretensions, Malinowski felt a natural affinity for the chiefly sub-clan of Tabalu, the highest-ranking Trobrianders and 'owners of the soil', so it is understandable that he was immediately attracted to Omarakana, centre of the richest and most fertile district in the islands. It would have been perversely egalitarian of him to camp anywhere else, and Touluwa himself would have been mightily offended had he done so. Tabalu families occupied more than half the village of some three hundred people, and there can be little doubt that the anthropologist's long sojourn among them coloured his perspective of Trobriand society. His rhetorical choice of terms to describe the polity of Omarakana ('aristocrat', 'commoner', 'vassal', 'court', 'tribute', 'insignia') was more appropriate for feudal Europe than for Melanesia. But if he tended by the use of such words to exaggerate the rank and glorify the power of the so-called paramount chief (a designation applied with some reservation by Seligman), it was not for lack of detailed concrete evidence on Trobriand chieftainship, of which Malinowski recorded a good deal more than he actually published.

Even local white traders paid their dues to Touluwa, though not with the deference he would have wished. The scornful manner in which Billy Hancock wrote to Malinowski about him says it all:

> Old Touluwa called one day . . . he anchored his stern on the verandah & grunted twice. I was busy at the time & took no notice of him; after about two minutes he grunted some more & when I looked at him he calmly remarked TAPWAK BUA [tobacco, betel nut], so I gave him one stick & some bua & he got up saying 'Bili Kaione' [goodbye] and I haven't see his royal highness since.[22]

As a guest in his village, Malinowski was obliged to render Chief Touluwa more demonstrative respect. Their relationship did not always run smoothly (to the ethnographer's annoyance Touluwa refused to take him on Kula expeditions), but Malinowski generally referred to him with affection as well as esteem. This tall but stooped and aging man was shrewd and dignified. 'He was a conspicuous presence in the village, sometimes squatting on the ground in front of his hut or storehouse, sometimes perched high on his *kubudoga* (raised platform) . . . so as to allow his subjects to move freely about', for his rank obliged him always to be in a physically higher position.[23] Since his imprisonment by Bellamy, however, 'his pride had been broken . . . and he had retired from most of his offices'. The most important of these was the supervision of an elaborate system of garden magic which he had delegated to his sister's son and heir apparent, Bagidou.

Another of Malinowski's favourites, Bagidou was 'a man of outstanding ability and intelligence' who suffered from 'some internal wasting disease, probably tuberculosis' which kept him more or less housebound, and hence an easy prey for the resident ethnographer. With 'one of the best minds in the Trobriands' and an excellent memory, Bagidou was a repository of tradition. He was certainly one of Malinowski's most fruitful sources of information on magic:

> For he not only allowed me to be present at every rite in the garden, but usually advised me some days beforehand, explained the rationale of most of his arrangements, invited me to his own house while he was reciting spells in the solemnity of actual performance, dictated them to me with unusual patience and capability, and helped me to translate them – by no means an easy task for him or me.[24]

Bagidou's wife had left him for a younger man. 'The comic side of this otherwise sad story was that Bagidou had the reputation of being the greatest expert in the magic of love.'[25] His younger brothers, Towesei and Mitakata, were his acolytes, and the latter would eventually succeed Touluwa as chief, a position he held until his death in the 1950s, long after Malinowski had predicted the demise of the office.

No fewer than eighteen of Touluwa's sons by various wives lived in Omarakana. His five sons by his first and favourite wife were particularly useful as informants. The eldest, Namwana Guyau, taught Malinowski sorcery spells. Gilayviyaka, the secondborn, was 'a fine and intelligent native' who died in 1916. He achieved local notoriety by being discovered by his wife *in flagrante delicto* with one of his father's wives, and after 'a dreadful public scandal' he was banished by his father for a time. The third son was

Yobukwau – 'one of the finest-looking, best-mannered, and really most satisfactory fellows of my acquaintance' – who was conducting an affair with
Ilakaise, a 'model of a Melanesian beauty' and the youngest of his father's
wives.[26] There were also Kalogusa and Dipapa, 'pleasant and clever, attractive and enterprising'. All these young men, in fact, delighted Malinowski
with their 'aristocratic' dignity and good manners. Another name that crops
up frequently in his earliest Kiriwina notebooks is Tomeda, 'a handsome
man from Kasanai, famous for his strength, his efficiency in gardening and
his skill in dancing'.[27]

It was among such people, then, that Malinowski spent most of his first
field trip to the Trobriands. After introductory diplomatic overtures to the
chief (if the date on a sketch plan of the village can be trusted he was there
on 29 June, just two days afer his arrival in the Trobriands), he returned in
mid-July with, one may imagine, a line of carriers from the Losuia gaol.
Although Omarakana is situated near the eastern coast, there are no anchor-
ages, so he was obliged to walk the ten level miles across the central plain,
through 'monotonous stretches' of low scrub, past several small villages and
the occasional yam garden with its staked vines, looking 'like an exuberant
hop-yard'.

Omarakana itself, surrounded by groves of fruit trees, is built according
to a pleasingly symmetrical plan. An outer ring of dwelling huts and an
inner ring of more solidly constructed yam storehouses encircle a broad
central plaza, the *baku*, which serves as meeting place, dancing ground and
cemetery (at least it did so until Bellamy outlawed burials within the confines of the village). The chief's enormous yam house, the largest in the
islands, is situated in the middle of the *baku* and takes pride of place in this
civic arrangement, while his decorated dwelling hut, with its pitched gothic
façade, is slightly to one side.[28] His wives and children had their own houses
in a segment of the outer ring. The street that encircles the village between
the two rows of houses Malinowski described as 'the theatre of domestic
life and everyday occurrence'. If the central place was largely associated with
men's activities, the street was the domain of women.

The ethnographer was directed to pitch his tent in alignment with the
outer ring of dwelling houses, just a few yards behind Touluwa's large
dwelling. Bagidou was another close neighbour, so there could be no mistaking the honorary rank accorded to the visitor. Like all dwellings in the
village, the door of his tent was oriented towards the central plaza. The tent
– a 'fragile canvas artifact of civilized Europe' that would become not only

a famous icon of Malinowski's legendary fieldwork but also the subject of a hoax – was in fact borrowed from Bellamy's store in Losuia, Malinowski having decided that the one he had bought in London was too small.[29] This site in Omarakana would be his home for the next six months, and he would return to it for several weeks in 1918. Today the exact spot is marked by a phallic stalactite, broken from the roof of a coral cave, by which the villagers suggestively commemorate the author of *The Sexual Life of Savages*.

Enter the Ethnographer

In the romanticized 'arrival scene' that introduces *Argonauts of the Western Pacific*, Malinowski asks the reader to imagine 'making your first entry into the village'.[30] In this 'first engagement', an audience gathers around the visitor, who hands out tobacco, inducing 'an atmosphere of mutual amiability'. Proceeding to business, the ethnographer begins 'with subjects which might arouse no suspicion' such as technology. In this case, the inadequacy of pidgin English in early inquiries soon gave rise to the 'uncomfortable feeling that free communication in it will never be attained'. But until Malinowski could converse with them in their own language, 'I knew well that the best remedy for this was to collect concrete data, and accordingly I took a village census, wrote down genealogies, drew up plans and collected the terms of kinship.' Such documents remained 'dead material', however, and 'their real comprehension can be gained only from the knowledge of real life'.[31] 'As to obtaining their ideas about religion, and magic, nothing was forthcoming except a few superficial items of folk-lore, mangled by being forced into pidgin English.'[32] Yet Malinowski's earliest Trobriand fieldnotes indicate that he went in active pursuit of such material, superficial though he knew it to be, and the 'mangled' cadences of pidgin are evident on every page ('There seems to be a belief in reincarnation. When a male or female has been for a long time in Tuma and he dies again there, he comes back to "belly belong a woman"').[33]

His sense that 'the native is not a natural companion of the white man' was probably reciprocated, despite the many friends he claimed among the menfolk of Omarakana. Mutual tolerance and occasional 'rapport' (the catchword for smooth ethnographic engagement with the subjects of one's study) were established – after a fashion. But he was under no illusion that they truly welcomed him in their midst. 'In fact, as they knew that I would

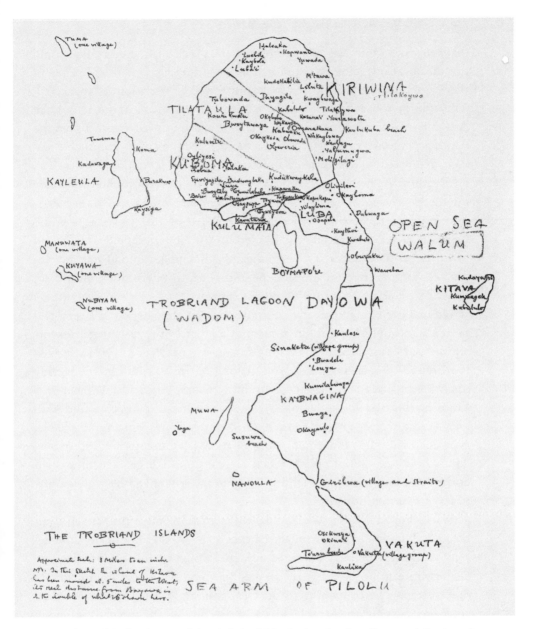

Map 3   Malinowski's sketch map of the Trobriand Islands, showing the villages and districts of Kiriwina. European settlements are not marked. Losuia, Oiabia and Gusaweta are between Kavataria and Teyava; the Kiribi plantation is just to the south of Oburaku.

thrust my nose into everything, even where a well-mannered native would not dream of intruding, they finished by regarding me as part and parcel of their life, a necessary evil or nuisance, mitigated by donations of tobacco.'[34] The role of tobacco in his fieldwork was fundamental. Manufactured in Australia in the form of sticks of black, molasses-cured twist, it was the common colonial currency in Papua, used to pay for most goods and services required by whites: in Malinowski's case, local foodstuffs as well as information. As he had complained to Atlee Hunt in April when reporting on the penny-pinching of his Mailu expedition: 'I had to be very economical with tobacco, a feature greatly disliked by the natives in a white man's character.'[35] More liberally funded for his Trobriand field trips, he did not stint on trade tobacco when ordering his supplies in Samarai, and his invoices indicate that his annual expenditure on this item was almost £50, about 20 percent of his total fieldwork budget.

He quickly became an object of attention to the curious villagers, and he remarked upon the confident manner and lack of reserve that Kirwinians showed. 'As soon as an interesting stranger arrives, half the village assembles around him, talking loudly and making remarks about him, frequently uncomplimentary, and altogether assuming a tone of jocular familiarity.'[36] Or as he put it in his notebook: 'Always a number of people around both ends of the tent. Men and women. Girls much more easily approachable. Not offended when looked at or even handled (ethnologically!) in public. The whole *baku* full of people when arriving in a village.'[37] In time, such constant and importunate attention became an irritant and he would complain of a 'surfeit of native'.

What they saw was a tall, balding white man of indeterminate age. His beard and disconcerting green-tinted eyeglasses would have made an unattractive impression. Baldness was considered a sign of old age, while beards (as he wrote in his notes) were 'very ugly – men who wear [them] simply don't want to have anything to do with women'.[38] His own beard, then, advertised his celibacy. Later he would write: 'Europeans, the natives frankly say, are not good-looking. The straight hair . . . the nose "sharp like an axe blade"; the thin lips; the big eyes "like water puddles"; the white skin with spots on it like those of an albino – all these the natives say (and no doubt feel) are ugly.' But his Polish features partly exempted him. 'More polite than truthful', they made a 'meritorious exception' of him, tactfully telling him that he 'looked much more like a Melanesian than like an ordinary white man' by crediting him with 'thick lips, small eyes' and a blunt nose.

They were 'discreet and honest enough', however, not to compliment him on his forehead and hair.[39]

As to his behaviour, Raphael Brudo agreed with the people of Sinaketa in 1918 that the Doctor was rather strange.

> Here is a man who comes from a country far away to fulfil an aim that they thought futile. Neither missionary nor magistrate, neither buying nor selling, always asking questions and giving tobacco in exchange for words. . . . And then at regular hours, towards the fall of night, he went to the beach and performed certain movements similar to mysterious incantations (these were physical exercises). All this was suspicious to them, and I had often to reply to their anxious inquiries about this man whom they thought strange. . . . In a word, he appeared to them not to be overburdened with sense.[40]

Much later, a Catholic missionary who came to the islands in the 1930s would report that Malinowski was 'remembered by the natives as the champion ass at asking damnfool questions, like, do you bury the seed tuber root end or sprout end down?' The local whites 'got back at him by referring to him as the anthrofoologist and his subject as anthrofoology'. They were all, natives and whites alike, made uneasy because 'they did not know what he was at'.[41]

'The kaleidoscope of tribal life'

If the people of northern Kiriwina were preoccupied with the *taitu* harvest during the weeks of July, Malinowski's interests were more wide-ranging. He was covering warfare, stone implements, insults, courtship expeditions, dances, ghosts, witches, burial, mourning, modes of cooking, times of eating, soil types, counting methods, perfumes and colour categories – to mention only some of the topics of his inquiries. He also sketched the most prominent features of Trobriand society: local and descent-based groupings, clan totemism, gardening, land tenure, chieftainship. But if he was working to a plan of investigation it is not evident from the surreal concatenation of subjects in his notebooks. As in Mailu he was opportunistic, taking notes from anyone willing to talk to him authoritatively about anything. When there were no 'expert' informants available, he resorted to *Notes and Queries* and did it by the book, like painting by numbers. Time was short; he expected to sail off soon to the Mambare, so his principal aim was to achieve comprehensive coverage, to 'know' as much as possible about Trobriand culture. His survey strategy was not unlike that of his mentors, his model an amalgam of Seligman and Rivers, and the sheer catholicity of his interests give a kaleidoscopic effect to the pages of his notebooks. There are *imponderabilia* galore: 'I saw a lady washing her hands before preparing food: she took some water into her mouth and let it run over her hands in a fine jet.'

Initially, then, Malinowski worked on a very broad front. He had already renounced physical anthropology (as he had told Hunt earlier that year), and his measuring stick, calipers, skin-colour gauges and other instruments he had purchased in Berlin remained unused in his tent and would later lie forgotten in Billy Hancock's store. He collected not a jot of the anthropometric data Haddon and Seligman would have recorded. He had not yet rejected their 'antiquarian' interests in technology and material culture, however, and his first Kiriwina notebooks reveal a preoccupation with stone tools and their classification, and he collected a great number in various stages of manufacture. With the Melbourne Museum in mind, during the first couple of months he conscientiously amassed as many artifacts as he could lay his hands on – probably with the aid of the magistrate, who could have ordered them to be brought to the station for sale. The flurry of artifact-collecting eased as his projected trip to the Northern Division was indefinitely postponed. Aided by Billy Hancock, however, he remained on the alert for good specimens, and by the end of his last visit to the Trobriands he had accumulated almost three thousand items. By the exacting standards of the ethnologists and museum anthropologists of the day he was a somewhat careless collector.[42] His most serious failing was as a 'housekeeper' and his documentation was sketchy and incomplete. Housekeeping was for servants. His heart was no more in collecting than it was in photography, and he treated them both as 'secondary occupations of fieldwork'.[43] His interest in arts and crafts ('primitive technology') was principally in their economic and social aspects, and he railed against the 'museum moles' who studied disembodied objects torn from the cultural contexts that gave them life and meaning. Such views were integral to Malinowski's temperament, and they are reflected in his earliest thinking about the kind of anthropology that most interested him: 'primitive sociology' rather than 'ethnology'.

The most important tool of Malinowski's trade as an ethnographer was his notebook. The custom-made notepads that he had ordered in London characterize the first period of his fieldwork in Kiriwina, just as loose-leaf, foolscap sheets characterize the second. The pads consisted of a hundred pages of unlined white bond paper. They opened vertically (one lifted the page rather than turned it) and, with the pages serrated at the top, looked rather like invoice books. On the first page of each pad there was an index, which Malinowski dutifully completed. The pages were numbered consecutively, and when he began his Trobriand fieldwork he was halfway thorough his seventh pad at page number 748. This page is headed 'Ubuia, 23.vi.15'. He wrote most of his notes with a thin-nibbed fountain pen; occasionally he used a pencil.

Malinowski filled thirteen such notebooks between June 1915 and February 1916. His movements can be reconstructed from them, for he generally noted the village location as well as the date of his investigations. In early July he visited Sam Brudo in Kavataria and the mission sisters at Oiabia, where Miss Jamieson explained how women's banana-leaf skirts were made. He was in Omarakana on 19 July to watch the *taitu* being brought into the village for the harvest displays of Milamala, an event he described in colourful detail in his '*Baloma*' essay. Under the personal tutelage of Chief Touluwa, he visited the gardens frequently (his rough handwriting and resort to pencil testify to the discomfort of his working conditions), and he began to photograph activities and compile the detailed eyewitness notes on gardening that would finally bear fruit in *Coral Gardens and their Magic*.

Omarakana was Malinowski's field base from July to December 1915. From there he made forays to neighbouring villages of northern Kiriwina. In November he spent a few weeks at Billy Hancock's place, working in the nearby villages of Teyava and Tukwaukwa. After spending Christmas with Billy, early in the new year he visited the chiefless, low-ranked villages of Bwoitalu and Bau, home of the most virulent sorcery. By the middle of January 1916 he was back in Omarakana, where he spent another month. In mid-February he visited the southern part of Kiriwina to look at coral caves where skulls of the deceased were deposited. On 25 February he was back in Losuia, waiting for the *Misima* which would take him to Samarai. Of a total of eight months on Kiriwina he spent almost six in Omarakana, rather fewer than he later claimed.[44]

Much of the early information he recorded was flawed and incomplete. He revisited all his notes, however, sometimes weeks, sometimes months and even years later, checking the statements and correcting his initial observations. His term for this checking process was 'control' and the word 'controlled' occurs, like a stamp of authenticity, on many pages of his notebooks, together with a date and the informant's name or initials indicated in red, blue, orange or purple pencil. In this way the notebooks became palimpsests of temporal deposits, lightly worked over in different-coloured pencils. His choice of colour appears to have been arbitrary, though it is tempting to suppose that he deployed a code linking colour to groups of topics or to the dates of their revisiting.

There are scarcely a few score words of Polish in these notebooks; only very occasionally did he use a Polish phrase. (Interestingly, he abandoned English when searching for anatomical terms for describing the butchering of a pig.) An early entry illustrates the clumsy generalizing that he would soon forsake for 'concrete' instances: 'If a married man wants to fuck with another girl he would go with her to the *bukumakula* [bachelors' house], but his wife, on learning this, would be very wild & would very likely thrash the "correspondent", the girl in question.'[45]

The term 'Kula' appeared in his notes within days of his arrival, when he described it as the 'circular transmission of *bagis* [shell necklaces]'.[46] He sketched their general route on the map that Bellamy had drawn for Seligman, and in the opposite direction he indicated the trajectory of *mwali*, armshells. 'The principle of this exchange,' he noted in an unpromising aside, 'is entirely vanity.' These notes were 'controlled' by an informant in Omarakana a few weeks later: 'Two kinds of jewels: those who [sic] were owned individually and did not make the Kula, and the travelling ones.'

The first death to occur while he was in the vicinity of Omarakana was that of a youth named Kimai, who on 6 July had fallen to his death from a coconut tree in the village of Wakailuva. The demonstrative, emotional force of the mourning impressed Malinowski, and his lengthy and lucid account displays some characteristic ingredients of his style: keen, concrete observation combined with an awareness of his own role as witness. (At this date, of course, he could understand only a few words of the language.) It was just before sunset, and men were 'sobbing and slobbering; women keening and wailing. . . . I noticed the squeezing of the noses by the men & smearing the mucus excretia on the ground.' He watched the 'adopted mother' of the dead youth and was 'struck by the mixture of real grief & the ritual frame in which she put it. She was actually crying, yet she did it the whole time in the ritual sing-song, in the typical melody.' Here he sketched the dying fall of the lament from a prolonged G, then to D, back to G, then D, and finally G, or sometimes F. 'She was nursing a piece of mat, like a child, & singing . . . "My child, my belly is sore." There could be no line drawn between the artificial & the genuine in her grief. . . . She accepted my tobacco with quiet dignity.'[47] Only months later did Malinowski learn that Kimai had leapt to his own death.

By the fourth Trobriand notebook, begun in early September, he was using vernacular phrases and inserting short texts. As might be expected, the proportion of matter in Kiriwinian gradually increased, though Malinowski never abandoned English altogether. By November he was collecting sorcery spells (*silami*) from his Omarakana friends: 'They are all afraid of my tent being infected with *silami*. They all dread when I begin to sing one out. . . . The force resides in the voice . . . one should not transmit them face to face, but with each person on either side of a tree.'[48]

The juxtapositions are often surreal as Malinowski ranged from topic to topic. All of human life is here, and there is a resonant parallel between Malinowski's notebooks of this year and his diary of 1917–18. He does not discriminate between things or events according to their salience or relative importance; there is no hierarchy of topics. Nothing is too trivial to record. Every sensation, every observation, is grist to the diarist-ethnographer's mill. The same generosity of observation, the same promiscuity of attention, is evident in both kinds of document. His eye was a camera with variable depth of field, or a bifocal lens that combined the diarist's eye for subjective detail with the anthropologist's eye for social context. It was an essential quality of his genius as an ethnographer that he was able to combine them: to observe an act in close-up, register its unique properties, then draw back to apprehend its general setting, the context that gave the act its meaning. His passionate concern, in ethnography as in his diary, and in anthropology as in his life, was to plumb the depths. 'Try to find out the deeper aspects (native psychology) of these things,' he urged himself. 'By noting everyday observations in diary form agglomerate sufficient number of actual "small facts", e.g. about daily routine.'[49] As for his diary: 'Principle: along with external events, record feelings and instinctual manifestations; moreover, have a clear idea of the metaphysical nature of existence.'[50]

Some of the most densely written pages of his fieldnotes were devoted to a single, dramatic occurrence in Omarakana one night in early December.[51] Malinowski invested this event with great significance. In retrospect it came to have an almost mythical import, and he twice described it in considerable detail – in *Crime and Custom* and in *The Sexual Life of Savages*. Indeed, it would be hailed as a pioneering use of the 'case-study method', according to which exemplary cases of a quasi-juridical nature are analysed for the light they shed on customary rules.[52]

For Malinowski, there was a personal dimension to his fascination with the expulsion from Omarakana of the chief's favourite son. A poisonous rivalry between Namwana Guyau (the chief's eldest son) and Mitakata (the chief's sister's son) led to the ceremonial explusion of the former by the Tabalu 'owners' of the village. It was a complex case involving adultery, deadly insults and the mutual antagonism between sons and maternal nephews, who were true heirs under the system of matrilineal succession. Malinowski theorized it as the enactment of an inherent conflict between two principles: the legal one of Mother-right and the sentimental one of Father-love. The quarrel caused 'a deep rift in the whole social life of Kiriwina' and its political reverberations were felt for years to come. It incidentally affected Malinowski's fieldwork, for his sympathies clearly lay with Namwana Guyau, one of his best informants. Thereafter, the chief retreated into a brooding silence, his favourite wife (Namwana Guyau's mother) died of 'a broken heart', and Mitakata avoided the ethnographer.

Beyond the drama, political import and anthropological lessons of the event, it echoed Malinowski's own plight as an outsider in Papua, a potential *persona non grata*. He already suspected that Chief Murray favoured his expulsion. Namwana Guyau's banishment was a reminder of his own vulnerable status as an enemy alien; conversely, he was trapped in aching exile from Poland. Where did he belong? What was he? Among other identities: prisoner of war, temporary government employee, unfulfilled scientist, frustrated artist and pining lover.

'Sensual temptations'

Persistent themes emerged in his notebooks after a month or two, broad topics that he worried about repeatedly. These were magic and religion, gardening, sex and Kula trade. Sex was a healthy preoccupation of

Trobrianders, both young and old, and Malinowski could scarcely avoid the subject. Healthy or morbid, it was a preoccupation of his own, too, and it is needless to suppose that the frequency – and raunchiness – of his notebook inscriptions concerning sexual behaviour were in some way sublimatory. He clearly relished such observations, just as he relished obscene language. ('I suppose you will learn all the "wicked" words first,' Annie had written.)[53] Within days, he was recording salacious details that fifteen years later would delight or scandalize readers of *The Sexual Life of Savages*.

Courting expeditions, he noted, could 'lead to trouble'. 'Row when the girls return if the boys from their own village catch them: "Why you fuck in another village!" In olden days . . . the revenge of the men might be accompanied by a kind of violation. This was done in public on the road; some boys holding a girl & fucking her in turn.'[54] On the custom of biting eyelashes and scratching each other's backs (*kimari*) in love play: 'Tom says that they do not make *kimari* during copulation', only before or after; and Bellamy had told him that scratches on the back were often adduced as proof of adultery – they were therefore of forensic interest to the medically minded magistrate.

Local Europeans were an inexhaustible source of smutty stories, which Malinowski gleefully noted. Billy Hancock told him about a complaisant husband (a minor chief of Sinaketa) who used to take his wife out to the boats of itinerant white traders then wait in Billy's cookhouse until the visitors had finished with her – an example that Malinowski later cited in *The Sexual Life of Savages* to question the existence of jealousy.[55] The trader Ted Harrison of Fergusson Island told him about the steepled yam houses of Sewa Bay on Normanby. 'The shape of the house from the front suggests the female external organs. From the side it reminds one of the male organ in a state of erection,' Malinowski wrote. 'Only good looking girls are allowed into these houses', where they receive one man after another 'till she can't stand it any longer.'[56] (Géza Róheim would call it 'ceremonial prostitution' when he worked in the area many years later.) To amuse himself, Malinowski sometimes wrote of the Trobrianders as if they were Europeans: 'Mr G. was caught copulating with Mrs D. in a garden. Mr G. was ashamed and killed himself with *tuva* [derris root fish poison].'[57] Whites themselves were not exempt from scurrilous gossip: 'None of the missionaries have *kaita'ed* [copulated with local women]. Brudo's accusation of Mr Ballantyne is considered to be a lie. MacGregor never fucked. [Resident Magistrate] Moreton did and so did Bellamy.'[58]

After six weeks in Kiriwina, Malinowski was bantering obscenely in the vernacular. 'When I used the word *wila* [vagina] in the presence of Sam's wife she had a hearty laugh. When Mrs Mitakata heard Tokulubakiki's obscene pantomime of fucking she was amused. Gomaya simulated being offended, when yesterday, I called him *"suvasova kuim"* ("incestuous cock") in the presence of ladies.'[59] To differentiate himself from the prudish missionaries, perhaps, Malinowski was being deliberately crude, flouting the courtesies of a culture he had barely begun to comprehend. But his hosts appeared to enjoy his ribaldry, and later there was 'laughter like a group of gentlemen in a smoking room' when he dropped into a conversation the name of the legendary hero who had had his enormously long penis chopped off.[60] In fairness, Gomaya had provoked him by boasting of his sexual adventures, including those with clan 'sisters'. With 'his doglike face', Gomaya amused and attracted Malinowski.[61] 'When I reproach him with Don Giovani-ism he told me with much conviction that this is the net result of knowing magical means for attracting females.' As Malinowski knew from his own experience, one didn't have to be strikingly handsome to win a woman's favours. Gomaya features repeatedly in *The Sexual Life of Savages* as 'a very capable and useful informant', valuable 'because of certain shortcomings in his character'. He was 'vain, arrogant and wilful', lazy, dishonest and an 'incurable braggart' but 'a great *coureur de femmes*'. A talented mimic, he performed a brilliant caricature of the European mode of copulation 'in a clumsy reclining position, and in the execution of a few sketchy and flabby movements'.[62]

From Gomaya, Malinowski learned that 'a breach of clan exogamy . . . is a rather desirable and interesting form of erotic experience' which figured in village life in much the same way as adultery did in French novels.[63] It was one example of many that enabled him to turn conventional anthropological wisdom on its head. The norms of conduct shaped people's statements, though not necessarily their behaviour. As for Gomaya's irresistible love magic: 'I am ugly, my face is not good-looking. But I have magic, and therefore all women like me.' Perhaps with his own experience in mind, Malinowski commented: 'A man of intelligence, of strong will, personality, and temperament, will have greater success with women than a soulless dullard – in Melanesia as in Europe.'[64]

And what of Malinowski's 'sensual temptations' (as Annie called them) in this land of sexual freedom where so many pretty and petite young women – gloriously bare-breasted, scantily skirted and sweetly scented with mint and fragrant blossoms – flaunted themselves with 'friendly familiarity'? Teasingly, he had sent Annie (who confessed to feeling 'so middle-aged & stale & stodgy') some photographs from his first expedition, perhaps ones of Suau belles. Annie intuitively understood him as well as anyone at that time, and her barbed commentary on his sexual predicament went straight to its target.

> Those native girls seem so very well set up, good looking girls – I wonder whether St Joseph has protected you thus far. I am afraid my praying to him would not be of much avail – especially as the 'goods' are so cheap, always a recommendation to you. Are they free from disease? I think it is quite wonderful that the 'dream of your youth' has not yet been realized with regard to them or at any rate hadn't been up to the time you wrote. I wonder if the realization will exceed the anticipation – I think there would be an after feeling of disgust![65]

There was the rub. It was a residual Catholic conscience, a fear of racial or caste pollution, and, not least, a horror of physical disease that enabled him to keep the nubile sirens of Omarakana at arm's length, despite recurrent surges of lust for them. What Malinowski needed, the Trobrianders lacked – a magic of abstinence.

'My Dear Seligman'

Malinowski had been in Kiriwina for little over a month when he wrote his first letter to Seligman. He could already claim to have a more comprehensive view of Trobriand culture than his supervisor had achieved. In September 1904, Seligman had spent only a week on Kiriwina, mainly in the missionized village of Kavataria where Gilmour was based. Much of his information he had received from his correspondence with Bellamy, and much of the rest he took from the reports of the Rev. Fellowes and the administrator Sir William MacGregor in the *British New Guinea Annual Reports*. But, Malinowski wrote authoritatively,

> there are lots [sic] to be done yet and things of extreme interest. There is their whole system of 'ceremonial gardening' – almost an agricultural cult . . . there are several beliefs and ceremonies about the spirits . . . the unusual harvest feast MILAMALA . . . a regular All Souls day. Then

trading is much more peculiar and interesting, as it might appear at first sight. But I am only sketching things and I propose to do the N. Massim together with Misima and Panaiati and perhaps Dobu . . . they all belong together, in a way.

As for his plans: 'I am going by the next boat to the Mambare district where I shall stay for at least 6 months – then if I am very seedy I'll go South again.' [66]

A few weeks later he confirmed this general plan in a letter to Atlee Hunt. 'If the war still lasts,' he concluded, 'I should very much like to return to Papua again having finished my library work in Australia.' His postscript was diplomatic: 'I need hardly add that I am paying special attention to Land Tenure, native authority and law and in general questions which may perhaps be of some practical interest.'[67]

His letter provoked a flurry of official exchanges between Melbourne and Port Moresby. Hunt accepted it as 'tantamount to an application for a continuance of the subsidy' into 1916, and he approached his minister, who sought Murray's advice. Already mistrustful of Malinowski, Hubert Murray had earlier advised against extending his 'contract' beyond 1915, and he now recommended that 'the present arrangements be not continued'.[68] He felt that since Malinowski was being paid from the Papuan budget he should be subject to his control. As it was, he protested, 'it is only by accident I hear where he is or what he is doing'.[69] The upshot of the official exchange was that Malinowski would be permitted to return the following year, but would receive no further funding from the Papuan government.

Towards the end of September Malinowski wrote to Seligman again, almost apologetically, telling him of his revised plans. 'I am not a little cross with the fact that I am working here on a field which you have done before. I was, as you know, practically pushed into it by circumstances.' He was probably referring to the disruption of boat schedules, but now he told Seligman that Copland King, the Anglican missionary in Mambare, had been called to Dogura, the Anglican headquarters in Papua, as Henry Newton's replacement. Newton had been appointed bishop of Carpentaria in Queensland ('worse luck for me!' Malinowski cursed lightly. 'All Bishoprics be d–d'). Still, he was beginning to speak the vernacular and was 'getting such damned good stuff' in Kiriwina that he hoped Seligman would forgive him anything.

He proposed to send Seligman an article for the *Journal of the Royal Anthropological Institute*. Would he like something on land tenure and gardening ('very good information; have watched 60% as an eye-witness'), including garden magic? Or would he prefer something on death, burial, mourning and the afterlife (he had already 'seen 3 deaths, one almost immediately after expiration, 2 in wailing stage; 1 burial & any amount' of mortuary exchanges)? He tactfully pointed out that 'this information would encroach on your stuff', though he felt that Seligman's chapter on death was 'the only one that needs serious amplification'. Finally, he proposed a 'short article about reincarnation; ideas about conception and pregnancy'. In the event, what he completed a year later was his groundbreaking essay '*Baloma*: The Spirits of the Dead in the Trobriand Islands', which dealt in some measure with all of these topics.

As for his immediate plans, he now intended to stay in the Trobriands until November. Kiriwina, he judged, was 'absolutely necessary' if he was to deal next time with Misima, Sudest and Rossel, the main islands of the Louisiade Archipelago. As yet no ethnographers had worked on them, and Seligman was especially keen for him to visit Rossel. Malinowski proposed to 'do Rossel' in 1916, adding, 'Jenness did only Goodenough and I should love to do Dobu & the Amphletts in connection with Kiriwina.'[70]

It was December by the time Seligman received this letter, so it was not until Malinowski was on his way back to Australia that he learned of his supervisor's encouraging response.

> It's a most important area and I am delighted you are working there; the fact that I lightly scratched the soil has nothing to do with it. Please get out of your head any idea about 'encroaching' on my stuff, the whole of my Massim work was the merest preliminary survey, and I shall not feel in the least sore if even much of it does not hold. Your business is to go ahead and publish the right stuff, no matter whom you may contradict, but I agree there is no hurry as to publication.[71]

This was magnanimous. To this day anthropologists are territorial animals, and apt to feel threatened when their colleagues or students wander into preserves they have marked as their own. Long before receiving this reassurance, however, Malinowski had again written to Seligman offering Christmas greetings, and with uncanny good luck his letter reached its destination on Christmas morning. He still felt uneasy about working on the Trobriands without Seligman's explicit sanction. He had now been on Kiriwina for four months, and his work was 'going fairly smoothly' despite the fact that he had recently sacked his interpreter, who was 'a bloody scoundrel in personal relations'. He still intended to go to Mambare the following year 'to get a glimpse of the mainland *pure Papuans*'. His health was 'fairly good', although, he said:

> at times I feel damnably 'sick' (in the metaphorical sense) & I long to get away. Mind you, I am absolutely alone amongst niggers & at times they get on your nerves & add to it a bit of feverishness – any one would drink whisky under such circumstances. Now I don't use neither [sic] whisky nor the other 'white man's solace' – and such double abstinence makes life less merry'.[72]

Although it arrived too late to be of much consolation, Seligman's answer offered sympathetic advice. 'I know that "nerves" feeling you write about; although I was never very long alone in New Guinea I had a good deal of time by myself in Borneo. I expect the thing is for you to get South for a bit and get some decent grub, see the magazines and talk to people at the clubs.'[73]

In October, Malinowski also wrote to Rivers, telling him of his 'intensive work in the Trobriands'. In a covert boast he added:

> my linguistic facilities are some use in this, though my experience has shown me that it is possible to do almost as good work with an interpreter, though one looses [sic] much time; when one begins to understand the natives talking among themselves, the old men discussing your questions, of the people gossiping in the evening, lots of things crop up automatically.

Rivers might well have flinched, for he had learned the vernaculars of none of the people he worked among. As if to console him, Malinowski continued:

> I have your last book [*The History of Melanesian Society*] with me and am paying special attention to many points raised by you. As far as method of inquiry is concerned, I am of course following your advice of 'getting everything through concrete facts'. Genealogies, village census, plans of land in land tenure etc. are means which allow gaining possible knowledge.[74]

Haddon had written to him in late June, congratulating him on getting his Mailu work into press; he would write to Atlee Hunt to thank him for the financial support, 'a kindly as well as a wise action'. He urged Malinowski to continue 'for some time' to confine his attention to the Papuo-Melanesians of the east. He agreed with Seligman that 'Rossel Is. needs doing very badly'. There was an ethnological puzzle to be solved there, he believed, 'since Elliot Smith, Rivers, & Perry are very keen just now on the megalithic problem − or "heliolithic" as they term it as they are satisfied that megaliths go with a sun cult. . . . As this question is so much to the fore, it might not be a bad plan if you definitely worked at it in New Guinea.' In pursuit of this problem, he even suggested that it might be worthwhile for Malinowski to go over the same ground Seligman had covered.[75]

Malinowski would have been delighted to have his efforts approved by such a high authority, one that actually encouraged him to work in the same area as Seligman. He was proceeding according to his own agenda, however, and had no intention of being distracted by the British diffusionists' search for traces of an ancient sun cult. He replied to Haddon in the obsequious tones he had used since first meeting him. 'It was very kind of you to write in such encouraging terms and to show so much interest in my work. And I value it all the more, as it comes from you and I know well how much I owe you in connection with this journey.' The year's work, he promised, ought to yield 'somewhat better than the Mailu stuff'.[76] As for megaliths ('stone circles'), he would 'try to investigate them in the d'Entrecasteaux Islands'. He never did so, but he would surely have been less dismissive of megaliths had he only known of several that would be discovered on Kiriwina and Kitava some twenty years later.

'My dearest little son'

News of the war filtered through. From Losuia, Campbell sent him terse notes about terrible battles in France. In November, Marjorie Peck wrote from Melbourne:

> You must feel so sad − desolate − for your country which has always suffered so and now has been fought over again and again. . . . The letters we get from our men at Gallipoli make us weep − they are so tragically cheerful − making the best of a pitiful business − and our streets are full of maimed and broken looking men who till now have taken life more or less as a picnic.[77]

Józefa Malinowska wrote regularly to her 'dearest little son', constantly worried that her letters were not reaching him. Seligman did his best to keep her informed, and wrote to her directly whenever he heard from Papua. Occasionally she received these reassuring messages. One reported Haddon's visit to her son in Mailu, and she gratefully acknowledged that 'even such news though short and imprecise brings me great joy'.[78] She was overjoyed to receive two letters from Bronio in August, one via Washington D.C. that took three months to reach her, another that took only half that time. But she feared that now he was back in New Guinea the letters would be indefinitely delayed again. News of her sister had come at last, but it was not good and told of her privations. Dr Konrad Dobrski (who had attended young Bronio) had died in Warsaw, and Jerzy Żuławski (who had joined the Polish legion) had succumbed to typhus in a military hospital. The only good news came from Professor Estreicher, who had assured her that her son's book on primitive religion would soon be in the bookshop window.

In October she told Bronio that six of his letters had reached her in the previous months, each by a different route. The last one came 'as an official document from the Ministry of External Affairs' – which could only have been sent through an obliging Atlee Hunt. She was well, but 'unspeakably sad for many, many reasons'. She had finally managed to visit her sister at the Janiszów estate. The situation was heartbreaking. The stables, pigsties and hen coops had been burned down, the mill badly damaged, the horses and cattle were gone. Although the manor house remained intact it had been comprehensively pillaged.

> What couldn't be taken was destroyed, burnt down or smashed. The portraits of Zygmunt [Malinowski's cousin, who had died in 1912] and others were shredded – the eyes pierced. Nothing survived of our things. We lost all the beautiful linen, sheets, lots of important papers, books, my clothes, two fur coats, some silver and jewelry, a huge box of china, so now we have nothing whatsoever. Also some very important family papers of my father have been lost, all the big photographs of your father and my parents, your beautiful portrait painted by Witkiewicz, and a whole lot of other things I can't enumerate.[79]

In a later letter she added:

> All that pillaging was by our countryfolk! They carried Auntie away during a battle, almost by force, and as soon as she left, the peasants plundered the

house and carried away cartfuls of things! One would need thousands to replace what we've lost, but the worst sorrow is over the things that can't be bought! Even your doctor's diploma has been torn to pieces.

His imperial gold ring was safe in Warsaw, however, along with a small cache of other valuables.[80]

By February 1916 she had heard almost nothing from her son since the previous June. 'I'd be so happy if you . . . moved south, to healthier conditions! After all, you've done enough in that place! And Miss Stirling is so nice!'[81] She could not know that he was indeed about to sail back to Australia. She had received an undated letter from him via California, for which she gently rebuked him: 'Please, my dear, always write the date. Even though I know you don't do it out of forgetfulness but on purpose, to make me think it's more recent, this is precisely why it's less meaningful to me.'[82] In another of his letters he told her about the Trobrianders, who were 'nicer, more intelligent, excellent carvers, and generally better culturally developed' than the Mailu. 'So generally speaking, they're more attractive than the local "savages". Now the word "savage" seems very funny to me, if applied to the people whom I came to treat like good acquaintances. Some of them are quite nice and decent.'[83]

Mama's letter of 3 April 1916 informed him that she had set aside a hundred gold coins for his return journey. (The value of their money in Russian Poland had already been halved.) She pestered him about the sulphur treatment for his hair: 'I'm worried that for all kinds of reasons you stubbornly refuse to do it.'[84] The previous year he had obediently followed the odoriferous cure: 'I treat my hair and will continue every day,' he told her, 'but with sulphur in alcohol, because the ointment, particularly in summer, melts, drips, and goes rancid.'[85]

Nina the muse

Malinowski had mentioned to his mother his feelings for Nina Stirling. He had also told Annie, who wanted to know more. 'I was very pleased to hear about her & would be really glad to know that you were in love with a nice girl like she must be.'[86] Annie offered her frank opinion.

I daresay anyhow that some day you will be less fond of change & more disposed to be true to one person, especially if you are really in love with

them – although I must own I don't recognize you in the role of a steadfast & true lover. . . . What about the New Guinea 'temptations'? The
thought of that 'British girl' ought to be enough to keep you from yielding – I daresay you must find it hard at times – the loneliness must make
it worse.[87]

As much as absence, loneliness did make his heart grow fonder. It was
important for him to keep a desirable woman in mind as he endured the
inner solitude of the field. Curiously, although Nina's letters fed his desire,
they did not inspire him to resume his diary. He had vowed, in his single
entry of 1 August, to 'start another diary' and 'fill the empty blank pages of
these last five months', but he failed to do so.[88] Yet all his significant love
affairs to this point had been accompanied by the kind of minute scrutiny
of his soul that a journal allowed. Perhaps the very distance that lay between
Adelaide and Kiriwina obviated the emotional oscillations that had characterized his other affairs. He had known Nina for too short a time to spin
resentments and concoct jealousies, so he was spared the storm and stress
that close proximity engendered.

As his principal love object during this period, Nina was the only con-
tender for the role of muse. His letters to her (perhaps diary-letters as he
had written for Annie and Żenia) might have been a satisfying substitute
for an intimate journal, though later we hear him complaining that her
letters did not satisfy his craving for 'subjective depth'. Almost certainly, too,
he talked to her in his head. It was an enjoyable indulgence and kept his
love on the boil, though he sometimes despised the habit as 'telesenti-
mental monomania'.[89] To Nina Stirling, then, went the honour of being the
imaginary companion who sustained him throughout this productive
period of fieldwork. He needed such spiritual succour: a guiding light,
someone to work for and to impress. His mother could no longer adequately fulfil this role, though she had set the pattern. Memories of Tośka
were fading; she was far beyond reach and their love had wilted for lack of
nourishment. Annie Brunton was now 'the past' and also impossibly far
away.

He had made a few other female friends during his brief and busy stay
in Melbourne, notably the five Peck sisters who lived with their recently
widowed mother in a comfortably large house called 'Warton' in St Kilda.
It was perhaps through Nina that Malinowski met the Pecks, for she was
a close family friend, having been nursed through a girlhood illness by

Muriel, the eldest sister. Malinowski fancied Leila, the third sister, who cut a voluptuous figure. Even after committing his soul to Elsie Masson he lusted secretly after her. 'Malina dear,' she would address him in her letters, suggesting that they had enjoyed an affectionate flirtation. Like many of her female friends – unmarried, upper-middle-class Anglo-Australians – Leila dabbled in paints and clay-modelling, read the latest novels, went to concerts and public lectures, looked after the children of others and spent part of the year 'resting' in country houses on the Mornington Peninsula or in the Dandenong Range. These young women were moderately cultivated, serious-minded and as well educated as women of the period could expect to be. They hungered for self-improvement and, vaguely dissatisfied with their leisure, sought useful employment in the 'caring professions'. The war in Europe had given them a fresh urgency, even as it delivered opportunities – Muriel Peck, for instance, sailed for France as a military nurse. But the loss of so many young men left a proportionate number of spinsters; Leila and one of her sisters would be among them.

The Peck family were well aware of Malinowski's courtship of Nina Stirling; it was Mrs Peck who fondly referred to Nina as his Galatea. Marjorie (or Madge), the second eldest, initially disapproved of the potential match. Writing to Malinowski in November 1915, she admitted that she had seen 'nothing but tragedy in it' for them.[90] During his months in Kiriwina, he had lived with the knowledge of others' misgivings – he even shared some of them – so it must have come as sweet relief and vindication that Marjorie confessed to having 'misunderstood'.

> You see Nina had not told me then all you were to her and she to you – Idiot that I was – I thought you were just strongly attracted – yes possibly I meant physically not that wasn't by any means all. But then you didn't understand that she was absolutely just awakening . . . till she met you she really knew nothing.

Nina brought out protective instincts in other women. In courting her, Malinowski was treading on very dangerous ground.

Within six months Nina had been transformed by his epistolary attentions. 'You have done for her what no one else could,' Marjorie told him. 'She is independent and oh, most delightfully in love. . . . Your letters to her and the fact that she can speak openly to you has made the difference. . . . she is such a glowing splendid *woman*.' But Majorie Peck still had reservations about the relationship, and hinted at them by asking Malinowski 'to read between the lines a little'. He always did so, avidly, and would complain to his female correspondents when there was nothing to be read there. Marjorie, though, left little unsaid. She managed both to congratulate him as a Prince Charming for awakening Nina to life, and to warn him that the battle for her was far from over. A thorn of reproach lay concealed in the bouquet of praise she offered him.

> Nina tells me that you may return in February and I wonder what that will mean. She so dreads another parting & it will be so hard for you both. I agree with her that where love comes in it seems so dreadful that marriage is the only solution. – Marriage is such a final sort of business and I expect *you'd* say 'stodgily *British*' but here it is the only solution. Oh please, please forgive me but I am writing so crudely.[91]

To help him through his 'dark hours', Marjorie sent him a new novel by Conrad's erstwhile friend and collaborator, Ford Madox Ford. It was *The Good Soldier*, a melancholy tale of an upright man destroyed by passion – 'the saddest story' of an appalling betrayal that led to three deaths and the madness of an innocent girl. 'I wonder how it will impress you,' wrote Marjorie mischievously.

At the beginning of March 1916, as Malinowski sailed for Port Moresby aboard the *Misima* he drafted a letter to Seligman. 'Your letters were most welcome – as I have been feeling very depressed lately. The life I led in Omarakana was trying enough, and as I told you, I began to feel "queer" about the natives. I got to such a loathing of them that I was unable to work.'[92] He was perhaps referring to the imbroglio in Omarakana following the expulsion of the chief's son.

Although Annie expressed it awkwardly, she put her finger on an important aspect of Malinowski's achievement. As it would be defined nowadays, this was his acquisition of 'ethnographic authority'. 'Don't you feel,' she wrote,

> now that you have been on the spot and done research work yourself that it is almost absurd for anyone to set up as an authority on your particular science who has never been out of civilized (!) Europe? You remember I used to laugh at you about it. At any rate you must feel that whatever you write and say now must carry a great deal more weight than it did before.[93]

Precisely – he had been there.

Chapter 21

Melbourne Maladies

'Only integrate'

In November 1917, while stranded on Samarai waiting for a boat to take him to the Trobriands, Malinowski conducted two experiments. He discovered a talent for designing and carving combs out of turtleshell, which was an amusement he abandoned soon enough, but the second experiment was momentous. He constructed a retrospective, synoptic diary of great technical significance for his Trobriand ethnography and for the subsequent development of his functional method. The importance of this 'diary' was less in its content than in the mode of its presentation: he drew up a series of neatly designed charts, comprising several columns under various headings. They were synoptic charts of remembered events.[1]

He had not kept a journal since his return to Australia in early March 1915. An impossibly long time had elapsed for him to be able to summarize past events with all the nuances he needed in order to understand the braided strands of his life. He compromised by drawing an imaginary line under his first period of fieldwork in the Trobriands. For purposes of recollection, that phase was well covered by his voluminous fieldnotes. He could always read between the lines of any dated and situated page of his notebooks and bring to mind 'the face of the day', its emotional tone and mental undercurrents. His Trobriands existence was ordered by the exigencies of his ethnography (or so it would seem with the dispassionate distance of time), but in November 1917 he felt the need to bring order to his recollections of the thirty months he had spent in Melbourne. It was a longer period than he would spend in total in Papua, and a period every bit as important for his future as his time mining the material for his monographs at the Kiriwina coalface. First, he exercised his memory and drew up a month-by-month chronology of events. Next, he classified the events, bringing them to order under different rubrics. Finally, he transferred them to a series of three charts. In this way he systematized his 'Life in Melbourne in Retrospect' (the title of his first chart) by tabulating it, in approximate chronological order, under several aspects. The first chart, covering what he called the 'First epoch, April–November [1916]', comprised six columns. Reading from left to right their headings were: 'Scientific Work'; 'External Events'; 'Health'; 'N.S.'; 'M.W.'; and 'E.R.M.'.

These categories, devised to classify the separable but interdependent elements of his life, were, analytically speaking, 'functional'. On this view he treated autobiography as a species of ethnography, and vice versa, a realization that struck him afresh, when, on the first day of 1918, he wrote at the back of his diary: 'Main thing to do, is to reflect on the two branches: my ethnological work & my diary & to take the clue from both. They are well-nigh as complementary as complementary can be.' The development and deployment of what he called synoptic charts was one of the most significant innovations of his fieldwork method, and it suited his later functionalism perfectly. Indeed, his charts, with their two axes and numerous 'cells', were graphic instantiations of functional relations. Their final, formulaic apotheosis in *A Scientific Theory of Culture* encapsulated his monumental scheme, and there is an analogical relationship between objective, impersonal categories such as 'Commissariat', 'Recreation' and 'Reproduction' and the subjective, personal categories of his diary-charts. 'Only integrate' could have been Malinowski's motto.

Amplifying their complementarity in another way, the attempt to classify lived experience was a parallel task to that of classifying ethnographic facts. They were retrospective exercises, for it is as difficult to understand life in the living as it is to comprehend a culture in the moment of its ethnographic recording. The interesting thing, however, was how Malinowski's intuitions converged and cohered in patterns that could be represented in the form of charts. His creative act lay in the manner of synthesis: 'functionalism' was a synthetic way of viewing his experience as well as his anthropological data. Charts enabled him to integrate 'fragmenting themes' into higher syntheses of comprehension.

It is significant, too, that this innovation occurred to him in Samarai, where he found himself 'in retreat' with ample time for reflection. It was that becalmed liminal space, known to all fieldworking anthropologists, that lay between 'home' and 'the field': a time of waiting – impatiently or with resignation – on the threshold of 'real' life.

Fig. 2   Facsimile of Malinowski's third synoptic diary-chart, 'Retrospect of Life in Melbourne, 3rd Epoch'.

'The first epoch'

Aboard the *Marsina* on the return voyage to Australia, Malinowski was having doubts about Nina. Desires and expectations had crystallized around her, though he had felt 'strong fluctuations' while in Kiriwina. Her letters didn't always satisfy him, and what he called a 'reaction' persisted almost until his departure from Papua. By February, however, he was longing for her again and even 'anticipating a life in Mt Lofty'. Encouraged by Marjorie Peck's rambling letter, he probably felt that a third party's acknowledgment of their love confirmed its reality, if not its respectability.

In a bad mood during much of the journey, he suffered frequent headaches. Disembarking at Sydney docks on Wednesday 15 March, he took a room at the Metropole Hotel and for the next fortnight spent the mornings in the Mitchell Library and the afternoons with Charles Hedley at the Australian Museum. A garrulous marine zoologist, Hedley spoke about 'golden opportunities' in America and later wrote about Malinowski's visit to his old friend Haddon:

> He was a bit troubled by the military supervision, he seems to have enough funds to exist on but nothing more. His last trip must have been a profitable one. Scientifically his work seems very thorough. But public feeling is here turning very bitter and I fear that poor Malinowski is at times very uncomfortable.[2]

On 27 March 1916, Malinowski reported to the military commandant for permission to travel to Melbourne. The officer noted his 'brown hair (thin on top), brown whiskers and moustaches'. Two days later he arrived in Melbourne and booked into the Federal Hotel on Collins Street – its letterhead proclaiming it to be the largest hotel and coffee palace in Australasia. He was given a light and pretty room that smelled of mothballs. Thus began what Malinowski would call the worst year of his life.

With the charisma of a traveller returned from exotic places, he was in social demand during the first week or two. He dined at 'Darley' with the Spencers on Friday, at 'Warton' with the Pecks on Saturday, and at 'Chanonry' with the Massons on Sunday. Marnie Masson remembered him from the British Association meetings as 'an elegant man of the world and a good dancer'.[3] This new social whirl, in which he doubtless entertained his hosts with stories from New Guinea, probably contributed to the heady mood of '*Schampagnesque*' he alluded to in his diary jottings: 'Fantastic *Stimmung* [atmosphere]; dry clean air.' There was perhaps another reason too. On the diary page an arrow connects '*Schampagnesque*' with the name Mim Weigall. Marianne ('Mim') was taking courses at the university and blossoming intellectually in a way that Malinowski found irresistible. She wrote sonnets and reawakened in him poetic yearnings. He renewed his acquaintance with the all-female Peck family and became a weekly visitor to

'Warton'. But after two years of bitter warfare and horrendous losses, Australian attitudes towards foreigners were hardening. Upper-middle-class Melburnians were increasingly reluctant to invite 'enemy aliens' into their homes, and within a few weeks Malinowski was feeling the chill of rejection.

Immediately on arriving in Melbourne, he notified Atlee Hunt, and on 31 March presented himself at the administrator's Spring Street office. One of Malinowski's priorities was to escape the irksome demands of the Department of Defence, so he asked to be relieved of the necessity to report to the police each week. Hunt inspected Malinowski's birth certificate and passport; he noted with satisfaction that Malinowski's father had been a university professor and that his mother was the daughter of 'a senator of the one-time Kingdom of Poland'. Hunt concluded that he had no reason to doubt Malinowski's sincerity when he expressed 'strong anti-German sympathies'. For the present, he was once again a comparatively free man in a comparatively free country. He was required only to inform the police or the military if he left the Melbourne district he resided in and to apply for a permit whenever he wished to leave the state of Victoria.[4]

Malinowski was as free, that is, as he would permit himself to be. There was much work to be done. He had a mass of field materials to re-read, sort and reflect upon. On his first day in Melbourne he had seen Baldwin Spencer at the museum. They had an amiable talk and Spencer gave him the use of an office next to his own, though at some stage he was also allocated an alcove and desk in the adjoining library. 'The Reading Room is marvellous,' he told his mother. 'The same rotunda as in London, but even bigger and with much more light.'[5]

By 19 April he had left the Federal Hotel and moved into lodgings at 128 Grey Street, East Melbourne. The house overlooked Fitzroy Gardens, and it was a pleasant fifteen minutes' walk to the museum-library at the top of Swanson Street. Mim Weigall would remember his room as 'poky', but Malinowski described it with affection as he hung up his Trobriand 'trophies': 'The walls covered with light green and yellow stripes with designs; the window facing East and Southeast; a wardrobe with a mirror . . . ; a table with a red cloth; the bed leans against the North wall.'

Poky or not, Malinowski was content to use Grey Street as his base for the remainder of his stay in Melbourne. He soon developed a routine, and on a typical day during 'the first epoch' of his life in Melbourne he worked in the library until 6 p.m., having lunched 'for a shilling' in the refectory. Then he took a tramcar to St Kilda for a walk by the placid waters of Port Phillip Bay. In the middle of July he wrote to his mother:

> It is very cold here, in an unheated apartment, so I didn't feel too well for the last six weeks, but in the last ten days I've been feeling much better and started working very hard. A few days ago I sent an article to London for Seligman, some hundred pages, the result of my latest expedition. I think it's quite good. Apart from that my life here is very monotonous. I have a few friends, but none like the Stirlings in Adelaide.'[6]

Why had he not gone to Adelaide to see Nina at the first opportunity? A letter from her sister Harriet suggests he had been welcome in February, but the situation had changed by the time he arrived in Melbourne.[7] The notes he jotted in his retrospective diary under the heading 'N.S.' are tantalizingly cryptic, but they hint at an emotional impasse. 'I think about her a lot exclusively, and maintain "purity of soul". . . . I'm in love with her and I construct an ideal N.S. based on her ideal character and personal charm.'

Sir Edward Stirling wrote to him soon after his arrival in Melbourne, sym-pathizing with his feelings and lauding his 'honourable intentions', but asking that future correspondence with his daughter 'shall not be too frequent and that they shall contain nothing that will in any sense aggravate anew an impossible situation'. It was the stiffly polite letter of a protective patriarch. 'You will I am convinced realize that it would not be fair to her, or to any young and inexperienced girl that she should face the future years under anything of the nature of an obligation the fulfilment of which you must admit appears quite hopeless.'[8] There was no hint here that the suitor had overstepped the bounds of decency; indeed, he was commended for his honour, in which the wary father had complete trust. But it is clear that the Stirlings were alarmed by rumours of their daughter's engagement to an 'enemy alien'. Malinowski appears to have been complicit in the impasse, for Stirling's letter was a reply to one of his own (of 30 March, now lost) concerning the delicacy of his position.

More can be gleaned from letters Malinowski wrote to Sir Edward and Lady Stirling two years later. His drafts of these letters survive, scribbled in blue ink on the backs of pages of a carbon copy of the *Mailu* typescript (which, by a nice coincidence, deals with sex, shame and in-laws).[9] These letters confirm that parental opposition was at work, probably from the very beginning. Despite the good impression he had made on the Stirlings in 1915, they obviously baulked at the idea of a Polish son-in-law. Like his friend Baldwin Spencer, who became increasingly anti-German (and there-fore anti-Austrian) as the terrible war dragged on, Stirling regarded Mali-nowski as an unacceptable suitor. Enlightened men of science though he and Spencer claimed to be, they were not immune to popular prejudice.

Spencer had written a long letter to Haddon the previous November, commenting bitterly on the 'fatal place' of Gallipoli, where so many of his old students had fallen to no purpose:

> Melbourne is a very changed place from what it was when you saw it. The streets are full of khaki men . . . nothing but the war is thought of & gradually the people are realizing that Australia's battles are being fought out in Europe & that she must send her men home & on top of that there has always been a very strong feeling for the Empire.[10]

John Layard had just passed through on his way back to England, having 'evidently done really good work in Malekula', and he was now about 'to do something in connection with the war'. As for Malinowski, he had ruffled the Papuan authorities and 'made rather a nuisance of himself'. The letter was about Australia's heroic war effort, the sacrifice of its young men and the helplessness of their elders who saw them off to their deaths. Of all those mentioned by Spencer, only Malinowski – the foreigner of uncer-tain loyalty – was vaguely reprehensible. In this exalted, patriotic company he was the odd man out.

Friends in need

While settling down to work, Malinowski made several new friends. In the library he met Ernest Pitt, a senior librarian of Irish descent. Pitt was reticent, formal, efficient, and would become one of Australia's most distinguished librarians. His friendship, Malinowski reflected, was 'heavy and constant like a rather empty woman. I talk, he agrees, understands; reacts, but without any initiative. But I'm always pleased to see him.' Another friend was Robert Broinowski, whom he had met casually in the street one day. Tall, lean and balding, they shared a passing physical resemblance. Broinowski was a public servant in the federal department of the Senate;

eventually he would be elevated to the position of Clerk of the Senate in Canberra. His father had fled Russian Poland and worked his passage to Australia in 1854.[11] Although Malinowski was several years his junior, he saw a younger version of himself in Bob Broinowski, whose attitudes he likened to his own fifteen years earlier: 'romantic idealism and contempt for the business aspect of life; intensity and emptiness; lack of experience; the tendency to take himself very seriously.' He wrote poetry, which Malinowski greatly admired, and was a dedicated bush-walker. They enjoyed gossipy, ribald conversations and sometimes Ernest Pitt would join them for lunch at the Café Florence.

Malinowski's friendships with women typically preoccupied him more than did those with men. He felt an 'attachment' to three of the Peck sisters, though it was an 'attraction mixed with resistance' and they sometimes bored him. But he grew particularly fond of Leila and for a period they created a companionable routine. Once or twice a week she came to find him in the library, then they strolled the streets, ate supper and went to a concert. He liked her for, among other things, allowing him a 'discharge of anti-British feelings'. Later, erotic images of 'L.P.' would come unbidden to him under the mosquito net in Kiriwina.

Mim Weigall appears to have been the first of Malinowski's Melbourne lady friends, and they came perilously close to having an affair. Their relationship was important enough for him to dedicate a column to her (alongside 'N.S.' and 'E.R.M.') in his diary chart. Mim was the daughter of Theyre à Beckett Weigall, a distinguished high court judge of 'simple tastes and boyish enthusiasms' who played tennis and bicycled everywhere.[12] Her mother was the daughter of Sir Robert Hamilton, a governor of Tasmania. Mim was probably in love with Malinowski, and before he took up seriously with Elsie Masson he admitted to 'a moment' when he could have fallen in love with her.

Fifty years later, Mim recalled that it had been her father who had invited Malinowski to 'St Margarets', their house in St Kilda. It was a memorable event 'as my father rarely brought home a *man* to the family'.[13]

Bronio came – slender, serious, well-dressed, erect – stopping at the drawing room door to bow gravely to Mother before approaching to shake hands. His finely chiselled face was pale and his expression solemn. He seemed to be nearly bald and certainly not young (we thought!), but it was hard to see what he was really like because his eyes were almost completely hidden by a pair of enormous round green-tinted spectacles (large spectacles were unusual in those days) with very thick glasses. [H]e was extremely polite and spoke English perfectly, not at first saying very much.

Mim's younger sister was there too; as Joan Lindsay, she would one day write the best-selling novel *Picnic at Hanging Rock*. Joan and another young friend nicknamed the intellectual foreigner 'Professor Popoff'. Mrs Weigall had also invited 'a learned and rather pedantic scholarly house-friend'. He was Archibald Strong, an Oxford-educated man of letters who taught at Melbourne University and was influential in local literary circles. Thick-set and bull-necked, Strong was a commanding figure, eight years older than Malinowski. As an ardent believer in the British Empire he spoke at recruiting rallies and campaigned for compulsory military service. Eventually he became professor of English at Adelaide University and a knight of the realm.[14] Mim remembered:

> Archie's way of talking about literature was rather ponderous, but his learning impressed me and he had always been one of the heroes of my childhood and youth. Mother, who talked easily and was a kindly hostess, soon had the conversation growing round our dinner-table. . . . Bronio played his part well, laughed in the right places and pleased Mother and me.

In the drawing room afterwards, Mother and Archie launched upon some literary topic.

> I can't remember that Bronio said much, but I began to have an awful feeling that Archie was not impressing him. Gradually it came over me that this stranger's contributions to the conversation were cleverer and more stimulating than anything of Archie's. It was a terrible moment for my youthful hero-worship. . . . [Strong] was being quietly and subtly de-throned before my very eyes.[15]

Malinowski was soon cultivating an intellectual love affair with Mim. 'I think for her and develop definitive theories for her. . . . To begin with she doesn't attract me physically. Then, a strong liking; her nice smile, her honest and open sympathy for me. I like her as a companion, and she stimulates my mind.' They walked the banks of the Yarra, discussing poetry. Later, as they sketched specimens together in the museum, there was 'some physical closeness, and a gentle attraction begins'. Mim reminded him how he would come to find her in the library: 'through the swing door, with your felt hat & green glasses & oldest suit and umbrella on your arm, shoulders squared, chin up, serious expression, narrowed eyes, quick step; you came up to me, stopped, bowed, discreetly smiled.'[16] They exchanged sonnets and attended concerts together. At a Paderewski performance he was 'completely remote, staring and listening as though in another world'. She was grateful for his intellectual attentions, awed by his mental powers, and he taught her to read in a disciplined way. Once she invited him to attend a philosophy lecture at the university. They sat in the front row and, like other students, passed notes to one another during the lecture. Malinowski scribbled: 'This man of yours is a fool.' Mim was horrified. 'Afterwards Bronio thanked the lecturer very politely and we walked out with the others.'

Mim's oldest and best friend was Elsie Rosaline Masson, Marnie's younger sister. Early in May the Massons invited Malinowski for supper at 'Chanonry', their Gothic house on Professors' Row. It was not an auspicious occasion. Elsie regarded him simply as 'a relic of the British Association' and 'an interesting friend of Marnie's'. She saw 'a tall man with a square reddish beard, big glasses, an impenetrable expression, might have been any age between 30 or 40'. He looked 'very foreign'. As she told him later: 'You made the impression of someone very grave and intellectual, with very good manners and very sincere, only saying a thing when you had something to say. . . . I didn't suspect you of humour, or liveliness, and certainly not of being at all sentimental or romantic.'[17]

Under the 'E.R.M.' column of his retrospect, Malinowski charted the beginning of their relationship. 'On Good Friday I read her book [*An Untamed Territory*]. . . . I hear her story. . . .' It was about the fiancé who had been killed at Gallipoli the previous August. On other scraps of paper he elaborated: 'Beginning of May: an evening at the Massons; her black dress. . . . A very good and deep impression. Attitude of deepest respect and reservation with well-masked adoration.'[18] He recognized in himself 'a religious respect for suffering' (surely a legacy of his Catholic upbringing), which coloured all his early meetings with Elsie. Malinowski knew also that she was completing a demanding four-year course in nursing at the Melbourne Hospital. He would have seen a petite young woman of twenty-six, with delicate features, high cheekbones and large green eyes. Her long thick hair, which she wore atop her head, was a rich red. But there was no mistaking her aura of grief. 'Empty and miserable' was how she described her life at that time.

It was Elsie who took the initiative, however, and on 11 June she wrote to 'Dr Malinowski' asking to see his 'New Guinea photographs' which had so impressed Mim. He replied promptly, praising *An Untamed Territory*, Elsie's lively memoir about the town of Darwin and the Northern Territory that had been published the previous year.[19] Of their meeting in the library later that week he remembered: 'A navy blue dress. Delicate, elegant. Strong impression. I try to kindle her interest. Photographs in the tea room. . . . In the Reference Room I develop the deepest and greatest sociological theories. . . . I try to get her interested in my materials. . . . I lend her *Mailu.*' Elsie recalled quite different things about this meeting:

> At first I felt shy, but not ill at ease, and immediately interested. I think it was after you had shown me the collection that we went for a walk to Yarra Bank, and you said it was the same thing to you as a Beethoven Quartette. We talked very easily and sincerely and coming back you said you felt a kind of reaction of having talked too much, and I said 'You are very analytical' which you laughed at.[20]

She cried that night, at having found herself 'once more walking with a man and talking gaily and intimately with him'. But Malinowski did not measure up to her image of Charles, the soldier-farmer from Leederville, who still represented for her 'tenderness and passion and the physical ideal'. Malinowski seemed to her 'just a mind that marvellously stimulated' her own.

They met once or twice a week after that, for coffee and for walks, usually in the late afternoons before Elsie went on her night shift. He gave her his '*Baloma*' manuscript, which she read at night in the silent hospital ward. 'I could hardly believe my criticisms were any use,' she told him later. In those early days she detected in him 'a kind of cold egotism – I don't think consideration of my feelings would make you do anything that was a nuisance to yourself'.[21] She imagined him as 'a man who had very definite ideas about women, and had had many love affairs, had been in love with countesses and milkmaids in an experimental kind of way'. She liked the 'dignified simplicity' of his manner towards waitresses, and she liked him all the better for hearing him swear in Polish in the library one day when his papers became disordered. Her heart warmed to him when he spoke passionately about his exile and Poland's plight, and she pitied him because he seemed so 'lonely and melancholy'.

Still, she was ready to poke fun at him. While reading his manuscript she had discovered his parsimonious habit of recycling old letters for his drafts. On 24 July she wrote to him, squeezing her message into the top quarter of the page and concluding: 'The cramped mode of this letter is due to my generosity and thoughtfulness. Observe that you have *all* the rest of the paper as well as the back to write on. In fact, you might drop a hint to all your correspondents to follow my example.'

On 26 July their meeting went wrong. Malinowski had shaved off his beard in order to look 'less foreign', and his eyes were troubling him. Elsie was feeling tired and stupid and they parted without arranging a further meeting. He remembered:

> She talks about 'having to get used to' my new face. We go for a cup of coffee. . . . Her failure to say she wants to see me. . . . I say a pathetic goodbye to her and go to see Dr Stawell with a broken heart. Worries about the eyes. I feel very unnerved and forlorn. I miss her friendship terribly.

Later she told him that his clean-shaven appearance affected her idea of him: 'I saw you as a younger man, and your face became much more expressive to me.' They had begun meeting again by the end of the month, but there were more misunderstandings. One evening over dinner at Café Sergeant, he confessed some of his 'weaknesses' in what Elsie perceived as an impersonal way. Deceived by his 'grave and aloof manner', she suspected that he 'might have a passionate or romantic love affair going on after all'.[22] Malinowski's version of the evening reveals the difference in their characters, a difference that could be caricatured in terms of ethnic stereotypes: soulful Slav (or passionate Pole) meets sensible Scot (or down-to-earth Aussie).

> I try to pose as a hero *à la* Dostoevsky, or rather I try to awaken her interest in this way. One evening in Café Sergeant I 'confess' some grave sins. She has absolution for me, an uplifting power, and deep wisdom. I see her as socially 'superior'; as a person sanctified by suffering and beautiful with spiritual taboos.

The taboos defined Elsie's state of mourning. Charles Adams Matters, Elsie's rightful man, was a ghostly presence at her meetings with Malinowski. On first being told about him, he felt 'deep sorrow', though it took him a while to extract the full story. Her tale was a kind of allegory that evoked conflicting emotions. He became obsessed by it. The picture he formed of the tragic young soldier was an idealized one: 'an extraordinary character, simple, pure, heroic.' Having confected this image of Charles, he assigned the role of tragic heroine to Elsie.

As one 'sanctified by suffering and beautiful with spiritual taboos' she was out of reach, and Malinowski kept himself at a respectful distance during August, the anniversary of Charles's death. In late September, Elsie sailed to Western Australia to pay a visit of respect to his family and to say farewell to Marnie, who was bound for England. In his diary-chart, Malinowski summarized: 'After her departure I think of her only as a spiritual entity.' Elsie did not know it then, but he was ill, 'approaching that state of apathy and indifference that comes to sick people'.[23]

About this time a mysterious Mrs Cummings appeared on Malinowski's horizon. She came from New Zealand and had been married to a Jewish solicitor by whom she had a daughter; little else is known about her, not even her Christian name. She lodged in the adjoining house at 130 Grey Street (an address Malinowski also used sometimes during this period). 'I spend the days and evenings with her,' he wrote in his retrospective diary. 'Flirting with her. She goes to hospital, I live in her room.' An unusually long entry fleshes out the relationship a little:

> She often comes about 4 or 5 when I get back home weak with a headache, unable to work. She pets me, puts a blanket over me, feeds me, gives me hot water bottles. Straightforward conversations v. personal and intellectual. The woman's not stupid, with an unchecked temperament, lack of restraint and cultivation. We move on to kissing and petting. I almost sleep with her. I'm not romantically in love with her, but I like her, she works on me, charms me, and she's good to me.

A succouring relationship, in short. Malinowski had again found a good woman to care for him. If she was intelligent as well as physically attractive, so much the better, and if she was married but estranged from her husband, best of all, for she would be mature enough to understand a man's needs and yet be less inclined than a single woman to seek a complicated amatory relationship.

Writing 'Baloma'

As he had promised Seligman, Malinowski's first scholarly task was to write an article for the *Journal of the Royal Anthropological Institute*. Seligman had cautioned that to deal adequately with mortuary practices would require a description of the 'general sociology' of the people; this would be difficult to do 'without practically writing a monograph'.[24] Malinowski was not one to be deterred by questions of length, and he decided to write a treatise on the sociology of Trobriand belief. '*Baloma*: The Spirits of the Dead in the Trobriand Islands' would deal, in exuberant detail, with universal themes of sex, death and religion. When printed, it filled seventy-seven pages of the journal – he had 'practically' written a monograph which did more for Malinowski's reputation as an ambitious, up-and-coming theoretical anthropologist than anything he had published hitherto. It grew, naturally enough, out of his earlier preoccupations with magic and religion and with the teasing topic of the 'ignorance of the physiology of reproduction'. It grew, too, out of his obsession with fieldwork method. The methodological self-consciousness of '*Baloma*', indeed, marks it historically as a foundation text, 'the first truly modern ethnological monograph'.[25] Not least, while it dealt with topics dear to Sir James Frazer, it subverted the Master's methods. '*Baloma*' was a brilliant performance. Malinowski had found his ethnographic voice.

The previous year he had dashed off his Mailu monograph in six weeks, an achievement facilitated by closely following his fieldnotes and adhering to a conventional *Notes and Queries* format. Now, in a comparable burst of concentrated writing, similarly interrupted by at least one bout of illness, and in a similar period of time, he dashed off his *baloma* monograph. In this instance the achievement was all the more remarkable, for he did not slavishly follow his notes, nor was there any template to guide him. '*Baloma*' was created *ab initio*. Nothing quite like it had appeared before in the annals of ethnology and it initiated a new style of ethnographic analysis, one characteristic of what has come to be regarded as the classical era of social anthropology. Although functional analysis plays only a minor role in the theoretical underpinning of '*Baloma*', it can be detected as a subtext and a compositional device.

Beginning with the Trobrianders' conceptual contrasts between ghosts (*kosi*), witches (*mulukuausi*), and ancestral spirits (*baloma*), Malinowski explored the ideology and sociology of Trobriand religion. He tracked the shadowy *baloma* through different sets of beliefs associated with different institutions. He sought their presence in mortuary practices, in dogmas of the afterlife on the island of Tuma, in myths and magic spells, in notions of communication with the living through dreams and visions, and during their annual attendance at the 'all souls' day' harvest festival of Milamala. He traced them in beliefs about reincarnation and examined their role in human procreation. The themes of the essay radiate from the master concept of *baloma* like spokes from a wheel.

Malinowski's analysis was subtle and sophisticated. No monolithic dogma was described here, rather the documentation of variations in belief. He implicitly demonstrated the redundancy of the crude anthropological assumption, current at the time, that tribe A believed X and tribe B believed Y. The working assumption of one set of dogmas per tribe crumbled under his analysis. His investigative thrust pointed in a new direction: inwards towards variation within the same culture, instead of tacking across gross variations between cultures. He went beyond what he called 'one-dimensional account' ethnography (simply recording what informants said) by persistently challenging his informants' statements through cross-examination, by confronting them with what others had said on the same topic, and by presenting them with contradictions in their stated beliefs.

The aggressive manner of his interrogation (he spoke of forcing his informants 'against a metaphysical wall') involved asking 'leading questions' of the kind that *Notes and Queries* warned against. Malinowski's dismissal of this piece of conventional wisdom is typical of his methodological jousting: 'The dread of "leading questions" . . . is one of the most misleading prejudices.' Leading questions, in his experience, were 'dangerous with a new informant. . . . But any work done with a new, and consequently bewildered, informant is not worth being recorded.' After that, a good informant will 'contradict and correct you'. Leading questions were also dangerous 'when dealing with a lazy, ignorant, or unscrupulous informant – in which case the best thing is to discard him altogether'. Again, ethnographic work proceeds incrementally, 'in statement of actual details', and here too there is no danger from leading questions. In fact they are 'essential when one wants to know what an informant's views are about something, or when the questions turn upon matters that cannot be directly observed, such as customs of war or intimate sexual behaviour'. The strategy was to coach the informant into adopting 'an "ethnographical perspective" then one day it will be possible to ask "What is your interpretation of such and such a ceremony?" '.[26]

Anecdotes concerning his own participant observation enlivened Malinowski's descriptions. He deployed what Clyde Kluckhohn later described – with a hint of disdain – as the 'well-documented anecdote set firmly in a ramified context'.[27] Malinowski placed his observing eye at the centre of village proceedings, with the other eye reflexively monitoring the scientific status of the observer. Facts did not exist until theories could vouch for them. He never allowed the reader to forget the epistemological basis of his descriptions of events or social facts: they were framed by him, in that time and this place, with this or that named informant to hand. The passive voice of the positivist, of the dispassionate laboratory experimenter, had no place here. The reader is constantly reminded that rigorous anthropology is being conducted by a disciplined observer who shares his humanity with those under his scrutiny. The ethnographer as observer was a fiction in one sense, of course, a literary device that compelled authority and quelled any suspicion of untrustworthiness.

Malinowski's mode of presentation was also innovative as, for example, in his use of dramatic irony. He first gave a straight-faced account of what a number of informants had told him about the *ioba* ceremony, when the visiting *baloma* were drummed out of the village at the end of the harvest period and 'chased' back to the afterworld on Tuma. He followed this with a detailed description of what he had witnessed in the village of Olivilevi where he had 'made the sacrifice of getting up at three in the morning to see the ceremony'. He noted a fair congruence between report and reality, but the emotional 'tone' of the proceedings was utterly unexpected. Instead of awe and piety, he found in the *ioba* ceremony 'no traces of sanctity or even seriousness'. Instead of a gathering of solemn villagers 'there remained to farewell the *baloma* only five or six urchins with the drums, myself and my informant'. In an 'undignified performance', it was the small boys who beat the retreat for the ancestral spirits and chanted the formulaic farewell ('O spirits, go away, we shall remain'). 'They spoke with the same characteristic mixture of arrogance and shyness, with which they used to approach me, begging for tobacco, or making some facetious remark, in fact, with the typical demeanour of boys who perform some nuisance sanctioned by custom.'[28]

Malinowski drew the obvious lesson that such events must be witnessed at first hand by the ethnographer before they could be properly described and understood; it was not good enough to rely on hearsay. Participant observation was the key. It also yielded mundane details that allowed him to de-mythologize romantic notions of the primitive. At the ritual burning of the gardens, for instance, the torches of the officiants were lit 'quite without ceremony (by means of wax matches, produced by the ethnographer, not without a pang)'. Thus participant observation became the watchword of his fieldwork method. It pulled a substantial rug from beneath the kind of generalizations made by armchair anthropologists who relied solely on second-hand reports.

A centrepiece of the essay was the role of *baloma* in human reproduction. The observation that Trobrianders were ignorant of physiological paternity was made by Raynor Bellamy as early as 1906; in view of his medical and census work, he was in a better position than any missionary to uncover this ethnographic fact. Seligman had given Malinowski a copy of the letter Bellamy wrote to Administrator Barton, in which he stated: 'It would seem that in the native's mind childbirth is not necessarily connected with sexual intercourse'. Malinowski proved him wrong on the narrower point, for it was known that virgins could not have children, and sexual intercourse was one of the acknowledged means by which a woman was 'opened up' in order that a spirit-child from Tuma could enter her. He took the reader through the stages of this particular investigation, through the seemingly hopeless 'contradictions and obscurities in the information', down and out of 'the desperate blind alleys, so often encountered in ethnographical field work, where one comes to suspect that the natives are untrustworthy, that they tell tales on purpose'.[29] There was no final consensus among his informants, but Malinowski nonetheless reached a common denominator of belief.

The ignorance of physical fatherhood was no great mystery, Malinowski argued, and it required no 'far-fetched explanations' to account for it. He seemed almost prepared to endorse the 'illustrious opinion' of James Frazer that such ignorance was 'universal among early mankind'.[30] After all, one must imagine the 'absolutely insurmountable difficulties which a native "natural philosopher" would have to overcome if he had to arrive at anything approaching our embryological knowledge'. Furthermore, the causal connection between sexual intercourse and pregnancy is by no means obvious. Malinowski modified his views slightly in later publications, though he never quite came to terms with Billy Hancock's 'discovery' (conveyed to him by letter after he had left the Trobriands in 1918) that *baloma* did not recycle themselves through women. Malinowski's style of questioning women may well have been counterproductive: they told him what they thought he wanted to hear – that is, confirmation of what he had learned from the men.[31] Malinowski's final formulation smoothed over some of the difficulties: 'we are left with a composite picture which, though blurred in some of its details, presents a strong outline when viewed from a distance. Thus all spirits rejuvenate; all children are incarnated spirits; the identity of sub-clan is preserved throughout the cycle; the real cause of childbirth is the spirit initiative from Tuma.'[32] More recent ethnographers in the Trobriands have found no reason to contradict this general statement. Indeed, Annette Weiner, the first female anthropologist to work there (with access to women as informants on a scale and in a manner denied to Malinowski), constructed an ideological reading of Trobriand culture that owed everything to the doctrine of the reincarnation of *baloma*.[33]

Malinowski concluded his essay with a disquisition on method. He rehearsed the obstacles he had encountered in trying to penetrate native belief. Initially, he had abided by Rivers's basic rule, 'to gather pure facts, to keep the facts and the interpretations apart', but he learned that some preliminary interpretation was necessary to separate the essential from the irrelevant. He aimed a shaft at his mentors' mode of ethnography:

> The often fragmentary, incoherent, non-organic nature of much of the present ethnological material is due to the cult of 'pure fact'. As if it were possible to wrap up in a blanket a certain number of 'facts as you find them' and bring them all back for the home student to generalize upon and build up his theoretical constructions upon.

This procedure was 'quite impossible', because 'the ordering, the classifying, and interpreting should be done in the field with reference to the organic whole of native social life'. This allusion to what he would later call 'the functionalist viewpoint' clearly demanded of the fieldworker some skill as a theorist, one capable of synthesis as well as analysis.

> In the field one has to face a chaos of facts, some of which are so small that they seem to be insignificant; others loom so large that they are hard to encompass with one synthetic glance. But in this crude form they are not scientific facts at all; they are absolutely elusive, and can be fixed only by interpretation, by seeing them *sub specie aeternitatis*, by grasping what is essential in them and fixing this. *Only laws and generalizations are scientific facts*, and fieldwork consists only and exclusively in the interpretation of chaotic social reality, in subordinating it to general rules.

This was a brave statement; it gave an epistemological underpinning to fieldwork method that implicitly dismissed the plodding, empirical mode of 'collectioneering' characteristic of his teachers. In stark contrast to his agree-able and sometimes ingratiating manner in personal correspondence with his elders, Malinowski seemed unafraid of sniping at them in print. Rivers's 'concrete method' was clearly a target, and in scoring a sophisticated point he was proclaiming himself an equal if not better theorist than Rivers.

> All statistics, every plan of a village or of grounds, every genealogy, every description of a ceremony – in fact every ethnological document – is in itself a generalization, at times quite a difficult one, because in every case one has first to discover and formulate the rules: what to count and how to count; every plan must be drawn to express certain economic or sociological arrangements; every genealogy has to express kinship con-nections between people, and it is only valuable if all the relevant data about the people are collected as well. . . . All this may appear almost as a truism, yet the unfortunate stress on keeping to 'pure facts only' is constantly being used as the guiding principle in all instructions for field work.[34]

The sociology of belief had exercised Malinowski throughout his essay. He claimed to have had no theoretical guidance in tackling 'the difficulties and discrepancies' that beset him in Kiriwina. Now, after raising more awkward epistemological questions concerning the nature of belief, he out-lined a methodological procedure for dealing with them. It was a theoreti-cal scheme that had been forged in the field, 'bit by bit, through actual experience'. He had found it necessary to distinguish between 'social ideas or dogmas' on the one hand, and 'theology or interpretation of the dogmas' on the other. The first comprised beliefs embedded in customs, institutions, magico–religious formulae, rites and myths; they elicited emotional responses and were expressed in behaviour. The second comprised three types of interpretations: the orthodox views of specialists such as magicians; 'popular' or public opinions held by a majority of villagers; and finally, the idiosyncratic speculations of individuals. The distinctions seem obvious enough, but few other ethnographers of the period had bothered to make them. In a lengthy footnote, Malinowski delivered a glancing blow to Durkheim, again rejecting his 'philosophical basis of sociology' with its 'untenable' metaphysical postulate of a 'collective soul'. (In his diary he scoffed that he had 'never met' a collective soul.) 'In the field . . . one has to do with a whole aggregate of individual souls, and the methods and theoretical conceptions have to be framed exclusively with this multiplex material in view. The postulate of a collective consciousness is barren and absolutely useless for an ethnographical observer.'[35] Rather, the awkward fact of inconsistency had to be incorporated into theory. 'Two beliefs, quite contradictory to each other, may co-exist, while a perfectly obvious inference from a very firm tenet may be simply ignored. Thus the only safe way for an ethnological enquirer is to investigate every detail of native belief and to mistrust any conclusion obtained through inference only.' Frazer and others engaged in the enterprise of gross comparisons were put out of business by methodological demands of this kind.

But what *had* Malinowski discovered about belief? In addition to a showcase of exotic and curious items, he found there was considerable variation in beliefs; that dogmas (institutional beliefs) were compartmentalized and not necessarily consistent with other dogmas; that Trobrianders were 'all too human' in their ability to say one thing and do something different (there was slippage between the stated norm and actual behaviour); that the cake of custom was not, ideologically speaking, all of a piece. This last 'discovery' became a substantial plank in his theoretical understanding of primitive society. It resonated with his own individualism. It was as if he relished the waywardness of humans, their impulse to flout the rules. The institutional realm of culture, he would argue, was forever being subverted and suborned by individuals who wriggled to be free. Variation in belief was simply one instance of this. Cultures were not homogeneous, and there would always be conflict between rule and impulse, structure and sentiment. Society was forever making compromises with itself to accommodate this internal struggle. 'Savage society', as he put it later, is 'not a consistent logical scheme, but rather a seething mixture of conflicting principles'.[36]

Ancestral approval

Seligman had virtually guaranteed publication. He not only submitted 'Baloma' to the editor of the *JRAI* on Malinowski's behalf, but also reported upon it as a reader. Then, together with his faithful research assistant Mary Jonas, he edited it for publication. He was 'very pleased with it', he told Malinowski:

I should call it all good, and some of it very good. Your linguistic abilities have given you an immense pull over all the rest of us with regard to magic, and what you have written about it seems to me the most important statement that has yet appeared on Melanesian magic. I think you have got even Rivers beat here.[37]

Seligman had considered sending it to *Folk-lore*, but judged that it was much too long (and 'much too good', added Mary Jonas). Besides, 'I expect . . . it would have been too shocking. They have just turned down quite a good little paper of Landtman's because it upset the chaste feelings of the old women of both sexes on the committee.' He perhaps had in mind Malinowski's forthright statement: 'In Kiriwina the unmarried girls from six upwards are generally supposed to practise licence well-nigh every night. It is immaterial whether this is so or not; it matters only that for the natives of Kiriwina sexual intercourse is almost as common an occurrence as eating, drinking, or sleeping.'[38] On the strength of '*Baloma*', Seligman had been able to mention Malinowski's name 'with a good deal of effect' at the recent meeting of the British Association.[39] He also showed the manuscript to Haddon, who wrote to congratulate Malinowski on 'a very good piece of work'.[40]

On one issue, however, Seligman did tamper with Malinowski's text: 'I have purposely softened down what you say about [Carl] von Strehlow; I have allowed you to impute incompetence to him, as I believe he is a missionary, and most missionaries are incompetent, but I have not allowed you to call him unintelligent.'[41] Seligman's softening imputed 'insufficient mental training' to Strehlow, but allowed Malinowski's pungent criticism to remain:

> You can no more expect good all round ethnographic work from an untrained observer than you can expect a good geological statement from a miner, or hydrodynamic theory from a diver. It is not enough to have the facts right in front of one, the faculty to deal with them must be there.[42]

'*Baloma*' duly appeared in a bumper issue of the journal featuring distinguished contributors whose names put Malinowski's in the shade. Among them were the Royal Anthropological Institute president Arthur Keith, H. J. Fleur, H. Peake, P. Amaury Talbot, H. D. Skinner, H. Ling Roth, A. C. Haddon and R. S. Rattray. Coincidentally, there was also a paper on Papuan war magic by Malinowski's Finnish contemporary Gunnar Landtman, but it was a conventional ethnographic report that offered little competition to '*Baloma*'. Most notably, the issue featured Sir James Frazer's

Huxley Memorial Lecture on 'Ancient Stories of a Great Flood'. Malinowski might well have joked that it was an antediluvian piece, but he was pleasantly surprised when Frazer himself wrote to him with warm appreciation of 'the thoroughness of your methods and the soundness of your conclusions'. He did not seem to mind that the young ethnographer had demolished his comparative method. 'Social anthropology,' he wrote, 'is no doubt only in its beginning, and as it progresses it will employ methods of inquiry ever more exact and thorough. From your paper I judge that you are one of those who will lead the way in this direction.'[43]

With this magisterial endorsement of his research efforts Malinowski must have been deeply gratified. A copy of the letter found its way onto his official file held by Atlee Hunt's department, so we may imagine its recipient proudly tendering it to his Australian patron. Frazer was not dispensing praise gratuitously. He was pleased to infer that his own pet theory concerning the ignorance of physiological paternity had been confirmed in the field by an ethnographer of Malinowski's calibre. This academic point aside (which preoccupied Malinowski more than his general empirical and anti-historical stance logically warranted), to have Frazer so firmly on his side at this stage of his career – with all its present uncertainties – was alone worth the effort that '*Baloma*' had cost him. In characteristically cadenced prose, Frazer went on to commend Malinowski's attack on Durkheim:

> I am pleased also to see that you prick the bubble of the 'collective unconscious' which has been blown to such height by some French writers and also (I fancy, for I have not paid serious attention to these vagaries) by their followers in this country. The simple fact is that there is no such thing as a collective consciousness; it is an abstract idea which has no concrete reality corresponding to it, and therefore all conclusions drawn from its assumed reality must be fallacious. In short it is a myth invented by learned but not wise men in their study.

In his response some months later, Malinowski said he was pleased that Frazer approved of his 'sally' against the 'Collective Consciousness' and he renewed the onslaught begun in '*Baloma*' with a battery of mixed metaphors that outdid Frazer.

> Such metaphysical concepts, shrouded in the worn out rags of Hegelian pomp, only slightly trimmed and repainted to suit the modern craving

after greater sobriety, are bound to play havoc with field work: they
obscure the real issues and, if blindly followed, would produce artificial
and twisted methods of observation.[44]

Frazer referred also to Baldwin Spencer, who had visited him in London
the previous winter to Frazer's 'great pleasure and refreshment'. Spencer, he
wrote, 'spoke most highly of the work you have done and are doing in the
Trobriands, so that I look forward with the keenest interest to the publication of your book'.

Indiscretions, calumnies and restrictions

Malinowski wrote to his mother in August, telling her of his plans. Since
despatching '*Baloma*' to Seligman, he had been working on a draft monograph that would encompass his Trobriand materials.

> I'm going to finish the whole book before I set off again, so I'll prob-
> ably spend the summer here, till March, when autumn sets in, and for
> the winter I'll go again to New Guinea. I've got enough money for two
> years, so I'm not worried about it. The winter here was very severe, and
> this hindered my work. . . . Now it's much warmer, so I can get down
> to work again. Prof. Spencer (now ennobled as Sir Baldwin Spencer)
> reads my manuscript with me and is very helpful and, as far as I can tell,
> interested.[45]

Supportive though he was, Spencer had been less than frank with
Malinowski. In November 1915 he had written to Haddon, warning him
that all was not well with their Polish protégé. 'Malinowski I hear has rather
come up against the Authorities and has made somewhat of a nuisance of
himself.'[46] In early February he elaborated:

> He is a strange fellow – very capable as I found out when I went through
> his material with him – really good stuff. He evidently knows what to
> look for but I am sorry to say that he has been somewhat indiscreet and
> has come across Murray in NG with the result that there will be no
> further assistance given to him in his work out here. I fancy that his sym-
> pathies are rather with the German than the Russian Poles. However he
> will be down in Melbourne again before long & I will do my best to
> restrain him if necessary & to keep him out of gaol.[47]

Rumours reverberated through the corridors of London University and wheels began to turn behind Malinowski's back. None of his letters to Seligman during 1916 has survived, so we can only infer from Seligman's replies what Malinowski told him, but he appears to have been unaware of the predicament he was facing with 'the Authorities' in Papua – or, indeed, of the global reach of Haddon's surveillance network. Even on his remote South Sea isle Malinowski was not beyond the concern of British thought police.

Haddon alerted Seligman to Spencer's warning, and when Seligman received word from Malinowski that his Australian grant would not be renewed he leapt to the conclusion that it was something to do with his 'indiscretion'. Seligman was disappointed, because on Malinowski's urging he had already written to Adelaide in the hope that Stirling would use his influence to assist in getting the grant renewed. (He knew nothing, of course, of the strained relations between 'Papa' Stirling and the man who had captivated his daughter.) Malinowski had also hinted that Haddon might be able to help, for he had 'an immense sway over Atlee Hunt'.[48] Not knowing the exact nature of Malinowski's misdemeanour, however, Haddon seemed reluctant to act. The University of London Senate committee soon learned that Malinowski had 'come up against the Government folk' (as Seligman phrased it), and the consternation in London and Cambridge now turned upon whether he would be prevented from doing further fieldwork. Staunchly supportive as ever, Seligman reasoned with Haddon:

> We'll allow that he has been indiscreet . . . but he can't have done anything very dreadful, for all the Government has done is to withdraw its unusually kind and generous allowance. There does not seem to be anything whatever to show that if he had the money he would not be allowed to work in New Guinea, and I must say that until there is evidence to this effect, it does not seem to me that it would be in any way prejudicing anthropology, or your power to push anthropology with the Australian Government, if you helped to get him a grant from the Sladen Fund.[49]

The secretary of the LSE, Miss MacTaggart, who confessed to 'a certain affection' for Malinowski, also appealed to Haddon to write to the chairman of the Sladen Trust.[50] Seligman begged Haddon yet again: 'I do feel very strongly that if the money can be found from this country he will probably be allowed to go on with the work.'[51] The university approached the Australian authorities asking if there would be any objection to Malinowski being granted further funding to continue his research in Papua. 'No objection' was Hunt's welcome reply.[52]

Concerning Malinowski's 'indiscretion', of which the various committees were keen to learn more, Seligman had lately received news from William Strong in Port Moresby, and he quoted the relevant passage to Haddon. Although still ambiguous, it gave more substance to the rumour. 'I have pretty good reason,' Strong had written in January,

> for believing that he expressed certain views (views which are unpopular and not understood outside of purely scientific medical circles) and that these views have got round to the powers that be, possibly in an exaggerated form, and may have influenced them in discontinuing help. I do not think the fact of his being an Austrian Pole has anything to do with it.[53]

This was surely an allusion to Malinowski's unguarded remarks about homosexuality, recalled so many years later by Hubert Champion. It was all 'a regrettable muddle', commented Seligman.

Meanwhile, he had written to Malinowski to say that he was trying to get him £100 from the Dixon Fund. If this failed, he would turn again to Robert Mond, who had 'admitted cheerfully that like all other big manufacturers he was making money out of the war'. If he got the financial support, he expected Malinowski 'to make every attempt to get to Rossel', which he regarded as 'the most important thing to be now done in New Guinea'.[54] The attempt to milk the Dixon Fund failed. Seligman's case was 'thrown out by the Senate', following what Graham Wallas reported were 'disgraceful speeches' concerning Malinowski's nationality. The Sladen Trust also decided against him, reluctant 'to send £100 out of the country for work which might not be allowed to proceed'.[55] So it fell to Mond, the war profiteer, to come to Malinowski's aid with £150.

By May, Seligman had heard Malinowski's version of his 'indiscretion', which he immediately relayed to Haddon: 'some of his trouble has apparently arisen from the fact that Bellamy has left the service, and the new magistrate [Campbell] is an Australian "patriot", with little geography & less history, who insists on regarding the Poles as "bloody Austrians". I can imagine how this would try Malinowski.'[56] But there was more to the 'indiscretion' than that, as Haddon, Seligman, Strong and Spencer well knew.

Seligman had already decided it was time to tell Malinowski, as tactfully as possible, what Strong had written about him:

Strong says that you are doing excellent work, but that you have rather come up against people, so he hears, not on account of your nationality, but on account of some views you have expressed on subjects of a scientific medical nature, as he phrases it. . . . Haddon too has had hints that you are considered to have been indiscreet. I expect the whole matter is absolutely trivial with regard to what actually happened, or what you actually said, but people, whether anthropologists or government officials, easily get irritated in the tropics, especially in times like this, and I think you ought to go very slowly and cautiously, and if necessary now be prepared to eat a certain amount of humble pie.[57]

Later Malinowski spoke of 'calumnies'.[58] While this unsettling letter was on its way, he wrote to Haddon, sending him an offprint of his 'short article' on the Mailu. He was currently 'working out' his material on art in the Trobriands, he said, and had found Haddon's work on Massim decorative art 'extremely useful & suggestive'. As for his own modest achievement: 'I have spent over 8 months in one village in the Trobriands, and this proved to me, how even a poor observer like myself, can get a certain amount of reliable information, if he puts himself into the proper conditions for observation.'[59]

Malinowski wrote to Seligman in June to tell him of his plans. It was 'absolutely essential' to 'work out' his data before returning to Kiriwina 'for two or three months' in January or February 1917. Then, of course, he would have a crack at Rossel.[60] His frugality impressed Seligman: 'I think £10 or £12 a month, which is what you say you are spending in Australia, must require great care and forethought.'[61] Despite his financial worries Malinowski's luck held. Not only was Mond's £150 more than expected, but Baldwin Spencer made another appeal on Malinowski's behalf. He wrote directly to the Minister of External Affairs, praising Malinowski's work ('the best of its kind yet done in Papua') and urged that he be granted a further sum of £100 pounds.[62] Lt-Governor Murray was invited to comment. His reply was predictably hostile:

I do not feel justified in raising any objections to Dr Malinowski's return to Papua, although I have heard disquieting rumours as to his moral character. . . . I doubt the sincerity of Dr Malinowski's expression of sympathy with the cause of the allies – but this is a question which has doubtless been fully considered by the Department of Defence. If Dr Malinowski returns to Papua he should, I think, be confined to the Trobriands, and the term of his stay should be limited – say to twelve months.

'There would,' he added, 'be the strongest objection to the payment by the Papuan Government of any part of Dr Malinowski's salary or expenses.'[63]

Atlee Hunt duly conferred with his minister and offered his own recommendation that a further grant of £100 be made. Siding with Hunt rather than Murray, the minister approved.[64] At the end of August, Hunt wrote formally to Spencer about the 'supplementary grant' for Malinowski. 'This would be conditional on his continuing to work within the limits of the Trobriand Group and on the assumption that his further stay in Papua will not exceed 12 months.'[65] Murray had won some concessions; the net could be tightened around the objectionable and possibly perverted Pole.

A grateful Malinowski formally responded to Hunt via Spencer. But he continued to push for greater freedom, asking that after completing his work on the Trobriands he be permitted to go to Rossel as Seligman had advised. 'Malinowski returning Trobriands,' Hunt cabled Murray. 'Expect finish there about four months then desires work Rossel Island in accordance with Seligman's instructions. Is there any objection?'[66] There was indeed from Murray: 'Strongly urge arrangements be adhered to and that he leave Papua on completion of his work at Trobriands.'[67]

Seligman commiserated:

Murray is of course technically correct as he has supreme power in time of war, but I can imagine nothing meaner than to take action against you as he has, without giving you an opportunity of setting matters right. It is sad how this war is gradually corroding away one's trust and belief in so many of one's fellow countrymen, or at least in their possession of such virtues as fair play.[68]

Fair play had little to do with it, however, and Murray certainly did not regard Malinowski as a fellow countryman. Indeed, he found another reason to feel aggrieved. He had still not received complimentary copies of *The Natives of Mailu* and he would not be placated by the single copy belatedly forwarded to him by Spencer.[69]

Undeterred, Malinowski continued to wriggle for concessions. Accepting that he would now be unable to go to Rossel, he politely inquired whether he might visit 'the islands to the north of Dawson Strait' – Dobu, Sanaroa and the Amphletts. 'These places are lying on the way from Samarai to the Trobriands and from the ethnological point of view, their study is quite essential as a complement to any work done in the Trobriands proper.'[70] The justification was sound, as Murray would have known, for these islands participated in the 'regular circle' of ceremonial exchange to which he had alluded in his own book.[71] Malinowski won this particular dispensation, but he would be more constrained than on previous expeditions – though it was stretching the meaning of the word to claim, as do some versions of his legend, that he was 'interned' in the Trobriands. With hindsight, by restricting Malinowski's movements, Hubert Murray did social anthropology a singular favour.

'Health: the basic element'

Malinowski expected to be ready to return to Papua by March 1917, but he gradually came to realize that his health would not allow it. 'Health' was one of the categories under which he entered notes in his tabulated diary. It is a log of ill-health and punishing sickness, beginning with the pitiful entry: 'Health: the basic element. Makes my whole stay in Melb. and the whole year one of the worst in my life. Aggravates the rancour caused by social ostracism. Thus the abandonment and the lack of a friendly atmosphere is all the more painful.'

While it took weeks, even months for the stigma of his enemy status to become fully evident (he noted at one point that Spencer did not invite him to dinner any more), his health began to fail soon after he arrived in Melbourne. He was at the Federal Palace Hotel when he suffered his first bout of influenza. The Melbourne winter, notorious for its damp chill, set in. As always when sick, Malinowski felt acutely sorry for himself. 'Frequent catarrh and influenza . . . theory of rheumatism and arthritis. Sunbathing with salt. Theory of mental illness; headaches, excitation.' On a separate page he elaborated:

> I can't bear the cold. One Sunday I catch a cold at the Weigalls. I go to the Pecks; headache. I take quinine (malaria hypothesis) and arsenic. Getting headaches. I have long periods of depression with headache and eye pain (cannot bend down, cannot write . . .). About 15 August I go to see the eye specialist.

His health grew worse as the winter yielded to the antipodean spring. By September he was going to bed every afternoon, and by October he felt 'worse and worse; deeper resignation, lack of faith in the future and the possibility of working'. He began to have suicidal thoughts. By November: 'It's clear I'm sick, I stay at home. Go to see Stawell. Consumption?' Richard Stawell, later knighted, was one of Melbourne's most eminent physicians, a specialist in diseases of the nervous system and a pillar of the community. He had a practice on Spring Street and his fees were steep.[72]

Malinowski told Elsie Masson about his headaches and the pain in his eyes, and she tried to warn him that he 'lived a very unhealthy life'. Good nurse that she was, she recommended nothing stronger than aspirin ('her constant recommendation of aspirin annoys me a bit,' he admitted). The eye specialist was reassuring in that he found no evidence of disease, but the headaches continued. Malinowski considered several hypotheses to explain his worsening illness, of which he rejected the malaria hypothesis as the least likely. The others were symptomatic of a rampant hypochondria:

> Hypothesis of mental illness. I take lots of iodine in milk. Hypothesis of rheumatism: salt baths; they help to some extent. Hypothesis of lack of sexual intercourse: I get irritable easily and develop spinster-like peevishness. Longer and longer periods of depression. The same indescribable headache I got in London (in the light of pyrotea, heartburn, and the streptococcal infection, probably antrum and forehead sinuses).

He spent feverish days in bed, no longer comforted by Mrs Cummings (though he was using her room) since she was herself in hospital with some malady. But his other friends were solicitous: 'Leila and Broinowski come every day, in the afternoon, we talk, read poetry – I still have fever; chronic state of excitement and slackness; my head is burning and every thought is an effort.' His friends' sympathetic attentions did little to alleviate his condition. He suffered 'terrible dejection and despair' and 'the threat of blindness returns for a time' and also the 'threat of mental deterioration'. He had 'moments of complete despondency' and 'mindless resignation' and suspected that he might never finish his work on the Trobriands. He thought 'lustfully about suicide'. 'Every sign of improvement fills me with optimism, but I relapse over and over again. When I'm better I don't believe in illness; when I'm not well I can see death and decay within the next six months.' At the beginning of September he felt strong enough to go walking in the Dandenong Ranges with Ernest Pitt and Bob Broinowski, but he caught cold and suffered another relapse. 'I feel absolutely dreadful; "consumptive". . . . Then I practically give up work completely, I give in and stay at home. I go to see Stawell. The phase of consumption. I can't walk. Constant temperature.'

He had alarmed Annie Brunton, who wrote to sympathize with the 'rotten time' he was having.

> I can picture you going out in the middle of the day, looking miserable and dejected, & as you say, unwashed . . . as you used to be in those days in London – as white as a ghost, muffler up to the throat & looking the picture of misery. It is really no joke being ill & without friends.[73]

Courageous Annie was enduring her own misery: her favourite nephew Brian had been killed at Ypres at the beginning of June. During his first hour of action a shard of shrapnel from an exploding shell had pierced his brain. Annie was inconsolable, but 'proud that Brian wanted to go & fight'.[74] She could no longer bear to listen to music, though she had many pupils to teach. Annie then had nightmares of anxiety about Justin, Brian's twin brother, who was still 'in the thick of it' in France. It came almost as a relief in November when he was seriously wounded ('his leg from hip to knee being practically blown away') and invalided out of the war.[75] This was not the last of Annie's worries. The value of her pension was reduced by inflation. Her brother's wife fell ill, and her eighty-year-old mother was becoming demented. Despite these cares, however, she found room in her heart to worry about Malinowski. 'I wish you had someone to look after you a little bit,' she wrote, 'you need it so much with your dreaming, impractical nature.'[76] She was even more distressed to learn of his 'consumption hypothesis'.

> I can't bear to think of you ill & run down with no one you really love at hand to try & cheer you & tender you the loving services one longs for when one is weak & depressed. If only you were nearer to me & I could do something for you how happy it would make me! . . . Remember Niusiu that you need good nourishing food & fresh air more than anything. Don't sleep with your head under the blankets breathing in the same bad air, always have your windows open.[77]

Malinowski would never be short of advice from good women concerned about his health.

In October, Melbourne treated Malinowski to its fickle changes of weather. 'You can't imagine a climate like this,' he wrote to his mother on

1 November. 'One day tropical heat . . . the next day the temperature drops
to ten degrees, rain, mud, and winds that blow through these badly built
houses as if through a sieve. As I result I had some influenza and a bit of
malaria.'[78] By chance, his mother wrote to him on the same day. She told
him his cousin Mancia had given birth to another boy and that Father
Pawlicki had died. According to the hazy rumours that reached her, Staś
Witkiewicz had 'suffered a general contusion' and was recovering in a
military sanatorium; but he was reported to be painting, so presumably his
condition was not critical. She added sadly, 'You won't find many friends
left when you come back.'[79] To avoid worrying her, Malinowski told his
mother little about his problems. His letter of mid-November, referring to
Melbourne's inhospitable weather, reached her with unusual speed. She
replied at the end of January 1917, suspecting the worst. 'I'm begging you,
don't think of going North again, but start researching some tribe from
middle Australia. . . . If you have malaria you should take even more care
of your baldness; hopefully you can rescue at least a little hair on the sides.
I'm begging you!'[80]

At the end of October a diversion of sorts was provided by an invitation
to Parliament House. It was probably at the suggestion of Atlee Hunt that
Malinowski was asked to testify on labour conditions in Papua before an
inter-state commission investigating British trade in the South Pacific. He
was sworn and examined on Friday 27 October 1916 and his verbatim
testimony was subsequently published.[81] His retrospective diary makes no
mention of this event, though it was during the period when he was beginning to entertain suicidal thoughts. His sour mood might explain some of
his jaundiced opinions, though these were consistent with the entrenched
paternalistic, if not downright racist, views expressed by the Australian
planters and manufacturers who also testified on that day.

Malinowski told the commission that he had seen many plantations at
first hand and had talked with many natives about their experiences of
working on them. The raw statements in his evidence (typically delivered
in staccato fashion and prefaced by 'I think', 'I expect', 'I know' or 'I believe')
focused on work and sex.

On labour, for example: 'I think that the native Papuan is not very keen
on working for a white man. . . . I conclude that very much depends on
the manner in which the natives are managed on the plantations, as they
certainly prefer some plantations to others.' On sex:

I could not say whether it is common for boys on plantations to take up with other [local] women. But it was pointed out as a fact that they had intrigues. It is an abnormal state of things, and the sexual problem is important, because it is almost impossible to think that a young native would spend three years of his life without having sexual intercourse without degenerating into sexual abnormality.

(Nor yet a young Polish anthropologist? Although they were too polite to say so publicly, and although there was not a shred of evidence other than Malinowski's own incautious badinage, Murray and others in Papua were clearly of the opinion that he too had degenerated into 'sexual abnormality'.)

On the industrial potential of Papuans:

I believe they will be able to make copra. I do not think it would be possible to induce the natives to engage in any other form of industry. No native will plant coconuts voluntarily, but this [Bellamy's] experiment on Trobriand Island [sic] shows that they are extremely glad for having done so.

On their indigence and lack of incentive: 'The native Papuan cannot really see even seven or eight days ahead, though he may be very intelligent in many matters; he has no mental grasp of a further perspective. . . . There is no incentive to the native except some present desire.' Such bizarre judgments were not only unworthy of Malinowski, they flew in the face of his own evidence concerning the agricultural cycle, Kula trading and mortuary feasting – all of which required complex strategic planning and considerable forethought.

Regarding depopulation Malinowski told the committee: 'There is not much likelihood of the native Papuans and of the natives of other Pacific Islands dying out if left alone. . . . Broadly speaking, I think it would be best to leave them to their own conditions.'

A boost to his shaky self-esteem came with the award of his doctor of science degree. Once again, it was the faithful Seligman who set the wheels in motion by submitting *The Family among the Australian Aborigines* and *The Natives of Mailu*. 'It could go through within a couple of months,' he wrote in October, 'but be sure if any excuses for delay can be found they will be taken full advantage of.'[82] The exorbitant fee of £20 (two months' living expenses) was deducted from his university scholarship but Malinowski did not cavil. And it was Seligman once more who steered his protégé through. He was appointed one of the examiners, the other being Captain T. A. Joyce of the British Museum.[83]

When the DSc was awarded in December, Malinowski was pleased to receive 'most hearty congratulations' from Baldwin Spencer, who had gone to England to be knighted by the king and honoured by his Oxford college. Spencer conveyed welcome news: he had lunched with Robert Mond and encouraged him to provide Malinowski with £250 per annum for the next two years. 'This will make your mind easy on money matters,' Spencer wrote. He had also had 'a long talk' with George Macmillan about Malinowski's work. 'I feel quite sure that when the war is over he will publish your book. In connection with this I have also seen Sir James Frazer who will I feel sure support what I have said to Mr Macmillian when he sees your forth-coming paper.'[84]

In early December Malinowski's doctor, Frank Andrew, recommended a spell in the country. A new 'epoch' began for him. 'I lead a monotonous and regular life' was how he summarized it under the heading 'Nyora' on the second diary-chart. He took the train to Healesville, a resort in the hills to the northeast of the city, and there he spent the following weeks at a fashionable guesthouse. He was 'absolutely worn out and barely able to walk' on arrival, and had to sit down in order to shave. He slept for sixteen hours at a stretch. It was now summer and he spent days lying on the grass or in a deckchair gazing at the 'enchanting' valley. In the warm haze scented by aromatic sassafras, the trees seemed to be 'submerged in a grey-green mist topped with tiny leaves'. Under the heading 'Reading and Thoughts' he recalled:

> I can neither read nor think clearly. Mim gives me [Conrad's] *Under Western Eyes* and *Sunshine Sketches* by Leacock. I read them with pleasure. Also a load of rubbish from cheap magazines. Gradually I become interested in Anglo-Saxon mentality: the anatomy of the open and french-polished uncouthness and stupidity. The appetite for feeble and sentimental songs.

While at 'Nyora' he embarked upon a 'rigorous treatment for tuberculosis', monitoring his temperature several times a day and spraying his nose and throat. But there was no improvement and he ceased to observe the regime. The phlegm analysis proved negative, so the cause of his malaise must have lain elsewhere. Arsenic helped, as did the appearance at the guest-house of a number of attractive women. Among others, Cathie Johnson took his fancy, and by Christmas he had found the strength to flirt and even to dance. 'Women & Entertainment' was another heading in his synoptic chart of the 'Nyora epoch'. The column largely comprises a list of names and sobriquets ('flappers', 'two little intelligent Jewish girls', 'the Spaniard') and cryptic references to 'episodes'. The most coherent statement is revealing: 'I'm unnerved by the fact that the women don't understand my wit and my "superiority".' On New Year's Eve he was seedy and unsociable. 'I felt very dejected and "shrouded in my own misery",' he told Elsie Masson later. Despite the 'gay and noisy crowd' he 'just wanted to be left alone and vegetate'.[85]

But he often thought of Elsie during his stay at 'Nyora'. 'You existed very much for me, but somewhere quite beyond my reach, somewhere whence you could not even give me comfort or pity.' She was back at work in the surgical ward of the hospital, absorbed in her patients' broken lives. Overworked, dispirited and tired, she felt 'as if everything of one's youth were being snatched away'. Her unsympathetic father 'regarded it as one's duty . . . to keep cheerful', but December brought news from France of the death of her dashing young cousin, Jim Struthers. She could admit then that she had lost her nerve.[86]

Chapter 22

Elsie Rosaline

The Massons

Elsie Rosaline (as she signed her early letters to Malinowski) colourfully described herself as 'the descendant of Dutch wine merchants, Northumbrian linen manufacturers and Highland cattle-lifters'.[1] More prosaically, and more recently, the Massons and the Struthers (her mother's family) were Scottish academics. Elsie's father, David Orme Masson (1858–1937), was a dominant figure in Australian science. A portrait painted in the year of his retirement shows a dark-suited man with the serious mien of a company director. Together with his two professorial colleagues, Baldwin Spencer and Thomas Rankin Lyle, Masson brought international recognition to the University of Melbourne. Among his other achievements were the foundation of the Australian National Research Council and the Australian Chemical Institute. Over a period of two decades he had a direct involvement in the heroic age of Antarctic exploration, in which Australia had a national interest. While Malinowski was sweating in Papua, Masson's friend Douglas Mawson was freezing in the Antarctic.[2]

Orme (as he preferred to be called) belonged to a large family of distinguished academic achievers. His father, David Mather Masson, had held the chair of English literature at University College London, and from 1865 the Regius chair of rhetoric and English literature at Edinburgh, where he also became the historiographer royal for Scotland. After labouring for twenty-one years on the definitive, six-volume *Life of John Milton*, he produced another thirteen volumes on Scottish history. His wife, Emily Rosaline Orme (descended through her mother from eminent clergy with distant connections to John Wesley), was the daughter of a wealthy brewer and distiller. Two of Orme's sisters, Flora and Rosaline, became notable authors. The youngest sister, Nell, married George Gulland, professor of medicine at Edinburgh. As a child Orme had been surrounded by literary figures, though he was one of the few members of his family never to write a book. Among those who visited the family home in Hampstead were Tennyson, Carlyle, Emerson, the Rossettis, Holman Hunt, Coventry Patmore (Orme's mother's sister's husband) and the exiled Italian revolutionary Mazzini. As a student in Edinburgh, Orme became acquainted with T. H. Huxley, Robert Browning, Lord Kelvin and Robert Louis Stevenson.

Having turned to chemistry, Orme did doctoral work on nitroglycerine and taught at Bristol under the physical chemist Sir William Ramsey. In 1886, he married Mary ('Molly') Struthers, the petite daughter of another distinguished academic, Sir John Struthers of Aberdeen. Almost immediately, the couple sailed for Melbourne, where Orme had been appointed to the chair of chemistry. 'Moral character' and 'gentlemanly manners' were among the selection criteria for the position. By the age of forty-five Orme Masson had been elected a Fellow of the Royal Society.

Molly Masson's sister Christina ('Tina') married a professor of music; another sister, Lucy, married a professor of English, while John Struthers, their medically trained brother, became president of the Royal College of Surgeons. Orme and Molly's three children, Irving Orme, Flora Marjorie and Elsie Rosaline, continued the family tradition. Irving, who married his father's sister's daughter, became a professor of chemistry, and was later knighted as vice-chancellor of the University of Sheffield. Marnie (as Flora Marjorie was better known) wrote fiction, memoirs, travel books and a celebrated history of the Australian wool trade. In 1923 she married Walter Bassett, a mechanical engineer whose 200-foot jet of water still gushes spectacularly from Canberra's Lake Burley Griffin. Elsie, the youngest sibling, married 'a penniless Pole', Bronislaw Malinowski.

Born into a family so richly steeped in academic and scientific excellence, Elsie was ready to be impressed, but not awed, by a central European savant like Malinowski. For his part, he could conceive of Elsie's extended family in Polish terms as *inteligiencja* and landless *szlachta* of the kind that would have summered at Zakopane.

Melbourne University had admitted women since 1889 and was one of the first universities to admit women to its medical school – political achievements for which Orme Masson was partly responsible. In this he was continuing another family tradition, for his own parents as well as Molly's had been active supporters of higher education for women. Curiously, though, the Massons did not encourage their own daughters to enter university. The Massons and the Weigalls, and most other families that they knew, had governesses who taught their daughters at home. The Masson sisters shared their tutor with Baldwin Spencer's two daughters. Brother Irving went to Melbourne Grammar, but their mother did not think it proper for Marnie and Elsie to travel across the city to attend Merton Hall, the sister school of the boys' establishment.

Mim and Elsie had been friends since their early teens and visited one another frequently, using the trams that trundled between Carlton and St Kilda. The girls had literary leanings and wrote *faux*-poems and parodies of popular novels. Their parents told them to spend more time in the fresh air and save their scribbling until they were older. Mim found Professor Masson 'gentle and kind' and everyone agreed he had great personal charm. An 'inveterate cigarette smoker', Orme cycled when it was fashionable and (as a founding member of the Royal Melbourne Golf Club) played golf when it was not. Mim was fond of Mrs Masson, too, but 'sometimes a little frightened of her' as she could be domineering. At 'Chanonry' she was a formidable housekeeper who colour-coded the maids' dusters.

In 1906 Molly took her daughters on a visit to Europe. They spent an autumn in the Scottish Highlands followed by a winter studying music and language in Germany and a spring studying paintings and architecture in northern Italy. On their return to Melbourne, the girls began a spell of formal schooling, and after matriculation Marnie took courses in French and history at the university. She learned typing and shorthand and for a few years acted as secretary to her father when he was president of the professorial board and chairman of the BAAS organizing committee.

Meanwhile, in 1912, Elsie went to the Northern Territory as tutor and companion to the daughters of the newly appointed administrator, John Gilruth, a professorial colleague of Orme. For Elsie, at twenty-two, the trip was a rite of passage. On expeditions into the bush with her host, she came into contact with Aborigines for the first time (most Melburnians had never seen one), and was excited by the wild colonial town of Darwin. She wrote vivid letters home about her experiences, followed by a series of newspaper articles. These formed the basis for a book, which she wrote in a burst of youthful confidence. When she ignored her father's literary advice it led to their first disagreements and her parents realized that she was 'headstrong'. John Macmillan in London (probably on Baldwin Spencer's recommendation) published *An Untamed Territory* in 1915. It was an unfortunate year for first authors, as Malinowski knew from his Polish experience. The book did, however, snare the imagination of her future husband, and he told her later that had it not been for *An Untamed Territory* they would perhaps have never met.[3]

The outbreak of war turned Elsie's thoughts to nursing. Her 'obstinacy' in taking on a rigorous four-year training was against her parents' advice. They feared she was not physically strong enough to endure the twelve-hour shifts, and they were probably right. The work involved menial tasks of sweeping and cleaning as well as the demands of caring for the sick and wounded. Many trainees resigned, exhausted, before the end of their course. 'Elsie, sometimes ill and nearly always tired, doggedly stuck it out to the last, but I think her health suffered in the end,' recalled Mim.[4]

Marnie sailed for England from Perth on the *Arabia* on 3 October 1916. After leaving Suez, the ship was torpedoed. Its passengers were rescued and reached Marseilles safely, Marnie's chief loss being a cherished violin. In London she worked for the Ministry of Defence, while brother Irving worked on munitions at Woolwich Arsenal. Meanwhile, their father conducted laboratory research on the development of gas masks for the army and their mother engaged in war-related community work. In 1918, three members of the Masson family were honoured: Molly and Orme with CBEs and Irving with an MBE. Marnie was almost indignant when she wrote to her father: 'You deserve everything, not a silly old CBE.' Five years later he was rewarded with a knighthood.

Trotsky of the wards

Feminism was beginning to take root in Australia. The state of Victoria had been enlightened enough to grant women the vote in 1908 – six years after South Australia – but suffragettes were still active in 1916 under the militant leadership of Adela Pankhurst, daughter of the notorious Emmeline. Socialism was a sturdy growth, having been planted by the Labor Movement in the 1850s, and trade unions cultivated a social role as well as industrial clout. Malinowski would have endorsed the banner of the movement's first successful struggle: 'Eight hours' labour; eight hours' recreation; eight hours' rest.' Much later he would say that Australia was the most socialist country he had ever lived in.

Malinowski's 'epoch' in Melbourne was one of unusual political turbulence. The syndicalist revolutionary movement, popularly known as the Wobblies (Industrial Workers of the World), focused the radical Left's disenchantment with the reformist Australian Labor Party government. (It had been a Labor prime minister, Andrew Fisher, who pledged at the outbreak of war that Australia would defend the mother country 'to our last man and our last shilling'.) The IWW was also supported by assorted anti-war activists. Malinowski and Elsie referred to this increasingly vocal and influential political movement as 'the Socialists'. Although his enemy status precluded him from active partisanship, as a reader of the daily press Malinowski could not fail to be aware of issues — such as the momentous conscription debate — that were dividing the Australian nation. Significantly, however, there is scant reference in his diary notes to any political events except those to which Elsie Masson had responded. In short, it was mainly through her political activities that Malinowski's own interest became engaged.

Elsie was by nature a principled political creature. Her father found this hard to accept and her activities provoked an ambivalent response. While he was proud of her courage and independent spirit, he was disconcerted by the passionate manner in which she expressed her views and by the dubious company she kept. In early February 1917 he wrote to Marnie, telling her how Elsie had inadvertently become 'a stump orator' on Yarra Bank. It was Melbourne's Speakers' Corner, where dissidents mounted their soapboxes on Sunday afternoons.

> Well, Elsie began by asking awkward questions which were evaded, and then she seems to have been dared to mount the table and address the crowd; and she did it! . . . But — though I admired her pluck (and it required a lot) . . . I have told her I very much hope she won't make a practice of it. . . . Moreover the I.W.W. is an organization which is pretty powerful and quite unscrupulous, and it should be fought by the law and not by our little Elsie. I believe she would tackle a tiger with D.T.s if she saw a chance, but a man with a rifle would do better.[5]

Elsie was convinced that 'working people' were being duped by the radical socialists' insistence that the war was being fought wholly for the benefit of the capitalists. For one thing, their arguments left German militarism out of the equation. Her father's attitude was to remain aloof and condemn the dupes of the IWW from his privileged social position, but Elsie believed that she could 'show them they were working against their own interests'. She publicly debated with Adela Pankhurst, who was also speaking out against the war.

Elsie did give up stumping after a few attempts, but only to enter the lists of more formal debate in a less rambunctious venue. She began to attend meetings of variegated anti-war dissidents at Socialist Hall on Exhibition Street, and on Friday 15 June, after much preparation, she spoke there herself. A handbill advertised her talk as 'Our Attitude towards the War'. She endorsed the humanitarian principles of socialism and 'the need for universal solidarity in the struggle for Freedom'. Although Malinowski had helped her prepare the speech, he was required by the Enemy Aliens Ordinance to keep well away from such meetings.

On 19 July Orme wrote again to Marnie: 'Elsie is to lecture again to the Socialists. . . . I believe she does it extremely well and I should like to hear her, but I hate those people and all their ways and can't bring myself to go there.' He left no doubt which side he was on in the class war. He became even more anti-socialist after it became apparent that the Russian Revolution had succeeded. He suspected the socialists, unionists 'and other disloyal elements' of conspiring to bring down the Australian government.

From London, Marnie remonstrated with her father. 'You Daddy darling, are reluctant that Elsie should do this work, but you cannot bar anyone from sharing in the universal service campaign in its wider sense. . . . The Yarra Bank crowd deserves more attention than your fastidiousness – your personal silver aristocraticness, will allow.'[6] The lines drawn between the Left and the Right on the matter were not distinct. While tilting to the Left on many issues, Elsie and Marnie were at one with their class in supporting conscription.

Orme Masson, however, suspected organized conspiracy: 'In the past there has been far too much tame giving in to the Unions. They, or at least their leaders, have no policy beyond purely selfish class warfare, and it is high time they were given a severe lesson.' Prime Minister Billy Hughes, he believed, was not capable of 'anything stronger than talk'.

> Most of our misfortunes come from the fatal habit of giving malcontents their own way. It is a species of cowardice – the British species. Hence the Irish troubles; hence also the various labour troubles. As to Elsie's socialist friends one fourth of them should be in jail and three fourths of them in idiot asylums.[7]

Presumably, Orme Masson would have been happy to see Malinowski in gaol or in an asylum.

Although he was on the State Referendum Council, Masson's view was anti-democratic: 'Fact is, I don't believe in the voice of the people and have very little hope of the result of their appeal to it.'[8] In another letter denouncing the radical Catholic archbishop Daniel Mannix, he concluded: 'If we win this war it will be in spite of – not because of – democracy. Now what do you think?'[9] It was a few months later, from the perspective of the imperial capital, that Marnie told him what she thought: 'Yes, I believe in democracy, not because I think there is any divinity in the majority but simply because I think it is the only form of government that is morally justifiable.'[10] Orme bounced back: 'What of Russia now and its messy revolution and its rotten socialists of all grades? That country requires an autocracy and won't be happy till it gets it. . . . Do you begin to see the inherent weakness of democracy – or what passes by that name? Too many cooks in excelsis!'[11] As the war approached its end, Marnie had a final say:

> Each of us is optimistically inclined either to the Right or to the Left: the complete pessimist, who believes there is no hope anywhere, hardly exists. No, all I ask is a certain amount of sympathy for and generosity of belief in the 'underdog' as you call him. People can wear any political badge they like, or none, as long as they have an open heart.[12]

There is little enough evidence for the colour of Malinowski's 'political badge' at this troubled time, but he would probably have agreed with Marnie that while his class naturally inclined him to the Right, his temperament tilted him to the Left. There was also the fermenting milieu of his Polish youth. He had, after all, drunk tea with Lenin in Poronin and argued with his socialist friends in Zakopane. He had mingled with the Webbs, Hobhouse, Graham Wallas and other Fabians at the LSE. Although he despised party machinations and never belonged to a political party, and although he probably never voted in a general election, Malinowski was a democrat who breathed the air of the champagne socialism that permeated London's Holborn and Hampstead. In Australia, his political convictions had 'crystallized' (as he put it) during his 'third epoch' in Melbourne. This was largely due to the stimulus of Elsie's engagement with the socialists, though there were also the interminable discussions with his intellectual companions Paul Khuner, Elton Mayo and Bob Broinowski. Long afterwards, Marnie recalled how he had excoriated the Russians from his Polish perspective: ' "They are animals!" he said, enunciating the last word as only Europeans can, the syllables evenly spaced and the final "s" hissed. . . . It was the Austrians he liked, Germans he could stand, but Russians – no.'[13]

After jousting with the socialists, Elsie turned in 1918 to do battle with the hospital board. Her 'obstinacy' now upset the autocratic superintendent, Matron Jane Bell, a martinet whose rigidity of rule made the nurses' lives a misery. Elsie resented the regime's injustices and at the risk of dismissal agitated for better working conditions, most crucially for three shifts a day instead of two. She led a group of like-minded nurses and presented a petition to the state parliament. Matron Bell strongly disapproved. It was tantamount to militant unionism, and on the wards Elsie was nicknamed 'Trotsky'.

Malinowski had learned about Elsie's political debut when he met her at Yarra Bank on 11 February 1917. It was their first meeting since her visit to Perth the previous October. 'She tells me about her new hobby,' he recalled. 'I encourage her and decide myself to join the Socialists.' In spirit, at least. He resolved 'to work for her'. Elsie was impressed by his 'understanding' and by the fact that he took her seriously. It seemed to her 'ironical that my only helper in work I considered patriotic should not be a Briton'.[14] As she got to know him better, he seemed less impersonal, 'much livelier, more sprightly and quaintly witty'.

In late February he went to Sorrento, a seaside resort on the Mornington Peninsula. Elsie had written to him and included a newspaper cutting about Marnie's narrow escape in the Mediterranean. On the boat to Sorrento his double revealed himself: 'I read her letter religiously, and then I paw and kiss one anaemic plump seamstress.' The following week, still feeling poorly, he joined his new friends the Khuners at 'Nyora' before returning to Melbourne for an operation on 6 March. Dr Andrew had advised the extraction of all his teeth. The previous August, Seligman had written: 'You must not be careless about these. . . . You might easily get so much toothache or septic absorption in New Guinea that your health would go to pieces.'[15]

The loss of half of his teeth marked the beginning of what Malinowski termed 'the third epoch' of his life in Melbourne, which would end with his departure for Papua on 20 October. The events he noted under the five columns of his tabulated diary are a sure guide to what he believed to have been significant. At the top of the chart he identified the 'Main Themes –

Health and treatment; friendship with the Khuners; emergence of clear political and social opinions together with E.R.M.; work taken up anew; and most importantly, the love for E.R.M. and the tragedy of N.S.' In this final chart Elsie Rosaline Masson's column is the widest and longest. Elsie, the most important, the greatest love of his life and the mother of his children, was his investment in the future.

The Clan

The protracted and hesitant start to their love affair was linked inseparably with Elsie's stumping on Yarra Bank and her debates with the socialists. For a few months, in the face of growing parental opposition to their friendship, Elsie's political activities provided her with an excuse – if not a fully legitimate pretext – to be seen with Malinowski in public. There was another important factor that facilitated their courtship: their close friendship with the Khuners.

Although Malinowski was no longer required to report weekly to the police, the sense of being an enemy alien dogged him. Subtle forms of ostracism restricted his social life. Just as ostracism was occasioned by war paranoia, so were its victims infected by paranoia induced by their ostracism. One result of this was the blossoming of otherwise unlikely friendships, as marginalized aliens made the best of one another's company in mutual commiseration. In Malinowski's case, the most profoundly joyful and materially beneficial friendship he was ever to create with any man began in this way. He met Paul Khuner towards the end of 1916 and their friendship endured until death. It was a serendipitous meeting of hearts and minds, and in the generous space created by their mutual affection they delighted in the complementarity of their personalities. To Malinowski's mercurial persona, Paul presented a more solid disposition; his gravitas was the perfect foil for Bronio's intellectual playfulness. They influenced one another enormously.

Paul Khuner was a Viennese Jewish industrialist, a partner in a successful family business called Khunerol which manufactured soaps, margarine and chocolate. He and his wife Hedwig ('Hede') had been caught by the outbreak of war while visiting copra plantations in German New Guinea. Within days an Australian battalion had seized the capital, Rabaul, and all German and Austrian citizens were rounded up and shipped to Australia.

The Khuners' business credentials allowed them to avoid internment, though as enemy aliens their movements were restricted for the duration. Their camera was confiscated and for a time the military authorities denied them a telephone. On moving to Melbourne from Sydney in September 1915, they lived in reasonable comfort on remittances from Switzerland. Their eight-year-old son Hans had been left in Vienna in the care of an aunt and it would be six years before he saw his parents again.[16]

Paul and Malinowski first met through a Russian charmer, Juliette Grebin, with whom Malinowski had flirted in the library. 'The Khuners on the horizon,' he noted in his retrospective diary. But it was during his second visit to 'Nyora' in February 1917 that their friendship truly blossomed and became one of the 'main themes' of his life in Melbourne. At the end of March, he introduced Elsie to the Khuners, and his deepening friendship with them moved in tandem with his deepening love for Elsie. Without the Khuners, his courtship of Elsie, fraught as it was, would have encountered even greater obstacles. 'Carinya', Paul and Hede's rented house at 6 Canberra Grove, East Malvern, provided a neutral meeting place that was also a protective home base.

Elsie remembered how Malinowski had introduced her to Paul as someone who could help write speeches for her campaigning. They met outside the Reading Room, and she saw 'the figure of a small man, something like Napoleon, but with an expression of beaming good-will'. As they talked their way down Little Bourke Street, 'in the midst of severe criticisms of Germany and the Germans' he excused himself to dive into a shop to buy a German sausage. Elsie telephoned Mim later and told her about 'the loveliest people, an Austrian couple – he took me to their house and imagine, they had sausages for afternoon tea!'[17]

Elsie's first impression of Paul was astute: 'I thought him very clever, with a grasp of all things, a quick, keen, but also solid intellect, very sincere, very kindhearted, liking to see people about him happy but also impersonal and difficult to get at.'[18] As they helped her with speeches, Elsie wondered at Bronio and Paul's attention to detail and the trouble they took, how they gave 'everything its due value. . . . Nothing was ignored, however trivial.' On approaching anything new, her fellow countrymen were apt to 'close their minds with a snap'.

At 'Carinya', the hospitable Khuners created a suburban salon – an impoverished antipodean counterpart of Bloomsbury – where a coterie of friends

gathered to enjoy conversation and music. Later they referred to their circle
as 'the Clan'. At its core were the Khuners, Malinowski, Marianne Weigall
and Elsie Masson. (When Hede gave birth to a daughter in 1919 she was
named Elsie Marianne.) The Clan's outer circle comprised Bob Broinowski,
Edward Pitt, Carmen and Pierre Teppema (a Flemish-Dutch diplomat),
Frankel and Henry Schapper (a schoolteacher), Olga Ivanov, Jessie Masson
(a concert pianist) and Leila Peck. In the background was Ivy Forsythe, the
pretty housemaid from whom Malinowski occasionally stole kisses. There
were musical evenings, centred on the Khuners' piano, when Paul played
Beethoven and Schumann duets with Elsie, Jessie dazzled them with César
Franck and Saint-Saëns, or when Carmen Teppema brought her violin and
insisted on playing Sarasate, Paganini and (to Paul's disgust) 'a sprinkling of
Handel'.

More frequent were the conversational evenings at which Malinowski
was in his element, filling the cramped sitting room with his argumenta-
tive exuberance, his outrageous generalizations and coarse humour. The
conversation bubbled wickedly. Contesting received opinions was the main
agenda, and Mim and Elsie were often spellbound by the 'European' flavour
of these events, and sometimes abashed (Mim more so than Elsie) by the
witty savaging of sacred cows. Mim recalled: 'Bronio, a born teacher, began
almost as soon as we knew him, to "improve our minds", telling us girls
that the kind of conversation we indulged in was undisciplined and led
nowhere – we must learn to "formulate" our ideas, he said.' It was a word
he used often.

'Wowser' was another word they bandied about, referring to prudes and
killjoys who assumed the moral high ground. Henry Schapper was a
wowser. He protested at Malinowski's habit of swearing in company, and
Elsie archly suggested that 'perhaps his objection to "bloody" is allied to the
sentiments which make him a vegetarian'.[19] Broinowski, on the other hand,
would swear simply to prove that he was not a wowser. As Paul Khuner
wrote to Malinowski later:

> Poor Bob is horribly scared – probably mainly by you – that he would
> do anything to avoid being called a wowser. . . . He even went so far as
> to write quite a voluptuous sonnet – just to show how this sort of thing
> can be done properly. I can already see a future Privat-docent at
> Melbourne University writing a thesis on BM's influence on Australian
> poetry.[20]

Together Paul and Malinowski generated intellectual heat. Not that they disagreed about many things, rather they relished mental sparring for its own sake. Paul's command of English was the equal of Malinowski's, but they often resorted to other European tongues to conduct their arguments. Mim recalled how Malinowski insisted that 'often an idea can only be really accurately expressed by drawing on the resources of more than one language'.

Malinowski's eroticized friendship with Mim waned during 1917. In the new year they read psychology together – perhaps he was reminded of those times with Żenia – and he attended a few university lectures with her. As he became more and more absorbed by Elsie, he noted that he needed 'less and less' of Mim. She even began to bore him a little, and by the time he was ready to depart for Papua they were 'undoubtedly drifting away' from each other. 'Once or twice Mim makes a faint complaint,' he observed, 'but she really behaves like a true Lady.' Of course, Mim saw their drifting apart rather differently, and later she reproached Malinowski for the way he tried to hide his feelings for Elsie, her oldest friend. It was insulting to their friendship, 'a silly pretence that deceived neither of us'.[21] Unwittingly or not, he had created yet another love triangle.

Elsie and Mim continued to see Paul and Hede Khuner after Malinowski returned to New Guinea. The Massons and the Weigalls, however, disapproved of their daughters' association with the Khuners and never invited the Viennese couple to their homes. Elsie felt sorry for her mother, vainly fighting what she believed to be 'inimical influences', when 'it only has the effect of throwing me more violently into the Khuner-Mim-Malinowski camp'.[22] Hede Khuner felt 'quite touched, thinking of the old Massons . . . yearning for "Home" for more than twenty years . . . somehow ossified in their old English insular traditions'.[23] Recalling the kind of people who got on his nerves ('Prussian officers, religious maniacs, and nut-food cranks'), Paul, too, could feel sorry for the Massons. 'It must be quite dreadful for parents to see their child attached to people they dislike, or, at least, don't approve of.'[24] In the end, Elsie and Mim ceased to mention the Khuners to their families.

Troublesome triangles

While Malinowski was recovering from his first dental operation, Elsie visited him at Grey Street. She found him in bed, sick and deeply despondent, as she recalled. 'You didn't want to be cheered with prophecies false or true, you didn't want to pose about it. . . . You held my hand and looked into my face as I longed to be able to do something. . . . I did pity you so, alone in your room.'[25]

He was not alone for too long, and at Easter he returned to 'Nyora' for a fortnight. He felt much better and read psychology intensively, intending to help Mim through her university course. At 'Nyora' there were 'lots of strangers, great wenches, feasting, dances' and he felt himself 'going downhill' with Cathie Johnson. But looking over the valleys he thought often of Elsie and 'her debut' on Yarra Bank and after his return to Melbourne in mid-April he began to see her more regularly. She remembered:

> You told me about the various complications at Nyora, and we spoke of what 'honour' meant. You disclaimed any sense of moral obligation (I did not believe this), but said you at least would never make love to the wife of a man who was at the front fighting for her.[26]

These were sensitive issues, both personally and politically, and Malinowski was fully alert to them. His own occasional 'resentment and aversion' towards Elsie, and his fluctuating 'Dostoevskian reactions' (as he called them) were fuelled by a third party: Sergeant Charles Adams Matters of the 6th Battalion, killed in action at Lone Pine along with two thousand other ANZAC soldiers and five thousand Turks. Elsie's grief was so visible, Charles's heroic spirit so palpable, that Malinowski was both awed and appalled. It was a triangle with a difference; the ghostly presence of Elsie's dead sweetheart was an obstacle of a kind he had never encountered before. Her mourning not only placed her under taboo, but set her apart as 'sacred'. In a curiously abject projection, Malinowski placed the dead Charles on a pedestal. Contemplation of the heroic image was acutely painful for him, and engendered some of the most poignant passages in his retrospective diary.

After Malinowski's second operation, in which the rest of his teeth were extracted, he went to the Khuners to recuperate. Elsie found him there, his head 'wound up in a rug, saying nothing'.[27] Others would remark on Malinowski's capacity to feel acutely sorry for himself when sick, to dramatize his illness and resort to the most theatrical demonstrations when taking to his bed. Mim remembered:

> When Bronio was ill he would wrap his head in a towel and wander through the Khuners' house groaning extravagantly till the Khuners sent

him to bed in their ever-hospitable spare room. One late afternoon I can remember him appearing in the sitting room in Paul's dressing gown and slippers with a towel around his head, mumbling disconsolately that he had had a bath and was going to get up, but 'these Khuners, they don't even make your bed!'.

His complaint became a standing joke among the Clan.

From June onwards he saw Elsie almost daily. After recovering from his second dental operation he resumed the drafting of his monograph on Kiriwina, and in her spare time Elsie joined him in a small room at the museum, where his papers and notebooks were spread out. She sat by his side, reading his chapters and posing questions about his material: they called it 'Kiriwining'. In return, he helped her to prepare her speeches for the socialists.

Their growing intimacy was proceeding slowly, just as Malinowski wished. They were learning a great deal about each other, 'always hankering after the personal element, but not yielding too easily'. This, he judged, was 'the surest basis for a perfect friendship and a deep love'. He pondered the irony that his friendship with Elsie had begun with his admiration – 'adoration' was the word he used – for Charles's heroic memory. He even experienced vicarious grief and a 'religious respect for suffering'. One of the incidents that awakened Elsie from the lingering stupor of grief was when Malinowski looked directly at her and asked, 'Where is this metaphysical shadow?' Elsie confessed, 'I felt a most peculiar thrill. . . . I didn't think you were in love with me. . . . I thought that by your own confession you were a fickle and wandering Pole. But I *was* disturbed, and it began with that look!' Alone at 'Carinya' one day as they sat reading together, she leaned towards him and rested lightly on his arm. Their first kisses would be etched in his memory. Friday the thirteenth was a day of ill omen for the superstitious streak in him, yet he remembered it was the day that he had first kissed Elsie.

Another 'first kiss' occurred after a concert given by Mrs Ernest Scott on 21 July. It was an occasion that he later used to illustrate the difficulty of selecting what to record in his diary – a problem he also encountered in his ethnography.

By the sea, a cool damp evening; rain clouds hastening across the green waters; ships swinging far away in the mist – the same view, if repeated a thousand times, gives you a thousand different experiences. If repeated in your memory, it gives you also a thousand different associations. – The evening I sit with her on a jetty; the first kiss. What an infinity of feelings is connected with this one memory. The thing is not to lose the facts. To remember all the physical, objective circumstances; the evening; the moon; the smell of the sea. In the course of life we are so strongly limited by the unpredictablity of the psychological happening: a most external detail can stand in the way of the essential insight into the meaning of an experience. As when she suddenly threw her arms around me saying: '*Poor Charles*' and sobbing, and I had just noticed someone approaching.

Elsie remembered this event, too, not analytically, but simply as one of their happiest moments in what was a distressing period. 'We left early, walked by the shore and sat on the little Brighton pier and you kissed me. I was quite ready then; I just felt as if our spirits were melting together. I hardly felt as if we had bodies.' She does not mention sobbing in his arms.

'I still felt troubled,' she told him later. 'I didn't see where we were going; it seemed hopeless, and we helpless.' Convention dictated that they should have been formally engaged before they had begun to kiss passionately.

But it had all come so naturally, I could not feel I was behaving wrongly. At the end of that evening you told me about Adelaide and your intending to visit there. I felt deeply depressed, but of course wanted you to go. I felt all the same as if a farewell had sounded.

On 13 June Malinowski had received a letter from Lady Stirling inviting him to Mt Lofty. Nina was ill with tuberculosis and the family hoped that his visit would cheer her. It was well over two years since they had seen one another, though they had kept up a steady correspondence and a wistful pretence that they were still – albeit unofficially – engaged. Although he was now reluctant to go to Adelaide, it would be an opportunity for him to set matters right.

In April he had 'confessed' to Elsie his confused relationship with Nina, whom Elsie had never met. At the time, she was vaguely understanding: 'a great many men have such entanglements.' In June, however, a second confession had stunned her, though he was still sparing of details. She even suspected wildly that he might be married. For Elsie this was a crisis; something had shifted between them. But she was astonished when he seemed prepared to carry on as if nothing had happened. She thought then that she should give him up: 'it was useless to talk of mere friendship; we would only have been insincere.'[28]

Perceptively, she guessed that he must be having similar doubts about her. 'I still could not think of you and Charles in the same thought, one always excluded the other.' Yet it struck her as strange that Bronio's story and Charles's were similar, though Charles had behaved 'as a man should' with regard to the woman he broke with. But Elsie could no longer persuade herself that she did not love Bronio.

> I realized almost with alarm how much. It wasn't only the delight I had in you as a companion, but I began to love *you*, your ways & voice & touch. . . . I didn't know how much you really loved me; I thought at any moment it might end. So I still clung to my vision of Charles.[29]

It had been in January 1914 that Charles, semi-conscious with typhoid fever, was admitted to the Melbourne hospital. He was one of Elsie's first patients. She nursed him back to health and they fell in love. He proposed to her and then in April 1915 he went off to war, leaving Elsie to feel it had all been a dream. He wrote her long letters from Gallipoli, and then abruptly, in August, the telegram came to say that he was dead.

Little by little, Malinowski had learned that Charles's story was more complicated. In Perth he had been involved with another woman who was reluctant to let him go. After his death the woman claimed that *she* had been engaged to Charles, a claim that added indignation to Elsie's grief. 'What a sordid affair,' her father had commented dismissively. Her mother was more sympathetic, but even she had declared that Elsie's engagement 'should never have happened'.

Malinowski was deeply moved by this latest version of her story. He admired her for the understanding she had shown towards 'the other woman' when they finally met in Perth. Indeed, he loved her the more for her touching confession, though some of the shine had been removed from Charles's saintly image. The picture of him as 'one of those smooth, wholemeal, simplified colonial Englishmen' was no longer quite accurate. But overwhelming his ambivalent feelings was his sheer admiration for Charles. 'He is something very lofty to me, he's my hero,' he noted in his diary. 'So I'd like to keep him on a pedestal.'

'There were times of extreme reaction,' remembered Elsie. 'Reaction' was their word for estrangement, disharmony and mutual irritation. Although due in part to the friction generated by two independent spirits of very different national and family circumstances, such 'reactions' were precipitated by the uneasy awareness that they each had secret pasts. Indeed, they were still being held emotional hostage by others – a sick woman in Malinowski's case and a dead man in Elsie's. As in some *fin-de-siècle* drama, sickness and death haunted the early years of their relationship.

Of his bleak, 'Dostoevskian' moods, Elsie wrote: 'I don't to this day know exactly what they were, except that in some way, mentally or physically, I got on your nerves. . . . I felt you were unstable but you could not help that.'[30] By calling them Dostoevskian he identified them as essentially Slavic. Thin-blooded Britons would not be troubled by such angst. They belonged to a dark side of him that perhaps only Staś Witkiewicz understood, for they also entailed an element of theatrical pose. Reductively, he now tried to explain them to Elsie as a kind of brooding over the intractable contradictions of their respective attachments to Nina and Charles. 'I am certain that all the Dostoyevski [sic] moods were on this basis.' But he did not sound convinced.[31]

The superstitious belief persisted that she was under taboo, and that by making love to her he would be 'trespassing or committing a sacrilege'. He sensed that he could not break the taboo without being punished, that he was perhaps courting 'a nemesis'. On the first occasion that he undressed Elsie in his lodgings he was reminded of this. The gold medallion she wore around her neck had always 'unnerved' him, and during their embrace the chain broke and fell to the floor. After that she did not wear it again. The taboo broken, Charles would be forgotten. 'E.R.M. becomes mine and her past is in the past.'

The test of Adelaide

On 5 August, Elsie went with her mother to a guesthouse in the Dandenongs for a week's holiday. Sherbrooke was renowned for its towering stands of mountain ash and tame lyrebirds. In gentle rain on Yarra Bank the previous evening, Malinowski had held her in his arms and whispered 'sweet Polish names'. He gave her parting gifts of a watch bracelet and expensive chocolates. The letters they exchanged during this brief separation were shyly self-conscious. It was their first sustained correspondence.

With the disclaimer that he did not want her to take them seriously, he sent her some poems. After glancing at them she joked: 'I would like some biographical notes with them. "This was written when the poet was suffering from a bad cold in the head in his 19th year etc." I think I can tell you now that they are better than Mr Broinowski's.' In truth, they were not, as both Malinowski and Mim Weigall knew. Bronio's ponderous versifying was drearily romantic, testimony to a sentimental nostalgia he summoned whenever he picked up his poet's pen. A typical couplet from *Twilight Stimmung*: 'The past lay there forgotten, a thing dead and passed o'er/ With ghosts of joy ill-gotten and loves that count no more.' This four-stanza poem concludes: 'Bathed in the light of dreaming, sunk in the depths of rest/ The present shone redeeming the vainness of life's quest.'

In commenting on Elsie's story about an Indian rajah who was admitted to the snooty Melbourne Club but not to the 'aristocratic' Sydney Club, Malinowski anticipated Groucho Marx's joke about not wanting to belong to any club that would accept him as a member:

> [T]here are worse fools than those who consider themselves exclusive (in a place where everybody's grand-dad might be a convict) and these are those who want to be admitted to a society which kicks them out. So I have as little time for the Rajah as for the hidalgoes [sic] of the Sydney Club.

In this letter he signed himself Bronisław Kasper z Kalnicy Pobóg-Malinowski ('to show that I have blue blood also, though I'd have been blackballed even in the Melbourne Club').[32] Elsie kept up the banter in her own letters. She pictured him 'regarding the couples on Yarra Bank with Nietzschean scorn', and later, how she had glimpsed a man at the library 'with a jaunty step and his head held very far back like B. Malinowski, PhD. (I suppose he was shortsighted and streptococcal)'.[33]

It was the second anniversary of Charles's death, and just as she felt ready to let go of him she feared for Bronio. He was about to go to Adelaide, determined to end the relationship with Nina, but she wondered if instead he might rediscover his love for her. She looked upon the coming encounter 'as a kind of test'. She decided that if things remained the same she must part from him.

His mouth aching with a new set of teeth fitted that very morning, he departed Melbourne on 9 August. The day before he had presented himself to the Victoria Barracks for permission to leave the state. The 'Aliens' form he signed described him as of slight build with light brown hair and a sallow complexion; his height was now recorded as 5 feet 7 inches – four inches shorter than in 1915.[34] He looked with sudden nostalgia through the train window at the Dandenong Range to the east, wishing he was going there, to Elsie, instead of chugging in the opposite direction. He felt as if he was 'approaching a precipice', and indeed, the visit to Mt Lofty augured a moral fall. Nina suspected nothing, continued to trust him and, he surmised, continued to nurture hopes for the future. Hospitable as ever, Lady Stirling treated him graciously, and asked kindly after the Massons. In Sir Edward's library he saw Elsie's book sitting cosily close to his own.

Sensing Nina's fragile condition, he faltered in his resolution. The deception remained, and their correspondence would pursue its false course until the inevitable day when she discovered his betrayal. He had failed Elsie's unspoken 'test', and when he returned to Melbourne on 17 August it was with deep remorse. On their usual seat by the Yarra, Elsie heard his account of what had happened in Adelaide. She remembered: 'when you said things were the same, I felt a sinking of the heart, and almost a sensation of being tricked.' But she accepted his excuse that Nina was too ill to be confronted with the truth: 'We were too much to each other by then, and I had to give in.' A few days later, following an evening together at a Franck symphony concert, he made love to Elsie for the first time. Later she said, 'We were like two people swept together out of a shipwreck, weren't we?'[35]

'Kiriwina', a monograph unborn

Malinowski's health picked up during August. He was taking arsenic and other tonics and by the end of the month felt strong again. He had resumed work, and Leila Peck helped him to finish cataloguing the Trobriand artifacts that he would later present to the Melbourne Museum in Robert Mond's name.

By this time he was telling Elsie: 'my work is absolutely soaked with your personality and when ever I plan something or write something down I find that I am addressing you.'[36] In short, she was fully installed as his muse and well on the way to becoming his amanuensis. She was also his chief editor. While at Sherbrooke, Elsie edited an article of three thousand words that Malinowski had been invited to write for *The Australian Encyclopaedia*. He had toyed with it during the previous months, and had already sent a copy to Seligman who 'touched up the phraseology here and there'.[37] The article, entitled 'The Papuo-Melanesians', was a concise account of

Trobriand ethnology. Elsie read it twice, and sent Malinowski four pages of comments and corrections. These are of interest in showing the nature of her editorial interventions, for they were typical of the commentaries she made on his subsequent writings.

Mindful of his sensitivity to criticism, she conveyed her suggestions with diplomatic touches of humour. Her editorial hand was sure yet subtle; she guided his style, corrected misspellings and malapropisms, and occasionally polished his prose. Tactfully, she praised him before suggesting how he might improve the piece by 'crisper' writing.

> I thought it quite wonderful what a comprehensive idea you had given in such a small space. . . . In writing not meant to be popular, it is much more important of course to get the very exact shade of meaning even if it means making a sentence clumsy than to get finish of style.[38]

In years to come, Malinowski would endeavour to write in a manner both popular and academic. Elsie's advice helped him to strike a balance that would make his writings accessible to lay readers. On this occasion she encouraged him to avoid the passive voice ('pigs are also kept') and she poked gentle fun at his clumsier constructions ('"the ethnologically interested traveller" . . . I am sure Archie [Strong] & others would prefer you to say "the traveller who is interested in ethnology"'). Malinowski made further changes, but the finished article was not published until 1926.[39]

The book on which Malinowski had been working intermittently since mid-1916 was shaping up to be a monumental work – 'of at least a thousand pages', as he told Atlee Hunt. 'KIRIWINA: A Monograph on the Natives of the Trobriand Islands (Robert Mond Ethnographical Research Work in British New Guinea)' was how he styled it in his diary in November 1917.[40] It would contain everything he had learned about the Trobrianders. 'The aim of this work is to give a clear and complete account of a native tribe,' runs the opening sentence – in Elsie's hand – of a late version of chapter 2, entitled 'The Islanders'. It occupied him especially during the 'third epoch' of his stay in Melbourne. As he summarized in his retrospective diary: 'I thoroughly review the materials. Elsie helps me increasingly. I edit almost everything, working by *gusts*.'

Several handwritten synopses survive among his papers.[41] According to the most detailed of these, probably dating from late 1918, the book would consist of eight parts. Following a methodological 'Introduction', six parts were to be devoted to Social Structure (or Sociology), Tribal Life, Economics, Magico-Religious Ideas and Practices, Knowledge, Sorcery and Art, and Language. Part eight would contain five or six bulky appendices, and Malinowski visualized a 'pocket for Documents' attached to the inside back cover. The parts of 'Kiriwina' consisted of many chapters subdivided into sections.

It might seem curious that after writing '*Baloma*' − an innovative, theoretically focused and methodologically alert 'mini-monograph' − Malinowski would be inclined to revert to the model of a conventional ethnographic blockbuster. The synopses promised exhaustive coverage, the fulfilment of a Haddonesque prescription to be comprehensive, down to the last item of recondite technology. Looming over the book's very conception was the long shadow of *Notes and Queries on Anthropology*. No complete manuscript of 'Kiriwina' exists, however, and without the evidence of a full draft criticism is unjustly proleptic. Malinowski himself appeared to believe that his 'Kiriwina' would break fresh ground. When Elsie went to Sherbrooke he sent her Emile Zola's *La Terre*, because, as he awkwardly put it, 'it strikes me as somewhat akin in its tendency to my Kiriwinian efforts'.[42] As she began reading this 'ethnographic' novel about the travails of nineteenth-century French peasantry, Elsie agreed:

> It has a tremendous central idea, and everything expresses this idea, and has a bearing on it. Therefore nothing described seems trivial. . . . The reader is not just presented with a jumble of fact . . . but a philosophy is constantly placed before him. . . . It *is* just the same as in your work, only of course instead of being able to select just what you want, as the novelist can, you must present *all* facts, and then it is much more difficult to give their bearing on the central idea.[43]

While this can well be said of *Argonauts of the Western Pacific*, it is not at all obvious from the synopses of 'Kiriwina' what the 'tremendous central idea' might have been. Unless, like Zola, Malinowski vaguely had in mind the cycle of the seasons, agricultural and human, in thrall to Mother Earth. This, if anything, would become the 'central idea' of *Coral Gardens and their Magic*. Zola had defined his art as 'a corner of nature as seen through a temperament'. His novelistic realism does foreshadow Malinowski's ethnographic realism, while Malinowski's temperament stamped everything he wrote.

Although the proposed format of 'Kiriwina' promised little in the way of innovation, there were at least two exceptional features. First, the methodological introduction was almost certainly meant to be a field-worker's manifesto, a blueprint for the pioneering Introduction that would launch *Argonauts* some years later. A second innovation is suggested by the detailed notes that Malinowski assembled for a capacious appendix entitled 'Black and White'. It reproduced the eight-part structure of the monograph as a whole, as Malinowski revisited every chapter under the aspect of social and cultural changes that colonial contact had brought about in Kiriwina. Although in telegraphic form, there is a great deal more substance in these few dozen pages than Malinowski ever managed to publish on the topic. Anthropological projects of the time were, in Malinowski's words, 'mainly interested in the "real savage" as representative of the Stone Age'.[44] The documentation of post-contact change was not even on the academic agenda. At the end of his last great Trobriand monograph, Malinowski made the rueful admission that this neglect had been 'the most serious shortcoming' of his field research.[45] Although the 'Black and White' appendix, by definition, was not central to the plan of the monograph, the systematic coverage Malinowski meant to give to European impact and native response was, in conception at least, profoundly innovative. It was important, he noted, that changes 'wrought by new conditions' were neither 'ignored nor glossed over'. It was equally important for the ethnographer to state what was 'actually seen to be going on and what [was] reconstructed and how [it was] reconstructed' – not, he added, in the 'underhand' manner of reconstructing defunct customs 'as done by Spencer and Gillen'. His intention was to view changes from several different perspectives: those of the government officer, trader and missionary, as well as that of the native villager. The ethnographer's perspective would be the objective, disinterested one that brought the partial views into synthetic focus. More's the pity, then, that he never realized this aim of writing a systematic account of contact-induced change in Kiriwina.[46]

As if to demonstrate that he had not entirely lost touch with the antiquarian interests of ethnology, Malinowski proposed to precede the 'Black and White' appendix by one devoted to a speculative reconstruction of Trobriand culture as it might have been created by a succession of immigrant Austronesian seafarers. '*Kulturkreise* and History' would attempt to place Trobriand culture in its wider Massim context. The sketchy notes for this appendix, too, were never written up into publishable form, though they are of specialist interest today in the light of recent archaeological investigations on Kiriwina.

The dozen or so months that Malinowski spent laboriously drafting chapters of 'Kiriwina' were not wasted. Ultimately, the incomplete and abandoned monograph was dismembered, its chapters detached from their parts and scattered throughout his papers. They provided pre-digested ethnographic substance for his other books. The more immediate significance of 'Kiriwina' was twofold. Writing it was an extended preparation for his return to the Trobriands. As he worked on it he identified gaps in his material and drew up long lists of questions as well as points that needed elaboration in the text. The greater significance of the draft monograph, however, lay in its role as an explicit guide to the research Malinowski would conduct on his return to the field. Armed with this document and the set of questions it generated he simply had to check facts, test interpretations and fill gaps. With its cut-and-dried categories 'Kiriwina' set limits on what he would investigate; rethinking the entire research agenda was out of the question. To this extent 'Kiriwina', the stillborn monograph, determined the course of his next expedition.

Malinowski had become reconciled to Hubert Murray's insistence that his movements be confined to the Trobriands and nearby islands. The command was liberating in its way, for he was relieved of the obligation to satisfy Seligman and Haddon's oft-repeated wish for him to 'do Rossel'. Instead, he would turn the restriction to advantage and delve deeper into Trobriand life; he would learn to think and feel like a Trobriander. To accomplish this he would need to improve his command of the language, and during his stay in Melbourne he began to sketch a grammar and compile an annotated lexicon of Kiriwinian. He wrote to Seligman for books, and Seligman consulted Sidney Ray, but neither was of much help. 'The fact is we ordinary folk over here are unaccustomed to linguistic prodies [sic],' Seligman told him. 'Ray no doubt knows a great deal about grammar and morphology, but I have been with him in the field, and I know how extremely slow he is at picking up even a few words of a new language.'[47]

According to his own admission, Malinowski 'entirely failed' in this early attempt to analyse the language; it was a 'miscarriage' that led him to 'a good deal of linguistic reading and reflection'.[48] When he returned to the Trobriands he would need only 'a month or two's practice' before he was able to follow conversations easily and take down notes directly in Kiriwinian.[49] He had already discovered the value of vernacular texts, so he would record more and more of them, texts on all and every subject. Here would lie the main achievement of his fieldwork: its depth as well as breadth of coverage and its consummate documentation made possible by mastery of the vernacular.

Reluctant departures

The time for his departure was drawing close. Edward Pitt organized 'a send off', and Malinowski called on Atlee Hunt on 25 September with the assurance that he was sailing from Sydney later that week on the *Marsina*. In truth, he was reluctant to leave Melbourne. Although his health was restored and his troublesome dentures had been fixed for the third and last time, his involvement with Elsie had reached the point where parting from her would be painful. They spent their last evening together and she helped him to pack on his day of departure. Malinowski was distracted, his mind 'on lists and details of the journey', and Elsie was worried about his 'complication of feelings' which made her still uncertain of him.[50]

Elsie, Mim, the Khuners and Leila said goodbye, and he took the train to Sydney on 27 September. Elsie wrote him a loving letter that evening with a postscript: 'I forgot to tell you – be TACTFUL.' But it was a false departure. He had neglected to reserve a berth, and on arrival at Sydney docks he discovered that the *Marsina* was fully booked. On Saturday 29 September, with the joy of a reprieve, he returned to the love and companionship of Melbourne. 'Many happy returns,' Elsie greeted him. To celebrate they went to a Brahms concert with two of the Peck sisters. 'I settle down in Melb. as if I had to live there a lifetime,' he recalled later.[51]

On learning from Baldwin Spencer that Malinowski had missed the boat, Atlee Hunt was displeased. In an icy letter he summoned Malinowski to an interview to explain himself.[52] Once again, there is a sense that this generous official was doing all he could to help an enemy alien whose work he respected, but who was seemingly unaware of how slender was the thread of trust that ensured his liberty. Hunt had struggled to protect Malinowski and secure for him the freedom and funding to continue his research; for his part, Malinowski seemed careless of the privileges he had been granted and ignorant of the degree to which Hunt was compromising his own position by seeking them. At the interview, held on 9 October, Hunt insisted that he secure a berth on the next boat to Port Moresby. The noble Polish anthropologist was in the ludicrous position of being ordered back into the field by an Australian bureaucrat.

Malinowski's extra weeks in Melbourne enabled him to read up on some economics, engage again with members of the Clan and intensify his courtship of Elsie. He spent the late afternoons and early evenings with her before walking her back to the hospital. One happy afternoon they took a tram to Port Melbourne, walked along the shore and marvelled at the sunset. Seeing 'silhouettes of ships misty in the distance', they dreamed of voyaging in a sailing boat to South America. It was 'one of the rare occasions', Malinowski noted, 'when we assume that we are engaged'. He had begun to call her Złotko, 'Gold'.[53]

The week before he was due to leave, he felt 'simply rotten' again and on 16 October consulted Dr Stawell. 'I have made a medical examination of Dr. Malinowski,' Stawell wrote to Hunt. 'I find that he is not well enough to undertake work in New Guinea at present. It seems advisable to me that he should postpone undertaking work until the hot season is over.'[54] This letter is to be found among Malinowski's papers – not Atlee Hunt's – suggesting that he had thought twice about malingering. If Malinowski nursed a secret hope of postponing his departure until the following April, it was Baldwin Spencer who thwarted it. He strongly disapproved of Malinowski's relationship with Elsie Masson and now wished to see the back of him.

The day of departure, 20 October, was a fiasco, though Elsie's word for it was 'nightmare'. To be 'together for the last time', she had gone directly from her night shift to Grey Street. Matron Bell had her own means of surveillance. She had telephoned 'Chanonry' and asked to speak to Elsie. An alarmed Molly Masson said that her daughter was not there, but guessed where she might be. The scandal would be the talk of the hospital for days. It was under the cloud of this 'vulgarizing' row that Malinowski departed for Sydney. At the Massons' and the Spencers' his name would be taboo.[55]

Chapter 23

Samarai

The voyage of the Makambo

Malinowski contemplated 'the majestuous Pacific' crashing onto Sydney's surf beach at Manly. It elevated his soul but made his stomach sink: there was seasickness in store. Infected with Elsie's matter-of-factness, he dealt efficiently with his baggage, cargo and departure procedures. Six men in khaki escorted him aboard, and 'plain cloth men' (sic) inquired if he was carrying any correspondence. The scent of spying was in the air. As he told Elsie, 'you feel that all the ship's crew and stewards and passengers look at each other suspiciously.' (There were dark rumours that the *Matunga*, which had disappeared in August, had been sunk by a German raider.) And as they left the harbour he noted the 'Conradesque contrast between the "last glimpse of civilization"; the crammed storehouses of the Sydney Docks, with their assurances that Buchanan whisky is the best, and the opening seas beyond the heads'.[1]

The *Makambo*, 'a small tub' of 1,159 tons, was short of beam and rolled in the smoothest seas. Malinowski's invocation of Conrad was more appropriate than he knew, for the passage of the *Makambo* up the eastern seaboard of Australia replicated that of the *Otago*, an iron sailing barque that Conrad skippered from Sydney to Mauritius in 1888.[2] As usual, Malinowski was captivated by coastal seascape. It was 'like listening to some music, of which you could not seize the meaning'.[3]

Going ashore at Brisbane on the evening of 25 October 1917, he was ushered from the docks by six marines. He took a cab to the university, where Elton Mayo had invited him to join a seminar on the sociology of religion.

I was unshaven, dirty and very tired so I did not quite feel an ornamental piece, especially as there was four girls and one man only. . . .

[But] I proffered some awful nonsense with utmost composure, sang-froid and self-assurance and Mayo says that I made an impression of great depth on my hearers![4]

As the *Makambo* sailed north on the inside of the Great Barrier Reef, Malinowski was reminded of the myth-imbued coasts of Homer's Greece and he projected onto the mountains of the mainland reclining figures of gods and goddesses. It was no coincidence that he had spent the days on deck composing a belated reply to Sir James Frazer's letter of congratulation on his '*Baloma*' essay.[5] He gave it his best, for he was anxious to convey what an inspiration Frazer had been to his own thinking about ethnographic writing.

> Through the study of your works mainly I have come to realize the paramount importance of vividness and colour in descriptions of native life. . . . In fact I found that the more scenery and 'atmosphere' was given in the account . . . the more convincing and manageable to the imagination was the ethnology of that district. I shall try to give the local colour and describe the nature of the scenery and *mise-en-scène* to the best of my ability.

Malinowski would demonstrate the extent to which he had absorbed this lesson when writing *Argonauts*.

He then presented Frazer with a homely account of his participant-observation method by generalizing his own induction into British society.

> The comprehension of an institution in a foreign country can be measured by an individual's ability to 'live' in that country, that means to fit into its institutions. A foreigner in England, who would not understand the language, the temperament, the current ideas, the tastes and fads of the outlook there, would not be able to live in English institutions: to enjoy their sports and amusements, to fit into English schools and universities, to make himself at home in English social life or take part in English politics. On the other hand, he would never be able to penetrate into the depths of the British mentality, if he kept aloof of the British institutions. The same refers, *mutatis mutandis*, to native society, as far as I can see.

Malinowski's overdrawn analogy was a somewhat patronizing illustration, for he knew that Frazer's first-hand knowledge of contemporary Others was limited to the citizens of France, Italy and Greece. Given his circumstances, the image of the fieldworking anthropologist as a fifth-column spy deploying close surveillance seems apt. If one cannot assume a native identity, one can at least – by learning the foreigners' language and trying to do as they do – understand as much about them as any outsider possibly can. This basic insight, as old as Herodotus, was ignored by current ethnology which, with its natural-history model of specimen collection and 'salvage ethnography', overlooked the intricacies and imponderables of social existence. Malinowski was in the business of rediscovering those intricacies and making them the foundation of a new kind of anthropology, one of everyday, practical concerns. By all means investigate the seemingly bizarre notions underlying magic, for example, but ask also – or rather ask first of all – what magic does to help people earn their living. ('Magic helps those who help themselves,' became one of his memorable *mots*.) Frazer had not even begun to think along these lines. For Malinowski, speculation about the evolution of human thought in a universal framework was less interesting than what people thought in the here and now, and, to pursue the empirical question, the effects of what they thought on what they *did* in the here and now. Thus was he able to develop a fresh approach to primitive economics, one that escaped the straitjacket of postulated evolutionary phases.

With tactful deference, Malinowski continued:

> I am personally most interested in the mental life of the natives, in their beliefs and their ideas of the Universe. But I realise that this can be understood only after the concrete manifestations have been studied. The study of your works, and most especially of *The Golden Bough*, has convinced me of the intimate relationship between magic and religion on the one hand and economic pursuits, such as gardening, fishing and hunting, on the other.[6]

He was committed to 'the psychological method' – though this he derived from Wundt and Westermarck more than he did from Frazer – but he would eventually drop the phrase and disguise his Continental theoretical roots. He would overthrow the old regime: not only Haddon, Rivers, and Elliot Smith, but Divine King Frazer himself. The palace revolution in anthropology fancifully begins with this letter written between Brisbane and Cairns, the pretender to the throne giving covert warning to the incumbent as he resumed his search for the ethnographic riches that would confer upon him the mantle of supreme anthropological authority. Jason would return with his Golden Fleece.

There is an engaging parallel between Malinowski's mythopoeia and a tale told throughout the northern Massim of a Kula hero with a dual identity. Tokosikuna belongs to the island of Digumenu, to the east of the Trobriands. He is crippled and scabrous, so ugly that women shun him. He voyages in search of a fabulous, magical flute that many men have sought in vain. After many adventures and 'through cunning and daring', he succeeds in gaining it. He returns to Digumenu and charms everyone, for he is utterly transformed – now youthful, smooth-skinned and strong. The village chief surrenders his position to him, and women leave their husbands for him. Embarking on a Kula voyage with his rivals, he wins the best shell valuables. The jealous menfolk of Digumenu plot his death, but despite their ruses Tokosikuna seems invincible. Finally, they manage to sink his canoe and maroon him on a coral islet. He swims to the nearby Amphletts, curses his rivals and remains in resentful exile.[7]

The first part of the myth tells of the hero's winning of the flute, his transformation from a diseased and disabled outcast to a resplendent seducer – one of several double-skinned heroes of Massim mythology.[8] The second part tells of his success in Kula exchange against the challenge of his rivals; thus the association between the magic of love and the magic of Kula. The myth's function, as Malinowski perceived it, was to provide a charter for the system of Kula magic that invoked Tokosikuna's name as redolent with power. Besides its Freudian signification (of which Malinowski was not unaware), the magic flute is a symbol of the personal charisma that enabled him to seduce women and woo Kula exchange partners. The devious hero who captures it becomes 'endowed with extraordinary powers, due to his knowledge of magic': just as Malinowski's own extraordinary powers as the charismatic leader of anthropology were due finally to what he called 'the ethnographer's magic, by which he is able to evoke the real spirit of the natives, the true picture of tribal life'.[9] He mirror-wrote this in *Argonauts*, and whether we picture it as a wooden flute or as a Golden Fleece, if there is any single symbol of Malinowski's success it must be his charmed ethnography of the Kula, arguably the most influential monograph in the history of social anthropology. But now, as he sailed for the last time to his 'promised land', success was still uncertain. Like Tokosikuna, he yearned to shed his flawed skin and assume a pure, irresistibly powerful and undivided identity that would enable him to defeat his rivals and win women, wealth and fame.

The odyssey resumed

The first breath of the tropics had greeted Malinowski at Cairns, but Port Moresby was insufferably hot. Following days of 'disgusting seasickness', he told Elsie, he was now ready to curse 'all the damned "protectors" who have been feeling "responsible" for me against all dictates of common sense'.[10] His resentment against Spencer ('Baldy') and Hunt (whom they codenamed 'Nestor' after the platitudinous King of Pylos of the *Iliad*) simmered for weeks. He blamed them for sending him to the tropics in the hottest season; he and Elsie were convinced that one could do only half the work that was possible in the cooler dry season. Besides the threat to his health, he was dismayed at being so abruply parted from Elsie. 'I suddenly realized how happy I'd been,' he told her later, 'especially towards the end, when I tried by hook and by crook to remain in Melbourne.'[11] Incurably nostalgic, whenever he thought of Melbourne it was with 'that Paradise Lost feeling'.[12]

Chief Medical Officer Strong came aboard the *Makambo* as it berthed and accompanied Malinowski ashore. The ship would make a short detour to the west before returning to Port Moresby and sailing east to Samarai. Despite the unpleasant impression Strong made upon him ('apathetic, empty, characteristic tropical paralysis progressiva individualitatis'), Malinowski camped on his verandah.[13] William Strong was a reluctant host: 'he feeds me and helps me in many other ways but I feel that my buoyant and aggressive individuality gets on his nerves.'[14] It is perhaps as well that the collaboration Malinowski had once planned with him did not eventuate. He had written to Strong in April 1916 proposing 'joint work'. Strong had replied positively, suggesting either Binandele (in the Mambare District which Malinowski had failed to reach in 1915) or Sudest Island, the largest of the Louisiades.[15] Sudest was more urgent in view of its depopulation and disappearing customs, but Binandele promised more ethnographic riches. By November 1917, however, all plans for teamwork had long since been abandoned owing to Strong's appointment to the position of chief medical officer. A few months later Malinowski wrote to him from Kiriwina for medical advice. The latter's reply betrays no hint of a quarrel. He suspected that Malinowski was 'suffering only from hypochrondrical symptoms' and was sceptical concerning his fear of hookworm. He offered some gratuitous advice:'I suppose the Trobriands are a rather solitary place; but you should get some exercise every day, also keep the bowels moving properly; and make use of whatever congenial society is available.You will feel much better if you do.'[16] It was a patronizing remedy at best.

Concerning his 'Odyssey in the savage and dangerous island of New Guinea' (as Malinowski teased Elsie), it was initially a matter of checking his provisions and borrowing a new tent from the government. Everywhere he went in the town he was accompanied by her image or, as he would soon refer to it, her double. 'I am constantly seeing you, rowed along in a whaleboat across the harbour, trudging along the dusty, glaring roads, looking with amused yet keen interest at the niggers, and more amusedly at the whites.'[17] One day he made an excursion to Tatana, a Motu village tucked into a corner of the harbour where fine shell discs were manufactured. It was his first spell of fieldwork for almost two years. His old informant Ahuia accompanied him, and it 'was delightful to sail again in a native canoe . . . and hear the monotonous chant of the Motuan sailing song'.[18] Tatana was still traditional in aspect, a pleasing contrast to the modernized tin-roofed and refuse-littered Hanuabada, 'the most miserable village in the Territory'. During the excursion Malinowski talked to Elsie's double in didactic mode and 'formulated things' for her. The imaginary involvement of Elsie in his work ('our common ground') would become a persistent theme of his diary. 'You are following me in all my bodily wanderings and mental excursions,' he told her.[19]

Elsie was not his only imaginary companion, however. About this time he summed up his recent career under the heading 'Scientific Work' and admitted to a broader imagined audience:

> I begin to realize clearly my talent for precisely this kind of work. Ambition is a strong motive for my actions, as well as the drive to form the material and create new facts, to discover new aspects in sociology. . . . The role of E.R.M., Mim W., & Spencer as my audience. Seligman as the main *accomplice during the fact and before*.[20]

A prisoner of conscience

The *Makambo* landed Malinowski at Samarai on Tuesday, 6 November 1917. The picture-postcard island, with its coconut-fringed paths of crushed coral, its heady scents of frangipani, hibiscus and rich red bougainvillea, enchanted him afresh. Once again he was struck by the duplicitous tropical ambience of eastern New Guinea. 'Everything is so radiant and smiling and innocent,' he wrote to Elsie, but behind it he sensed 'hidden evil intentions'.[21] Of Samarai itself he told her: 'It is the contrast between this wonderful little island bathed in light and sea . . . and the miserable existence of the white men absolutely out of harmony with all this.'[22] These were Conradian perceptions of moral ambiguity: the canker in the rose, the evil lurking behind the smiling surface.

Installing himself in the Samarai Hotel, he settled down to wait for a boat to take him to the Trobriands. He was feeling 'strong and efficient' and enjoyed doing the practical things he generally regarded as a waste of time: 'compiling lists, buying, arranging etc.'[23] Yet somehow he contrived to miss a boat leaving for the Trobriands a few days later. Paul Khuner was incredulous: 'You really are a specialist in missing boats, from the sumptuous Burns Philp liners down to the smallest motor launch. How did you manage it this time, being on the spot already some days before the boat left?'[24] Hede suspected it was because she was not there 'to pack, un-pack and re-pack your scattered belongings'.[25]

Now he was waiting for the Auerbach brothers' cutter-rigged launch from Kiriwina. Ted Auerbach waited too, 'marching up and down the verandah, swearing and groaning and looking North for the Ithaca'.[26] Marooned on minuscule Samarai, Malinowski felt captive. In pragmatic mood, he looked upon his temporary imprisonment there 'as inevitable and desirable, provided I use this time to collect myself and prepare for ethnological work'.[27] In metaphysical mood, however, he felt imprisoned within himself and the island came to represent 'imprisonment in existence'. Thrice daily he paced the footpath around the island as a prisoner paces his cell.[28]

After a week he began to feel at home. Breakfast was at eight: 'rice, steak, jam – the usual heavy, peppery sort of tropical breakfast; to spoil your appetite they dump a dozen jars and bottles with chutney, worcester sauce, piccalilly and other horrors in front of you.'[29] His daily routine included taking morning and afternoon tea with the women of the hotel, listening to their gossip and occasionally playing bridge with them. Although he referred to them in his diary by a slightly disparaging Polish term (*baba*), he enjoyed their company while deploring his own predatory behaviour. 'I shower them with compliments and behave in a way that hints at the crudest desire on my part.'[30] He devoted several hours a day to his diaries, current and retrospective. It was a form of meditation. On the day he resumed his daily journal he wrote to Elsie: 'Instead of fretting and killing the time with novel reading and running around talking to windbags, I decided to "concentrate", write up a sort of dairy of my last year in Melb. (at least in vague outline) and get "in order with myself".'[31] During the following weeks he arranged his jottings into the prototype of the synoptic charts that would prove such an important analytical aid to his ethnography.

Elsie shared Malinowski's admiration for Joseph Conrad and was toying with some short stories of her own which she liked to call 'Conradesque'. In his letters Malinowski fed her enthusiasm with anecdotes about the colonial types he met. They had also discussed a tropical travel book that he fancied writing one day, and to this end he was collecting eccentric characters and colourful vignettes. Ted Auerbach was one such character: 'a little whizened [sic] looking fellow, suggestion of a monkey about him; a drunkard, liar, braggart, totally irresponsible and a dirty chap but not necessarily nasty.'[32] Another was Harry Osbourne, a trader from Rossel Island, a small, wiry, foxy man, who 'looks at you with suspicious, bloodshot eyes, you are sure he was drunk the night before. *De facto*, a theosophist; every day stands motionless watching the rising sun; vegetarian; believes that natives possess mystical knowledge.'[33] Malinowski's sketches of Melanesians are pallid and clichéd by comparison. He interrogated Osbourne's 'boys' and learned enough about Rossel Island to whet his ethnographic appetite (though he found Rossel phonemes formidably difficult). 'I liked the look and manner of these boys very much: serious, not cheeky, yet not morose, attentive and intelligent.'[34]

During his weeks in Samarai Malinowski devoted far more time to his diaries, current and retrospective, than he did to ethnology; indeed, he devoted more time to the crafting of turtleshell combs than to ethnology. This was a wholly unexpected preoccupation for one who had shown so little interest or talent in handiwork of any kind. It was as improbable as if he had taken up tennis. Yet this self-confessed clumsy and impractical man became intoxicated with his own artistic success at working the thin, translucent shell: so delighted and astonished that he coined a mongrel word for it: *szyldkretomania* ('turtleshell mania').[35] The incentive, he told Elsie, was her habit of losing combs. He had watched a certain Mr Smith carve turtleshell and was inspired to copy him. Soon he had made a paperknife for Paul and a shoehorn for Hede; then he began to carve combs for Elsie. With Smith he planned to launch 'a new Papuan style' and scurried from store to store seeking the best bargain for raw turtleshell. Proud of his combs, he went around showing them to people like a child with a new toy.

If Elsie was constantly in his mind as he worked on the combs, Nina was there too, for he had discovered the private pleasure of a handicraft and finding 'that *joy of small things*, just as she, poor girl, used to'.[36] Whatever the subconscious significance of this displacement activity, it paid an ethnographic dividend by sharpening his appreciation of Massim carving – the elegant, curvilinear style that had been described by the indefatigable Haddon before the turn of the century.[37] On a visit to Rogea, Malinowski noted that his scientific and artistic interests coincided as he sketched the carvings on the washboards of seagoing canoes. Later he incorporated some of these motifs into the combs and hairpins that he sent to Elsie. 'I think I shall have to dress up to them,' she teased him. 'They are slightly above my station.' She would treasure them for many years and her daughters remember them clearly. The combs seemed to symbolize Malinowski's determination to win and to be worthy of her.

Diaries

As do isolated prisoners who are granted the means, Malinowski communed with his diary and confronted his divided nature. He devised an epigraph for this latest of his diaries. On the inside front cover of the black notebook he inscribed 'A diary in the strict sense of the term', and immediately beneath 'Day by day without exception I shall record the events of my life in chronological order. – Every day an account of the preceding: a mirror of the events, a moral evaluation, location of the mainsprings of my life, a plan for the next day.' And beneath that: 'The over-all plan depends above all on my state of health. At present, if I am strong enough, I must devote myself to my work, to being faithful to my fiancée, and to the goal of adding depth to my life as well as to my work.' So begins the notorious diary that – lightly censored and published by his widow, Valetta, in an English translation twenty-four years after his death – scandalized his friends and pupils.

The first entry is dated 'Samarai 10.11.17'.[38] Familiar moral exhortations punctuate the pages that follow. First the ledger listing the sins, then the judgments. Sexual temptations were highest on the list. They were to be found both at the hospital, where the matron was 'an attractive dish', and at the hotel, which Mrs Kate Young's daughters helped to run. The eldest was Mrs Flora Gofton, two years Malinowski's junior. With the death of her husband in France she was about to become Samarai's merry widow. On the opening page of his diary Malinowski had three peccadillos to confess: he had 'mentally caressed' the matron; he had had 'lecherous thoughts' about Leila Peck; and he had made up to Flo Gofton ('I fondled her and undressed her in my mind, and I calculated how long it would take me to get her into bed'). 'In short,' he wrote, 'I betrayed Złotko [Elsie] in my mind.' He gave himself a minus for these lapses, which offset the plus he allowed himself for not reading novels.

There was also 'a disastrous tendency' to punish with imaginary humiliations those 'rascals' who had thwarted or pestered him, especially Spencer, Murray, Strong, the Burns Philp manager, and resident magistrates Campbell and Higginson. He recognized that this was a ridiculous form of mental revenge and resolved to stop it.[39] And, of course, there was the lapse of concentration caused by 'slackness', by being too relaxed and inattentive. Self-dispersal was the main enemy, for it brought with it an inner emptiness, as on the previous afternoon when he hadn't known what to do with himself. As before, the diary was an instrument of self-discipline, a means of bringing his 'moral anarchy' under control and of integrating himself. Self-reflection brought his failings into stark relief, however, and writing the diary induced an urge to confess to Elsie his 'deepest' experiences. His 'primordial feeling' for her had an unmistakably religious tinge: 'my deep faith in her, my belief that she has treasures to give and the miraculous power to absolve sins.'[40]

'Writing a retrospective diary suggests many reflections,' Malinowski wrote on 13 November, 'a diary is a "history" of events which are entirely accessible to the observer, and yet writing a diary requires profound knowledge and thorough training . . . we cannot speak of objectively existing facts: theory creates facts. Consequently, there is no such thing as "history" as an independent science.'[41] It was a preliminary formulation of his conception of history as a 'charter' that serves present purposes. Historical facts do not exist without a theory by which to perceive them. He had argued similarly in his '*Baloma*' article the previous year, and it would become a cornerstone of his mature functionalism. So too, of course, would be his epistemological suspicion of history. The essence of a diary 'is a look into the past, a deeper conception of life'.[42] Keeping such a diary was in itself a creative act, for 'training the understanding of the daily passage of life through the diary changes the technique of living'.[43]

He drew up a chronology of his acquaintance with Elsie. The 'facts' of this personal history were defined by his feelings for her in the present. As he told her later:

> A diary means simply recording the dates of happenings, their outward shape, some sign by which the corresponding pieces of life can be brought back to memory. When you read it again, it is not what you have written that surges in your memory but complex visions of what you have lived through at that time, and many other associations. If I had written a diary at the time I saw you for the first time in the street, near the Town Hall, I would simply have noted: 'a slight looking girl in blue, with fair hair' and a few antecedent and following happenings. And now re-reading it I would see that moment shine and iridesce with all the colours of the over-rich future it was to beget.[44]

Why did Malinowski think of his diary and his ethnography as 'well nigh as complementary as complementary can be'?[45] As texts they could scarcely be more different in character: one profoundly subjective, the other aspiring to be objective. Both documents comprise descriptions: one of a fractious ensemble of inner selves, the other of an alien 'primitive' society. But by means of introspection Malinowski described himself as objectively as he could (therein lies the astonishing frankness and confessional honesty of his diaries) – as if he were an alien being whom he was dedicated to interrogate and understand. Conversely, he believed that if he could write about the Trobrianders 'from the inside', an intimate ethnography would be created, one that revealed the psychological mainsprings of their culture. This he would later claim to have done in his monographs, despite the yawning gulf that remained between private confessional diaries and public scientific ethnography.

The issue of the diary was becoming doubly reflexive. Not only was he piecing together a retrospective diary of his period in Melbourne, but also 'deepening' the journal of his Samarai existence. At the same time, he urged Elsie to write a retrospective of the period since she had met him – an intimate chronicle of their relationship – as well as a diary-letter of her current activities and feelings. His plan was for them to exchange their diaries. Not entirely, however, for his was in Polish and inaccessible to her. ('Why did you go into Polish, into that strange land where I can't follow you?' she asked.)[46] Instead he would write abridgments of his daily journal and include them in his letters — as he appears to have done for his previous lovers. But the exercise was constrained by self-censorship and the entries became so abbreviated that they left little space for subjective explorations. His appetite for 'the examined life' was insatiable, however, and he urged Elsie to tell him everything, and not to skimp on the details of her existence.

> There are different layers in the things we do, life flows in different currents and though the deepest stream matters most and I would like you always to try to give me the trend of your innermost feelings and your real metaphysical life, the ripple on the surface will also interest me always.[47]

Recalling his 'Nietzschean period', he told Elsie of his belief in the value of diaries as a secular substitute for the Roman Catholic 'retreat'. 'After all, if religion has any good in it, it consists in compelling people to deeper reflection over themselves and to pauses in everyday life. This would be an enormous boon to the human soul, if it led to a *free* exam. of conscience.'[48] He admitted there was some danger in keeping diaries, however. 'They naturally tend to interfere with the normal technique of life: to develop autoanalysis, constant criticism of oneself, constant shifting of values.'[49] His own self-analysis was sometimes so extreme as to be pathological:

> Not only do I always try to get at the lining of the very underneath, to ransack the obscurest nooks and corners of instinct and motive and subconscious reaction, but in this very process I have got a tendency to morbid exaggeration. . . . There is a craving in me for the abnormal, the sensational, the queer, and my imagination (with a slight admixture of pose perhaps) runs always that way. I am always likely to suspect people, to imagine dreadful possibilities, to suffer from a mania of persecution. This hangs together with my poor health and especially with my bad nerves. . . . When I am feeling quite strong and fit, all this vanishes almost completely.[50]

Auto-eroticism had sinful overtones for him; his ironic codeword for masturbation was 'Bible'. When he succumbed to temptation he sometimes excused himself by citing physiological factors: having eaten too much spicy food or feeling unwell. Except for what he termed a 'heaviness in the head and body – the *tropical increase in specific gravity*', during his weeks in Samarai he felt in good health.[51] But a feverish spell lasting a few days led to 'moral collapse' and 'attacks of lecherousness'. His description of this negative state is revealing for what he conceived to be its opposite: the health that he sought throughout his life. The symptoms he lists are often psychological rather than physical. For Malinowski, just as thought and emotion were inseparable, so too were mental and bodily maladies. 'Indifferent, tired, feverish, almost without emotional tonus'; again, 'physical and mental sluggishness', irritability, 'weak grasp of reality; shallow associations or absence of thoughts; total absence of metaphysical states'.[52] To counter these tendencies he uttered a philosophical mantra: 'To submerge myself in the deeper metaphysical stream of life, where you are not swept by undercurrents or tossed about by the waves. . . . There I am myself, I possess myself, I am free.' On this occasion the mantra was ineffective: he drowned in 'a lewd excess of the imagination and adulterous lusts' and fantasized luridly of gentle deflowerings.[53]

Recalling his Dostoevskian moods in Melbourne, he ventured a somewhat different interpretation than previously, one that placed Elsie in the double bind of a double standard:

> By contracting a personal relation with me, she lost the charm of absolute loyalty, as well as the charm of something inaccessible and objective. On the other hand, so suddenly did she stand in front of me as a lover that I wasn't ready to desire her enough when I had her.[54]

Poor Elsie slipped from the pedestal he had placed her upon. The romantic in him had wanted her to remain under taboo, a paragon of virginal virtue and unbending loyalty to the memory of a dead man.

Doubles

Malinowski spent much time in his hotel bedroom during these weeks, writing his diaries. From his verandah there was a fine view of the bay and its boats, the island of Sariba and the passage northwards – his 'gate to the field'. As he wrote, his image stared back at him from the dressing-table mirror. His routine was shared by Elsie's double, who lived in his heart. He was aware of the risk of idealizing the beloved in this way, 'because the "double" is bound to differ more and more from the original as time goes on'. But he respected Elsie's strong individuality, and was sure that he was not projecting his own image 'onto some psychologically formless space, into a purely passive, receptive mentality'.[55]

'I am already jealous of that Double,' Elsie replied, making light of what he took so solemnly. 'Do be careful of her. I am sure she is a Cat. Don't let her turn you against the real me.' And later she wondered 'if the Double is prettier or plainer than I. Prettier I suppose, the little brute.' Although she communed with the double he had left behind in Melbourne, 'he isn't as nice as the real you', and 'when letters from the real Bronio come, I find he is better than his Double in every way.'[56] She was beginning to realize that temperamentally she was a happier and more optimistic person than her 'dear pernicious Pole'. She lived more in the moment, for 'what is the use of only tasting happiness in retrospect?'[57]

The imaginary doubles of which they wrote were projections of passionate longing, nourished by a rich diet of love letters. The duality Malinowski experienced though was an internal phenomenon. 'It is as if we harboured in ourselves a double personality,' he had written to Elsie with Nina guiltily in mind.[58] Now he promoted the moralistic, monogamous self who wanted to be faithful to Elsie in thought as well as deed, against the amoral, lecherous self who 'mentally undressed' and sometimes even 'pawed' every attractive woman who crossed his path. Re-reading his letters to her he could see that she would never suspect him of such duplicity, so he decided to tell her. He wanted to edge their love into deeper waters, expose to her *his* double, by confessing all his doubts, antipathies and 'emotional low tides'.[59] There was hubris in this urge to confess, as if he also wanted to impress her with the heroic effort it was costing him to remain faithful. These were dangerous waters indeed, and he recklessly presumed upon the unconditional nature of Elsie's love.

He was still composing a confessional letter on the day he left Samarai.[60] He referred to 'strong returns in memory to some former experiences' and admitted, 'I also had some temptations out here: not brown skins of course.' Without naming her, he described Flo Gofton as 'very fine', though 'just beginning to be on the descending line', and 'coarsened and banalized in these [colonial] conditions'. He hastened to add: 'I did not make any advances, but I could not help admiring her and thinking what a pity it is that she is wasted.'[61] He mentioned no other lapses of erotic fantasy, and was silent about Nina and Leila. Ideally, of course, there would be 'no other woman at all' to whom he might feel attracted – nor any other man for Elsie – but he also felt that 'we both have too much imagination and too much novelistic curiosity and too intense human interests'. While he thought it was unfair to her that he had had 'so much more previous "life" there is a difference in a man and a woman in this respect and chastity can perhaps be regained by a man to a certain extent'.[62]

On 25 November Elsie went into hospital to have her tonsils removed, so it was perhaps as well that Malinowski's letter did not reach her until late in December. She was hurt and dismayed by his confession. In her reply she ignored the explicit double standard, but explained how insecure in his love she now felt. It had not occurred to her that it would be possible for him 'to return in mind to other attachments'. 'I'm not satisfied with not giving you everything. . . . I don't want any artificial faithfulness, but somehow I miss the feeling I had with Charles of an absolute haven of safety. I feel as if I might suddenly find myself adrift. It frightens me.' She had formulated the thought, if indistinctly, that marrying Malinowski would entail a risk.

> I feel that if I do not represent for you the physical ideal, there is danger in that for the future. And now of all times would be the time I would fill your mind to the exclusion of others. If I do not do it then there is some fundamental reason. Then I begin to wonder if perhaps your falling in love with me was mainly due to the fact that to be in love is almost a necessity for you, and that I was the most available and the most suited to you.[63]

If Malinowski responded directly to these misgivings, the letter has not survived. His diary continued to affirm his intense love for her and he thought about her 'with tenderness, deep friendship, and passion'. As he read her letters her personality filled him 'with music'. And if he did wonder occasionally whether she was the 'complete woman' for him, he kept such doubts to himself.[64]

On 21 November, Governor Murray and his nephew, Leonard Murray, made a sudden appearance in Samarai. Malinowski's immediate impulse was to hide from them. There had been talk on the island about the case of the pearl trader C. A. Verebelyi, a British subject of Hungarian origin who had previously worked in the Trobriands. On the basis of a secret denunciation Murray had denied him a permit to leave Samarai and he was effectively imprisoned there for the duration of the war.[65] To Malinowski, Verebelyi's fate was a discomforting reminder of the tenuous nature of his own freedom.

Although Murray greeted him with civility the following day, Malinowski's nervousness must have showed. 'I spoke too fast, and arrogantly. I was not myself. I had no *dignity*. Too chummy. He didn't mention my work or anything serious, except for my health.' Leonard Murray was 'almost flattering' about his work, however, and in return Malinowski fed him compliments about Australia. He was relieved by Leonard's amiability. It removed 'unpleasant personal tension' and offered some hope that he would be granted an extension of his residence permit. In his letters to Seligman and Frazer written aboard the *Makambo* he had informed them of this possibility, hoping they would use their influence to gain him an extra six months in Papua.

For his part, Hubert Murray continued to suspect that Malinowski was a pro-German pederast, though it was clear that he had no proof. As he admitted to his sister-in-law, May Murray: 'My objection to him is partly unreasoning (I can not stay in the same room with him) and partly because he is suspected of introducing habits – or at any rate of being likely to introduce habits – among the natives which they are very much better without.'[66] Fortunately, this poisonous innuendo did not stand in the way of Malinowski's later friendship with May's husband, Gilbert Murray.

Another acquaintance renewed during his last week in Samarai was Will Saville, the missionary from Mailu. Malinowski had not seen him since December 1914, when their parting had been distinctly cool. Now there was 'obvious embarrassment and exaggerated politeness on both sides'. After exchanging guarded apologies for their earlier behaviour, they discussed Malinowski's report on the Mailu ('I depreciated it, he praised it, not too sincerely'). Malinowski then accompanied Saville and his wife to Kwatou, and even laid plans for further collaboration on Mailu ethnography. But their reconstructed relationship fell apart the very next day. While discussing the war, Saville remarked tactlessly: '*I wonder that you haven't been interned.*' Malinowski replied 'fairly sharply' and released a torrent of invective in his diary against the contemptible 'petty greengrocer'.[67] Relations between them would not be resumed until Saville attended the London School of Economics in 1924.

'Signing on'

Although he conducted some desultory fieldwork while in Samarai, working through 'vile' pidgin English, Malinowski's heart wasn't in it. The limbo of waiting for 'something to happen' while poised on the threshold of the real theatre of action was unconducive to research. He picked up scraps of information on Kula from itinerant natives, but for the most part he shunned them. 'The half-civilized native loitering in Samarai is to me something a priori repulsive and uninteresting; I don't feel the slightest urge to work on them.'[68] Still, he gathered information on the regional extent of Kula, which in the light of his previous knowledge was 'quite usable'.[69]

He visited the adjacent island of Rogea for a couple of days' work on canoes. There was a magnificent specimen from Woodlark Island, which he measured, sketched and photographed; but he was unimpressed by the 'characterlessness' of the local villages and did not intend to wait around for the *toreha* pig feast that was being planned. He noted his apathy concerning the 'thanklessness of such sporadic work'. Another day he hired a launch to take him to Sariba. Sitting on a house platform he had that 'feeling of disorientation' that assailed him in any 'new, unfamiliar place among natives'. The village scene stimulated him, but he felt frustrated by the shortness of the visit. Productive ethnography needed time.

His immediate objective in going to Sariba was to recruit a man to serve as his 'butler, cook, and personal attendant'. Derusira had been recommended by Ted Auerbach as 'a Samarai boy of a fair degree of civilization'.[70] Nicknamed Ginger for his mop of reddish hair and golden-brown skin, he spoke adequate Kiriwinian though his pidgin English was poor. A *so'i* feast was in preparation, however, and Ginger was reluctant to leave home. Malinowski bargained with him and eventually persuaded him to 'sign on' for fifteen shillings a month. The incident caused him to wonder:

> What is the deepest essence of my investigations? To discover what are his [the native's] main passions, the motives of his conduct, his aims? (Why does a boy *'sign on'*? Is every *boy*, after some time, ready to *'sign off'*?) His essential, deepest way of thinking. At this point we are confronted with our own problems: What is essential in ourselves?[71]

To this fundamental question, which in various guises echoes throughout his diaries with their Freudian and Machian subtexts, Malinowski had no concise or final answer, though it surely entailed a combination of love and labour, sex and work, which he took to be universal human motivations.[72]

The possibility of his own 'signing on' for an additional six months' field-work was worrying him at the time. He was weighing work and ambition against love and happiness: he could satisfy both sets of needs only by deferred gratification. On 26 December he submitted a formal request for an extension to Atlee Hunt and Herbert Champion, the government sec-retary, explaining that the delays caused by his ill-health, by the exigencies of the wet season, by missing the important seasonal activities that took place in Kiriwina between August and October, would make it impossible for him to complete his work by April. In view of his fragile health, too, he was anxious about the prospect of leaving a Papuan summer for a Melbourne winter.[73] As he formulated it to Elsie, he was 'philosophical' as to the outcome of his application:

> If they don't grant it, it will be . . . a damned pity, but after all I'll be able to go quickly over the material & thus I'll avoid making any glaring errors. And personally I shall be damned glad to be back in Melbourne six months sooner (you understand the equation is Philosophical Equa-nimity = damned glad in instinctive & emotional wishes + damned sorry in ambition and intellectual schemes). But fairly indifferent I feel as to the issue. On the whole, I reckon they will grant it to me.[74]

And so they did. On Hunt's recommendation, the minister ignored Murray's contrary advice and gave his approval.[75] Insofar as Malinowski's fieldwork achievement was cumulative and contingent rather than strategically planned, the extra six months (five as it happened) were crucial for the quantity and quality of his field data.

Although she was disappointed that Bronio would not be returning in April, Elsie accepted his decision. Her limbo was more prolonged than his. 'I just feel as if I were in a state of waiting, and everything is suspended,' she wrote to him on 3 December, 'the kind of life I am leading now isn't life at all really; it seems to be just a getting through the time.'[76] She con-ceded that his work took priority over her own. It formed 'the link in the chain of the various phases' of their evolving relationship and nourished their mental affinity. Still, the issue touched upon her independence and what nowadays would be called her feminist convictions, and she responded sharply to his crudely expressed desire that she abandon suffragette prin-ciples. 'I hope darling,' he had written, 'you will never feel a suffragette again in your inmost heart. Why force a begrudged equality upon the male and never be accepted into real comradeship on these terms, when you can be his mate and more than equal on the terms of mutual inequality?'[77]

She replied with a rhetorical question of her own:

> Why must it be suffragette versus woman? Of course I do not think the sexes are equal. I feel more strongly than I did that sex affects psychology profoundly, and as the sexes are, leads to a kind of inequality in which perhaps the man must play a dominating part in some things. But I don't regard the vote as anything to do with this. It seems almost a technicality.

If women could be educated to the level of men, it was illogical to prevent them from using their qualifications at Oxbridge, for example, or at the Bar. 'On these practical grounds I shall always be a suffragette,' she wrote.[78]

Released from his captivity on Samarai, Malinowski sailed with Ted Auerbach aboard the *Ithaca* (or *Itaka*) late in the evening of 29 November. It was a voyage that he would retrace in his romantic description of the Dobu district in *Argonauts*.[79] Mick 'the Greek' George, the original owner of the *Ithaca*, had nostalgically named it after the island of his birth. When Malinowski awoke at daybreak the cutter was off East Cape and he could now see Bwebweso, the Land of the Dead, a sinister bare mountain that crouches darkly on Normanby Island. The landscapes and seascapes of the Massim are 'impregnated with legendary meaning', and this insular reach of the Solomon Sea is as richly populated with supernatural beings as the Aegean. He would write in *Argonauts*: 'What was a mere rock, now becomes a personality; what was a speck on the horizon becomes a beacon, hallowed by romantic association with heroes; a meaningless configuration of landscape acquires a significance, obscure, no doubt, but full of intense emotion.'[80]

Entering Dawson Strait, he sketched the silhouettes of the mountainous islands of the D'Entrecasteaux. The populous Dobu district is 'studded with spots of special, mythological interest'; it is 'the land and sea where the magically inspired sailors and heroes of the dim past performed feats of daring and power'. Next day they sailed up the eastern coast of Fergusson, past the island of Sanaroa where two black rocks stand, the brothers Atu'a'ine and Aturamo'a, and a little way off, their sister Sinatemubadiye'i who lost her comb.[81] On they sailed, past the rocky island of Tewara where the petrified figure of Kasabwaibwaireta, another skin-changing Kula hero, stands poised to dive for Muyuwa. They sailed on beneath the majestic twin peaks of Koyatabu (or Oya Tabu, 'Taboo Mountain'), on towards the domes, pagodas and pyramidal forms of the Amphlett Islands. In the late afternoon, the *Ithaca* anchored at Gumasila, where resentful Tokosikuna cursed his enemies and turned himself to stone.

Malinowski was enraptured by the picturesque forms of the Amphletts. He prepared to go ashore to inspect and photograph the 'little grey, pinkish huts' and the stone walls that protected them from the tides. Anthropologically speaking, these tiny rugged islands were virgin territory, and it was with this in mind that he inscribed in his diary: 'Feeling of ownership: It is I who will describe them or "create" them.'[82] The secondary myth that many commentators have elaborated about this proprietorial, even imperialistic claim assumes that he was referring to Kiriwina, which in a sense he did 'create' for succeeding generations of anthropologists through his Trobriand ethnography. But the narrower fact is that this claim referred only to the Amphletts, which he intended to study in the near future.

As they sailed through rain squalls towards Kiriwina, Malinowski swaddled himself in the canvas of a sail and dozed – dreaming perchance of the heroes of Kula, or of Tokosikuna's Greek cousin, Jason, sailing to Colchis with his Argonauts to seize the Golden Fleece. Soon the waters of the vast lagoon turned deep green and 'the subtle thin line of the horizon' broke up, growing thicker 'as though drawn with a blunt pencil'.[83] The line resolved itself into several low grey-green coral islands whose shimmering palms seemed to grow directly out of the water. George Auerbach, in yellow shirt and khaki trousers, greeted him as he stepped ashore at Sinaketa. His exile was over, he was home – back among the traders.

Chapter 24

Return to the Islands

The traders' Trobriands

At the Auerbachs' plantation, Gomaya greeted him and cadged tobacco. Observing that his dog-faced friend's feelings for him were − not unlike his own − 'utilitarian rather than sentimental,' Malinowski interrogated him for news. After an absence of twenty-one months he was keen to pick up the threads of recent events. Returning to the islands was like revisiting a dreamscape, for during his months of sickness he had despaired of resuming fieldwork. As he told Elsie later, 'I believed that I should never see Kiriwina again, nor did I want very much to go.'[1]

The *Ithaca* ferried him across the familiar green lagoon to Losuia, where he reported to Assistant Resident Magistrate Campbell. 'Old 30 percent' seemed less loathsome than before. Still, aware of his supreme authority in the islands, Malinowski was nervous. Billy Hancock's other nickname for Campbell was 'PC 49' − a Londoner's joke. It was a year since Billy had written to the Doctor in Melbourne, imploring him to make his headquarters at Gusaweta on his return, so it was to Billy's place that Malinowski sailed from Losuia.[2] He spent a week there, sorting out his gear and trying to readjust to the strangeness of Kiriwina. He became reacquainted with Billy and his nasal cockney voice. In Australia, Billy had worked on railways, in mines and stores; in Papua he had made and lost money on the Mambare goldfields before building up his pearling business at Gusaweta. He consolidated this by marrying the daughter by a village woman of another lagoon trader, Mick George. 'I always keep in mind Bill's basic problem,' Malinowski noted, 'his marriage with Marianna; his love for their children. He treats Marianna as a native, stressing her bronze complexion. . . . I thought that this was perhaps very clever on his part, that he expected the worst.'[3]

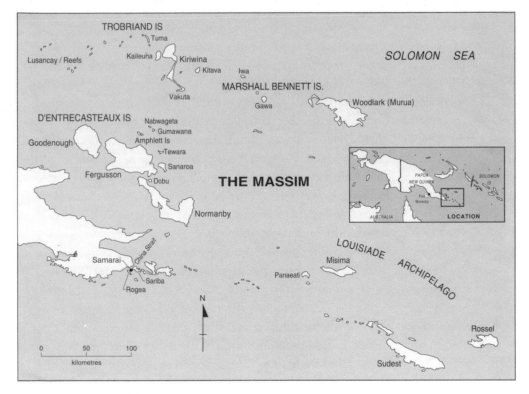

Map 4   The islands of the Massim.

Reluctant to begin work, Malinowski was overcome by 'emotional lethargy'. He dosed himself with quinine and calomel and sought distraction in trashy novels. 'During the first few days I was most disgustingly absorbed with myself,' he confessed to Elsie. On the fourth day he forced himself to visit the nearby village of Tukwaukwa, though he 'couldn't imagine' what he would do there. He struck up a conversation, however, and was soon surrounded by a chattering group. At his instigation an old woman began to recite a ribald folktale; others interjected with indecent jokes and 'the whole village roared with laughter'. Malinowski felt 'a bit vulgar', but at least it was a start.[4]

Next day he examined some fishnets and took notes on fishing techniques, dismayed to realize that his previous information had been inadequate, for it was now too late to supplement the short article he had already submitted to the Royal Anthropological Institute's journal *Man*. The 'feeling of absurdity' that had dogged him since his arrival began to fade, though it was disconcerting to learn that the Teyava villagers were speculating about his identity – was he the same *dimdim* who came before, or his brother?

On his last day at Gusaweta he was granted a stroke of ethnographic luck. Teyava held a *wasi*, a ceremonial exchange of fish for taro, which he observed closely and photographed. Later Billy 'corrected and supplemented' his notes.[5] Billy helped Malinowski a great deal on this final field trip, and his presence on Kiriwina was perhaps the most striking good fortune of all. Not only did he shelter the native-surfeited ethnographer for weeks on end and provide the setting for those 'Capuan days' when they drank beer together and talked about (if not indulged in) the spicy pleasures of whoring; not only did he serve as Malinowski's agent, storeman and packer in acquiring and safeguarding 'curios'; not only did he provide a mail service and free passage on his cutter; but when the Doctor was settled in Oburaku, Billy regularly supplied him with fresh eggs and milk, home-baked bread, bags of betel nut and stick tobacco. Again, not only did Billy proffer technical advice and provide darkroom facilities for the photography that Malinowski pursued so conscientiously yet with so little enjoyment, but had it not been for Billy there would be few if any photo-graphs of the ethnographer at work in the Trobriands. Those classic shots that ornament the monographs were Billy's work: an imperiously posed Malinowski with the bewigged sorcerer Togugua; a squatting, pith-helmeted Malinowski observing children at play; a gaitered, white-attired Malinowski sitting with his aristocratic Tabalu friends, dangling a priceless *soulava* from his wrist.[6] Such images illustrated the methodological principle of participant observation and they were worth pages of text. For such services and 'many acts of friendship' Malinowski acknowledged Billy in *Argonauts* and again in *The Sexual Life of Savages* as 'a trader of exceptional intelligence and one of the finest men I have known'.[7]

Not least, of course, Billy shared with Malinowski the ethnographic observations he had made over many years in Kiriwina. Yet it was another pearl trader, Raphael Brudo, who later put to paper an account of his own amateurish forays into Trobriand ethnography. Raphael and his Parisian wife, Simone, had been in the Trobriands for several years, Raphael having come to work the other side of the lagoon as Sam Brudo's partner. 'The trader is one who lives closest to the life of the native,' wrote Raphael. 'Obliged by his work to speak the language of the neighbouring villages . . . he would be without doubt in the best position to undertake their ethnography.' It was an illusory expectation, however, for even the best-intentioned trader lacked the training to pursue ethnographic studies, and in time he succumbed to the 'habitual lassitude' of the tropics. Nor was the government official any better placed to do ethnography, for he 'represents the authority which inflicts fines and terms of imprisonment, and in his case, more than any other, it would be difficult for him to know the native because the latter must always humble himself before him'. For these reasons, Brudo concluded, 'so many details had escaped observation in the Trobriand Islands until Dr. Malinowski came along'.[8]

Malinowski would loftily denigrate the other white residents who were 'for the most part, naturally enough, full of the biassed and pre-judged opinions inevitable in the average practical man, whether administrator, missionary, or trader, yet so strongly repulsive to a mind after the objective, scientific view of things'.[9] (He was prepared to make 'delightful exceptions' of Billy Hancock, Raphael Brudo and the Rev. Gilmour.) These views were for public consumption and presumed a readership sympathetic to the aims of anthropology; but there were other reasons why Malinowski felt uncomfortable in the company of his own kind, despite the 'solidarity of identity' based on a common European heritage. As he explained to Elsie, he oscillated between the two worlds of the 'official' whites and the natives. The government officers represented 'red tape, lack of imagination, abuse of power, banalization of opportunities', the missionaries 'wowserism, inherent falsehood about main aims in life' and 'nefarious influence over the natives'. White company was also a distraction and a drain on his precious energy. 'Tropical non-sociability' was a phrase he used to excuse his resentful response whenever whites appeared at the door of his tent: 'purely and simply, it annoyed me to have other white men about, especially in "my" place.'[10] 'I go to these people out of my purely brown company, with the impulse of something happening, of being moved out of my inertia. And I run away from them, because they have "rubbed me the wrong way".'[11]

If the native was 'not the natural companion of the white man', neither was the government officer or the missionary the natural companion of the anthropologist. When Campbell dropped by, it irritated him 'like a customs search on the border; a little afraid he might cause me some unpleasantness'.[12] Traders, too, tended to keep to themselves and generally resented the officials who regulated their activities. 'I never go near him unless it's on business,' said Billy of Campbell, and the sentiment was probably reciprocated.

Concerning missionaries, Billy judged them according to their nonmissionary behaviour. He wrote approvingly of the Rev. Davies: 'a real good sort, absolutely none of the wowser about him, like Johns he is more interested in his cows and calves than he is in the welfare of the nigg's soul.'[13]

Malinowski captured something of the flavour of trader–missionary relations in a pithy vignette. Ted Auerbach developed pustules on his penis and approached the Rev. Gilmour for medication. 'I have the clap.' 'What is clap?' asked the innocent missionary. 'Bloody pox!' replied Ted impatiently.[14] As for anthropologist–missionary relations, a cynical Malinowski described for Elsie one of his rare visits to the mission station at Oiabia.

> The three men [were] dressed in spotless white tunic coats. . . . I was in ragged trousers with white socks tucked over the trousers, pyjama coat, no tie, & a dirty coat over the pyjamas. . . . The conversation soon ebbed down & it was a kind of spiritual communion between the elder and the two adepts with a varnish of mystery & unction & something that remained unexpressed. A stifling atmosphere of a well organized secret society. . . . for the fostering of mutual welfare. They talked much about the war. . . . Then after the meal was over, came the prayers & Gilmour got off his chest a little improvised sermon, Methodist fashion, 'blessing God' because he makes things so comfy & secure & you always know that at the bottom of things there is a Jack in the Box specially favourable to Methodists. Then came a prayer for the Governor & all that make laws, that these laws might be good & a prayer for the good of the British Army (that it might behave decently) etc.[15]

Malinowski's scornful criticisms of the whites in authority, including the missionaries, contrasted with his generally bemused tolerance of the traders. Although he knew himself to be a cut above them in the social order, his alien status brought him into sympathetic alignment with them in their mistrust of the government. They formed an alliance of snapping underdogs. His association with traders, however, exposed him to their irredeemably racialist views and invective. Neither Murray nor Gilmour would have used the disparaging term 'niggs' in their letters home. It is telling that both Malinowski and Elsie seem to have adopted it without compunction.

For Elsie's amusement, Malinowski was inclined to portray the local traders as Conradian characters eking out their sad, betrayed existences in tropical squalor. Norman Campbell, for instance, had been 'a beautiful, fresh, energetic Scotch lad' when he had come to the islands twenty years before. 'Now he is gone half native, chewing betel nut, drinking whiskey whenever he can, absolutely cut off from civilization and – like the most loathsome niggers – covered with sores on his legs so that he moves about on the floor of his verandah in a sitting position.' Campbell remained gentle, hospitable, generous and honest, though married to 'the most disgusting native hag, who has made of his trading house the brothel of the Trobriands'.[16] Elsie saw 'pure Conradian romance' in such relics of the colonial frontier.

Mick George, Billy's father-in-law, was another such figure. Once the most successful trader in the islands, he was now almost incapacitated by asthma and sat crouched on his verandah 'like Achilles in a drawing by Wyspianski'.[17] According to present-day Oburaku legend, Miki Gumagiriki ('Mick the Greek') had bought the land at Kiribi for one steel axe, a bag full of clothes and a box of twist tobacco.[18] In addition to pearling, Mick opened a trade store, planted coconuts and established a piggery. His fat European pigs, *Miki buluwka*, were soon in great demand – despite the displeasure of the Kiriwina chiefs. Mick exchanged piglets for pearls and agisted others with local villagers, allowing them to keep one or two from each litter. If government officer Raynor Bellamy undermined the chiefs' power by abolishing their monopoly on coconuts, trader Mick George did likewise by breaking their monopoly on pigs. Hitherto, chiefs had also controlled access to betel nut, but white pearl traders soon supplied commoner villagers' insatiable demand by importing betel nut from other islands. The chiefs naturally objected to these economic assaults on their prerogatives, but government officers overruled them.

Mick consolidated his relations with Oburaku by marrying a local woman, Ilumedova, thereby ensuring the pick of the pearls from local reefs. In time the villagers became dependent on his store goods and largesse, and Malinowski noted that he treated his wife's village as 'a kind of feudal dependency'. Mick evoked Malinowski's youthful dreams of Greece:

> I have got a latent yearning for the Mediterranean and his huge, lean, stooping figure and haggard, clumsily but characteristically cut face, make me think of some prehistoric Greek *Stimmungen* – of the followers and comrades of Odysseus. . . . Mick also has his yearnings and we feel a kind of freemassonic [sic] community of souls on the grounds of this Mediterranean Kultur-influence.[19]

Malinowski gave no such detailed description of any individual Kiriwinian. His thin caricatures of his Trobriand friends suggest that the cultural and colonial divide was too profound to allow of any 'community of souls'.

Despite Mick George's longing for the 'fine days of yore', when all the traders were 'like brothers' it is doubtful that there was ever any *esprit de corps* among them.[20] Malinowski frequently noted their mutual backbiting. Mick spoke of Raphael Brudo as 'that bloody Jew', and Raphael reciprocated with 'that bloody Greek'. Traders often poached on one another's pearling sites. Thus Billy, in early 1919, writing of Kavataria: 'I go and anchor on the patch & collect most of the pearls. [Sam] Brudo is some wild [sic], & tells the boys that he is going to "break" me next season, poor Sammy, he's not a sport at all.'[21]

A sensible government regulation forbade traders to dive for pearl-oysters themselves. Malinowski noted that for the five village communities on the lagoon, pearl-diving provided a source of income that 'produced a revolution in native economics'. Payment for pearls was in cash or a combination of European trade goods and native valuables.

> For really good pearls the trader has to give native objects of wealth in exchange – armshell, large ceremonial blades, and ornaments made of spondylus shell-disks. . . . So nowadays each trader keeps a retinue of native workers who polish large axe-blades, rub spondylus shell into the shape of small disks, occasionally break up and clean an armshell – so that for savage ornaments civilized 'valuables' may be exchanged.[22]

It is clear from Billy's letters to Malinowski that, like Kula, the pearling industry was driven by devious bargaining and double-dealing. First one had to compete for native labour, then for the best pearls, and finally for the best prices the metropolitan pearl-buyers could offer. It made good business sense to have a working knowledge of Kula. Pearl traders were in direct competition with one another, just as Kula traders of the same Trobriand village competed for shell valuables when they visited their exchange partners. An analogous system bound and divided them both – something that Malinowski did not seem to appreciate at the time. For their part, white traders inadvertently democratized Kula by giving 'commoners' access to the valuables they manufactured or imported, enabling them to 'buy into' Kula. Within a generation it ceased to be a pursuit exclusive to men of rank.

On Sunday 9 December, Malinowski sailed with Billy across the lagoon to Kiribi. Mick's rambling house was surrounded by coconut palms and sat high on stilts facing the beach. Malinowski's arrival was serendipitous, for Mick was about to hold a *sagali* food distribution in Oburaku. He intended to sponsor a *kayasa*, a pearling competition. Despite this novelty, during his few days at Kiribi Malinowski felt an 'increasing aversion' to the natives.

Lots of people had gathered from all over the island, but he was disappointed by his own ethnographic performance. He confessed to Elsie: 'I found that my knowledge of the lingo is much less perfect than I imagined; then, suddenly, there cropped up lots of things of which I had not the slightest idea and which I could not work out with my informants.'[23] If he had been disheartened at Billy's, he was even more so at Mick's.

Billy accompanied him to Oburaku where they prepared to take photographs of the *sagali*. With 'mixed feelings of cruelty and indignation', he watched squealing pigs being singed alive, and while they were being butchered he elicited anatomical terms. During the spectacular *sagali* distribution, he observed that most of the villages of Kiriwina, Vakuta and even Kitava were called to receive their share of pork and vegetables. That evening Mick boasted how 'Kiriwina had never seen such a *sagali*'. Malinowski did not comment on the interesting ethnographic fact that a resident white man had successfully deployed two Trobriand institutions, *kayasa* and *sagali*, to advance his business interests.

It is clear that the traders were an important and integral part of the social landscape of the islands, and Malinowski spent much longer in their company than he later cared to admit. Although this mixed bunch of Europeans (German-born Australians, 'Turkish' Jews from Paris, Scotsmen, a Cockney and a Greek) featured in his Conradian fantasies at that time, they are absent from the myth he confected about his life as an anthropologist in Kiriwina. Understandably, with hindsight they seemed irrelevant to any estimation of his achievement. For the record, however, Malinowski's own final statement concerning his association with the traders must be contested. At the end of *Coral Gardens* he wrote, doubtless referring to both Trobriand field trips: 'Only for brief intervals, all in all not more than six weeks, did I enjoy the hospitality of my friend Billy Hancock of Gusaweta, and of M. and Mme Brudo of Sinaketa. The rest of the time was spent right among the natives where I used to pitch my tent.'[24] For want of any diary it is impossible to check the 1915–16 trip, but according to his journal for 1917–18 (and where this is absent, his letters to Elsie), he spent eight weeks with Billy at Gusaweta, and three weeks with the Brudos at Sinaketa. He spent a further five weeks in Sinaketa staying in an old house of Billy's, a short walk from the Brudos with whom he dined in the evenings. The nights he slept at Kiribi add up to yet another week. In the light of these figures it would be charitable to suppose that the 'six' in Malinowski's statement 'all in all not more than six weeks' was a misprint for 'sixteen'. It can be calculated that he dwelt in his tent 'right among the natives' for only twenty-two of the forty-one weeks he spent in the islands between December 1917 and September 1918. To put it another way, his tent was folded for almost half his time in Kiriwina.

Tenting in Oburaku

On Thursday 13 December, Malinowski returned to Oburaku. Guided by the village policeman, he chose a site for his tent a few yards from the muddy mangrove shore, next to the house of Toyodala and his pretty wife, Ineykoya. Mick's wife introduced her three brothers, who helped him with his first ethnographic task: to draw a plan of the village with its individual households. Oburaku was not arranged with the pleasing concentric symmetry of Omarakana, but consisted of an irregular cluster of seven *dala*-based hamlets. The sketch map was preparatory to a detailed census and genealogical mapping of the community that would intermittently occupy him during the weeks to come. He was soon complaining to Elsie that the census was 'damnably tedious work and my head is splitting after 2 hours of it', and to his diary that it was 'monotonous, stupid work, but indispensable'.[25]

It was in this settlement, conveniently close to Kiribi, that Malinowski chose to live for almost three months. His principal ethnographic objectives appear to have been threefold: to compare a non-ranked village with the chiefly village of Omarakana; to study a lagoon village reliant on fishing; and to explore the subtle differences between Oburaku and Omarakana in their horticultural and associated magical systems.[26] In addition, he sought to improve his command of the vernacular and apply more discipline to his methods of gathering and sorting information. As he told Elsie:

> It was one of the main faults of my previous work that I worked on without any control whatever of what was done and what had to be done still. . . . I am going to set aside one day every week and go over the material and check it with our 'plans and problems' and see what there is gaping still and what must be filled out most urgently.[27]

He was referring to the many pages of questions he had compiled with Elsie's help. These often took the form of imperative instructions (such as 'describe landscape on the spot, so as to get the right *Stimmung*'). He had also drawn up check lists of particular artifacts to collect and photographs to take, of places to visit and tasks to complete in each of them.

His susceptibilty to the torpor of the tropics was about to be severely tested. Oburaku was tucked into the lee side of the island and, during the north-west monsoon, when the tepid air 'rolled along in clammy, indolent puffs', it had 'the atmosphere of a Turkish bath'.[28] He enjoyed 'tent life' more this time – he had 'simply hated' it on his first trip. 'It is rather nice to wake up and see through one end of the tent the blue lagoon and the green stripe of mangroves on the opposite island of Boimapou and to have a peep into the village through the other gable.'[29] But there was a disconsolate aspect to the lagoon that gradually oppressed him. Oburaku induced melancholy. Skyscapes provided some visual compensation, however, and he never tired of penning painterly descriptions of 'clouds with dirty-bronze reflections', of early mornings with 'chalcedony-coloured sky with patches of tea-rose', of sunsets of 'blazing brick-colour'.[30] Moonlight on the lagoon seemed to create an 'enormous space for thoughts and feelings' and gazing over it his thoughts would dissolve into shapeless reverie.

It was an hour's walk across the pinched waist of the island to Wawela on the sea side. On his first visit he 'cried with joy' at seeing the 'trans-parent water with a dark steely sheen in the distance and a line of black and white breakers'. The generous view 'created a kind of background of holiday spirits' quite absent on the lagoon. Once a large thriving village, Wawela had shrunk to a mere twenty huts; it was sad- and deserted-looking and surrounded by overgrown coconut groves. Even so, it promised to yield ethnographic gems. Wawela was an important centre of calendrical knowl-edge based on 'star-gazing', and its ritual experts dabbled in rain magic. Wawela was also reputed to be the home of flying witches, and walking back to Oburaku that night he sang 'Kiss my ass' to a Wagnerian melody to discourage the *mulukwausi*.[31]

Overcoming his fear of the dark, he would take out Mick's borrowed dinghy at dusk to row on the lagoon for exercise. 'I am always happy to be there in a melancholy and sentimental fashion,' he told Elsie. 'I can be myself and dream and long. . . . I can also think more freely and take a more "synthetic" view of my work.' In addition to the contemplative pleasure it brought him, there was a profound physical satisfaction to be derived from rowing. It was an activity that verged on sport – something he generally despised.

To row in a dinghy, on a slightly rough sea, with plain oars and rowlocks is simply heavenly. . . . Yachting on a small sailing boat makes me almost weep at the idea that I have missed it for 33 years of my life, and shall miss it probably for the rest of it. This and mountaineering (also a paradise lost for me) are the two sports I should love most.[32]

On 20 December he participated in what Europeans would have regarded as another kind of sport, though fishing was a matter of livelihood to the inhabitants of the lagoon. Malinowski was exhilarated at joining 'the most important ethnological event of this season' so soon after his arrival, and he thrilled with romantic joy at 'being with real *Naturmenschen*'. He outlined for Elsie the principle of participant observation:

It was another cardinal error in my previous work that I talked too much in proportion to what I saw. This one expedition . . . has given me a better idea of the Kiriwinan [sic] fishing than all the talk I heard about it before. It was also a more fascinating though not necessarily an easier method of working. But, it is *the* method.[33]

'I let the time do the rest'

Christmas did not begin well. He awoke on 24 December to find that all the men had gone fishing. He tried to take photographs of women making mourning skirts but he 'blundered' with the camera and spoilt a roll of film. His frustration turned to 'rage and mortification' and by lunchtime he was in a chronic state of irritation. When he gave orders to Ginger it was with tears in his voice. In the late afternoon, two white visitors from Samarai appeared. Displeased, he endured their company on the long walk to Gusaweta, the 'poetic trip through the mangroves spoiled by their chatter'. Worse, his perceptions were influenced by what he imagined to be theirs: 'I saw and felt the utter drabness of the Kiriwina villages; I saw them through their eyes (it's fine to have this ability), but forgot to look at them with my own.'[34]

He arrived at Billy's place to find it besieged by villagers on the way to Oiabia. Wherever they established stations in Papua, the Methodist missionaries held sporting contests on Christmas Day; at Oiabia the tradition was at least a dozen years old. Malinowski peevishly complained to Elsie that there was a 'whole horde camped under Billy's house, the chosen ones sleeping even on the verandah, snoring, chatting, chewing betelnut and making themselves a general nuisance'. There was no mail and his Christmas promised to be 'dull and monotonous and aimless'. He particularly longed for Elsie that night, reminding himself remorsefully of the sparkling Christmas celebrations of his Polish youth.

> I have a chronic, almost subconscious pang of conscience about my mother, my friends in Poland and my country in general. I mean the callousness in which I am able to wrap myself up. . . . At every mail I am awaiting some bad news from Poland – I worry in a gloomy, dumb, philosophical manner.[35]

His premonition would be realized. His mother was unwell. Family legend has it that she cut her finger while killing a chicken for the pot and the wound festered. In what was the last of her letters to survive, dated 6 December 1918, she wrote: 'I'm weak, I have a problem with my hand – and at present I don't go out or write by myself.' She was anxious to know whether he was in New Guinea or Australia. 'What are you doing? How are you? Send me your photograph, even if self-made. Hugging you a million times.'[36] A cruel trick of fate delivered this letter to Malinowski several weeks after he had learned of his mother's death.

On Christmas Day, Billy went to Oiabia to watch the sports. Malinowski remained at Gusaweta and spent most of the day writing to Elsie. To escape the noisy household he sat outside in an easy chair, shaded by an umbrella held by a bored Ogisi. His Dobu manservant must have yearned to be at the mission compound, watching the canoe races and tugs-of-war, watching especially the short-skirted maidens in their holiday finery flirting seductively under the pained gaze of the missionaries. It did not trouble Malinowski that he too missed the spectacle. His general antipathy to sports, crowds and missionaries was enough to keep him away from Oiabia. But it was a curious dereliction of ethnographic duty to ignore what was going on there, to rely solely on Billy's account of what had already become a 'customary' event in the annual calendar. By confining his ethnographic interests entirely to 'traditional' Trobriand culture, he was inadvertently adhering to the agenda of the 'antiquarian' ethnologists he scorned.

On 27 December he reported to the government station at Losuia. Campbell and his immediate superior, Symons from Woodlark Island, made 'stupid, unpleasant jokes' about Malinowski's Austrian nationality. He hit back in his diary. 'These fellows have such fabulous *opportunities* – the sea, ships, the *jungle*, power over the native – and don't do a thing!'[37] That night he returned to Oburaku and the four-hour walk gave him an opportunity to ruminate on his unsatisfactory attitude to work. 'As for ethnology: I see the life of the natives as utterly devoid of interest or importance, something as remote from me as the life of a dog.' Pulling himself together, he 'made it a point of honour' to think about what he was there to do. 'I have a general idea about their life and some acquaintance with their language, and if I can only somehow "document" all this, I'll have valuable material. – Must concentrate on my ambitions and work to some purpose.'[38]

Looking beyond his fieldwork, he felt a strong 'spiritual impulse' to 'lead an intellectual life and live in seclusion, with E.R.M. for my *companion*. I visualize the happiness of possessing her so intensely that I am seized with polycratic fear lest something so perfect actually come true.'[39] As he put it to Elsie: 'Fate cannot be too good to us without planning some dreadful revenge.' Yet he also had a vague, equally irrational conviction that they had 'already paid the ransom to fate'.[40] Introspective insights such as this informed his anthropological theory of religion, which held that beliefs in Providence and Immortality were fundamental. If he found it impossible to believe in the latter, he obscurely believed in the first.

After the disruptions of the holiday period – as inescapable in the Trobriands as they were in Zakopane, London or Melbourne – Malinowski's life in Oburaku settled into a routine. Although tedious it was conducive to productive work. On a typical day he would rise between six and seven and, after taking tea and biscuits for breakfast, would make a round of the village. For a week or two he kept an ethnographic diary of daily village life, a running record of what people were up to. But he was soon dissatisfied with it for (as he explained to Elsie) 'it is not minute enough and does not record the *normal* so much as the *abnormal* and it is the first that really matters'.[41] Some mornings he attended *kayaku* – moots or meetings held by the men to discuss community matters concerning gardening, fishing and forthcoming exchanges and other celebrations. Then he returned to his tent to write his personal diary for the previous day. Beginning about ten o'clock, he worked for a few hours with selected informants. He was collecting as many magic formulas as he could – Trobriand culture was infinitely rich in them – having discovered that in the process of laboriously translating them with his informants, word by word and line by line, many different things came to light: 'lots of superstitions, beliefs, taboos, technicalities and traditions [are] embedded there.'[42] Magic formulas, he believed, were the royal road to the Melanesian mind.

After a lunch prepared by Ginger, he would read a novel and take a nap (on particularly lethargic days he would take several); then he would work with pen and paper again in the late afternoon before taking Mick's dinghy out for a vigorous stint of rowing. Drifting awhile, he would dream of Elsie, the Clan and Melbourne. On other afternoons he would walk to the *raibwag* with Ginger and bathe in one of the blue pools of the limestone ridge. More often he would do Swedish gymnastics at a quiet spot just outside the village. In the evening, after what was usually a light supper – sometimes he only drank tea – he would work for another hour or two with informants before retiring under his mosquito net between ten and eleven, perhaps to read again. At least once a week he reviewed his notes and 'set in order' his papers, and at least once a week he visited other local villages for one reason or another: a *sagali*, a death, or in pursuit of an informant reputed to know a particular myth or magic spell. Occasionally he would row to Kiribi to see Mick, returning the same evening after a sumptuous supper.

He complained frequently of the tedium and monotony of the work in Oburaku. 'Writing down information, I have (1) a pedantic feeling that I must do *a certain measure (3 pages, 2 hours, fill out a blank space in Chap. X or Y* [of his draft monograph], (2) too great a desire to skip wherever possible.'[43] When his interest waned, such time-serving was the greater part of ethnographic investigation. 'Work does not go brilliantly but I keep on without pressure and *I let the time do the rest*.'[44]

He had finished the notebooks he used on previous trips, and now used loose-leaf pages in a more efficient way. He began the systematic practice of drawing up schematic tables or synoptic charts after the model of his retrospective diaries. Such charts enabled him to picture his material and identify gaps. He now took down texts in 12-by-8 inch sketchpads. He wrote with the page in a horizontal position, leaving a wide margin on the left-hand side – just as he had made notes on his reading in Zakopane in 1912. Over time, each sheet – carefully numbered in an arcane mixture of Roman and Arabic numerals according to its place in the synoptic scheme of his draft monograph 'Kiriwina' – acquired in its left-hand margin a rich deposit of ethnographic and linguistic notes and *scholia*. In blue, red, orange or purple pencils, Malinowski cross-referenced these to numbered pages of

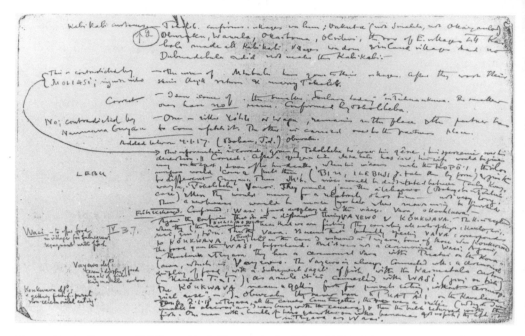

Fig. 3 Facsimile page of Malinowski's field notes in English and Kiriwinian, January 1918, illustrating his method of working. For an exegesis of this page see M. W. Young, *Malinowski's Kiriwina*. Chicago: Chicago University Press, 1998, pp. 143–4.

his notebooks, or to yet other texts. In this way, the sheets inscribed with verbatim texts became dense palimpsests. Heavily worked over, the texts sometimes became buried beneath their commentaries and expanding marginalia. No detail appeared to be too insignificant for his attention; vernacular terms sprout everywhere – in the margins and between the lines. These ostensibly untidy pages reveal Malinowski's infinite capacity for taking pains. As he wrote many years later, the ethnographer's 'supreme gift' was the ability to 'integrate the infinitely small imponderable facts of daily life into convincing sociological generalization'.[45]

He had returned to the Trobriands better equipped intellectually than two years before. His methods had been refined and he had discovered the integrating power of synoptic charts. His theories too had been sharpened. Language was the key to almost everything, and the sociology-of-knowledge approach that informed '*Baloma*' promised a great deal. His aims were more clearly defined: 'the native's point of view' presented in terms accessible to Western readers, and the final theoretical goal of formulating 'laws' of social psychology that would accurately describe the human condition in whatever cultural guise it appeared.

In tandem with his ethnographic recording, he gave thought, as always, to method. On 18 December he noted concisely: 'Yesterday while walking I thought about the "preface" to my book: Jan Kubary as a concrete [i.e. Riversian] methodologist. Miklouho-Maclay as a new type. Marett's comparison: *early ethnographers as prospectors*.'[46] Maclay, the aristocratic Russian scientist, deserves rather more credit. In addition to the year (1871) he had spent in pre-colonial New Guinea – in conditions incomparably more hazardous than those faced by Malinowski – he had actually visited the Trobriands for a few days in 1879, five years before Malinowski was born. Still, the latter acknowledged his fellow Slav as a precursor, a 'new type' of ethnographer – one, moreover, who documented the tribulations of life in New Guinea in detailed diaries.[47]

By now Malinowski was fully aware of the pioneering nature of his own fieldwork. He was not a 'prospector' or surveyor scratching the surface for ethnographic traces, but a miner digging for the mother lode, the wellsprings of a culture. Ever since his student days in London (with Rivers in mind as a mentor), one of his broader objectives had been to place ethnography on a scientific basis, to give it the authoritative rigour of chemistry or physics. He would go beyond Rivers, whom he now regarded as having betrayed the cause by embracing ethnology as a quasi-historical discipline. In his diary he kept pondering the difference between history and sociology. The historical point of view was one of 'causality as in respect of *extraordinary*, singular things', whereas the sociological point of view sought '*law* in the sense of the laws of physics and chemistry'. In analogous fashion, ' "Historicists" à la Rivers' investigated 'geological history' by viewing societies as layered stratigraphically by discrete deposits of culture in time. For Malinowski, 'the physics and chemistry of history and ethnography' was social psychology.[48] Oburaku, then, was a laboratory in which he imagined himself to be conducting a kind of anthropological experiment.

'The condition of the performer'

'Anthropology is the science of the sense of humour,' wrote Malinowski in his introduction to Julius Lips's *The Native Hits Back* (1937). 'For to see ourselves as others see us is but the reverse and the counterpoint of the gift to see others as they really are and as they want to be. And this is the *métier* of the anthropologist.'[49] There is a cynical aphorism in the professsion that anthropologists get the people they deserve (it can be inverted with equal validity). In Malinowski's case, he found in the Trobriands a society of tricksters and 'show-offs' with interesting sex lives, a passion for dancing and a keen interest in magic.

One of several nicknames given to him by Oburaku people was *Tosemwana*. It is a teasing sobriquet and was unlikely to have been used in his presence, so he was perhaps unaware of it. The prefix *to-* means 'man', the verb *semwa*, 'to put aside'. The-man-who-puts-aside refers to a person who suspends his own identity in order to assume a different one, as does an actor. *Tosemwana* has mocking connotations, however. It is said of those who mimic their social superiors – as when a little boy struts around clutching betel-chewing equipment, or when a villager pretends to a grammatical command of English he does not possess. Thus *Tosemwana* can be a childish imitator, an amusing buffoon or a contemptible fool who affects to be someone he is not.[50] Malinowski perhaps appeared in all of these guises as he struggled with the vernacular, affected to chew betel nut, told ribald *kukwanebu* and in other ways emulated the behaviour of his bemused hosts. In a more sinister light, they saw how he closed the flaps of his tent whenever sorcery spells were being recited to him. While Oburaku people probably missed the irony of his performances, the nickname was a sharp and perhaps unflattering judgment on his participant observation. Would it have amused Malinowski, twenty years later, if this perception of him had somehow found its way into *The Native Hits Back*?

There is another sense in which Malinowski was a performer. 'Magic,' he wrote, 'is composed of three essential ingredients . . . the formula, the rite, and the condition of the performer.'[51] It is 'surrounded by strict conditions: exact remembrance of a spell, unimpeachable performance of the rite, unswerving adhesion to the taboos and observances which shackle the magician. If any one of these is neglected, failure of magic will follow.'[52] Being the receptacle of magic and the channel of its flow, the human body must be properly conditioned and purified. 'Thus the magician has to keep all sorts of taboos, or else the spell might be injured.'[53] Canonically, such interdictions concerned eating and sex.

Malinowski was well aware of his superstitious turn of mind and his propensity for magical thinking. His introspective monitoring of subconscious impulses nurtured, if not seeded, his theories concerning magic and religion, both of which, he believed, arose and functioned in situations of emotional stress. Magic, he wrote, is a 'pseudo-science . . . based on specific experiences of emotional states in which man observes not nature [as in science] but himself, in which the truth is revealed not by reason but by the play of emotions on the human organism.'[54] Again, magic 'provides the spiritual strengthening of the individual mind and that discipline and preparation of the group which are necessary whenever the natives are confronted with a task difficult and not altogether controllable by knowledge and skill.'[55]

Performing as a pioneering ethnographer, inventing his role as he went along and not at all certain of the outcome, he was indeed confronted with a difficult task not altogether controllable by his own knowledge and skills. Regarding himself as an instrument of research – a keen eyewitnessing, participant observer – 'the condition of the performer' was crucial to his success as an ethnographer. Ever since his sojourn in the Canary Islands, if not before, he had tried to temper his physiology, master his body and subject it to his mind's control in service to an inchoate spiritual ambition. His ideal was a healthy body subservient to an alert, concentrated mind, perfectly atuned to its environment. There was a moral dimension to his instrumentality too: 'The fact that, in order to attain magical efficacy, we must pay undivided attention to our spiritual communion, demands what every theologian as well as the anthropologist or the man in the street would call a "clean heart".'[56] As he reminded himself in his diary, he was 'perfectly capable of an all but ascetic life' (desirable for a clean heart). Sensual enjoyment was acceptable in its place but it was important 'not to let it interfere with essential things'.[57] Among the most essential things, in his view, were the striving for integration, the 'deepening' of his subjective life, the mind's triumph through the economy of thought to theoretical clarity, and ultimately 'the smile of the Buddha' and a nirvana-like contentment.[58]

Towards the perfection of the performer he deployed his diary as a monitoring device. The purpose of keeping a diary 'must be to consolidate life, to integrate one's thinking, to avoid fragmenting themes'.[59] The chief instrument of investigation was his own observing, analytical self. Some components of this human apparatus he knew to be faulty. His physical body was recalcitrant, too often sluggish and distracted by wayward emotions. His health, the most fundamental aptitude, could not be guaranteed. (He suffered two bouts of incapacitating sickness while at Oburaku, and for at least a week was quite unable to work.) His linguistic facility fell short of what was needed. His mental attitude – another vital component of the research apparatus – was sometimes 'wrong', his motivation fickle. Elsie was at once a mental support and a distraction. It was partly on her account that he wanted to 'succeed' in Kiriwina, but it was largely because of her that he yearned to be somewhere else. Yet other distractions conspired to prevent his full immersion in the field: the nagging question of his political status, the presence of the white traders, his obfuscating informants and rebellious servants. A sense of dislocation rarely left him – the jarring contrast between his dreams of civilization and his daily life among 'the savages'.[60] Whatever he later came to claim about his fieldwork experience (as one 'whose heart is in Melanesia,' he would write),[61] his immersion in Trobriand culture was only ever tentative and incomplete. It was impossible for him to transgress his profession's code and go native, and it would have seemed inconceivable to him even to try. It wasn't just the 'niggrophobia' – euphemistically, 'surfeit of native' – that occasionally gripped him, it was an inability to slough the skin of his European identity in the cause of ethnography. To that extent he was an incomplete Trickster, a failed Tokosikuna.

The irrefutable fact that 'man has a body subject to various organic needs' was a fundamental axiom of his mature theory of culture.[62] He dealt with his own body in a number of instrumental ways while in the field. He had to eat, sleep and exercise, and to some extent he could control the satisfaction of these needs. Although his body often betrayed him, the goal was to keep it in sound health. To this end, his faith in medications seemed boundless. He took calomel, Epsom salts and enemas to regulate his bowels, dosed himself regularly with quinine, aspirin and arsenic, and applied eye-drops daily. In moderation, physical exercise prevented listlessness and kept him alert: 'it calmed my nerves, restored my balance and put me in an excellent mood.' Gymnastics were also 'an essential form of solitude and mental concentration', though if overdone they induced 'a certain nervous tension' and even insomnia.[63] He bathed in the sea, too, though with some hesitation. He enjoyed the sensation of salt and sunshine on his skin, imagining that he felt 'the effect of salt on bones and muscles', but ever since he had almost drowned in the Canaries he had been a timid swimmer. 'As soon as I realize there is no bottom under my feet I lose my head,' he told Elsie. Fear of sharks deterred him from bathing in the placid lagoon, for 'it is well known that though blacks are practically immune, a white man runs a certain risk'.[64]

His diet was varied, a combination of local foods and European imports, though he appeared to eat little of the canned food that he had ordered so lavishly in London. On 19 December he noted: 'What I eat at present: morning, cocoa, lunch relatively varied, and almost always *fresh food*. Supper very light, banana compote, *momyapu* [pawpaw]; once I ate a lot of fish and felt no ill effects.'[65] He taught Ginger ('yelling and swearing') how to fry scrambled eggs in lard, and besides Billy's weekly loaf of bread, there were fried taro, crab soup, cucumbers and rice. He told Elsie that the three fresh foods he liked best were bananas, eggs and pawpaw.[66] He also relished taro: 'a splendid thing & I thank God for having created it, but even the best thing gets monotonous.'

It was one thing to regulate his bodily functions, it was quite another to control his sexual impulses. His excited imagination teetered between Dionysian surrender – letting nature have its way with him – and Apollonian balance. The refrain 'dirty thoughts under the mosquito net' was usually followed by a stern resolve 'absolutely to avoid all lecherous thoughts and achieve spiritual purity'.[67] But he forgave himself masturbatory fantasies that did not involve living women – they were not 'betrayals' of Elsie but mere physiological release, and although he did not approve of such weakness it was morally neutral. The part of his erotic imagination that he deplored was the one that conjured past lovers and other desirable women he had known: Annie, Żenia, Tośka, Etonka, Nina, Leila and latterly Flo Gofton. Just occasionally did he rebel against his self-imposed moral strictures: 'I said to myself: "I don't regret my sins of the past, I wish I had committed more!"'[68]

'The shadow of death'

On his first evening in Oburaku, Malinowski had been startled by a mournful dirge issuing from a nearby house – it was *walamsi*, 'a melodious, monotonous chant'. A woman had recently lost her son, and she punctuated the nights with her laments. Next day there was a torrential downpour and the crash of terrifying thunder, and two days later he was awakened by 'deafening *walamsi* in two voices'. The entire period of his stay in Oburaku was shadowed by death, for which the season of damp heat and violent squalls provided its own pathetic fallacy.[69]

Several deaths in Oburaku and neighbouring villages provided opportunities for the exhaustive investigation of mortuary matters. He was already armed with a battery of questions formulated in Melbourne. The list testifies to his thoroughness. 'Go over consecutive account of death & mourning and inquire into native psychology of each detail.' Some of the details were unsavoury: why is mucous so avidly displayed by mourners; why is the corpse washed and by whom; why are its orifices stuffed before burial; why are certain kin unable to touch the corpse or grave; why do mourners stroke the corpse and fondle the nose and mouth; why are certain valuables buried with the body; why are certain bone relics treasured and others not? Under pressure from the missionaries, some of the more lurid practices had been abandoned and his notes to himself include: 'Go over a mimic representation of dying, so as to get the old customs, re stuffing of holes etc.' One cannot imagine Malinowski enacting the role; rather the hapless Ogisi would be induced to play dead. As for the innumerable mortuary distributions, the problems to be 'thrashed out' were legion, and in dialogue with the material from his first field trip they kept piling up. Another instruction to himself reads: 'Construct synoptic chart of definite death and mourning series.'[70]

Weathering fits of nostalgia, on 3 January he fell under the spell of Swinburne's poem 'Tiresias'. 'It is the most forcible and clear expression of the feeling about heroic death,' he enthused to Elsie. He was thinking of Charles Matters and it brought his spirits to a low ebb. He saw his surroundings that day as from a great inner distance. A canoe gliding across his line of sight, the woman wailing next door: 'All this is so inexpressibly sad in its remoteness and detachment from my own life – I am stranded here far away from all that makes life.'[71] It was one of his periodic moods of alienation and 'a strong feeling of irreality'. Under the mosquito net that night he wondered if he would ever see Elsie again. 'Death, the blear-eyed visitor, I am ready to meet,' sang sightless Tiresias. And the next day, Malinowski told Elsie that he was 'feeling almost hysterical . . . in such a mood, as would make a child capricious and crying'. His informants had been dispersed by a downpour; heavy low clouds crawled across the sky; there was a drumbeat of thunder, and he was irritated by the 'useless niggers' hanging around his tent. It attracted 'cripples, idiots and other sorts of drones, almost like a church gate in (civilized) Roman Catholic countries'.[72] Next day he reflected that his 'pessimistic temperament' never allowed him 'to enjoy life in a simple, unsophisticated manner' and he was full of forebodings. As he told Elsie, 'one always dreads all sorts of evils and especially death and annihilation, at a time when life is at an ebb.'[73]

26. Malinowski in the tropics, *c.* 1914.

27. Elsie Masson, *c.* 1916.

28. The *Makambo* leaving Samarai wharf, November 1917.

29. A Dobuan canoe in the Amphlett Islands *en route* to Kiriwina for Kula, March 1918.

30. J. H. P. Murray at Government House. Port Moresby, 1907.

31. Malinowski watching children at play, Teyava village, Kiriwina, May 1918.

32. Malinowski's tent (*left*) in Omarakana. Chief Touluwa is on the right, his house behind him.

33. Mick George's house at Kiribi. Kiriwina Island, 1918.

34. Ilakaise, the youngest of Chief Touluwa's wives, standing in front of her annual 'dowry'. The yam-houses have been filled by her maternal kinsmen. Omarakana, July 1918.

35. The decorated corpse of Ineykoya, supported by her husband Toyodala. Oburaku, 25 January, 1918.

36. Billy Hancock inspecting pearls outside his store at Gusaweta.

37. Chief Touluwa ceremonially receiving a *soulava* necklace from his favourite son, Namwana Guyau. Next in line is Yobukwau with a conch shell, followed by Kalogusa with the chief's limepot, and an empty-handed Dipapa. Omarakana, November 1915.

38. Malinowski, Hede Khuner, Elsie Masson and Mim Weigall outside 'Carinya'. Melbourne, late 1918.

39. Paul Khuner.
Melbourne, c. 1918.

40. Elsie Malinowska in her wedding dress on the steps of the Melbourne Museum and Public Library, 6 March 1919.

41. Elsie Malinowska relaxing in
Whitfield, late 1919.

42. Marnie Masson bidding farewell
to the *Borda*. Melbourne,
26 Feburary 1920.

Superficially, his work seemed to be going well; he was recording magic formulas and translating them with excellent informants such as the *towosi* Navavile and the village policeman, Yosala Gawa. But he was dissatisfied with his 'mechanical' approach and lacked the feeling of 'the ultimate mastery of things'. Time-serving is the enemy of good ethnography. 'Toward the end of the day's work hidden longings come to the surface,' he noted; longings for Melbourne's 'elegant, well-dressed women' and most of all for Elsie.[74]

The day before he had seen some young Oburaku women, their heads shaved and their bodies charcoal-blackened in mourning, one of them 'with an animal like, brutishly sensual face. I shuddered at the thought of copulating with her.'[75] About his own face he was brutally honest.

> The other day, when I looked at myself, with my face unshaven and my hair shorn, I saw the picture of one of those raw, impudent looking German prisoners of war, with its bulging, bald forehead, the small myopic bespectacled eyes, the small receding chin and badly designed nose, without shape, without line or meaning. Only lit up by this instrument-like, mechanical intelligence. 'A face like a scientific instrument of sorts' as Witkiewicz described Dr Ignatius Wasserberg.[76]

Not unlike, too, Staś's lampoon of Malinowski as the Duke of Nevermore.

On 19 January a man died in Kwabulo, and Malinowski, although feeling unwell, was taken there in a canoe. 'I went to the grave and talked about the cutting of trees and the wrecking of houses after a man's death.' Next day, the condition of his neighbour's ailing wife deteriorated. Ineykoya, tragically youthful, had tuberculosis and could scarcely breathe; she haemorrhaged, 'groaned horribly, and was apparently dying'. He thought about poor consumptive Nina and suddenly felt that he was deserting her. 'I wanted to be with her at any cost, to allay her sufferings.' He thought also of Elsie: 'I told myself: "*the shadow of death is between us and it will separate us.*" My betrayal of N.S. confronted me in all its starkness. . . . Kabwaku [a bird of ill omen] sings melodiously and clearly. – Death – all this is like an ebb tide, a flowing off into nothingness, extinction.'[77]

On 23 January another bag of mail arrived, bringing with it 'emotional turmoil'. A long letter from Elsie included her diary of their meeting, their blossoming friendship and eventual love. On his first avid reading the diary unnerved him: 'My portrait in it is not sympathetic, as I see it. I don't like this fellow and I feel that she does not like me.'[78] Letters from Nina pierced him with guilt. Sitting in a canoe on the lagoon he felt 'that this funda-mental error casts a shadow over my life, over my relation with E.R.M. I shouldn't have started anything with her before definitively breaking off with N.S.' Her letters were 'especially beautiful and affectionate' and he 'simply howled with despair'.[79]

Ineykoya was laid out in the house, waiting for death and the voyage to Tuma. She had been decorated with shell valuables, her lips painted red with betel juice. Her husband, Toyodala, was crouched behind her, holding her pathetically in his arms and stroking her. She was almost unconscious and mumbled incoherently as the people who surrounded her tried to keep her thoughts clear. 'You can imagine,' Malinowski told Elsie, 'that the purely human aspect of the events got hold of me much more strongly than the ethnological.'

> It was a mixture of the hideous and the touching, the publicity of it, the ingredients of human belief distorting and banalizing the tragic depth of natural events, the mixture of the inevitable real feelings and of a histri-onic display dictated by custom. Again the sight of these two, clinging to each other – in true fondness or in obedience to tribal law? – threw such an unexpected and such a strong light on my thoughts of love and affection. Of two people, who love each other, one is bound to die in the arms of the other, or to die away from the beloved one, yearning and missing her or him.[80]

Ineykoya lingered for a few more days. Her shrieks tore at Malinowski's insides. 'The moon had struggled through the clouds and shone on the village from among the high palm-tops. . . . and somehow the whole serene, beautiful scene seemed to recede into a darkness to become engulfed by the shadow of approaching death.'[81] He thought: '*Desertion in the face of the enemy*', and felt that if Nina's life depended upon it he would have to sacrifice Elsie (and himself) and go back to her. He was confused as well as distressed. 'More clearly than ever I feel now that I love them both. . . . Aesthetically, I should never go back to Australia. Death, the ebb tide of reality, does not seem as terrible as a few days ago.'[82]

On Thursday 24 January, the day of his mother's death in distant Poland, he recorded a secret myth about canoe-carving, and after lunch took photographs of men roasting fish. Then he set out for Gusaweta. Restless at Billy's, he returned to Oburaku the next day. Ineykoya died during that night. Some hours earlier, Józefa Malinowska had died, too, and although news of her death would not reach him for almost six months, Malinowski grieved through the vicarious death of a pretty young Papuan woman. At 3.30 a.m. he visited Ineykoya's deathbed. 'Deep impression. *I lose my nerve.* All my despair, after all those killed in the war, hangs over this miserable Melanesian hut.'[83]

'The heroic struggle against illness'

Elsie had sent Malinowski an edition of Robert Louis Stevenson's letters. He identified immediately with the sickly Scot who lived a tropical idyll in Samoa with his wife and his mother, one who exemplifed 'the heroic struggle against illness and exhaustion'.[84] To Elsie he wrote:

> Stevenson's egotistic interest in his health and in his work is, alas, so damnably like my own case that I cannot help finding passages which I almost have said myself. . . . I was very much struck by a passage in which he sings the praise of his enduring, patient heroism in the continuous struggle with ill health and in his striving to do the work in spite of sickness and depression and failing forces. I felt like that myself so often and indeed had I not felt this note of heroism in this ignoble battle . . . it would have been impossible to go on.[85]

On Sunday 27 January he awoke with his skull throbbing and the feeling that something was wrong. 'Subjectively I am very indifferent, I don't believe in the possibility of danger, but if I died, it would be *an excellent way out of the muddle.*' On Monday he felt worse, and in the afternoon he collapsed, wracked by fever. He was beginning to believe that he might die. 'A sense of having perfect conditions for dying. Alone, calm, *air of finality.*'[86] He dosed himself with several medications and the quinine possibly saved him, though he preferred to believe it was a purgative. By Thursday he was feeling well enough to believe that he would recover. He felt an unjustified resentment against Elsie, and the 'complication' with Nina weighed heavily upon him. On Friday there was another mail delivery, with more loving letters from Elsie. But there was further aggravation in store with her account of Baldwin Spencer's 'slanders'. She was being circumspect, and Malinowski did not yet know the worst. With this mail came notification that Hubert

Murray had granted him an extension of his stay in Papua until 31 October. Until this point he had been in a state of uncertainty.

After a few recuperative days at Gusaweta, feeding on cow's milk and other fresh food, by 5 February he was able to concentrate again and resume his diary. It had been almost two weeks since he had written to Elsie. 'All this period lived literally from day to day. Impulse to read trashy novels. Through all this strong, unexpressed longing for E.R.M. Now I really can say she is the only woman for me.'[87] One night he dreamed he was living with Nina in Mały Rynek. 'Mama surprised and reproachful because I am not married to N.S. "She has only two weeks left to live." I, too, was very sad.'[88] Another ambivalent betrayal featured in his dreams the following night. He was in Germany 'fraternizing' with two crippled cavalry officers. He expressed his sympathy for German culture and told them that he had been a prisoner of war in England. A few days later, in an imaginary conversation with William Strong, he spoke about the shortcomings of the English: 'the embodiment of self-assurance . . . the whole world *in the palm of their hands*, yet how they lack enthusiasm, idealism, purpose. The Germans have a purpose, possibly lousy and thwarted, but there is an *élan*, there is a sense of mission.' Spencer's meddling in his affairs was undermining Malinowski's Anglophilia.[89]

Although at first he felt 'incomparably better' back in Oburaku, his fever soon returned. He fasted for a few days and again dosed himself heavily with aspirin and quinine, and purged himself with salts and an enema. He put hot compresses on his chest, too, for the sudden rises in temperature affected his lungs. This time, he told Elsie, he suspected 'regular malarial fever', though in his diary he proposed the more fanciful hypothesis of septicaemia. Still, he reflected, a high temperature 'is a wonderful invention of Providence: it narrows down your consciousness to a mere thread and you do not mind a bit if this snaps.'[90] On 11 February he felt well enough to eat toast and indulge himself with Charlotte Brontë's *Villette*. Like *Pride and Prejudice*, it charmed him with its 'feminine tact, intuition, grasp of *inwardness of things* and longing for life' – though one of its less pleasant effects was to remind him of how 'wicked' he was.[91]

For another week he remained feeble, sweated at night, and suffered insomnia. He was tired and grumpy and lacked that 'vital thread'. *Villette* was his only solace. But he forced himself to work with the garden magician Navavile, and found that even short spells of concentration banished his dejection and helped him break out of his 'prison mood'. He worked also with Molilakwa on sorcery texts and with Niyova on flying witches. Niyova, he told Elsie, was 'quiet, respectful, without any "dog" or other form of self importance . . . nicely spoken, volunteering information and relatively very uncadging'.[92] One evening he visited Tomwaya Lakwabulo, a seer who reminded him of Sir Oliver Lodge. The old man was in a trance – presumably communicating with his spirit wife-cum-daughter in Tuma. Malinowski had already recorded what Tomwaya purported to be the speech of *baloma*, and tried to determine whether it was an invented language or, as he suspected, mere gibberish. Tomwaya's dealings with the afterworld fascinated him, and he returned to the topic in several publications, always with jocular scepticism.[93] As if subconsciously thinking about the traffic of spirits to and from Tuma, the next day he wondered what would happen if Charles Matters 'came back' to claim Elsie. It jolted him to realize anew how much she meant to him.[94]

There followed another cycle of physical debility and mental dullness. For several days he rose late, feeling as if he had been 'put through a wringer'. But he forced himself to work intensively for the sake of his self-respect: there were mortuary exchanges to observe and analyse with the help of informants' commentaries. The ethnography of death was proving productive, and he sketched a completely new outline of the 'Disease and Death' chapter for his monograph. 'I told myself that although my work was not amusing and not glamorous, it was not entirely pointless.'[95] He was also completely reworking his material on sorcery, telling Elsie that his earlier information was not only incomplete 'but downright incorrect'.[96] She was surprised, and her reply put into simple words the main plank of his revolutionary fieldwork methodology. 'It made me think how much absolutely false there must be in nearly all ethnology. So few know the language and stay a long time in the country, camping alone among the niggs, but still fewer, I should think, ever go back to test their conceptions with reality.'[97]

'I simply loathe the whole village and all its inhabitants,' he told Elsie on 21 February. It was a 'monotonous empty existence' and he could hardly bear the prospect of another eight months' fieldwork. He was only now recovering from the 'fits of terrible mental depression' for which work had become the only cure.[98] His depression was joined to a profound pessimism, and his paranoid hypersensitivity was detrimental to fieldwork – as he was fully aware:

Here, in my dealing with the natives, one bloody nigger who does not want to come & give me information or says that I don't pay them well enough (which is true, because I pay them miserably) will spoil my whole day & I imagine at once a general mutiny of the whole village, I get suspicious & irritable, swear at all the niggers & spoil really my chances of getting good informants.[99]

The work of ethnography itself was beginning to bore him, and he longed to be back in a library doing 'some theoretical work': 'I am a philosopher by temperament and I like "pure thinking" better than anything else and moreover I believe in its value. Just this work here teaches me that general ideas are the only thing for fertilizing observation and experimental research.'[100]

On Friday 22 February, he rowed to Gusaweta with Ginger. The place seemed sad and deserted. Mick George and Marianne were there, but Billy was in Samarai attending his sick son. Mick was supposedly looking after Gusaweta but Malinowski found pandemonium. 'The niggers have completely invaded the verandah, betel chewing, spitting, putting their blackened skins (those in mourning & always 50% are in mourning) on every conceivable place.'[101]

He had been pondering his reaction to Elsie's diary-letter: why had it 'unnerved' him so? One reason, he told her, was that he found himself 'most unromantic and uncongenial' in her description and could not understand how she could have come to care for him. 'It is almost as if this ungainly foreigner had used some *megua* [magic] and not acted by his own personality.'[102] But it also occurred to him that Elsie might have begun to love him precisely because – not being in khaki and not marching off to war – he had felt unworthy of her. His love for her was still intricately ambivalent. So it would remain until he could exorcise Charles, against whose imagined heroism he measured himself. At least he could admit to himself that his lack of heroism was the cause of her devaluation: 'I loved her in relation to C.A.M. and I believed in her eternal faithfulness.'[103]

The turmoil of letters

Between January and March the monotony of Malinowski's life in Oburaku was broken by irregular mail deliveries. He anticipated them with nervous strain, for they invariably agitated him. As he read and re-read his letters the world beyond the islands crowded in. While they satisfied what he called 'a craving for strong and complicated impressions' and delivered 'a condensed dose of a friend's personality', the intrusion of another's presence was deeply unsettling.[104]

> It is quite a magic effect which a mail has, at a long distance: suddenly all things visible and palpable vanish. The crowd of niggers around my tent become blurred and unreal; Wawela and Oburaku cease to be local-ized in space and time, and I see only the bundle of papers which exhale a peculiar spiritual fluid.[105]

While personal letters – Elsie's especially – reaffirmed his identity and main-tained his morale, they were apt to increase rather than allay his yearning for civilization. Paul Khuner gently played upon his friend's nostalgia for Melbourne and for the life that used to be:

> If you were to enter 'Carinya' just now you wouldn't notice much of a change. I am sitting in the study, Hede is lying on the front verandah reading Masefield's 'Gallipoli' . . . Your room, still officially called 'Malinowski's Room', is waiting for you, the *Schlafrock* [dressing gown] is hanging on the doornail. . . . Your spirit is constantly hovering over the place, whatever 'important' happens in the household is judged and discussed under the aspect 'what would Malina say?'[106]

On opening his mail bag, Malinowski would sort the letters to read in a certain order. Mama's first, scanned with urgency despite its being several months old, followed perhaps by Seligman's for news of his finances and the fate of his publications. Then the 'less important ones' from Leila, Mim, the Khuners, the Mayos, Pitt and Broinowski. (The trickle of Annie Brunton's letters had all but ceased, but he would have placed them in this category.) Finally, in a 'crescendo of sentimental intensity', he would open Elsie's neatly numbered envelopes, each bearing the censor's sinister stamp. Or he would leave until very last Nina's letter, dreading its innocently affec-tionate message. After reading them all, he would feel deflated, a 'charac-teristic dissatisfaction and restlessness'.[107] Mim Weigall caught the mood when she wrote: 'Don't you sometimes feel even worse just after you've read your mail and laid it down, than you did before? There is such a ghastly period of flatness after the reading, when the voices one has been listening to so eagerly suddenly cease, and silence falls for another month.'[108] Mim was among those he chided for not baring their souls to him. She wittily repaid his reproach with a protest that Elsie would have endorsed:

> My soul does not like going abroad without a concrete covering. Remember, please, that I am a British plum-pudding after all, with all the somewhat unappetizing mysteriousness of the genus. Prod in me patiently enough, & you might occasionally be rewarded with a plum; but do not be angry with the poor pudding because it does not flow & froth all over you like champagne.[109]

By far the largest correspondence was with Elsie, and between October 1917 and September 1918 they exchanged well over five hundred pages. Often her letters transported him; he read and re-read them 'in a trance, drunk – the *niggers* don't exist. I don't even want to eat or drink.'[110] Then he would spend the whole of the following day writing to her. He confessed that her letters threw him 'off balance', evoking a mad, restless longing for her.[111] She also sent him packets of newspapers. The *Argus*, redolent of Melbourne and thus fodder for his nostalgia, was also a form of local currency, for islanders used it to roll their cigarettes of black twist. 'You can buy virtue, extort secrets, pervert chastity with a number of newspapers,' he told her.[112] The arrival of the mail reminded him of his dislocated relationship to time. 'I have been brought out of equilibrium by this mail and put in touch with Actuality and the war and the outer world.'[113]

The news that Malinowski received in this way was weeks, sometimes months, out of date. Such delay added to his sense of alienation, of being outside the orderly passage of time. 'I just wait, endure, and time flows along beside me,' he complained to his diary.[114] His longing to be with Elsie simply aggravated the condition. 'Sometimes I can screw myself up to a kind of philosophical quietism and feel that it won't do to fret through this time of separation. And then again I cannot: I feel that I am here not living but waiting.'[115] The sense of being stranded appears to have been most acute in the parochial backwater of Oburaku. In Omarakana he could at least fancy himself to be drifting in the island's political mainstream, while in Gusaweta and Sinaketa his everyday intercourse with other Europeans connected him to a measured colonial time with its clocks and calendars, its determined routines and regularities.

In the limbo of Samarai he had been waiting to enter the field; in the limbo of Oburaku he was waiting to leave it. It is one of the most telling paradoxes of his fieldwork that he experienced such chronic ambivalence about 'being there'. He had a persistent, worrying sense that 'real life' was going on elsewhere without him, that he was being bypassed by 'actualities', marooned in an ox-bow river bend. He was out of the war, out of civilized life, and the stream of time flowed around him. He waited like his homeland, the inert nation of Poland sidelined by Hegelian History, waiting for liberation and for real life to begin again. Yet it is arguable that his best ethnography was done during such periods, when he felt that time was annulled, when he could suspend his imaginary life elsewhere and enter wholeheartedly into the present moment of the islanders. Those were rare moments of immersion, when a joyful enthusiasm for ethnography took him out of himself.

It is arguable, too, that the key to his epoch-making ethnography and theoretical anthropology was a concept grounded in his dislocating experience of time suspended. Synchrony was the atemporal condition – the very bedrock – of his functionalism. Time present, not time past, was of the essence in his here-and-now ethnography. Synchrony, not diachrony, provided the methodological purchase, the Archimedean point, for his descriptive exploration of social institutions. Functionalism subordinated history to sociology. So his sense of being out of time in the field surely enabled his understanding of the perfect scientific ethnography as one grounded empirically in the ethnographic present, a timeless sociological construct rather than a conjectural historical sequence. Malinowski himself would claim that the 'functional method . . . was very largely born in the field'.[116] So it must be allowed that personal experience, too, led him to conceive of myth and history as ideological 'charters' for present-day social and political arrangements.

As Malinowski well understood, history was being made with a vengeance on the other side of the world. Battlefields were blazing while he fiddled with magic formulas for sailing and sorcery. Aside from the dull anguish he felt for his mother, what troubled him most was 'the problem of heroism' and a 'definitive regret' that he could not put himself to the test of war. It stung him afresh with every mention of Charles in Elsie's letters.

> I recalled my superstitious feeling that if E.R.M. fell in love with me, I would have *mala sombra* in N[ew] G[uinea] – For one moment I thought that there is no room for me in her heart in the shadow of his glory. I wished that he had come back and that I had never met her.[117]

Elsie half-believed 'that fate had sent her and broken her to give happiness to Charles' before his violent end. Malinowski drew his own humbling lesson from this. What he was suffering in the islands was as nothing compared to the unimaginable horrors of Gallipoli.

> I know that if I had had to go to war, I would have gone calmly without too much inner fuss. Now: place my everyday life in that heroic frame; be ruthless in relation to appetites and weakness; not to yield to depression and such digressions as the inability to take photos. Shake off clumsiness, yearning, sentimentalism. My love for E.R.M. can be, must be, based on the feeling that she has faith in my heroism.[118]

Many of his letters to Elsie at this period include expurgated transcriptions of his diary. It was as if he invited her to eavesdrop on his daily conversation with himself; though he allowed her to hear only snatches, of course, and the real diary was in a language she could not understand. In both diary and letters he frequently pondered his Polish identity and obliquely examined the roots of his patriotism. 'I'll surely be "an eminent Polish scholar",' was one of the more comforting thoughts that occurred to him while drifting in the dinghy. 'This will be my last ethnological escapade. After that, I'll devote myself to constructive sociology: methodology, political economy etc., and in Poland I can realize my ambitions better than anywhere else.'[119]

It sometimes worried him that he would be 'estranged from Polishness' if he married Elsie.[120] At one point he regretted that Elsie was not Polish, but then decided that it did not matter: 'I shall go back to Poland and my children will be Poles.' She had few such doubts about him. 'I'm so glad you are a Pole,' she told him. 'I couldn't imagine you anything else really.'[121] In time, Elsie would help him to achieve his ambitions and, crucially, help him decide that Poland was not, after all, the best place to realize them. Yet it had been his idea that she would adopt Polishness to the degree that he had already adopted Britishness. At the time he was testing her willingness to live in Poland:

> you represent for me all that I like best in English culture, and none of its drawbacks . . . I almost feel that with us two, it will be a mutual adoption of our countries, the exchange of patriotisms. . . . I wonder how you feel about your adopted country? You see, Poland is more in need of 'people' than Australia. On the other hand, life there must be much harder & the task more thankless.[122]

Much of the emotional turmoil that attended mail deliveries was due to Baldwin Spencer. From 8 January, each successive delivery brought more disturbing news from Melbourne, news relayed by Elsie of 'Baldy on the warpath'. On the last day of the old year she told him how Spencer had informed her of Malinowski's multiple entanglements.

> One was that of N.S. (spoken of finally by name) and, he said, there were others — 3 other girls with whom you had relations, or had had in the very near past. He thought, and wanted me to think, that I was one of a series of dupes, to all of whom in turn you made a confession of your 'pasts'.[123]

Spencer always had a soft spot for her and wanted to protect her from a man whom he regarded as a scoundrel. Elsie knew Malinowski would be 'in a fearful rage' with him but begged him not to take any action — a letter of protest to Spencer would only make matters worse.

> I must say I do feel slightly indignant when I remember how generously you have behaved towards his weaknesses. But I do not want any open rupture to come between you and those who can influence your fortunes. . . . owing to the war you are at a tremendous disadvantage, and I am so anxious for you to steer clear of any rocks while this is so.[124]

The weaknesses Elsie alluded to concerned Spencer's immoderate drinking. This had become increasingly noticeable — to the Massons at least — since the British Association meeting at the beginning of the war. He was under enormous pressure of work, combining several jobs, occupying prominent positions in the university, the museum and the art gallery, as well as fulfilling self-imposed civic duties. His marriage was under great strain, and Lady Spencer seemed to be of little comfort to him. Whisky consoled, or so he believed, though it shortened the fuse of his explosive Lancastrian temper. Malinowski was just one of several provocations.

Malinowski replied to Elsie in early February, admitting that the news had depressed him but assuring her that he would not act rashly. Still, the thought of his private affairs being 'hawked about' was loathsome, and he even wondered whether Spencer had hired a detective to spy on him. Elsie was right to blame him about Nina; as to the other three girls, he had already told her that he had not behaved 'in a puritanic manner' at Nyora the previous Easter. He concluded his confession with a declaration, as true to himself as he could make it: 'You are the only woman in the world for me. I do not expect that I shall have never any lapses or regrets. But to my ideal of faithfulness it is necessary that there should be the "only one" feeling between the two people.'[125]

Elsie's next letter brought more unwelcome news. She had learned that Spencer now had documentary evidence of Malinowski's several entanglements, and he intended to tell Edward Stirling and David Orme Masson, for the sake of their daughters, just what he thought of his character. 'He also is seriously thinking of writing Home [England] in order to disclaim all responsibility for you personally, and discourage further supplies [of funds].' She now pleaded with Malinowski to write immediately to Nina or to her father. 'No hesitation can spare her any pain now, or me either, and you may simply ruin your own position here.' He saw the wisdom of her advice but continued to procrastinate.

Malinowski suspected Spencer was acting out of pure malice – but why the hatred? As he told Elsie, somewhat disingenuously: 'I usually either make friends or enemies and it sometimes astonishes me, how suddenly & without any provocation on my part there crop up around me sworn enemies, people who go out of their way to do me harm.'[126] He feared that Spencer had already written with 'calumnious insinuations' to Mond and Frazer, perhaps even to Seligman. He was depressed, too, by the painful scrutiny of his conscience, forced upon him by this 'unsympathetic intrusion' into his private life. It coincided with Ineykoya's final days, with the arrival of heart-rending letters from Nina, and with his own morbid slide into sickness. Now, for Elsie alone, he accurately nailed his moral flaw:

> I may be furious with that man, but none the less I must own that I have behaved abominably both to N.S. and to yourself. . . . I ought to have wound up the other affair. But I am most damnably weak, sentimental and soft – & very egotistically so: it is very hard for me to tell people definitely that I must give up any claims to their affection & friendship. Coupled with a congenital fickleness, it produces that abominable combination, of which I am an example.[127]

The Ethnographer's legend

On Monday 11 March 1918, Malinowski packed up his things and dismantled his tent. He reflected sourly that he had no sentimental feelings about his departure. He noted dismissively: 'I am glad that the Oburaku *niggers* are behind me, and that I'll never again live in this village.' A group of 'friendly' people had come to his tent the previous evening, presumably to bid him farewell, but at noon he left the village without fanfare. He was irritated by the difficulty of finding a canoe to carry his gear to Gusaweta, and complimented only Morovato, who 'helped me loyally to the end'.[128]

Malinowski's attitude towards the people who had hosted him for three months seems ungracious and churlish. He had imposed himself upon them uninvited, yet they had provided him with priceless information on their way of life. They had taken him into their houses and gardens and on their fishing expeditions. Oburaku elders and ritual specialists had taught him their secret lore: their myths and complex magical formulae which accompanied gardening, village prosperity, fishing, canoe-making and other technical tasks. His collection of sorcery spells was larger and more varied than could be claimed by any single villager. He had been allowed to penetrate the mysteries of their cosmological beliefs and their mortuary customs. Despite the cycles of tropical ennui, the bouts of sickness and the oscillations of his energy levels, his months in Oburaku had been hugely productive. Yet he gave no hint of gratitude in his diary for the villagers' gifts of knowledge, and it was with obvious relief that he left them.

What the people of Oburaku really thought of their ethnographer in 1918 is beyond recovery. But almost eighty years later one of their descendants could tell stories about him that had been orally transmitted across three generations. Although the veracity of such testimony must remain suspect, the gist of the anecdotes is curiously positive. Oburaku people appear to have liked the *dimdim* who lived among them. In June 1995, Linus Digim'Rina interviewed an Oburaku man of some seventy years named Kewaiyabisila.[129] He was the maternal grandson (sister's daughter's son) of Kadilakula, one of Malinowski's informants. Three brief references to Kadilakula occur in his diary. On 25 February 1918 a gale blew: 'The palms swayed, the leaves like arms flailing madly, or wild locks of hair tossed in passion. . . . Kadilakula sat bravely and performed the *megwa* [to still the wind].' Two days later, his head 'bursting with fatigue', Malinowski took down from him the magical formula. On 6 March they discussed a *sagali* in Kaytuvi.[130] The following account of what Kewaiyabisila remembers being told by his grandfather and other elders contrasts markedly with what Malinowski recorded in his diary.

It was Mick the Greek who introduced him to the villagers of Oburaku. They helped him pitch his tent a few yards from the shore by a tall *natu* fruit tree, long since fallen. The site of his tent is well remembered, though not commemorated by any sign as in Omarakana. Malinowski's knowledge of the language was said to be defective, and he arrived with an 'interpreter' (*toropeta*), thought to have been a Suau man. (Ginger was in fact from Sariba, though he would have spoken a Suau dialect.) Malinowski was correctly said to have worked mostly with Navavile, the *towosi*, investigating gardening techniques and magic. Kewaiyabisila had been told that the ethnographer had not explained the purpose of his stay, but simply assumed that everyone he asked would tell him everything he wanted to know. Kewaiyabisila patiently listed 'everything' from net-fishing rites to the *mwasila* magic of Kula. Malinowski was also said to have accompanied Kadilakula, Molilakwa and Navavile on Kula trips to Kitava – though by his own account, he never went to Kitava. He was remembered to have witnessed the funeral procession, burial and mortuary ceremonies for Ineykoya, and to have taken photographs of her decorated corpse. He did indeed, and published one of them in *The Sexual Life of Savages*.[131] Touches of authenticity also occur in Kewaiyabisila's account of how the young men of Oburaku would paddle Malinowski to Kwabula to visit Tomwela 'the seer' and accompany him to Wawela to consult the stargazers.

The name Malinowski meant nothing to Kewaiyabisila, for he was known by the sobriquet *Tolilibogwa*, 'the man of *libogwa* or *liliu*' (myths, legends, folklore).[132] A more concise translation would be 'Historian'. As we have seen, another nickname was *Tosemwana* which might freely be translated as 'Performer', 'Show-Off' or 'Exhibitionist'. The name implies that he was 'proud' of the way he affected certain Trobriand mannerisms. Kadilakula was said to have given him a handsomely decorated, cassowary-bone lime spatula. The gift indicated that Malinowski was accorded the noble status of *guyau*, and he was thought to have enjoyed flaunting the spatula in public.[133] He was also said to have carried a coconut-leaf basket in which he stored his betel nuts and chewing equipment. In truth, he refers in his diary very rarely to partaking of this narcotic, and the precarious state of his dentures would have made betel-chewing a risky if not uncomfortable exercise. He could, of course, have ground his betel, lime and pepper leaf in a mortar as did the toothless elders, but made not a single reference to having done so. Yet another engaging nickname alluded to his funny habit of hitching up his trousers while peering through the lens of his camera: he was a 'man of laughter', *Topwegigila.*

Oburaku legend records that Malinowski was unusual for a white man in that he employed no cook or other servants, except for his 'Suau' interpreter. Ogisi the Dobuan and the informal retinue of hangers-on (whom Malinowski referred to collectively as 'the boys') appear to have been forgotten. This modest lack of servants (at least in legend) endeared him to the villagers, but Kewaiyabisila maintained that, far from being self-sufficent, Malinowski relied on village women to cook his yams and taros and to bring him bananas and fish. 'They looked after him,' he said. The diary maintains otherwise. Apart from those occasions when he shared feast food with the villagers, it was the much-abused Ginger who purchased or bartered for local produce and prepared his daily meals.

Even so, Malinowski's supposed generosity in doling out tobacco in exchange for gifts of food, together with his considerate treatment of people (by invidious comparison with the bullying tactics of traders, government officers and missionaries), form an essential part of his legend. Kewaiyabisila said: '*Tomota sena tombwelisi. Pela bikikatupoi, e ibigatonasi e mapela bilokeyesa wala tuta tuta. Tau bwena. Gala iluluki tomota, o kena iwaweya.* [People liked him very much. Because whenever he asked questions, they responded and therefore enjoyed paying him visits time and again. He was a nice man. He did not berate people, nor beat them.]'

Asked about Malinowski's sexual behaviour in Oburaku (a question that can be put in Kiriwina without undue indecorum), Kewaiyabisila declared that the visitor did have a few intrigues with village women. His verbatim testimony is blunt: '*Sena kaduwanoma isisu. Iulatila. Iseki tobaki vivila, mapusi. Pela tovau e sena wala magisi vivila.* [He lived here for a long while. He had affairs. He gave tobacco to women as payment for sexual favours. Because he was new, the women were very fond of him.]' Against this, however, there is no evidence whatsoever in his diary (including in those elisions demanded by his widow before its publication) that Malinowski ever did more than 'fondle', 'pat' or 'paw' the Trobriand sirens who inadvertently aroused him. His disgusted reaction to his own responses are honest enough, and his evident fear of caste-based sexual pollution – not to mention his commitment to 'purity' for the sake of Elsie – tell convincingly against the Oburaku legend.

The most remarkable fabulation, however, concerns Malinowski's departure, convincingly represented in his diary as unsentimental and ill-tempered. One would expect his leaving to have been equally unmourned by the villagers of Oburaku. But their generosity extended to imagining that they had feasted one another, and his departure was reconstructed as an emotional and spectacular event. Initiated by Kadilakula, the villagers staged a grand farewell feast for him. Kewaiyabisila relished the description. Many taros were harvested, cooked and mashed to make *mona* pudding; bunches of yellow betel nuts were gathered and laid by the cooking pots; and three pigs were slaughtered for the occasion. At the conclusion of the feast Malinowski distributed farewell gifts to his favourites. Kadilakula himself received a tomahawk, a bush knife and canvas from the ethnographer's tent. Finally, in blatant contradiction to Malinowski's dismissive version of his departure ('Looking for a *waga* in the village irritated me'), Kewaiyabisila said that when *Tolilibogwa* boarded the boat the people of Oburaku 'wailed as if someone had died'.

Chapter 25

Fear, Love and Loathing

'Creating' the Amphletts

On Wednesday 13 March 1918, Malinowski finished packing at Billy Hancock's, obtained a permit from Campbell at Losuia, and boarded the *Kayona* bound for the Amphlett Islands. Among his belongings was a box of medications containing quinine, calomel, iodine, bromide, smelling salts, bay rum, glycerine, vaseline, magnesia, eye-drops, arsenic and extra aspirin. He expected the worst: 'brackish water, swarms of mosquitoes or sandflies, no mails, no fresh food.' But as long as he kept his health, he believed he could tolerate such discomforts and even 'enjoy them as a kind of lark'.[1]

Ginger and Ogisi accompanied him; the skipper was Monauya, a Sariba islander, and the crew were from Suau. As the cutter sailed southwards across the shallow sea-arm of Pilou, heading directly for the Koya and 'the fabulous world of the little islands', Malinowski was exhilarated by a sense of freedom. By late afternoon they were approaching the oriental shapes of the Amphletts in pastel shades of pink and green. Gumasila, 'a tall, steep mountain with arched lines and great cliffs, suggest[ed] vaguely some huge Gothic monument'.[2] To the left of it loomed the massive pyramid of Domdom.

Darkness had already fallen and the *Kayona* was cruising between Gumasila and Domdom when a violent northwesterly squall forced it to run before the wind. There was clamour on the deck, and from the stifling cabin where he lay, queasy with seasickness, Malinowski heard the cry: 'Look out for the reef!' He was soon 'in a state of unmitigated funk'. Ginger and Monauya could see witches flickering over the masthead, and when the wind shredded the mainsail, Malinowski realized their situation was serious. For the first time in his life (he told Elsie) he literally trembled with fear. His first thought was that it had been foolhardy to sail on the thirteenth of the month, and he recalled the nightmarish premonition he had had about the Amphletts ever since Ernest Johns, the missionary at Oiabia, had told him about his near-fatal shipwreck there some years before. It suddenly seemed to be 'the absolute logic of fate' that he should be drowned in these islands, as if the entire course of his life had led to this particular 'appointed term'. His second thoughts were for his mother and for Elsie. His reflex pessimism conjured another superstition: he was afraid to be optimistic because he secretly believed it brought bad luck. 'I felt this astonished shock,' he told Elsie. Out of a drowsy grey afternoon 'there emerged a Finality . . . with which I could not cope, because I was seasick . . . & I could only lie down and *tremble!*'[3]

He was ashamed of his funk. 'I *had* lost my nerve entirely!' he confessed. In due course Elsie replied that only one without imagination felt no fear. She would have prevented herself from losing her nerve only 'by a kind of fatuous, self-deceiving optimism, perhaps also a kind of superstitious fatalism'. How could she despise him, then? She would mind if his courage were to fail when something was demanded of him, but she trusted it would not do so. 'Your self control and sense of dignity would conquer your imaginings.'[4]

The brush with shipwreck had some ethnographic value. It enabled him to appreciate the hazards that Kula traders confronted in their fragile canoes. When he came to write *Argonauts* he devoted a chapter to the natural and supernatural perils of sailing on the sea of Pilou, and another to the story of a shipwreck. He referred to his own experience matter-of-factly and without heroics, for he wanted to illustrate a point about the fear of flying witches.

> Except for myself, all the members of the crew saw clearly the flying witches in the form of a flame at the mast head. Whether this was St Elmo's fire I could not judge, as I was in the cabin, seasick and indifferent to dangers, witches, and even ethnographic revelations.[5]

The candid appeal to his own infirmity was an ironic form of heroism, perhaps, but there was no allusion to his own fear, or to its aggravation by superstitious premonitions.

The danger of shipwreck, of flying witches that eat the insides of floundering sailors, dogged the *Kayona* for several hours that night. Then, 'broken and discouraged by seasickness', Malinowski awoke to find they had been driven well south of the Amphletts and were testing the shores of the low green island of Sanaroa. The boat found sanctuary in a calm inlet, beyond which lay a maze of sago swamps. They were already halfway to Dobu and the mountains of Normanby Island were visible to the south. Thunder growled and lightning sparked over the sinister black hump of Bwebweso, Land of the Dead.

After sleeping until late afternoon, Malinowski sought white company aboard a motor launch that had moored nearby. It belonged to a Finnish trader, another Conradian character whom Malinowski had met in Port Moresby. He was blond and gaunt and wore a 'pendant, tow-coloured mustache' that reminded Malinowski of the classical figure of *The Dying Gaul*. They took tea together, talked politics and listened to the gramophone. The strains of Harry Lauder and Viennese waltzes floated above the indifferent mangroves. There were other encounters with itinerant whites during these days, traders and recruiters who plied between Samarai and the Trobriands. Far from being isolated, Malinowski wondered ruefully, the Massim seemed to be only a 'little less peopled with boats than the English Channel'.[6]

When the sea had smoothed, the *Kayona* tacked north, back towards the Amphletts. The squall-driven diversion brought Malinowski some ethnographic compensations. In Sanaroa he had observed preparations for a Kula expedition to the Trobriands and, for the first time, witnessed sago-making. Now he was permitted a serendipitous glimpse of northeast Fergusson islanders, whom Trobrianders feared as cannibals. The people they knew as Basima lived beneath the twin peaks of majestic Koyatabu ('Sacred Mountain'), which soared above the jungle 'like a somewhat tame juxtaposition of the Matterhorn and Wetterhorn'. Skipper Monauya found an anchorage and Malinowski went ashore to inspect a couple of settlements. Only recently descended from the foothills at the behest of the government, the people seemed 'small, sickly looking, frightened'; they gave him the 'feeling of "savages"'. The men understood the language of Dobu and he spoke to them through Ogisi. In a second hamlet of four or five houses he observed people 'covered with Sepuma [ringworm], all scratching themselves, or scratching their dogs'. Their houses were set on stilts and looked more primitive than those of Kiriwina, which had been modified since European contact. He sat with the Basima villagers for a while, but (as he told Elsie) 'did not attempt much ethnographying and my few attempts were met with smiles which meant "don't try these silly jokes on us"'.[7]

Malinowski's brief encounter with some of the inhabitants of the hitherto blank and mysterious Fergusson Island gave to it a human face. When Trobrianders next spoke of *Wa Koya*, he would bring to mind those faces and places. Twelve years later, a New Zealander named Reo Fortune – a pupil of both Haddon and Malinowski – would spend a month among Basima people. And seventy years after Malinowski's visit, a young Trobriand anthropologist named Linus Digim'Rina would conduct a more thorough and intensive study, in precisely the manner advocated by the Master in *Argonauts*.[8]

On 19 March, the *Kayona* sped for the Amphletts on a fresh southeasterly wind. It was Józefa Malinowska's saint's day, and her son believed it would bring him luck. This clutch of rugged islets was the Canaries in miniature – if 'savage' rather than 'civilized', pagan rather than Christian. With memories of the Canaries came thoughts of his mother ('O *Mamusiu, Mamusiu,* will we ever travel again by *carretera* from Tacoronte to Icod de los Vinos?').[9] He did not know that she was already two months in the grave.

As they neared the islands from the south the view was just as splendid as that from the north: 'the pyramid of Domdom with the cupola on top. . . . Gumasila, with the double hump. The three cupolas of Nabwageta, further along the wooded hills of Kwatouto and Yabwaya.' These were the inhabited islands – occupied by fewer than three hundred people – but there were a score of barren satellites among them. Monauya found a sheltered anchorage on southwest Gumasila, and by mid-afternoon Malinowski was landing at Nuagasi with all his gear. The village was a line of houses strung between the mountain and the sea, and there was scarcely room for his tent on the narrow strip of beach. Ginger and Ogisi disembarked with him in the dinghy while the *Kayona* and its crew sailed off to Samarai. The strangers' sudden appearance stunned the tiny community and normal life was suspended as the women and children fled into the bush.

The dwellings fascinated Malinowski. Perched on posts, their gable roofs arched almost to the ground. Like the Basima houses, they struck him 'as very old, very "deep-rooted"'. He was already familiar with Amphlett pottery in Kiriwina. The women were expert potters and produced some of the most elegantly shaped and tastefully decorated cooking pots in Papua. The men traded the clay pots throughout the region in exchange for garden produce, sago, pigs and betel nuts. From the Trobriands they imported wooden dishes, lime-pots, three-tiered baskets and women's fine leaf skirts.[10]

At first the prospects for serious ethnographic work were unpromising. The men of Nuagasi were reluctant informants. Tovasana, the leading headman of the islands, 'looked like an old gnome' with a 'large aquiline nose sticking out from under an enormous turban-like wig'.[11] His profile put Malinowski in mind of Sir Edward Stirling. Kipela was a singlet-clad youth who had spent time in white men's service where he 'acquired the art of speaking pidgin and of lying'. A second young man was Anaibutuna: sweet-faced, innocuous, honest, decent, willing and well-mannered, but, for all these virtues, not very intelligent. Although they all spoke the language of the Trobriands, Malinowski spoke it better, and without this Kiriwina asset he would have accomplished little. Then he was joined by Tobawona and began to do 'excellent work on the language' – though within a week Tobawona went stale on him. As for the other men of Gumasila, a single Polish-English image from the diary will suffice: 'The fellows sat dully on stones, *independent, sulky, unfriendly – true islanders!*'[12]

Malinowski's objectives were precise: to document the language and local technology, sketch the settlement pattern and relations of kinship and marriage, investigate the Amphlettans' role in Kula, their religious beliefs and mortuary practices. In short, he aimed to gather information for a general ethnographic description for the solid appendix he planned to write for his magnum opus. (When he abandoned 'Kiriwina' the material instead came to form the basis of a chapter on the Amphletts in *Argonauts*.) It was for the sake of situated description, he explained to Elsie, that he tried to impress the scenery upon his mind. He was certainly stimulated by the fresh surroundings and by the new ethnological challenge. 'This kind of work – superficial, without going into details – is much lighter and more amusing than the work in Kiriwina.' He now understood 'the charm of "*survey study*" à la Rivers, the encompassing of broad areas as a single whole'.[13]

Elsie entertained her own fantasies about doing fieldwork with Malinowski. Mindful of their romantic appeal, she had jumped at his dreamy suggestion that the Amphletts would be an ideal place to make their fieldwork début as a team. 'Together we will pitch a tent not far from one of their villages, and I shall learn from one of the women how to make their pots.'[14] She had Robert Louis Stevenson in mind when she later wrote: 'I feel we would have a right to withdraw for a while from this sad, turbulent world to an islet of our own, because we would be working also.'[15] Elsie would have been a considerable asset, but Malinowski now decided that the islands were 'just a small side-show to Kiriwina' and that if they worked '*à deux*' they would need to tackle larger islands such as Rossel or Misima.[16] But Elsie dreamed on:

> I shall write a popular book called 'A Woman in the Field,' of which the publishers will say 'A unique account of the marvellous adventures of this daring woman amongst the cannibalistic savages of Australian New Guinea. . . . Extract: 'It was not long before my little tent became the central point of attraction in the Trobriands. The white traders frequently came to visit me, generally bringing me pearls and tortoiseshells as offerings. They would remain for an hour or two, confiding to me the story of their lonely lives, while a ring of natives formed a sort of bodyguard around us, awaiting a word or a smile from the beautiful Miss with a turned-up nose. . . .' Don't you think we would make our fortune?[17]

At times Malinowski longed desperately for Elsie: 'I felt I wanted her the way a child wants his mother.' To his diary he also confessed a 'fierce, almost religious yearning' for her. The religious overtones of his love are manifest. He referred to 'the sacramental sacredness of the marriage bed', tabooing the phrase by placing it in quotes.[18] It was a mental talisman against the 'dirty thoughts' that came unbidden in the night. 'Spiritual purity' was his impossible goal: 'I realise that purity in deeds depends on purity of thought, and I resolve to watch myself down to the deepest instincts.'[19]

Good ethnography requires the alertness of every sense. Enthralled by the romantic beauty of the islands, Malinowski enjoyed a heightened awareness of his surroundings. Just a few steps from the sea, he could hear from his tent 'the sound of gentle plashing, and the noise of torrents up above in the lofty green wall'. He went for daily rowing excursions with Ginger, absorbing the scenery from the drifting dinghy. His diary is replete with painterly descriptions. Expressions of 'joy' sprinkle the pages. For a few days he was happy and felt strong and healthy. The scatter of ornately figured islands against the purple profiles of the high mountains of Fergusson – the visual rhythms of sea, sky, rock and jungle – enraptured him and engaged his musical sensibilities. When caught in sheeting rain he roared Wagnerian melodies; another time he recalled his old friend, the composer Szymberski. He felt the harmonic synergies of music and seascape. Wanting to tell Elsie about the magical light, he repeated: '*This is quite like a symphony.*' The sense of smell too, contributed to his delight: 'yesterday moss, seaweed and flowers, the wind was from the island; today the fragrance of tuberoses on the beach.'[20]

Sight is the primary sense for the ethnographer and, impaired though his vision was, Malinowski indulged his appreciation of colour and form. The sky above the village at dusk yielded 'a black shadow slowly strangling the yellowish light blended with the silvery glow of the moon behind clouds'. Another evening he saw the gold and silver of the rippling sea at sunset, 'when the light seems to materialize into liquid metal and shrink, vanish and again appear'. So 'charmed' and 'spellbound' was he by the scenic glories of the Amphletts that he was granted occasional epiphanies, moments of altered consciousness in which he saw the Platonic world of Ideas beyond the world of Appearances. Rowing quietly one evening when the moon was lurking behind lacy clouds, he felt that, 'next to this actual ocean' with its changing moods, 'there is an Absolute Ocean, which is more or less correctly marked on the map but which exists outside all maps'.[21]

An explorer's epiphany occurred while rowing around Gumasila following a misty sunset. Ginger pulled on the oars while Malinowski studied the uninhabited coast. He 'rejoiced in the feeling of recognition', adding: 'This island, though not "discovered" by me, is for the first time experienced artistically and mastered intellectually.'[22] Such imperialist arrogance discounted the Massim inhabitants' unfathomably different perception of their island; by what Eurocentric measure was he able to claim that they could neither aesthetically experience nor cognitively master it?

Lies and superstitions

On Sunday 24 March, half a dozen men arrived in Gumasila from the Trobriands. Malinowski observed them initiate Kula transactions, and he was struck again by the nonchalance of the visitors and by the matching indifference of their hosts. Studied unconcern ordered the protocols of gift exchange. Malinowski sat with them and listened to their conversation, their 'jocular haggling' and creative 'lying' about their shell valuables.[23] The following day the men of Gumasila departed abruptly for the Trobriands to engage in Kula. Although he had been warned that an expedition was imminent, its suddenness caught him by surprise. 'Whether because of *secretiveness* or superstition, they always conceal their departures from me,' he complained. It had happened in Mailu and in Omarakana, too, and it always angered him.

It was as if he thought he had every right to be informed of their plans, as if he had been betrayed. Had he reflected on his own cautionary superstition concerning 'unlucky' departures on the thirteenth of the month, he might have been prepared to concede Massim people their belief that departures announced were departures threatened – by witches, or by the ill will of the living. To inform others of your travel plans was to invite misfortune.

With the departure of most of the men from Gumasila there was 'not a single good informant to be found'. He had worked hard since arriving and felt intellectually and emotionally fatigued. An aphorism provided him with a wise excuse for indolence: 'Rest is one of the most important forms of work.'[24] The news from the nearby island of Nabwageta next day was that they too were about to depart for Kiriwina. He was annoyed at the disruption of his own plans, felt 'hatred for the *niggers*' and suppressed a resentful impulse to leave the Amphletts altogether.[25] He was pleasantly surprised, then, to find Nabwageta 'pulsating with intense life'. The men would not leave for a few more days, so he decided to camp there rather than go to Domdom. As he well knew, the men of Gumasila wanted him gone from their island. They did not trust him and his 'boys' enough to leave them alone with the women.

Informants on Nabwageta disappointed him, however. They did not know the terms for design-elements of canoe carvings and they denied that they had any garden magic. He grew irritated and sought out other informants, with similar results; whenever he touched on questions of magic he sensed they were 'telling lies'. Assuming a right to be told the truth, he complained repeatedly of Amphlett men's 'lying' – as he had of people in Mailu and elsewhere. Yet he was not innocent of the odd, casual lie himself in order to lead informants on. In this way he made an accidental discovery of cannibalism in the Amphletts. '*Old man* asked me: "Do you eat dogs?" "Of course, some dogs and people." "We don't, but Domdom and Kwatouto did." '[26]

The thirteenth day of his sojourn in the Amphletts was 1 April – an inauspicious day in its own right, he believed. Fate had played some nasty tricks on him on that day in previous years. In 1914 he had quarrelled painfully with Tośka in London; in 1915 it had been the day of his arrest and brief imprisonment in Adelaide; in 1916 it had been the 'rupture' with the Stirlings; and 1 April 1917 was the day he was told that he must lose the rest of his teeth.[27] (Elsie joked later about his return to Melbourne: 'Don't come on the 13th, or you will simply force yourself to have bad luck. . . . Nor 1st April, or you might have another rupture with a lady.')[28]

Almost certainly, it was superstition that made him decline the invitation to sail with the *Kayona* which called early that morning on its way back to Gusaweta. It was not simply a matter of 'missing the boat', at which he was a past master, but of deliberately refusing to board it on 1 April. (The cryptic note in his diary merely hints at incipient 'funk': 'The boat and the noise unnerve me and I *retreat.'*) As soon as the cutter had departed, however, he regretted his decision. By avoiding one risk he had courted another, for he might now be marooned in the Amphletts for weeks. It was ethnographic folly, too, for the Nabwageta canoes were about to follow the Dobuan fleet and he was in danger of missing a major event: the convergence on Sinaketa of the largest overseas Kula expedition that he was ever likely to witness. Later, he candidly admitted his 'mistake' in *Argonauts*: 'I was left in the village with a few cripples, the women, and one or two men who had remained perhaps to look after the village, specially to keep watch over me and see that I did no mischief.'[29]

After another fretful day Malinowski won an undeserved reprieve. Providentially, the Auerbach brothers called into Nabwageta in the *Ithaca*. He hurriedly packed and boarded, sorry only that he had not taken more photographs and made a better study of pottery-making. He had spent precisely two weeks in the Amphletts (not 'about a month' as he later claimed)[30] and, despite its near-disastrous beginning and abrupt ending, despite too his irrational fears and the surly evasions of some of his informants, the trip had been fruitful and he had enjoyed some of the most picturesque scenery in Papua. Although he would disparage these islands as 'ethnographically barren', he had gathered enough material to write a concise account of the Amphletts, enough to 'create' them for the record.[31] More important, perhaps, he had learned much about Kula and could begin to see it from the perspective of Dobu, a task that he could now complete by joining the fleet in Kiriwina.

Tempering joy at the prospect of a return to 'the middle of things' was his dismay on learning of the terrible news concerning Germany's fresh offensive on the Western Front. It roused his pro-British feelings, though not for the first time did he wonder how Elsie could continue to love him, given his own unheroic circumstances. Yet anthropological posterity would come to view his fieldwork achievement as singularly heroic, and the recursive pattern of his charter myth is discernible even in his brief expedition to the Amphletts. The hero sails to unknown shores, confronts natural and supernatural dangers, overcomes obstacles with trickery and magical help, and returns safely with the treasures he has won. In the manner of such heroes, too, he would claim a wife and rightful fame. Did it perhaps occur to him that his own quest for ethnographic riches mirrored the heroic quest for fame and fortune of the Kula traders who plied these islands?

Francophilia in Sinaketa

Eager to pick up his mail, he sailed first to Gusaweta. There was only one letter from Elsie, but several from Nina which he could not bring himself to open. The next day he sailed to Kiribi and then on to Sinaketa, where the Kula fleets from the south and from Kitava were about to converge. He made himself as comfortable as possible in a ramshackle old house belonging to Billy on the edge of the village, then he turned to review his material on the phase of Kula that he was about to witness. Later, he turned the exercise into a lesson in methodology:

> If . . . as it often happens in ethnographic field-work, one gets the opportunity only once of witnessing a public ceremony, it is necessary to have its anatomy well dissected beforehand, and then concentrate upon observing how these outlines are followed up concretely, gauge the tone of the general behaviour, the touches of emotion or passion, many small yet significant details which nothing but actual observation can reveal, and which throw much light upon the real, inner relation of the native to his institution.[32]

On 5 April, the Dobuan canoes were sighted on the horizon, 'their triangular sails like butterfly wings'. Joined by smaller fleets from the Amphletts and Kitava, more than eighty canoes were now approaching Sinaketa. With a surge of 'ethnographic joy' Malinowski hurried to the shore with his camera and persuaded Tovasana to paddle him to a nearby promontory.[33] There he watched the fleet make its mandatory halt, the men of each canoe performing their final magical preparations for the ceremonial landing. Sinaketa soon resembled 'a summer resort' as men from several islands and dozens of villages mingled on the beach – over two thousand in all, Malinowski judged.[34] The event was one of the highlights of his fieldwork and he was 'engrossed – as an ethnographer – in all the goings-on'.[35] Writing to Elsie a few days later, he likened the Kula gathering to an enormous garden party and struck a note of blasé condescension: 'a typically English garden party seems to me always entirely pointless and inherently tedious, quite as much as the *Kula.*' He could understand why people indulged in such social activities, 'but subjectively I could find happiness and joy in neither'.[36]

Still, it was a unique opportunity and he worked furiously at photography ('which I hate above all other things'), taking two dozen plates and dozens more shots with his Graflex 'snapshot' camera. He also made countless sketches of canoe carvings. By Sunday 7 April – his thirty-fourth birthday – he had exhausted himself and was so tired that he almost fainted. The note-taking was less productive. He couldn't work well with the visitors as they were 'all self-conscious and excited' and 'strangers are never willing to open up in a distant village'. As for eavesdropping, he was at a disadvantage because everyone was speaking the lingua franca of Dobu. Yet he was pleased about what he had seen and done. 'I think my account of it will have much more "body".'[37] Sure enough, his portrayal of the event in *Argonauts* bears the authentic stamp of close ethnographic engagement.[38]

After the Dobuans had gone – abruptly as usual – Malinowski returned to Gusaweta to develop and print his photographs in Billy's darkroom. Sailing back to Sinaketa by canoe, he whiled away the afternoon by re-reading his diary. It prompted moral reflections. His present mode of life was unsatisfactory: 'I turn in too late, I get up at irregular hours. Too little time devoted to observation, contact with niggers, too much barren collecting of information. I rest too frequently, and indulge in "demoralization" as in Nabwageta.' He gave thought also to the 'problems of keeping a diary':

> How immensely difficult it is to formulate the endless variety of things in the current of a life. Keeping a diary as a problem of psychological analysis: to isolate the essential elements, to classify them (from what point of view?), then, in describing them indicate more or less clearly what is their actual importance at the given moment.[39]

In what is the most analytical presentation he ever gave of his prescriptions for writing an ideal diary, he listed four essential components. First, there were 'external impressions; landscape, colours, mood, artistic synthesis'. Second, were 'dominant feelings in respect to myself, to my beloved, to friends, to things'. Third, 'forms of thought; specific thoughts, loose associations; obsessions.' Fourth, 'dynamic states of the organism; degree of concentration; degree of higher awareness; programs.'[40] In the light of his observation that his diary and his ethnography were complementary to one another, these four 'essential' psychological elements of the exemplary diary can be detected, if only faintly, in an exemplary ethnography such as *Argonauts*. Description of surroundings and 'artistic synthesis' appear most prominently in his adaptation of a Frazerian *mise-en-scène* to present an ethnographic setting. 'Dominant feelings' are less relevant, except as they occasionally enliven his ethnographic anecdotes by constrasting his own emotional reactions to an event with those of the islanders. Thoughts and associations appear in crystallized, formal guise as theoretical statements and generalizations. The reflexive question 'to what extent introspective analysis modifies psychic states' could well be reformulated for the eyewitnessing fieldworker: to what extent did his presence modify the behaviour of those islanders under his observation? There is scant evidence, however, that this question bothered him. Finally, his ethical programmes for self-improvement have an analogue in the methodological prescriptions he laid down for aspiring ethnographers.

He returned to Billy Hancock's dilapidated house on the outskirts of Sinaketa. Seated at his camp table on the narrow verandah he wrote to Elsie in what he called his morning dress, 'which consists of pyjama trousers and socks, the rest being exposed to the fresh air and stray mosquitoes'.[41] He told her:

> I like to think that all my work is just for you and that the publishing of it is only a secondary product. This attitude makes also for greater honesty and sincerity, because there would be no point in deceiving you even for a hairbreadth as to the degree of my certitude or conceal deficiencies.[42]

There were degrees of honesty in ethnography, he continued, 'and there are just small touches which one can give to the phrasing, to the arrangement of facts etc. that will give an additional lustre to things.' There were many such touches in Baldwin Spencer's books. 'My two short articles are also full of them, though the "Baloma" less than the first one. I'll try to be as stern as a Quaker in my *Magnum Opus* and my Elsie will help.' To this protestation of scientific scruple she replied:

> It would be really good if we were able to make absolute sincerity our goal. It strikes me more and more how inaccurate most ethnological

work must be, how hopelessly off the track. If you knowing the language and with your training find many holes in your own work on your return, and had it not been for the unusual circumstances, that return itself would have never taken place.[43]

This insight invites the 'what if?' reflection that without the restrictions imposed upon Malinowski by the circumstances of the war and by Hubert Murray's decision to curtail his movements, he would probably have cut short his Trobriand work and gone to Rossel Island instead. The contingency of his illness in 1916 and his enforced stay in Melbourne was also to benefit his work in the long run.

Although he slept and sometimes worked in Billy's house, he fell into the routine of dining each evening with the Brudos. After the culinary privation of Oburaku and the Amphletts, the appeal of French cooking was irresistible. On his return from Gusaweta on 11 April, he told Elsie:

> The Raffaels [sic] kept a Lucullus meal for me (fish boiled with a nice sauce, fresh beans, chocolate blancmange and lemonade) and then we began to talk French literature and R. read some Alfred de Musset. It was a very un-Kiriwinian evening and we spoke much of Paris and Racine, Corneille etc.[44]

Elsie would like the Brudos, he felt, for they were in some ways 'replicas of the Khuners' and worthy of admittance to the Clan. Raphael was 'tall and well-built, bald with a broad forehead and prominent, brilliant black eyes . . . pale complexion and nervous expression'. Simone was shorter, fatter and aggressively French – despite the insinuations of the other traders that she was Turkish. Raphael was

> intelligent, half-educated with lots of crude and funny ideas, but with very sound instincts of real and independent thinking & with a real interest in things. He speaks Kiriwinian relatively well and he is capable of constructing native problems (like the *Kula*) in a manner far beyond what anyone else here would do.[45]

Malinowski told Elsie he was in a happier frame of mind than he had been in Oburaku. He had entered a new, more mobile phase of his fieldwork:

> It is infinitely more attractive to move about and one completely escapes the feeling of loneliness and hopeless 'being left behind' by all the world. The Raffaels [sic] will make a good deal of difference to my welfare &

most likely I am going to put in as much as a couple of months in Sinaketa, later on, as information seems to be very easily available here.[46]

In Sinaketa he enjoyed the best of both worlds. The rigours of the field were tempered by the civilized comforts of good cooking and intelligent conversation. The Brudos provided an atmosphere in which he could relax, be entertained by readings from Racine, Hugo and Chateaubriand, and where he could leaf through risqué issues of *La vie parisienne*. He even played croquet with his hosts. Although it was intensive, his fieldwork during his seven weeks in Sinaketa did not entail the immersion he advocated. It recalled his period in Mailu rather than his months in Omarakana; it was a retreat to the verandah from which colonial masters viewed their subjects, and where he indulged in 'armchair work'.

From the later perspective of 1932, Raphael Brudo romanticized their friendship and its exotic setting:

> Can you imagine our evenings? After having each finished our daily tasks, he preparing his notes, and I carrying on my work as trader, we were together at the meal table. . . . I read aloud verses of poetry or a chapter of a good author on whose work we commented. On other evenings the fancy for music gripped us, and we hummed passages of Wagner or a sonata of Beethoven under the gaping regard of my native boys.[47]

Although Malinowski's acquaintance with him ripened into a lifelong friendship, it was only a matter of days before he found the Frenchman's company too much of a good thing. The gravitational pull of another's personality upset his psychological balance. 'Everything is in the shadow; my thoughts are no longer characteristic in themselves, and they take on value *qua* conversation with Raf.' His individuality leaked, and he noticed again how intensive social intercourse made it impossible for him to write his diary. He needed to recover his solitude.[48]

Tiberius in Vakuta

On Sunday 14 April, Malinowski left Sinaketa for a week's visit to Vakuta, the boomerang-shaped island that hangs from the bottom of Kiriwina. He had tried to sail with the Kitavan Kula traders who were returning to their own island via Vakuta, but fearing he would bring them misfortune they refused to take him. The crew of a Vakutan canoe reluctantly accepted him instead. The trip did not begin well. That morning Malinowski had a violent altercation with Ginger and in his rage punched him in the jaw. Not usually given to violence, he scared himself, afraid the assault could degenerate into a brawl. Ginger took the punishment on the chin, so to speak, though his resentment can be imagined.[49]

With only two hours' notice, Malinowski packed his gear and left with his party in mid-afternoon. Punting and paddling, the canoe hugged the shallow margins of the broken shore. It was his first opportunity to venture so far south on Kiriwina, and he was keen to see the coast with his own eyes. 'There is something attractive in this craving,' he wrote to Elsie later, 'to translate an extremely abstract idea, that of a geographical spot, into concrete experience.'[50] He minutely described the slowly changing scene, striving for artistic synthesis. Then, 'with threatening clouds and distant thunder', darkness fell and he sensed rather than saw the coral ridge – the *raybwag* – add its thickening mass to the blunt end of Kiriwina as the hammering chorus of frogs gave way to the chirping of crickets. Before the rain came they reached Giribwa, 'a miserable village of 11 huts' situated on the narrow passage between the main island and the 'fairylike promontory' of Vakuta. He retired to a partially completed hut and that night, with deliberate pornographic intent, he read Montesquieu's *Lettres persanes*.[51]

Next morning he was paddled across Vakuta's lagoon to a tidal creek, then through a mangrove swamp to a clearing shaded by high forest trees. Nearby was a dilapidated mission compound which Malinowski commandeered as his quarters: the teacher's old house would serve as his kitchen, the abandoned church as his bedroom. A short walk away was the new house of the native missionary, Samsoni, and just beyond were the hamlets of the main village of Vakuta. That evening he paid a diplomatic visit to the local *guyau*. While his rank was inferior to that of the Kiriwina chiefs, Kouligaga was 'not a bad chap' who accepted 'as much tobacco as you give him and does not impudently beg for more'. Cadging tobacco was the shameless practice of most *guyau*.

Malinowski was delighted to submit himself to new impressions. As he walked to Kaulaka, an inland village picturesquely situated in a palm-lined hollow, he took an anticipatory pleasure in an 'unsettled consciousness, where waves of new things . . . flow from all sides, break against each other, mix, and vanish'.[52] It was like listening to a new piece of music, or the thrill of a new love. And next day he was feeling contentment with his solitude and the prospect of keen concentration. For the moment at least, fieldwork was rewarding enough to take its place in the wider spectrum of intellectual life. 'Since I left Oburaku,' he told Elsie, 'I have almost enjoyed the free, independent extemporized existence here, full of discomfort and petty annoyances, yet giving full scope for creative mental expansion and at the same time affording wonderful artistic impressions.'[53]

He was now intent on investigating the similarities and differences between Vakuta and Kiriwina, particularly with respect to gardening, mythology, religion and the sailing magic associated with Kula. Vakuta was one of the most important canoe-building and wood-carving centres in the islands, and Malinowski was also keen to learn more about the design motifs that mastercarvers (*tokabitam*) painstakingly worked into the prowboards and transverse splashboards (*tabuyo* and *lagim*) of new canoes. Both Haddon and Seligman had urged him to pursue this line of inquiry in the Massim, but although he learned a good deal more in Vakuta than he had in the Amphletts about the magic of carving and the significance of ornamental motifs, he was disappointed with the piecemeal nature of the information. Like his British mentors, he had expected to discover a magico-religious symbolic system. He might as well have chased moonbeams. 'I am now quite certain,' he told Elsie, 'that the natives have neither mythological nor individual explanations as to the meaning of their compositions.' While they could name motifs, they could not tell him why they were combined in particular ways. 'For me,' he confessed, 'their decorative art is a real mystery, which I (privately) solve by assuming that this art has been handed down by members of a much superior culture.'[54] This kind of explanation, he well knew, was a tacit admission of failure. Had he been more patient and apprenticed himself to a mastercarver, he would have learned a great deal more, though he still would not have found the kind of grand explanatory system that he sought.[55] While he despaired of finding an ideological key to their art, he nevertheless documented it conscientiously by sketches, rubbings and photographs, and by noting whatever exigeses were offered to him. He never found occasion to publish this material, so it lies forgotten in his archived fieldnotes.

During the first part of the week the weather continued wet and sultry, 'everything floating in a thick soup of fog, mist, and smoke'. It induced a claustrophobic mood of nervous tension, a 'superirritability and supersensitiveness of mental epidermis'.[56] Impatient with being cooped up by the rain, on Wednesday evening he walked to Kaulaka, an exercise that proved

inspirational. Returning between the walls of sodden vegetation, he conceived the idea of a 'New Humanism' based on an anthropology of 'living
man, living language, and living full-blooded facts'. The 'twin pillars' of the
New Humanism, he told Elsie, would be philosophy and sociology, the latter
being 'the science of your fellow human beings'. It would 'take its inspiration from ethnography, mainly, or the study of living societies, and not from
archaeology, history etc. or dust and death'.[57] His idea was to rescue humanism from its moribund association with petrified thinking centred on
classical Greece and Rome. In Vakuta, it seems, he was beginning to imagine
a broader, public role for anthropology. His 'revolution' would not be confined to academe. While the founding of 'a kind of humanistic R[oyal]
S[ociety]' was too extravagant a hope, he did float the idea of a sociology-
based humanism in a seminal article he wrote on returning to England.[58]

Thursday dawned fine. He worked well for several hours and in the late
afternoon took a long walk to the seashore beyond Kaulaka.

> A pretty, finely built girl walked ahead of me. I watched the muscles of
> her back, her figure, her legs, and the beauty of the body so hidden to
> us, whites, fascinated me. Probably even with my own wife I'll never have
> the opportunity to observe the play of back muscles for as long as with
> this little animal. At moments I was sorry I was not a savage and could
> not possess this pretty girl.[59]

Soon he was also 'admiring the body of a very handsome boy', and observed
in his diary: '*Taking into account* a certain residue of homosexuality in human
nature the cult of the beauty of the human body corresponds to the definition given by Stendhal.' Beauty is the promise of bliss. In the village that
evening he 'pawed' another pretty girl, a lapse for which he was punished
by remorse that night. 'That lousy girl . . . everything fine, but I shouldn't
have pawed her. . . . Resolve: absolutely never to touch any Kiriwina
whore. To be mentally incapable of possessing anyone except E.R.M.'[60] He
mentioned none of these mental lapses in his diary-letter to Elsie. Another
revealing incident occurred a few weeks later. He visited George Auerbach
one evening and danced to the gramophone with a local woman named
Jabulona. He confessed to his diary that he had 'pawed' her. He felt suitably
guilty afterwards, and attributed this lapse mainly to 'a desire to impress the
other fellows'. He wanted to show George in particular that he was attracted
to women. The rumour that he fancied 'boys' had probably reached the

Trobriands (if indeed it did not begin there), and he might have felt some need to disprove it. His diary for this year mentions several moral lapses when he 'pawed' young women; but there is not a single reference to his having 'pawed' young men; and for every reference to male beauty there are a dozen that admire female forms. If he did show any homosexual inclination during his fieldwork it was weakly motivated and heavily outweighed by his unsatisfied longing for female flesh. Only once in his New Guinea diaries did he allude to a homoerotic encounter – with Diko, the Sinaugolo man.[61] More telling – and inadvertently comical – testimony to Malinowski's narcissism is the dream that he recorded in Port Moresby on 20 September 1914. It featured a homosexual act with his own double. 'Strangely autoerotic feelings; the impression that I'd like to have a mouth just like mine to kiss, a neck that curves just like mine, a forehead just like mine (seen from the side).'[62]

Friday 19 April was another productive day – one of those rare days when ethnographic work delivered emotional rewards, as in Nuagasi when 'the veil was rent' and information flowed. Walking along the beach that evening he was flushed with optimism. Ogisi lit a fire on the beach and they sat watching the flames flickering redly on the tree trunks.

> I also had the real joy of creative work, of overcoming obstacles, new horizons opening up; misty forms take on contours, before me I see the road going onward and upward. I had the same upsurges of joy at Omarakana – then they had been even more justified, for that was my first success and the difficulties were greater.[63]

Working at his present pace, he considered, he would return to Melbourne as 'laden with materials as a camel'. He was in splendid health: 'For nothing in the world would I read trashy novels, and I think with pity about people who keep taking medicine all the time! Health!!'[64]

On Sunday morning he made a rare attendance at a church service. He did not bother to describe it, dismissing it lightly as 'just another ethn[ographic] experience'. Then he continued his diary-letter to Elsie. 'I am quite in love with Vakuta,' he told her. 'The information is not pouring in but simply gushing & instead of worrying for informants & losing time for lack of niggers, I have an *embarras de richesses* & I am almost crushed by the opportunities streaming in, overtaking me, begging to be taken.'[65] He was getting more in a single, teatime conversation than he had in a day's

hard work at Oburaku. The difference, he suspected, was due to the civilizing influence of the local mission and to the Vakutans' willingness to 'sign
on' and work for white men. They were less secretive, less inclined to evasion
and dissimulation. Paradoxically, the deracinating effects of colonial contact
worked in anthropology's favour, and Malinowski admitted to being 'almost
reconciled to mission work'. Indeed, Samsoni, the mission teacher, proved
to be an excellent informant on traditional religion.

On Monday his concentration began to waver and he felt 'frankly seedy'.
His elation was turning to rancour. He intended to leave Vakuta next day
and had already hired a canoe (for ten sticks of tobacco, plus two sticks per
head for its four crew); but in the morning the men offered a variety of
excuses ('a dying child, or a headache, or a sore toe') and refused to go.
'This drives me to a state of white rage and hatred for bronze-coloured
skin, combined with depression, a desire to "sit down and cry", and a furious
longing "*to get out of this*".' He decided to make the best of the delay,
however, and spent the day working in the village. The next day, 'after much
ado', he managed to assemble a crew, but he was so angry that he 'simply
couldn't look at the *negroes*' and spent the four-hour trip to Sinaketa reading
and sulkily watching the coastline glide slowly by.[66]

In his letter to Elsie he was even more vehement about the incident than
in his private diary.

> Today I am in a black rage against all the niggers, the Mission, the British
> System of pampering the blacks etc. etc. . . . . It certainly makes you feel
> that you would like to have a revolver in your hand and drive the swine
> at its point or else you would love to have here the system, so denounced
> by E.R.M. at the Socialists [meetings] & be able to send any or all of
> them to some office, where they would receive 10–20 sticks not of
> tobacco but of good solid cane![67]

To this outburst of white-supremacist pique at 'spoilt natives' Elsie
responded with a veiled reprimand, though she tried hard to excuse his
attitude.

> Of course the British laws exist just to protect the niggs from similar
> attacks of spleen from white men in the tropics when thwarted by the
> niggs whom they must regard as naughty children. I know that one is
> very prone to such attacks in the tropics when all ordinary standards
> dissipate, and I can imagine one's horror of oneself if one gave way and

looked back on it afterwards from civilization. I don't think I could ever feel quite the same towards someone who had sent a nigg to have a government beating, worse than I would if he drew a revolver on him. Of course, in your case it was a matter of very important work being stopped by the whim of silly children, but next time it would be a trader.[68]

It was a gentle enough deflation, but Malinowski returned aggressively to the subject after his return to Omarkana in early July.

> I had a row with some of the niggs – they crowd round the tent: to ask them to get away is of no avail, to swear at them in fury or to hit them is dangerous, because they'll swear back or even hit back & as you have more to lose by loss of prestige than they have, you are the weaker in the contest. No, Elsie, I see no way out of this problem – it is either slavery for them or for us & out of the two, I prefer slavery for them. It is all very well for the *New Europe* to write about self-determination of niggers & for Mr Lloyd George to announce the principle quite as seriously & for Elsie R. Masson to endorse them both. . . . But you all have *not* lived with niggs. Billy, who is the only decent man out here[,] is just the man who openly yearns, like I do, for the institution of flogging the niggs. I am awfully sorry that you will not be able to like me after this admission; but I have committed the sin mentally, if not actually – my omission being due to lack of opportunities. If I were living under the wise rule of Dr Hahl in Rabaul [German New Guinea], I *would* have sent Ginger to be flogged & this not once, I expect. Or perhaps I would not have, because Ginger would have behaved different [sic]. And here lies the crux of the question. When the niggs are afraid, they will be manageable. But it is an illusion to imagine that they can respect a white man, without being afraid of him. And the decent white man (like myself), who does not want to get into a scrape with the niggers or flog them personally – is absolutely at the mercy of any lazy & cunning nigg. . . . But the Papuan system is *rotten* & every white resident will tell you so.[69]

Malinowski's advocacy of the legal flogging of recalcitrant natives is starkly at odds with his professional commitment to anthropology and to his vision of a New Humanism. Although on both occasions he was writing in the heat of the moment's frustration and fury, his intemperate words betray a blatant racism. That he was perfectly serious there can be little doubt, and months of exposure to the bigoted views of white traders appear to have hardened his attitude. In what he wrote to Elsie next there is no apology for his obduracy, only a flippant attempt to explain it by his ancestry.

> Remember that the Prussians are a bastard mixture of Teutons & Western Slavs & that I am a Western Slav with Teutonic culture. Again: I am sure that if I had been born to be a Roman Emperor I would have been like Tiberius or Nero or at best like Hadrian, who had intervals of enlightened benevolence mixed with despotic cruelty. And my national (as Slav in general, not as Pole) hero is Ivan the Terrible (Iwan Groźny). So take this warning in time![70]

There is more than a hint of hyperbole here – and the mischievous desire to shock – of the tactless kind that put him into the bad books of Sir Hubert Murray's administration and invited the calumnies of Sir Baldwin Spencer.

A linguistic interlude

On his return to Sinaketa on Wednesday 24 April, Malinowski stayed with the Brudos, sleeping on their verandah and enjoying 'excellent physical comforts'. He also took renewed pleasure in French language and literature. Raphael Brudo, 'who really is an *inteligentny* fellow', proved to be quite a competent linguist. For a week or two, Malinowski worked intensively for a few hours each day with him on Kiriwinian grammar.

Coincidentally, another inspiring letter arrived from 'the congenial Egyptologist' Alan Gardiner, containing twelve pages of pertinent linguistic advice. The two men's views were remarkably similar, and Malinowski felt he was making important steps forward in his understanding. He noted down Gardiner's words as instructions in the back of his diary.[71] Most importantly: one should give 'the *ipsissima verba* of a statement. Try to find epigrammatical statement illustrating fundamental ideas of native belief. Characteristic views of nature; characteristic sociological views. Also give rep[resentative] answers verbatim.' Second, one should pay special attention to abstractions embodied in speech, such as classifiers, for the light they shed on semantics.

Malinowski was becoming increasingly confident about the value of his linguistic work. As he told Elsie:

I am by no means sure whether I shall be able to 'live up' to my linguistic principles. That is, whether I shall be capable of collecting sufficient material to substantiate my general assertions. But if I do, even somewhat imperfectly, it ought to make a hit in ethnographic linguistics and possibly in linguistic theory in general.

He had sketched out a rough grammar, beginning with a general classification of everyday speech contexts. 'If you want to analyse language as an instrument for the transmission of thought, emotion, etc. you must first inquire under what circumstances this transmission takes place, how far is the use of language necessary and what are the other means of conveying a meaning.' Although tentative, his grammatical sketch had alerted him to many aspects of speech behaviour that he had hitherto ignored. 'From now onward,' he told Elsie, 'I am going to collect a few native phrases and descriptions every day, as well as complete my dictionary.'[72]

Towards the end of April he began working with a middle-aged man named Motagoi. So good did the latter prove to be that Malinowski decided to return to Sinaketa for an even longer period in July. He enthused to Elsie that Motagoi was 'by far the best [informant] I ever had in precision of answers and in the ability to gauge exactly the point I am driving at'. He excelled in discussions of trading relations and the complexities of *sagali*. He was that rare find, a conscientious informant with a 'schoolmaster's point of view' who enjoyed making things clear to his pupil.[73]

Despite the satisfaction he derived from this work, Malinowski's second period in Sinaketa fell prey to familiar discontents. 'Ethnographical problems don't preoccupy me at all. At bottom I am living outside of Kiriwina, although strongly hating the *niggers*.' His precious individuality was also under threat from what he called 'an unnecessary communion of souls' with Raphael. The moral he drew: 'Preserve the essential inner personality through all difficulties and vicissitudes: I must never sacrifice moral principles or essential work to "posing", to convivial *Stimmung*, etc. My main task now must be: work. *Ergo*: work!'[74]

Chapter 26

'A Most Damnable Lack of Character'

Children of Teyava

On 7 May Malinowski left the Brudos to rejoin Billy Hancock's riotous *ménage* at Gusaweta. While in Vakuta he had resolved to 'eliminate Capuan days in Sinaketa and Gusaweta', implicitly likening himself to a conquering Hannibal debilitated by the luxuries of Rome.[1] He wrote as if he did not regard his time in Gusaweta as being in the field. Sites corrupted by European traders — Gusaweta, Kiribi and Sinaketa — were liminal spaces for him, neither in the field nor out of it. He intended to spend a couple of weeks with Billy, but ended up staying a month — though gracious living and Capuan self-indulgence were not to blame.

Compared to the civilized ambience of the Brudos, he told Elsie, 'Billy's place has all the flavour of a bachelor home & in a way it is nicer . . . but the two are complementary to each other.'[2] His liking for Billy did not extend to other members of his household and he found it almost impossible to work amid the constant hubbub. 'Billy never gets on my nerves personally, & as he has no nerves himself, I cannot get on his.' But he had the faults of his qualities: kindness, tolerance, meekness and an unconditional adoration of his sons, who were therefore 'dreadfully spoilt'. Five-year-old George was a little pest whose animal spirits drove a neurasthenic Malinowski to imagine the infliction of cruel punishments. 'I am suffering terribly at seeing the little brat wandering about my papers, linen etc.,' he told Elsie, wondering hopefully 'what sort of babies we shall have and if they will be angels and quite unable to get on anyone's nerves'.[3]

At Gusaweta the 'spirit of dissipation and the desire for actualities' tended to take hold of him, manifesting itself in harmless though time-consuming sessions of magazine-reading. 'I must try not to waste a single minute in my present work,' he had admonished himself before leaving Sinaketa. 'Too much *moving about* won't give good results.' But he needed to spend more time in Omarakana, Liluta (where Namwana Guyau lived) and Kabwaku. Then he planned to spend a week in Bwoytalu, another couple of weeks in Sinaketa, and a few days on the islands of Kitava and Kaduwaga.[4]

With almost five months to go, these were precise and exacting plans for covering the rest of the Trobriands. He was still concerned to map local variations in social organization, Kula participation, mythological traditions and – what by now had become a consuming interest – the various systems of garden magic that accompanied horticultural practice. In addition, there was the vital topic of land use and land tenure. But his plans remained flexible, and in the event he changed them. He was unable to visit the islands of Kaileula and Kitava, but he managed to spend about a month in Omarakana and several more weeks in Sinaketa. Now he would also spend a month at Gusaweta, making frequent excursions to the nearby villages of Teyava and Tukwaukwa.

This was an unexpected twist to his research, for he had hitherto shown little interest in this narrow coastal district of Kulumata, and none of its villages appear in the list of places to visit that he had drawn up in Melbourne. He had probably been inclined to ignore Kulumata because it was thick with colonial deposits. In addition to the government station at Losuia and the Wesleyan mission at Oiabia, there were the trading compounds of Norman Campbell, Sam Brudo and Billy Hancock. Tucked into the neck of the bulging head of Kiriwina, this district was the most directly influenced by the comings and goings of missionaries, schoolteachers, nursing sisters, government officers, armed native policemen, medical orderlies, commercial traders, pearl-buyers and other itinerants. Malinowski wanted little to do with any of them, but they were a fact of colonial life.

Owing partly to Billy's presence, he spent a good deal of time and effort taking photographs. He also prepared a campaign to study children's games, and during the weeks that followed he recorded and photographed many Teyava children at play. Most of the games were demonstrations, enacted at his bidding for the benefit of the camera.[5] He also carefully described the games – as he had described dances in 1915 – and took down the songs and ditties that accompanied them. In his '*Baloma*' essay he had commended ethnographic work with children: 'The mental volubility, lack of the slightest suspicion and sophistication, and, possibly, a certain amount of training received in the Mission School, made of them incomparable informants in many matters.'[6]

His investigations did not always go according to plan and he was beset, as usual, by mishaps and aggravations. In Teyava one day he made some coarse jokes, at which 'one bloody nigger made a disapproving remark, whereupon I cursed them and was highly irritated'. On 11 May, while taking photographs, he somehow broke his upper dental plate ('Consternation, followed by a philosophical calm: after all I did live without teeth for two months'). Apart from such annoyances, he was in good spirits: 'I simply live in and for my work.'[7]

One evening he went to Teyava to record *kasaysuya*, games that involved song and dance. In a proactive form of participant observation he began to *kasaysuya* by himself, thereby encouraging others to join in.

> I needed exercise, moreover, I could learn more by taking part personally. . . . Here at least there is movement, rhythm, and moonlight; also emulation, *playing of parts*, skill. I like naked human bodies in motion, and at moments, they also excited me. But I effectively resisted all thoughts I would be ashamed of or would fear to disclose to Elsie. I thought about her, as the human body always makes me think about her.[8]

Everything led back to Elsie. In an earlier incident he had watched some Teyava women drawing water at the spring. 'One of them very attractive, aroused me sensually. I thought how easily I could have a *connection* with her. Regret that this incompatibility can exist: physical attraction and personal aversion.' He followed her back to the village, admiring the beauty of the human body in movement. 'The poetry of the evening and the sunset permeated everything. I thought about how marvellously E.R.M. would have reacted to this, and I realized the gulf between me and the human beings around me.'[9] The sequence was typical of his suppression of base desire. On feeling illegitimate lust he subjected it to intellectual scrutiny then spiritualized it into a celebration of natural beauty – an aesthetic prompt that brought Elsie ineluctably to mind. He had jested to her about the tawdry tendency of his imagination: 'your imagination is moral & sentimental, Paul [Khuner]'s romantic & rational, whereas mine is mean & dirty, it revels in brothels, stinks & indignities.'[10]

The thirteenth of the month wrought its usual superstitious charm: 'I don't dare to plan anything important and I am at bottom convinced that whatever I may begin today will be *cursed and blighted*.'[11] It also brought a mail delivery with its burden of joy and dejection. Until then he had felt well at Gusaweta; now he began to feel poorly with 'dryness and pressure in eyeballs, lack of energy and initiative'. As usual Nina's letters evoked pity and remorse. He wished he could devote his life to her, 'console her and lighten her illness'; but he knew quite well it would be a mistake: 'happiness in a little whitewashed house' was not for him.[12] As usual, too, there were remarks in Elsie's letters that irritated him. 'Only after reading them 2 or 3 times did I recover my balance – all the shadows vanished and I felt the music of her individuality.' Her letters were six or seven weeks old and he was concerned that she might be ill. 'If anything happened to you,' he wrote, 'I would be a broken man for the rest of my life. I have such an intense feeling of the impermanency of things, of youth and health & security – & I also just long to be with you again & never separated.'[13]

Letters never failed to remind him of the ignominy of his exclusion from the war, though there was a faint chance that he might be able to remedy this later. As he told Elsie:

> I heard of Polish Legions being formed in America & at times, I feel that it might be my duty to volunteer – for clerical or suchlike work, because with my eyes & general health they would never take me into the firing line. . . . After all I believe sincerely & deeply that the bloody Deutschlanders must be beaten, both for the sake of Poland & Australia & the rest of humanity, including themselves. But we shall not allow ourselves to be 'swept into the current' as you put it, unless we see that it is quite necessary, shall we?[14]

He preferred to believe that he would be able to continue his academic career. 'I trust that with the publication of Kiriwina & other things I ought to have good chances of getting some endowment for further work.' It was quite likely that he could 'find an academic position in Poland, as soon as the war is over, which would be poorly endowed . . . but we both do not mind poverty, do we?' Still, he sometimes envisaged a gypsy existence. 'We may remain migratory birds the best part of our common life.'[15]

He was as demanding as ever of Elsie's epistolary efforts, reminding her that she was 'still a bit too objective' with 'still too much of the British pose at impersonality'. Although he lamented that his own letters lacked the passionate intensity of his imaginary conversations with her, hers brought to heel the playful Double that dwelled in his heart.

Double never thinks of teasing me, though she often makes me feel ashamed of myself & is very critical. . . . She is less witty than you & her looks vary immensely from perfect beauty to a modest & attractive plainness. She is sweet, playful & elusive & she comes and goes like music. I love her very, very much. I wonder: if you suddenly entered this room, would I not want, after an hour or two, to escape from the company of this Miss & seek my own Elsie (= Double)?[16]

'I am extremely ambitious'

Malinowski planned to go to Omarakana on 16 May. He began to pack the day before and sent Ginger ahead to prepare the way, but a violent cold and a sore throat laid him low for several feverish days and he languished at Gusaweta, unable even to write his diary. He starved himself, recalling Elsie's theory that he may have 'a septic centre' in his intestines. He was also alarmed by a new pain in his lumbar region, and his 'nerves' played havoc. A cantankerous patient at best, he 'suffered horribly in this pandemonium of children and negroes'.[17]

Melancholy set in as the fever retreated, but he resumed his diary and resolved not to surrender to sluggishness. Writing in English, he exhorted himself:

Work easily, without effort and heroism. Work ought to be for you a matter of course and a matter of play. You ought to love to see your papers round you, plunging into the depths of work. Again, don't get lured by byways, by a stray novel lying about, by some food being displayed on the table. The main thing now is to return to your full working capacity.[18]

He was feeling guilty about the waning of his scientific interests and had 'a metaphysical remorse' about wasting time. After all, he had a duty to Elsie and to their prospective children to work hard in order 'to be someone who really accomplished something', someone who made his 'mark in this world'. He fretted about his demoralizing back pain, his physical torpor and mental listlessness in his letter to her that week, declaring that his dread of becoming a permanent invalid hinged on the fear of losing her.[19] In his diary he was even more perversely, comically pessimistic: 'if I am to be a useless cripple, I will commit suicide or at all events won't marry her.'[20] He was oppressed by practical tasks, too, for Billy's verandah and store groaned reproachfully under his luggage and his curio collection. His remedy was to procrastinate and, 'with a terrible regret', read novels. It was all too easy to read two or three a day, and by the following week he was nauseated by a surfeit of them.[21]

By 24 May he was feeling better and dipped into Rivers 'as a sort of warm-up' before resuming work. *The History of Melanesian Society* now seemed 'less absurd'.[22] Soon he would cautiously agree with Brenda Seligman's comment that 'it is quite the most wonderful book I have ever read . . . every page gives you something fresh to think about'.[23] His response to Brenda was a significant statement of his own view:

> Modern ethnology (= historical school) seems to ignore that to a really scientific mind facts do not matter a bit: it is only what can be squeezed out of facts in the way of generalizations that really matters. History as a sequence of facts is material and not theory. History explains nothing. And that is where I cannot accept the foundations on which Graebner, Fay [Cooper Cole], and Rivers want to build.

In case he sounded too dogmatic and too scornful of facts, he added: 'At present I am as slavishly bound to fact and detail as possible. I trust I have not made you suspect that I'll return with a bagful of generalizations only! Indeed I am feeling almost swamped with detail.'[24]

He began another marathon letter to Elsie on 28 May. He was still in Gusaweta, 'partly because up to this very moment I have not quite recovered my full energy, partly because I can do a lot of useful work here'. But he was running out of excuses; the weather had been fine for several days and the roads were dry again. 'I have always this damned tendency to lag behind, to "miss the bus", to let things drag on,' he told Elsie, expatiating on his failings, his self-contradictions, his addiction to self-examination.

> I certainly need a woman to manage me. You will be an efficient manageress of me, won't you? I always have to 'keep myself well in hand' to control myself, as naturally I am indolent and have a tendency to let time slip away between my fingers. I have an awful inborn penchant to just lying down & dreaming. I could make an ideal Turk, smoking the narghile all day, enjoying a few good hours in my harem at night & sleeping or idly talking away the rest of the time.

On the other hand:

> I am extremely ambitious . . . I have the need for development and self-
> expression and a dread of stagnancy and of the same horizons for ever
> and ever. I don't think that everybody is cursed with such radical con-
> tradictions. With me, this one of indolence and activity (or activeness?)
> is probably also very much fostered by my poor health combined with
> a gifted mind. . . . for me it is essential to be always on the alert, always
> to control, whether things are going well & whether I am up to the
> maximum my health allows.

For this reason, he added, 'the writing of a diary is absolutely indispensable'. It compelled him to make a daily examination of his conscience and
his character.

> This again keeps me aware, constantly, that there is an Eye of Providence
> (= my diary writing self) open & it gives me an extra incentive to hold
> myself together. Again, by writing it down, reflecting on it, getting con-
> trite & wanting to reform, I am driven to analyse the mental mechanism
> of my lapses and to be able better to control them. I think 'character'
> might be defined as 'persistence of the same real self in one person'.[25]

During his last week at Billy's he continued to work on children's games
in Teyava, though these became tiresome when he was the hunted instead
of the hunter. 'I got mad at some little girls. I tried to chase them away, but
they wouldn't go.'[26] In Tukwaukwa he worked intensively on sorcery. It was
a week of intellectual ferment. 'I read Rivers; theoretical work attracts me.
I thought wistfully: when shall I be able to meditate quietly in some library
and spin philosophical ideas.' Rivers's arguments stimulated ideas which he
began to formulate for Elsie. This exercise, in turn, gave him the notion of
writing a layman's 'Introduction to Comparative Sociology' which 'would
differ in tone from usual textbooks – much freer, more informal. . . .
Written in a strong, striking, amusing style.' If he must spend another year
in Melbourne he could write an outline of the work and hold a weekly
seminar to discuss it.[27] In his verso diary notes he listed the reasons for
writing such a book. Its urgency derived in part from the 'imperative need
of studying the dying out of races'. There was also the need to formulate
new conceptions showing the practical utility of sociology. 'Social action in
democratic countries' depends upon the informed opinions of citizens, and
opinions 'must be based on "being in touch" with facts'. He sketched what

he would write in a preface to the book; he was determined to keep it informal, and to give 'the confidential information which a teacher usually gives *viva voce* but which it is unusual to give in books'. He intended to break the stuffy academic mould by admitting his mistakes and exposing gaps in his material: 'I want to be confidential, colloquial and attractive.'[28] His Introduction to *Argonauts* and his appendix 'Confessions of Ignorance and Failure' in *Coral Gardens* partly fulfil these early prescriptions.

Despite the erratic state of his health, on 6 June he prepared to leave for Omarakana. He was thinking about what to investigate and the methods he would use. As before, he resolved to be thorough. 'The main principle of my work in the field: avoid artificial simplifications. To this end, collect as concrete materials as possible: note every informant; work with children, *outsiders, and specialists. Take side lights and opinions.*'[29] Pondering a methodological introduction to 'Kiriwina', he added in verso: 'Explain the details of taking notes. Show specimens. . . . Say ab[out] methods of working in the field. . . . Its relation to bookkeeping.' These thoughts led him to reflect again upon the nature of his ambition and what he wanted to accomplish:

> An ambition stemming from my love of work, intoxication with my own work, my belief in the importance of science and art . . . ambition stemming from constantly seeing oneself – *romance of one's own life.* . . . When I think of my work, or works, or the revolution I want to effect in social anthropology – this is a truly creative ambition.[30]

Mourning in Omarakana

On Friday 7 June, Malinowski finally wrenched himself free from Gusaweta and walked the eight miles to Omarakana accompanied by a small team of carriers. The exercise banished his sluggishness and he soon felt 'as fit as a fiddle'. He was excited at the prospect of going back to the capital of Kiriwina. It had been three years to the month since his first visit.

It gave him a thrill to see all the old places and to greet familiar faces. 'I recognized almost everybody,' he told Elsie, 'although some of the boys have grown up and changed in these three years quite perplexingly . . . and girls, who were children & now are "blossomed" into pronounced wh*s [whores].'[31] For their part, villagers would have noticed that his command of the vernacular was more accomplished, that he looked older, balder and toothless. Some even wondered whether he was really the same *dimdim*, or perhaps his elder brother. Many of his old friends greeted him: honest Tokulubakiki, tobacco-cadging Touluwa, sickly Bagidou and the scoundrel Tom who used to extort money from him. As he toured the village, he dispensed bits of twist tobacco with invitations to visit his tent to work with him. The harvest was in full swing, and the villagers had begun to build a massive new yam house for Chief Touluwa. Malinowski promised five sticks of tobacco towards the enterprise, fifteen if they would give him the finely carved lintel board from the old yam house. The previous site of his tent by Touluwa's imposing house was now occupied by Bagidou, so the ethnographer was obliged to accept an inferior site a few yards to one side, though it still commanded a view of the central *baku*. That evening he wrote to Elsie while a few of his *guyau* friends hung about the tent, 'perched on my boxes, all round my table, looking at my writing and from time to time passing some remark *sotto voce* about some of my things'.[32]

That night he slept badly and had two 'horrid' wet dreams. One was 'of the Freudian type' accompanied by a 'feeling of sinfulness, evil, something loathsome, combined with lust – repulsive and frightening'.[33] At some level his residual Catholic conscience was troubling him. The dreams were a prelude to his worst emotional crisis for many years. On Tuesday 11 June he received two registered letters from his aunt Eleonora with news of his mother's death.

Dazed, he stumbled about, 'went here and there and sobbed'. Then he retreated to his tent and, in 'phrases which rise to the surface of emotions like foam', he wrote to Elsie.

> I do not know, almost, how I shall live through the immediate future. Life has changed for me completely and I am cut adrift. . . . The link between my past and present has been broken and my life will now be incomplete. Oh – all the terrible regrets with which I shall look back to the many years past, when I could have given and received from mother infinitely more than I did!

Remorse, too, that he did not try to bring her to Australia after the war had broken out; that he had neglected to write to her as often as he might have done; that she would never know Elsie; that Mama had been 'cheated by Fate of everything that would have made her happy'. Distraught and disoriented, he was unable to continue his diary.

> My mother was such an essential element in my life, though I did not even feel it explicitly. It is this accursed bent in my character to take for granted all that I have and to yearn for that which is not there. I feel cut off from my country, from all that is stable and permanent, from the earth almost.[34]

For several days he was quite unable to work and found escape in *The Brothers Karamazov* and *Jane Eyre*. He took exhausting, aimless walks, blindly striding the tracks between the monotonous green walls, pausing now and then to weep in the privacy of the bushes. In random fashion, he visited the villages surrounding Omarakana, villages whose very names – Okaykoda, Obweria, Kabwaku, Kwaibwaga, Kaulagu – mockingly echoed his cries of grief.

Plots and counter-ploys

The shock of his mother's death broke the impasse with respect to Nina Stirling. Since December he had been telling himself he must write to her once and for all concerning Elsie. He had tried in May, but had still not told her the whole truth for fear that it would destroy her. He was mindful perhaps of the tragic suicide of Staś Witkiewicz's fiancée. 'My chief guilt,' he confessed to Elsie,

> lies in not having thought of the difference between myself and Miss N.S. in the quality of our emotional constitution: that I could plunge very deep into a real and true and even fine sentiment and then come out unscathed, whereas she ought not to have been submitted to such experiments.[35]

It had been one such 'experiment' that led to the death of Jadwiga Janczewska. On the day after receiving the news about his mother, he steeled himself to write two lengthy letters to Nina's parents – one to each – though the tone of both, like the substance, was essentially the same. (The anguished drafts survive among his papers.) He sent the fair copies to Elsie, who approved them and gave them to Paul Khuner for typing, and they were eventually despatched to Adelaide in late August. Although he felt more guilt than he admitted in either letter, he rehearsed what the Stirlings already knew – his infatuation with Nina, his hopeless position as an unwanted foreigner, their frequent correspondence despite Sir Edward's disapproval, his being politely but firmly kept away from Adelaide, his dilemma once he had 'befriended' Elsie Masson, his protective silence on learning of Miss Nina's illness, his subsequent procrastination. But there was another delicate issue that had to be broached: Baldwin Spencer's 'machinations'.

On 21 June he wrote to Seligman. Elsie gasped when she read some of the phrases he had used to excoriate Spencer; they were 'certainly quite libellous', she thought, but she obediently asked Paul to type the letter.[36] Paul had read Seligman's last letter to Malinowski and was touched by his kindness and amused by his fatalism: 'I couldn't help smiling when I recognized the old Jewish trait of saying good-bye to one's family and giving instructions about the funeral when one has a bit of a headache.'[37] Malinowski mounted his defence:

You may take it for Gospel truth that Baldwin Spencer is my enemy. He has personal reasons for disliking me – not to his credit at all – and he seems bitterly to hate me and to be determined of harming me and my work. He has already played a number of dirty tricks on me, really dirty tricks, the more so, as he obviously waited till I left Melbourne, to deliver his kick from behind. What he may be up to still, I don't know. . . . I may just as well tell you that he even threatened to take steps to get me interned on account of my 'anti-British utterances'. This latter, I need not add, the result of his (of late chronically alcoholized) imagination. But it shows you the length to which he will go.

His main worry now, he continued, was not that he would be incarcerated or forbidden to leave Papua (for he had some influential friends in Melbourne like Atlee Hunt and, so he hoped, the Massons), but rather of what mischief Spencer might cause in England with Frazer, Mond and Macmillan, the publisher. Frazer was the key, as his opinion would weigh most with the others. Malinowski therefore begged Seligman to find out whether Frazer had been 'infected' by Spencer, and to put his case before him. He then outlined 'the plot on which B.Sp.'s intrigues are hingeing', a sensational plot worthy of 'some of the more lurid pages in Dickens, or out of a penny dreadful'. Without naming Nina or Elsie (he referred to them as Miss A and Miss B), he sketched the whole sorry saga and the 'tragic complication' of his growing affection for Miss B. just as Miss A. became seriously ill, and he was unable to confront her with the truth. As for Spencer's part in the plot:

> He had the impudence of rummaging [among] my private papers. . . . He found some of Miss A's letters (written to me in Papua three years ago!) which I mislaid among my scientific MSS. . . . Under the charge of my playing a double game, he showed the letters left and right. . . . Parents of both ladies were warned. . . . B.Sp. is tacking on to this charge that Papuan gossip, and probably hints that I am a German spy, a Saddist [sic], etc. etc.

The only card Seligman could play on Malinowski's behalf was the value of his work.

> I believe it would be a great pity if through any mean machinations my work should be hampered. If you don't mind perjuring yourself just a little bit, you may describe it as 'the best ethnographical book on the Pacific', and you would not hit wide off [sic] the mark.[38]

Malinowski also penned a pre-emptive missive to Haddon, sparing of detail but vaguely warning him of Spencer's perfidy.[39]

It was several months before Seligman replied. He advised tactfully that, while 'it may be that your Melbourne ethnological friend is as down on you as you think, I still have my doubts'. Even so, Malinowski need not worry about Spencer influencing people against him in England. Mond was 'absolutely sound' and Frazer was a confirmed admirer of Malinowski's work. Besides, Spencer had 'let us all know that your work would be the best thing on the Pacific'.[40] This was hardly the verdict one would expect of a man consumed by hatred or jealousy.

As presented by Baldwin Spencer's biographers, the record confirms that he fully backed Malinowski, both in his efforts to fund him by eliciting the support of Atlee Hunt in the teeth of Murray's protests, and in promoting Malinowski's reputation as a brilliant ethnographer. D. J. Mulvaney and J. H. Calaby remark that there is 'no evidence that Spencer carried on any vendetta against Malinowski'.[41] But Elsie Masson's testimony reveals that Spencer had indeed threatened to discredit him and that the vendetta was by no means a figment of Malinowski's paranoid imagination. In her warning letter to him of 10 April, Elsie confirmed his suspicions:

> I think your extreme mind has hit it for once when you say it is personal jealousy, and perhaps not altogether platonic. I knew this last year,

but didn't tell the Irascible Foreigner. . . . But it made me feel sad that through me anything like misfortune could come to you. . . . Now don't go and let the extreme mind jump to its furthest reach – I only mean there was a flavour of the unplatonic and is still, which influences him.[42]

Elsie defended Malinowski in a series of angry confrontations with Spencer. He maintained that breaking with the scoundrel was in her own best interests, but she responded that if he considered himself her friend he would do no harm to Malinowski. 'He said, "O nonsense, child!" and bolted into his lab for his lecture.' On learning that Spencer had sent the incriminating letters to Adelaide, Elsie became thoroughly alarmed. 'I felt sure Sir B. would make use of any influence he could,' she told Malinowski, 'and I imagined he might attempt to detain you in New Guinea, or at any rate prevent your return to Melbourne, or at the very least prevent any renewal of your grant.' Bearding Spencer again, she delivered an ultimatum by threatening to 'throw everything over and go where you were, marry you even if it meant starving, and therefore that in harming you he would be directly harming, in fact ruining, *me*, and there could be no pretence that he was doing it for my good'. Spencer replied, 'This is sheer obstinacy.'

> I said, 'You may call it what you like, there it is, I mean it, I'll do it.' He said, 'You may be putting us in a very awkward position.' And I said, 'Well that *is* the position. And if you harm him you will have a lot to answer for.' Then he said he never had intended to take any action politically or in any way of that kind, but that it would be simply a personal matter. . . . He would simply drop you.[43]

As for the evidence of Malinowski's two-timing, Spencer insisted on showing Elsie the exact spot where he had found the incriminating letters that he had shown to Sir Edward Stirling. 'Bronio dear,' wrote Elsie,

> it was on the window ledge in the room off the Children's Museum where you kept your things. . . . I am sure it was absolutely accidental and carelessness is not a crime however dire the consequences. . . . It gave me such a constricted feeling in my heart to be there amongst your things, your dear familiar handwriting about me, and your enemy beside me.[44]

Later she learned that Sir Edward had burned the letters without showing them to his daughter, though by that time Nina knew about Elsie. By then, too, Spencer appeared to Elsie as 'old and feeble and the mere shell of his former self'. Her anger became tempered with pity.[45]

'Truly I lack real character'

The painful problem of Nina Stirling refused to go away. The death of Malinowski's mother caused him to feel his betrayal more acutely. He had managed the love triangle so badly it had almost wrecked his career. Nina had been an ethereal muse during his fieldwork in 1915; two years later Elsie had replaced her as a more tangible and sustaining helpmeet. Indeed, in this respect she was like his companionable, down-to-earth mother. How could he work 'for' the childlike Nina in the way he worked 'for' Elsie-cum-Mama?

He turned to Elsie for consolation in this matter too, wanting her to understand how a 'platonic brotherly affection' for Nina persisted. He offered clumsy explanations for their temperamental differences and their unsuitablity for one another owing to their constitutional weaknesses: 'My life is going to be rough & I really know that I need protection rather than I should give it.' As to why he did not stop writing to her when it became clear to him that he was in love with Elsie: 'I have showed throughout the whole thing a most damnable lack of character & foresight.' Nevertheless, although he had no wish to see Nina again, he would like to hear from her 'from time to time' and he asked Elsie whether she would mind if he continued to correspond with her.[46] He was therefore devastated afresh and 'morally squashed' on 1 July when the inevitable letter arrived from Nina terminating their friendship. As he abjectly confessed to Elsie:

> I feel an absolute brute & unworthy of anyone's friendship, not to speak of love. I almost feel, as if you would turn away from me, not because everybody else does, but because my character has been shown up. . . . At the bottom of my heart, I realize how tragically superficial my character is, compared to N.S.'s feelings and character. She has a perfect right to consider me dishonourable & so has her family & they will not spare me in their feelings.[47]

Yet he soon discovered ('as one makes a discovery amidst a continuous stream of feelings') that, despite his sorrow and humiliation, 'I was not a thoroughly unhappy man, that there was a bottom to my unhappiness so to say.' He was hugely relieved that the deception was finally over. 'It was terrible to go on abusing her confidence and in a way lying to her the whole time. . . . And I really did & do love her as unselfishly as I ever loved anyone.'[48] It was not until August that Elsie told Malinowski that Nina had written to her three times since April, when Nina first learned of his duplicity. Nina confessed it was 'incomprehensible' to her, as he had given her 'a faithful promise to tell her everything, even the lightest flirtation'. Nina's letters pierced Elsie's heart. She admired Nina for being brave enough to write: 'a noble soul and a heroine in some ways'. Elsie added, 'You will not love me the less because I am the "attainable", will you?' She enclosed a fragrant sprig of Boronia in her letter: 'It always reminds me of you. You wore a sprig in your coat and its browns and yellows are like you, and the name abounds in Bs and Ns.'[49]

Malinowski's remorse over Nina joined his equally deep remorse over his mother. The grief and guilt overshadowed everything, and for weeks he worked with a heavy heart, mechanically and apathetically. All his hopes, schemes and plans for the future were diminished. He was counting the days to his reunion with Elsie, but could not rejoice in the thought of returning to Melbourne for 'every new sensation, every emotion will have in it the poison of regret & grief that my Mother will never share it with me'. When the most acute stage of mourning had passed, he wrote to Elsie again about the unreal world he seemed to be living in. He experienced a detachment, a disconnection which allowed him to function, though a part of him was shocked at his own callousness in not being able to face the dreadful truth at every moment. Although it was months before he received them, Elsie wrote consoling letters, wishing she could be there to put her arms around him and soften his grief. She intuited that he might learn to feel for her what he had felt for his mother: 'There is such a lot of the maternal in what I feel for you at times, Bronio.' Her loss of Charles enabled her to sympathize: 'To live on and think on is the only way we can give the dead immortality.'[50]

After a week of anguished mourning, Malinowski had resumed intensive work. The stimulus was a rowdy competitive food exchange between neighbouring villages that became so heated that it almost led to bloodshed.[51] With this concentrated bout of work his worldly ambitions returned. They crawled over him 'like lice' as he dreamed again about founding the New Humanism, about the eminence he would achieve and the honours that would follow: Fellow of the Royal Society, Companion of the Order of the Star of India, a knighthood, an entry in *Who's Who*. (In time he would be granted only the last of these.) Yet he knew such ambitions were hollow, that such titles would mean nothing to him, that at bottom he despised distinctions.[52]

As for fieldwork, the 'craftsman's interest in getting things done is there, though the deeper interest, the real ambition is undermined,' he told Elsie on 19 June. 'I am getting old material into new perspective and it is marvellous how things are gaining in plasticity, how they get new life and new depth through my better methods and better knowledge of the language.'[53] The next day brought a violent squall which flooded his tent and was in danger of toppling Touluwa's hut and crushing the old chief ('what a "windfall" that would have been for an ethnologist!' he joked). The harvest had been a rich one, and Touluwa had declared a competitive display of yams, a *kayasa*. People were bringing baskets of taitu into the village 'in an orgy of conchshell blowing'.[54]

But sorrow and grief returned and saturated everything. Having resumed his diary, he noted on 24 June, 'I know that if I lost my eyesight or my health now, I could easily commit suicide.' There was a bitter comfort in the thought of his own mortality.[55] The villagers were still harvesting taitu and displaying them in large pyramidal heaps; he photographed them and worked 'to the point of complete exhaustion'. Keeping busy was a defence against woeful remorse.

> The moment I let myself go, my thoughts go back to Poland, to the past. I know that I have a black abyss, a void in my soul. . . . A feeling of the evil of existence. – I think constantly about the shallow optimism of religious beliefs: I'd give anything to believe in the immortality of the soul.[56]

Fieldwork was becoming meaningless and absurd. Without thoughts of Elsie to sustain him he might have packed up and left the Trobriands. He continued to be demoralized by grief and self-pity to the very end of his diary. The last few entries build to a dirge-like coda, haunted by childhood memories, infinite regret, thoughts of death and the pathetic insufficiency of religious consolation. He regressed. 'At night, sad, plaintive dreams, like childhood feelings. . . . Everything permeated with Mother.'[57]

On 2 July he wrote a four-page letter to Elsie. 'I have lost the sense of happiness. I am doing my work almost normally, with keen interest & I am unable to suppress outbursts of hilarity (when working with the niggs.) even, at times; but I feel as if I were going over hollow ground all the time.' Elsie had remarked on his similarity in character to the eponymous hero of Romain Rolland's *Jean-Christophe*, a musical genius. Malinowski demurred. 'I am not an artist & I do not create. That is, I must create the artistic constructions I have in me (as everyone has) in my own life. And that makes the whole difference. For me, life cannot be mere material for a *chef d'oeuvre*, it must be the *oeuvre* itself.' He begged Elsie to forgive him his faults, and accept him as he was, though perhaps he could still change for the better. 'I know that my character is not very deep. Small ambitions & vanities & a sense for intrigue & spite are more rampant there than the real, true feelings. Will this ever change? With better health my character would improve, I know this.'[58]

Thoughts of his mother inevitably took him back to his schooldays in Cracow, to the whitewashed classroom, the brown benches, the faces of his school companions. Her death robbed him of this past: 'As long as my mother was alive, I never felt that my past life was gone – she had it in her & all the possibilities of a future to make up & replace the past.' This realization could have brought him to a fresh sense of his maturity, of being able to renew himself, but he was not yet ready to relinquish his grief. He remained as preoccupied as ever with his unfinished, fragmented self, his weak 'integrity'.

His work was now 'beginning palpably to round off', he told Elsie. There were several chapters of his manuscript that he had effectively closed to further inquiry: 'war, all parts of sociology, decorative art, spirits.' The rest, 'gardening, Sorcery, wind & rain magic, sex & marriage, children, games, *kula* etc. etc. need only an energetic effort of a couple of days each to get into almost perfect shape.'[59] His health was good and his capacity for work excellent. His mood had lifted, too, and with Tokulabakiki he made 'great progress in magic and linguistics'.[60]

He was about to go back to Sinaketa. 'I was doing splendid work in Omarakana,' he explained to Elsie, 'but I wanted specially to polish up the *kula*, external trading, canoe building, and I could do this much more easily in Sinaketa'. He was also oppressed by the monotonous landscape of northern Kiriwina. The green waters of the lagoon enticed him, as did the prospect of literary evenings at the Brudos'. He was about to abandon his diary, too, completely this time. His daily inscriptions had been faltering since he had returned to Omarakana in early June and there had been a fortnight's gap from the beginning of July.

Malinowski's final diary entry is a meditation on loss and on his own ambivalent hold on life. It is crowded with memories of his childhood in Poland, of his relatives and his teachers at the gymnasium, above all of his mother and of their last unhappy moments together in London. His own death was becoming more real to him: 'to go to Mother, to join her in nothingness.' Yet all was not lost, and at moments he felt it was only the death of something within him. '[M]y ambitions and appetites have a strong hold on me and tie me to life. I shall experience joy and happiness (?) and success and satisfaction in my work' – even though it had become meaningless and the world had lost colour. Wallowing in nostalgia, he ended his diary:

> All the tender feelings of my childhood come back: I feel as when I had left Mother for a few days, returning from Zwierzyniec with Father. – I go back in my thoughts to Annie Br. – how utterly everything has vanished from my life! – Staś's betrayal, and N.S. Truly I lack real character.

'A state of metaphysical instability'

On Friday 19 July 1918, Malinowski left Omarakana for Gusaweta. There he suffered his 'customary two days of sickness'. Mick George was sick, too, and they lay on adjacent mattresses, groaning, sighing and complaining to one another 'in a very Levantine & East European & entirely unBritish manner'. After reporting to Campbell at Losuia and paying off the long-suffering and now redundant Ginger, Malinowski was paddled and punted to Sinaketa.[61]

Arriving with high expectations, he took a few days to rediscover his fondness for the Brudos. He saw more clearly that much of their glamour was due to their cultivated European tastes in a place where no one else longed for music, theatre, cathedrals and cafés. But he reacted soon enough to the surfeit of their society: 'I talk with Raffael [sic] and we argue and I am "superficial" . . . I just talk and joke and forget my sorrow and my real life.'[62] His suffering self was more real to him than his sociable self, and he withdrew from the 'transient home' of pleasant company in order to find it.

He spent a further five weeks in Sinaketa, working furiously on Kula and garden magic. He wrote few letters, and was even sparing in his communications to Elsie, from whom he had had no word since the end of May. He could not say why he had not written. His diary too remained closed and he had been 'living on the surface'. The loss of his mother had placed him in what he called 'a state of metaphysical instability'. But he had been physically fit and worked at such a rate as never before. As he told Elsie on 14 August:

> In many respects I have reached the end of my vista and I see nothing beyond, that is, nothing but clearing up of more or less irrelevant details. . . . I shall leave Kiriwina with the general feeling of having left exactly half of the things undone, but it can't be otherwise.[63]

On 21 August there was a big mail, the first since 1 July. The glut triggered an attack of his usual nervous complaint; he felt exactly as he did during the latter stages of seasickness. He cured it by fasting for three days, a cure that had the virtue of cheapness. Despite his superstitious dread of further bad news, there was nothing too drastic in this mail. He got a sad shock on receiving his mother's last letter, which had taken eight months to reach him. He was upset, too, by Mim Weigall's letter, which lavished admiration upon a soldier friend recently returned from the Western Front. As he told Elsie: 'Such personal touches bring the war & the ignominy of being a "stay behind" . . . more pungent. All these three letters depressed me – in various ways – horribly, & even Paul's Olympian placidity & friendliness could not quite obliterate the hopeless feeling of utter worthlessness & loneliness.' The letters were uncomfortable reminders of his weakness, his perfidy and lack of 'character'. By the time he turned to read Elsie's letters he was despondent: 'I had the apprehension that on any page I may find you breaking off our relations and of pure general contempt for me & I read them almost as if receiving all your love & friendship under false pretences.'[64]

He had now had 'almost enough' of fieldwork and longed to do some theoretical work. As for his Kiriwina monograph:

> It must be as perfect as I can possibly do it. I would not remain another summer here, even if I had the money & the permission to do it. But these cool months are excellent for work & I am seeing more & more how my material rounds up. In fact if I were obliged to leave the Trobs. today, I could do it with a light heart.

He resumed his letter to Elsie on Friday 30 August, his last day in Sinaketa. He was off to Gusaweta again, and planned to spend another three weeks in Omarakana before sailing for Australia in October. But after talking to Billy Hancock he changed his mind, though he did not explain why he now had 'no choice but to leave the Trobriands in the middle of September'. Having decided to cut short his ethnographic polishing, he could hardly sleep for excitement. 'I shall be on the move in two weeks and then be steadily approaching you.'[65]

Nine months later, Billy Hancock sent Elsie his congratulations on their engagement:

> I can assure you the Doctor kept his secret well guarded, and it was not until the day before he was leaving that he told me of you; when I gave him the few small pearls he said 'I will present these to my fiancée', and in answer to my look of inquisitiveness he told me all about you; I had suspected for some months previous that there was a 'Lady in the case', for towards the latter part of the Doctor's stay he would sit on the front verandah for hours, looking across the ocean, towards the South, suddenly he would jump up and coming inside to me would say that he wished it was October, so he could get away south. Once I said 'Why not stay another twelve months there is plenty of work to do,' the look he gave me and the tone in which he shouted 'What!' at me, I never suggested such a thing again. I suppose ere this reaches you, you will have made him a happy man.[66]

Chapter 27

Marriage

Leaving the field

Steaming between Samarai and Port Moresby aboard the *Morinda*, Malinowski began a marathon letter to Elsie. She was now clearly in his sights and, although he was three weeks earlier than he had led her to expect, he was growing impatient. His decision to catch an earlier boat had put him into a frenzy and, 'instead of flowing along at the usual Kiriwinian pace', life in the islands had 'rushed along with Moving Pictures speed'.[1]

He had spent a final busy week in Omarakana adding some finishing touches to his work. In Elsie's phrase, he had 'almost scraped Kiriwina clean'. On 12 September, after 'a not very sentimental last look around Omarakana', he walked to Gusaweta and during the following days he reported to A. R. M. Campbell at Losuia, said goodbye to the missionaries at Oiabia, and had final talks with his favourite *guyau* informants, Tokulubakiki and Yobukwau. Billy judged that, weather permitting, the *Kayona* could make Samarai in a week or so. 'Do not miss the steamer in your usual manner,' Elsie had pleaded, and to be certain of catching the *Morinda* on 3 October they sailed from Kiriwina on 16 September.

Billy took him first to the Kiribi plantation, where he shared a farewell meal with Mick George. 'I was sitting there in Mick's store and I suddenly looked on all the quaint mixture of Greek and Melanesian barbarism with Anglo-Saxon trade-culture, as one looks at a memory – it was receding fast into the realm of remembrances.'[2] Then they sailed down the lagoon to Sinaketa, where Malinowski took one last walk through the village. The Brudos hosted another farewell dinner, though 'there was little romance now in the "civilized" atmosphere of villa Raphael'. The *Kayona* departed for Samarai that evening. The trip took thirteen days ('your lucky number,'

Billy drily observed) and there were some agonizing delays. Becalmed off Normanby Island one day, Malinowski became fretful, convinced that he would miss the steamer and be marooned again on Samarai.[3]

Cruising down the Queensland coast, he dreamily contemplated his future with Elsie. Their destinies would soon merge and he felt swept towards her on a tide of tumultuous feelings. He wrote to her about his plans. Providing that Robert Mond continued to fund him for a couple more years, he and Elsie could live comfortably enough on £250 a year. He had that amount in the bank, while the £250 that Mond had promised for 1918 was still to come. 'With our well known economic faculties, this should be quite enough for us. Then the war cannot last more than 2 years & after that I'll have my book ready & a fairly good chance of a position in Poland or America.' He would not dream of 'touching' his future parents-in-law for money. 'After all,' he teased, 'if things were hopelessly black, you could do some work & I could apply for free board and lodging in a Concentration Camp.'

He drafted a letter to Seligman on the voyage, reporting in general terms on the success of his fieldwork.

> I have done some work & the results are satisfactory. The linguistic material will be ample and gained almost entirely as by-product, through writing almost all my informants' statements in native [Kiriwinian]. This will also enrich the documentary evidence & illustrate their means of expressing themselves on almost all subjects.
>
> There are of course gaps & enormous ones & I see them and should I begin in another field, I expect I'd do twice as much & go twice as deep in the same time. But now I need some 18 months to write it out & think it over. My material is appallingly copious & it gives me the shivers to think of working it out!
>
> Of course, as I told you I want to offer my services for any Polish work in the USA, though I doubt that they'll have any use for me. So I'll be able to give you more details about my plans after I've gone South. Moreover, as you know from my last letter, there are certain complications pending, which may influence the future course of my personal affairs.[4]

His personal affairs, of course, were to do with his forthcoming marriage, and the pending complications concerned his relations with Orme and Molly Masson. Elsie was prepared to go it alone if need be, but Malinowski hoped to win their acceptance if not their favour. His foreigner status was the main issue; aside from this there was his social status, for Molly was a snob. But then, Malinowski admitted to Elsie, so was he.

> I also would look a man up in Who's Who to see whether his letters are A.I. at Snob's Lloyds & whether his College is incorporated or only affiliated. . . . In loving you, I *was* influenced at first by the glamour cast over you by Massonic tradition and distinguishedness. But now this has vanished altogther.[5]

Elsie was still concerned about their disparities of mood. 'Your unhappiness has always been more a matter of temperament than of circumstances,' she had written to him. '[P]erhaps better health will make a difference, but it suddenly struck me with a pang the other day that you may still think of life as the meaningless void slightly veiled by the curtain of your interests, your work, and art and friendship.' She wondered if his mother's death had 'shocked away that sense of unreality', adding: 'Oh let us be as happy as we can togther, Bronio, for we may lose each other some day.'[6] Sailing towards her now, he replied:

> I will have my ups and downs in all phases of my emotional life. . . . I yearn for you to become everything to me, to take partially the place of the affection I had for my mother. I have realized, since her death, how meaningless life becomes when there is no one who shares intimately all our good and bad fortunes.

The voyage to Sydney was uneventful; the weather was fair, the sea calm, and he was spared seasickness. The ship's company was tolerable, but he was disinclined to socialize. At Brisbane he spent a couple of hours with the Mayos and the conversation with Elton gave him an idea: 'I felt the sacred fire of philosophical propensities fanned up & I am planning a kind of seminar in which we two with Paul and Mim if possible will do some reading on psychology etc.' Elton − destined to become a notable industrial psychologist − promised to send him copies of his lectures.[7]

As he sailed further south he poured out his love and his anxiety. There was still time for something to go wrong, and her parents' resolute opposition to their marriage was a real possibility. He would follow Elsie's lead in his conduct towards them, try heroically to be congenial, but if her father was abrasive and spoke about Baldwin Spencer's calumnies, they would have to adopt a 'take us or leave us' attitude. There was nothing he wanted from

Orme and Molly Masson; nothing, that is, except their daughter. Yet he could sympathize with Orme's views and perfectly understood the attitude of a bourgeois paterfamilias who looked down upon the interloper 'with a hostility & instinctive contempt, such as I might feel for a dirty Jew or for a half-caste'. Defiantly, he added: 'Your father feels instinctively, almost physiologically that you are soiled, polluted by your bodily union with me. And that makes me feel "proud" (as a high-flown half-caste might feel) & averse to accept any material benefits from their hands.' Then he conceded:

> I have entirely given up the idea of marrying into the Masson clan & indeed I feel that personally I'd prefer you to marry out of it. But for your sake I'll stand any amount of parlaying & arguing & dissecting of any past, present, & future humiliation & flattery etc.

The more he thought about Baldwin Spencer, however, the more his ire and indignation mounted. 'The fellow is unaccountable and you have seen what his promises are worth. . . . He is a *mala fide*, unscrupulous & dirty adversary of mine.' His paranoid hostility to Spencer verged on the hysterical.

> I am evolving an intense hatred for the type of middle class sufficiency, as represented by Stirling, Orme, Spencer, Hunt – with its cult of established fact, established values & established calumnies. On the other hand, against this feeling . . . works my philosophical spirit of impartiality, which rebels at the unfairness of my attitude & despairs at the utter instabilty of my sentiments.

He added that he wasn't going to change this aspect of his character. Elsie would need to show him patience, and let him 'unload the occasional burden of resentment in an outburst of abuse – that afterwards I always shall repent & be the nicer for it. But you must know how to manage me.'

He telegraphed Elsie from Sydney on 11 October: 'After energetic scramble got clear and arrive tomorrow Melbourne.'[8]

An unsuitable suitor

Of the reunion of Malinowski and Elsie, almost a full year since they had parted, nothing is on record. It is likely that, as he had requested, she was alone when she met him at Spencer Street Station on Saturday 12 October.

Elsie expected they both would be 'as stiff as a poker' but would quickly recover themselves.[9] Perhaps it was as Malinowski had romantically imagined their meeting, his pessimism ironically subverting the vision: 'Probably it will turn out quite prosaic – lost luggage, drunken porter, no cabs there, uncertainty where to find lodgings, Show Day & other such calamities.'[10]

The letters cease, and the couple fades into the Melbourne streets. Malinowski appears dimly at his old Grey Street lodgings (he had wired Elsie to reserve him a room, his old one if possible, at a rent of not more than 8/6d. a week) and Elsie resumed her semi-surreptitious visits to him there. Within days of his return Malinowski succumbed to a bad cold and took to his bed. Elsie's mother wrote him a thoughtful note of commiseration: 'After so long in the tropics one must be liable & sensitive to such infections.'[11]

A heavily corrected draft survives of Malinowski's letter to Orme Masson, asking for Elsie's hand in marriage. The fair copy was probably posted on 17 October. Stiff and stilted, defensive yet not undignified, the letter gives an honest appraisal of his own worth as a future son-in-law. Wisely, he omitted all mention of Baldwin Spencer. He addressed each objection that he knew the Massons held against him as 'liabilities': his foreign nationality, his relative poverty, his uncertain career prospects, his indifferent health. The biggest asset he could put into the balance was a loving commitment to Elsie – though the word 'love' nowhere appears in the letter; rather, banal phrases of admiration and regard 'for the character and talent of your daughter' and her 'altogether exceptional personality'. He crossed out other phrases referring to his feeling of inferiority and his worship of her, and also deleted an abject admission that began: 'I would have never drempt [sic] of allowing myself to. . . . ' The draft reeks of a quiet desperation. 'I very well realize how unworthy I am of the great privilege of having won your daughter's friendship and regard. . . . I cannot but strive to attain my aim, and that it is to marry your daughter.'

David Orme Masson's frank reply, of 18 October, seemed resigned to a *fait accompli*.

If the choice rested with me, the difference of nationality would be a fatal objection; for, rightly or wrongly, I have a strong feeling against mixed marriages.

But Elsie has the right to decide for herself and – which is more to the point – it is too late to be raising objections when she and you have made up your minds. Elsie's happiness is really the only consideration that counts with her mother and me, and that now rests with you.

So come on Sunday and let us talk things over. And of course what I have said means that we shall welcome you here as one of ourselves.[12]

With this show of magnanimity the Scottish paterfamilias relented, and all further hostility to Malinowski was, if not expunged, then politely muted. The Massons reluctantly accepted him as a prospective son-in-law. He had fortified himself against rejection. He was like a man tensed to charge through a locked door only to find that it was, if not wide open, then at least ajar. Social invitations followed. Among the first was one from Lady Spencer to Elsie: 'Will you and Dr Malinowski come to tea at the Lyceum at 4 p.m. Friday?' Atlee Hunt sent a chilly acknowledgment: 'I have your letter of 27 October and am interested to learn that you are engaged to Miss Masson.'[13] The Mayos sent a congratulatory telegram followed by a letter to express their delight that the 'so-distinguished anthropologist has joined the human majority'. The lucky man was

destined to marry the most charming lady in Melbourne – the affair has most obviously been arranged in whatever is your sociological substitute for heaven. Our abiding sorrow is that you will both 'flit', leaving Dorothea and myself a pair of disconsolate Anglo-Saxons – gazing towards the steam smoke on the horizon. Please express my thanks and delight to Miss Masson in that she has graciously consented to rescue a well-loved friend from the depths of sociologico-Slavic gloom. For from now on, you should tread the sunlit way.[14]

The path to marriage, however, was neither sunlit nor smooth. It was as if, on charging with such resentful energy through the door the Massons had quietly opened for him, he stumbled on the threshold. His paranoia erected a fresh obstacle. Within weeks of his return he was suspecting Elsie and Paul Khuner of 'squeezing him out'. He imagined they had formed a 'sentimental attachment' to one another during his absence and, once the idea had taken hold, he saw evidence of it in every glance and gesture. He fell into despair, and on Sunday 17 November quarrelled bitterly with a perplexed Elsie. He wrote to her the following day, proposing a cooling-off period of two days' separation. She replied immediately with patent anguish. 'I was very upset by your letter. . . . You must remember that the relationship we have contemplated for the future won't allow of such artificial separations as you suggest now, and if they are necessary between us, it is not a good look-out.' She signed herself plainly, 'Elsie'.

On 20 November he vented his jealousy and resentment in a long, repetitive letter to her — which he sensibly decided not to send lest it inflame matters further. Still, the pained and painful letter demonstrates not only Malinowski's hypersensitivity but also his propensity for making enemies out of friends. 'The situation is quite impossible,' he wrote. 'You compel me crudely to speak about my jealousy — a thing unpleasant in itself, but could you not see it coming plainly?' He had tried to hide his resentment, not wanting to offend Paul.

> My grievance the whole time was due to a feeling of acute awareness that something was happening between you and him. . . . Can't you understand, could you not have foreseen that it is poisonous to my feelings, can't you understand that I don't want to have a three-cornered tragedy when I hoped for a honeymoon?

Whether or not there were any objective grounds for Malinowski's suspicion of betrayal by his fiancée and his best friend — and it seems utterly unlikely — there is a prototypical aspect to the case. It would become an occupational hazard for anthropologists who absented themselves on fieldwork, in his fashion, for a year or more. They risk their lovers' constancy, yet they secretly expect the world to stand still for them, patiently awaiting their return.

'A definite methodological mission'

Before leaving Kiriwina, Malinowski had made a bet with Raphael Brudo that the war would outlast the year. He lost his £1. The armistice was signed on 11 November 1918, just four weeks after his return to Melbourne. On 2 December, from the Maghull Military Hospital near Liverpool, Seligman wrote to Malinowski, asking if he intended to go back to New Guinea. He was suggesting that the continuation of Robert Mond's funding might depend upon the need for further fieldwork. Malinowski would remain an enemy alien until the peace treaty was signed, but thereafter, Seligman supposed, 'you will be able to move about New Guinea as you like, in fact as a national of the Greater Poland that is to come, you will almost be an ally'.[15]

Three weeks after despatching this letter, Seligman received one from Malinowski announcing his intention to marry. Seligman hastily replied with coy congratulations: 'there is really nothing one can say on these occasions, but I think you know that Brenda & I really do wish you & Miss Masson all the happiness that can come to two people.' He added a pragmatic postscript: 'Glad to hear you're at the book – the sooner you're married the quicker you'll work.'[16] In an earlier letter Seligman had told him that Frazer would surely commend Malinowski to his publisher, though 'no amount of backing will persuade Macmillan to publish unless they can see their expenses back'. Seligman reminded him that London University still had first refusal, so he should not pledge himself to anyone in the USA for his 'big book'.[17] In the event, Malinowski's attempts to interest Americans in 'Kiriwina' came to nothing. Clark Wissler, curator of anthropology at the American Museum of Natural History, replied dismissively that the museum's publication funds would 'not permit our printing papers not based upon the results of our own explorations'.[18]

Malinowski was dismayed by Seligman's expectation that he might wish to return to New Guinea, and even more alarmed that the flow of Mond's money might dry up if he did not. On 21 January 1919, he wrote to Seligman at considerable length. 'I am sorry,' he began, 'that my letters to you are so often concerned with sordid questions of lucre, but in your last letter I find a statement which did send a chill through my bones.' He could not forgo the last instalment of Mond's grant. His work would not be at an end until his book was in the press.

> Remember it took Rivers about 4 years to write and print his 'Melanesians'. My material is certainly bulkier, my theoretical ambitions quite as far reaching, and the care with which I propose to bestow on style and finish, I trust not less than Rivers'. I hope to finish my work in half the time, owing to a considerable extent to the help which I am sure to receive from my wife.

He reviewed his options. First, if he were to return to New Guinea it would be with his wife (whose assistance would 'more than repay the extra expense'). But he had decided it would be most unwise to return ('unless you insist on it') and thereby postpone the publication of the ample material that he already had. His second option would be to remain in Australia indefinitely to finish his manuscript. He would be able to live for a couple of years on his own and his wife's assets: 'then I would be practically penniless, unable to return to Europe, and with a great difficulty to find a position here which would not be an impasse; probably cut off from scientific work for a time or for good.' Anthropology had yet to find a niche in Australian universities (by a happy coincidence, when it did so several years later it was thanks largely to Malinowski's father-in-law), so it was only realistic of him to regard an indefinite sojourn in Australia as death to his budding career. His third option was to return to Europe as soon as practicable. 'This would be the most desirable on account of my work (your counsel, libraries, etc.) and because of my duty as a Pole, which might call me for some time to my country.' The drawbacks were the high cost of fares ('I could not travel steerage with my wife except in extremis'), and the likelihood that they would find themselves penniless soon after arriving in England. But if he were to receive further assistance from Mond, this was the alternative he would choose.

He appealed to the disinterested scholar in Seligman. He was working as hard as he could towards 'a definite scientific aim, without troubling much about any prospects of career, remuneration, etc.' An assertive note of self-confidence emerged:

> I believe in the value and importance of my work, I feel that I have a 'message' to bring, and I want to give my work a fair chance. As you know I am 35 years old, and now I am just within sight of bringing forth the first important product of my labours. I feel morally entitled to clamour for help in my work. I do need to feel that I am insured at the very least until my book is out. Then I trust that my work will speak for itself.

He humbly believed that he had 'the right to marry', and argued that his marriage would not make a great deal of financial difference. As a trained nurse, his wife might even temporarily earn a living for them ('her calling is much more liquidable than any of my talents').[19]

He wrote also to Robert Mond, using many of the arguments he had put to Seligman in pleading for the work and not for himself. Regarding his ambitions for 'Kiriwina', he told Mond:

> I estimate that my future publication will be voluminous, roughly three volumes of 500 pages each at 500 words per page. It will take me about two years to get the MS ready and see it through the press. My material is now a chaotic mass of notes. To work it out and put it into the right theoretical frame is perhaps the most difficult, exacting and

important stage of research. To work it out efficiently I must give all my time to it.

Maintaining a modicum of modesty, he added:

I believe in the value of my work, and I see clearly that it is not altogther unimportant. Indeed I feel that I have a definite methodological mission, and I know that I shall be able to make a solid addition to fundamental problems of method and scope of ethnology; to make it less a matter of idle speculation and pure curiosity and more a definite branch and adjunct discipline of theoretical social science.

He summarized:

To put it put it crudely: I feel confident that the money spent on me so far and the future assistance I am asking for will be returned in really good value of scientific fact and method. But if I am compelled now to earn my living by other means, the result of my four years' work assisted by your generosity may be seriously jeopardized.[20]

It is clear from his reply that Mond had little understanding of Malinowski's scientific objectives. As a naïve evolutionist he seemed to think that Malinowski had spent several years in New Guinea obtaining 'facts which may be of fundamental importance as regards the evolution of ideas and customs'. But as long as he was prepared to put up the money his ignorance did not greatly matter.

I very heartily approve of your suggestion that you should now devote a couple of years to digesting the very valuable material you have accumulated. This is essential not only for the proper regard to the observations you have already made but also for learning in what directions further research may become necessary.

He would have much pleasure, he concluded, in continuing his contribution for the next two years. This must have been as music to Malinowski's ears when he received the news at a low point in wintery June. To a penurious scientist Mond was a saviour.[21]

Keeping the vigil

Elsie completed her training at the Melbourne Hospital in January. At the celebration, in addition to her nursing certificate, she received a gift and a signed scroll from the Labour MP John Lemmon for the part she had played in nursing reform ('Lemmon-aid,' Malinowski called it). But her health was suffering again, and in the searing heat of early February she accompanied her parents for three weeks' holiday at Mt Buffalo in northeastern Victoria. With its two horned peaks, the mountain is a rocky, granitic hump that resembles a buffalo in repose. The government-built Chalet, perched on a cliff-top below the summits, offered superior accommodation to its well-connected guests.[22] 'Well, my vigil has begun on the top of this strange mountain away from the world,' Elsie wrote to Malinowski that night. 'I am keeping it so far in the regular knightly [sic] way, as I have eaten practically nothing all day.'[23] She and Malinowski exchanged letters every day, but only Elsie's have survived.

The Chalet's guests were dull, respectable people – 'dapper, mustachioed gents & their massive ladies' – and, despite the Wangaratta belles who sang comic songs, a kind of torpor seemed to hang over everyone. The main recreations were walking, riding, and scrambling over the gigantic rocks. Elsie also went rowing on the mountain lake, joking that in Australia 'nothing could be safer than to go for a row with a priest and a married man, whereas for you Continentals I presume nothing could be more risky'. Conversation also passed the time, much of it with her parents. His name was often mentioned: 'Father calls you "er-Malinowski" and Mother calls you "Broh-nioh".'

Elsie had begun to study Polish. Malinowski was delighted, but had warned her of its difficulty. It was almost a year since he had written:

> To give you a first lesson, there are seven cases of declension in Polish nouns. Whenever you address anyone you must use the fifth case vocative. Thus, it is not Pan Malinowski when you speak to me, but Panie, and not Bronio, but Broniu. The other abbreviation of my Christian name is spelled Bronius, 's' with an accent sign. But the vocative is Broniusiu. A damned hard lingo, isn't it?[24]

Elsie's days of vigil were brightened when Mim Weigall joined the Massons. They walked and read together, and studied Polish for an hour each day. 'I hug the thought of you to myself,' Elsie told Malinowski. She did not want to talk to Mim about him lest she strike 'a complex rock'. By this she meant a subterranean seam of jealousy that she sensed in Mim. It was an intellectual fad of their circle to identify and dissect 'complexes' – gestalts of ideas, suppressed and tinged with emotion, that conflicted with more acceptable ideas and feelings. Malinowski was having trouble with his dentures again and admitted to 'a dentist complex'; about this time he bit the bullet, so to speak, and had his loose palate replaced by a tighter one. Elsie confessed to a petty complex of her own. She realized that she did not want Mim to study Polish, though having dragged the complex from her subconscious she made the effort to invite Mim to participate. 'I'm sick of complexes,' she wrote to Malinowski. 'I agree with you that they must be cleared up, but then again there comes a point when they must be dropped, and I trust your psychoanalytic judgement to know when this moment arrives, the moment when we are pursuing complexes for the amusement and excitement of the game, not for the good it does.'[25] Paul had wearied of them, too, and suggested that 'any member of the Clan mentioning a complex will be fined one shilling, the proceeds to go to the Wesleyan Mission to Papua'.

Inevitably, the Massons' conversation was dominated by the forthcoming marriage. 'Mother is more inclined to talk about you than Mim, but from a practical and externalizing aspect.' Malinowski was 'the Husband-to-Be, a rather terrifying person'. Elsie sensed a 'vague loving reproach' as her mother put a brave face on her daughter's choice of mate. Molly Masson objected 'rather tartly' to Mrs Malinowska: 'You cannot have your name *different* from your husband's here, dear.' Mim thought 'Madam Malinowska' sounded more international. Elsie told them that Bronio would decide what the world would call her.[26]

'Mother's idea of marriage,' Elsie reflected,

seems to be a kind of decent partnership which forms a practical excuse for love, which otherwise is something which should be repressed; the husband's business in the firm lies in doing work which will raise him in repute and give him weight in the eyes of the world, and the wife's duties consist in helping him to get on.

But, Elsie told Malinowski, 'I'm sure I cared more for your work than she has ever really cared for father's, and I care for yours because I believe in its worth and value, not for what it will bring you.' He had said that 'love is like art and is really an end in itself and one of the things making life worthwhile'. Molly Masson held the sternly Calvinist view that 'love is only permissible when it is rendered disciplinary by the bringing up of children'. In other words, the only proper sex was procreational; the only proper means of birth control was continence.[27]

Orme had already given Elsie a wedding present of £250 invested in a war loan, and a great aunt had given another one of £100 in her name.

(Later, Malinowski would be abashed when Baldwin Spencer made a wedding gift to Elsie of £50.) Paul Khuner had offered the couple financial support, which Malinowski indignantly refused. Elsie commented gratefully: 'But if we were in straits I would far rather turn to the Khuners than to anyone else because they would be more truly generous in their manner of giving.'[28]

On 16 February 1919 Malinowski went to 'Nyora' for ten days and kept his 'knightly' vigil there, though, like Elsie, he found it difficult to 'vigilize' in company. More practically, he sought to escape the Spanish influenza epidemic that was beginning to take its toll in the city. Brought from Europe by returning soldiers, the virus would claim more than twelve thousand lives in Australia. While Malinowski remained in Melbourne, Elsie advised him to 'avoid closed atmosphere, trams with windows shut, etc.' and 'do try to walk everywhere, and wear an overcoat, scarf, and good boots'. Now she teased him about flirting with the ladies of 'Nyora', comparing its liveliness with the staidness of the Chalet, where 'there are no houris . . . to give you furtive kicks or teach you the pop-slide dawdle'. There was a sedate nightly dance at the Chalet, but Elsie danced only with Mim. She did not want another man's arm around her.

Bush fires were sweeping the ranges beyond 'Nyora', and Malinowski described one for Elsie in great detail; he sensed there was 'a dread purpose' in its awesome fury. Elsie was struck by his descriptive style – it was Dickens to her Kipling.

> You carefully pile up one effect after another, giving, in the most deliberate and awfully well selected language the entire history of the scene as it unfolds before you, and describing it action by action, each a bit at a time. I am more impressionistic. I really only seek to convey an impression, you to convey the whole scene as it happened.'[29]

Whether or not Malinowski's narrative style was that of a Dickens, a Zola or a Conrad, it was more suited to ethnographic description than Elsie's.

An unhappy contention arose between them over Elsie's epistolary style, or rather over what she omitted from her letters. Malinowski made his old complaint that his beloved's letters were not sufficiently self-searching. He wanted more subjectivity, more unpacking of psychological baggage. Elsie could not meet this demand and felt that she had failed him. 'It is more a fault in myself, perhaps, than a technical fault of letter writing,' she protested.

'You cannot imagine that I do not have metaphysical crises and *Stimmung* as much as you do, and you believe that only reserve and stiffness prevent me from expressing them.' If she had to invent feelings and confect precious sentiments in order to please him, the cost would be 'a letter writing complex'. Her letters show that she could be his equal in feisty wit, and in that two independent intellects agreed on so many important things, theirs was a marriage of minds. But her inability to match his Polish 'emotionalism' depressed her, and his psychological bullying inhibited her to the point where she became almost afraid to write to him. There was a tyrannical possessiveness to Malinowski's love; he wanted to reach to the bottom of her soul, but Elsie feared his disappointment at finding so little there.

She identified another difference between them. 'You love me most when we are away from each other. You have to get things into the land of thought before you feel them intensely.' For her, reality lay in the unmediated present: she loved him most when he was with her.

> It is almost frightening to me dear Broniu how much more intensely you feel a thing when it ceases to become reality and is only thought. What you say of feeling love so deeply in absence is something like what you told me once, that you were immediately more interested in the war when it was over.[30]

She had also a half-formed fear that she would be less attractive to him once they were married. 'I wonder if "your wife" can have the same charm for you as Elsie R. Masson. . . . I am sure women are more tenacious of loving than men. . . . No husband who is loved is in the hinterland, he simply *is* the landscape.'[31]

Elsie's despondency was cured by her sister's arrival a few days later. Orme had gone to meet Marnie's ship and bring her to Mt Buffalo for a joyful reunion. She had seen the Seligmans before she left London and was delighted to talk to Elsie about Malinowski.[32] In time, however, Marnie came to dislike him. That her parents did not like him either, she thought, was

> because their temperaments were so different, his so complex, introspective, emotional, theirs so much simpler, their attitude to people much kinder – he could be any sort of person towards others if he found it expedient to be so, but could say cleverly analytical things about them if that's how he really felt.

Marnie suspected that he always felt as if he were unacceptable to the Massons. Her father had once written to her: 'There are always two sides to a family, but they should not be the *inside* and the *outside*.' Malinowski, it seems, would always remain on the outside, forever the alien.[33]

The wedding

The worst drought in Melbourne's history broke during the first week of March. After five inches of torrential rain the city was awash, the Yarra rose above its banks and low-lying suburbs were flooded. The hospitals were also flooded – with the victims of Spanish 'flu. Nursing auxiliaries combed the streets in face masks, carting off the stricken to an emergency hospital set up in the Royal Exhibition Building. Theatres, cinemas, libraries and other public buildings had been closed as a precautionary measure. It was certainly not the most auspicious week in which to marry.

The Massons remained at Mt Buffalo until Monday 3 March. Malinowski had already returned to Melbourne and rented a room at 156 Powlett Street, a broad, tree-lined street that sloped gently down to the Yarra. It was just one street away from his Grey Street lodgings. He would have been quite happy to stay there after their marriage, but Elsie objected; although Grey Street had sentimental associations for her too, it seemed better to start afresh. As for the honeymoon: 'We won't tell anyone where we are going exactly, even if it's only in town.'

They had decided on a civil wedding, which most people thought unromantic, though, to an idealistic Elsie, 'it is real romance to transform the dull and incongruous into something wonderful by the strength of what lies within your own feelings. I keep wishing it were to be just you and I there, and we would call in utter strangers from the street to be our witnesses.'[34]

They were married on Thursday 6 March, at Melbourne's registry office in Collins Street. Such was the significance of this rite of passage in the life of Bronislaw Malinowski that the ceremony might have been one to compare with the imperial conferral of his doctorate in Cracow some eleven years earlier. Yet it could not have been more different. On the marriage certificate Malinowski modestly recorded his occupation as 'student', as if his status had remained unchanged for the past decade. Marnie's is the only eyewitness report of the wedding, apart from a few lines in the social column of a local newspaper. There the anonymous reporter cheerfully noted that 'the bride wore a travelling costume of fawn cloth, with self-coloured stockings and shoes set off with a smart hat in variegated straw'. Elsie was described as 'a highly cultured girl with strong intellectual gifts'. The groom had been doing scientific work in the Trobriand Islands, and 'was now engaged in compiling all the valuable scientific facts gleaned by studying his dusky neighbours in the tropics'.[35] (*His* dusky neighbours? Luckily, the reporter did not mention the groom's enemy alien status.) In addition to the three Massons and their faithful servant Jessie Inglis, those present at the wedding were Mim Weigall, Paul Khuner (perhaps Hede, too, though she had only recently given birth), and the doleful librarian Edward Pitt, who served as best man. Marnie remembered 'a dreary room, dust and a general feeling of bowler-hatted legality but no sentiment, and my heart sank to see the two just walk away afterwards, in spite of my knowing that this was what they wanted'. She was happy for Elsie 'but dispirited at the coldness of the ceremony and, more seriously, at the knowledge that she did not have the warmth of parental support'.[36] After the ceremony the happy couple walked hand in hand down Collins Street to begin their secret honeymoon.

Marnie often visited the newlyweds in Powlett Street, of which her recollections were as sour as those of the wedding. Their room was 'undeniably sordid, but order, disregarded by Bronio, was achieved as far as possible by Elsie'. Marnie had a clear memory of her sister standing at the window, gazing out pensively over the kitchen sink, and she wondered then whether Elsie realized what she had taken on in marrying Dr Bronislaw Malinowski.[37]

While at Mt Buffalo, Elsie had received two letters from Nina Stirling. Her father was terminally ill, but Nina was also distressed that Malinowski had not sent her his personal assurance that he had destroyed all her letters and photographs. His letter to Nina was to have been concealed inside one from Leila Peck – a necessary subterfuge after her family's pact to have no further communication with him. He would finally destroy all but one of Nina's letters and many of her photographs; but some of them – accomplished prints of bushland and the gardens at St Vigeans – he kept. Now Elsie rebuked him for his procrastination. She would reply to Nina, and she hoped that he would too. 'I *do* think it was awfully unkind to weakly put this off just for want of a little self-discipline, and I felt all the time that it could only lead to everyone involved having some additional hurt, and so it has turned out.'[38]

It was on the eve, if not on the very day, of his wedding that Malinowski sent Nina a letter of sympathy concerning her father. A draft of it survives.[39] 'Dear Friend,' he addressed her.

> You and your family have shown me more heart and kindness after I left home, & however badly I may have acted towards you all, does not mean that I have no feelings of gratitude. I am grieved deeply at your present trouble and it makes me feel sad that I have forfeited the right of giving a friend sympathy.

He might have left it there, but could not resist another stumbling apology, another limp excuse for his conduct.

> Whatever my guilt was, I never have been callous regarding your feelings & in the way in which I have acted towards you – partly through my fault and partly through a fatal coincidence of circumstances – has left me very unhappy with remorse. And in all the minor details – as writing to your mother instead of to you – I never acted so as to spite you or show you that I don't suffer or care.

He did not refer to his imminent marriage to Elsie.

Nina replied promptly. Her final letter, of 8 March, was in part an acknowledgment of his sympathy and an account of her father's suffering and her mother's endurance (Edward Stirling would die within a fortnight); but in larger part it was a bitter reproach. Its wounded innocence must have lacerated him; but he kept this letter, perhaps as a prickly reminder of his perfidy.

> I can never understand why [Nina wrote] . . . when you asked me 'not to be single on my account' why you hadn't the pluck to tell me. Further back than that your coming over [to Adelaide] at all was *so* cruel, I do not know how you could have added this torture. . . .
>
> Apart from all, we were friends, such jolly good pals & you had this friendship, apart from all else, & threw it away, for I should never have hurt you & it nearly killed me to think that you didn't confide in me & that my family knew & it was common property for a month before I knew. . . .
>
> It was funny how it nearly did kill me bodily I mean, & I have often thought since, how you'd have had another bond with your Polish friend, if I had pegged.

I sincerely hope & almost pray you will not be remaining in Australia. It is my own wish that someday or somehow I may hear of your possible departure. This is purely selfish – if it were for your own advantage to stay of course you should do this. . . .

You may feel you have your side to say so you can feel in your conscience you have made all amends & enjoy your married life, but it is so late now & the Past must be buried entirely as you will have Another to consider now – & it is absolutely necessary that St Vigeans & all it has meant – must be another Past.

I awfully hope you will be happy.
Nina

A mute memento of their past can be seen today in the South Australian Museum – a woman's leaf skirt from the Trobriand Islands, donated by Miss Nina Stirling.

Seminars on 'social ideas'

Settling into the new regime of married life, Malinowski went back to work on 'Kiriwina' while Elsie continued to assist John Lemmon in the struggle to improve nurses' working conditions. Despite a touch of neuritis, Malinowski continued to review his Trobriand materials and throughout April and May began to formulate ideas about their theoretical significance. On the back of a letter from Lemmon to Elsie he sketched 'Historical hypotheses: *Kulturkreise*' for the Massim, which he intended to elaborate in one of the appendices to 'Kiriwina'. A 'historical perspective was necessary', he noted, to order the 'stratification of various cultural elements', though he was conscious of the limited value of such hypotheses. He listed gross culture traits of Kiriwina (settlement pattern, clanship, chieftainship, agriculture, warfare, religious belief, decorative art, material culture, etc) and made snap comparisons with their analogues in other districts of the Massim. These were perhaps the 'problems of the Rivers type' to which he referred in his 1918 diary. He was clearly uncomfortable with this kind of ethnological analysis, and the four 'layers' of culture he purported to find in eastern New Guinea are hedged with cautionary question marks. He never published these speculations, but the notes belie the conventional assumption that Malinowski gave no thought to the kind of problems that preoccupied contemporary ethnology.[40]

It was probably towards the end of 1918 – when Elton Mayo paid a fleeting visit to Melbourne – that Malinowski inaugurated 'a kind of seminar' for the airing of views, philosophical, psychological and sociological. The seminar was revived in April and attended by the Khuners, Elsie, Mim, Ursula McConnell (sister of Dorothea Mayo), and perhaps Bob Broinowski and Ernest Pitt. Their meetings were held in 'Nizza', the Khuners' spacious home at 439 Victoria Parade. They had moved from suburban Malvern in January, just before Hede gave birth to their daughter – whom they named after Elsie and Mim. In such congenial domestic surroundings Malinowski thought through his intellectual positions. He and Paul led discussions on economics; Paul was still preoccupied with theories of currency, and he surely influenced Malinowski's thinking at this time about the money-like valuables that circulated in Kula. Ursula, who had studied psychology at the University of Melbourne and was thought by others to have 'an unbounded respect for herself', brought her lecture notes along for discussion.

Between 10 and 16 April 1919, Malinowski assembled many pages of notes under the heading 'Social Ideas'.[41] They outlined his current thinking on 'sociology', and although he modified his terminology in later years, these dense pages contain the essentials of what he would call his 'scientific theory of culture'. Thus, in a few autumn days in the 'undeniably sordid' lodgings that he shared with Elsie in East Melbourne, Malinowski erected the grand framework of his functionalism. It marked an important stage in the evolution of his anthropological thinking. He would work out the ideas in the years to come, but here in a nutshell was the combination of methodological and biological functionalism that grew into the edifice that was unveiled in its final form in the United States some twenty years later.

According to these notes from Powlett Street, he conceived the idea of an ideal ethnography conducted by an omnipresent, omniscient 'Perfect Being'. This Ideal Ethnographer (like the latter-day 'Anthropologist from Mars') would comprehend in its totality the society under scrutiny. Slipping into the role of an all-knowing Big Brother, Malinowski gave a fair summary of what he believed he had accomplished in the Trobriands.

Imagine a society being studied by a Perfect Being able to record all regularities in social grouping and behaviour by objective means of collecting data (including by kinematograph and phonograph). By these means our Perfect Being could objectively 'fix' the diverse aspects of a Culture (such as religion, economics, law, war etc.) and its primary groupings – in fact *all* social groupings underlying each specific activity or institution. He would also collect all material items of the Culture . . . describing them in relation to the physical environment: that is, what natural materials are used and how they are used. And he would, of course, learn the language of the people and collect innumerable texts. In sum, our Perfect Being would get to grips with the entire sociology: all social action and individual behaviour would be recorded insofar as they were regular and socially conditioned and not merely idiosyncratic.

In notes for a second seminar, Malinowski pared his system to the bone and structured his presentation according to five leading points. Psychobiological functionalism comes clearly to the fore.

1. Kultur [sic] is the sum of institutions; that is, means of satisfying human needs through social co-operation.

2. Kultur can be analysed broadly into a series of Aspects, each fulfilling a definite role in satisfying needs. . . .

3. Institutions. Sometimes these embrace a whole aspect of Kultur, sometimes there are several institutions in a single aspect. . . . An institution is based upon products of material civilization, including such collective expressions of human organization as language, and it consists of a group of human beings forming its social basis.

4. Each institution thus possesses a material, objective aspect and a human, subjective one.

(a) To understand the material, objective side we must construct the functional, teleological meaning of an institution as a means of satisfying a definite human purpose. . . .

(b) To understand the subjective side, we must allow that the individuals who constitute the group have definite Social Ideas with regard to their institution. It is these Ideas which drive them and form the cement that unites them. . . .

5. Each institution fulfills a certain function, each has its teleology. . . . For example, magic in primitive society, religion in the Middle Ages, modern Christianity, all satisfy a human craving for the mastery of Fate, for the mastery of natural or supernatural forces. They have this aim, which we recognize by taking . . . a philosophical view of human nature.

This philosophy would deal with Man as an Animal with physical and mental needs and institutions as mechanisms to satisfy them.

In a third seminar, Malinowski introduced the problem of the relationship of history to ethnology and sociology, a topic he had repeatedly pondered in his last Trobriand diary.

> History is the everchanging stream of happenings. When do they happen? In what medium? Surely only in human society. There must be rules or laws, proper to the medium, according to which historical events happen. History is the undulating stream between two banks, physical hard-and-fast rule and the more plastic embankment of human mental nature. If we want to enjoy the vicissitudes of the stream – the novelist's interest – well and good; but if we want to understand the general course of history, then we must study its matrix: the lie of the land, the nature of the banks. . . . Whether we study the amours of Louis XIV or the exploits of Bonaparte or the schemes and ambition of Bismarck, we are always brought back to the big social forces: organization, military, economic factors etc., which lend their influence to the *dramatis personae*.

He concluded with a prophetic flourish. 'The development of History leads to Sociology. History is bound to die a painless death. Part of its inheritance will go to Antiquarianism; part to Sensationalism; part to Romantic Sentiment. But its scientific heir will be Sociology.'

Chapter 28

Country Retreats

Under the cupola

The end of the war to end all wars had not brought peace to Australia, and the armistice augured the most violent year in its history. Nineteen nineteen was the year in which Lenin announced the imminent triumph of the proletarian revolution, which would stalk triumphantly from country to country. Although the turmoil in Australia was as nothing compared to the revolutionary violence in the collapsed empires of Germany, Austria, Russia and Turkey, Australian soldiers returned to find intensified class warfare and a country torn by strikes, riots and mutinies. The cheering crowds, brass bands, flag-waving and patriotic speeches could not conceal a fractured society, a condition that Prime Minister Billy Hughes called 'war neurosis'. The war had divided the nation over conscription and brought unemployment and increased poverty; now the spread of Bolshevism threatened bourgeois civilization. The War Precautions Act of 1915 had delivered a limited form of martial law, but such was the social unrest that it was extended to the middle of 1919. Until then Malinowski and the Khuners would remain enemy aliens. Before the war, Australian politics had been preoccupied with welfare and reform; after the armistice it was preoccupied with the spread of Communism. The average weekly wage for men in 1919 was £3.14.11, but a Royal Commission had declared the subsistence minimum to be £5.16.0. On this reckoning Malinowski and Elsie were barely above the breadline.

The Spanish influenza epidemic fed the popular fear that Australia was beset by foreign evils. It was a metaphor for the pestilence of Bolshevism that had infiltrated the factories and was infecting the entire society. Medical auxiliaries patrolled the city in ghostly white garb, searching for victims. In the second week of June, when Elsie and Malinowski went down with the virus, there were eight hundred sufferers in Melbourne hospitals.

Molly Masson sent in the family doctor, Dunbar Hooper, who packed Elsie off to the makeshift hospital in the Royal Exhibition Building.[1] Although feeling 'seedy', Malinowski thought at first that he might have escaped. He hung on in Powlett Street for a week, fasting and feeling increasingly sorry for himself. Paul, the go-between, popped in twice a day to light the fire and make tea. Then he would visit Elsie, carrying a letter from Malinowski, and when she was well enough to write, Paul conveyed her missives back to him. Their letters during this brief period of separation – the first of so many in their marriage – were fugue-like in their contrapuntal exchange, playing variations on a theme of mutual concern. Malinowski's twice-daily résumés of his minutely monitored symptoms were reciprocated by Elsie with similar bulletins; their recitatives alternated with loving arias.[2]

'I had a slight temperature of 99.2 last night, and a slightly sore throat,' Malinowski wrote to her the day after she was admitted to hospital.

I would feel nearer to you there, under the law of association by contiguity, but here I feel nearer under the law of remembered complexes, where 'complex' is not used in the Freudian sense. . . . I took an assortment of drugs (empirin, paraffin, vaseline, calomel, smelling salts, spray, inhaler, mentholin, and eye-drops), and not much over a dozen vitamins.

Otherwise, he was ingesting only milky tea and biscuits. He lay in bed with pyjama bottoms wrapped turban-wise around his head. 'I would feel a pasha in sweet heaven were it not for the absence of my houri,' he told her.

'My poor dear lonely one,' Elsie wrote on Tuesday from her bed under the cupola. The 'usual Exhibition din' was going on around her: 'the clatter of auxiliaries in the pantry, washing dishes, scraping pots and singing at the tops of their voices, children shouting and screaming, hammers hammering, feet tramping etc.' It was the first time she had been able to sit up. Her gastric complication appeared to be quite common, 'and if it does nothing else it must remove your cruel suspicion that I have, not Spanish, but Australio-Polish influenza'. Lady Spencer had sent flowers: 'I would send them all via Paul to you, but you would only swear.' Mim had also gone down with the 'flu, and now Paul was their only link. She lay thinking how happy they had been: 'I feel as if every day we spent together at Powlett St. ought to be paradise, and so many of them were.' But she remembered some of their differences too. 'I wonder if such things must come about & who is most to blame, or rather, how we are both to blame.'

As his temperature mounted Malinowski's paranoid jealousy returned. 'Paul came at 10.30 after I'd turned out the light,' he wrote to her on Wednesday.

> A feeling of grievance, no doubt the flu depression is mostly to blame. But reverse our positions and substitute you for me, Marnie for Paul and think hard: how would you feel if you knew that as soon as you went off with your sickness Marnie had taken your place by my side as a comforter and companion. That night after night she sits till all hours by my side and is mistaken by observers for my wife. . . . I wrote you a long and bitter letter during the night but I could not possibly send it.

As he continued the letter that afternoon, an obscure fury gripped him, and he launched into a mock Zarathustrian tirade:

> My own darling. Goddam you, goddam Paul, goddam Hooper! All of you! What is it, Oh light of my heart, that turns your head into that of a stupid sheep or an unwieldy ass. What words do I hear from the patient messenger who toils between us like an unfortunate mangy mule or camel, beaten here, kicked there, abused everywhere.

His temperature had climbed to 100.8 and he was undoubtedly feverish, but Elsie was injured by his tone and indignant at his supposition:

> I have just got your letter and I am very unhappy indeed. . . . I only know I have only been thinking of you. . . . Last night Paul came here about 8, and stayed till *a quarter to ten*, no longer. . . . But 'taken your place by my side' he has not, no, no, no, not in the very least. . . . I would rather have been alone from beginning to end of this wretched time than have had this happen.

Malinowski was contrite, and replied: 'I felt lonely . . . so sentimental and so unsatisfactory after having written those semi-jocular stupid letters to you.' It was on 20 June that Dr Hooper finally diagnosed his influenza. Conveyed at last to the Exhibition Building, he slept for twelve hours. Although still physically separated from Elsie by screens, he could gaze up at the copula knowing that she lay beneath it too. He could also reflect that he was being nursed in the grandiose building that had housed the first Australian Commonwealth Parliament, beneath the very dome where, in May 1901,

Federation had been declared before a great assembly. An Austrian enemy alien for five years, he was soon to become a free citizen of Poland. It was under a similar dome in London that he had soaked himself in British scholarship, and it was under the replica dome of the Melbourne Public Library nearby that he had begun to work on his Mailu and Trobriand fieldwork materials. Now, under this third dome, his work in mining ethnography at the coalface lay behind him, but the writing had hardly begun. He despaired that, owing to illness yet again, he was losing precious time.

Malinowski and Elsie missed the street celebrations on 28 June, the day the Versailles peace treaty was signed. Edward Pitt wrote to him: 'I pictured you in fancy [dress] rushing down Bourke St. waving a huge flag and trying to push a tramcar off the line, with your distracted wife hanging on to your coat-tails. But alas, it is not to be.'[3]

Escape to Wangaratta

On being discharged from hospital, they were persuaded by Molly to begin their recuperation at 'Chanonry'. They gave up their room in Powlett Street and planned an escape from cold, gloomy Melbourne. On 6 July Malinowski wrote to the military authorities to inform them that he and his wife had been ordered by their doctor to leave Melbourne immediately. He begged permission to travel to Wagga Wagga in the Riverina district of New South Wales. Permission was instantly granted, although as he was still on parole the permit forbade them to break their journey at any intervening station. Malinowski baulked at this petty restriction, and a modified permit – the last document in the military's file – was reissued on 8 July: 'Dr Malinowski is required to notify the Police in Victoria prior to leaving for N.S.W. and secure the proper police forms. He is then to report to the Police in N.S.W. at the first place where he leaves the train and is to comply with the War Precautions Act.'[4] Much later, Marnie remembered 'what pleasure and entertainment Bronio got from his reporting visits to the police. . . . I can see his amused face and hear his and Elsie's laughter about the formality, so softened by Australian friendliness on the part of the Arm of the Law.'[5] Friendly or not, Malinowski preferred to see as little of the police as possible, so he and Elsie decided to remain within Victoria.

They travelled by train to Wangaratta, a farming town on the Ovens River some way short of the New South Wales border. There they found

accommodation in a sturdy house on a broad boulevard lined with eucalyptus. A short walk took them to the centre of town and an even shorter
one to the river flats, where they could watch myriad water birds, glimpse
the occasional platypus, and hear the raucous laughter of kookaburras. With
rugs over their knees they spent many contented hours on the house verandah, bathed in the winter sunshine. Malinowski picked up his Trobriand
texts again, and together they worked on them.

The texts loomed large in Malinowski's conception of the kind of anthropology he wanted to promote. In the methodological credo he wrote two
years later, vernacular texts underpinned 'the third commandment of fieldwork', which was to discover 'the typical ways of thinking and feeling, corresponding to the institutions and culture of a given community'. Such texts
comprised: 'A collection of ethnographic statements, characteristic narratives, typical utterances, items of folk-lore and magical formulae [which
have] to be given as a *corpus inscriptionum*, as documents of native mentality.'[6] An encouraging endorsement of this approach had been provided by
Britain's leading Egyptologist, Alan Gardiner, with whom Malinowski had
begun corresponding in 1917. It is likely they had met in London several
years earlier, for Gardiner's wife was Finnish and well acquainted with
Tancred and Anna-Mi Borenius. Gardiner and Malinowski became friends
and significantly influenced one another's thinking about the pragmatics of
speech and language (which to them were effectively one and the same
thing). Together they inspired J. R. Firth and what became known as the
London School of Linguistics. Their collaboration remained informal,
however, as Gardiner was an independently wealthy scholar who held no
academic positions; consequently, he left no disciples and his linguistic work
received less recognition than Malinowski's.

It was aboard the *Marsina* on 26 October 1917 that Malinowski wrote to
Gardiner, praising his work on Egyptian inscriptions and explaining his own
use of vernacular texts to authenticate his Trobriand ethnography. Gardiner
replied in early January 1918 and a six-page fragment of his letter has survived.[7] He had read 'Baloma' and admired Malinowski's deployment of vernacular texts. He was disappointed with anthropological works that quoted
verbatim statements of informants in translation only. The ethnographer had
the advantage over the student of mute, ancient texts in that he could cross-
question the native speaker for commentaries on the verbatim text he
wished to interpret.

He thus obtains what are in effect glosses (*scholia*). But none the less one feels that one would have liked to have the *ipsissima verba* of the original statement in all its obscurity and vagueness, since that is the way that people think, and precisely the glosses and skolia are not really the *meaning* of the original statement, but an improvement upon it called forth by the fact that the question is (if you will pardon me saying so) unusually importunate and troublesome.

Gardiner also pleaded for the unadorned native text of 'important assertions made in your hearing, or replies to your questions', to be given in footnotes or in an appendix. 'These would always serve you and others as points of repair whenever . . . doubts arise as to the correctness of an interpretation, or when a new synthesis suggests itself.' Malinowski reproduced these prescriptions when discussing his *corpus inscriptionum Kiriwiniensium* in the methodological introduction to *Argonauts*.[8]

Gardiner's second major point went to the heart of what would come to be known as linguistic philosophy. He had 'a hazy kind of notion' that the philosophers he read 'never asked themselves exactly the meaning of the words they are using'. They seemed to forget 'that all language, even the simplest, is a mass of daring abstractions, and that philosophy ought to be, to a large extent, the consideration of the validity of these abstractions; or if not their validity, their usefulness – the two things, I take it, are one'. Some years later Ludwig Wittgenstein would say something very similar. 'As a philologist,' Gardiner concluded, 'I am supremely dissatisfied with the whole position of *semantics*.' So too was Malinowski, and he found in Alan Gardiner an intellectual soulmate – an empiricist and a pragmatist who held that language was the product of acts of speech and that it was the context of an utterance that provided its meaning.

In Wangaratta, and later in Whitfield, Malinowski struggled with the translations of texts that he intended to incorporate into his 'Kiriwina' monograph. It was perhaps to preserve the legibility of the originals that Malinowski made handwritten copies of the texts he was working on. With characteristic parsimony, he frequently made these copies on the backs of letters – from Leila Peck, the Seligmans, Baldwin Spencer, Robert Mond and many others – or on the backs of carbons of his own articles. The letters date the texts on their verso to this period, during which Malinowski transcribed, translated and commented upon at least 125 numbered texts.[9]

Among the first dozen were versions of the myth of Tudava, and texts of varying length and complexity on erotic dreams, *baloma*, cannibalism, conception theory, flying witches, *sagali* feasts and a freak tidal wave that swept across the narrow waist of Kiriwina long ago.

Nursing Paul

Scarcely had Elsie and Malinowski begun to enjoy the open skies of Wangaratta when news reached them that Paul Khuner was ill. On 26 July Malinowski hastened back to Melbourne by the afternoon train. He had just missed two days of rioting in the city. Of this alarming civic crisis, however, he said nothing in his letters to Elsie, so preoccupied was he with the private crisis of Paul's illness. Although he was uncertain whether he could be of any use, he felt he owed it to their friendship to be at his side; it was also an opportunity to repay Paul's ministrations during his own illness. Elsie remained in Wangaratta to continue her convalescence; it was their second separation in only four months of marriage. Their letters – each wrote twice a day – were filled with concern for Paul and for one another. They conjured a culture of illness and cure in a syncretic discourse of scientific and folk medicine. Fahrenheit temperatures sprinkle the pages. Neither of them trusted their doctor. Nurse Elsie Rosaline abetted Bronio's hypochondria, and occasionally outdid him. In their epistolary duet, which echoed that of the month before, Elsie sang with the confidence of her medical training, Malinowski from his rich experience of malaise.[10]

As soon as he had gone she began to worry about him. 'Go to bed early,' she begged, 'take salts every morning, and don't go on the outsides of trams.' Dr Hooper had said that Paul's chill was not due to influenza, but Elsie did not believe him, and advised Malinowski to treat it as if it were.

> That means: stay in bed, back to the light, fire in the room if it is cold; flannel or wool next to the skin; nothing solid to eat till the temp. is normal, but drink plenty of milk, tea, cocoa, coffee etc.; a purgative every night or morning, salts preferred. *Do not set foot to the ground.* If Paul had done this from the first it would have been much better.

Now into her stride as a business-like nurse, Elsie urged her husband to be severe and consistent in making sure that Paul followed her instructions.

Personally, I don't believe in a wash first thing in the morning for patients, I should say first a cup of tea and then a rest and then wash them about ten, first taking temp. Perhaps if Paul gets really ill it would be better to move his bed into the sitting room.

Malinowski found himself amid a confusion of contradictory medical diagnosis and practical advice, to which he added his own *ad hoc* folk wisdom. Paul's high temperature, he suspected, was due to

a 'flu infection directed on the stomach and liver. . . . But there is here a brothel of lunatics. . . . Mim believes that Paul should sleep, so we all talk in whispers and walk without boots in the next room. Hede thinks Paul should *not* sleep in daytime, so she goes into his room every few minutes.

Malinowski slept in Paul's room, kept him covered in case he began to sweat and in the morning gave him an enema and a bowel pump, ministering to him as would a male nurse. Dr Hooper came and 'overhauled' Paul yet again as the women had been making a fuss about his persistent temperature. After Hooper had gone Mim arrived, and then Bob Broinowski. Mim wanted to consult a second doctor, and Leila Peck also called later with a message from her sister to the effect that Hooper was no good, so they decided to get another doctor on the case as well. The Clan was rallying around Paul as a chief at death's door, though according to Malinowski he was only 'slightly languid, but by no means looking or seeming really ill'. He was also looking after himself, he reassured Elsie: 'I spray my threat and wash my hands constantly.'

Elsie was maintaining a low-grade temperature; she was still weak and it depressed her. On Sunday she wrote to her husband, 'I remember how you once said that the life you had to lead would never do for an invalid wife, but I never thought I would be one.' She had strolled into town and weighed herself: 7 stone 7 pounds, a modest gain of half a pound. (The week before, it seems, Malinowski had weighed 10 stone 9½ pounds – a healthy weight for a man of his height.) It distressed her that she was not at 'the Pauls' to help. 'What a mockery my training has been, just when I could turn it to some account.' But she was proud of Bronio, 'the supposed impractical man stepping into the breach and pulling things together. But I knew he could and would.' Paul liked being nursed, Malinowski told her, 'and I thought, how nice it would be to be sick and to be nursed by you, darling.

You never nursed me so far, in the strict sense of the word?' To this she replied, 'I would just love to nurse you, and I could do it couldn't I?'

By Wednesday Paul was out of danger. Dr Hooper had finally decided that his illness was 'pure pneumonia, not influenza in type'.[11] Elsie could hardly wait for Malinowski's return. It had been cold, windy and rainy, and impossible to sit outside. 'So I have a good fire and the window wide open,' she wrote.

Before returning to Wangaratta, he visited some foreign consulates. There was no Polish consul in Melbourne and obtaining a Polish passport proved to be a frustrating process. He complained to Elsie: 'I simply loathe all touch with officialdom and red tape & I am in the same state of concentrated fury as I was when I had to run about the Defence Dept.' In August he wrote to the newly appointed Polish consul-general in Sydney, asking for recognition of his Polish nationality.

> Apart from feeling that the rights of my nation should be recognized in my person, I want to have a full legal status, as my non-defined position may lead to discomfort or difficulties. Again, I may be obliged to leave Australia soon, and I want to travel under a Polish Passport, and not as a 'subject of the Emperor of Austria'.[12]

In the end, it was Seligman who somehow secured a Polish passport for Malinowski in London and posted it to him by registered mail.[13]

Particles in Whitfield

Although warmer than Melbourne, Wangaratta was damper than Malinowski believed to be healthy and they looked around for a more elevated and scenic spot. Late in August they decided on Whitfield, a secluded farming village on the King River at the end of a trolley line from Wangaratta. It was from Whitfield that Elsie and her parents had taken a coach to Mt Buffalo in February, and the long dark hump of the mountain could be seen thirty miles to the east. Malinowski and Elsie now found cosy accommodation at Mrs Tyrell's timbered Mountain View Hotel. The Khuners joined them in September, and together they rented a cottage across a paddock from the hotel. The friendship of the two couples deepened and became poignant with the knowledge that they would soon be parted. Having waited several months for a passage, the Khuners were due to sail for Europe at the end of November. In the meantime they were visited separately by Marnie, Mim and Elsie's friend Jean Campbell. It was a happy springtime for the Malinowskis, perhaps the happiest they would ever know. Bronio was in the pink of health and Elsie had shaken off her fevers. In November she conceived.

It was a fertile period for Malinowski, too. With Paul he returned to the study of economics and psychology; library renewal notices indicate that in October they were reading Alfred Marshall's *Principles of Economics*, Irving Fisher's *Purchasing Power of Money* and Hugo Munsterberg's *Psychology*.[14] But it was his linguistic study of Kiriwina texts that preoccupied Malinowski, and he began to draft an article.[15]

Having discovered that 'most branches of linguistics and classical philology [were] useless to the anthropologist', he set himself the task of formulating an ethnographic theory of language, though it would be several years before he was satisfied with it. Beginning with Sidney Ray's first principle that 'a scientific study of language is essential to a full ethnographic description', he adduced a basic principle of his own that foreshadowed his later functionalism.

> All aspects of tribal life play into each other; to sunder a few of them from the rest results in a mutilation of the whole, and language is not an exception in this respect. The study of the linguistic aspect is indispensable, especially if we want to grasp the social psychology of the tribe, i.e. their manner of thinking, in so far as it is conditioned by the peculiarities of their culture.

Malinowski's principal interest was in *meaning*, but all the works on language he had studied neglected semantics. Yet 'it is only from the development of Semantics . . . that the ethnographer can look for real help'. The analysis of meaning invariably led to ethnographic descriptions. 'Thus linguistics without ethnography would fare as badly as ethnography would without the light thrown on it by language.'

In his article – the only technical linguistic description he ever published – he focused on a particular exotic feature of the language of Kiriwina, namely its use of parts of speech that classify and quantify nouns. 'Classifiers', 'formatives' or (as Malinowski preferred to call them) 'classificatory particles' define grammatically what kind of entity a speaker is referring to. When he distributed tobacco, for instance, 'the natives would ask for their portions with different words, according as to whether I would twist off the "stick" with my fingers and tear off pieces, or cut off portions with a knife'. To disregard this kind of usage was as improper as to misuse gender in an Indo-European language, 'and the natives might laugh, as rude people, uncorrupted by good manners, do laugh when their language is mutilated by a foreigner'.

Malinowski was fascinated by the semantic function of noun classes in framing thought. Classifiers offered clues to the Trobrianders' worldview because they ordered perception, and he recognized their pragmatic, discriminating function as an aid to achieving that 'economy of thought' required by all human minds. The categories that Trobriand people use to think with are encoded in their classifiers. They create semantic domains, as for example: persons, animals, trees and wooden things, yams, body parts, quantities, fire, proper names, time, quality, shape, utensils, dress and adornment, and ritual items.[16] Some twenty years before Ludwig Wittgenstein, Malinowski recognized that each language provided a unique window on the world.

The main problem he faced was how to describe the meaning of particular classifiers. The analysis of their meaning led to 'excursions into ethnography' in order to make sense of them. He identified eight groups consisting of forty-two particles altogether, though later students of the language – today called Kilivila – have discovered many more. Fr Baldwin, a Catholic missionary in the 1930s, listed seventy-five; Ralph Lawton, a Methodist missionary in the 1960s, found 147; and most recently a German linguist, Gunter Senft, has described 177. The discrepancy in numbers is no reflection on Malinowski's research and language-speaking competence; it is rather a question of deciding what to call a classifier, and it is clear that the later linguists have cast their nets wider than Malinowski. There is also the inconvenient fact that new classifers are continually being created by Kilivila speakers.

Throughout his article Malinowski urged the need for a sound linguistic theory, one that would reveal

what is essential in language and what therefore must remain the same throughout the whole range of linguistic varieties; how linguistic forms are influenced by physiological, mental, social, and other cultural elements; what is the real nature of Meaning and Form, and how they correspond; a theory which, in fine, would give us a set of well-founded plastic definitions of grammatical concepts.

He promised a Kiriwina grammar, but he never wrote one. This pioneering article on classificatory particles was nonetheless important in signposting the direction of his later work. Lurking within it is the key concept of his ethnographic theory of language as expounded in *Coral Gardens and their Magic*. Paradoxically, he observed:

> The real difficulty of this language consists not in the complexity of the grammatical apparatus but rather in its extreme simplicity. Its structure is on the whole what might be described as telegraphic; the relation of the words, as well as the relation of the sentences, has mainly to be derived from the context.

'Context of situation' would become the cornerstone of the pragmatic theory that characterized the London School of Linguistics in the 1930s.

It was December by the time Malinowski finished the article – 'Classificatory Particles in the Language of Kiriwina'. Elsie helped him 'a great deal with style & plan' and typed up half of it. Malinowski dictated the other half to Bob Broinowski, who typed it on 'the Senatorial machine, stopping occasionally to argue about the use of certain words, semi-colons etc.'[17] As if to prove Malinowski's contention that anthropologists did not take linguistics seriously enough, the article was rejected by the *Journal of the Royal Anthropological Institute*. Instead it appeared in 1922 in the newly founded *Bulletin of the School of Oriental Studies*.

A museum display

In late November, the Malinowskis returned to Melbourne to say farewell to the Khuners aboard the S.S. *Van Cloon*, bound for Valparaiso. 'At the moment of parting,' Bronio wrote to Paul, 'I felt most awfully sentimental, in fact Leila and myself, of the whole party, had to use a surreptitious handkerchief. Then I felt as if the main cable holding us – Elsie and me – to Australia had snapped & I became keen on leaving this country as soon as possible.'[18]

They stayed at 'Chanonry' during December, doubtless relieved that the Massons were away on vacation. Malinowski had one more important task to complete. Soon after his return to Melbourne in October 1918, he had written to Baldwin Spencer promising to select and catalogue the collection of Trobriand artifacts commissioned by Spencer in 1915. He proposed to donate them to the National Museum of Victoria in Seligman's name. He also proposed to return the £30 he had been granted by the museum trustees, as 'it will be simpler if a free gift is made to the Museum of the specimens, as well as of my personal work in collecting, arranging and cataloguing them'.[19] Unaware that an obscure point of honour was at stake, Spencer replied that it would be best if he kept the money 'as a slight recognition of the great value of your work done for the Museum'.[20] However, 'for personal reasons' that he did not spell out, Malinowski insisted that he was unable to keep the money. Recalling the vengeful fantasy in his diary ('I'll present the collection and reproach him with the promise he did not keep'), it would appear that he wanted to 'shame' Spencer.[21] Returning the grant was perhaps a way of paying him back for his damning judgment of Malinowski's character. It was a devious moral retaliation that would have been readily understood by a Trobriander, though it was probably lost on Spencer, who simply pointed out that there would be technical difficulties in returning it. A happy compromise was reached when Malinowski persuaded Spencer to remit the £30 to Mr W. Hancock, 'trader & pearler in the Trobriand Is.', who 'gave a considerable amount of his time & took great trouble in assisting me to collect, pack & transport the specimens'.[22] Honour was satisfied, and Billy was the beneficiary.

The twenty-seven cases of 'curios' that had been packed for Malinowski by an obliging Billy were not shipped from Samarai until May 1919, and it was the last week of November by the time Malinowski began to catalogue the 282 items that he had selected for the museum. Seligman had earlier written to say, with typical modesty, that he thought the collection should commemorate, not himself, but Malinowski's chief benefactor, Robert Mond.[23] The greater part of the collection would be shipped, at the National Museum's expense, to the British Museum in London.

With the help of James Kershaw, the curator of ethnology, Malinowski arranged the specimens in a large display case. He checked and redrafted the descriptive labels – on stone tools and women's leaf skirts, for instance – that Leila Peck had helped him to write in August 1917. These, together with a number of his best photographs, enhanced the value of the exhibition. He completed it the week before he left Australia, and it must have given him quiet satisfaction to write to Spencer: 'I have the honour to inform you that the Collection of Ethnological Specimens from the Trobriand Islands has been arranged and exhibited in accordance with the instructions received from you.'[24] In March Kershaw reported to the

museum trustees: 'By far the most important addition to the Ethnographical collection during the year is a valuable collection of native objects
obtained by Dr. Bronislaw Malinowski, during a long visit to the Trobriand
Islands.'[25] It was the first and last museum display Malinowski curated.

Malinowski and Elsie returned to Whitfield for three weeks on 10 January.
The days were fiercely hot, and they lounged in the shade of the willow
trees outside the Mountain View Hotel. 'Here we are in Whitfield,' wrote
Elsie to the Khuners, 'or rather, in the remains of Whitfield . . . it is simply
haunted by your ghosts, and is nothing but an empty background now.
Everything we do is just a mere echo of what it used to be.'[26] Malinowski
wrote to Paul while sitting in the little parlour of the hotel. He was missing
his friend dreadfully: 'Mrs Tyrell's courtyard simply screamed for Paul. Paul
sailing along with a tray, running for lemons or surreptitiously carrying a
claret bottle – Paul as Bacchus or in any of his gift-bringing capacities. The
verandah without Hede's voice or the baby's screams seemed empty and
inhospitable.' The political climate in Australia had become inhospitable,
too, as conservatives gained the ascendancy.

> As to our political ideas, it happened as could be foreseen: since Paul
> went away & there is no Principium Contradictionis in being moder-
> ately pro-Ally, we have developed into vehement Bolsheviks & Hinden-
> burgians & our feelings are so venomous that Paul's would seem meek
> & compromising. . . . It is really dreadful & I am quite a Communard
> International.[27]

Mim Weigall joined them for a few days, followed by Bob Broinowski
and his new lady friend, Jenny McCowan. They hired horses and set out
across the countryside. Malinowski followed on a white steed next day
in order to chaperone Bob and Jenny to Mt Buffalo. Mim returned to
Whitfield to keep Elsie company. Being pregnant, the latter was unable to
ride with the others.

It was unseasonably cold and blustery. Elsie wrote to Malinowski late that
night, with 'the old, bereft feeling'. It was their first separation since he had
attended Paul the previous July. 'It will be very lonely in the big bed outside,
& I'll think of Bronius battling with fleas & cursing, & wishing he were
with his Elsie.' After riding all day through the bush, the party slept at a
farmhouse; Bob Broinowski slept on the floor, leaving Malinowski a luxurious double bed. Next day they climbed, gently at first but then up 'incredibly steep, rocky & overgrown slopes'. At one point they lost the track and

Malinowski 'felt like sitting down and weeping', but Broinowski the resourceful bushman found it again. After walking their horses for six hours they gained the broad summit ridge of the mountain, and after another two hours reached the cliff-top Chalet. 'It was a revelation to see the gorge,' Malinowski enthused, imagining how Elsie, a year ago, had stood above the same precipice while on her vigil. Next day they cantered to the mountain lake and beyond it to the 'horn'. The scramble to the craggy summit was a fitting farewell to this strange continent. Atop the peak, the two Poles surely gave thought to their heroic eighteenth- and nineteenth-century compatriots, the soldier Kosciuszko and the explorer Strzelecki, whose noble names are linked to Australia's highest mountain.[28]

Adieu to Australia

The Malinowskis returned to Melbourne at the beginning of February and spent their last three weeks at 'Chanonry', empty at first of all but the maids. Their preparations for departure preoccupied them, and there were bureaucratic obstacles to the end. To disembark in England they needed a permit which had to be issued by the Australian prime minister's office. The paperwork was delayed because Billy Hughes was on holiday. A bemused Elsie exclaimed: 'what bad business management that such details have to wait for the Prime Minister himself!'[29]

On 25 February they sailed on the *Borda*, a war-weary vessel of some 11,000 tons that had served as a troopship. It was third class only, Malinowski had told Paul, 'but we have a deck cabin, so it will not be so bad'. They boarded the ship at night, 'a grievous parting', recalled Marnie, who was there to say farewell to them, together with her parents, Mim and the remaining members of the Clan. Marnie went down to the wharf again early next morning and glimpsed Elsie at the top of the gangway: 'I'll never forget her face when she saw me. . . . Bronio was not visible when I got there, and I don't remember seeing him when the ship drew away from the wharf, but he could have been with her – surely he was? But not in my mind now.'[30] Marnie never saw her sister again.

The voyage was far from idyllic, Elsie told the Khuners. The *Borda* was overcrowded, 'walking almost an impossibility, & the sixty children filling the air with one continuous hoot'. They sailed via South Africa and the couple enjoyed seeing something of Durban ('went right into the country

& walked about among dinkum kaffir kraals'). After Cape Town there were no further port calls, but on their passage through the Canary Islands they sailed tantalizingly close to Tenerife.

> We could see the peak floating far above a wisp of cloud, striped with snow, & then the green, treeless slopes going down to the shore, sprinkled with villages of white houses, & odd tramp steamers & sailing boats beating about on the blue sea. We passed close enough to Santa Cruz to see the cathedral & bull fight ring, & we longed to be able to get ashore.

Of their fellow passengers, Elsie best remembered a boorish Dr Borghetti whose table manners disgusted them. He treated his children abominably, and 'carried frankness to such a point that even Bronio winced and squirmed and implored him if he must describe his ailments or pass scandalous comments on the passengers to do so in Italian!'[31] Malinowski was weighing the prospects of his own fatherhood. Neither he nor Elsie could quite imagine themselves as parents.

> But I think I'll love the little brat when it arrives. So will Bronio, with moments of severe exasperation. It was funny to see him noticing with great intentness the children on board ship. I saw a devoted father rocking a child to sleep in its pram for over an hour, & Bronio kept looking at him with a more & more woe-begone expression, & finally turned to me & said in the meekest, but most miserable tone – 'is all that necessary?' I had to promise him that his child would not be rocked at all by anyone.[32]

Elsie thought she had deteriorated mentally on the voyage. 'I read such things as the *Conquest of Mexico* & a short modern history of England, but even those languidly. Perhaps my brains will revive in Oxfordshire.' The Seligmans had thoughtfully invited the couple to stay with them at Thame, near Oxford. Sligs had advised Malinowski to write to William Beveridge, the new director of the London School of Economics, to remind him of his existence as a research scholar of the School, and to tell him 'that you have a mass of material to work up, and [ask] whether you can have a room for some months in the Autumn'. He should also drop a friendly line to Miss MacTaggart, the School secretary. 'No doubt the matter will be referred to me,' added Seligman, 'and of course I will blow your trumpet.'[33]

Returning to an uncertain future in England after six years at the other end of the world, Malinowski was comforted by such assurances. A new chapter of his life was about to begin. He would soon become a family man, concerned with providing for his wife and child. He was confident that he could build upon the promising reputation he had gained in Britain with his most recent publications. These he had listed in a letter to Atlee Hunt, written the day before he sailed. It proved to be the last document placed in Malinowski's thick government file, a file that tells the story of his volatile relationship with Australian officialdom. Yet with this final report to the man who, more than anyone in that country, had helped Malinowski bring his fieldwork projects to fruition, there is a satisfactory, almost triumphant closure. Despite his years of living under the opprobrium of his status as an enemy alien, despite too the scurrilous rumours that had circulated about him, he had prevailed. Hunt's dogged, if sometimes ambivalent, support had been vindicated.

Malinowski tendered his thanks, and listed his seven Australian writings. In addition to *The Natives of Mailu* and '*Baloma*', there were two articles in *Man* and three as yet unpublished articles, two of them for encyclopaedias and one on classificatory particles. He mentioned the award of the DSc and the honorary title of 'Local Correspondent of the R.A.I. for Papua' which had been bestowed upon him in December 1919. He referred also to the ethnographic specimens and photographs he had presented to the National Museum as 'The Robert Mond Collection'. He concluded: 'Within the next two years, after I have finished writing up my materials, I expect to have it published as one treatise.'[34]

It was probably during the two-month voyage to Europe that Malinowski decided to abandon the treatise called 'Kiriwina' and extract from its voluminous bulk a more essential monograph, one that could be completed within a year. He left no clue as to why he chose to focus on the ceremonial trading system of Kula, but it is tempting to imagine that the ocean voyage itself, with its romantic Conradian associations, encouraged him to think about those brave seafarers of the Massim he would fancifully describe as Argonauts of the Western Pacific. There was a kind of closure, too, in sailing through the Canary Islands, where sad memories of his mother would have been awakened. In his luggage were gifts from Billy Hancock – a handful of pearls and a priceless Kula trophy, the only *soulava* shell necklace he possessed. But more precious by far were the ethnographic riches contained in his notebooks. Jason was returning with his fleece, Tokosikuna with his magic flute.

Abbreviations

AHPNLA	Atlee Hunt Papers, National Library of Australia
AT	*Anthropology Today*
BAAS	British Association for the Advancement of Science
HOA	*History of Anthropology*
HPCUL	Haddon Papers, University Library, Cambridge
JASO	*Journal of the Anthropological Society of Oxford*
JPH	*Journal of Pacific History*
JRAI	*Journal of the Royal Anthropological Institute*
MERNAA	'Dr B. Malinowski, Ethnological Research, Papua', 1914–20, A1 21/866, National Archives of Australia
MFNAA	Malinowski File, Intelligence Section, General Staff, 3rd Military District (Victoria), 15/3/406, National Archives of Australia
MPLSE	Malinowski Papers, British Library of Political and Economic Science, London School of Economics
MPUMA	Masson Papers, University of Melbourne Archives
MPY	Malinowski Papers, Yale University Library, New Haven
NAA	National Archives of Australia, Canberra
NLA	National Library of Australia, Canberra
NMA	National Museum of Australia, Melbourne
PR	*Polish Review*
SPLSE	Seligman Papers, British Library of Political and Economic Science, London School of Economics
WAAA	Westermarck Archive, Åbo Akademi, Turku, Finland

Notes

Introduction

1. A. Kuper, *Anthropologists and Anthropology: The Modern British School*, London: Routledge, 1973, p. 23.
2. B. Malinowski, *Argonauts of the Western Pacific: An Account of Native Enterprise and Adventure in the Archipelagoes of Melanesian New Guinea*, London: Routledge, 1922, p. 25.
3. *Islands* 16 (5), 1996. (See also Tony Wheeler and Jon Murray, *Lonely Planet Guide. Papua New Guinea: A Travel Survival Kit*. 5th edition, Lonely Planet, 1993.)
4. *Oceania* 40 (4), 1970, p. 347.
5. C. Geertz, 'Under the Mosquito Net', *New York Review of Books*, 14 Sept. 1967.
6. See Bibliography under Cech, Clifford, Ellen, Firth, Flis, Forge, Geertz, Gellner, Gross, Jerschina, Kardiner and Preble, Koepping, Kubica, Métraux, Murdock, Paluch, Panoff, Payne, Audrey Richards, Skalník, Stocking, Symmons-Symonolewicz, Thornton, Urry, Wax, Wayne, and Young.
7. Frazer, 'Preface' in *Argonauts*, 1922, p. ix.
8. Bronisław Malinowski, *Dziennik w ścisłym znaczeniu tego wyrazu* [A Diary in the Strict Sense of the Term], ed. Grażyna Kubica, Kraków: Wydawnictwo Literackie, 2002.
9. M. Mead, *An Anthropologist at Work: Writings of Ruth Benedict*, London: Secker & Warburg, 1959, p. 305. A. Montagu, review of H. Wayne (ed.), *Story of a Marriage*, in *Nature* 374, April 1995. R. H. Lowie, *The History of Ethnological Theory*, New York: Farrar & Rinehart, 1937, p. 242.
10. H. Wayne, 'Foreword', in R. Ellen et al (eds), *Malinowski between Two Worlds: The Polish Roots of an Anthropological Tradition*, Cambridge: Cambridge University Press, 1988, pp. xi–xii.

Chapter 1

1. Dedication to Sir James Frazer, 'Myth in Primitive Psychology', in B. Malinowski, *Magic, Science and Religion*, ed. R. Redfield, New York: Doubleday, 1954, pp. 93–4. Although he says here that he read *The Golden Bough* himself, in a letter to Frazer dated 25 May 1923, Malinowski credits his mother with having read it aloud to him.
2. South Africa Union Education Department, State Archives, Pretoria. Ref: UOD 1086 (E46/58/16).

3. Helena Wayne, 'Bronislaw Malinowski: The Influence of Various Women on his Life and Works', *JASO* 15 (3), 1984, p. 193.

4. B. Malinowski, *Sex and Repression in Savage Society*, London: Routledge, 1927, pp. 16–17.

5. Hilda Kuper, *Sobhuza II: Ngwenyama and King of Swaziland*, London: Duckworth, 1978, p. 5.

6. Józef Szymański (ed.), *Herbarz sredniowiecznego rycerstwa polskiego*, Warsaw: Wydawnictwo Naukowe PWN, 1992, pp. 222–3.

7. The phrase is from a poem by Vladimir Nabokov.

8. A. Zajączkowski to Helena Burke (later, Helena Wayne), 30 July 1972.

9. Ibid.

10. Norman Davies, *Heart of Europe: A Short History of Poland*, Oxford: Oxford University Press, 1986, p. 332.

11. Wayne, 'Bronislaw Malinowski', p. 193.

12. B. Malinowski, *Freedom and Civilization*, London: Allen & Unwin, 1947, p. 336.

13. A. Zajączkowski to H. Burke, 14 June 1972.

14. Ibid.

15. Malinowski to Elsie Masson, 5 Feb. 1918, in Helena Wayne (ed.), *The Story of a Marriage*, 2 vols, London: Routledge, 1995, vol. 1, p. 109.

16. Malinowski to Elsie Masson, 6 Sept. 1918, MPLSE; see Wayne, *Story*, pp. 172–3. Stefan Jabłoński to Malinowski, correspondence of 1927–28, MPY I/301.

17. The main source for the following biographical sketch is Hieronim Łopaciński, 'Lucjan Malinowski (1839–1898)', *Kurjer Niedzielny*, Warsaw, 1898. Translation by Marc Heine. See also Maria Zagórska-Brooks, 'Lucjan Malinowski and Polish Dialectology', *PR* 30 (2), 1985, pp. 167–70.

18. Łopaciński, 'Lucjan Malinowski'.

19. Davies, *Heart of Europe*, p. 262.

20. Ibid.

21. Among them Bolesław Prus, Henryk Sienkiewicz, Aleksander Świętochowski, Juljan Ochorowicz, Jan Baudouin de Courtenay (a linguist colleague of Lucjan Malinowski), Piotr Chmielowski, Bronisław Chlebowski, Adolf Dygasiński and Wiktor Gomulicki (see ibid., p. 263).

22. 'Lucjan Malinowski', in *Słownik folkloru polskiego* (Dictionary of Polish Folklore), Warsaw, 1965, p. 217.

23. Łopaciński, 'Lucjan Malinowski', p. 15.

24. Although there is some dispute among Conrad's biographers whether it was St Anne's (whose records show no trace of him) or St Jacek's (the other gymnasium in Cracow at the time, whose records were destroyed during the last war), Fredrick Karl argues convincingly in support of Conrad's own claim to have attended St Anne's in 1870–72 (see *Joseph Conrad: The Three Lives*, London: Faber & Faber, 1979, p. 90).

25. Łopaciński, 'Lucjan Malinowski', p. 17. See also Ewa Borowska, 'Lata polskiej młodości Bronisława Malinowskiego', MA thesis, Jagiellonian University, Cracow, 1971, p. 3.

26. Łopaciński, 'Lucjan Malinowski', p. 18.

27. Document dated 30 June 1875, reproduced in Borowska 'Lata polskiej'.

28. L. Malinowski to J. Goll, 27 Oct. 1887, Stanisław Sochacka *Listy Lucjana Malinowskiego do Jarosława Golla*, Opolu: Wydawnictwo Instytutu Śląskiego, 1975. I am grateful to Grażyna Kubica for bringing these letters to my attention and for translating the excerpts cited in this and the following chapters.

29. Lucjan's other pupils of note were Jan Hanusz, Roman Zawiliński, Józef Kallenbach, Szymon Matusiak, Jan Biela and Bolesław Szoma among the older generation, and R. Koppens, Jan Rozwadowski, Zygmunt Paulisch, Stanisław Dobrzycki and Stanisław Zathey among the juniors.

30. Grażyna Kubica, 'Malinowski's Years in Poland', in R. Ellen et al, (eds), *Malinowski between Two Worlds*, p. 88. (This is a slightly modified version of Kubica's earlier article in *JASO* 17 (2), 1986.)

31. B. Malinowski, review of *Kwartalnik Etnograficzny*, *Lud* 16, 1910, in *Folk-lore* 22, Sept. 1911, pp. 382–5.

32. MPLSE Culture 1/139.

33. Ibid. The document is variously titled 'What Is Culture?' 'The A.B.C. of Culture: A Text-Book of Comparative Anthropology and Sociology' and 'An Introduction to the Study of Social Sciences from the Anthropological Point of View'.

34. In 1880, according to a gazetteer, Ponice's population of 843 dwelt in 136 houses. There was one Jew; the rest were recorded as Roman Catholics.

35. Almost certainly Conrad's *A Personal Record*, 1912.

36. In *Sex and Repression in Savage Society*, Malinowski contrasted the child-rearing practices of Eastern European peasants with those of the educated classes, and both with those of the Trobriand Islanders: 'My personal knowledge of the life, customs and psychology of Eastern European peasants has allowed me to ascertain deep differences between the illiterate and the educated classes of the same society as regards the mental attitude of parents to children and vice versa' (p. 14n).

37. Reproduced in Ellen et al, *Malinowski between Two Worlds*, p. 70.

38. B. Malinowski, *A Diary in the Strict Sense of the Term*, London: Routledge, 1967, p. 298.

39. Malinowski to Elsie Masson, 11 June 1918, MPLSE. Wayne, *Story*, p. 153. (Unless indicated otherwise all references are to vol. 1 of *Story*.)

40. Wayne, 'Bronislaw Malinowski' p. 190.

41. *Sex and Repression*, p. 28.

42. Ibid. I agree with John Wengle's observation that 'Malinowski's characterization of the "typical" Western father . . . is so extreme, harsh, and contrary to reality that it cries out to be read as (auto)psychobiography'. John Wengle, *Ethnographers in the Field: The Psychology of Research*, Tuscaloosa: University of Alabama Press, 1988 p. 179.

43. B. Malinowski, 'Parenthood – The Basis of Social Structure' (1930), in *Sex, Culture, and Myth*, London: Rupert Hart-Davies, 1963, p. 42.

44. *Sex and Repression*, p. 27n. While Malinowski allowed that there was a 'biological' component in the affection and tenderness that an 'average man' feels towards his children, he believed that the social (or cultural) configuration of the family was decisive in whether this was given expression. He was inclined to argue that the 'paternal instinct' of affection was more freely expressed in a society like that of the Trobriands where there were no legal impediments to its expression: that is, where the father was not succeeded by the son and the son did not expect to inherit from him. The Trobriand father lacked legal authority over his offspring, a fact that meant that his love for them was unencumbered by material considerations. On the other hand, he had to earn the affection of his children; it was not his right or prerogative. Conversely, in the patriarchal regimes of the West the father's 'natural affections' are hampered by the consideration that 'the children should be there for his benefit, pleasure and glory', and Father-Right 'tilts the balance against a happy equilibrium of natural affection and natural impatience of the nuisance' (ibid., pp. 31–2). The

assumption that all fathers, of whatever culture, find their children 'a nuisance' is surely a revealing one.

45. Ibid., pp. 37–8.
46. Ibid., p. 38.
47. Malinowski to Elsie Masson, 12 Jan. 1929. in Wayne, *Story*, vol. 2, p. 129.
48. *Sex and Repression*, p. 38.
49. On the other hand, too much might be made of the Oedipal battles Malinowski is supposed to have fought with Frazer; see Ernest Gellner, ' "Zeno of Cracow" or "Revolution at Nemi" or "The Polish Revenge: A Drama in Three Acts" ', in Ellen et al, *Malinowski between Two Worlds*. For a critique see Michael W. Young, 'Young Malinowski: A Review Article', *Canberra Anthropology* 17 (2), 1994, pp. 103–22.
50. MPY II/218.
51. Cited by G. Kubica, 'Bronislaw Malinowski's Years in Poland', *JASO* 17 (2), 1986. p. 141.

Chapter 2

1. L. Malinowski to J. Goll, 11 Oct. 1882, in Sochacka, *Listy*, p. 60.
2. 14 Nov. 1881, ibid., p. 44.
3. 4 June 1883, ibid., p. 64.
4. 17 Dec. 1884, ibid., p. 71.
5. Adam Dubowski, 'Z tradycji rodzinnej' (From a Family Tradition), *Tygodnik Powszechny*, 8 April 1984. Translated by Annamaria Orla-Bukowska.
6. Davies, *Heart of Europe*, p. 333.
7. Wayne, 'Bronislaw Malinowski', p. 190.
8. Ibid., p. 191.
9. Ibid., p. 193. Malinowski to Frazer, 25 May 1923: 'You know how my first love of Anthropology is associated with *The Golden Bough*, read to me aloud by my mother.' Frazer Papers, Trinity College, Cambridge. MS b.36:185.
10. S. I. Witkiewicz, *The 622 Downfalls of Bungo*, excerpted in Daniel Gerould (ed.), *The Witkiewicz Reader*, Evanston, Ill.: Northwestern University Press, 1992, p. 53.
11. Wayne, 'Bronislaw Malinowski', p. 190.
12. L. Malinowski to J. Goll, 17 May 1884, in Sochacka, *Listy*, p. 69.
13. 29 April 1885, ibid., p. 75. Lucjan is quoting Mephistopheles in Goethe's *Faust*.
14. 16 Nov. 1885, ibid., p. 77.
15. 22 Feb. 1886, ibid., p. 79.
16. 17 Oct. 1886; 27 Oct. 1887; ibid., pp. 84, 95–6.
17. 14 May 1888, ibid., p. 100.
18. 14 Nov. 1888, ibid., p. 105.
19. 2 July 1889, ibid., p. 112.
20. 19 Oct. 1889, ibid., p. 113.
21. 1 Nov. 1890, ibid., p. 117.
22. 7 Aug. 1891; 5 March 1892; ibid., pp. 128, 135.
23. 25 July 1892, ibid., p. 141.
24. 13 Feb. 1893, ibid., pp. 148–9.
25. 10 Feb. 1894, ibid., pp. 158–9.
26. 13 Oct. 1895, ibid., p. 167.
27. 17 Oct. 1895, ibid., p. 171.

28. 10 Aug. 1897, ibid., p. 186.

29. 11 Oct. 1897, ibid., p. 187.

30. Malinowski to Elsie Masson, 24 Dec. 17, in Wayne, *Story*, p. 76.

31. 5 Feb. 1918, ibid., p. 109.

32. Józefa Malinowska to Bronislaw Malinowski, 20 Aug. 1915, MPY I/406.

33. Janina Marchwicka to Helena Michaniewska, Dec. 1970, MPLSE.

34. Witold Truszkowski, unpublished lecture delivered in Cracow in 1984. Translation by G. Kubica. Zofia Krzyżanowska was Truszkowski's mother-in-law.

35. J. Malinowski to J. Goll, 11 Jan. 1899, in Sochacka, *Listy*, pp. 194–5.

36. Truszkowski, unpublished lecture. Cited by Kubica, 'Malinowski's Years', in Ellen et al, *Malinowski between Two Worlds*, p. 89.

37. B. Średniawa, 'The Anthropologist as a Young Physicist: Bronislaw Malinowski's Apprenticeship', *Isis* 72, 1981, p. 614.

38. Andrzej Paluch, 'Introduction: Bronislaw Malinowski and Cracow Anthropology', in Ellen et al, *Malinowski between Two Worlds*, p. 5.

39. Robert J. Thornton and Peter Skalník (eds), *The Early Writings of Bronisław Malinowski*, Cambridge University Press, 1993, p. 258. He praised Dargun for his 'highly modern approach' and as a 'guide for the future direction of scientific sociology in the proper sense of the word'.

40. Paluch, 'Introduction', p. 5.

41. Ibid., p. 6.

42. Ibid., p. 28.

43. Foreword to the Polish edition of *The Sexual Life of Savages*. (This foreword was written in 1937 but published only in 1980.) Cited by Kubica, 'Malinowski's Years', p. 94.

44. From an application Malinowski made in 1907 to Emperor Franz Jozef; Andrzej Flis, 'Bronislaw Malinowski's Cracow Doctorate', in Ellen et al, *Malinowski between Two Worlds*, Appendix 1.

45. L. Malinowski to J. Goll, 27 Jan. 1892, in Sochacka, *Listy*. p. 119.

46. Borowska, 'Lata polskiej', and repeated by Wayne, 'Bronislaw Malinowski', p. 190.

47. F. Gross, 'Young Malinowski and his Later Years', *American Ethnologist* 13 (3), 1986, p. 556.

48. Malinowski to Emperor Franz Joseph, 1907. Flis, 'Bronislaw Malinowski's Cracow Doctorate', p. 196.

49. Gross, 'Young Malinowski', p. 557.

50. Flis, 'Bronislaw Malinowski's Cracow Doctorate', p. 196.

51. On the calculation that each semester of sixteen weeks totalled about five hundred hours of classes, there would have been some six thousand class hours for the six years that Malinowski attended school. His absences (all of them 'justified' as the record declares) totalled 836 hours, or 14 percent of the optimum. If the number of class hours is increased beyond these rather conservative figures (as one might well expect of a 'demanding and difficult' curriculum), then the percentage of time Malinowski was absent from school decreases proportionately. Of course, if we add the two years for which he was not even enrolled, his total rate of absence from school amounts to more than one-third of the optimum.

52. L. Malinowski to J. Goll, 6 Aug. 1897, in Sochacka, *Listy*, p. 185.

53. J. Malinowska to J. Goll, 11 Jan. 1899, ibid., pp. 194–5.

54. 10 Feb. 1900, ibid.

55. *Diary*, p. 297.

56. W. L. Benedict to Franklin H. Maury, 23 Dec. 1938, MPLSE.

57. Malinowski to Secretary, New Lodge Clinic, 20 Apr. 1932. MPLSE.

58. Freud would have been delighted by this uncanny conjunction of events. Oedipus blinded himself in atonement following his discovery that he had slain his father and married his mother. But to follow Freud here would be to assume that Malinowski's temporary blindness was in some sense self-inflicted. Malinowski was handicapped by weak eyesight all his life, and in his fifties was diagnosed with choroiditis: inflamation of the network of small blood vessels between the retina and the sclera. This may cause blurred vision, but is usually painless. Complications such as detached retina and glaucoma are more serious effects, and Malinowski did in fact suffer a detached retina in 1940.

59. J. Malinowska to J. Goll, 10 May 1901, in Sochacka, *Listy*, p. 196.

60. 7 July 1901, ibid. pp. 197–8.

61. Kubica, 'Malinowski's Years', p. 90, citing Truszkowski.

62. Dubowski, 'Z tradycji rodzinnej'. See also Kubica, 'Malinowski's Years', p. 90.

63. Wayne, 'Bronislaw Malinowski', p. 190.

64. J. Malinowska to J. Goll, 14 Feb. 1903, in Sochacka, *Listy*, pp. 198–9.

65. Elsie Masson to Malinowski, 17 Aug. 1918, in Wayne, *Story*, vol. I, p. 163.

66. Paul Khuner to Malinowski, 17 Aug. 1918, MPY I/325.

67. *Sex and Repression*, p. 17.

68. Ibid., pp. 60–1.

69. Malinowski to Elsie Masson, 2 July 1918, in Wayne, *Story*, p. 159.

70. Wengle, *Ethnographers in the Field*, p. 109.

71. *Diary*, p. 253.

72. Ibid., p. 297.

73. Ibid., p. 296.

74. Ibid., p. 293.

75. Ibid., p. 291.

76. Malinowski to Elsie Masson, 11 June 1918, in Wayne, *Story*, pp. 153–5.

Chapter 3

1. Joseph Conrad to John Galsworthy, 25 July 1914, in Joseph Conrad, *Collected Letters of Joseph Conrad*, vol. 5, 1912–16, eds F. Karl and L. Davies, Cambridge: Cambridge University Press, 1996, p. 407.

2. One thinks, for example, of Marx, Shaw, Wittgenstein and Eliot in England, of Joyce, Lawrence and Pound in Italy. Among Malinowski's colleagues and pupils at the LSE were dozens of such exiles.

3. Joseph Conrad, *A Personal Record*, London: J. M. Dent, 1946, p. 122. Malinowski also substituted 'British' in his own quotation of this remark, thereby confusing it with Conrad's statement on an earlier page: 'if I was to be a seaman then I would be a British seaman and no other.' Ibid., p. 119.

4. 'Rivers is the Rider Haggard of anthropology; I shall be the Conrad' was reported by Raymond Firth on the hearsay of Brenda Seligman (R. Firth, 'Introduction: Malinowski as Scientist and Man', in R. Firth, *Man and Culture*, London: Routledge & Kegan Paul, 1957, p. 6). It is a statement that has been seized upon frequently by commentators with postmodern points to make about ethnographic writing strategies.

5.   MPLSE Language 3/289. The single-page carbon copy is headed 'Biography of Dr B.M'.

6.   Gross, 'Young Malinowski', pp. 557–8.

7.   Ibid., p. 558.

8.   Conrad, *A Personal Record*, p. 13.

9.   Wayne, 'Bronislaw Malinowski', pp. 190–1.

10.   Kubica and Wayne give 1899 as the year of the first trip to Biskra, but in a letter to Goll of 10 Feb. 1900 Józefa Malinowska specifically states: 'Last year was very peaceful for us and we did not undertake anything new.' She writes that they spent the summer in Zakopane and spent Christmas and Easter in Warsaw. Stanisław Witkiewicz confirms that Bronio spent the summer of 1900 with Staś in Zakopane. (S. Witkiewicz to his son, 13 July 1900, in S. Witkiewicz, *Listy do syna*, (eds. Bozena Danek-Wojnowska and Anna Micińska) Warszawa: Państwowy Instytut Wydawniczy, 1969.) Thornton and Skalník (*The Early Writings*, p. 10) imply that Malinowski went to Algeria in 1901 following his 'eye operation'. Józefa tells Goll only that they went to Trenczyn. It is clear from Malinowski's letter to Aniela Zagórska (see below) that his first visit to the Mediterranean was in autumn 1901.

11.   MPLSE Culture 1/139.

12.   Malinowski to his daughter Józefa, 17 Nov. 1937, MPLSE.

13.   Gross, 'Young Malinowski', p. 557.

14.   B. Malinowski to J. Malinowska, 20 June 1914, MPY I/408.

15.   2 July 1914, ibid.

16.   Draft introduction to textbook, MPLSE Culture 1/139.

17.   B. Malinowski, 'Myth as a Dramatic Development of Dogma', in *Sex, Culture and Myth*, 1963, p. 248.

18.   L. Malinowski to J. Goll, 19 Oct. 1891, in Sochacka, *Listy*. p. 130.

19.   See Malinowski's BBC talk 'Science and Religion', delivered in 1930; published in *Sex, Culture and Myth*, pp. 256–65.

20.   J. Malinowska to J. Goll, 11 Jan. 1899, in Sochacka, *Listy*. pp. 194–5.

21.   Seligman to Malinowski, 30 Dec. 1915, MPY I/565.

22.   Karl, *Joseph Conrad*, p. 91.

23.   He understood spoken Russian but did not speak it with any fluency.

24.   Firth, 'Bronislaw Malinowski', in S. Silverman (ed.), *Totems and Teachers: Perspectives on the History of Anthropology*, New York: Columbia University Press, 1981, p. 109.

25.   MPLSE Linguistics 3/294.

26.   Introductory notes to 'What Is Culture?', MPLSE Culture 1/139.

27.   Henri Peyre of Yale told Helena Wayne that her father cursed in French with greater fluency than any native speaker he had ever heard.

28.   Unpublished lecture given to the Psychological Society of the University of London, 24 Nov. 1935. MPLSE Linguistics 3/293.

29.   The letter-essay of about twenty handwritten pages was found among those of Malinowski's papers taken to Mexico by his widow. It is not a conventional letter for it lacks a salutation (and, being unfinished, a farewell), but it is stated clearly at the top of the first sheet: 'Written for Miss Aniela Zagórska in Zakopane' and dated London, 25 Feb. 1913. Although it addresses her directly in the text, it does so without any reference to her own life or to their personal relationship in Zakopane. Its essay character derives from its literary tone, its discursive psychological asides, ruminations on national character and other general observations. The translation from the Polish is by Marc Heine. The document has been published by Zbigniew Benedyktowicz in

Konteksty 54 (1–4), 2000, pp. 66–79, and by Grażyna Kubica in her definitive edition of Malinowski's diaries. B. Malinowski, *Dziennik w ściłym znaczeniu tego wyrazu*, ed. Grażyna Kubica, Cracow: Wydawnictwo Literackie, 2000, pp. 128–41.

30. This approach to language, following the word 'magic' in the previous sentence, lies at the heart of Malinowski's scholarly analysis of the language of magic in the Trobriands (see *Argonauts*, and especially vol. 2 of *Coral Gardens and their Magic: The Language of Magic and Gardening*, London: Allen & Unwin, 1935).

31. J. Conrad, *The Mirror of the Sea* (1906), London: J. M. Dent, 1946, p. 154.

32. Ibid., p. 152.

33. Thomas Mann, *Death in Venice* (1912), Harmondsworth: Penguin Books, 1955, p. 24.

34. Wayne, 'Bronislaw Malinowski', p. 191.

Chapter 4

1. J. Malinowska to J. Goll, 14 Feb. 1903, in Sochacka, *Listy*. pp. 198–9.

2. Published in *Za i przeciw* 38, 17 Sept. 1967.

3. Plate 7 of Ellen et al, *Malinowski between Two Worlds*.

4. Peter Skalník, 'Bronislaw Kasper Malinowski and Stanisław Ignacy Witkiewicz', in H. F. Vermeulen and A. A. Roldán (eds), *Fieldwork and Footnotes: Studies in the History of European Anthropology*, London: Routledge, 1995, p. 140.

5. *Diary*, p. 29.

6. Malinowski to Gustaw A. Mokrzycki, 6 Jan. 1941, MPLSE.

7. Gerould, *Witkiewicz Reader*, p. 27.

8. Karol Estreicher, 'Zakopane – Leur Amour', *Polish Perspectives* 14 (6), Warsaw, June 1971, p. 36.

9. Anna Micińska, *Witkacy: Life and Work*, trans. Bogna Piotrowska, Warsaw: Interpress Publishers, 1990, p. 58.

10. S. I. Witkiewicz to his mother, Jan. 1889. Cited in ibid., p. 53.

11. Gerould, *Witkiewicz Reader*, pp. 28–9.

12. Ibid.

13. S. Witkiewicz, *Listy do syna*, 1969.

14. S. I. Witkiewicz to Aniela Jałowiecka, June 1903. Cited in Micińska, *Witkacy*, p. 74.

15. S. I. Witkiewicz to Maria Witkiewicz, June 1903. Cited in ibid.

16. S. Witkiewicz to his son, summer of 1903. Cited in ibid.

17. Gerould, *Witkiewicz Reader*, p. 31.

18. S. I. Witkiewicz to Malinowski, 10–15 Sept. 1903. (Unpublished letter, translated by D. Gerould.)

19. 31 July 1900, in Witkiewicz, *Listy do syna*, p. 39. (See K. Cech, 'Malinowski: Edgar, Duke of Nevermore', *JASO* 12 (3), 1981, p. 179.)

20. Cited by Gerould, *Witkiewicz Reader*, p. 8.

21. 17 June 1909. Cited by Kubica, 'Malinowski's Years', p. 91; also Cech, 'Malinowski', p. 180. As given here, my quotation is an amalgam of both translations.

22. Karol Estreicher, *Leon Chwistek – biografia artysty*, Kraków: Państwowe Wydawnictwo Naukowe, 1971, pp. 7–8. Cited by Borowska, 'Lata polskiej', p. 4; also Kubica, 'Malinowski's Years', p. 91.

23. Dated St Petersburg, Oct. 1914. Cited in Gerould, *Witkiewicz Reader*, p. 103.

24. *Diary*, p. 34. (2 Nov. 1914.)

25. Cited by Gerould, *Witkiewicz Reader*, p. 1.

26. S. Witkiewicz to his son, 1904. Cited by Estreicher, 'Zakopane', p. 44.

27. Estreicher, 'Zakopane', p. 34.
28. Translated by Basia Plebanek.
29. A. Flis, 'Cracow Philosophy of the Beginning of the Twentieth Century and the Rise of Malinowski's Scientific Ideas', in Ellen et al, *Malinowski between Two Worlds*, pp. 114, 127.
30. Wayne, 'Foreword', in Ibid., p. xvii.
31. Gross, 'Young Malinowski', p. 561.
32. Ibid., p. 568.
33. Kazimiera Żuławska's recollection is quoted by A. Waligórski in his appendix to the first Polish translation of *Argonauts*, 1967, p. 675. Cited by Kubica, 'Malinowski's Years', p. 92.
34. Estreicher, 'Zakopane', p. 44.
35. T. Miciński, *Nietota*, Warsaw, 1910, p. 243. I am grateful to Grażyna Kubica for this translation.
36. Plate 76, Sztaba Wojciech, *Stanisław Ignacy Witkiewicz*, Warszawa: Auriga, 1985.
37. Arthur Rubinstein, *My Young Years*, London: Jonathan Cape, 1973, p. 119.
38. Estreicher, 'Zakopane', p. 43.
39. Gross, 'Young Malinowski', p. 561.
40. Malinowski to Elsie Masson, 5 Feb. 1918, in Wayne, *Story*, p. 109.
41. Ibid.
42. Principal sources for this section on Young Poland are Jan Jerschina, 'Polish Culture of Modernism and Malinowski's Personality', in Ellen et al, *Malinowski between Two Worlds*, pp. 128–48; Manfred Kridl, *A Survey of Polish Literature and Culture*, Gravenhage: Mouton & Co., 1956; Harold B. Segel, '"Young Poland", Cracow and the "Little Green Balloon"', *PR* 5 (2), 1960, pp. 74–97.
43. Kridl, *Survey*, p. 408.
44. Ibid.
45. Ibid.
46. These appeared in 1902 and 1905 in the elite Warsaw journal *Chimera*.
47. Joachim T. Baer, 'Nietzsche and Polish Modernism', *PR* 38 (1), 1993, p. 72. See also Kridl, *Survey*, pp. 447–8.
48. Berent, as quoted by Baer, 'Nietzsche', p. 72.
49. Segel, '"Young Poland"', p. 79.
50. S. Wyspiański, *The Wedding*, trans. Gerard T. Kapolka, Ann Arbor: Ardis, 1990, p. 14.
51. Quoted by Estreicher, 'Zakopane', pp. 42–3.

Chapter 5

1. Stanisław Witkiewicz to his son, Sept. 1903. Cited in Micińska, *Witkacy*, p. 77.
2. Document cited in Borowska, 'Lata polskiej'. In 1905 Malinowski also received the Potocki Foundation stipend for Polish noblemen, worth 315 Austrian crowns a year.
3. Ibid., p. 7. These regulations were changed after Poland regained independence in 1918. Students were then required to pass annual examinations. The master's degree and other qualifications were also introduced.
4. A. Korzybski to Malinowski, 4 Dec. 1932, MPY I/334.
5. B. Russell, *Portraits from Memory and Other Essays*, London: Allen & Unwin, 1956, p. 20.
6. Ray Monk, *Bertrand Russell: The Spirit of Solitude*, London: Jonathan Cape, 1996, p. 26.

7. MPLSE Culture 1/139.
8. Średniawa, 'The Anthropologist as a Young Physicist', p. 614. This section owes much to Średniawa, who is professor of theoretical physics at the Jagiellonian University.
9. Ibid., p. 615.
10. W. Matlakowski, 'Wolni słuchacze w Krakowie', *Za i Przeciw* 38, 17 Sept. 1967.
11. Flis, 'Cracow Philosophy', p. 109.
12. Cited in ibid. For 'fop' Feliks Gross translates 'buffoon', 'Young Malinowski', p. 559.
13. Flis, 'Cracow Philosophy', p. 111.
14. G. Kubica, Appendix 2, in Ellen et al, *Malinowski between Two Worlds*, p. 202. Kubica dates this letter 1906, but it must refer to a philosophy seminar held the previous year. By 1 Nov. 1906 Malinowski and his mother had already left Cracow for the Canary Islands.
15. There is some confusion in the records as to whether Malinowski took several other courses in 1903–04. In her list of lectures for which Malinowski was registered during the first semester, Borowska, 'Lata polskiej', includes general botany, survey of cryptogamous plants, classification of plants, basic concepts of philosophy, animal evolution, twenty-five centuries of the development of philosophy, Polish lyrical poetry in the nineteenth century, Polish literature and microbiology. If the list is accurate, the heady mix of natural sciences and humanities (amounting to twenty-five hours of lectures a week) would suggest that Malinowski had become intoxicated with knowledge during the autumn of 1903. Unfortunately, there is no confirmation that he actually attended any of these courses, and other Polish authorities who have studied Malinowski's student record fail to mention them, as does the entry for 1903–04 in Malinowski's own *Index Lectionum* (MPY IV/32).
16. Flis, 'Cracow Philosophy', p. 109.
17. Ibid., p. 108.
18. Średniawa, 'The Anthropologist as a Young Physicist', p. 616.
19. Flis, 'Cracow Philosophy', pp. 108–9.
20. A. Paluch, 'Introduction: Bronislaw Malinowski and Cracow Anthropology', in Ellen et al, *Malinowski Between Two Worlds*, p. 4; Kubica, 'Malinowski's Years', p. 102; Borowska, 'Lata polskiej'. Malinowski's *Index Lectionum* in the Yale archive confirms Kubica but not Borowska on this matter.
21. Flis, 'Cracow Philosophy', pp. 105–27.
22. E. Mach, *The Analysis of Sensations and the Relation of the Physical to the Psychical* (1906), New York: Dover Publications, 1959, p. 12.
23. E. Mach, *Popular Scientific Lectures* (1895), trans. Thomas J. McCormack, La Salle, Ill.: Open Court, 1943, pp. 186, 196, 191, 197.
24. E. Mach, *Knowledge and Error: Sketches on the Psychology of Inquiry* (1905), trans. T. J. McCormack and P. Foulkes, Dordrecht: D. Reidel, 1976, p. 120.
25. Mach, *The Analysis of Sensations*, p. 25. Cited by John Blackmore, *Ernst Mach: His Life, Work and Influence*, Berkeley: University of California Press, 1972, pp. 123–4.
26. E. R. Leach, 'The Epistemological Background to Malinowski's Empiricism', in Firth (ed.), *Man and Culture*, pp. 121–2. Malinowski had apparently read James by 1914 (see Witkiewicz to Malinowski; Gerould, *Witkiewicz Reader*, p. 79).
27. Thornton and Skalník make this claim for an essay Malinowski devoted to Nietzsche's *The Birth of Tragedy*, which they believe to have been written in 1904 (*The Early Writings*, p. 16). They are mistaken, however, and proof that it was written in 1912 is to be found in Malinowski's diary of that year.

28.   The original thesis, housed in the Jagiellonian University Archives, is entitled 'O zasadzie ekonomii myślenia'. It was first published in 1980 in vol. 1 of the *Dzieła* (Works) of Bronislaw Malinowski. The translation I refer to is by Ludwik Krzyżanowski, published as chapter 2 in Thornton and Skalník, *The Early Writings*. For other commentaries on the thesis, see Andrzej Paluch, 'The Polish Background of Malinowski's Work', *Man* 16 (2), 1981, pp. 276–85; George W. Stocking, Jr, 'Anthropology and the Science of the Irrational: Malinowski's Encounter with Freudian Psychoanalysis', in *HOA*, vol. 4, Madison: University of Wisconsin Press, 1986, pp. 15–17; Flis, 'Cracow Philosophy', pp. 114–19; Thornton and Skalník, *'The Early Writings'*, pp. 26–38.

29.   Coincidentally, the Austrian novelist Robert Musil (1880–1942) also submitted a thesis to Berlin University on Mach's epistemology and was awarded a doctorate the same year as Malinowski.

30.   Mach, *Popular Scientific Lectures*, pp. 15–16.

31.   Ibid., p. 186.

32.   In Thornton and Skalník, *The Early Writings*, p. 113.

33.   Cited by Flis, 'Cracow Philosophy', p. 114.

34.   Paluch, 'The Polish Background', p. 279.

35.   B. Malinowski, 'Totemism and Exogamy (1911–13),' in Thornton and Skalník, *The Early Writings*, p. 127.

36.   Manuscript notes, MPY II/266.

37.   Manuscript notes, MPY II/239.

38.   A. Asermely, 'Directing Pure Form: "The Pragmatists"', *PR* 18 (2), 1973, pp. 136–7.

Chapter 6

1.   S. Witkiewicz to his son, Zakopane, June 1905. Cited by Micińska, *Witkacy*, p. 78.

2.   May 1906. Cited in ibid., p. 79.

3.   Malinowski to Pawlicki. Cracow, 1 Sept. 1906, cited in Ellen et al., *Malinowski between Two Worlds*, pp. 201–2. Translation by Grażyna Kubica. The works Malinowski refers to are probably Clodius Piat (ed.), *Les grands philosophes*, Paris, 1903; Eduard Zeller, *Die Philosophie der Griechen in ihrer geschichtlichen Entwicklung*, Tübingen, 1856–62; and F. Ueberweg, *Grundriss der Geschichte der Philosophie*, Berlin, 1876–80.

4.   Józefa Malinowska to Malinowski, 27 Aug. 1906, MPY I/405. Translation by Basia Plebanek.

5.   21 Sept. 1906, ibid.

6.   S. I. Witkiewicz to Malinowski, n.d., 1906, in Gerould, *Witkiewicz Reader*, pp. 50–1.

7.   S. I. Witkiewicz, *622 Upadki Bunga, czyli demoniczna kobieta* (Warsaw: Państwowy Instytut Wydawniczy) was published in a handsome edition in 1972, with an editorial introduction by Anna Micińska. Twenty-five thousand copies were printed, an indication of Witkacy's growing popularity in Poland at that time. There is still no English edition, though Daniel Gerould's *The Witkiewicz Reader* contains translations of several chapters. See also D. Gerould, 'Review Article: Witkacy's Portrait of the Artist as a Young Man', *PR* 18 (2), 1973, pp. 139–5.

8.   Robert B. Pynsent (ed.), *Decadence and Innovation: Austro-Hungarian Life and Art at the Turn of the Century*. London: Weidenfeld and Nicholson, 1989, pp. 178ff. Otto Weininger was a misogynistic homosexual Viennese Jew, whose book *Sex and Character* had a baleful influence on Ludwig Wittgenstein. Weininger committed suicide in 1903.

9. Allen Tate, 'Our Cousin, Mr Poe', in A. Tate, *The Man of Letters in the Modern World*, London: Meridian Books/Thames & Hudson, 1957.

10. Gerould, *Witkiewicz Reader*, pp. 55–6. Unless otherwise indicated, all quotations from *The 622 Downfalls of Bungo* are from this source.

11. Passage translated by Cech, 'Malinowski: Edgar, Duke of Nevermore', p. 180.

12. Estreicher, 'Zakopane', p. 36.

13. MPY I/146. There are about thirty-eight letters, written between late May and 20 September 1906. Averaging one every three days, the frequency of Zofia's letters is indicative of the emotional intensity of her correspondence. Many were diary-letters, written over a period of days then posted with a covering note. I am grateful to Matthew Ciolek for a preliminary reading, to Jadwiga and Daniel Gerould for summarizing it, and to Grażyna Kubica for further commentaries on this correspondence.

14. According to the *Catalogue of Picture Exhibition and Incomplete List of Zofia Dembowska Romer's Works* (M.K. Čiurlionis State Museum of Art, Kaunas National Museum, Warsaw, 1991), Zofia's debut was in Cracow in 1909, and years later, under the name of Zofia Romer (in 1911 she had married Eugeniusz Romer, a wealthy Lithuanian landowner), she exhibited in Vilnius, Lwów, Riga and Kowno. Deported to Siberia in 1941, Zofia survived by painting children's toys. On her release in 1943 and following the death of her husband, she lived for a time in Tehran, Cairo, London (where she was reunited with her children), Washington D.C. and ultimately Montreal. She died in 1972 at the ripe age of eighty-seven.

15. Daniel Gerould, personal communication, 9 July 1997.

16. S. I. Witkiewicz to Malinowski, in Gerould, *Witkiewicz Reader*, pp. 50–1. Although not precisely dated, this letter cannot have been written later than May 1906.

17. MPY I/146. Translation by Elizabeth Tabaka.

18. Estreicher, 'Zakopane', p. 34.

19. Gerould, 'Review Article', p. 151, citing Micińska's introduction to *The 622 Downfalls of Bungo*.

20. Ibid., p. 74. I have inserted the title of the Duke's fictional work, omitted by Gerould but present in other translations of this passage.

Chapter 7

1. Malinowski to Pawlicki, 4 Jan. 1907. Translation by G. Kubica. Cited in Ellen et al. *Malinowski between Two Worlds*, p. 203.

2. Malinowski to Elsie Masson, 24 Nov. 1917, in Wayne, *Story*, pp. 63–4.

3. F. Nietzsche, *The Will to Power*, Translation by W. Kaufmann. New York: Vintage Books, 1968 (1901), p. 689.

4. There are undated and partly illegible jottings on *Zarathustra* towards the end of the diary. The most coherent lines are:

   Zarathustra *observations.*
   I. The problem of creativity for oneself and for others. In N[ietzsche] one can see a need for comrades . . .
   II. Living in a new, unusual, undefined state of mind. A basis of artistic creativity.
   III. Image of a man going off to find himself. The camel: the need to assume burdens – my generalized asceticism. . . . The lion joined with him. . . . Thread

binds us – the life of the appetites, vanity . . . each of the little threads. . . . All together they render even a giant powerless.

5. The translation is by Marc Heine. The document itself is a pocket-sized black note-book. Published as 'Dziennik Kanaryjski', in Malinowski, *Dziennik*, pp. 37–69.

6. Compare André Gide's *Journal*, especially that of 1893 when Gide, then twenty-four, was the same age as Malinowski. For example: 'La Roque, 14 July. . . . I have lost the habit of lofty thought; this is a *most regrettable* thing. I live in a facile manner, and this must not go on. Everything in life must be intentional, and the will constantly taut like a muscle.' *Journals 1889–1949*, Harmondsworth: Penguin Books, 1967, p. 28.

7. Some of Malinowski's phrasing with respect to his objectives is reminiscent of the esoteric teachings of George Gurdjieff and his Russian disciple P. D. Ouspensky: for example, their injunctions to 'work' by practising 'self-remembering' and avoiding 'identification' in order to raise consciousness above that of the 'mechanical', 'sleep-walking' state of the average human being. As Gurdjieff did not come to Moscow until 1912 and his teachings were not propagated (in Europe at least) until the 1920s Malinowski could not have known of them in 1908.

8. George W. Stocking, Jr., *After Tylor: British Social Anthropology 1888–1951*, Madison: University of Wisconsin Press, 1995, p. 269.

9. He later claimed to have been introduced to his theories 'about 1902', but I believe this to be a misprint for 1912 (MPY II/153), in which year he was exposed to a heavy dose of Freudianism in Zakopane.

10. Malinowski to Elsie Masson, 24 Nov. 1917, in Wayne, *Story*, p. 64.

11. Malinowski's undated letter is reproduced in Flis, 'Bronislaw Malinowski's Cracow Doctorate', pp. 195–200.

12. Ibid. Additional details are from a copy of the official programme, of which there is a translation among Malinowski's papers. MPLSE.

13. To commemorate the centenary of Malinowski's birth, this photograph was published on the cover of *Anthropology Today* 1 (5), Oct. 1985.

14. Truszkowski, cited by Kubica, 'Malinowski's Years', p. 95.

Chapter 8

1. Grażyna Kubica, 'Bronislaw Malinowski's Years in Poland,' *JASO* 17 (2), 1986, p. 146. Her source is S. I. Witkiewicz, 'Listy do Heleny Czerwijowskiej', *Twórczość*, 9, 1971, p. 49.

2. Malinowski's Leipzig diary, 13 Dec. 1908. Translations are by Marc Heine.

3. Kubica, 'Malinowski's Years', in Ellen et al. *Malinowski between Two Worlds*, p. 96.

4. Museum für Völkerkunde to Helena Burke, 17 July 1973, MPLSE.

5. Brunton to Malinowski, 6 April 1916, MPLSE.

6. James Edward McCarthy, Annie's father, died in East London in 1874 at the age of forty-nine, leaving a wife and four young children. Their names – Christopher, Richard, Mary and Annie – appear on their father's death notice, so Annie cannot have been born later than 1874. Her birthday was 21 October, but in her correspondence with Malinowski she never once reveals her exact age.

7. *Diary*, p. 241: 'I thought of mother. . . . I also recall N who was always very kind to me and very loyal.'

8. Published in Malinowski, *Dziennik*, pp. 70–118. Although it spans a period of six months (13 Dec. 1908 to 20 May 1909) the first diary contains entries for only forty days. The longest consecutive sequence is from 12 March to 19 April 1909.

9. None of Annie's letters from this period has survived.
10. *Diary*, p. 297.
11. Ibid., p. 140.
12. Malinowski to Elsie Malinowska, 23 Oct. 1933, in Wayne, *Story*, vol. 2, p. 184. His claim to have lived in Leipzig for nearly two years is a characteristic exaggeration. At most he was there for fifteen months (Dec. 1908 to March 1910), even fewer if the summer months of 1909 are subtracted.
13. The second Leipzig diary covers the period 13 Oct. to 22 Nov. 1909. Translation by Marc Heine.
14. Brunton to Malinowski, 2 Sept. 1914, MPLSE.
15. A fairly recent example is Thornton and Skalník, *The Early Writings*, p. 14. These authors give more attention than others as to how Bücher's and Wundt's theories might have influenced Malinowski's thinking.
16. E. G. Boring on Wundt in *International Encyclopedia of the Social Sciences*, vol. 16, London: Macmillan, 1968, p. 349. Wundt's chief work was published in Leipzig in 1874: *Grundzüge der Physiologischen Psychologie* (translated into English as *Principles of Physiological Psychology*, London: Macmillan, 1905).
17. University Library, Karl-Marx University (as the University of Leipzig was renamed) to Helena Burke, 11 Aug. 1971, MPLSE.
18. Wilhelm Wundt, *Elemente der Völkerpsychologie*, Leipzig, 1912. This was a summation of his ten-volume work. English translation by E. L. Schaub, *Elements of Folk Psychology*, London: Allen and Unwin 1916.
19. Malinowski's epistolary essay to Aniela Zagórska, 25 Feb. 1913, MPLSE.
20. René Girard has examined the structure of 'triangular desire' in the novels of Dostoevsky, Stendhal, Proust and others in *Deceit, Desire and the Novel*, Baltimore: Johns Hopkins Press, 1965.
21. This address is the one heading his letter of 5 Jan. 1910 to Father Pawlicki.
22. Brunton to Malinowski, 29 May 1914, MPLSE.
23. Olcza retrospective diary, Sept. 1911, MPLSE. Published in Malinowski, *Dziennik*, pp. 150–8.
24. Brunton to Malinowski, Feb. 1915, MPLSE.
25. Olcza diary, MPLSE.
26. Malinowski to Pawlicki, 5 Jan. 1910, translation by G. Kubica, in Ellen et al, *Malinowski between Two Worlds*, pp. 204–5.
27. Ibid., p. 209 n. 10. For comparison, in this pre-war period the caretaker of the city hall in Cracow earned 950 crowns a year, a night watchman 350 (personal communication, G. Kubica).
28. Olcza diary, MPLSE.

Chapter 9

1. Essay-letter to Aniela Zagórska, 25 Feb. 1913, MPLSE. Translation by Marc Heine.
2. Retrospective diary written in Olcza, Zakopane, Sept. 1911, MPLSE.
3. Number 16 Fitzroy Street and several adjacent houses were swallowed up in the 1960s by a concrete University of London dormitory called Carr-Saunders House. By a happy coincidence the Royal Anthropological Institute is today located at 50 Fitzroy Street where it joins Fitzroy Square.
4. Robert Skidelsky, *John Maynard Keynes: Hopes Betrayed, 1883–1920*, London: Macmillan, 1983, pp. 242, 252.

5. Saville Street no longer exists. The site is occupied today by the Royal Orthopaedic Hospital.
6. His letter to Staś Witkiewicz of 12 Aug. 1911 gives this address, 'c/- Mrs A. Brunton, flat G'.
7. Ted Morgan, *Maugham: A Biography*, New York: Simon & Schuster, 1980, p. 77.
8. Ibid., p. 78.
9. Stocking, *After Tylor*, p. 98.
10. *Argonauts*, p. xv.
11. Cited by A. Hingston Quiggin, *Haddon the Head Hunter*, Cambridge: Cambridge University Press, 1942, p. 94.
12. Anita Herle and Sandra Rouse (eds), *Cambridge and the Torres Strait: Centenary Essays on the 1898 Anthropological Expedition*, Cambridge: Cambridge University Press, 1998. The best account of the expedition remains the original one by A. Haddon, *Head-Hunters: Black, White and Brown*, London: Methuen, 1901.
13. Quiggin, *Haddon*, p. 97.
14. Graham Richards, 'Getting a Result: The Expedition's Psychological Research 1898–1913', in Herle and Rouse, *Cambridge and the Torres Strait*, pp. 136–75.
15. C. S. Myers, 'Charles Gabriel Seligman, 1873–1940', *Royal Society Obituary Notices*, 1939–41, 3. Raymond Firth, 'Seligman's Contributions to Oceanic Anthropology', *Oceanias* 45 (4), 1975, pp. 272–82.
16. From this point in the biography I shall use the post-1914 spelling of his name.
17. W. H. R. Rivers, *The Todas*, London: Macmillan, 1906, p. v.
18. R. Slobodin, *W. H. R. Rivers*, New York: Columbia University Press, 1978, p. 29.
19. Rivers, *Todas*, p. 2.
20. W. H. R. Rivers, 'A Genealogical Method of Collecting Social and Vital Statistics', *JRAI* 30, 1900, p. 74.
21. Rivers, *Todas*, pp. 11–12.
22. Ibid., p. 465.
23. E. R. Leach, 'W. H. R. Rivers', in *International Encyclopedia of the Social Sciences*. Vol. 13 London: Macmillan, 1968, p. 527.
24. *Man* 10, 1910, p. 139.
25. Malinowski to Haddon, 20 March 1910, HPCUL 3/concertina file.
26. Malinowski to Haddon, 23 June 1910, HPCUL 5/7. This letter was addressed as from 16 Fitzroy St.
27. Malinowski to Haddon, 8 Aug. 1910, ibid. Nothing is known about this visit Malinowski made to Poland. The Warsaw address on his letter, 153 Marszalkowska, was the home of his great uncle, Kazimierz Szpotański.
28. *L.S.E. Calendar*, 1909–10, p. 164.
29. 'Anthropology', *Encyclopaedia Britannica*, 13th edn, supplement 1, vol 29–30, 1926, p. 131.

Chapter 10

1. Michael Holroyd, *Bernard Shaw: The Search for Love, 1856–1898*, Harmondsworth: Penguin Books, 1988, p. 176.
2. Cited by Stocking, *After Tylor*, p. 160.
3. Ralf Dahrendorf, *L.S.E.: A History of the London School of Economics and Political Science, 1895–1995*, Oxford: Oxford University Press, 1995, pp. 102–3.

4. Ibid., pp. 104–6. Stefan Collini, *Liberalism and Sociology: L.T. Hobhouse and Political Argument in England 1880–1914*, Cambridge: Cambridge University Press, 1979. p. 209. Stocking, *After Tylor*, p. 160.

5. *Argonauts*, p. xvii.

6. Haddon to G. Howes, 19 May 1901, HPCUL Envelope 3.

7. Stocking, *After Tylor*, p. 116.

8. Ibid., p. 172.

9. R. R. Marett, in H. Balfour et al (eds) *Anthropological Essays Presented to Edward Burnett Tylor in Honour of his 75th Birthday*, London: Routledge, 1907, p. 219.

10. *L.S.E. Calendar*, 1910–11, p. 77.

11. Raymond Firth, 'A Brief History of the Department (1913–63)', Pamphlet published by the Department of Anthropology, LSE, 1963, p. 1. In March 1909, a deputation of academics and senior colonial officers petitioned Prime Minister Asquith for a modest annual sum (£500 was suggested) for the establishment of an Imperial Bureau of Anthropology within the Royal Anthropological Institute. The argument turned on the training of colonial administrators 'to increase the efficiency of the Empire in all directions; to lessen friction with native races and stimulate and help our commerce'. Asquith was sympathetic but gave no assurances and referred the matter to the Chancellor of the Exchequer, who presumably shelved the submission (see *Man* 9, 1909, pp. 85–7).

12. *L.S.E. Calendar*, 1910–11, pp. 190–1, and 1911–12, pp. 207–8.

13. Cited by Firth, 'A Brief History', p. 2.

14. *L.S.E. Calendar*, 1910–11, pp. 191–2.

15. MYP II/245.

16. Timothy Stroup, 'Westermarck, Edward Alexander', in C. Winters (ed.), *International Dictionary of Anthropologists*, New York: Garland Publishing, 1991, p. 750.

17. Dahrendorf, *L.S.E.*, pp. 106–7.

18. Timothy Stroup, 'Edward Westermarck: A Reappraisal', *Man* 19 (4), 1984, p. 582.

19. B. Malinowski, 'Anthropology of the Westernmost Orient', *Nature* 120, 17 Dec. 1927, p. 867.

20. Malinowski's acknowledgment of Westermarck appears in his 'Foreword' to Ashley Montagu's *Coming into Being among the Australian Aborigines*, London: Routledge, 1937, p. xxiii. Montagu dedicated this work to both Westermarck and Malinowski.

21. G. C. Wheeler, *Mono-Alu Folklore*, London: Routledge, 1926.

22. Haddon's reference is dated Jan. 1940, HPCUL 7/9.

23. D. Collins and J. Urry, 'A Flame Too Intense for Mortal Body to Support', *AT* 13 (6), 1997, pp. 18–20.

24. R. R. Marett, Obituary for Maria Czaplicka, *Man* 21, 1921, p. 106.

25. Borenius's daughter, Clarissa Lada-Grodzicka, gave a lecture to the Anglo-Finnish Society in the 1970s. The quotations are from the unpublished, undated TS. See also Denys Sutton, 'Tancred Borenius: Connoisseur and Clubman', *Apollo Magazine*, April 1978, pp. 294–309.

26. Much of what follows is extracted from typescript notes of an interview Helena Burke conducted with Anna-Mi Borenius on 4 Nov. 1970. Anna-Mi was then eighty-four.

27. Anna-Mi Borenius to Helena Burke, 16 Sept. 1971.

28. London: John Murray, 1910. Westermarck contributed a 'prefatory note'. Malinowski's review appeared in *Man* 11, 1911, pp. 25–8.

29. Westermarck in Wheeler, *The Tribal*, p. v.

30. B. Malinowski, 'Sexual Life and Marriage among Primitive Mankind', *Nature* 109, 22 April 1922, pp. 126–30. Reprinted in *Sex, Culture, and Myth*, pp. 117–22.

31. B. Malinowski, *The Family among the Australian Aborigines: A Sociological Study*, London: University of London Press, 1913, p. 1.

32. L. R. Hiatt, *Arguments about Aborigines: Australia and the Evolution of Social Anthropology*, Cambridge: Cambridge University Press, 1996, p. 139.

33. J. A. Barnes, 'Introduction', in B. Malinowski, *The Family among the Australian Aborigines*, New York: Schocken Books, 1963, p. xii.

34. Ibid., p. xxi.

35. Hiatt, *Arguments*, p. 51.

36. Malinowski to Haddon, 19 June 1911, HPCUL 5/7. Written as from Passmore Edwards Settlement, Tavistock Place.

37. Seligman to Haddon, 9 Oct. 1911, HPCUL 5/7.

38. *Man* 14, Feb. 1914.

39. Malinowski to Witkiewicz, 16 June 1911. The letter is in the Tatra Museum, Zakopane. Translation by G. Kubica, who cites part of it in Ellen et al, *Malinowski between Two Worlds*, p. 96.

40. Ibid., p. 97.

41. Translation by Basia Plebanek. First published in Malinowski, *Dziennik*, pp. 721–2.

42. This is just one stanza of twenty-two in a poem dedicated to Nalepiński; it was probably written during the autumn of 1911. Published in Malinowski, *Dziennik*, pp. 702–6. Translation by B. Plebanek.

43. S. I. Witkiewicz, 'Listy do Heleny Czerwijowskiej', *Twoczosc* 9, p. 46. Malinowski's letter was dated 12 Aug. 1911. Cited by Kubica in Ellen et al, *Malinowski between Two Worlds* p. 96.

44. B. Malinowski, 'The Economic Aspect of the *Intichiuma* Ceremonies', in *Festskrift tillegnad Edvard Westermarck i anledning av hans femtiarsdag den 20 November 1912* (in homage on his fiftieth birthday), Helsingfors: Simelli, 1912, pp. 81–108. Reprinted in Thornton and Skalník, *The Early Writings*, pp. 209–27.

45. *The Times*, London, Thursday, 7 Sept. 1911.

46. 'The Economic Aspect', p. 209.

47. Ibid., p. 220.

48. Ibid., p. 224.

49. Ibid., p. 226. Firth criticized Malinowski for failing to deal with the problem of the 'assembly cost' of such large ceremonies; Firth, *Man and Culture*, p. 211.

50. Malinowski, 'The Economic Aspect', p. 227.

51. Firth, *Man and Culture*, p. 212.

52. Slobodin, *W. H. R. Rivers*, p. 45.

53. W. H. R. Rivers, 'The Ethnological Analysis of Culture', *Science* 34, 1911, pp. 385–97. Reprinted in W. H. R. Rivers, *Psychology and Ethnology*, ed. G. Elliot Smith, London: Kegan Paul, 1926, p. 121.

54. Ibid., pp. 124–5. There were those German scholars who continued to adhere to Bastian's doctrine of independent origin, though they had adopted the biological notion of convergence, a topic on which Rivers also wrote (see 'Convergence in Human Culture', in *Psychology and Ethnology*, pp. 141–50).

55. Rivers, 'The Ethnological Analysis', pp. 131–2.

56. G. Elliot Smith, 'Preface', in Rivers, *Psychology and Ethnology*, p. viii.

57. Rivers, 'The Ethnological Analysis', p. 132.

58. *Argonauts*, p. xv.

59. Malinowski to Westermarck, 14 Sept. 1911, WAAA.
60. The 'Leipzig to London Retrospect' was written in Polish on six loose folio sheets and labelled 'Records IX–11', i.e. Sept. 1911, MPLSE. Translation by Marc Heine. Published in Malinowski, *Dziennik*, pp. 122–7.
61. Olcza diary, 25 Sept. to 8 Oct. 1911, MPLSE.

Chapter 11

1. Malinowski to Bolesław Ulanowski, 16 Jan. 1912 and 1 Feb. 1912; Ulanowski to Malinowski, 30 Jan. 1912. Translations by Annamaria Orla-Bukowska. Archives of the Polish Academy of Sciences and Arts, Cracow.
2. Malinowski to S. Estreicher, 14 Aug. 1912. Translation by Annamaria Orla-Bukowska. Jagiellonian University Archives.
3. Malinowski to Seligman, 22 Feb. 1912, MPLSE.
4. Seligman to Malinowski, 29 April 1912, ibid.
5. Seligman was a poor linguist and relied on Brenda to learn whatever lingua franca was needed for their field trips.
6. Malinowski to Seligman, 14 June 1912, MPLSE.
7. Seligman to Reeves, 20 June 1912, ibid.
8. Seligman to Malinowski, 1 July 1912, ibid.
9. Malinowski to Seligman, 10 July 1912, ibid.
10. 9 March 1918, *Diary*, p. 219.
11. This diary consists of thirty-five closely written, double-sided sheets. It begins on 4 Aug. 1912 and continues almost uninterruptedly until 30 Jan. 1913. MPLSE. Translation by Marc Heine. Published in Malinowski, *Dziennik*, pp. 158–292.
12. B. Malinowski, 'Observations on Friedrich Nietzsche's *The Birth of Tragedy*', in Thornton and Skalník, *The Early Writings*, pp. 67–88.
13. Malinowski to Elsie Masson, 8 Jan. 1918, in Wayne, *Story*, p. 94.
14. Malinowski to Elsie Masson, 3 Oct. 1918, MPLSE.
15. He cites Fustel de Coulanges only once, in his German essay on the 'Sociology of the Family' which he was drafting at this time. He does not cite Simmel at all.
16. 'Observations', p. 67.
17. Cambridge University Press used this portrait as the dust-cover illustration for Thornton and Skalník's *The Early Writings*.
18. Malinowski, *The Family*, pp. 305–9.
19. Stocking, *After Tylor*, p. 173.
20. Review in *Nature* 12, Jan. 1928. Reprinted in *Sex, Culture, and Myth*, pp. 122–9. A schoolmaster by profession and an amateur ethnologist by inclination, Crawley (1869–1924) was a classics scholar, a prize-winning golfer and tennis player, and a sports commentator for *The Times*.
21. *Sex, Culture, and Myth*, p. 129.
22. Ibid. Malinowski worked out this argument more fully in *Sex and Repression in Savage Society*.
23. Gerould, *Witkiewicz Reader*, p. 33.
24. 'Observations', p. 73.
25. Ibid., p. 76.
26. Today the ground floor of this building boasts a garish video shop.
27. Brunton to Malinowski, 24 Nov. 1912, MPLSE.

28. MPY II/244. Translated and published as 'Religion and Magic: *The Golden Bough*', in Thornton and Skalník, *The Early Writings*, pp. 117–22. The editors arbitrarily assign this undated document to 1910, but it was almost certainly written in late 1912.

29. Ibid., p. 39.

30. Malinowski to Westermarck, 31 Dec. 1912, as from 16 Fitzroy Street, WAAA.

31. Karola Zagórska, 'Under the Roof of Konrad Korzeniowski', in Z. Najder (ed.), *Conrad under Familial Eyes*, Cambridge: Cambridge University Press, 1983, pp. 230–46 (originally published in *Kultura* 2–3, Warsaw, 1932).

32. John Conrad, *Joseph Conrad: Times Remembered*, Cambridge: Cambridge University Press, 1981, pp. 195–6.

33. Conrad to Marynowski, 8 Sept. 1921, in Z. Najder (ed.), *Conrad's Polish Background: Letters to and from Polish Friends*, London: Oxford University Press, 1964, p. 271.

34. John Conrad, *Joseph Conrad*, p. 196.

Chapter 12

1. Adam Kuper, *The Invention of Primitive Society: Transformations of an Illusion*, London: Routledge, 1988, p. 121.

2. Malinowski's epistolary essay to A. Zagórska, 25 Feb. 1913, MPLSE.

3. Malinowski to Westermarck, 2 Feb. 1913, WAAA.

4. Brunton to Malinowski, 24 Feb. 1914, ibid.

5. Brunton to Malinowski, 3 March 1914, ibid.

6. McCarthy to Malinowski, 20 March 1914, ibid.

7. Malinowski to Fischer, 29 May 1913, translated and published by G. Kubica in Ellen et al, *Malinowski between Two Worlds*, pp. 205–6.

8. Malinowski to Nitsch, 30 June 1913, Jagiellonian Library. Translation by Annamaria Orla-Bukowska.

9. Cited by Stocking, *After Tylor*, p. 127.

10. B. Malinowski, 'Sir James George Frazer: A Biographical Appreciation', in *A Scientific Theory of Culture, and other Essays*, Chapel Hill: University of North Carolina Press, 1944, p. 181.

11. Ibid., p. 184.

12. E. Gellner, 'James Frazer and Cambridge Anthropology', in Richard Mason (ed.), *Cambridge Minds*, Cambridge: Cambridge University Press, 1994, p. 204.

13. Raymond Firth, personal communication. Firth referred to Malinowski's 'somewhat contemptuous affection for Frazer'. See also M. W. Young, 'Young Malinowski: A Review Article', *Canberra Anthropology* 17 (2), 1994, p. 114.

14. All quotations are from Malinowski's essay, 'Totemism and Exogamy (1911–1913)', in Thornton and Skalník, *The Early Writings*, pp. 123–99. The end of Part II is dated 'London 1912' so Malinowski must have completed it during the brief visit he made to England on 30 Dec.

15. Stocking, *After Tylor*, p. 150.

16. Claude Lévi-Strauss, *Totemism*. Translated by Rodney Needham, Boston: Beacon Press, 1963.

17. *Nature* 141, March 1938; reprinted in *Sex, Culture, and Myth*, pp. 277–82.

18. Ibid., p. 281.

19. Malinowski to Elsie Masson, 18 June 1920, in Wayne, *Story*, vol. 2, p. 4.

20. *Sex, Culture, and Myth*, pp. 95, 154.

21. David Schneider, 'Rivers and Kroeber in the Study of Kinship', in W. H. R. Rivers, *Kinship and Social Organization*, London: Athlone Press, 1968, p. 10.

22. MPY II/256. An abstract of Rivers's paper and Malinowski's handwritten notes are in the same folder. The abstract was published as 'Survival in Sociology', *Sociological Review* 6, 1913, p. 293.

23. W. H. R. Rivers, 'Sociology and Psychology', *Sociological Review* 9, 1916, pp. 1–13.

24. Malinowski, *A Scientific Theory of Culture*, p. 29.

25. Rivers, 'The Ethnological Analysis of Society'. Cited by Slobodin, *W. H. R. Rivers*, p. 162.

26. Cited in ibid., p. 163.

27. Brilliantly fictionalized by the novelist Pat Barker in a prize-winning trilogy: *Regeneration*, *The Eye in the Door* and *The Ghost Road*. See also Rivers, 'On the repression of war experience', *The Lancet*, 2 Feb. 1918; and Rivers, *Conflict and Dream*, London: Routledge, 1923.

28. W. H. R. Rivers, 'Anthropological Research outside America', in *Reports on the Present Condition and Future Needs of the Science of Anthropology*, Washington D.C.: Carnegie Institute, 1913, p. 7. Although Malinowski did not cite it directly, he was obviously familiar with Rivers's statement. In 1922 he wrote: 'To borrow the terminology of Dr Rivers and his opinion: in the present state of ethnography intensive field work is even more urgently needed than survey work' ('Ethnology and the Study of Society', *Economica* 2, Oct. 1922, p. 218).

29. Malinowski to Haddon, 5 May 1916, HPCUP 5/7.

30. Firth, 'Introduction', in *Man and Culture*, p. 6. Historians and other commentators who have seized upon this statement as a key to Malinowski's ambition are too numerous to mention. Two of the most thoughtful are C. A. Thompson, 'Anthropology's Conrad', *JPH* 30 (1), 1995, and Stocking, *After Tylor*, p. 268.

31. Stocking, *After Tylor*, p. 268.

32. Malinowski to Brenda Seligman, 21 June 1918, MPLSE.

33. Keith to Malinowski, 31 Oct. 1933, ibid.

34. Evidence for the gift is circumstantial. In *Conrad's Polish Background* (p. 21) Najder notes that the book, bearing an inscription in Polish by the author, was discovered in W. Heffer and Sons of Cambridge (Catalogue of Second-hand Books, 1925, No. 251).

35. B. Malinowski, 'Culture', in *Encyclopaedia of the Social Sciences*, vol. 4, New York, 1931, p. 623.

36. Robert Ackerman, *J. G. Frazer: His Life and Work*, Cambridge: Cambridge University Press, 1987, p. 225.

37. Stocking, *After Tylor*, p. 249.

38. Malinowski's review appeared in *Folk-lore* 24 (4), Dec. 1913, pp. 525–31. Reprinted in *Sex, Culture, and Myth*, pp. 283–88.

39. *Wierzenia pierwotne i formy ustroju społecznego* was republished in Poland in 1980 in the first volume of Malinowski's collected works. (*Dzieła*, Warzawa: Państwowe Wydawnictwo Naukowe.)

40. 'Magic, Science and Religion', in J. A. Needham (ed.) *Science, Religion and Reality*, London: Macmillan, 1925. Reprinted in B. Malinowski, *Magic, Science and Religion, and other Essays*, Boston: Beacon Press, 1948, p. 54.

41. Ibid., p. 57.

42. E. Durkheim. *The Elementary Forms of the Religious Life*, trans. J. W. Swain, London: Allen & Unwin, 1915, p. 225.

43. Malinowski, *Coral Gardens*, vol. 2, p. 236.
44. B. Malinowski, '*Baloma*: The Spirits of the Dead in the Trobriand Islands', JRAI, 46, 1916. Reprinted in Malinowski, *Magic, Science and Religion*, p. 274.
45. Frazer to Malinowski, 5 July 1917, MERNAA.
46. Malinowski, *Coral Gardens*, vol. 2, p. 236.
47. Malinowski, *A Scientific Theory of Culture*, p. 19.
48. Approximately 420 pages in Polish to 360 pages in English.
49. Malinowski to Nitsch, 18 July 1913, Jagiellonian Library. Translation by Annamaria Orla-Bukowska.
50. Anna-Mi Borenius to Helena Burke, 4 Nov. 1970, MPLSE.
51. Micińska, *Witkacy*, p. 26.
52. Władysław Matlakowski, cited in ibid., p. 99.
53. Ibid.
54. Stuart Baker, 'Witkiewicz and Malinowski: The Pure Form of Magic, Science and Religion', PR 18 (1–2) 1973, p. 81.
55. S. I. Witkiewicz, *Metaphysics of a Two-Headed Calf* (1921), trans. D. and E. Gerould, in *Tropical Madness*, New York: Winter House, 1973.
56. B. Malinowski, *The Foundations of Faith and Morals*, London: Oxford University Press, 1936: Reprinted in *Sex, Culture and Myth*, p. 336.
57. The full title of the lecture was 'The Relationship of Primitive Beliefs to the Forms of Social Organization' (in Thornton and Skalník, *The Early Writings*, pp. 229–42). It was originally published in Polish by the academy in 1913.
58. Postcard, Malinowski to J. Żuławski, 24 Oct. 1913, Jagiellonian Library.
59. Brunton to Malinowski, 1 Oct. 1914, MPLSE.
60. Brunton to Malinowski, 4 April 1916, ibid.
61. *L.S.E. Calendar*, 1913–14, p. 238.
62. Malinowski to Westermarck, 23 Dec. 1913, WAAA.
63. Westermark to Malinowski, 9 Jan. 1914, MPLSE.
64. Malinowski to Haddon, 17 Nov. 1913, HPCUL 5/7.
65. Seligman to Haddon, 24 Nov. 1913, ibid.
66. R. R. Marett, Address, 13 July 1942, in *Professor Bronislaw Malinowski: An Account of the Memorial Meeting Held at the Royal Institution in London on July 13th 1942*, London: Oxford University Press, 1943, p. 7.
67. Malinowski to Westermarck, 23 Dec. 1913, WAAA.

Chapter 13

1. *Diary*, p. 133.
2. Ibid., p. 27. *Romance* (1903) was written in collaboration with F. M. Hueffer (Ford Madox Ford).
3. Ibid., p. 42; Guterman's translation modified by Basia Plebanek.
4. Ibid., p. 133.
5. Conrad to Sir Sidney Colvin, n.d. (probably late 1912), *The Collected Letters of Joseph Conrad*, eds F. Karl and L. Davies, vol. 5, Cambridge: Cambridge University Press, 1996, pp. 141–2.
6. Interestingly, in 1948 Zofia Dembowska-Romer (Malinowski's old girlfriend) painted Retinger's portrait in London.
7. Joan Givner, *Katherine Anne Porter: A Life*, New York: Simon and Schuster, 1982, p. 151.
8. Ibid., p. 152.

9. Jeffrey Meyers, *Joseph Conrad: A Biography*, London: John Murray, 1991, p. 293. Meyers states that Anderson 'broke up' the Retingers' marriage, but Malinowski's diary indicates clearly that it was in deep trouble several years before Anderson became Retinger's mistress.

10. See Joseph Retinger, *Memoirs of an Eminence Grise*, ed. John Pomian, Sussex: Sussex University Press, 1972; concerning Conrad and Jane Anderson, see Meyers, *Joseph Conrad*.

11. Conrad to Retinger, 19 March 1917, in Najder, *Conrad under Familial Eyes*, p. 229; and 22 June 1917, ibid., pp. 229–30.

12. Joseph Retinger, *Conrad and his Contemporaries*, New York: Roy Publishers, 1943. Tola Zubrzycka, 'A Son of Two Countries: Some Reminiscences of Joseph Conrad Korzeniowski' (originally published in *Iskry* 8–10, 1931), in Najder, *Conrad under Familial Eyes*, pp. 201–10.

13. It is accessible from central London via the underground station at Chalk Farm, which also lends its name to the surrounding area. Malinowski wrote, for example: 'I think of the little room with the door locked in Chalk Farm.' See *Diary*, p. 65, where Chilt should read Chalk.

14. Ibid., p. 65.

15. 'Polish Diary', 17 May 1914. MPLSE.

16. Brunton to Malinowski, 10 Feb. 1914, MPLSE.

17. *L.S.E. Calendar*, 1913–14, p. 239.

18. Brunton to Malinowski, 19 March 1914, MPLSE.

19. *Diary*, p. 21.

20. Ibid.

21. Ibid., p. 68. Translation amended by Basia Plebanek.

22. Brunton to Malinowski, 20 Feb. 1914, MPLSE.

23. As told to Helena Burke in an interview with Anna-Mi Borenius on 4 Nov. 1970.

24. Brunton to Malinowski, 11 March 1914, MPLSE.

25. Brunton to Malinowski, 19 March 1914, ibid.

26. Brunton to Malinowski, 12 March 1914, ibid.

27. Brunton to Malinowski, 28 March 1914, ibid.

28. Ibid.

29. White notebook labelled 'Polish Diary T-L', 12 April to 30 July 1914. MPLSE. All quotations in this chapter not otherwise attributed are from this diary. Translation by Marc Heine. Published in Malinowski, *Dziennik*, pp. 299–357.

30. Brunton to Malinowski, 7 May 1914, MPLSE.

31. Hutton Webster, *Rest Days: A Sociological Study*. Malinowski's review is in *Man* 14, March 1914, p. 46.

32. This diary covers his last months in England, a return visit to Poland and the journey to Australia: a total of 108 days. It ends abruptly in Western Australia on 30 July, just before the outbreak of war.

33. Translation by K. Symmons-Symonolewicz in *PR*, 5, 1960, p. 40.

34. Gerould, *Witkiewicz Reader*, undated letter of March–April 1914, pp. 82–3.

35. Witkiewicz to Malinowski, c. 28 February 1914, in Gerould, *Witkiewicz Reader*, p. 80.

36. Brunton to Malinowski, 28 March 1914, MPLSE.

37. Gerould, *Witkiewicz Reader*, p. 80.

38. Brunton to Malinowski, 28 April 1914, MPLSE.

39. Joseph Conrad, 'The Return' (1897), in *Tales of Unrest*, London: J.M. Dent 1947, p. 172.

40. Ibid., p. 183.
41. Zubrzycka, 'A Son of Two Countries', p. 208.
42. Ibid.
43. MPY I/689 and 690.
44. A. Grimble, *A Pattern of Islands*, London: John Murray, 1952, p. 85.
45. Since Malinowski's day the Army & Navy has shed some of its imperial image while retaining its reputation for quality – a social notch below Harrods, but more upmarket than Marks & Spencer.
46. See Appendix 1, 'Malinowski's Photographic Equipment', in Young, *Malinowski's Kiriwina*, pp. 275–6.
47. MPY I/565.
48. *Diary*, p. 297. After divorcing Retinger, Otolia did not remarry. She remained mostly in Poland where she reared her daughter, taught foreign languages and produced a children's programme on Polish radio. She died in 1981 at the age of ninety-two (Grażyna Kubica, personal communication).

Chapter 14

1. D. Gerould, 'Witkacy's Journey to the Tropics and Itinerary in Ceylon', *Konteksty* 54 (1–4), Warszawa: Instytut Sztuki Polskiej Akademii Nauk, 2000, p. 216.
2. Józefa Malinowska to Malinowski, 18 June 1914, MPY I/405. All translations of Malinowski's correspondence with his mother are by B. Plebanek.
3. Gerould, *Witkiewicz Reader*, 1992, p. 84.
4. Witkiewicz to Malinowski, 15 June 1914, in Gerould, *Witkiewicz Reader*, pp. 86–7.
5. Malinowski to Józefa Malinowska, 17 June 1914, MPY I/408.
6. Malinowski to Józefa Malinowska, 20 June 1914, Ibid.
7. 18 June 1914. This translation is by K. Zdziechowski. Also published in *Konteksty*, pp. 258–60.
8. Gerould, *Witkiewicz Reader*, pp. 85–6.
9. Witkiewicz to Beaurain, c. 20 June 1914. This translation is by K. Zdziechowski. Also published in *Konteksty*, p. 303.
10. Gerould, Introduction, *Witkiewicz Reader*, p. 9.
11. Malinowski to Józefa Malinowska, 26 June 1914, MPY I/408.
12. Józefa Malinowska to Malinowski, 24 June 1914, MPY I/405.
13. Brunton to Malinowski, 16 July 1914, MPLSE.
14. Witkiewicz to his father, 29 June 1914, in Gerould, *Witkiewicz Reader*, p. 88.
15. Ibid., p. 90.
16. Malinowski to Józefa Malinowska, 2 July 1914, MPY I/408.
17. Letter dated Anuradhapura, 2 July 1914; for a corrected English version, see Gerould, *Witkiewicz Reader*, pp. 90–1.
18. Malinowski to Józefa Malinowska, 18 July 1914, MPY I/405.
19. Gerould, *Witkiewicz Reader*, p. 96.
20. Ibid.
21. See Micińska, *Witkacy*, plate 93.
22. Malinowski to Józefa Malinowska, 18 July 1914, MPY I/408.
23. Malinowski to Józefa Malinowska, 12 July 1914, Ibid.
24. Entitled 'Z podróży do Tropików' ('A Journey to the Tropics') it appeared in the *Echo Tatrzańskie* (a Zakopane magazine) in 1919. Republished with an English translation

in *Konteksty*, 2000, pp. 226–35. Written in characteristically extravagant prose, the essay is steeped in tropical melancholy and riddled with racial prejudice.

25. Malinowski to Józefa Malinowska, 16 July 1914, MPY I/408.
26. Malinowski to Józefa Malinowska, 18 July 1914, Ibid.
27. Malinowski to Józefa Malinowska, 19 July 1914, Ibid.

Chapter 15

1. BAAS, *Report on the 84th Meeting: Australia 1914*, London: John Murray, 1915, p. 685.
2. Ibid., p. 712.
3. He unwittingly echoed Baldwin Spencer's appraisal of Australia in 1898, 'there is so much that is new', which D. J. Mulvaney and J. H. Calaby adopted as the title of their biography of Spencer.
4. Gerould, *Witkiewicz Reader*, 1992, p. 97.
5. Malinowski to Józefa Malinowska, 27 July 1914, MPY I/408.
6. *The Western Mail*, 27 July 1914.
7. E. Le Souef to Malinowski, 27 Aug. 1914, MPY I/357.
8. Malinowski to Józefa Malinowska, 2 Aug. 1914, MPY I/408a.
9. S. I. Witkiewicz to his parents, 3 Aug. 1914, in Gerould, *Witkiewicz Reader*, pp. 91–2.
10. Malinowski to Józefa Malinowska, 3 Aug. 1914, MPY I/408a.
11. Conrad's return to Poland in July 1914 has been documented by several of his biographers.
12. Anna-Mi Borenius to Helena Burke, 18 April 1972, MPLSE.
13. Zubrzycka, 'A Son of Two Countries' in Najder, *Conrad under Familial Eyes*, p. 207.
14. E. Le Souef to Malinowski, 27 Aug. 1914, MPY I/357.
15. Gerould, *Witkiewicz Reader*, pp. 92–3.
16. Brunton to Malinowski, 6 Aug. 1914, MPLSE.
17. BAAS, *Report*, p. 697.
18. Ernest Scott, *Australia during the War*, Sydney: Angus & Roberton, 1937, p. 32.
19. Peter M. Last, 'Stirling and the Biology of the Family', 47th Edward Stirling Memorial Lecture, Unpublished TS, Medical Sciences Club of South Australia, Adelaide, 1986.
20. E. C. Stirling and F. J. Gillen, 'Part IV, Anthropology', in B. Spencer (ed.), *Report on the Work of the Horn Scientific Expedition to Central Australia*, London: Dulau and Co., 1896, p. 2.
21. *The Adelaide Advertiser*, 12 Aug. 1914.
22. Gerould, *Witkiewicz Reader*, p. 96.
23. Ibid., p. 98.
24. For example, Malinowski doubted the adequacy of Spencer and Gillen's facts concerning the *pirrauru* ('wife-sharing') institution among the Urabunna tribe (*The Family*, p. 108).
25. D. J. Mulvaney and J. H. Calaby, *'So Much That Is New': Baldwin Spencer 1860–1929*, Melbourne: Melbourne University Press, 1985, p. 316.
26. Brunton to Malinowski, 13 June 1915, MPLSE.
27. Brunton to Malinowski, 14 Aug. 1916, ibid.
28. Michael Allen, 'Some Extracts from John Layard's Previously Unpublished "The Story of my Life"', *Australian Anthropological Society Newsletter*, 73, Sept. 1998, p. 14.
29. BAAS, *Report*, p. 532.
30. Mulvaney and Calaby, *'So Much That Is New'*, p. 267.

31. 'Dr B. Malinowski, Ethnological Research, Papua', MERNAA.
32. Pemberton Reeves to Cook, 11 June 1914, ibid.
33. AHPNLA MS 52/338–42.
34. Hunt to Murray, 14 Aug. 1914, ibid., MS 52/388.
35. Strong's letters are all dated 27 June 1914, MPY I/677.
36. Ray to Holmes, 29 June 1914. Ray had also written earlier to the Rev. Riley of Daru, 22 May 1914, MPY I/677.
37. Seligman to Dauncey, 27 June 1914, MPY I/677.
38. Malinowski to Józefa Malinowska, 23 Aug. 1914, MPY I/408a.
39. Haddon's report to the Percy Sladen Trust, HPCUL 7/10.
40. Malinowski to Józefa Malinowska, 24 Aug. 1914, MPY I/408a.
41. BAAS, *Report*, p. 522.
42. Ibid., p. 535.
43. Ibid., p. 710.
44. Ibid., p. 713.
45. *Diary*, p. 34.
46. F. Golding to Malinowski, 13 Sept. 1914, MPY I/224.
47. Witkiewicz to Malinowski, 14 Sept. 1914, in Gerould, *Witkiewicz Reader*, pp. 100–1.
48. *Diary*, pp. 29–30.
49. Witkiewicz to Malinowski, 1 Oct. 1914, in Gerould, *Witkiewicz Reader*, pp. 101–2.
50. *Diary*, p. 22.
51. F. Golding to Malinowski, n.d. (Dec.) 1914. Cited without attribution by Gerould, *Witkiewicz Reader*, p. 102.
52. Witkiewicz to Malinowski, n.d. Oct. 1914, in Gerould, *Witkiewicz Reader*, pp. 102–5.
53. Ibid., p. 103.
54. Ibid., p. 105.
55. *Diary*, p. 298.
56. Rivers to Hunt, Sept. 1914, AHPNLA MS 52/1960.

Chapter 16

1. *Diary*, pp. 7–8.
2. J. H. P. Murray, *Papua or British New Guinea*, London: T. Fisher Unwin, 1912, p. 46.
3. *Diary*, pp. 14–15.
4. Francis West, *Hubert Murray: The Australian Pro-Consul*, Melbourne: Oxford University Press, 1968, p. 97.
5. Ibid., p. 34.
6. *Diary*, p. 8.
7. H. Murray to G. Murray, 5 Oct. 1914, in Francis West (ed.), *Selected Letters of Hubert Murray*, Melbourne: Oxford University Press, 1970, p. 83.
8. Lord Hailey, 'Introduction', in L. P. Mair, *Australia in New Guinea*, London: Christophers, 1948, p. xvi.
9. West, *Hubert Murray*, p. 163.
10. See Hank Nelson, 'European attitudes in Papua, 1906–1914', in *The History of Melanesia*, Second Waigani Seminar, Port Moresby: University Press; N.G. and Canberra: R.S.Pac.S., 1969.
11. Kenneth Mackay, *Across Papua*, London: Witherby, 1909, p. 54.
12. M. Staniforth Smith, *Handbook of the Territory of Papua*, 2nd edn, Melbourne: J. Kemp, 1909.

13. Ian Stuart, *Port Moresby: Yesterday and Today*, Sydney: Pacific Publications, 1970, p. 95.
14. C.G. Seligmann, *The Melanesians of British New Guinea*, Cambridge University Press, 1910.
15. Murray, *Papua*, p. 146.
16. Ibid., p. 114.
17. Ibid., p. 156.
18. West, *Hubert Murray*, p. 68.
19. Seligmann, *The Melanesians*, p. 59; Barton's photograph of Ahuia in full regalia is reproduced as plate III.
20. F. E. Williams, 'The Reminiscences of Ahuia Ova', *JRAI* 60, 1939, p. 12.
21. *Diary*, p. 9.
22. Malinowski to Seligman, 20 Sept. 1914, MPLSE.
23. New Guinea Field Diary, 1903–04, SPLSE 1/2/2.
24. Williams, 'Reminiscences', p. 32.
25. *Diary*, p. 10.
26. Hanuabada Fieldnotes, MPY II/197.
27. Ibid.
28. The notebooks were probably transcribed by a research assistant during the late 1920s.
29. Hanuabada Fieldnotes, MPY II/197.
30. Ibid.
31. Malinowski to Józefa Malinowska, 20 Sept. 1914, MPY I/408a.
32. New Guinea Field Diary, SPLSE 1/2/2.
33. Murray to Mahon (his minister in Melbourne), 27 Oct. 1914, in West, *Selected Letters*, p. 84.
34. Williams, 'Reminiscences', p. 27.
35. Malinowski to Seligman, 20 Sept. 1914, MPLSE.
36. *Diary*, p. 13 (27 Sept. 1914). The alternative translation was suggested by B. Plebanek: 'their own language' might refer to the fact that Koita is a non-Austronesian language and therefore very different from Motu. Still, the sense of Malinowski's being at a linguistic disadvantage is identical.
37. Ibid., p. 15. Translation modified by B. Plebanek.
38. Józefa Malinowska to Malinowski, 23 Sept. 1914, MPY I/405.
39. Malinowski to Józefa Malinowska, 11 Oct. 1914, MPY I/408a.
40. *Diary*, p. 21. Translation modifed by B. Plebanek.
41. Malinowski to Hunt, 12 Oct. 1914, MERNAA A1 21/866.
42. Undated typed postscript in Malinowski file, Ibid.
43. Malinowski to Seligman, 3 Nov. 1914, MPLSE.
44. Seligman to Malinowski, 14 Jan. 1915, MPLSE.
45. *Diary*, p. 24.
46. *Argonauts*, p. 4.
47. Mary Louise Pratt, 'Fieldwork in Common Places', in J. Clifford and G. Marcus (eds), *Writing Culture: The Poetics and Politics of Ethnography*, Berkeley: University of California Press, 1986, p. 38.

Chapter 17

1. *Papua Annual Report*, 1914–15, p. 64.
2. Malinowski to Józefa Malinowska, 24 Nov. 1914, MPY I/408a.

3. Saville to his brother, 8 Oct. 1902, Saville Papers, Mitchell Library, Sydney. For the complete list of Saville's 'laws' see M. W. Young, *Malinowski among the Magi: 'The Natives of Mailu'*, London: Routledge, 1988, p. 44.

4. *Diary*, p. 136.

5. Ibid., p. 16.

6. Ibid., pp. 26–7.

7. Ibid., p. 16.

8. Malinowski, 'Foreword', in W. J. V. Saville, *In Unknown New Guinea*, London: Seeley Service, 1926, p. 8.

9. In Papua in 1908, for instance, of a total European 'workforce' of 516 there were seventy-eight government officials and seventy-five missionaries.

10. Seligman to Malinowski, 30 Dec. 1915, MPY I/565.

11. Mailu Fieldnotes, p. 270, MPY II/194.

12. *Diary*, p. 31.

13. Ibid., p. 32.

14. Ibid., p. 35. Translation modified by B. Plebanek.

15. Malinowski to Seligman, 3 Nov. 1914, MPLSE.

16. Malinowski to Józefa Malinowska, 5 Nov. 1914, MPY I/408a.

17. *Diary*, p. 36. Translation modified by B. Plebanek.

18. See ibid., p. 155 for the prospecting/mining trope. M. W. Young, 'The Ethnographer as Hero: The Imponderabilia of Malinowski's Everyday Life in Mailu', *Canberra Anthropology* 10 (2), 1987. Stocking, 'Ethnographer's Magic', p. 104.

19. Malinowski to Józefa Malinowska, 24 Nov. 1914, MPY I/408a.

20. Malinowski to Seligman, 24 Nov. 1914, MPLSE.

21. Mailu Fieldnotes, p. 280, MPY II/194. *Diary*, p. 37.

22. Mailu Fieldnotes, pp. 240–1, MPY II/194.

23. See Christina Thompson, 'Anthropology's Conrad', *JPH* 30 (1), 1995, p. 68.

24. *Diary*, p. 41.

25. Malinowski to Hunt, 24 Nov. 1914, MERNAA.

26. 15 Dec. 1914, ibid.

27. *Argonauts*, p. 54.

28. *Diary*, p. 43.

29. *Argonauts*, p. 35.

30. Ibid., p. 36.

31. *Diary*, p. 43.

32. Seligman, Field Diary, p. 62, referring to his first visit in April 1904, SPLSE 1/2/2.

33. Mackay, *Across Papua*, p. 47.

34. *Diary*, p. 112.

35. *Argonauts*, pp. 10n, 31n.

36. *Diary*, p. 47.

37. Ibid., pp. 50–1.

38. Ibid., p. 52.

39. Ibid., p. 54.

40. M. W. Young, 'The Careless Collector: Malinowski and the Antiquarians', in M. O'Hanlon and R. Welsch (eds), *Hunting the Gatherers: Ethnographic Collectors, Agents and Agency in Melanesia, 1870s–1930s*, Oxford: Berghahn Books, 2000.

41. *Diary*, p. 58

42. Ibid., p. 49.

43. Ibid., p. 58.
44. Brunton to Malinowski, 4 Nov. 1914, MPLSE.
45. Józefa Malinowska to Malinowski, 27 Dec. 1914, MPY I/405.
46. Józefa Malinowska to Malinowski, 4 Jan. 1915, MPY I/406.
47. *Diary*, p. 63.
48. Ibid., p. 65.
49. Ibid., p. 66. Italizied phrase in English in original.
50. Haddon to Hunt, Dec. 1914, AHPNLA 52/1965.
51. Haddon to Hunt, 6 Sept. 1914, AHPNLA 52/1959.
52. Chinnery had already served in Papua as a field officer. After the war he studied under Haddon at Cambridge. In spite of Haddon's support, Chinnery was rejected for the post of government anthropologist because Murray distrusted him.
53. *Diary*, p. 69.
54. Ibid., p. 72.
55. Ibid., p. 74.

Chapter 18

1. *Diary*, p. 75.
2. Malinowski to Seligman, 25 Jan. 1915, MPLSE.
3. *Diary*, p. 78.
4. Seligmann, *Melanesians*, p. 17.
5. *Diary*, p. 79.
6. Ibid., p. 82.
7. Ibid., p. 80. Some lines censored by Valetta Malinowska restored by B. Plebanek.
8. Mailu Fieldnotes, p. 656, MPY II/196.
9. Malinowski, *The Natives of Mailu*, in Young, *Malinowski among the Magi*, p. 108.
10. Ibid., p. 176n.
11. Malinowski to Seligman, 4 May 1915, MPLSE.
12. *Diary*, p. 83.
13. HPCUL 5/7.
14. H. Champion to Helena Burke, 17 Nov. 1971. Helena dismisses her father's reported remark as one of his 'unfunny' attempts to shock.
15. See *Diary*, p. 90. Translation revised by B. Plebanek.
16. See ibid., pp. 89, 92. Translation revised by B. Plebanek and elisions restored.
17. *Argonauts,* p. 477.
18. Malinowski to Hunt, 26 Feb. 1915, MERNAA.
19. *Diary*, p. 97.
20. Dated 27 Feb. 1915. The letter fragment was discovered among his manuscript poems, MPLSE. Translation by Daniel and Jadwiga Gerould.
21. Józefa Malinowska to Malinowski, 28 Feb. 1915, MPY I/406.

Chapter 19

1. *Diary*, p. 98.
2. Malinowski to Józefa Malinowska, 14 March 1915, MPY I/409.

3. Malinowski to Hunt, 2 April 1915, MERNAA.
4. Hunt to Malinowski, 7 April 1915; Secretary of Defence to Hunt, 13 April 1915, MERNAA.
5. Scott, *Australia during the War*, p. 137.
6. MFNAA.
7. *Diary*, p. 261.
8. Stirling Papers, Matlock Library, Adelaide, PRG 388.
9. For a detailed analysis of the writing of *The Natives of Mailu*, see Young, *Malinowski among the Magi*. (Page references to Malinowski's monograph refer to this edition.)
10. Malinowski to Hartland, 20 Sept. 1914, Hartland MSS 16889, National Library of Wales, Aberystwyth; *Natives of Mailu*, pp. 192–204.
11. *Argonauts*, pp. 3–4.
12. *Natives of Mailu*, p. 174.
13. Mailu Fieldnotes, MPY II/195, pp. 242–3; *Natives of Mailu*, pp. 175, 306.
14. Young, Introduction to *Natives of Mailu*, pp. 35–9.
15. *Natives of Mailu*, p. 184.
16. Ibid., p. 109.
17. Ibid.
18. Ibid., p. 275.
19. Malinowski to Rivers, 15 Oct. 1915, HPCUL 129/12055.
20. Malinowski to Haddon, 15 Oct. 1915, HPCUL Envelope 7.
21. Culture boxes, MPLSE.
22. S. H. Ray, review of *The Natives of Mailu*, *Nature* 100, 1917, pp. 335–6.
23. Stirling to Haddon, 28 Aug. 1915, HPCUL 8/24.
24. Frank A. Norick, 'An Analysis of the Material Culture of the Trobriand Islands Based on the Collection of Bronislaw Malinowski', PhD thesis, University of California, 1976, p. 5.
25. Martha Macintyre, personal communication.
26. Malinowski to Seligman, 4 May 1915, MPLSE.
27. Ibid.
28. Malinowski to Hunt, 28 April 1915, MERNAA.
29. Hunt to Minister of External Affairs, 28 April 1915, ibid.
30. Hunt to Malinowski, 4 May 1915, ibid.
31. Malinowski to Hunt, 7 May 1915, ibid.
32. Spencer to Haddon, 11 Nov. 1915, HPCUP Envelope 3. Cited by Mulvaney and Calaby, *So Much That Is New*, p. 322.
33. Haddon to Hunt, 15 March 1915, AHPNLA MS 52/1975. Hunt to Haddon, 7 May 1915, HPCUL 8/24.
34. Young, 'Introduction', in *Malinowski among the Magi*, pp. 23–4.
35. Murray to Hunt, 30 Oct. 1916, MERNAA.
36. *Daily Telegraph*, Sydney, Wednesday 19 May 1915. The column bears the double heading: 'For Poland. Why Germany Is Hated'.
37. Brunton to Malinowski, 13 June 1915, MPLSE.
38. MPY IV/27.
39. Malinowski to Józefa Malinowska, 15 June 1915, MPY I/409.
40. Draft letter to Lady Stirling, MPY I/590.
41. *Diary*, p. 99.
42. Malinowski to Seligman, 13 June 1915, MPLSE.
43. *Argonauts*, p. 53.

44. Rev. J. Wesley Booth to Helena Burke, 20 March 1972, MPLSE.
45. Diane Langmore, *Missionary Lives: Papua, 1874–1914*, Honolulu: University of Hawaii Press, 1989, p. 160.
46. Ibid., p. 119.
47. Ibid., p. 120.
48. *Coral Gardens*, vol. 1, p. 212.
49. The date of the first entry is 23 June 1915. Trobriands Fieldnotes, pp. 746ff., MPLSE.
50. Malinowski, *Argonauts*, p. 500. Rev. M. Gilmour, 'A Few Notes on the Kiriwina (Trobriand Islands) Trading Expeditions', in *British New Guinea Annual Report*, 1904–05, pp. 71–2. Malinowski said that he found it 'substantially correct, and on the whole formulated with precision' (*Argonauts*, p. 500).
51. *Diary*, pp. 183–4.
52. Wayne, *Story*, vol. 1, p. 105.

Chapter 20

1. Plate 8 in M.W. Young, *Malinowski's Kiriwina: Fieldwork Photography 1915–18*, Chicago: University of Chicago Press, 1998, p. 49.
2. *Diary*, p. 143.
3. Robert H. Black, 'Dr Bellamy of Papua', *The Medical Journal of Australia*, 11 (6), 24 Aug. 1957, p. 283.
4. *Papua Annual Report*, 1914–15, pp. 37–9.
5. Ibid., 1911–12, p. 125.
6. Ibid., 1913–14, pp. 46–53; Young, *Malinowski's Kiriwina*, pp. 81–2.
7. Mackay, *Across Papua*, pp. 71–2.
8. R. L. Bellamy, 'Notes on the Customs of the Trobriand Islander', *Papua Annual Report*, 1907–08.
9. Black, 'Dr Bellamy', p. 279.
10. Ibid.
11. Malinowski to Prisk and Jamieson, 8 Sept. 1915, MPLSE.
12. '*Baloma*', p. 386n.
13. Trobriand Fieldnotes, pp. 776ff., MPLSE.
14. Malinowski to Seligman, 30 July 1915, ibid.
15. Black, 'Dr Bellamy', p. 279.
16. *Sexual Life*, p. 28n. A later assistant resident magistrate, Leo Austen, agreed with Malinowski that Bellamy's imprisonment of Touluwa had damaged his prestige and reduced his authority. In the 1930s Austen dedicated himself to reconstituting the chief's power – initially by giving him an annual 'income' of tobacco. (Austen to Malinowski, 22 Sept. 1933, MPY I/28.)
17. Malinowski to Murray, 19 June 1929, NAA G69, item 16/14.
18. Campbell to Malinowski, 3 Aug. 1915, MPLSE.
19. Malinowski to Elsie Masson, 15 Jan. 1918, in Wayne, *Story*, p. 104.
20. *Sexual Life*, p. 7.
21. *Coral Gardens*, vol. 1, p. 393.
22. Hancock to Malinowski, 8 Feb. 1919, MPY I/245.
23. *Coral Gardens*, vol. 1, p. 84.
24. Ibid., pp. 85–6; see also vol. 2, pp. 222, 244.
25. *Sexual Life*, p. 317.
26. Ibid., p. 118.

27. Ibid., p. 266.
28. Ibid., p. 8.
29. Stocking, 'Ethnographer's Magic', p. 97. J. Urry, 'Item #[4]355: Malinowski's Tent', *AT* 12 (5), Oct. 1996, p. 20. M.W. Young, 'Malinowski's Second Tent', *AT* 12 (6), Dec. 1996, pp. 24–5. J. Benthall, 'That Tent,' *AT* 16 (3), June 2000, pp. 18–19.
30. *Argonauts*, p. 5.
31. *Sexual Life*, p. 240.
32. *Argonauts*, p. 5
33. Fieldnotes, p. 810, MPLSE.
34. *Argonauts*, p. 8.
35. Malinowski to Hunt, 28 April 1915, MERNAA.
36. *Argonauts*, p. 52.
37. Fieldnotes, p. 887, MPLSE.
38. Ibid., p. 1507.
39. *Sexual Life*, pp. 258–9.
40. Original text in F. E. Williams Papers, Papua New Guinea National Archives, Box 2989, item 22. Published by Ira Bashkow, '"To Be His Witness If That Was Ever Necessary": Raphael Brudo on Malinowski's Fieldwork and Trobriand Ideas of Conception', *History of Anthropology Newsletter* 23(1), 1996, p. 8.
41. B. Baldwin, 'Traditional and Cultural Aspects of Trobriand Islands Chiefs', *Canberra Anthropology* 14 (1), 1991, p. 84.
42. Young, 'The Careless Collector', in O'Hanlon and Welsch, *Hunting the Gatherers*, pp. 181–202.
43. *Coral Gardens*, vol. 1, pp. 461–2.
44. *Argonauts*, p. 16.
45. Fieldnotes, p. 804, MPLSE.
46. Ibid., p. 764.
47. Ibid., pp. 819ff. See *Sexual Life*, pp. 475–6.
48. Fieldnotes, p. 1545, MPLSE.
49. Kinship Boxes 127, MPLSE.
50. *Diary*, p. 130.
51. Fieldnotes, p. 1717, MPLSE.
52. B. Malinowski, *Crime and Custom in Savage Society*, London: Routledge, 1926, pp. 100–5. *Sexual Life*, pp. 10–13.
53. Brunton to Malinowski, 9 Jan. 1915, MPLSE.
54. Fieldnotes, pp. 873–4, MPLSE.
55. *Sexual Life*, p. 272.
56. Fieldnotes, p. 1001, MPLSE.
57. Ibid., p. 976.
58. Ibid., p. 1400. Malinowski referred to this 'house of prostitution' in *Sexual Life*, p. 234n, though he mistakenly located it on 'the southern shores of Normanby Island'. Sewa Bay is on the west of the island.
59. Fieldnotes, p. 1170, MPLSE.
60. Ibid., p. 1583.
61. *Diary*, p. 143. *Sexual Life*, pp. 91, 122, 316.
62. *Sexual Life*, p. 284,
63. Ibid., pp. 430–1.
64. Ibid., p. 316.

65. Brunton to Malinowski, 15 Aug. 1915, MPLSE.
66. Malinowski to Seligman, 30 July 1915, ibid.
67. Malinowski to Hunt, 16 Aug. 1915, MERNAA.
68. 15 Oct. 1915, ibid.
69. 16 Aug. 1915, ibid.
70. Malinowski to Seligman, 24 Sept. 1915, MPLSE. Diamond Jenness had also intended to study 'trade relations' between the islands of the Massim, including the Trobriands and Rossel (Field Programme, 27 May 1911, Jenness Papers, UDC/C/2/4, Bodleian Library, Oxford). His plans were thwarted by the unreliability of sea transport.
71. Seligman to Malinowski, 2 Dec. 1915, MPY I/565.
72. Malinowski to Seligman, 19 Oct. 1915, MPLSE.
73. Seligman to Malinowski, 30 Dec. 1915, MPY I/565.
74. Malinowski to Rivers, 15 Oct. 1915, HPCUL 129/12055.
75. Letter fragment, Haddon to Malinowski, 30 June 1915, MPLSE Culture 11/166.
76. Malinowski to Haddon, 15 Oct. 1915, HPCUL 5/7. (Later catalogue number is 7/8.)
77. Marjorie Peck to Malinowski, 18 Nov. 1915, MPY I/496.
78. Józefa Malinowska to Malinowski, April 1915, MPY I/407.
79. Józefa Malinowska to Malinowski, 20 Oct. 1915, ibid.
80. Józefa Malinowska to Malinowski, 28 Dec. 1915, ibid.
81. Józefa Malinowska to Malinowski, 3 Feb. 1916, ibid.
82. Józefa Malinowska to Malinowski, 31 March 1916, ibid.
83. Malinowski to Józefa Malinowska, probably Aug. 1915, MPY I/409.
84. Józefa Malinowska to Malinowski, 2 April 1916, MPY I/407.
85. Malinowski to Józefa Malinowska, 15 June 1915, MPY I/409.
86. Brunton to Malinowski, 15 Aug. 1915, MPLSE.
87. Brunton to Malinowski, 25 Oct. 1915, ibid.
88. *Diary*, p. 99.
89. ibid., p. 181.
90. Marjorie Peck to Malinowski, 18 Nov. 1915, MPY I/496.
91. Ibid.
92. Letter fragment, incorrectly dated 3 Feb. as the *Misima* sailed in early March. Verso of fieldnotes, Language Boxes, MPLSE.
93. Brunton to Malinowski, 22 Feb. 1916, MPLSE.

Chapter 21

1. The charts and related retrospective diary notes, all in Polish, were found among miscellaneous fieldnotes in MPY II/204. Unattributed quotations in this and the following chapter refer to these charts and diary notes. Basia Plebanek accomplished the heroic task of reading the barely legible pages and translating them into English.
2. Charles Hedley to Haddon, 9 May 1916, HPCUL 5/7.
3. Marnie Bassett (Masson) to Helena Burke 28 Sept. 1970.
4. Hunt to Secretary of Defence Department, 2 April (?) 1916, MERNAA.
5. Malinowski to Józefa Malinowska, 1 Nov. 1916, MPY I/409.
6. Malinowski to Józefa Malinowska, 15 July 1916, ibid.
7. Harriet Stirling to Malinowski, 12 Feb. 1916, MPY I/590.
8. Stirling to Malinowski, 2 April 1916, ibid.
9. Malinowski to the Stirlings, 12 June 1918, ibid.

10. Spencer to Haddon, 11 Nov. 1915, HPCUL Envelope 3.

11. Richard Broinowski, *A Witness to History: The Life and Times of Robert Broinowski*, Melbourne: Melbourne University Press, 2001.

12. *Australian Dictionary of Biography*, vol. 12, p. 435.

13. Mim's letter of invitation to Malinowski (dated 14 April 1916) refers only to her mother, MPLSE.

14. *Australian Dictionary of Biography*, vol. 12, p. 125.

15. Weigall to Helena Burke, 27 April 1971, MPLSE.

16. Weigall to Malinowski, 8 April 1918, ibid.

17. Elsie's diary-letter, in Wayne, *Story*, p. 1.

18. All unattributed quotations in this section are from the fragmentary diary notes written by Malinowski in Nov. 1917, MPY II/204.

19. Elsie R. Masson, *An Untamed Territory*, London: Macmillan, 1915.

20. Wayne, *Story*, p. 2.

21. Ibid., p. 3.

22. Elsie's diary-letter, MPLSE.

23. Wayne, *Story*, p. 6.

24. Seligman to Malinowski, 2 Dec. 1915, MPLSE.

25. John W. Bennett, *Classic Anthropology: Critical Essays, 1944–1996*, New Brunswick: Transaction Publishers, 1998, p. 173.

26. B. Malinowski, 'Baloma: The Spirits of the Dead in the Trobriand Islands', *JRAI* 46, 1916, p. 383n.

27. Clyde Kluckhohn, 'Bronislaw Malinowski', *Journal of American Folklore* 56, 1943, p. 214.

28. 'Baloma', pp. 381–2.

29. Ibid., p. 412.

30. Ibid., p. 414n.

31. Cf. G. W. Stocking, 'Contradicting the Doctor: Billy Hancock and the Problem of Baloma', *History of Anthropology Newsletter* 4 (1), 1977, pp. 4–7.

32. *Sexual Life*, 1932 edn, p. 152.

33. A. Weiner, *Women of Value, Men of Renown: New Perspectives on Trobriand Exchange*, St Lucia: University of Queensland Press, 1976.

34. 'Baloma', pp. 418–19.

35. Ibid., p. 423n.

36. *Crime and Custom*, p. 121.

37. Seligman to Malinowski, 6 July 1916, MPY I/565.

38. 'Baloma', p. 417.

39. Seligman to Malinowski, 12 Oct. 1916, MPY I/565.

40. Haddon to Malinowski, 4 Oct. 1916, MPLSE.

41. Seligman to Malinowski, 26 Oct. 1916, MPY I/565.

42. 'Baloma', p. 415n.

43. Frazer to Malinowski, 5 July 1917, MERNAA.

44. Malinowski to Frazer, 25 Oct. 1917. Frazer Papers, Trinity College, Cambridge, Ms.b.36/175.

45. Malinowski to Józefa Malinowska, 4 Aug. 1916, MPY I/409.

46. Spencer to Haddon, 11 Nov. 1915, HPCUL Envelope 3.

47. Spencer to Haddon, 2 Feb. 1916, ibid.

48. Seligman to Haddon, 24 Feb. 1916, HPCUL 5/7.

49. Seligman to Haddon, 26 March 1916, ibid.

50. MacTaggart to Haddon, 23 March 1916, ibid.

51. Seligman to Haddon, 24 and 31 March 1916, ibid.
52. Memo to Hunt confirming cables of 17 March 1916, MERNAA.
53. Strong to Seligman, 16 Jan. 1916, as cited in Seligman to Haddon, 26 March 1916, HPCUL 5/7.
54. Seligman to Malinowski, 3 March 1916, MPLSE. Fieldnotes, verso.
55. Herdman to Haddon, 9 April 1916, HPCUL 5/7.
56. Seligman to Haddon, 5 May 1916, ibid.
57. Seligman to Malinowski, 26 April 1916, MPLSE. Fieldnotes, verso.
58. Wayne, *Story*, p. 113.
59. Malinowski to Haddon, 25 May 1916, HPCUL 5/7.
60. Draft of letter to Seligman, probably 14 June 1916, MPY I/565.
61. Seligman to Malinowski, 15 Aug. 1916, ibid.
62. Spencer to Minister, 27 June 1916, MERNAA.
63. Murray to Minister, 29 June 1916, ibid.
64. Hunt to Minister, 31 July 1916; Minister's approval, 16 Aug. 1916, MERNAA.
65. Hunt to Spencer, 30 Aug. 1916, ibid.
66. Hunt to Murray, 8 Sept. 1916, ibid.
67. Murray to Hunt, 12 Sept. 1916, ibid.
68. Seligman to Malinowski, 16 Nov. 1916 (replying to Malinowski's of 26 Sept.), MPY I/565.
69. Murray to Minister of External Affairs, 10 Aug. 1916; Spencer to Hunt, 14 Sept. 1916, MERNAA.
70. Malinowski to Hunt, 29 Oct. 1916, ibid.
71. Murray, *Papua*, p. 125.
72. Malinowski paid him 4 guineas on 1 Sept. Verso notes on linguistics, MPLSE Ling. 178.
73. Brunton to Malinowski, 14 Aug. 1916, MPLSE.
74. Ibid.
75. Brunton to Malinowski, 25 Nov. 1916 and n.d. (probably Feb. 1917), ibid.
76. Brunton to Malinowski, 19 Sept. 1916, ibid.
77. Brunton to Malinowski, n.d. (probably Feb. 1917), ibid.
78. Malinowski to Józefa Malinowska, 1 Nov. 1916, MPY I/409.
79. Józefa Malinowska to Malinowski, 1 Nov. 1916; also 21 Dec. 1916, re. Witkiewicz, MPY I/407.
80. Józefa Malinowska to Malinowski, 29 Jan. 1917, MPY I/407.
81. B. Malinowski, 'Evidence by Bronislaw Malinowski, 27 October, 1916, on Pacific Labour Conditions', in *Parliament of the Commonwealth of Australia: British and Australian Trade in the South Pacific*. Report No. 66. Melbourne 1918.
82. Seligman to Malinowski, 12 Oct. 1916, MPY I/565.
83. Seligman to Malinowski, 9 Nov. 1916, ibid.
84. Spencer to Malinowski, 1 Jan. 1917, MPY I/460.
85. Malinowski to Elsie, 31 Dec. 1917, in Wayne, *Story*, p. 90.
86. Elsie's diary-letter, MPLSE. Also Wayne, *Story*, p. 6.

Chapter 22

1. Wayne, *Story*, p. 15.
2. Len Weickhardt, *Masson of Melbourne: The Life and Times of David Orme Masson*, Parkville, Victoria: Royal Australian Chemical Institute, 1989. Quotations in this section are from this source.

3. Wayne, *Story*, p. 98.
4. Memoir of Mim Weigall written for Helena Burke, 1973, MPLSE.
5. David Orme Masson (DOM) to Marnie Masson, 5 Feb. 1917, MPUMA.
6. Marnie to DOM, 18 June 1917. Cited by Weickhardt, *Masson*, p. 100.
7. DOM to Marnie, 15 Nov. 1917, MPUMA.
8. DOM to Marnie, 26 Nov. 1917, ibid.
9. DOM to Marnie, 29 Oct. 1917, ibid.
10. Marnie to DOM, 24 March 1918. Cited by Weickhardt, *Masson*, p. 101.
11. DOM to Marnie, 19 Feb. 1918, MPUMA.
12. Marnie to DOM, 13 Oct. 1918. Cited by Weickhardt, *Masson*, p. 102.
13. Marnie Bassett (Masson) to Helena Burke. 19 Dec. 1970.
14. Wayne, *Story*, pp. 7–8.
15. Seligman to Malinowski, 15 Aug. 1916, MPY I/565.
16. A substantial file on the Khuners was compiled by the Intelligence Section, General Staff, 3rd Military District (Victoria). NAA 15/3/133.
17. Wayne, *Story*, p. 8.
18. Ibid., p. 9.
19. Ibid., p. 16.
20. P. Khuner to Malinowski, 4 Feb. 1918, MPLSE.
21. Mim Weigall to Malinowski, 11 Feb. 1918, ibid.
22. Wayne, *Story*, p. 44.
23. H. Khuner to Malinowski, 26 Jan. 1918, MPLSE.
24. P. Khuner to Malinowski, 16 March 1918, ibid.
25. Wayne, *Story*, p. 11.
26. Ibid., p. 9.
27. Ibid., p. 11.
28. Elsie's diary-letter, 1916–17, MPLSE.
29. Ibid.
30. Ibid.
31. Wayne, *Story*, p. 18.
32. Ibid.
33. Ibid., p. 24.
34. MFNAA.
35. Wayne, *Story*, p. 19.
36. Ibid., pp. 14–15.
37. Seligman to Malinowski, 5 July 1917, MPY I/565.
38. Elsie Masson to Malinowski, 7 Aug. 1917, MPLSE.
39. B. Malinowski, 'The Papuo-Melanesians', in *The Australian Encyclopaedia*, vol. 2, Sydney: Angus and Robertson, 1926, pp. 260–2.
40. See Young, *Malinowski's Kiriwina*, p. 25.
41. MPLSE Coral Gardens Boxes, p. 446.
42. Wayne, *Story*, p. 13.
43. Ibid., p. 20.
44. *Coral Gardens*, vol. 1, p. 480.
45. Ibid., p. 481.
46. It was left to Leo Austen, an anthropologically trained resident magistrate in the Trobriands during the 1930s, to write 'Cultural Changes in Kiriwina' (*Oceania* 16 [1], 1945, pp. 15–60).

47. Seligman to Malinowski, 18 Jan. 1917, MPY I/565.
48. B. Malinowski, 'Classificatory Particles in the Language of Kiriwina', *Bulletin of the School of Oriental Studies* 1 (4), 1922, p. 74.
49. *Coral Gardens*, vol. 1, p. 453.
50. Wayne, *Story*, p. 23.
51. *Diary*, p. 105.
52. Hunt to Malinowski, 5 Oct. 1917, MERNAA.
53. *Diary*, p. 106.
54. Stawell to Hunt, 16 Oct. 1917, MPY I/281.
55. *Diary*, p. 107. Wayne, *Story*, pp. 25–6.

Chapter 23

1. Wayne, *Story*, pp. 29–30.
2. Meyers, *Joseph Conrad*, p. 85. Joseph Conrad, 'Geography and Some Explorers' (1924), in Joseph Conrad, *Last Essays*, London: J.M. Dent, 1926, pp. 18–21.
3. Wayne, *Story*, pp. 30–1.
4. Ibid., p. 32.
5. See Ackerman, *Frazer*, pp. 266–7. Frazer to Malinowski, 5 July 1917, MERNAA.
6. Malinowski to Frazer, 25 Oct. 1917, Frazer Papers, Trinity College, Cambridge, Ms.b.36/175.
7. *Argonauts*, pp. 308–9.
8. See M.W. Young, 'The Theme of the Resentful Hero: Stasis and Mobility in Goodenough Mythology', in J. W. Leach and E. R. Leach (eds), *The Kula: New Perspectives on Massim Exchange*, Cambridge: Cambridge University Press, 1983, pp. 383–94.
9. *Argonauts*, p. 6.
10. Wayne, *Story*, p. 34.
11. Malinowski to Elsie Masson, 23 Dec. 1917, MPLSE.
12. Wayne, *Story*, p. 47.
13. Ibid., p. 46. *Diary*, p. 108.
14. Wayne, *Story*, p. 35.
15. Strong to Malinowski, 7 May 1916, MPY I/595.
16. Strong to Malinowski, April 1918, ibid.
17. Wayne, *Story*, p. 35.
18. Ibid., p. 35.
19. Ibid., p. 47.
20. Diary notes, Nov. 1917, MPY II/202. Translation by B. Plebanek.
21. Wayne, *Story*, p. 45.
22. Ibid., p. 51.
23. Ibid., pp. 44–5.
24. P. Khuner to Malinowski, 5 Dec. 1917, MPLSE.
25. H. Khuner to Malinowski, 6 Dec. 1917, ibid.
26. Wayne, *Story*, p. 49.
27. *Diary*, p. 113.
28. Wayne, *Story*, p. 50.
29. Ibid., p. 48.
30. *Diary*, p. 123.

31. Wayne, *Story*, p. 47.
32. Ibid., p. 48.
33. *Diary*, pp. 124–5.
34. Wayne, *Story*, p. 63.
35. *Diary*, p. 116. Guterman mistranslates it as 'tortoise-shell mania'.
36. Ibid., p. 126. Italicized phrase in English.
37. A. C. Haddon, *The Decorative Art of British New Guinea: A Study in Papuan Ethnography*, Dublin: Royal Irish Academy, 1894.
38. Guterman transposed Malinowski's dates for the benefit of American readers, so the published diary has 11.10.17, etc.
39. *Diary*, p. 109.
40. Ibid., p. 110.
41. Ibid., p. 114.
42. Ibid., p. 121.
43. Ibid., p. 130. Guterman has: 'Of course, training myself to keep a diary affects my way of living.'
44. Wayne, *Story*, pp. 94–5.
45. Verso note dated 1.1.18. At the back of Malinowski's 1917–18 diary there are about a dozen pages of notes that were not included in the published version of *A Diary in the Strict Sense of the Term*. I refer to these notes as 'verso'.
46. Wayne, *Story*, p. 54.
47. Ibid., p. 50.
48. Ibid., p. 64.
49. Ibid.
50. Ibid.
51. *Diary*, p. 127.
52. Ibid., pp. 130–1, 135.
53. Ibid., p. 132. B. Plebanek's translation of omissions.
54. Ibid., p. 123. B. Plebanek's translation of omissions.
55. Wayne, *Story*, p. 53.
56. Ibid., p. 54.
57. Ibid.
58. Malinowski to Elsie Masson, 6 Aug. 1917, MPLSE.
59. *Diary*, p. 121.
60. Wayne, *Story*, p. 66.
61. In truth, Flo Gofton was far from being wasted. She already had two young children and much later, as 'Ma Stewart' of the Wau Hotel, would become a matriarch of the Morobe goldfields. Jan Roberts, *Voices from a Lost World: Australian Women and Children in Papua New Guinea before the Japanese Invasion*, Alexandria, N.S.W.: Millennium Books, 1996, pp. 50–1, 196.
62. Wayne, *Story*, p. 66.
63. Elsie Masson to Malinowski, 27 Dec. 1917, MPLSE.
64. *Diary*, pp. 169, 266, 196.
65. C. A. Verebelyi to Minister for Internal Affairs, 18 Jan. 1917, NAA G76-19-1917.
66. Hubert Murray to May Murray, 30 April 1918, Gilbert Murray Papers, Bodleian Library, Oxford.
67. *Diary*, pp. 133–6. Italicized sentence in English.
68. Ibid., p. 111.
69. Ibid., p. 127.

70. Wayne, *Story*, p. 61.
71. *Diary*, p. 119.
72. See George Stocking's perceptive footnote on this passage in 'Anthropology and the Science of the Irrational: Malinowski's Encounter with Freudian Psychoanalysis', in HOA 4, pp. 26–7.
73. Malinowski to Government Secretary of Papua and Atlee Hunt, 26 Dec. 1917, MERNAA.
74. Malinowski to Elsie Masson, 23 Dec. 1917, MPLSE.
75. Hunt to Minister, 18 Jan. 1918, MERNAA.
76. Wayne, *Story*, pp. 67–8.
77. Ibid., p. 52.
78. Ibid., p. 55, with additional text from Elsie's letter of 25 Nov. MPLSE.
79. *Argonauts*, pp. 38–48.
80. Ibid., p. 298.
81. Ibid., pp. 331–2.
82. *Diary*, p. 140. Guterman's translation omits the ironic quotation marks.
83. Ibid., p. 142.

Chapter 24

1. Wayne, *Story*, p. 81.
2. Hancock to Malinowski, 1 Dec. 1916, MPY I/245.
3. *Diary*, p. 148.
4. Ibid., p. 144.
5. Ibid., p. 145.
6. For a further selection, see 'Picturing the Ethnographer', in Young, *Malinowski's Kiriwina.*
7. *Argonauts*, p. xvii. *Sexual Life*, pp. 247, lxxxvii.
8. Bashkow, ' "To Be his Witness" '.
9. *Argonauts*, p. 5.
10. Wayne, *Story*, p. 187.
11. Ibid., p. 106.
12. *Diary*, p. 18
13. Hancock to Malinowski, 8 Feb. 1919, MPY I/245.
14. *Diary*, p. 165.
15. Malinowski to Elsie Masson, 28 May 1918, MPLSE.
16. Wayne, *Story*, p. 83, omissions restored.
17. *Diary*, p. 146.
18. Personal communication, Linus Digim'Rina.
19. Wayne, *Story*, p. 83.
20. Ibid.
21. Hancock to Malinowski, 8 Feb. 1919, MPY I/245.
22. *Coral Gardens*, vol. 1, pp. 19–20.
23. Wayne *Story*, p. 78.
24. *Coral Gardens*, vol. 1, p. 453.
25. Wayne, *Story*, p. 80. *Diary*, p. 156.
26. See *Coral Gardens*, vol. 1, pp. 233–9, 291.
27. Wayne, *Story*, p. 84.
28. *Diary*, p. 179.

29. Wayne, *Story*, p. 80.
30. *Diary*, pp. 155ff.
31. Wayne, *Story*, p. 84. *Diary*, p. 157.
32. Ibid., pp. 79–80.
33. Ibid., p. 85. Young, *Malinowski's Kiriwina*, plates 75 and 76.
34. *Diary*, p. 163.
35. Wayne, *Story*, p. 82.
36. Józefa Malinowska to Malinowski, 4 and 6 Dec. 1917, MPY I/407.
37. *Diary*, p. 167.
38. Ibid.
39. Ibid., pp. 167–8.
40. Malinowski to Elsie Masson, 28 Dec. 1917, MPLSE.
41. Wayne, *Story*, p. 80.
42. Ibid., p. 91.
43. *Diary*, p. 175. Italicized lines are in English.
44. Ibid., p. 185.
45. Malinowski, 'Introduction', in R. F. Fortune, *Sorcerers of Dobu: The Social Anthropology of the Dobu Islanders of the Western Pacific*, London: Routledge, 1932, p. xviii.
46. *Diary*, p. 155. Italicized phrase in English.
47. Baron Nikolai Miklouho-Maclay, *New Guinea Diaries 1871–1883*, trans. C. L. Sentinella, Madang. Kriston Press, 1975. These diaries were not accessible to Malinowski during his lifetime.
48. *Diary*, p. 161.
49. Malinowski, 'Introduction', in J. E. Lips, *The Savage Hits Back*, New Haven: Yale University Press, 1937, p. vii.
50. Personal communication, Linus Digim'rina, Nov. 2001.
51. B. Malinowski, 'Myth in Primitive Psychology', *Psyche Miniatures*, London: Routledge, 1926, in Malinowski, *Magic, Science and Religion*, p. 140.
52. Ibid., p. 85.
53. Ibid., p. 76.
54. Ibid., p. 87.
55. B. Malinowski, *The Foundations of Faith and Morals* (1936), republished in *Sex, Culture, and Myth*, p. 324.
56. Ibid., p. 332n.
57. *Diary*, p. 172.
58. Ibid., p. 186.
59. Ibid., p. 176.
60. Ibid., p. 161.
61. 'Introduction', in Fortune, *Sorcerers*, p. xvii.
62. *A Scientific Theory of Culture*, p. 36.
63. *Diary*, p. 187.
64. Ibid., p. 185, Wayne, *Story*, p. 104.
65. *Diary*, p. 156.
66. Malinowski to Elsie Masson, 13 Feb. 1918, MPLSE.
67. *Diary*, p. 156.
68. Ibid., p. 204.
69. Ibid., pp. 151–2.
70. Fieldnotes, MPLSE 11/166.

71. Wayne, *Story*, p. 91.
72. Ibid., p. 92.
73. Ibid.
74. *Diary*, p. 175.
75. Ibid., p. 177.
76. Wayne, *Story*, p. 103.
77. *Diary*, p. 192. Italicized phrase in English.
78. Ibid., p. 194.
79. Ibid.
80. Wayne, *Story*, p. 107.
81. Ibid., pp. 107–8.
82. *Diary*, p. 195. Italicized phrase in English.
83. Ibid.
84. Ibid., p. 160.
85. Wayne, *Story*, pp. 75–6.
86. *Diary*, p. 197. Translation amended by B. Plebanek. Italicized phrase in English.
87. Ibid., p. 199.
88. Ibid., p. 202.
89. Ibid., p. 208. Italicized phrase in English.
90. Wayne, *Story*, p. 109.
91. *Diary*, pp. 200–2. Italicized phrase in English.
92. Wayne, *Story*, p. 104.
93. See *Sexual Life*, p. 364. Young, *Malinowski's Kiriwina*, pp. 110–11.
94. *Diary*, p. 204.
95. Ibid., p. 206.
96. Malinowski to Elsie Masson, 21 Feb. 1918, MPLSE. See Wayne, *Story*, p. 111.
97. Elsie Masson to Malinowski, 10 April 1918, MPLSE.
98. Malinowski to Elsie Masson, 21 Feb. 1918, ibid.
99. Malinowski to Elsie Masson, 21 Feb. 1918, ibid.
100. Wayne, *Story*, pp. 111–12.
101. Malinowski to Elsie Masson, 22 Feb. 1918, MPLSE.
102. Wayne, *Story*, p. 113.
103. *Diary*, p. 209.
104. Ibid., p. 194.
105. Malinowski to Elsie Masson, 8 Jan. 1918, MPLSE. See Wayne, *Story*, p. 93.
106. P. Khuner to Malinowski, 24 Jan. 1918, MPLSE.
107. *Diary*, p. 194.
108. Weigall to Malinowski, 9 April 1918, MPLSE.
109. Weigall to Malinowski, 27 May 1918, ibid.
110. *Diary*, p. 178.
111. Ibid.
112. Wayne, *Story*, p. 95.
113. Ibid., p. 98.
114. *Diary*, p. 242.
115. Wayne, *Story*, p. 93 (11 Jan. 1918).
116. *Coral Gardens*, vol. 1, p. 480.
117. *Diary*, p. 179.
118. Ibid., p. 180.

119. Ibid., pp. 160–1.
120. Ibid., p. 174.
121. Wayne, *Story*, p. 86.
122. Malinowski to Elsie Masson, 15 Jan. 1918, MPLSE.
123. Wayne, *Story*, p. 88.
124. Ibid., p. 89.
125. Malinowski to Elsie Masson, 2–9 Feb. 1918, MPLSE. See Wayne, *Story*, pp. 108–10.
126. Wayne, *Story*, p. 113.
127. Malinowski to Elsie Masson, 21 Feb. 1918, MPLSE. See Wayne, *Story*, p. 112.
128. *Diary*, p. 220.
129. Personal communication, Aug. 1995.
130. *Diary*, pp. 210, 211, 217.
131. *Sexual Life*, plate 32.
132. See Wayne, *Story*, p. 128.
133. See Young, *Malinowski's Kiriwina*, Plate 14.

Chapter 25

1. Wayne, *Story*, p. 94.
2. *Argonauts*, p. 267.
3. Malinowski to Elsie Masson, 15 March 1918, MPLSE. See Wayne, *Story*, p. 115.
4. Elsie Masson to Malinowski, 30 April 1918, MPLSE.
5. *Argonauts*, p. 233; see also p. 377.
6. Malinowski to Elsie Masson, 15 March 1918, MPLSE.
7. Malinowski to Elsie Masson, 17 March 1918, ibid.
8. Fortune, *Sorcerers of Dobu*, p. 280. Linus S. Digim'Rina, 'Gardens of Basima: Land Tenure and Mortuary Feasting in a Matrilineal Society', PhD thesis, Australian National University, Canberra, 1995.
9. *Diary*, pp. 225–6.
10. *Argonauts*, p. 287.
11. Ibid., p. 270.
12. *Diary*, p. 230. Italicized phrases in English.
13. Ibid., p. 229.
14. Elsie Masson to Malinowski, 19 Jan. 1918, in Wayne, *Story*, p. 100.
15. Elsie Masson to Malinowski, 29 Jan. 1918, ibid.
16. Malinowski to Elsie Masson, 15 March 1918, ibid., p. 114.
17. Elsie Masson to Malinowski, 30 April 1918, MPLSE. Although Elsie was destined never to do fieldwork and never to set foot in the Trobriands, Art would imitiate Life imitating Art. Eighty years later, an Australian feature film, *In a Savage Land*, was made about a young couple from Adelaide who, in the months before the Japanese invasion of New Guinea, embark on fieldwork in Kiriwina, deliberately following in Malinowski's footsteps. After quarrelling with her husband, the beautiful anthropology student does independent research on another island, and by the end of the film – with her husband dead, buried and lavishly mourned, and her pearl-trader lover posted missing in the war – she has written a book about her experiences, *In a Savage Land*. Bill and Jennifer Bennett, the husband-and-wife team who wrote and directed this 1999 feature film, could have had no knowledge of Elsie's letter.
18. *Diary*, p. 237.
19. Ibid., p. 181.

20. Ibid., pp. 230–2. Italicized sentence in English.

21. Ibid., pp. 234–5.

22. Ibid., p. 236.

23. He reproduced the conversation between Tovasana and the visitors in *Argonauts*, pp. 270–2.

24. *Diary*, p. 237.

25. Ibid., p. 238.

26. Ibid., p. 239.

27. Wayne, *Story*, p. 122.

28. Elsie Masson to Malinowski, 30 April 1918, MPLSE.

29. *Argonauts*, p. 385.

30. Ibid., p. 284.

31. Ibid., p. 386.

32. Ibid., p. 387.

33. *Diary*, p. 244.

34. *Argonauts*, p. 390. His first estimate for Elsie was a thousand. Wayne, *Story*, p. 124.

35. *Diary*, p. 244.

36. Wayne, *Story*, p. 124.

37. Ibid., pp. 123–4.

38. *Argonauts*, chapter XVI.

39. *Diary*, p. 247.

40. Ibid., pp. 247–8.

41. Malinowski to Elsie Masson, 12 April 1918, in Wayne, *Story*, p. 126.

42. Ibid.

43. Elsie Masson to Malinowski, 19 May 1918, MPLSE.

44. Wayne, *Story*, p. 126.

45. Ibid., pp. 123–5.

46. Ibid., p. 127.

47. Cited by Bashkow, ' "To Be his Witness" '

48. *Diary*, p. 244.

49. Ibid., p. 250.

50. Malinowski to Elsie Masson, 16 April 1918, MPLSE.

51. *Diary*, p. 251.

52. Ibid., p. 253.

53. Wayne, *Story*, p. 128.

54. Ibid., p. 133.

55. Later researchers, Shirley Campbell in Vakuta and Giancarlo Scoditti in Kitava, have revealed an intricate web of meanings based on natural symbols and 'spiritual' values. See S. F. Campbell, *The Art of Kula*, Oxford: Berg, 2002 and G. Scoditti, *Fragmenta Ethnographica*, Rome: Giancarlo Serafini Editore, 1980.

56. *Diary*, p. 253.

57. Wayne, *Story*, p. 135. See *Diary*, p. 255.

58. B. Malinowski, 'Ethnology and the Study of Society', *Economica* 2, Oct. 1922.

59. *Diary*, p. 255.

60. Ibid., p. 256. Italicized phrase in English.

61. Ibid., p. 84. (See above, Chapter 18.)

62. Ibid., pp. 12–13.

63. Ibid., p. 257.

64. Ibid., p. 259.

65. Wayne, *Story*, p. 130.
66. *Diary*, pp. 261–2. Italicized phrases in English.
67. Malinowski to Elsie Masson, 24 April 1918, MPLSE.
68. Elsie Masson to Malinowski, 1 June 1918, MPLSE.
69. Malinowski to Elsie Masson, 4 July 1918, ibid.
70. Ibid.
71. Wayne, *Story*, p. 136. *Diary*, verso notes, 5 May 1918.
72. Wayne, *Story*, pp. 145–6 (14 May 1918).
73. Ibid., p. 136.
74. *Diary*, pp. 264, 265, 268.

Chapter 26

1. *Diary*, p. 259.
2. Malinowski to Elsie Masson, 10 April 1918, MPLSE.
3. Malinowski to Elsie Masson, 20 May 1918, ibid.
4. *Diary*, p. 269. Italicized phrase in English.
5. See Young, *Malinowski's Kiriwina*, chapter 11.
6. *Sexual Life*, pp. 44–6. 'Baloma', p. 428.
7. *Diary*, p. 272.
8. Ibid., pp. 280–1. Italicized phrase in English.
9. Ibid., p. 273. Italicized word in English.
10. Malinowski to Elsie Masson, 14 May 1918, MPLSE.
11. *Diary*, p. 274. Italicized phrase in English.
12. Ibid., p. 275.
13. Malinowski to Elsie Masson, 14 May 1918, MPLSE.
14. Ibid. (Wayne, *Story*, p. 147, with elisions restored).
15. Malinowski to Elsie Masson, 24 May 1918, in Wayne, *Story*, p. 150.
16. Malinowski to Elsie Masson, 14 May 1918, MPLSE.
17. *Diary*, p. 276.
18. Ibid., p. 277
19. Malinowski to Elsie Masson, 23 May 1918. See Wayne, *Story*, p. 149.
20. *Diary*, p. 278.
21. Malinowski to Elsie Masson, 24 May 1918. See Wayne, *Story*, p. 149.
22. *Diary*, p. 280.
23. Brenda Seligman to Malinowski, 19 March 1918, MPLSE.
24. Malinowski to Brenda Seligman, 21 June 1918, ibid.
25. Malinowski to Elsie Masson, 30 May 1918, ibid. *Diary*, p. 284.
26. *Diary*, p. 284.
27. Ibid., p. 286.
28. Ibid., verso notes, 2 June 1918.
29. Ibid., p. 290. Italicized phrases in English.
30. Ibid., p. 289. Italicized phrase in English.
32. Malinowski to Elsie Masson, 7 June 1918. See Wayne, *Story*, p. 151.
32. Wayne, *Story*, p. 153.
33. *Diary*, p. 290.
34. Wayne, *Story*, pp. 153–5.
35. Ibid., p. 156.

36. Elsie Masson to Malinowski, 21 Aug. 1918. See Wayne, *Story*, p. 164.
37. P. Khuner to Malinowski, 17 Aug. 1918, MPLSE.
38. Malinowski to Seligman, 21 June 1918, MPY I/565.
39. Malinowski to Haddon, 25 June, HPCUL Envelope 7. Cited by Mulvaney and Calaby, '*So Much That Is New*', p. 326.
40. Seligman to Malinowski, 24 Oct. 1918, MPY I/565.
41. Mulvaney and Calaby, '*So Much That Is New*', p. 325.
42. Elsie Masson to Malinowski, 10 April 1918, MPLSE.
43. Elsie Masson to Malinowski, 14 April 1918, in Wayne, *Story*, p. 142.
44. Elsie Masson to Malinowski, 14–16 April 1918, ibid., pp. 141–2.
45. Elsie Masson to Malinowski, 8 and 11 July 1918, MPLSE.
46. Malinowski to Elsie Masson, 12 June 1918, ibid.
47. Malinowski to Elsie Masson, 2 July 1918, ibid.
48. Malinowski to Elsie Masson, 4 July 1918, in Wayne, *Story*, p. 161.
49. Elsie Masson to Malinowski, 21 Aug. 1918, MPLSE.
50. Elsie Masson to Malinowski, 17 Aug. 1918, ibid. See also Wayne, *Story*, p. 163.
51. *Coral Gardens*, vol. 1, pp. 181–7.
52. *Diary*, p. 292.
53. Malinowski to Elsie Masson, 19 June 1918, MPLSE. See also Wayne, *Story*, p. 157.
54. Wayne, *Story*, p. 158.
55. *Diary*, p. 292.
56. Ibid., p. 293.
57. Ibid., p. 295.
58. Malinowski to Elsie Masson, 2 July 1918, in Wayne, *Story*, pp. 159–61.
59. Ibid.
60. *Diary*, p. 294.
61. Wayne, *Story*, p. 168.
62. Ibid., p. 170.
63. Ibid.
64. Malinowski to Elsie Masson, 24 Aug. 1918, MPLSE.
65. Wayne, *Story*, p. 172.
66. Hancock to Elsie Masson, 9 Feb. 1919, MPY I/704.

Chapter 27

1. Malinowski to Elsie Masson, 3–10 Oct. 1918, MPLSE. See also Wayne, *Story*, pp. 174ff.
2. Wayne, *Story*, p. 174.
3. Ibid., p. 177. Hancock to Malinowski, 5 Nov. 1918, MPY I/245.
4. Malinowski to Seligman, n.d. (Oct. 1918), MPY I/565.
5. Malinowski to Elsie Masson, 3–10 Oct. 1918, MPLSE. See Wayne, *Story*, p. 176.
6. Elsie Masson to Malinowski, 7 Aug. 1918, MPLSE.
7. Malinowski to Elsie Masson, 3–10 Oct. 1918, ibid.
8. Malinowski to Elsie Masson, 11 Oct. 1918, MPY I/673.
9. Elsie Masson to Malinowski, 6 Oct. 1918, MPLSE.
10. Malinowski to Elsie Masson, 24 May 1918, ibid.
11. Mary Masson to Malinowski, 20 Oct. 1918, MPY I/421.
12. D.O.M. to Malinowski, 18 Oct. 1918, Wayne, *Story*, pp. 177–8.
13. Hunt to Malinowski, 28 Oct. 1918, MPY I/281.

14. Elton Mayo to Malinowski, 6 and 23 Nov. 1918, MPY I/427.
15. Seligman to Malinowski, 2 Dec. 1918, MPY I/565.
16. Seligman to Malinowski, 21 Dec. 1918, ibid.
17. Seligman to Malinowski, 24 Oct. 1918, ibid.
18. Malinowski to Elsie Masson, 7 Aug. 1918, MPLSE. See Wayne, *Story*, p. 171. Wissler to Malinowski, 13 Nov. 1918, MPY I/14.
19. Malinowski to Seligman, 21 Jan. 1919. MPY I/565.
20. Malinowski to Mond, 21 Jan. 1919, MPY I/439.
21. Mond to Malinowski, 8 April 1919, ibid.
22. BAAS, *Handbook to Victoria*, Melbourne: Government Printer, 1914, p. 26.
23. Citations in this section are from Elsie's letters to Malinowski, 6–27 Feb. 1919, MPLSE. See Wayne, *Story*, pp. 179–86.
24. Malinowski to Elsie Masson, 5 Feb. 1918, MPLSE. See Wayne, *Story*, p. 109.
25. Elsie Masson to Malinowski, 8 Feb. 1919, MPLSE.
26. Wayne, *Story*, p. 183.
27. Ibid., p. 184.
28. Elsie Masson to Malinowski, n.d. 1918, MPLSE.
29. Wayne, *Story*, p. 184.
30. Elsie Masson to Malinowski, 20 and 22 Feb. 1919, MPLSE. See also Wayne, *Story*, p. 185.
31. Wayne, *Story*, p. 185.
32. Elsie Masson to Malinowski, 26 Feb. 1919, MPLSE.
33. Marnie Bassett to Helena Burke, 9 Aug. 1967; Orme Masson to Marnie, 16 Jan. 1917; MPUMA.
34. Wayne, *Story*, p. 183.
35. Ibid., p. 186.
36. Marnie Bassett to Helena Burke, 28 April 1954.
37. Marnie Bassett to Helena Burke, 28 Sept. 1970.
38. Wayne, *Story*, p. 186. Also Elsie Masson to Malinowski, 23 Feb. 1919, MPLSE.
39. MPY I/325. The undated, one-page draft was archived with Khuner correspondence because Malinowski wrote it as from the Khuners' address in Victoria Parade. Its content allows it to be dated precisely to 5–6 March 1919.
40. J. Lemmon to Elsie Masson, 23 April 1919, MPLSE Loose Fieldnotes 287. 'At a later date,' Malinowski wrote in *Argonauts* (p. 232n), 'I hope to work out certain historical hypotheses with regard to migration and cultural strata in eastern New Guinea.'
41. 'Sociological & Anthropological Notes,' MPLSE Culture III.

Chapter 28

1. Marnie Bassett to Helena Burke, 28 Sept. 1970.
2. Although undated except by day of the week, these letters cover the period 15–22 June 1919; MPLSE.
3. E. Pitt to Malinowski, 24 June 1919, MPLSE Fieldnotes, verso letter.
4. Malinowski to Military Controller, 6 July 1919, MFNAA. Malinowski to Minister for Home and Territories, 7 July 1919, MPLSE Language Box, verso letter.
5. Marnie Bassett to Helena Burke, 5 Oct. 1970.
6. *Argonauts*, pp. 23–4.
7. Alan Gardiner to Malinowski, 8 Jan. 1918, MPY I/676.
8. *Argonauts*, p. 24. A footnote on the same page refers to Gardiner's letter.

9. MPLSE, Loose Fieldnotes, 288.

10. These letters cover the period 27–31 July 1919; MPLSE.

11. D. Hooper to Elsie Malinowska, 5 Aug. 1919, MPLSE Fieldnotes. Verso letter.

12. Malinowski to Polish Consul, 9 Aug. 1919, ibid.

13. Seligman to Malinowski, Jan. 1920, ibid.

14. Melbourne Public Library to Malinowski, 29 Oct. and 7 Nov. 1919, MPLSE Language Box, verso letters.

15. Published as 'Classificatory Particles in the Language of Kiriwina', *Bulletin of the School of Oriental Studies* 1 (4), 1922, pp. 33–78. All quotations in this section are from this article.

16. See Gunter Senft, *Classificatory Particles in Kilivila*, Oxford: Oxford University Press, 1996, pp. 315–22.

17. Malinowski to Paul Khuner, 25 Jan. 1920; Elsie Malinowska to the Khuners, 12 Jan. 1920; MPLSE.

18. Malinowski to Paul Khuner, 25 Jan. 1920, ibid.

19. Malinowski to Spencer, 18 Oct. 1918 and 6 Nov. 1918, MPY I/460.

20. Spencer to Malinowski, 9 Nov. 1918, ibid.

21. *Diary*, p. 170.

22. Malinowski to Spencer, 18 Dec. 1918, MPY I/460.

23. Seligman to Malinowski, 21 Dec. 1918, MPY I/565.

24. Malinowski to Spencer, 17 Feb. 1920, MPY I/460.

25. J. Kershaw, 'Trustees Report of the National Museum, Melbourne', *Victorian Parliamentary Papers*, 10 March 1920, p. 473.

26. Elsie Malinowska to the Khuners, 12 Jan. 1920, MPLSE.

27. Malinowski to Paul Khuner, 25 Jan. 1920, ibid.

28. Elsie Malinowska to Malinowski, 27 Jan. 1920; Malinowski to Elsie Malinowska, 28 Jan. 1920; ibid.

29. Elsie Malinowska to the Khuners, 12 Jan. 1920, ibid.

30. Marnie Bassett to Helena Burke, 28 Sept. 1970.

31. Elsie Malinowska to the Khuners, 29 April 1920, MPLSE.

32. Elsie Malinowska to the Khuners, 15 May 1920, ibid.

33. Seligman to Malinowski, 6 Jan. 1920, ibid.

34. Malinowski to Hunt, 24 Feb. 1920, MERNAA.

Bibliography

Manuscript Sources

Atlee Hunt Papers, National Library of Australia
'Dr B. Malinowski, Ethnological Research, Papua', 1914–20, A1 21/866, National Archives of Australia
F. E. Williams Papers, Papua New Guinea National Archives, Port Moresby
Frazer Papers, Trinity College, Cambridge
Gilbert Murray Papers, Bodleian Library, Oxford
Haddon Papers, University Library, Cambridge
Jenness Papers, Bodleian Library, Oxford
J. P. H. Murray Papers, National Library of Australia
Malinowski File, Intelligence Section, General Staff, 3rd Military District (Victoria), 15/3/406, National Archives of Australia
Malinowski Papers, British Library of Political and Economic Science, London School of Economics
Malinowski Papers, Yale University Library, New Haven
Masson Papers, University of Melbourne Archives
National Archives of Australia, Canberra
National Library of Australia, Canberra
National Museum of Australia, Melbourne
Saville Papers, Mitchell Library, Sydney
Seligman Papers, British Library of Political and Economic Science, London School of Economics
South Africa Union Education Department, State Archives, Pretoria
Stirling Papers, Matlock Library, Adelaide
Westermarck Archive, Åbo Akademi, Turku, Finland
Witkiewicz Letters, Tatra Museum, Zakopane

References Cited and Select Bibliography

The most complete and accessible bibliography of Malinowski's writings can be found in R. Ellen et al (eds), *Malinowski between Two Worlds* (1988). See also R. Firth (ed.), *Man and Culture* (1957) and R. Thornton and P. Skalník (eds), *The Early Writings of Bronislaw Malinowski* (1993). A new edition of Malinowski's *Collected Works* has been published in ten volumes by Routledge (2002). It comprises most of his books but very few of his articles and other publications. Beginning in 1980, Malinowski's collected works have been appearing in *Dzieła* (Works), published in Warsaw by Państwowe Wydawnictwo Naukowe.

Ackerman, Robert. *J. G. Frazer: His Life and Work*. Cambridge: Cambridge University Press, 1987.

Allen, Michael. 'Some Extracts from John Layard's Previously Unpublished "The Story of my Life" ', *Australian Anthropological Society Newsletter* 73, Sept. 1998.

Asermely, A. 'Directing Pure Form: "The Pragmatists" ', *PR* 18 (2), 1973.

Ashley Montagu, M. F. *Coming into Being Among the Australian Aborigines*. London: Routledge, 1937.

———. Review of H. Wayne (ed.), *The Story of a Marriage*, in *Nature* 374, April 1995.

Austen, Leo. 'Cultural Changes in Kiriwina', *Oceania* 16 (1), 1945.

Austin-Broos, D. (ed.). *Creating Culture: Profiles in the Study of Culture*. Sydney: Allen & Unwin, 1987.

Australian Dictionary of Biography. Vol. 12, 1891–1939. Ed. J. Richie. Carlton: Melbourne University Press, 1990.

BAAS. *Notes and Queries on Anthropology*. 4th edition. London: Routledge, 1912.

———. *Handbook to Victoria*. Melbourne: Government Printer, 1914.

———. *Report on the 84th Meeting, Australia 1914, July 28–August 31*. London: John Murray, 1915.

Baer, Joachim T. 'Wacław Berent: A Writer for our Time', *PR* 37 (2), 1992.

———. 'Nietzsche and Polish Modernism', *PR* 38 (1), 1993.

Baker, Stuart. 'Witkiewicz and Malinowski: The Pure Form of Magic, Science and Religion', *PR* 18 (1–2), 1973.

Baldwin, B. 'Traditional and Cultural Aspects of Trobriand Islands Chiefs', *Canberra Anthropology* 14 (1), 1991.

Balfour, H., R. R. Marett and W. H. R. Rivers (eds). *Anthropological Essays Presented to Edward Burnett Tylor in Honour of his 75th Birthday*. London: Routledge, 1907.

Barnes, J. A. 'Introduction', in B. Malinowski, *The Family among the Australian Aborigines*. New York: Schocken Books, 1963.

Bashkow, Ira. ' "To Be his Witness If That Was Ever Necessary": Raphael Brudo on Malinowski's Fieldwork and Trobriand Ideas of Conception', *History of Anthropology Newsletter* 23 (1), 1996.

Bellamy, R. L. 'Notes on the Customs of the Trobriand Islander', *Papua Annual Report*. 1907–08.

Bennett, John W. *Classic Anthropology: Critical Essays, 1944–1996*. New Brunswick: Transaction Publishers, 1998.

Benthall, Jonathan. 'That Tent', *AT* 16 (3), June 2000.

Black, Robert H. 'Dr Bellamy of Papua', *The Medical Journal of Australia* 11 (6), 24 Aug. 1957.

Blackmore, J. *Ernst Mach: His Life, Work and Influence*. Berkeley: University of California Press, 1972.

Boring, Edwin G. 'Wundt, Wilhelm', *International Encyclopedia of the Social Sciences*, vol. 16. London: Macmillan, 1968.

Borowska, Ewa. 'Lata polskiej młodości Bronisława Malinowskiego', MA thesis. Jagiellonian University, Cracow, 1971.

Broinowski, Richard. *A Witness to History: The Life and Times of Robert Broinowski*. Melbourne: Melbourne University Press, 2001.

Bücher, Karl. *Arbeit und Rhythmus*. Leipzig: Teubner, 1899.

Campbell, Shirley F. *The Art of Kula*. Oxford: Berg, 2002.

Cech, Krystyna. 'Malinowski: Edgar, Duke of Nevermore', *JASO* 12 (3), 1981.

Clifford, James. 'On Ethnographic Self-Fashioning: Conrad and Malinowski', in T. Heller et al (eds), *Reconstructing Individualism: Autonomy, Individuality and the Self in Western Thought*. Stanford: Stanford University Press, 1986.

Clifford, J. and G. Marcus (eds). *Writing Culture: The Poetics and Politics of Ethnography*. Berkeley: University of California Press, 1986.

Collini, Stefan. *Liberalism and Sociology: L.T. Hobhouse and Political Argument in England 1880–1914*. Cambridge: Cambridge University Press, 1979.

Collins D. and J. Urry, 'A Flame Too Intense for Mortal Body to Support', *AT* 13 (6), 1997.

Conrad, John. *Joseph Conrad: Times Remembered*. Cambridge: Cambridge University Press, 1981.

Conrad, Joseph. 'The Return', in *Tales of Unrest*. London: J.M. Dent, 1947 (1897).

———. *The Heart of Darkness*. London: J. M. Dent, 1946 (1899).

———. *The Mirror of the Sea*. London: J.M. Dent, 1946 (1906).

———. *A Personal Record*. London: J.M. Dent, 1946 (1912).

———. 'Geography and Some Explorers', in Joseph Conrad, *Last Essays*. London: J.M. Dent, 1926 (1924).

———. *The Collected Letters of Joseph Conrad*. Vol. 5, 1912–16. Eds. F. Karl and L. Davies. Cambridge: Cambridge University Press, 1996.

——— and Ford Maddox Hueffer. *Romance*. London: J.M. Dent, 1949 (1903).

Crawley, Ernest. A. *The Mystic Rose: A Study of Primitive Marriage and of Primitive Thought in its Bearing on Marriage*. London: Methuen, 1902. (Enlarged edition by T. Besterman, 1965.)

Czaplicka, Maria. *Aboriginal Siberia: A Study in Social Anthropology*. Oxford: Clarendon, 1914.

Dahrendorf, Ralf. *L.S.E.: A History of the London School of Economics and Political Science, 1895–1995*. Oxford: Oxford University Press, 1995.

Davies, Norman. *Heart of Europe: A Short History of Poland*. Oxford: Oxford University Press, 1986.

Digim'Rina, Linus S. 'Gardens of Basima: Land Tenure and Mortuary Feasting in a Matrilineal Society', PhD thesis, Australian National University, Canberra, 1995.

Dubowski, Adam. 'Z tradycji rodzinnej' (From a Family Tradition), *Tygodnik Powszechny*, 8 April 1984.

Durkheim, Emile. *The Elementary Forms of the Religious Life*. Trans. J.W. Swain. London: Allen & Unwin, 1915 (1912).

Ellen, Roy. 'Poles Apart: Some Reflections on the Contemporary Image of Malinowski in his Homeland', *AT* 1(1), 1985.

———, E. Gellner, G. Kubica and J. Mucha (eds). *Malinowski between Two Worlds: The Polish Roots of an Anthropological Tradition*. Cambridge: Cambridge University Press, 1988.

Elliot Smith, Grafton. 'Preface', in W. H. R. Rivers, *Psychology and Ethnology*. London: Routledge, 1926.

Estreicher, Karol. 'Zakopane – Leur Amour', *Polish Perspectives* 14 (6), Warsaw, 1971.

———. *Leon Chwistek – biografia artysty*. Kraków: Państwowe Wydawnictwo Naukowe, 1971.

Firth, J. R. 'Ethnographic Analysis and Language with Special Reference to Malinowski's Views', in R. Firth (ed.), *Man and Culture*, 1957.

Firth, Raymond (ed.). *Man and Culture: An Evaluation of the Work of Bronislaw Malinowski*. London: Routledge, 1957.

———. 'Introduction: Malinowski as Scientist and Man', in R. Firth (ed.), *Man and Culture*. 1957.

―――. 'A Brief History of the Department (1913–63)', Pamphlet Published by the Department of Anthropology, LSE, 1963.

―――. 'Seligman's Contributions to Oceanic Anthropology', *Oceania* 45 (4), 1975.

―――. 'Bronislaw Malinowski', in S. Silverman (ed.), *Totems and Teachers: Perspectives on the History of Anthropology*. New York: Columbia University Press, 1981.

―――. 'Malinowski in the History of Anthropology', in R. Ellen et al (eds), *Malinowski between Two Worlds*, 1988.

―――. 'Second Introduction', in B. Malinowski, *A Diary in the Strict Sense of the Term*. Stanford: Stanford University Press, 1988.

Flis, Andrzej. 'Bronislaw Malinowski's Cracow Doctorate', in R. Ellen et al (eds), *Malinowski between Two Worlds* (Appendix 1), 1988.

―――. 'Cracow Philosophy of the Beginning of the Twentieth Century and the Rise of Malinowski's Scientific Ideas', in R. Ellen et al (eds), *Malinowski between Two Worlds*, 1988.

Forge, Anthony W. 'The Lonely Anthropologist', *New Society* 255, 1967.

Fortune, Reo, F. *Sorcerers of Dobu: The Social Anthropology of the Dobu Islanders of the Western Pacific*. London: Routledge, 1932.

Frazer, James G. *Totemism and Exogamy: A Treatise on Certain Early Forms of Superstition and Society*. 4 vols. London: Macmillan, 1910.

―――. *The Golden Bough: A Study in Magic and Religion*. Abridged edition. London: Macmillan, 1922.

Fustel de Coulanges, N. D. *The Ancient City: A Study on the Religion, Laws, and Institutions of Greece and Rome*. Trans. W. Small. New York: Doubleday, n.d. [1864].

Gardiner, Alan H. 'Some Thoughts on the Subject of Language', *Man* 19, 1919.

Geertz, Clifford. 'Under the Mosquito Net', *New York Review of Books*, 14 Sept. 1967.

―――. *Works and Lives: The Anthropologist as Author*. Stanford: Stanford University Press, 1988.

Gellner, Ernest. 'Malinowski and the Dialectic of Past and Present', *The Times Literary Supplement*. 7 June 1985.

―――. 'The Political Thought of Bronislaw Malinowski', *Current Anthropology* 28 (4), 1987.

―――. '"Zeno of Cracow" or "Revolution at Nemi" or "The Polish Revenge: A Drama in Three Acts"', in R. Ellen et al (eds), *Malinowski between Two Worlds*, 1988.

―――. 'James Frazer and Cambridge Anthropology', in R. Mason (ed.), *Cambridge Minds*. Cambridge: Cambridge University Press, 1994.

―――. *Language and Solitude: Wittgenstein, Malinowski and the Habsburg Dilemma*. Cambridge: Cambridge University Press, 1998.

Gerould, Daniel. 'Review Article: Witkacy's Portrait of the Artist as a Young Man', *PR* 18 (2), 1973.

―――. (ed.). *The Witkiewicz Reader*. Evanston, Ill.: Northwestern University Press, 1992.

―――. 'Witkacy's Journey to the Tropics and Itinerary in Ceylon', *Konteksty* 54 (1–4), Warszawa: Instytut Sztuki Polskiej Akademii Nauk, 2000.

Gide, André. *Journals 1889–1949*. Harmondsworth: Penguin Books, 1967.

Gilmour, Rev. M. 'A Few Notes on the Kiriwina (Trobriand Islands) Trading Expeditions', in *British New Guinea Annual Report*. 1904–05.

Girard, René. *Deceit, Desire and the Novel*. Baltimore: Johns Hopkins Press, 1965.

Givner, Joan. *Katherine Anne Porter: A Life*. New York: Simon and Schuster, 1982.

Grimble, Arthur. *A Pattern of Islands*. London: John Murray, 1952.

Gross, Feliks. 'Young Malinowski and his Later Years', *American Ethnologist* 13 (3), 1986.

Haddon, Alfred C. *The Decorative Art of British New Guinea: A Study in Papuan Ethnography*. Dublin: Royal Irish Academy, 1894.

————. *The Study of Man*. London: Bliss, 1898.

————. *Head-Hunters: Black, White and Brown*. London: Methuen, 1901.

————. (ed.). *Reports of the Cambridge Anthropological Expedition to Torres Straits*. 6 vols. Cambridge: Cambridge University Press, 1901–35.

Hailey, Lord. 'Introduction', in L. P. Mair, *Australia in New Guinea*. London: Christophers, 1948.

Heller, T. et al (eds). *Reconstructing Individualism: Autonomy, Individuality and the Self in Western Thought*. Stanford, Stanford University Press, 1986.

Herle, Anita and Sandra Rouse (eds). *Cambridge and the Torres Strait: Centenary Essays on the 1898 Anthropological Expedition*. Cambridge: Cambridge University Press, 1998.

Hiatt, L. R. *Arguments about Aborigines: Australia and the Evolution of Social Anthropology*. Cambridge: Cambridge University Press, 1996.

Hobhouse, Leonard T. *Morals in Evolution: A Study in Comparative Ethics*. London: Chapman & Hall, 1951 (1906).

Holroyd, Michael. *Bernard Shaw: The Search for Love, 1856–1898*. Harmondsworth: Penguin, 1988.

James, William. *The Principles of Psychology*. 2 vols. London: Constable, 1890.

————. *The Varieties of Religious Experience*. London: Collins, 1960 (1902).

Jenness, D. and A. Ballantyne. *The Northern D'Entrecasteaux*. Oxford: Clarendon, 1920.

Jerschina, Jan. 'Polish Culture of Modernism and Malinowski's Personality', in R. Ellen et al (eds), *Malinowski between Two Worlds*, 1988.

Kaberry, Phyllis M. 'Malinowski's Contribution to Fieldwork Methods and the Writing of Ethnography', in R. Firth (ed.), *Man and Culture*, 1957.

Kardiner, A. and E. Preble. 'Bronislaw Malinowski: The Man of Songs', in A. Kardiner and E. Preble, *They Studied Man*. London: Secker & Warburg, 1961.

Karl, Fredrick R. *Joseph Conrad: The Three Lives*. London: Faber & Faber, 1979.

Kershaw, J. 'Trustees Report of the National Museum, Melbourne', *Victorian Parliamentary Papers*, 10 March 1920.

Kluckhohn, Clyde. 'Bronislaw Malinowski', *Journal of American Folklore* 56, 1943.

Koepping, Klaus-Peter. ' "Tolilibogwo" Malinowski: Master of Myth or Narcissist?', *Journal of Humanities and Social Sciences* 7, Nagoya City University, 1999.

Kridl, Manfred. *A Survey of Polish Literature and Culture*. Gravenhage: Mouton & Co., 1956.

Kubica, Grażyna. 'Bronislaw Malinowski's Years in Poland', *JASO* 17 (2), 1986.

————. 'Malinowski's Years in Poland', in R. Ellen et al (eds), *Malinowski Between Two Worlds*, 1988.

————. 'Six Letters from Malinowski', in R. Ellen et al (eds), *Malinowski Between Two Worlds* (Appendix 2), 1988.

Kuper, Adam. *Anthropologists and Anthropology: The Modern British School*. London: Routledge, 1973.

————. *The Invention of Primitive Society: Transformations of an Illusion*. London: Routledge, 1988.

Kuper, A. and Kuper, J. (eds). *The Social Science Encyclopedia*. London: Routledge, 1997.

Kuper, Hilda. *Sobhuza II: Ngwenyama and King of Swaziland*. London: Duckworth, 1978.

L.S.E. Calendars 1909–14. British Library of Political and Economic Science.

Langmore, Diane. *Missionary Lives: Papua, 1874–1914*. Honolulu: University of Hawaii Press, 1989.

Laracy, Hugh M. 'Malinowski at War, 1914–18', *Mankind* 10, 1976.

Last, Peter M. 'Stirling and the Biology of the Family', 47th Edward Stirling Memorial Lecture. Unpublished TS. Medical Sciences Club of South Australia, Adelaide, 1986.

Leach, Edmund R. 'The Epistemological Background to Malinowski's Empiricism', in R. Firth (ed.), *Man and Culture*, 1957.

———. 'W. H. R. Rivers', in *International Encyclopedia of the Social Sciences*. Vol. 13. London: Macmillan, 1968.

Leach, J. W. and E. R. Leach (eds). *The Kula: New Perspectives on Massim Exchange*. Cambridge: Cambridge University Press, 1983.

Lévi-Strauss, Claude. *Totemism*. Trans. Rodney Needham. Boston: Beacon Press, 1963.

Lips, J. E. *The Savage Hits Back*. New Haven: Yale University Press, 1937.

Łopaciński, Hieronim. 'Lucjan Malinowski (1839–1898)', *Kurjer Niedzielny*, Warsaw, 1898.

Lowie, Robert H. *The History of Ethnological Theory*. New York: Farrar & Rinehart, 1937.

Mach, Ernst. *Popular Scientific Lectures*. Trans. T. J. McCormack. La Salle, Ill.: Open Court, 1943 (1895).

———. *Knowledge and Error: Sketches on the Psychology of Inquiry*. Trans. T. J. McCormack and P. Foulkes. Dordrecht: D. Reidel, 1976 (1905).

———. *The Analysis of Sensations and the Relation of the Physical to the Psychical*. New York: Dover Publications, 1959 (1906).

Mackay, Kenneth. *Across Papua*. London: Witherby, 1909.

Mair, L. P. *Australia in New Guinea*. London: Christophers, 1948.

Malinowski, Bronislaw. 'O zasadzie ekonomii myślenia' (On the Principle of the Economy of Thought), PhD thesis, Jagiellonian University, 1906. (Published in *Dzieła*, vol 1, 1980, also in R. Thornton and P. Skalník (eds), *The Early Writings of Bronisław Malinowski*, 1993.)

———. Review of J. Matthew, *Two Representative Tribes of Queensland*, in *Man* 10, 1910.

———. 'Totemism and Exogamy (1911–13)', in R. Thornton and P. Skalník, (eds), *The Early Writings of Bronisław Malinowski*, 1993.

———. Review of G. C. Wheeler, *The Tribal and Inter-Tribal Relations in Australia*, in *Man* 11, 1911.

———. Review of *Kwartalnik Etnograficzny*, *Lud* vol. 16, 1910, in *Folk-lore* 22, 1911.

———. 'Tribal Male Associations of the Australian Aborigines' (1912), in R. Thornton and P. Skalník (eds), *The Early Writings of Bronisław Malinowski*, 1993.

———. 'The Economic Aspects of the *Intichiuma* Ceremonies' (1912), in R. Thornton and P. Skalník, *The Early Writings of Bronisław Malinowski*, 1993.

———. 'Observations on Friedrich Nietzsche's *The Birth of Tragedy*' (1912), in R. Thornton and P. Skalník (eds), *The Early Writings of Bronisław Malinowski*, 1993.

———. *The Family among the Australian Aborigines: A Sociological Study*. London: University of London Press, 1913.

———. Review of W. B. Spencer and F. J. Gillen, *Across Australia*, in *Folk-lore* 24, 1913.

———. Review of E. Durkheim, *Les formes élémentaires de la vie religieuse: le système totémique en Australie*, in *Folk-lore* 24 (4), 1913. (Reprinted in *Sex, Culture, and Myth*. 1963.)

———. Review of H. Webster, *Rest Days: A Sociological Study*, in *Man* 14, March 1914.

———. 'Sociology of the Family' (1913–14), in R. Thornton and P. Skalník (eds), *The Early Writings of Bronisław Malinowski*, 1993.

———. 'A Fundamental Problem of Religious Sociology', in BAAS, *Report on the 84th Meeting*, 1914. (Reprinted in R. Thornton and P. Skalník (eds), *The Early Writings of Bronisław Malinowski*, 1993.)

———. *Wierzenia pierwotne i formy ustroju społecznego* (Primitive Beliefs and Forms of Social Organization). Kraków, 1915. (Reprinted in *Dzieła*. Vol. 1. Warszawa: Państwowe Wydawnictwo Naukowe, 1980.)

———. *The Natives of Mailu*, in *Transactions of the Royal Society of South Australia* 39, 1915. (Reprinted in Michael W. Young, *Malinowski among the Magi*, 1988.)

————. 'Baloma: The Spirits of the Dead in the Trobriand Islands', *JRAI*, 46, 1916. (Reprinted in *Magic, Science and Religion*, 1948.)

————. 'Evidence by Bronislaw Malinowski, 27 October 1916, on Pacific Labour Conditions' in *Parliament of the Commonwealth of Australia: British and Australian Trade in the South Pacific.* Report No. 66. Melbourne, 1918.

————. 'Fishing and Fishing Magic in the Trobriand Islands', *Man* 18, 1918.

————. 'War and Weapons among the Natives of the Trobriand Islands', *Man* 20, 1920.

————. 'Kula: The Circulating Exchange of Valuables in the Archipelagoes of Eastern New Guinea', *Man* 20, 1920.

————. *Argonauts of the Western Pacific: An Account of Native Enterprise and Adventure in the Archipelagoes of Melanesian New Guinea.* London: Routledge, 1922.

————. 'Classificatory Particles in the Language of Kiriwina', *Bulletin of the School of Oriental Studies* 1 (4), 1922.

————. Review of W. McDougall, *The Group Mind*, in *Man* 21, 1921.

————. 'Ethnology and the Study of Society', *Economica* 2, Oct. 1922.

————. 'Sexual Life and Marriage among Primitive Mankind' (review of E. Westermarck, *The History of Human Marriage*), *Nature* 109, 22 April 1922. (Reprinted in *Sex, Culture, and Myth*, 1963.)

————. 'The Problem of Meaning in Primitive Languages', in C. K. Ogden and I. A. Richards (eds), *The Meaning of Meaning*. London: Routledge, 1923. (Reprinted in *Magic, Science and Religion*. 1948.)

————. 'Magic, Science and Religion', in J.A. Needham (ed). *Science, Religion and Reality*, London: Macmillan, 1925. (Reprinted in *Magic, Science and Religion*, 1948.)

————. 'Anthropology', in the *Encyclopedia Britannica*. 13th edition, supplement 1, London, 29–30, 1926.

————. *Crime and Custom in Savage Society.* London: Routledge, 1926.

————. 'The Papuo-Melanesians', *The Australian Encyclopaedia*. Vol. 2. Sydney: Angus & Robertson, 1926.

————. 'Myth in Primitive Psychology', in C. K. Ogden (ed.), *Psyche Miniatures*. London: Routledge, 1926. (Reprinted in *Magic, Science and Religion*, 1948.)

————. 'Foreword', in W. J.V. Saville, *In Unknown New Guinea*. London: Seeley Service, 1926.

————. 'Anthropology of the Westernmost Orient' (Review of E. Westermarck, *Ritual and Belief in Morocco*), *Nature* 120, 17 Dec. 1927.

————. *Sex and Repression in Savage Society.* London: Routledge, 1927.

————. Review of E. Crawley, *The Mystic Rose*, in *Nature* 121, 1928. (Reprinted in *Sex, Culture, and Myth*, 1963.)

————. *The Sexual Life of Savages in Northwestern Melanesia.* London: Routledge, 1929. (Third edition with 'Special Foreword', 1932.)

————. 'Parenthood – The Basis of Social Structure', in V. F. Calverton and S. D. Schmalhausen (eds), *The New Generation*, New York: The Macauley Co. 1930. (Reprinted in *Sex, Culture, and Myth*. London: Rupert Hart-Davies, 1963).

————. 'Science and Religion', *The Listener* 4 (94), 1930. (Reprinted in *Sex, Culture, and Myth*, 1963.)

————. 'Culture', in the *Encylopaedia of the Social Sciences*. Vol. 4. New York, 1931.

————. 'Introduction', in R.F. Fortune, *Sorcerers of Dobu*. London: Routledge, 1932.

————. *Coral Gardens and their Magic: A Study of the Methods of Tilling the Soil and of Agricultural Rites in the Trobriand Islands.* Vol. 1: *The Description of Gardening*. Vol. 2: *The Language of Magic and Gardening*. London: Allen & Unwin, 1935.

————. *The Foundations of Faith and Morals.* London: Oxford University Press, 1936. (Reprinted in *Sex, Culture, and Myth,* 1963.)

————. 'Foreword', in Ashley Montagu, *Coming into Being among the Australian Aborigines.* London: Routledge, 1937.

————. 'Introduction', in J. E. Lips, *The Savage Hits Back.* New Haven: Yale University Press, 1937.

————. Review of J. G. Frazer, *Totemica: A Supplement to Totemism and Exogamy,* in *Nature* 141, March 1938. (Reprinted in *Sex, Culture, and Myth,* 1963).

————. *A Scientific Theory of Culture and Other Essays.* Chapel Hill: University of North Carolina Press, 1944.

————. 'Sir James George Frazer: A Biographical Appreciation', in *A Scientific Theory of Culture,* 1944.

————. *Freedom and Civilization.* New York: Roy Publishers, 1944. (Also London: Allen & Unwin, 1947.)

————. *Magic, Science and Religion, and Other Essays.* Ed. R. Redfield. Boston: Beacon Press, 1948.

————. 'Myth as a Dramatic Development of Dogma', in *Sex, Culture, and Myth,* 1963.

————. *Sex, Culture, and Myth.* London: Rupert Hart-Davies, 1963.

————. *A Diary in the Strict Sense of the Term.* Trans. N. Guterman. London: Routledge, 1967. (Reprinted by Stanford University Press, 1988.)

————. *Dziennik w ścisłym znaczeniu tego wyrazu.* Ed. Grażyna Kubica. Kraków: Wydawnictwo Literackie, 2000.

Mann, Thomas. *Death in Venice.* Harmondsworth: Penguin Books, 1955 (1912).

Marett, R. R. 'Obituary for Maria Czaplicka', *Man* 21, 1921.

————. Address in *Professor Bronislaw Malinowski: An Account of the Memorial Meeting Held at the Royal Institution in London on July 13th 1942.* Association of Polish University Professors and Lecturers in Great Britain. London: Oxford University Press, 1943.

Mason, Richard (ed.). *Cambridge Minds.* Cambridge University Press, 1994.

Masson, Elsie R. *An Untamed Territory.* London: Macmillan, 1915.

Matlakowski, Władysław. 'Wolni słuchacze w krakowie', *Za i przeciw* 38, 17 Sept. 1967.

Mead, Margaret. *An Anthropologist at Work: Writings of Ruth Benedict.* London: Secker & Warburg. 1959.

Métraux, Rhoda. 'Malinowski, Bronislaw', *International Encyclopedia of the Social Sciences* 9, London: Macmillan, 1968.

Meyers, Jeffrey. *Joseph Conrad: A Biography.* London: John Murray, 1991.

Micińska, Anna. *Witkacy: Life and Work.* Trans. Bogna Piotrowska. Warsaw: Interpress Publishers, 1990.

Mikloucho-Maclay, Baron Nikolai, *New Guinea Diaries 1871–1883.* Trans. C. L. Sentinella. Madang: Kristen Press, 1975.

Monk, Ray. *Bertrand Russell: The Spirit of Solitude.* London: Jonathan Cape, 1996.

Morgane, Ted. *Maugham: A Biography.* New York: Simon & Schuster, 1980.

Mulvaney, D. J. and J. H. Calaby, *'So Much That Is New': Baldwin Spencer 1860–1929.* Melbourne: Melbourne University Press, 1985.

Murdock, George P. 'Bronislaw Malinowski', *American Anthropologist* 45, 1943.

Murray, J. H. P. *Papua or British New Guinea.* London: T. Fisher Unwin, 1912.

Myers, C. S. 'Charles Gabriel Seligman, 1873–1940', *Royal Society Obituary Notices, 1939–41,* vol. 3.

Najder, Zdzisław. (ed.). *Conrad's Polish Background: Letters to and from Polish Friends.* Oxford: Oxford University Press, 1964.

———. *Conrad under Familial Eyes.* Cambridge: Cambridge University Press, 1983.

———. *Joseph Conrad. A Chronicle.* New Brunswick, N.J.: Rutgers University Press, 1983.

Needham, J. A. (ed.). *Science, Religion and Reality.* London: Macmillan, 1925.

Nelson, Hank. 'European Attitudes in Papua, 1906–1914', in *The History of Melanesia.* Second Waigani Seminar. Port Moresby: University Press; N.G. and Canberra: R.S.Pac.S., 1969.

Newton, Henry. *In Far New Guinea.* London: Seeley Service, 1914.

Nietzsche, Friedrich. *Thus Spake Zarathustra.* Trans. A. Tille and M. M. Bozman. London: Everyman's Library, J.M. Dent, 1950 (1883–1891).

———. *The Birth of Tragedy.* Trans. W. Kaufmann. In *Basic Writings of Nietzsche.* New York: The Modern Library, 1968 (1872).

———. *The Will to Power.* Trans. W. Kaufmann. New York: Vintage Books, 1968 (1901).

Norick, Frank A. 'An Analysis of the Material Culture of the Trobriand Islands Based on the Collection of Bronislaw Malinowski', PhD thesis, University of California, 1976.

Ogden, C. K. and I. A. Richards (eds). *The Meaning of Meaning.* London: Routledge, 1923.

O'Hanlon, M. and R. Welsch (eds). *Hunting the Gatherers: Ethnographic Collectors, Agents and Agency in Melanesia, 1870s–1930s.* Oxford: Berghahn Books, 2000.

Paluch, Andrzej. 'The Polish Background of Malinowski's Work', *Man* 16 (2), 1981.

———. 'Introduction: Bronislaw Malinowski and Cracow Anthropology', in R. Ellen et al (eds), *Malinowski between Two Worlds,* 1988.

Panoff, Michel. *Bronislaw Malinowski.* Paris: Payot, 1972.

Papua Annual Reports, Melbourne: Government Printer.

Payne, Harry C. 'Malinowski's Style', *Proceedings of the American Philosophical Society* 125, 1981.

Pearson, Karl. *The Grammar of Science.* London: Blackwell, 1900.

Pratt, Mary Louise. 'Fieldwork in Common Places', in J. Clifford and G. Marcus (eds), *Writing Culture: The Poetics and Politics of Ethnography.* Berkeley: University of California Press, 1986.

Powdermaker, Hortense. 'Further Reflections on Lesu and Malinowski's Diary', *Oceania* 40 (4), 1970.

Pynsent, Robert B. (ed.), *Decadence and Innovation: Austro-Hungarian Life and Art at the Turn of the Century.* London: Weidenfeld and Nicholson, 1989.

Quiggin, A. Hingston. *Haddon the Head Hunter.* Cambridge: Cambridge University Press, 1942.

Radcliffe-Brown, A. R. Review of B. Malinowski, *The Family among the Australian Aborigines,* in *Man* 14, Feb. 1914.

Rapport, Nigel. 'Surely Everything Has Already Been Said About Malinowski's Diary!', *AT* 6 (1), 1990.

Ray, Sidney H. Review of B. Malinowski, *The Natives of Mailu,* in *Nature* 100, 1917.

Redfield, Robert. 'Introduction', in B. Malinowski, *Magic, Science and Religion, and Other Essays,* Boston: Beacon Press, 1948.

Retinger, Joseph. *Conrad and his Contemporaries.* New York: Roy Publishers, 1943.

———. *Memoirs of an Eminence Grise.* Ed. John Pomian. Sussex: Sussex University Press, 1972.

Richards, Audrey. 'Bronislaw Kasper Malinowski', *Man* 43, 1943.

———. 'The Founding Fathers of Social Science: Malinowski, 1884–1942', *New Society* 41, 1963.

————. 'In Darkest Malinowski', *The Cambridge Review*, 19 Jan. 1968.

Richards, Graham. 'Getting a Result: The Expedition's Psychological Research 1898–1913', in A. Herle and S. Rouse (eds), *Cambridge and the Torres Strait*, Cambridge: Cambridge University Press, 1998.

Rivers, W. H. R. 'A Genealogical Method of Collecting Social and Vital Statistics', *JRAI* 30, 1900.

————. *The Todas*. London: Macmillan, 1906.

————. 'The Genealogical Method of Anthropological Inquiry', *Sociological Review* 3, 1910.

————. 'The Ethnological Analysis of Culture', *Science* 34, 1911. (Reprinted in *Psychology and Ethnology*, 1926.)

————. 'Anthropological Research outside America', in *Reports on the Present Condition and Future Needs of the Science of Anthropology*. Washington D.C.: Carnegie Institute, 1913.

————. 'Survival in Sociology', *Sociological Review* 6, 1913.

————. *The History of Melanesian Society*. 2 vols. Cambridge: Cambridge University Press, 1914.

————. 'Sociology and Psychology', *Sociological Review* 9, 1916.

————. 'On the Repression of War Experience', *The Lancet*, 2 Feb. 1918.

————. *Conflict and Dream*, London: Kegan Paul, 1923.

————. *Psychology and Ethnology*. Ed. G. Elliot Smith. London: Kegan Paul, 1926.

————. *Kinship and Social Organization*. London: Athlone Press, 1968.

Roberts, Jan. *Voices from a Lost World: Australian Women and Children in Papua New Guinea before the Japanese Invasion*. Alexandria, N.S.W.: Millennium Books, 1996.

Rubinstein, Arthur. *My Young Years*. London: Jonathan Cape, 1973.

Russell, Bertrand. *Portraits from Memory and Other Essays*, London: Allen & Unwin, 1956.

Saville, W. J. V. 'A Grammar of the Mailu Language, Papua', *JRAI* 42, 1912.

————. *In Unknown New Guinea*. London: Seeley Service, 1926.

Schneider, David. 'Rivers and Kroeber in the Study of Kinship', in W. H. R. Rivers, *Kinship and Social Organization*. London: Athlone Press, 1968.

Scoditti, Giancarlo. *Fragmenta Ethnographica*. Rome: Giancarlo Serafini Editore, 1980.

Scott, Ernest. *Australia during the War.* Sydney: Angus & Robertson, 1937.

Segel, Harold B. ' "Young Poland", Cracow and the "Little Green Balloon" ', *PR* 5 (2), 1960.

Seligmann, C. G. *The Melanesians of British New Guinea*. Cambridge: Cambridge University Press, 1910.

Senft, Gunter. *Classificatory Particles in Kilivila*. Oxford: Oxford University Press, 1996.

Silverman, S. (ed.). *Totems and Teachers: Perspectives on the History of Anthropology*. New York: Columbia University Press, 1981.

Skalník, Peter. 'Bronislaw Kasper Malinowski and Stanisław Ignacy Witkiewicz', in H. F. Vermeulen and A. A. Roldán (eds), *Fieldwork and Footnotes: Studies in the History of European Anthropology*. London: Routledge, 1995.

Skidelsky, Robert. *John Maynard Keynes: Hopes Betrayed, 1883–1920*. London: Macmillan, 1983.

Slobodin, Richard. *W. H. R. Rivers*. New York: Columbia University Press, 1978.

Sochacka, Stanisław (ed.). *Listy Lucjana Malinowskiego do Jarosława Golla*, Opolu: Wydawnictwo Instytutu Śląskiego, 1975.

Spencer, B. and F. J. Gillen, *Across Australia*. London: Macmillan, 1912.

Spencer, W. Baldwin and F .J. Gillen. *The Native Tribes of Central Australia*. London: Macmillan, 1899.

————. *Native Tribes of the Northern Territory of Australia*. London: Macmillan, 1914.

Spradley, J. P. *Participant Observation*. New York: Holt Rinehart & Winston, 1980.

Średniawa, B. 'The Anthropologist as a Young Physicist: Bronislaw Malinowski's Apprenticeship', *Isis* 72, 1981.

Staniforth Smith, M. *Handbook of the Territory of Papua*. 2nd edition. Melbourne: J. Kemp, 1909.

Stirling, E. C. and F. J. Gillen. 'Part IV, Anthropology', in B. Spencer (ed.), *Report on the Work of the Horn Scientific Expedition to Central Australia*. London: Dulau and Co., 1896.

Stocking, George W., Jr. 'Empathy and Antipathy in the Heart of Darkness', in R. Darnell (ed.), *Readings in the History of Anthropology*. London: Harper & Row, 1974 (1968).

———. 'Contradicting the Doctor: Billy Hancock and the Problem of Baloma', *History of Anthropology Newsletter* 4 (1), 1977.

———. 'The Ethnographer's Magic: Fieldwork in British Anthropology from Tylor to Malinowski', in *HOA*. Vol. 1. Madison: University of Wisconsin Press, 1983.

———. 'Anthropology and the Science of the Irrational: Malinowski's Encounter with Freudian Psychoanalysis', in *HOA*. Vol. 4. Madison: University of Wisconsin Press, 1986.

———. 'Maclay, Kubary, Malinowski: Archetypes from the Dreamtime of Anthropology', in *HOA*. Vol. 7. Madison: University of Wisconsin Press, 1991.

———. *After Tylor: British Social Anthropology 1888–1951*. Madison: University of Wisconsin Press, 1995.

Stroup, Timothy. 'Edvard Westermarck: A Reappraisal', *Man* 19 (4), 1984.

———. 'Westermarck, Edvard Alexander', in C. Winters (ed.), *International Dictionary of Anthropologists*. New York: Garland Publishing, 1991.

Stuart, Ian. *Port Moresby: Yesterday and Today*. Sydney: Pacific Publications, 1970.

Sutton, Denys. 'Tancred Borenius: Connoisseur and Clubman', *Apollo Magazine*, April 1978.

Symmons-Symonolewicz, K. 'Bronislaw Malinowski: An Intellectual Profile', *PR* 3 (4), 1958.

———. 'Bronislaw Malinowski: Formative Influences and Theoretical Evolution', *PR* 4 (4), 1959.

———. 'Bronislaw Malinowski: Individuality as a Theorist', *PR* 5 (1), 1960.

———. 'The Origin of Malinowski's Theory of Magic', *PR* 5 (4), 1960.

———. 'The Ethnographer and his Savages: An Intellectual History of Malinowski's Diary', *PR* 27 (1–2), 1982.

Szymański, Józef (ed.). *Herbarz sredniowiecznego rycerstwa polskiego*. Warszawa: Wydawnictwo Naukowe PWN, 1992.

Sztaba, Wojciech. *Stanisław Ignacy Witkiewicz*, Warszawa: Auriga, 1985.

Tate, Allen. 'Our Cousin, Mr Poe', in A. Tate *The Man of Letters in the Modern World*. London: Meridian Books/Thames & Hudson, 1957.

Thompson, Christina A. 'Anthropology's Conrad', *JPH* 30 (1), 1995.

Thornton, Robert J. ' "Imagine Yourself Set Down. . . ." ': Mach, Frazer, Conrad, Malinowski and the Role of the Imagination in Ethnography', *AT* 1 (5), 1985.

——— and Peter Skalník (eds), *The Early Writings of Bronisław Malinowski*. Trans. Ludwik Krzyżanowski. Cambridge: Cambridge University Press, 1993.

Urry, James. '*Notes and Queries on Anthropology* and the Development of Field Methods in British Anthropology, 1870–1920', in James Urry, *Before Social Anthropology*, 1993 (1972).

———. 'A History of Field Methods', in R. Ellen (ed.), *Ethnographic Research*. London: Academic Press, 1984.

———. *Before Social Anthropology: Essays on the History of British Anthropology*. Switzerland: Harwood Academic Publishers, 1993.

———. 'Item #[4]355: Malinowski's Tent', *AT* 12 (5), Oct. 1996.

Vermeulen, H. F. and A. A. Roldán (eds). *Fieldwork and Footnotes: Studies in the History of European Anthropology*. London: Routledge, 1995.

Wax, Murray L. 'Tenting with Malinowski', *American Sociological Review* 37, 1978.

Wayne, Helena. 'Bronislaw Malinowski: The Influence of Various Women on his Life and Works', *JASO* 15(3), 1984. (Reprinted in *American Ethnologist* 12, 1985.)

———— (ed). *The Story of a Marriage: The Letters of Bronislaw Malinowski and Elsie Masson.* 2 vols. London: Routledge, 1995.

Webster, Hutton. *Rest Days: A Sociological Study.* Lincoln: University of Nebraska, 1911.

Weickhardt, Len. *Masson of Melbourne: The Life and Times of David Orme Masson.* Parkville, Victoria: Royal Australian Chemical Institute, 1989.

Weiner, Annette B. *Women of Value, Men of Renown: New Perspectives on Trobriand Exchange.* St Lucia: University of Queensland Press, 1976.

Wengle, John. *Ethnographers in the Field: The Psychology of Research.* Tuscaloosa: University of a sociAlabama Press, 1988.

West, Francis. *Hubert Murray: The Australian Pro-Consul.* Melbourne: Oxford University Press, 1968.

———— (ed.). *Selected Letters of Hubert Murray.* Melbourne: Oxford University Press, 1970.

Westermarck, Edward. *The History of Human Marriage.* London: Macmillan, 1891.

————. *The Origin and Development of the Moral Ideas.* 2 vols. London: Macmillan, 1906–08.

————. *Marriage Ceremonies in Morocco.* London: Macmillan, 1914.

Wheeler, Gerald C. *The Tribal and Inter-Tribal Relations in Australia.* London: John Murray, 1910.

————. *Mono-Alu Folklore.* London: Routledge, 1926.

Williams, F. E. 'The Reminiscences of Ahuia Ova', *JRAI* 60, 1939.

Winters, C. (ed.). *International Dictionary of Anthropologists.* New York: Garland Publishing, 1991.

Witkiewicz, Stanisław. *Listy do syna* (Letters to a Son), (eds. Bozena Danck-Wojnowska and Anna Micińska) Warszawa: Państwowy Instytut Wydawniczy, 1969.

Witkiewicz, Stanisław Ignacy. 'Z podróży do Tropików' ('A Journey to the Tropics'), *Echo Tatrzańskie* (Zakopane), 1919. (Republished with an English translation in *Konteksty*, 2000.)

————. *The Pragmalists (Pragmatyíci).* Trans. D. and E. Gerould, in *Tropical Madness.* New York: Winter House, 1973 [1919].

————. *Metaphysics of a Two-Headed Calf.* Trans. D. and E. Gerould. In *Tropical Madness.* New York: Winter House, 1973 (1921).

————. 'Listy do Heleny Czerwijowskiej', *Twóczość* 9, 1971.

————. *622 Upadki Bunga, czyli demoniczna kobieta* (The 622 Downfalls of Bungo, or The Demon Woman). Warszawa: Państwowy Instytut Wydawniczy, 1972.

Wundt, Wilhelm. *Völkerpsychologie: Eine Untersuchung der Entwicklungsgesetze von Sprache, Mythus und Sitte.* 10 vols. Leipzig: Engelmann, 1900–09.

————. *Grundzüge der Physiologischen Psychologie.* 3 vols. Leipzig: Engelmann, 1874. (Published in English as *Principles of Physiological Psychology.* London: Macmillan, 1905.)

————. *Elemente der Völkerpsychologie.* 10 vols. Leipzig: Engelmann, 1912. (Published in English as *Elements of Folk Psychology.* Trans. E.L. Schaub. London: Allen & Unwin, 1916.)

Wyspiański, Stanisław. *The Wedding.* Trans. G.T. Kapolka. Ann Arbor: Ardis, 1990.

Young, Michael W. (ed.). *The Ethnography of Malinowski: The Trobriand Islands, 1915–18.* London: Routledge, 1979.

————. *Fighting with Food: Leadership, Values and Social Control in a Massim Society.* Cambridge: Cambridge University Press, 1971.

————. *Magicians of Manumanua: Living Myth in Kalauna.* Berkeley: University of California Press, 1983.

————. 'The Massim: An Introduction', *JPH* 18 (1), 1983.

————. 'The Theme of the Resentful Hero: Stasis and Mobility in Goodenough Mythology', in J. W. Leach and E. R. Leach (eds), *The Kula: New Perspectives on Massim Exchange,* 1983.

————. '"The Intensive Study of Restricted Areas"; or, Why did Malinowski Go to the Trobriand Islands?', *Oceania* 55 (1), 1984.

————. 'The Ethnographer as Hero: The Imponderabilia of Malinowski's Everyday Life in Mailu', *Canberra Anthropology* 10 (2), 1987.

————. 'Malinowski and the Function of Culture', in D. Austin-Broos (ed.), *Creating Culture: Profiles in the Study of Culture*. Sydney: Allen & Unwin, 1987.

————. *Malinowski among the Magi: 'The Natives of Mailu'*. London: Routledge, 1988.

————. 'Malinowski, Bronislaw', in C. Winters (ed.), *International Dictionary of Anthropologists*. New York: Garland Publishing, 1991.

————. 'Young Malinowski: A Review Article' (reviews of Ellen et al (eds), *Malinowski between Two Worlds*; Thornton and Skalník, *The Early Writings of Bronisław Malinowski*; Gerould, *The Witkiewicz Reader*), *Canberra Anthropology* 17 (2), 1994.

————. 'The Malinowski Papers', in *Laboratory of the Social Sciences: A Virtual Future*. London: British Library of Political and Economic Science, 1996.

————. 'Malinowski's Second Tent', *AT* 12 (6), Dec. 1996.

————. 'A Myth Exposed', *The Asia-Pacific Magazine* 3, June, 1996.

————. 'Bronislaw Malinowski', in A. Kuper and J. Kuper (eds). *The Social Science Encyclopedia*. London: Routledge, 1997.

————. *Malinowski's Kiriwina: Fieldwork Photography 1915–18*. Chicago: University of Chicago Press, 1998.

————. 'The Making of an Anthropologist: From Frazer to Freud in the Life of the Young Malinowski', *Anthropological Notebooks* 5 (1), Ljubljana, 1999.

————. 'Bronislaw Kasper Malinowski', in *American National Biography*. Vol. 14. New York: Oxford University Press, 1999.

————. 'The Careless Collector: Malinowski and the Antiquarians', in M. O'Hanlon and R. L. Welsch (eds), *Hunting the Gatherers: Ethnographic Collectors, Agents and Agency in Melanesia, 1870s–1930s*. Oxford: Berghahn Books, 2000.

————. 'Malinowski, Bronislaw (1884–1942)', in *International Encyclopedia of Social and Behavioural Sciences*. Vol. 14, article 90. Oxford: Pergamon, 2000.

Zagórska, Karola. 'Under the Roof of Konrad Korzeniowski', in Z. Najder (ed.), *Conrad under Familial Eyes*, 1983 (1932).

Zagórska-Brooks, Maria, 'Lucjan Malinowski and Polish Dialectology', *PR* 30 (2), 1985.

Zubrzycka, Tola. 'A Son of Two Countries: Some Reminiscences of Joseph Conrad Korzeniowski', in Z. Najder (ed.), *Conrad under Familial Eyes*, 1983 (1931).

Index

Works by Malinowski (BM) appear under title; works by others under author's name.